Sports Address Bible & Almanac

The Comprehensive Directory of Sports Addresses

Edward T. Kobak, Jr.

Global Sports Productions, Ltd.
1223 Broadway, Suite 102
Santa Monica, California 90404

Copyright © 2003 by Edward T. Kobak, Jr.

Fifteenth Edition

Copyright © 1980, 1983, 1987, 1990, 1991, 1994, 1995,
1996, 1997, 1998, 1999, 2000, 2001, 2002
& 2003 by Edward T. Kobak, Jr.

Printed and bound in the United States of America.
All rights reserved. No part of this book may be reproduced, or transmitted in any form or by any means, electronic or mechanical, including photocopying, recording, or by any information and retrieval system or otherwise, without the express written consent of the Author - except for the quotation of brief passages for the purposes of criticism and review for inclusion in a magazine, newspaper or broadcast.

Although the Author has made every effort to ensure the accuracy and completeness of information contained in this book, the Author assumes no responsibility for errors, inaccuracies, omissions, or any inconsistency herein. Any slights of people or organizations are unintentional.

2003 Fifteenth Edition

ISBN 1-891655-09-4
ISSN 0743-4561

www.sportsbooksempire.com

Introduction

Welcome to the *2003* edition of **The Sports Address Bible & Almanac,** *now* published annually. The **Bible** has rapidly becoming the most informative resource directory of its kind!

The **Bible** has continually grown since its inception back in 1980, when we first began the planning of the **Bible**. Since then, the book has changed over the years, due to the increase of information in the sports world!

What once was a book primarily for the sports collector, has now become a valuable resource bible for many people in the sportsworld! Each year, the **Bible** changes a little.

Now, with many people using the internet, our books have become a starting point for those who wish to save time surfing the web. They get their info here first, then hit the internet.

The sportsworld has rapidly changed each year. New leagues such as the outdoor pro lacrosse league and the expansion of existing leagues as well as the demise of old-time leagues such as the International Hockey League & the Continental Basketball Assn., and the re-birth of the CBA a year later along with leagues that merge together dramatically change the book each edition.

We are now entering a new era as the **Sports Address Bible & Almanac** is now listing *league champions* for most major, minor & amateur leagues as well as including a vast amount of *website & email addresses*, allowing the reader to use the **Bible** as a starting reference point to gain valuable information before hitting the internet and jumping off into the world wide web, creating an even greater need for **The Sports Address Bible & Almanac.**

A special "thank you" to my mother, Barbara, who spends most of her California vacation each year assisting with the data entry. A "thank you" to my special friends-Mike Boylan, Bristo Loving, George Hemat & Elvia Franco who have all contributed towards the growth of our books.

Lastly, a great "thank you" to all the sports administrators & publicists we have called upon, as well as our loyal subscribers. Your help & support has been greatly appreciated!

Printing
Mike Boylan/Boylan Printing

Data & Word Processing
Barbara Boldtmann Kobak

Publishing Operations
Greg Andrews

Book Layout & Pasteup
Elvia Franco/EC Graphics

Cover Printing
George Hemat/West Coast Printing

Mail Room Supervisor
Bristo Loving

www.sportsbooksempire.com

TABLE OF CONTENTS

SECTION I
Baseball
Major Leagues 1
MLB Spring Training Camps 4
Japanese Professional Baseball 6
Korean Professional Baseball 7
Chinese Taipei (Taiwan) Professional Leagues 8
Other Foreign Baseball 9
National Association Affiliated Minor Leagues 10
United States Fall/Winter Leagues 30
Minor League Independent Baseball 31
Caribbean Winter Leagues 37
Amateur Summer Leagues 41
Canadian Baseball 56
Organizations 59
Publications 62

SECTION II
Basketball
National Basketball Association 63
Women's NBA 66
Minor Leagues 67
Organizations 74
Publications 75

SECTION III
Football
National Football League 77
Canadian Football League 80
NFL Europe 81
Indoor/Arena Football 82
Women's Pro Football 88
Minor League/Semi-professional Leagues 89
Canadian Junior Football Leagues 92
Organizations 96
Publications 97

SECTION IV
Hockey
National Hockey League 99
Minor Leagues 102
Canadian Major Junior Leagues 114
Canadian Junior A Leagues 120
United States Junior A Leagues 133
Canadian Women's Pro League 137
Canadian Senior & Semi-pro Leagues 138
United States Senior Hockey 142
United States Junior B & C Leagues 143
Canadian Junior B & C Leagues 151
Organizations 157
Publications 158

SECTION V
Lacrosse
Professional Lacrosse Leagues..161
Canadian Lacrosse...163
Publications 170

SECTION VI
Soccer
Major League Soccer 171
Women's Division One Pro Soccer..172
Indoor Pro MISL..173
A-League Second Division..174
Division 3 Outdoor...176
Women's Tier II Outdoor..178
Organizations 186
Publications 187

SECTION VII
Women's Pro Softball/World Team Tennis...................................189
Womens Pro Volleyball USPVL...190

SECTION VIII
Individual Sport-by-Sport Listings
Air Sports...191
Archery...192
Arm Wrestling...192
Bicycling...193
Billiards...195
Boating/Sailing...196
Bocce..198
Bowling 198
Boxing 199
Broomball...200
Canoe/Kayak 200
Climbing/Alpine 201
Cricket..201
Croquet 202
Equestrian/Horse Racing 202
Exercise/Fitness...205
Fishing..207
Frisbee 208
Golf 208
Greyhound Racing 210
Gymnastics/Trampoling...211
Health & Sports Medicine..211
Ice Racing 213
Ice Skating/Speed Skating 213
In-Line Skating/Roller Hockey 213
Kiting...214
Martial Arts...214
Motor Sports 215
Orienteering..225

Paddle/Racquet Sports	225
Polo	225
Rodeo	226
Roller Skating	226
Rowing	227
Rugby	227
Running	228
Scuba Diving/Underwater Swimming	229
Shooting	230
Softball	230
Sports Acrobatics	231
Squash	232
Surfing	232
Swimming/Diving	233
Tennis	234
Track & Field	236
Triathlon	236
Volleyball	236
Water Skiing	237
Wind Surfing	238
Wrestling	239
Winter Sports	
Biathlon	240
Bobsledding	240
Curling	240
Luge	241
Skiing/Snowboarding	241
Sled Dog Racing	243
Snowmobiling	243
Winter Swimming	244

SECTION IX
Disabled Sports 245

SECTION X
Sports Organizations
Multi-Sport Organizations	247
U.S. Olympic Committee Sports Organizations	259
Canadian Olympic Committee Sports Organizations	262

SECTION XI
Sports Publications 263

SECTION XII
Sports Career Development
College Sports Administration Studies Programs 271
Placement & Job Opportunity Services 286

SECTION XIII
The Media
National Television Networks 287
National Cable TV Networks 288
National Radio Networks 289
Regional Cable TV Sports Networks 292
Television Flagship & Superstations 294
Pay-Per-View Television 295
Radio & TV Producers/Programmers/Syndicators 295
News Wire Services 296
International Media.. 297
All Sports Radio Stations... 298
Major United States Daily Newspapers 307
Major Canadian Daily Newspapers 332

SECTION XIV
Sports Museums & Hall of Fames.. 337

SECTION XV
Sports Commissions 351

SECTION XVI
Sports Facilities
United States Stadiums, Arenas & Ballparks 365
Canadian Sports Facilities 394
Sports Facility Service Companies 397
Sports Facility Architects/Engineers/Planners 398

SECTION XVII
Sports Business
Sports Agencies... 399

SECTION XVIII
Sports Collecting
Sports Card Manufacturers 405
Hobby Guides & Directories 406
Hobby Magazines 407
Hobby Periodicals & Newsletters 407
Foreign Collecting Periodicals & Societies 408
Collecting Clubs 409

SECTION XIX
International /Olympic Sports
International Olympic Committee 411
Olympic Games & Multi-Sport Games Committees 411

SECTION XX
Intercollegiate Athletics
College Athletic Associations 413
NCAA College Bowl Games & Basketball Tournaments 413
NCAA I & I-AA Member Conferences 415
NCAA II & III Member Conferences 421
NCAA I & I-AA Member Universities 427
NCAA Division II Member Universities & Colleges 457
Canadian Universities 481
Canadian Colleges 486

SECTION XXI
State High School Athletic Federations 495

SECTION XXII
Amateur State Games Committees 501
Senior Games 505

SECTION XXIII
Late Arrivals & Additions... 506

Baseball

Major League Baseball
245 Park Avenue
New York, NY 10167
T: (212) 931-7800
F: (212) 949-5654
www.majorleaguebaseball.com
Commissioner: Allan H. Selig
Exec VP: Sandy Alderson
PR: Richard Levin

Major League Baseball Players Association
12 E. 49th Street, 24th Floor
New York, NY 10017
T: (212) 826-0808
F: (212) 752-4378
Exec. Director: Donald Fehr
PR: Richard Weiss

Major League Baseball Properties
350 Park Avenue
New York, NY 10022
T: (212) 339-7900
F: (212) 339-7628
P: Robert Gamgort

American League

Anaheim Angels
2000 Gene Autry Way
Anaheim, CA 92806
T: (714) 940-2000
F: (714) 940-2205
www.angelsbaseball.com
CEO: Michael Eisner
GM: Bill Stoneman
PR: Tim Mead

Baltimore Orioles
333 W. Camden Street
Baltimore, MD 21201
T: (410) 685-9800
F: (410) 547-6272
www.theorioles.com
GM: Syd Thrift
PR: Bill Stetka

Boston Red Sox
4 Yawkey Way
Fenway Park
Boston, MA 02115
T: (617) 267-9440
F: (617) 236-6797
www.redsox.com
GM: Theo Epstein
PR: Kevin Shea

Chicago White Sox
333 West 35th Street
Chicago, IL 60016
T: (312) 674-1000
F: (312) 674-5116
www.chisox.com
GM: Kenny Williams
PR: Scott Reifert

Cleveland Indians
2401 Ontario Street
Cleveland, OH 44115
T: (216) 420-4200
F: (216) 420-4396
www.indians.com
GM: Mark Shapiro
PR: Bart Swain

Detroit Tigers
2100 Woodward Ave.
Detroit, MI 48216
T: (313) 471-2000
F: (313) 471-2138
www.detroit-tigers.com
GM: Randy Smith
PR: John Hahn

Kansas City Royals
PO Box 419969
Kansas City, MO 64141
T: (816) 921-8000
F: (816) 921-5775
www.kcroyals.com
GM: Allard Baird
PR: David Witty

Minnesota Twins
34 Kirby Puckett Place
Minneapolis, MN 55415
T: (612) 375-1366
F: (612) 375-7473
www.twinsbaseball.com
GM: Terry Ryan
PR: Sean Harlin

New York Yankees
Yankee Stadium
E. 161st Street & River Ave
Bronx, NY 10451
T: (718) 293-4300
F: (718) 293-8414
www.yankees.com
GM: Brian Cashman
PR: Rick Cerrone

Oakland Athletics
7000 Coliseum Way
Oakland, CA 94621
T: (510) 638-4900
F: (510) 562-1633
www.oaklandathletics.com
GM: Billy Beane
PR: Jim Young

Seattle Mariners
PO Box 4100
Seattle, WA 98104
T: (206) 346-4000
F: (206) 346-4400
www.seattlemariners.com
E: mariners@seattlemariners.com
GM: Pat Gillick
PR: Tim Hevly

Tampa Bay Devil Rays
One Tropicana Drive
St. Petersburg, FL 33705
T: (727) 825-3137
F: (727) 825-3111
www.devilray.com
GM: Chuck LaMar
PR: Rick Vaughn

Texas Rangers
PO Box 90111
Arlington, TX 76004
T: (817) 273-5222
F: (817) 273-5110
www.texasrangers.com
GM: John Hart
PR: John Blake

Toronto Blue Jays
1 Blue Jays Way, Suite 3200
Toronto, Ontario, Canada M5V 1J1
T: (416) 341-1000
F: (416) 341-1250
www.bluejays.ca
E: bluejay@bluejays.ca
GM: J.P. Ricciardi
PR: Howard Starkman

National League

Arizona Diamondbacks
Bank One Ballpark
401 E. Jefferson Street
Phoenix, AZ 85004
T: (602) 462-6500
F: (602) 462-6527
www.azdiamondbacks.com
GM: Joe Garagiola, Jr.
PR: Mike Swanson

Atlanta Braves
PO Box 4064
Atlanta, GA 30302
T: (404) 522-7630
F: (404) 614-1391
www.atlantabraves.com
GM: John Schuerholz
PR: Jim Schultz

Chicago Cubs
Wrigley Field
1060 W. Addison Street
Chicago, IL 60613
T: (773) 404-2827
F: (773) 404-4129
www.cubs.com
E: cubs@cubs.com
GM: Andy MacPhail
PR: Sharon Pannozzo

Cincinnati Reds
100 Main Street
Cincinnati, OH 45202
T: (513) 421-4510
F: (513) 421-7342
www.cincinnatireds.com
GM: James Bowden
PR: Rob Butcher

Colorado Rockies
Coors Field
2001 Blake Street
Denver, CO 80205
T: (303) 292-0200
F: (303) 312-2319
www.coloradorockies.com
GM: Dan O'Dowd
PR: Jay Alves

Florida Marlins
2267 NW 199th Street
Miami, FL 33056
T: (305) 626-7400
F: (305) 626-7302
www.floridamarlins.com
GM: Larry Beinfest
PR: Steve Copses

Houston Astros
PO Box 288
Houston, TX 77001
T: (713) 259-8000
F: (713) 259-8981
www.astros.com
GM: Gerry Hunsicker
PR: Warren Miller

Los Angeles Dodgers
1000 Elysian Park Avenue
Los Angeles, CA 90012
T: (323) 224-1500
F: (323) 224-1269
www.dodgers.com
GM: Dan Evans
PR: Derrick Hall

Milwaukee Brewers
One Brewers Way
Milwaukee, WI 53214
T: (414) 902-4400
F: (414) 902-4053
www.milwaukeebrewers.com
GM: Dean Taylor
PR: Jon Greenberg

Montreal Expos
PO Box 500, Station M
Montreal, Quebec HIV 3P2, Canada
T: (514) 253-3434
F: (514) 253-8282
www.montrealexpos.com
GM: Omar Minaya
PR: Matt Charbonneau

New York Mets
Shea Stadium
123-01 Roosevelt Ave.
Flushing, NY 11368
T: (718) 507-6387
F: (718) 639-3619
www.mets.com
GM: Steve Phillips
PR: Jay Horwitz

Philadelphia Phillies
PO Box 7575
Philadelphia, PA 19101
T: (215) 463-6000
F: (215) 389-3050
www.phillies.com
GM: Ed Wade
PR: Larry Shenk

Pittsburgh Pirates
PNC Park at North Shore
115 Federal Street
Pittsburgh, PA 15212
T: (412) 323-5000
F: (412) 325-4413
www.pittsburghpirates.com
GM: David Littlefield
PR: Jim Trdinich

St. Louis Cardinals
250 Stadium Plaza
St. Louis, MO 63102
T: (314) 421-3060
F: (314) 982-7399
www.stlcardinals.com
GM: Walt Jocketty
PR: Brian Bartow

San Diego Padres
PO Box 122000
San Diego, CA 92112
T: (619) 881-6500
F: (619) 497-5454
www.padres.com
GM: Kevin Towers
PR: Glenn Geffner

San Francisco Giants
24 Willie Mays Plaza
San Francisco, CA 94107
T: (415) 972-2000
F: (415) 947-2800
www.sfgiants.com
GM: Brian R. Sabean
PR: Jim Moorhead

2002 World Series
Anaheim Angels d *San Francisco Giants 4 Games to 3.*

2003 All Star Game, *Chicago, IL July 15, 2003 Comiskey Park*

Spring Training

Anaheim Angels
Tempe Diablo Stadium
2200 W. Alameda
Tempe, AZ 85282
T: (480) 350-5265

Arizona Diamondbacks
Tucson Electric Park
2500 E. Ajo Way
Tucson, AZ 85713
T: (520) 434-1111
www.tucsonbaseball.com

Chicago Cubs
HoHoKam Park
1235 N. Center Street
Mesa, AZ 85201
T: (480) 964-4467
F: (480) 461-0673

Chicago White Sox
Tucson Electric Park
2500 E. Ajo Way
Tucson, AZ 85713
T: (888) 683-3900
T: (520) 434-1300
www.tucsonbaseball.com

Colorado Rockies
Hi Corbett Field
3400 E. Camino Campestre
Tucson, AZ 85716
T: (520) 327-9467
F: (520) 322-4545

Kansas City Athletics
Surprise Stadium
15850 N. Bullard Avenue
Surprise, AZ 85374
T: (800) 326-4000

Milwaukee Brewers
Maryvale Baseball Park
3600 N. 51st Avenue
Maryvale, AZ 85031
T: (623) 245-5500

Oakland Athletics
Phoenix Municipal Stadium
5999 E. Van Buren
Phoenix, AZ 85008
T: (602) 392-0074

San Diego Padres
Peoria Sports Complex
16101 N. 83rd Street
Peoria, AZ 85382
T: (623) 878-4337
www.peoriaaz.com

San Francisco Giants
Scottsdale Stadium
7408 E. Osborn Road
Scottsdale, AZ 85251
T: (480) 990-7972
F: (480) 990-2643

Seattle Mariners
PO Box 999
Peoria Sports Complex
15707 N. 83rd Avenue
Peoria, AZ 85382
T: (623) 878-4337
F: (623) 412-7888
www.mariners.org

Texas Rangers
Surprise Stadium
15754 N. Bullard Avenue
Surprise, AZ 85374
T: (623) 266-9600

Grapefruit League

Atlanta Braves
Cracker Jack Stadium
Disney Wide World
of Sports Complex
700 S. Victory Way
Kissimmee, FL 34747
T: (407) 939-1500

Baltimore Orioles
Fort Lauderdale Stadium
1301 NW 55th Avenue
Fort Lauderdale, FL 33309
T: (954) 776-1921

Boston Red Sox
City of Palms Park
2201 Edison Avenue
Fort Myers, FL 33901
T: (941) 334-4700
F: (941) 334-6060

Cincinnati Reds
Ed Smith Stadium
2700 12th Street
Sarasota, FL 34237
T: (941) 954-4101

Cleveland Indians
Chain O' Lakes Park
Cypress Gardens Blvd.
Winter Haven, FL 33880
T: (863) 291-5803
F: (863) 291-4491

Detroit Tigers
Joker Marchant Stadium
Tigertown
PO Box 90187
2301 Lakeland Hills Blvd.
Lakeland, FL 33805
T: (863) 603-6278
F: (863) 688-9589

Florida Marlins
Roger Dean Stadium
4751 Main Street
Jupiter, FL 33458
T: (561) 775-1818
F: (561) 691-6886
E: info@rogerdeanstadium.com

Houston Astros
Osceola County Stadium
630 Heritage Parkway
Kissimmee, FL 34742
T: (407) 697-3200

Los Angeles Dodgers
PO Box 2887
Holman Stadium/Dodgertown
4101 26th Street
Vero Beach, FL 32961
T: (561) 569-4900

Minnesota Twins
Hammond Stadium
Lee County Sports Complex
14100 Six Mile Cypress Pkwy.
Fort Myers, FL 33912
T: (941) 768-4200
F: (941) 768-4207

Montreal Expos
Space Coast Stadium
5800 Stadium Parkway
Melbourne, FL 32940
T: (321) 633-4487

New York Mets
Thomas J. White Stadium
St. Lucie Co. Sports Complex
525 NW Peacock Blvd.
Port St. Lucie, FL 34986
T: (772) 871-2100
F: (772) 878-2181

New York Yankees
Legends Field
1 Steinbrenner Drive
Tampa, FL 33614
T: (813) 879-2244

Philadelphia Phillies
Jack Russell Stadium
800 Phillies Drive
Clearwater, FL 33755
T: (727) 441-9941
T: (727) 442-8496 Tickets
F: (727) 461-7768

Pittsburgh Pirates
Pirate City/McKechnie Field
(17th Ave. W & 9th St. E.)
1701 Roberto Clemente Dr.
Bradenton, FL 34208
T: (941) 748-4610
F: (941) 747-9549

St. Louis Cardinals
Roger Dean Stadium
4751 Main Street
Jupiter, FL 33458
T: (561) 775-1818

Tampa Bay Devil Rays
Al Lang Field
Progress Energy Park
180 Second Avenue SE
St. Petersburg, FL 33701
T: (727) 825-3250

Toronto Blue Jays
Dunedin Stadium @ Grant Field
373 Douglas Avenue at Beltrees
Dunedin, FL 34697
T: (800) 707-8269
T: (727) 733-0429

Foreign Professional Baseball

Japanese Baseball
Imperial Tower, 14F
1-1-1 Uchisaiwai-cho,
Chiyoda-ku, Tokyo 100, Japan
T: (81.3) 3502-0022
F: (81.3) 3502-0140
www.npb.or.jp
Commissioner: Hiromori Kawashima
Exec Sec: Kazuo Hasegawa
Media: Kunio Shimoda

Central League
Asahi Bldg. 3F, 6-6-7 Ginza
Chuo-ku, Tokyo 100-0011 Japan
T: (81.3) 3572-1673
F: (81.3) 3571-4545
www.npb.or.jp/cl/index.html
P: Hajime Toyokura
Sec Gen: Hideo Okoshi
Media: Kazu Ogaki

Chunichi Dragons
Chunichi Bldg., 6F, 4-1-1 Sakae
Naka-ku, Nagoya 460, Japan
T: (052) 252-5226
F: (052) 263-7696
www.dragons.co.jp
GM: Kazumasa Ito
PR: Mitsuo Kodama

Hanshin Tigers
1-47 Koshien-cho
Nishinomiya-shi, Hyogo-ken 663
T: (0798) 46-1515
F: (0798) 40-0934
www.hanshin.co.jp/tigers
GM: Katsuyoshi Nozaki
PR: Masaru Honma

Hiroshima Toyo Carp
5-25 Moto-machi
Naka-ku, Hiroshima 730, Japan
T: (082) 221-2040
F: (082) 228-5013
www.carp.co.jp
GM: Junro Anan
PR: Takashi Hamada

Yakult Swallows
Shimbashi MCV Bldg., 5F
5-13-5 Shimbashi, Minato-ku
Tokyo 105, Japan
T: (03) 5470-8915
F: (03) 5470-8916
www.yakult.co.jp/swallows
GM: Kesatoku Kurashima
PR: Shigeru Sugimura

Yokohama Bay Stars
Kannai Arai Bldg., 7F
1-8 Onoe-cho, Naka-ku
Yokohama 231, Japan
T: (045) 681-0811
F: (045) 661-2500
www.ifcnet.re.jp/baystars
GM: Yoshio Noguchi
PR: Mitsukuni Takeda

Yomiuri Tokyo Giants
Takebashi 3-3 Bldg.
3-3 Nishiki-cho, Kanda
Chiyoda-ku, Tokyo 101, Japan
T: (03) 3295-7711
F: (03) 3295-7708
www.yomiuri.co.jp/giants
GM: Makoto Doi
PR: Izumi Tanaka

Pacific League
Asahi Bldg., 9F, 6-6-7 Ginza,
Chuo-ku, Tokyo 104, Japan
T: (81.3) 3573-1551
F: (81.3) 3572-5843
P: Tadao Koike
Sec. Gen: Shigeru Murata

Chiba Lotte Marines
WBG Marive West, 26F
2-6 Nakase, Mihama-ku, Chiba-shi
Chiba-ken 261-8587 Japan
T: (043) 297-2101
F: (043) 297-2181
www.marines.co.jp
GM: Setsuo Goto
PR: Yoji Horimoto

Fukuoka Daiei Hawks
Fukuoka Dome 6F,
2-2-2 Jigyohama, Chuo-ku,
Fukuoka-shi, Fukuok-ken 810, Japan
T: (092) 844-1189
F: (092) 844-4600
www.hawkstown.com
GM: Ryuzo Setoyama
PR: Hiroshimi Kimura

Kintetsu Buffaloes
Midosuji Grand Bldg. 5F
2-2-3 Namba, Chuo-ku,
Osaka 542, Japan
T: (06) 6212-9744
F: (06) 6212-6834
www.buffaloes.co.jp
GM: Tetsuya Kobayashi
PR: Kiyoshi Onosaka

Nippon Ham Fighters
Roppongi Denki Bldg. 6F
6-1-20 Roppongi,
Minato-ku, Tokyo 106, Japan
T: (03) 3403-9131
F: (03) 3403-9143
www.fighters.co.jp
GM: Takeshi Kojima
PR: Takeshi Kagei

Orix Blue Wave
Green Stadium Kobe , Midoridai
Suma-ku, Kobe 654-0163 Japan
T: (078) 795-1203
F: (078) 795-1505
www.orix.co.jp/bw
GM: Kiyoshi Yano
PR: Syosaku Yokotai

Seibu Lions
Seibu Lions Stadium
2135 Kami-Yamaguchi,
Tokorozawa-shi,
Saitama-ken 359, Japan
T: (042) 924-1155
F: (042) 928-1919
www.seibu-group.co.jp/lions
GM: Kenji Ono
PR: Nozomi Kawakami

2002 Japan Series
Tokyo Yomiuri Giants d *Seibu Lions 4 Games to 0.*

Korean Baseball Organization
946-16 DoKok-Dong
Kangnam-Ku, Seoul, South Korea
T: (82.2) 3460-4643
F: (82.2) 3460-4649
www.koreabaseball.or.kr
E: jkj@koreabaseball.or.kr
Commissioner: Yong Oh Park
PR/BB Oper: Lee Sang-hyun

Doosan Bears
Chamsil Baseball Stadium
10 Chamsil-idong, Songpa-ku,
Seoul, South Korea
T: (82.2) 2240-1777
F: (82.2) 2240-1788
www.doosanbears.com
GM: Kun Koo Kang

Hanhwa Eagles
22-1 Yongjeon-dong
Daejeon, 300-200 South Korea
T: (82.42) 637-6001
F: (82.42) 632-2929
GM: Kyung Yon Hwang

Hyundai Unicorns
Hyundai Haesang Bldg., 9th Floor
1014 Kwonseon-dong, Kwonseon-ku
Suwon, Kyug-ki 441-390 South Korea
T: (82-32) 433-7979
F: (82-32) 435-3108
www.hyundaiunicorns.com.kr
GM: Yong Hwi Kim

KIA Tigers
Daebang-dong 266, 2FL
Kwangju-shi, Seo-gu 502-807 Korea
T: (82.62) 370-1878
F: (82.62) 525-5350
www.kiatigers.co.kr
GM: Jeong Jae-kong

LG Twins
Chamsil Baseball Stadium
10 Chamsil-1 dong, Songpa-ku
Seoul, South Korea 138-221
T: (82.2) 2005-5760
F: (82-2) 2005-5801
www.lgtwins.com
GM: You Song-min

Lotte Giants
930 Sajik-dong, Dongrae-ku
Pusan, South Korea
T: (82.51) 505-7422
F: (82.51) 506-0090
www.lottegiants.co.kr
GM: Chul Hwa Lee

Samsung Lions
184-3 Sunhwari, Jinryangyup,
Kyungsan, Kyung-Buk, Korea 712-830
T: (82.53) 859-3114
F: (82.53) 859-3117
www.samsunglions.com
GM: Jong Man Kim

SK Wyverns
1456-1 Kuwol-dong, Namdong-ku
Inchon, South Korea 405-220
T: (82.32) 422-7949
F: (82.32) 429-4565
www.skwyverns.com
GM: Myung Yung-chul

Baseball was first introduced to Korea in 1905. Professional Baseball began in 1982 with the current day KBO.

2002 Korea Championship Series
Samsung Lions d *LG Twins*
4 Games to 2.

2003 All Star Game, Suw-on
TBA

Chinese Taipei Professional Baseball League
2 F, No. 32, Pateh Road
Sec. 3
Taipei, Taiwan
T: (886.2) 2577-6992
F: (886.2) 2577-2606
www.cpbl.com.tw
Commissioner: T.C. Huang
Sec. General: Wayne Lee

Brother Elephants
No. 255, Sec. 3
Nanking East Road
Taipei, Taiwan
T: 886-2-712-1314
F: 886-2-717-3334
GM: Juei-ho-Hung

China Trust Whales
6F., No. 3, Sung Shou Road
Taipei, Taiwan
T: 886-2-722-2002 x 6941-6950
F: 886-2-723-0349
GM: Yu-Hsiu Chen

President Lions
No. 25, Hsinghua Street
Tainan, Taiwan
T: 886-6-228-8959
F: 886-6-228-8983
Pres: Juin-nan Kuo

Sinon Bulls
3F, No. 45, Wu-Chung Center St.
Taichung, Taiwan
T: 886-4-372-6202
F: 886-4-375-1141
GM: T.F. Yang

Established in 1990.

2002 CPBL Championship
Brother Elephants d *China Trust Whales 4 Games to 0.*

Taiwan Major League
9F, No. 1-1, Chong-Qing N Rd.
103 Taipei, Taiwan
T: (886.2) 2552-3668
F: (886.2) 2523 6440
www.naluwan.com.tw
P: Felix S.T. Chen
GM: George Chao
Sec. Gen: Robin Tseng

TML established in 1997.

2002 TML Series, Taichung Agan d Kaohsiung Fala 4 Games to 1.

Netherlands

Dutch Major League
Koninklijke Nederlandse Baseball
En Softball Bond
Twinstate II, Perkinsbaan 15
3439 ND Nieuwegein, Netherlands
T: (31.30) 607-6070
F: (31.30) 294-3043
www.knbsb.nl
P: Hans Meijer

Ado Baseball Club
Leen Volkerijk Stadion
Steenwijklaan 2
2541 RL Den Haag
T: (31.70) 366 97 22

Almere '90
Fanny Blankers Koen Sportpark
Almere
T: (31.36) 549 95 40

Amsterdam Pirates
Sportpark Ookmeer
Herman Bonpad 5
1067 SN Amsterdam
T: (31.20) 616 21 51
www.amsterdam-pirates.nl

HCAW Baseball Club
Mr. Cocker HCAW
Postbus 1321
1400 BH Bussum
T: (31.35) 693 14 30
www.hcaw.nl

Hoofddorp Pioniers
Sportspark Toolenburg
Hoofdweg 865
2131 MB Hoofddorp
T: (31.23) 561 35 57

Kinheim Baseball Club
Gemeentelijk Sportpark
Badmintonpad
2023 BT Haarlem
T: (31.23) 526 00 21

Neptunus Baseball Club
Familiestadion Neptunus
Abraham van Stolkweg 31
3041 JA Rotterdam
T: (31.10) 437 53 69
www.neptunussport.com

PSV Baseball Club
PSV Honkbal, Postbus 4057
5604 EB Eindhoven
T: (31.40) 211 19 84
www.psv-honk-softbal.nl

RCH Baseball Club
Heemsteedse Sportparken
Ringvaartlaan
2103 XV Heemstede
T: (31.23) 528 43 88

Sparta-Feyenoord Baseball Club
Postbus 9211
3007 AE Rotterdam
T: (31.10) 479 04 83
www.diertens.myweb.nl

2002 Dutch Major League Series
Neptunas d HCAW 3 Games to 0.

Italy

Italian Serie A/1
Federazione Italiana Baseball/Softball
Viale Tiziano 70
00196 Roma, Italy
T: (39.6) 368 58 130
F: (39.6) 368 58 201
www.baseball-softball.it
P: Everardo Dalla Noce
Sec Gen: Alessandro Pica

Anzio
Via delle Felci 4
00040 Lavinio (Roma)
T/F: (39.6) 981 90 87
www.anziobc.it
P: Roberto Monaco

Bologna
Piazale Atleti Azurri d'Italia
40122 Bologna
T: (39.51) 479 618
F: (39.51) 554 000
www.fortitudobaseball.tripod.com
E: fotitudobaseball@tin.it
P: Stefano Michelini

Caserta
Stadio del Baseball
81100 Caserta
T: (39.823) 472 003
F: (39.823) 322 686
E: caserta_baseball@yahoo.com
P: Sergio Musto

Grosseto
Via della Repubblica 2
58100 Grosseto
T: (39.564) 49 41 49
F: (39.564) 47 67 50
www.bbgrosseto.com
P: Claudio Banchi

Modena
Casella Postale 69
49010 Saliceto Panaro, Modena
T: (39.59) 371 655
F: (39.59) 365 300
E: modenabc@tin.it
www.modenabc.tripod.com
P: Giovanni Tinti

Nettuno
Stadio Steno Borghese
Via Scipione Borghese
00048 Nettuno-Roma
T/F: (39.6) 985 49 66
www.nettunobaseball.com
P: Cesare Augusto Spigoni

Parma
Via Donatore 4, Collecchio
43044 Parma
T: (39.335) 604 8969
F: (39.521) 802 601
www.eteamz.com/cusparma
E: parmabaseball@hotmail.com
P: Rossano Rinaldi

Paterno Warriors
Viale Dei Platani 15
95047 Paterno
T: (39.95) 623 590
www.warriors-cat.com
E: paternowarriors@hotmail.com
P: Nunzio Botta

Rimini Pirates
Via Monaco 2
47900 Rimini
T/F: (39.541) 741 761
www.baseballrimini.com
E: pirati@baseballrimini.com
P: Cesare Zangheri

San Marino
Dogana Via C. Cantu'
50 Republic of San Marino
T: (39.549) 909 678
F: (39.549) 909 656
www.sanmarinobaseballclub.sm
E: info@sanmarinobaseballclub.sm
P: Gian Paolo Giardi

2002 Italian Series
Rimini d Nettuno 4 Games to 1.

Canadian Baseball League
1140 W. Pender Street, Suite 440
Vancouver, BC V6E 4G1 Canada
T: (604) 689-1566
F: (604) 689-1531
www.canadianbaseballleague.com
E: info@canadianbaseballleague.com
CEO: Tony Riviera
Comm: Ferguson Jenkins
Media: Alex Klenman

Inaugural season is 2003. Teams are: Calgary Outlaws, Kelowna Heat, London Monarchs, Montreal Royales, Niagara Stars, Saskatoon Legends, Trois-Rivieres Saints & the Victoria Capitals. Clubs are owned by league.

2003 CBL All Star Game,
July 23 2003, Calgary, Alberta

Minor League Baseball

National Association of Professional Baseball Leagues
201 Bayshore Drive SE
St. Petersburg, FL 33701
Mail: PO Box A, 33731
T: (727) 822-6937
F: (727) 821-5819
www.minorleaguebaseball.com
President: Mike Moore
Exec DirBB Oper: Misann Ellmaker
Media Relations: Jim Ferguson
Asst. Media Rel: Steve Densa
Marketing Director: Rod Meadows

The following leagues are Affiliated Members of the National Association and operate as farm (developmental) clubs to Major League Baseball.

Class AAA Leagues

International League

55 S. High St., Suite 202
Dublin, OH 43017
T: (614) 791-9300
F: (614) 791-9009
www.ilbaseball.com
E: office@ilbaseball.com
President: Randy Mobley
League Secretary: Richard Davis

International League

The International League was founded in 1884, and is derived from three leagues: the Eastern, founded in 1884, the NY State League & the Ontario League, both organized in 1885 and merged into the IL in 1886.

The IL survived baseball's most expensive war of the time, when in 1890 major league players organized their own Player's (Brotherhood) League, in competition with the National and then, major American Association. Several teams jumped to the Brotherhood & the American Assn. & players jumped contracts.

Buffalo Bisons
PO Box 450, 275 Washington St.
Buffalo, NY 14205
T: (716) 846-2000
F: (716) 852-6530
www.bisons.com
E: info@bisons.com
GM: Mike Buczkowski
PR: Tom Burns

Charlotte Knights
2280 Deerfield Drive
Fort Mill, SC 29715
T: (704) 357-8071
F: (704) 329-2155
www.charlotteknights.com
E: info@charlotteknights.com
GM: Bill Blackwell
PR: Shannon Motley

Columbus Clippers
1155 W. Mound Street
Columbus, OH 43223
T: (614) 462-5250
F: (614) 462-3271
www.clippersbaseball.com
E: colsclippers@earthlink.net
GM: Ken Schnacke
PR: Chris Daugherty

Durham Bulls
PO Box 507
Durham, NC 27702
T: (919) 687-6500
F: (919) 687-6560
www.durhambulls.com
GM: Mike Birling
PR: Jessica Wucki

Indianapolis Indians
501 W. Maryland Street
Indianapolis, IN 46225
T: (317) 269-3542
F: (317) 269-3541
www.indyindians.com
E: indians@indyindians.com
GM: Cal Burleson
PR: Tim Harms

Louisville Bats
401 E. Main Street
Louisville, KY 40202
T: (502) 212-2287
F: (502) 515-2255
www.batsbaseball.com
E: info@batsbaseball.com
P: Gary Ulmer
PR: Mary Barney

Norfolk Tides
150 Park Avenue, Harbor Park
Norfolk, VA 23510
T: (757) 622-2222
F: (757) 624-9090
www.norfolktides.com
E: info@norfolktides.com
GM: Dave Rosenfield

Ottawa Lynx
300 Coventry Road
Ottawa, Ontario, Canada KIK 4P5
T: (613) 747-5969
F: (613) 747-0003
www.ottawalynx.com
E: lynx@ottawalynx.com
GM: Kyle Bostwick

Pawtucket Red Sox
PO Box 2365
Pawtucket, RI 02861
T: (401) 724-7300
F: (401) 724-2140
www.pawsox.com
E: info@pawsox.com
P: Mike Tamburro
PR: Bill Wanless

Richmond Braves
PO Box 6667
Richmond, VA 23230
T: (804) 359-4444
F: (804) 359-0731
www.rbraves.com
E: info@rbraves.com
GM: Bruce Baldwin

Rochester Red Wings
One Morrie Silver Way
Rochester, NY 14608
T: (585) 454-1001
F: (585) 454-1056
www.redwingsbaseball.com
E: info@redwingsbaseball.com
GM: Dan Mason
PR: Chuck Hinkel

Scranton/Wilkes-Barre Red Barons
PO Box 3449
Scranton, PA 18505
T: (570) 969-2255
F: (570) 963-6564
www.redbarons.com
E: barons@epix.net
GM: Rick Muntean
PR: Mike Cummings

Syracuse SkyChiefs
P&C Stadium, One Tex Simone Drive
Syracuse, NY 13208
T: (315) 474-7833
F: (315) 474-2658
www.skychiefs.com
E: baseball@skychiefs.com
GM: John Simone

Toledo Mud Hens
406 Washington Street
Toledo, OH 43604
T: (419) 725-4267
F: (419) 725-4368
www.mudhens.com
E: mudhens@mudhens.com
GM: Joe Napoli
PR: Brian Britten

2002 IL Governors Cup
Durham d *Buffalo 3 Games to 0.*

Pacific Coast League
1631 Mesa Avenue, Suite A
Colorado Springs, CO 80906
T: (719) 636-3399
F: (719) 636-1199
www.pclbaseball.com
E: office@pclbaseball.com
P: Branch B. Rickey
Dir. of Oper: George King III

Albuquerque Isotopes
1009 Bradbury Drive SE
Albuquerque, NM 87106
T: (505) 924-2255
F: (505) 242-8899
www.albuquerquebaseball.com
E: info@albuquerquebaseball.com
GM: Mel Kowalchuk
Oper: Drew Stewart

Colorado Springs Sky Sox
4385 Tutt Avenue
Colorado Springs, CO 80922
T: (719) 597-1449
F: (719) 597-2491
www.skysox.com
E: info@skysox.com
GM: Bob Goughan
PR: Michael Hirsch

Edmonton Trappers
10233 96th Avenue
Edmonton, Alberta, CAN T5K 0A5
T: (780) 414-4450
F: (780) 414-4475
www.trappersbaseball.com
E: trappers@trappersbaseball.com
GM: Dennis Henke
PR: Gary Tater

Fresno Grizzlies
700 W. Van Ness
Fresno, CA 93721
T: (559) 442-1994
F: (559) 264-0795
www.fresnogrizzlies.com
E: info@fresnogrizzlies.com
GM: Bill Gorman
PR: Chris Metz

Iowa Cubs
350 SW First St.
Des Moines, IA 50309
T: (515) 243-6111
F: (515) 243-5152
www.iowacubs.com
E: sbernabe@iowacubs.com
GM: Sam Bernabe
PR: Brett Dolan

Las Vegas 51's
300 S. 4th Street, Suite 1000
Las Vegas, NV 89101
T: (702) 798-7825
F: (702) 798-9464
www.lv51.com
E: info@lv51.com
GM: Don Logan
PR: Jon Sandler

Memphis Redbirds
175 Toyota Plaza, Suite 300
Memphis, TN 38103
T: (901) 721-6000
F: (901) 527-1642
www.memphisredbirds.com
GM: Dan Madden
PR: Richard Flight

Nashville Sounds
534 Chestnut Street
Nashville, TN 37203
T: (615) 242-4371
F: (615) 256-5684
www.nashvillesounds.com
E: info@nashvillesounds.com
GM: Glenn Yaeger
PR: Doug Scopel

New Orleans Zephyrs
6000 Airline Highway
Metairie, LA 70003
T: (504) 734-5155
F: (504) 734-5118
www.zephyrsbaseball.com
GM: Dan Rajkowski
PR: John Mooney

Oklahoma RedHawks
PO Box 75089
2 S. Mickey Mantle Drive
Oklahoma City, OK 73104
T: (405) 218-1000
F: (405) 218-1001
www.oklahomaredhawks.com
E: info@oklahomaredhawks.com
GM: Tim O'Toole

Omaha Royals
1202 Bert Murphy Drive
Omaha, NE 68107
T: (402) 734-2550
F: (402) 734-7166
www.oroyals.com
E: info@oroyals.com
GM: Doug Stewart
PR: Kevin McNabb

Portland Beavers
1844 SW Morrison
Portland, OR 97205
T: (503) 553-5400
F: (503) 553-5405
www.portlandbeavers.com
E: info@portlandbeavers.com
GM: Mark Schuster
PR: Chris Metz

Sacramento River Cats
400 Ballpark Drive
Sacramento, CA 95691
T: (916) 376-4700
F: (916) 376-4938
www.rivercats.com
E: info@rivercats.com
GM: Gary Arthur
PR: Mike Gazda

Salt Lake City Stingers
PO Box 4108
Salk Lake City, UT 84110
T: (801) 485-3800
F: (801) 485-6818
www.stingersbaseball.com
E: info@stingersbaseball.com
GM: Dorsena Picknell
PR: Michael Weisbart

Tacoma Rainiers
2502 S. Tyler Street
Tacoma, WA 98405
T: (253) 752-7707
F: (253) 752-7135
www.tacomarainiers.com
E: tacomapcl@aol.com
GM: Dave Lewis

Tucson Sidewinders
PO Box 27045
Tucson, AZ 85726
T: (520) 434-1021
F: (520) 889-9477
www.tucsonsidewinders.com
E: mail@tucsonsidewinders.com
GM: Rick Parr
PR: Ryan Elgenbrode

The PCL was formed in 1903.

2002 PCL Championship
Edmonton d Salt lake 3 Games to 1.

Mexican League
Angel Pola 16, Col del Periodista,
Mexico, D.F, C.P. 11220, Mexico
T: 525-557-1007
F: 525-395-2454
www.lmb.com.mx
E: mbl@prodigy.net.mx
P: Raul Gonzalez
PR: Nestor Alba Brito

The Mexican League was formed in 1955 and is a member of the National Association and is a Triple-A league.

Campeche Pirates
Unidad Deportiva 20 de Nov. Local 4
CP 24000, Col. Centro
Campeche, Camp., Mexico
T: (981) 816-6071
F: (981) 816-3807
E: piratasc@prodigy.net.mx
P: Gabriel Escalante Castillo
GM: Maria del Socorro Morales

Cancun Lobstermen
Blvd. Kukulhan Km 16, Zona Hotelera
Segundo Seccion, frente a retorno
Gucumatz, Cancun, Quintana Roo
T: (998) 885-2390
F: (998) 885-0516
P: Francisco Villanueva
GM: Maria Del Carmen Uc Chan

Cordoba Coffeegrowers
Av. 1 Esq. Calle 24 S/N
Cordoba, Veracruz C.P. 94560
Minatitlan, Veracruz, Mexico
T: (271) 716-5411
F: (271) 716-5570
www.cafeterosdecordoba.com.mx
P: Jose Antonio Mansur Galan
GM: Antelmo Hernandez Quirasco

Mexico City Red Devils
Av. Cuauhtemoc #451-101
Col. Piedad Narvarte, CP 03020
Mexico D.F., Mexico
T: (55.563) 9-87-22
F: (55.563) 9-97-22
www.diablos.com.mx
P: Roberto Mansur Galan

Mexico Tigers
Blvd. Diaz Ordaz, #811 Mezzanine A
Plaza Dorada, Col. Anzures,
CP 72530 Puebla, Puebla, Mexico
T: (222) 237-1670
F: (222) 237-01489
www.tigrescapitalinos.com.mx
E: tigres@tigrescapitalinos.com.mx
P: M. Rodriguez
GM: Alfonso Lopez

Monclova Steelers
Cuauhtemoc #1002
Col. Ciudad Deportiva, CP 25750
Monclova, Coahuila, Mexico
T: (866) 636-2334
F: (866) 631-1901
www.acereros.com.mx
P: Alonso Ancira Gonzalez

Monterrey Sultans
Av. Manuel L. Barragan S/N
Estadio Monterrey,
CP 66460, Monterrey,
Nuevo Leon, Mexico
T: (81) 8351-0209
F: (81) 8351-3964
E: sultanesrp@hotmail.com
P: Jose Maiz Garcia

Nuevo Laredo Owls
Degollado 235-G. 2210
Col. Independencia CP 88020
Nuevo Laredo, Tamaulipas, Mexico
T: (867) 712-2299
F: (867) 712-0736
www.tecolotes.com.mx
E: tecolotes@globalpc.net
P: Martin Reyes Madrigal

Oaxaca Warriors
Privada del Chopo No. 105
Fraccionamiento El Choppo
CP 68050, Oaxaca, Oaxaca, Mexico
T: (951) 515-5522
F: (951) 515-4966
www.guerrerosdeoaxaca.com
P: Vincente Perez Avella Villa

Puebla Parrots
Estadio Hermanos Serdan, Unidad
Deportiva 5 de Mayo, Calzada
Zaragoza s/n, CP 72220, Puebla
T: (222) 222-2116
F: (222) 222-2117
www.pericosdepuebla.com.mx
P: Ricardo Henaine Mezher

Reynosa Broncos
Hidalgo Norte 102,
Col. Adolfo Lopez Mateos, CP 88650
Reynosa, Tamaulipas, Mexico
T: (899) 924-1750
F: (899) 924-2695
www.losbroncos.com.mx
E: Broncos1@prodigy.net.mx
P: Mario Antonio Lopez Hinojosa

Saltillo Sarape Makers
Blvd. Nazario S. Ortiz Garza esq.
con Blvd. Jesus Valdez Sanchez
CP 25280, Saltillo, Coahuila, Mexico
T: (844) 416-9455
F: (844) 439-0550
www.saraperos.com.mx
E: aley@grupoley.com
P: Juan Manuel Ley

Tabasco Olmecas
Explanada de la Ciudad Deportiva
Estadio de Beisbol
Centenario 27 de Febrero
Col. Atasta de Serra, CP 86100
Villahermosa, Tabasco, Mexico
T: (993) 352-2787
F: (993) 352-2788
www.tabasco.gob.mx/olmecas
P: Angel del Campo Melo

Union Laguna Cotton Pickers
Calle Juan Gutemberg, S/N,
zona centro, Estadio de la Revolucion
CP 27000, Torreon, Coahuila, Mexico
T: (871) 718-5515
F: (871) 717-4335
www.unionlaguna.com.mx
P: Javier Cavazos Gomez

Veracruz Eagles
Jacarandas Esq. Espana
Fraccionamiento Virginia, CP 94294
Boca Del Rio, Veracruz
T: (229) 935-5004
F: (229) 935-5008
www.rojosdelaguila.com.mx
GM: Rafael Duran

Yucatan Lions
Calle 50 #406-B, Entre 35 y 37
Col. Jesus Carranza
CP 97109, Merida, Yucatan, Mexico
T: (999) 926-3022
F: (999) 926-3631
www.leones.yucatan.com.mx
Presidente: Gustavo Ricalde Duran

2002 Mexican League Series
Mexico City Red Devils d
Mexico Tigers 4 Games to 3.

Class AA Leagues

Eastern League
PO Box 9711
Portland, ME 04104
T: (207) 761-2700
F: (207) 761-7064
www.easternleague.com
E: elpb@easternleague.com
P: William B. Troubh
PR: Joe McEacharn

Akron Aeros
300 S. Main Street
Akron, OH 44308
T: (330) 253-5151
F: (330) 253-3300
www.akronaeros.com
E: info@akronaeros.com
GM: Jeff Auman
PR: Erin Wander

Altoona Curve
PO Box 1029, 1000 Park Ave.
Altoona, PA 16603
T: (814) 943-5400
F: (814) 943-9050
www.altoonacurve.com
E: curvekid@penn.com
GM: Todd Parnell
PR: Robin Wentz

Binghamton Mets
PO Box 598
Binghamton, NY 13902
T: (607) 723-6387
F: (607) 723-7779
www.bmets.com
E: bmets@bmets.com
GM: Bill Terlecky
PR: Scott Brown

Bowie Bay Sox
4101 NE Crain Hwy.
Bowie, MD 20716
T: (301) 805-6000
F: (301) 464-4911
www.baysox.com
E: info@baysox.com
GM: Jon Danos
PR: Dave Collins

Erie Seawolves
110 E. 10th St., PO Box 1776
Erie, PA 16501
T: (814) 456-1300
F: (814) 456-7520
www.seawolves.com
E: seawolves@seawolves.com
GM: John Frey
PR: Steve Glenn

Harrisburg Senators
PO Box 15757
Harrisburg, PA 17105
T: (717) 231-4444
F: (717) 231-4445
www.senatorsbaseball.com
E: hbgsenator@aol.com
GM: Todd Vander Woude
PR: Brad Sparesus

New Britain Rock Cats
PO Box 1718
New Britain, CT 06050
T: (860) 224-8383
F: (860) 225-6267
www.rockcats.com
E: rockcats@rockcats.com
GM: William Dowling
PR: Jeff Dooley

New Haven Ravens
252 Derby Avenue
New Haven, CT 06516
T: (203) 782-1666
F: (203) 782-3150
www.ravens.com
E: info@ravens.com
GM: Adam Schierholz

Norwich Navigators
PO Box 6003
Yantic, CT 06389
T: (860) 887-7962
F: (860) 886-5996
www.gators.com
E: tater@gators.com
GM: Brian Mahoney

Portland Sea Dogs
PO Box 636
Portland, ME 04104
T: (207) 874-9300
F: (207) 780-0317
www.seadogs.com
E: seadogs@portlandseadogs.com
GM: Charlie Eshbach
PR: Chris Cameron

Reading Phillies
PO Box 15050
Reading, PA 19612
T: (610) 375-8469
F: (610) 373-9570
www.readingphillies.com
E: info@readingphillies.com
GM: Chuck Domino
PR: Rob Hackash

Trenton Thunder
One Thunder Road
Trenton, NJ 08611
T: (609) 394-3300
F: (609) 394-9666
www.trentonthunder.com
E: office@trentonthunder.com
GM: Rick Brenner
PR: Dan Loney

The EL was formed in 1923.

2002 EL Championship Series
Norwich d Harrisburg 3 Games to 2.

Southern League
2551 Roswell Road, Suite 330
Marietta, GA 30062
T: (770) 321-0400
F: (770) 321-0037
www.southernleague.com
E: soleague@earthlink.net
P: Don Mincher
PR: Brian Benvie
Dir. Of Adm: Lori Webb

Birmingham Barons
PO Box 360007
Birmingham, AL 35236
T: (205) 988-3200
F: (205) 988-9698
www.barons.com
E: barons@barons.com
GM: Tony Ensor
Asst GM: Jonathan Nelson

Carolina Mudcats
PO Box 1218
Zebulon, NC 27597
T: (919) 269-2287
F: (919) 269-4910
www.gomudcats.com
E: muddy@gomudcats.com
GM: Joe Kremer
Asst GM: Eric Gardner

Chattanooga Lookouts
PO Box 11002, 201 Power Alley
Chattanooga, TN 37401
T: (423) 267-2208
F: (423) 267-4258
www.lookouts.com
GM: Frank Burke
Asst GM: Brad Smith

Greenville Braves
PO Box 16683
Greenville, SC 29606
T: (864) 299-3456
F: (864) 277-7369
www.gbraves.com
E: info@gbraves.com
GM: Steve DeSalvo
Asst GM: Jim Bishop

Huntsville Stars
PO Box 2769
Huntsville, AL 35804
T: (256) 882-2562
F: (256) 880-0801
www.huntsvillestars.com
E: Stars@traveller.com
GM: Bryan Dingo
Asst GM: Cliff Pate

Jacksonville Suns
PO Box 4756
Jacksonville, FL 32201
T: (904) 358-2846
F: (904) 358-2845
www.jaxsuns.com
E: jaxsuns@bellsouth.net
GM: Peter Bragan, Jr.

Mobile BayBears
Hank Aaron Stadium
755 Bolling Bros. Blvd.
Mobile, AL 36606
T: (251) 479-2327
F: (251) 476-1147
www.mobilebaybears.com
E: baybears@mobilebaybears.com
GM: Bill Shanahan
Oper: Travis Toth

Orlando Rays
PO Box 470818
Disney Wide World of Sports
Celebration, FL 34747
T: (407) 938-3845
F: (407) 938-3442
www.orlandorays.com
E: Orays@aol.com
GM: Mike Lukevics
Asst GM: Kevin Reynolds

Tennessee Smokies
3540 Line Drive
Kodak, TN 37764
T: (865) 286-2300
F: (865) 523-9913
www.smokiesbaseball.com
E: info@smokiesbaseball.com
GM: Brian Cox
Asst GM: Mark Seamen

West Tennessee Diamond Jaxx
4 Fun Place
Jackson, TN 38305
T: (731) 664-2020
F: (731) 988-5246
www.diamondjaxx.com
E: baseball@diamondjaxx.com
GM: Jeff Parker
Asst GM: Brian Cheever

2002 SL Championship
Birmingham d Jacksonville
3 Games to 0.

2003 SL All Star Game
July 8, 2003 Jacksonville, FL

The original Southern League ran from 1885-1899. The Southern Association 1901-1961, with the modern day league, 1964-present.

Texas League
2442 Facet Oak
San Antonio, TX 78232
T: (210) 545-5297
F: (210) 545-5298
www.texas-league.com
E: tkayser@iamerica.cvnet
P: Tom Kayser

The original Texas League was formed in 1888.

Arkansas Travelers
PO Box 55066
Little Rock, AR 72215
T: (501) 664-1555
F: (501) 664-1834
www.travs.com
E: travs@aristotle.com
GM: Bill Valentine
Asst GM: Hap Seliga

El Paso Diablos
9700 Gateway North Blvd.
El Paso, TX 79924
T: (915) 755-2000
F: (915) 757-0671
www.diablos.com
E: tickets@diablos.com
GM: Andrew Wheeler
PR: Rose Lucerno

Frisco Roughriders
7725 Gaylord Pkwy.
Frisco, TX 75034
T: (972) 731-9200
F: (972) 731-7455
www.ridersbaseball.com
E: info@ridersbaseball.com
GM: Mike McCall
PR: Shellie Johnson

Midland Rouckhounds
PO Box 51187
Midland, TX 79710-1187
T: (915) 683-4251
F: (915) 683-0994
www.midlandrockhounds.org
E: rockhounds@rouckhounds.org
GM: Monty Hoppel
PR: Jamie Richardson

Round Rock Express
PO Box 5309
Round Rock, TX 78683
T: (512) 255-2255
F: (512) 255-1558
www.roundrockexpress.com
GM: Jay Miller
PR: J.J. Gottsch

San Antonio Missions
5757 W. U.S. Hwy. 90
San Antonio, TX 78227
T: (210) 675-7275
F: (210) 670-0001
www.samissions.com
GM: Burl Yarbrough
PR: Jim White

Tulsa Drillers
4802 E. 15th Street
Tulsa, OK 74112
T: (918) 744-5998
F: (918) 747-3267
www.tulsadrillers.com
E: mail@tulsadrillers.com
GM: Chuck Lamson
PR: Brian carroll

Wichita Wranglers
PO Box 1420
Wichita, KS 67201
T: (316) 267-3372
F: (316) 267-3382
www.wichitawranglers.com
E: wranglers@wichitawranglers.com
GM: Steve Shaad
Asst GM: Chris Taylor

2002 Texas League Championship
San Antonio d Tulsa 4 Games to 3.

2003 TX League All Star Game
June 16, 2003 Wichita, KS

Class A Leagues

2003 California League/Carolina League All Star Game
June 24, 2003
Rancho Cucamonga, California

California League
2380 S. Bacom Ave., Suite 200
Campbell, CA 95008
T: (408) 369-8038
F: (408) 369-1409
www.californialeague.com
E: mail@californialeague.com
P: Joe Gagliardi
League Admin: Kathleen Kelly

Bakersfield Blaze
4009 Chester Avenue
Bakersfield, CA 93301
T: (661) 322-1363
F: (661) 322-6199
www.bakersfieldblaze.com
E: blaze1@bakersfiledblaze.com
GM: Jack Patton
PR: Doug Brackett

High Desert Mavericks
12000 Stadium Road
Adelanto, CA 92301
T: (760) 246-6287
F: (760) 246-3197
www.hdmavs.com
E: mavsinfo@hdmavs.com
GM: Brent Miles
PR: Stacy Maffei

Inland Empire 66ers
280 South E Street
San Bernardino, CA 92401
T: (909) 888-9922
F: (909) 888-5251
www.stampedebaseball.com
E:staff@stampedebaseball.com
GM: Dave Oldham
PR: Jason Ratliff

Lake Elsinore Storm
500 Diamond Drive
Lake Elsinore, CA 92530
T: (909) 245-4487
F: (909) 245-0305
www.stormbaseball.com
E: lestorm@pe.net
GM: Dave Oster
PR: Molly Stockwell

Lancaster Jethawks
45116 Valley Central Way
Lancaster, CA 93536
T: (661) 726-5400
F: (661) 726-5406
www.jethawks.com
E: ljethawks@qnet.com
GM: Mark Helminiak
PR: Bruce Battle

Modesto A's
PO Box 883
Modesto, CA 95353
T: (209) 572-4487
F: (209) 572-4490
www.modestoathletics.com
E: modestoa@aol.com
GM: Greg Coleman
PR: Adam Fox

Rancho Cucamonga Quakes
PO Box 4139
Rancho Cucamonga, CA 91729
T: (909) 481-5000
F: (909) 481-5005
www.rcquakes.com
E: quakewin@aol.com
GM: Pat Filippone
PR: Ron Buska

San Jose Giants
PO Box 21727
San Jose, CA 95151
T: (408) 297-1435
F: (408) 297-1453
www.sjgiants.com
E: sanjose-giants@mindspring.com
GM: Mark Wilson
PR: Dave Moudry

Stockton Ports
PO Box 8365
Stockton, CA 95208
T: (209) 644-1900
F: (209) 644-1931
www.mudville.com
E: casey@mudville.com
GM: John Katz
PR: Phil Elson

Visalia Oaks
440 N. Giddings
Visalia, CA 93291
T: (559) 625-0480
F: (559) 739-7732
E: visoak@aol.com
GM: Jennifer Whitcley

The California League began in 1941-1942, returning in 1946 after WW II.

2002 California League Final
Stockton Ports d *Lake Elsinore Storm 3 Games to 1.*

Carolina League
PO Box 9503
Greensboro, NC 27429
T: (336) 691-9030
F: (336) 691-9070
www.carolinaleague.com
E: office@carolinaleague.com
P: John Hopkins
Adm Asst: Marnee Larkins

Frederick Keys
PO Box 3169
Frederick, MD 21705
T: (301) 662-0013
F: (301) 662-0018
www.frederickkeys.com
E: info@frederickkeys.com
GM: Joe Pinto
PR: Heather Clabaugh

Kinston Indians
PO Box 3542
Kinston, NC 28502
T: (252) 527-9111
F: (252) 527-0498
www.kinstonindians.com
E: info@kinstonindians.com
GM: North Johnson
Asst GM: John Purvis

Lynchburg Hillcats
PO Box 10213
Lynchburg, VA 24506
T: (434) 528-1144
F: (434) 846-0768
www.lynchburg-hillcats.com
E: hillcatsbb@aol.com
GM: Paul Sunwall
Asst GM: Ronnie Roberts

Myrtle Beach Pelicans
1251 21st Avenue North
Myrtle Beach, SC 29577
T: (843) 918-6001
F: (843) 918-6002
www.myrtlebeachpelicans.com
E: info@myrtlebeachpelicans.com
GM: Matt O'Brien
PR: Bryan Dolgin

Potomac Canons
PO Box 2148
Woodbridge, VA 22193
T: (703) 590-2311
F: (703) 590-5716
www.potomaccannons.com
E: canonswin@aol.com
GM: Max Baker
PR: Mike Antonellis

Salem Avalanche
PO Box 842
Salem, VA 24153
T: (540) 389-3333
F: (540) 389-9710
www.salemavalanche.com
E: info@salemavalanche.com
GM: Stan Macko
Asst GM: Christian Carlson

Wilmington Blue Rocks
801 S. Madison Street
Wilmington, DE 19801
T: (302) 888-2015
F: (302) 888-2032
www.bluerocks.com
E: info@bluerocks.com
GM: Chris Kemple
PR: Mark Nasser

Winston-Salem Warthogs
PO Box 4488
Winston-Salem, NC 27115
T: (336) 759-2233
F: (336) 759-2042
www.warthogs.com
E: warthogs@warthogs.com
GM: Peter Fisch
Asst GM: David Beal

The Carolina League began in 1945.

2002 Carolina Mills Cup Finals
Lynchburg d *Kinston 3 Games to 1.*

Florida State League

PO Box 349
Daytona Beach, FL 32115
T: (386) 252-7479
F: (386) 252-7495
www.FSLbaseball.com
E: Bballleague@mindspring.com
P: Chuck Murphy
Office Sec: Peggy Catigano

The FSL was formed in 1919.

Brevard County Manatees
5800 Stadium Parkway
Melbourne, FL 32940
T: (321) 633-9200
F: (321) 633-9210
www.bcmanatees.com
E: mparkinson@flamarlins.com
GM: Andy Dunn
PR: Pat Hernan

Clearwater Phillies
PO Box 10336
Clearwater, FL 33757
T: (727) 441-8638
F: (727) 447-3924
www.clearwaterphillies.com
GM: John Cook
PR: Andy Shenk

Daytona Cubs
105 E. Orange Avenue
Daytona Beach, FL 32115
T: (386) 257-3172
F: (386) 257-3382
www.daytonacubs.com
E: dcubs@bellsouth.net
GM: Buck Rogers
Adm Asst: Kim Davis

Dunedin Blue Jays
PO Box 957
Dunedin, FL 34697
T: (727) 733-9302
F: (727) 734-7661
www.dunedinbluejays.com
GM: Ken Carson

Fort Myers Miracle
14400 Six Mile Cypress Pkwy.
Fort Myers, FL 33912
T: (239) 768-4210
F: (239) 768-4211
www.miraclebaseball.com
E: miracle@miraclebaseball.com
GM: David Burke
PR: Rob Malec

Lakeland Tigers
PO Box 90187
Lakeland, FL 33804
T: (863) 688-7911
F: (863) 688-9589
www.lakeland-tigers.com
E: tigers@lakelandtigers.com
GM: Todd Pund
PR: Zach Burek

Palm Beach Cardinals
PO Box 8929
4751 Main Street
Jupiter, FL 33468
T: (561) 775-1818
F: (561) 691-6886
www.rogerdeanstadium
GM: Chris Easom
Asst GM: Carole Ray Dixon

St. Lucie Mets
525 NW Peacock Blvd.
Port St. Lucie, FL 34986
T: (772) 871-2100
F: (772) 878-9802
www.stluciemets.com
E: slmets@gate.net
GM: Paul Taglieri
Mkt: Ari Skalet

Sarasota Red Sox
PO Box 2816
Sarasota, FL 34230
T: (941) 365-4460
F: (941) 365-4217
www.sarasox.com
E: sarasox@acun.com
GM: Todd Stephenson

Tampa Yankees
One Steinbrenner Drive
Tampa, FL 33614
T: (813) 875-7753
F: (813) 673-3174
www.legendsfieldtampa.com
E: sarena@yankees.com
GM: Sammy Arena
Asst GM: Eddie Robinson III

Vero Beach Dodgers
PO Box 2887
Vero Beach, FL 32961
T: (561) 569-4900
F: (561) 567-0819
www.vbdodgers.com
E: info@vbdodgers.com
GM: Trevor Gooby

2002 FSL Championship
Charlotte d Lakeland 3 Games to 2.

2003 FSL All Star Game
June 14, 2003 Fort Myers, FL

Midwest League
PO Box 936
1118 Cranston Road
Beloit, WI 53512
T: (608) 364-1188
F: (608) 364-1913
www.midwestleague.com
E: mwl@midwestleague.com
P: George Spelius
Adm: Kristin Oster

The Midwest League was established in 1947.

Battle Creek Yankees
1392 Capital Avenue NE
Battle Creek, MI 49017
T: (269) 660-2287
F: (269) 660-2288
www.battlecreekyankees.com
E: info@battlecreekyankees.com
GM: Tony DeSilveira
Asst GM: Kim Godek

Beloit Snappers
PO Box 855
Beloit, WI 53512
T: (608) 362-2272
F: (608) 362-0418
www.snappersbaseball.com
GM: Brian Schackow
PR: Dave Costello

Burlington Bees
PO Box 824
Burlington, IA 52601
T: (319) 754-5705
F: (319) 754-5882
www.gobees.com
E: staff@gobees.com
beesball@aol.com
GM: Chuck Brockett
PR: Randy Wehofer

Cedar Rapids Kernels
PO Box 2001
Cedar Rapids, IA 52406
T: (319) 363-3887
F: (319) 363-5631
www.kernels.com
E: Kernels@kernels.com
GM: Jack Roeder
Oper: Kelly Davis

Clinton LumberKings
PO Box 1295
Clinton, IA 52733
T: (563) 242-0727
F: (563) 242-1433
www.lumberkings.com
E: lumberkings@lumberkings.com
GM: Ted Tornow
Asst GM: Ben Giancola

Dayton Dragons
PO Box 2107
Dayton, OH 45401
T: (937) 228-2287
F: (937) 228-2284
www.daytondragons.com
P: Robert Murphy
Oper: Gary Mayse

Fort Wayne Wizards
1616 E. Coliseum Blvd.
Fort Wayne, IN 46805
T: (260) 482-6400
F: (260) 471-4678
www.wizardsbaseball.com
E: info@wizardsbaseball.com
GM: Mike Nutter

Kane County Cougars
34W002 Cherry Lane
Geneva, IL 60134
T: (630) 232-8811
F: (630) 232-8815
www.kccougars.com
E: info@kccougars.com
GM: Jeff Sedivy
PR: Marty Cusack

Lansing Lugnuts
505 E. Michigan Avenue
Lansing, MI 48912
T: (517) 485-4500
F: (517) 485-4518
www.lansinglugnuts.com
E: info@lansinglugnuts.com
GM: Greg Rauch
Mkt: Linda Frederickson

Peoria Chiefs
1524 W. Nebraska Ave.
Peoria, IL 61604
T: (309) 680-4000
F: (309) 680-4080
www.peoriachiefs.com
E: info@chiefsnet.com
GM: Rocky Vonachen
PR: Ed Beach

Quad City River Bandits
PO Box 3496
Davenport, IA 52808
T: (563) 324-3000
F: (563) 324-3109
www.riverbandits.com
E: bandit@riverbandits.com
GM: Dave Ziedelis

South Bend Silver Hawks
PO Box 4218
South Bend, IN 46634
T: (574) 235-9988
F: (574) 235-9950
www.silverhawks.com
E: hawks@silverhawks.com
GM: Christian Carlson
Asst GM: Jon Zeitz

West Michigan Whitecaps
PO Box 428
Comstock Park, MI 49321
T: (616) 784-4131
F: (616) 784-4911
www.whitecaps-baseball.com
E: playball@whitecaps-baseball.com
GM: Jim Jarecki

Wisconsin Timber Rattlers
PO Box 7464
Appleton, WI 54912
T: (920) 733-4152
F: (920) 733-8032
www.timberrattlers.com
E: info@timberrattlers.com
GM: Rob Zerjav
Oper: Rob Zerjav

2002 MWL Championship
Peoria d *Lansing 3 Games to 1.*

2003 MWL All Star Game
June 17, 2003 Comstock Park, MI

South Atlantic League
PO Box 38, 504 Crescent Hill
Kings Mountain, NC 28086
T: (704) 739-3466
F: (704) 739-1974
www.southatlanticleague.com
E: SALbaseball@telocity.com
P: John H. Moss
Adm Dir: Elaine Moss

Asheville Tourists
PO Box 1556
Asheville, NC 28802
T: (828) 258-0428
F: (828) 258-0320
www.theashevilletourists.com
E: touristbb@mindspring.com
GM: Ron McKee
Asst GM: Dave Meyer

Augusta GreenJackets
PO Box 3846, Hill Station
Augusta, GA 30914
T: (706) 736-7889
F: (706) 736-1122
www.greenjackets.net
E: grnsox@aol.com
GM: David Van Lenten
Asst GM: Scott Skadan

Capital City Bombers
PO Box 7845
Columbia, SC 29201
T: (803) 256-4110
F: (803) 256-4338
www.bomberball.com
E: info@bomberball.com
GM: Tim Swain
Asst GM: Mark Bryant

Charleston Alley Cats
PO Box 4669
Charleston, WV 25304
T: (304) 344-2287
F: (304) 344-0083
www.charlestonalleycats.com
E: team@charlestonalleycats.com
GM: Tim Bordner
Asst GM: Pat Twchig

Charleston RiverDogs
PO Box 20849
Charleston, SC 29413
T: (843) 723-7241
F: (843) 723-2641
www.riverdogs.com
E: dogsrus@awod.com
P: Mike Veeck
GM: Derek Sharrer

Delmarva Shorebirds
PO Box 1557
Salisbury, MD 21802
T: (410) 219-3112
F: (410) 219-9164
www.theshorebirds.com
E: jterrill@theshorebirds.com
GM: Jim Terrill

Greensboro Bats
510 Yanceyville Street
Greensboro, NC 27405
T: (336) 333-2287
F: (336) 273-7350
www.greensborobats.com
E: thebats@bellsouth.net
GM: Bill Blackwell

Hagerstown Suns
PO Box 230
Hagerstown, MD 21741
T: (301) 791-6266
F: (301) 791-6066
www.hagerstownsuns.com
E: info@hagerstownsuns.com
GM: Kurt Landes
PR: Michael Heckman

Hickory Crawdads
PO Box 1268
Hickory, NC 28603
T: (828) 322-3000
F: (828) 322-6137
www.hickorycrawdads.com
E: crawdad@abts.net
GM: David Haas
PR: Evan Malter

Kannapolis Intimidators
PO Box 64
Kannapolis, NC 28082
T: (704) 932-3267
F: (704) 938-7040
www.intimadatorsbaseball.com
E: info@intimadators.com
GM: Todd Parnell
PR: Buck Rogers

Lake County Captains
PO Box 7129
Eastlake, OH 44095
T: (440) 975-8085
F: (440) 975-8958
www.captainsbaseball.com
E: info@captainsbaseball.com
GM: Mike Edwards
Asst GM: Gary Thomas
PR: Katie Dannemiller

Lakewood Blueclaws
725 Airport Road
Lakewood, NJ 08701
T: (732) 901-7000
F: (732) 901-3967
www.lakewoodblueclaws.com
E: info@lakewoodblueclaws.com
GM: Geoff Brown
PR: Don Laney

Lexington Legends
PO Box 11458
Lexington, KY 40575
T: (859) 252-4487
F: (859) 252-0747
www.lexingtonlegends.com
E: alanm803@lexprobaseball.com
GM: Brad Redmon
PR: Tom Kenney

Rome Braves
PO Box 5515
Rome, GA 30162
T: (706) 368-9388
F: (706) 368-6525
www.romebraves.com
E: info@romebraves.com
P: Stan Kasten
GM: Michael Dunn

Savannah Sand Gnats
PO Box 3783
Savannah, GA 31414
T: (912) 351-9150
F: (912) 352-9722
www.sandgnats.com
E: gnatfans@aol.com
GM: Ken Shepard
PR: David Maloney

South Georgia Waves
1130 Ballpark Lane
Albany, GA 31705
T: (229) 420-5924
F: (229) 420-5925
www.sgwaves.com
E: info@sgwaves.com
GM: Gerry McKearney
Asst GM: Dean Sisler
PR: Tim Becwair

The Sally has operated from 1948-1952, then reorganizing in 1960 to the present.

2002 SAL Championship
Hickory Crawdads d Columbus Redstixx 3 Games to 2.

2003 Sally All Star Game
June 24, 2003 Lexington, KY

Short Season Class A

New York-Penn League
9410 International Court N.
St. Petersburg, FL 33716
T: (727) 576-6300
F: (727) 576-6307
www.minorleaguebaseball.com
E: NYPenn@attglobal.net
President: Ben Hayes
League Admin: Debbie Carlisle

Aberdeen Ironbirds
Ripken Stadium
873 Gilbert Road
Aberdeen, MD 21001
T: (410) 297-9292
F: (410) 297-6653
www.ironbirdsbaseball.com
www.ripkenbaseball.com
E: info@ripkenbaseball.com
P: Cal Ripken, Jr.
GM: Jeff Eiseman
PR: Steve Spadafino

Auburn Doubledays
130 N. Division Street
Auburn, NY 13021
T: (315) 255-2489
F: (315) 255-2675
www.auburndoubledays.com
E: auburndd@relex.com
GM: Tony Flores
PR: Kelle Renninger

Batavia MuckDogs
Dwyer Stadium, 299 Bank St.
Batavia, NY 14020
T: (585) 343-5454
F: (585) 343-5620
www.muckdogs.com
E: brrc@muckdogs.com
GM: Paul Marriott
PR: Adam Gerstenhaber

Brooklyn Cyclones
PO Box 608, 1904 Surf Ave.
Brooklyn, NY 11224
T: (718) 449-8497
F: (718) 449-6368
www.brooklyncyclones.com
E: info@brooklyncyclones.com
GM: Steve Cohen
PR: Dave Campanaro

Hudson Valley Renegades
PO Box 661
Fishkill, NY 12524
T: (845) 838-0094
F: (845) 838-0014
www.hvrenegades.com
E: info@hvrenegades.com
GM: Steve Gliner

Jamestown Jammers
PO Box 638
Jamestown, NY 14702
T: (716) 664-0915
F: (716) 664-4175
www.jamestownjammers.com
E: email@jamestownjammers.com
GM: Dave Wellenzohn

Lowell Spinners
450 Aiken Street, PO Box 778
Lowell, MA 01854
T: (978) 459-2255
F: (978) 459-1674
www.lowellspinners.com
E: generalinfo@lowellspinners.com
GM: Shawn Smith

Mahoning Valley Scrappers
PO Box 1357
Niles, OH 44446-1357
T: (330) 505-0000
F: (330) 505-9669
www.mvscrappers.com
E: mvscrappers@cboss.com
GM: Andy Milovich

New Jersey Cardinals
94 Championship Place, Suite 2
Augusta, NJ 07822
T: (973) 579-7500
F: (973) 579-7502
www.njcards.com
E: office@njcards.com
GM: Tony Torre
Asst GM: Herm Sorchar

Oneonta Tigers
95 River Street
Oneonta, NY 13820
T: (607) 432-6266
F: (607) 432-1965
www.oneontatigers.com
E: naderas@telenet.net
GM: Sam Nader
PR: Alice O' Conner

Staten Island Yankees
75 Richmond Terrace
Staten Island, NY 10301
T: (718) 720-9265
F: (718) 273-5763
www.siyanks.com
E: siyanks@siyanks.com
GM: Jeff Dumas
Asst GM: Jane Rogers

Tri-City ValleyCats
PO Box 694
Troy, NY 12181
T: (516) 283-4849
F: (516) 629-2299
www.tcvalleycats.com
E: info@tcvalleycats.com
GM: Richard Murphy

Vermont Expos
1 Main Street, Suite 4
Winooski, VT 05404
T: (802) 655-4200
F: (802) 655-5660
www.vermontexpos.com
E: mail@vermontexpos.com
GM: C.J. Knudsen
PR: Adrienne Wilson

Williamsport Crosscutters
PO Box 3173
Williamsport, PA 17701
T: (570) 326-3389
F: (570) 326-3494
www.crosscutters.com
E:mail@crosscutters.com
GM: Doug Estes
PR: Gabe Sinicropi

The NYP Lg. began in 1939.

2002 NY-Penn Championship
*Staten Island Yankees d Oneonta
Tigers 2 Games to 0.*

Northwest League
PO Box 1645
Boise, ID 83701
T: (208) 429-1511
F: (208) 429-1525
www.minorleaguebaseball.com
E: bobrichmond@worldnet.att.net
President: Bob Richmond

Boise Hawks
888 N. Cole Road
Boise, ID 83704
T: (208) 322-5000
F: (208) 658-9808
www.diamondsportsworld.com/hawks
E: gmbhawks@aol.com
GM: Jeff Walker
PR: Jack Cernefix

Eugene Emeralds
PO Box 5566
Eugene, OR 97405
T: (541) 342-5367
F: (541) 342-6089
www.go-ems.com
E: ems@go-ems.com
GM: Bob Beban
Asst GM: Mark Ruckwardt

Everett AquaSox
3802 Broadway
Everett, WA 98201
T: (425) 258-3673
F: (425) 258-3675
www.aquasox.com
E: aquasox@aquasox.com
GM: Mark Sperandio
Mkt: Brian Sloan

Salem-Keizer Volcanoes
PO Box 20936
Keizer, OR 97303
T: (503) 390-2225
F: (503) 390-2227
www.volcanoesbaseball.com
E: probasebal@aol.com
GM: Jerry Walker
PR: Pat Lafferty

Spokane Indians
PO Box 4758
Spokane, WA 99202
T: (509) 535-2922
F: (509) 534-5368
www.spokaneindiansbaseball.com
E: mail@spokaneindiansbaseball.com
GM: Paul Barbeau

Tri-City Dust Devils
6200 Burden Road
Pasco, WA 99301
T: (509) 544-8789
F: (509) 545-8064
www.dustdevilsbaseball.com
E: info@dustdevilsbaseball.com
GM: Brian Rogers

Vancouver Canadians
4601 Ontario Street
Vancouver, BC V5V 3H4 Canada
T: (604) 872-5232
F: (604) 872-1714
www.canadiansbaseball.com
E: staff@canadiansbaseball.com
GM: Jason Rowland

Yakima Bears
PO Box 483, 8 N. 2nd St.
Yakima, WA 98907
T: (509) 457-5151
F: (509) 457-9909
www.yakimabears.com
E: info@yakimabears.com
GM: Bob Romero
Off Mgr: De Anne Munson

The NWL organized in 1901-1922, reorganized in 1937-1942, & again in 1946 after WWII to the present.

2002 NWL Championship
Boise Hawks d Everett Aqua Sox 3 Games to 0.

Rookie Advanced Class

Appalachian League
283 Deerchase Circle
Statesville, NC 28625
T: (704) 873-5300
F: (704) 873-4333
www.minorleaguebaseball.com
E: appylg@directway.com
President: Lee Landers
Adm Asst: Bobbi Landers

The Appalachian was formed in 1921-1925, reorganized in 1937-1955 & 1957 to the present.

Bluefield Orioles
PO Box 356, Stadium Drive
Bluefield, WV 24701
T: (540) 326-1326
F: (540) 326-1318
www.bluefieldorioles.com
E: babybirds@inetone.net
GM: George McGonagle
Asst GM: Kim Long

Bristol White Sox
PO Box 1434, 40 Cherry Lane
Bristol, VA 24203
T: (540) 669-6859
F: (540) 669-7686
www.3wave.com/brisox
E: bwsox@3wave.com
P: Boyce Cox
GM: Bob Childress

Burlington Indians
PO Box 1143
Burlington, NC 27216
T: (336) 222-0223
F: (336) 226-2498
www.burlingtonindians.com
E: bindians@aol.com
GM: Mark Cryan

Danville Braves
PO Box 378
Danville, VA 24543
T: (804) 797-3792
F: (804) 797-3799
www.danvillebraves.com
E: dbraves@gamewood.net
GM: Dave Cross

Elizabethton Twins
136 S. Sycamore Street
Elizabethton, TN 37643
T: (423) 547-6440
F: (423) 547-6442
E: elztwin@preferred.com
President: Harold Mains
GM: Mike Mains

Johnson City Cardinals
PO Box 17
Johnson City, TN 37605
T: (423) 461-4866
F: (423) 461-4864
www.jccardinals.com
E: jccardinals@worldnettatt.net
GM: Vance Spinks
Mkt: Lori Weigel

Kingsport Mets
PO Box 1128
Kingsport, TN 37662
T: (423) 378-3744
F: (423) 392-8538
www.kmets.com
E: kingsportmets@aol.com
GM: Myra Mc Entire

Martinsville Astros
PO Box 3614
Martinsville, VA 24115
T: (540) 666-2000
F: (540) 666-2139
E: mastros@kimbanet.com
GM: Charlie Norton
Asst GM: Rachel Byrd

Princeton Devil Rays
PO Box 5646
Princeton, WV 24740
T: (304) 487-2000
F: (304) 487-8762
www.princeton-devilrays.com
E: devilrays@inetone.net
GM: Jim Holland

Pulaski Rangers
PO Box 676
Pulaski, VA 24301
T: (540) 980-1070
F: (540) 980-1850
www.pulaskirangers.com
E: info@pulaskirangers.com
P: Tom Compton
Oper: Dave Hart

2002 Appy Championship
Bristol d Bluefield
2 Games to 1

Pioneer League
PO Box 2564
Spokane, WA 99220
T: (509) 456-7615
F: (509) 456-0136
www.pioneerleague.com
E: fanmail@pioneerleague.com
President: Jim McCurdy
Adm Asst: Teryl Mac Donald

Billings Mustangs
PO Box 1553
Billings, MT 59103
T: (406) 252-1241
F: (406) 252-2968
www.billingsmustangs.com
E: mustangs@mustangs.com
GM: Bob Wilson
Asst GM: Gary Roller

Casper Rockies
PO Box 1293
Casper, WY 82602
T: (307) 232-1111
F: (307) 265-7687
www.casperrockies.com
E: baseball@casperrockies.com
GM: Mary Stanley

Great Falls White Sox
PO Box 1621
Great Falls, MT 59403
T: (406) 452-5311
F: (406) 454-0811
www.greatfallswhitesox.com
E: whitesox@greatfallswhitesox.com
GM: Jim Keough

Helena Brewers
PO Box 6756
1300 N. Ewing
Helena, MT 59604
T: (406) 495-0500
F: (406) 495-0900
www.helenabrewers.net
E: info@helenabrewers.net
GM: Paul Fetz

Idaho Falls Padres
PO Box 2183
Idaho Falls, ID 83403
T: (208) 522-8363
F: (208) 522-9858
www.ifpadres.com
E: padres@ifpadres.com
GM: Kevin Greene
Asst GM: Marcus Loyola

Missoula Osprey
137 E. Main Street
Missoula, MT 59802
T: (406) 543-3300
F: (406) 543-9463
www.missoulaosprey.com
E: info@missoulaosprey.com
GM: Matt Ellis

Ogden Raptors
2330 Lincoln Ave.
Ogden, UT 84401
T: (801) 393-2400
F: (801) 393-2473
www.ogden-raptors.com
E: homerun@ogden-raptors.com
GM: Jody Stein

Provo Angels
1 E. Center Street, Suite 205
Provo, UT 84606
T: (801) 377-2255
F: (801) 377-2345
www.provoangels.com
E: info@provoangels.com
GM: John Stein

The Pioneer League has operated from 1939-1942 and following WWII in 1946 to the present.

2002 Pioneer League Final
Great Falls d *Provo 2 Games to 1.*

Rookie Leagues

Arizona League
PO Box 1645
Boise, ID 83701
T: (208) 429-1511
F: (208) 429-1525
E: bobrichmond@worldnet.att.net
P: Bob Richmond

The Arizona League was established in 1988.

Gulf Coast League
1503 Clower Creek Drive, H-262
Sarasota, FL 34231
T: (941) 966-6407
F: (941) 966-6872
P: Thomas J. Saffell

The GCL has been in operation since 1964.

Dominican Summer League
Calle Segundo No. 14, Reparto Antilla
Santo Domingo, Dominican Republic
T: (809) 532-3619
P: Freddy Jana
Adm: Orlando Diaz

The Dominican League began in 1985

Venezuela Summer League
C.C. Caribbean Plaza Modulo 8 P.A.
Local 173-174
Valencia, Carabobo, Venezuela
T: (58.41) 24-0321
F: (58.41) 24-0705
www.venezuelasummerleague.com
Admin: Saul Gonzales
Coord: Ramon Fereira

2002 VSL Championships
Aguirre d San Felipe 2 Games to 0.

U.S. Fall/Winter Leagues

Arizona Fall League
10201 S. 51st Street, Suite 230
Phoenix, AZ 85044
T: (480) 496-6700
F: (480) 496-6384
www.mlb.com
E: afl@mlb.com
Exec. VP: Steve Cobb
Admin Mgr: Joan Mc Grath
Marketing: Larry Mackin

Grand Canyon Rafters
Scottsdale Stadium
7408 E. Osborn Road
Scottsdale, AZ 85251
T: (480) 941-1930
F: (480) 941-3060
GM: Jamie Jeffries

Maryvale Saguaros
3600 N 51st Avenue
Phoenix, AZ 85031
T: (623) 247-2727
F: (623) 247-9087
GM: Tim Martin

Mesa Solar Sox
1235 N. Center St
Mesa, AZ 85201
T: (480) 835-0184
F: (480) 835-0193
GM: Rob Mc Donald

Peoria Javelinas
16101 N. 83rd Avenue
Peoria, AZ 85382
T: (623) 486-2800
F: (623) 486-4366
GM: Mike Mollica

Phoenix Desert Dogs
5999 E. Van Buren
Phoenix, AZ 85008
T: (602) 681-9363
F: (602) 392-0225
GM: Greg Elliot

Scottsdale Scorpions
7408 E. Osborn Road
Scottsdale, AZ 85251
T: (480) 941-1930
F: (480) 941-3060
GM: Larry Mackin

The AZ Fall League was created by MLB, established in 1992.

2002 AFL Championship
Peoria Javelinas d Scottsdale Scorpions 7-1 in Championship Game

Mexican Academy Summer League
Angel Pola No. 16, Col. Periodista
CP 11220, DF, Mexico
T: (525) 577-1007
F: (525) 395-2454

Independent Minor Leagues

Atlantic League
401 N. Delaware Avenue
Camden, NJ 08102
T: (856) 541-9400
F: (856) 541-9410
www.atlanticleague.com
E: atlge@aol.com
Chmn: Frank Boulton
President: Bud Harrelson
Exec. Director: Joe Klein

The Atlantic League begins its sixth season in 2003.

Atlantic City Surf
545 N. Albany Avenue
Atlantic City, NJ 08401
T: (609) 344-8873
F: (609) 344-7010
www.ACSurf.com
P: Ken Sheppard
GM: Mario Perrucci

Bridgeport Bluefish
500 Main Street
Bridgeport, CT 06604
T: (203) 345-4800
F: (203) 345-4830
www.bridgeportbluefish.com
GM: Charlie Dowd
PR: Steve Schoenfeld

Camden Riversharks
Campbell's Field
401 N. Delaware Avenue
Camden, NJ 08102
T: (856) 963-2600
F: (856) 963-8534
www.riversharks.com
E: riversharks@riversharks.com
GM: John Brandt

Long Island Ducks
3 Court House Drive
Central Islip, NY 11722
T: (631) 940-DUCK
F: (631) 940-3800
www.LIducks.com
GM: Michael Hirsch

Nashua Pride
100 Main Street, Suite 1
Nashua, NH 03060
T: (603) 883-2255 (BALL)
F: (603) 883-0880
www.nashuapride.com
P: Chris English
GM: Billy Johnson
Manager: Butch Hobson

Newark Bears
450 Broad Street
Newark, NJ 07102
T: (973) 848-1000
F: (973) 621-0095
www.newarkbears.com
GM: Victor Rojas

Pennsylvania Road Warriors
Will operate as a road team until a stadium is completed for them. Contact league office for club info.

Somerset Patriots
1 Patriots Park
Bridgewater, NJ 08807
T: (908) 252-0700
F: (908) 252-0776
www.somersetpatriots.com
P: Michael Kalafer
GM: David Gasaway
Manager: Sparky Lyle

2002 Atlantic League Series
Newark Bears d *Bridgeport Bluefish*
3 Games to 0.

2003 Atlantic League All-Star Game
July 9, 2003 Nashua, NH

Central League

PO Box 2712
Colorado Springs, CO 87901
T: (719) 520-0060
F: (719) 520-0221
www.centralleaguebaseball.com
E: info@centralleaguebaseball.com
Commissioner: Miles Wolff
BB Operations: Dan Moushon
Bus Operations: Ryan Jamrog

Alexandria Aces
PO Box 6005, 1 Babe Ruth Drive
Alexandria, LA 71307
T: (318) 473-ACES
F: (318) 473-2229
www.acesbaseball.com
E: acesbaseball@centurytel.net
GM: Chet Cary
PR: Ryan Sachs

Amarillo Dillas
PO Box 311241, 501 W 9th
Amarillo, TX 79120
T: (806) 342-3455
F: (806) 374-2269
www.dillas.com
E: baseball@dillas.com
GM: Peggy Reed

Coastal Bend Aviators
1150 E. Main Avenue
Robstown, TX 78380
T: (361) 387-8585
F: (361) 387-3535
www.aviatorsbaseball.com
E: info@aviatorsbaseball.com
GM: George Stavrenos

Edinburg Roadrunners
PO Box 4119
Edinburg, TX 78539
T: (956) 289-8800
F: (956-289-8833
GM: Winston Ayala
www.roadrunnersbaseball.com
E: winstonayala@yahoo.com

Fort Worth Cats
PO Box 4411
Fort Worth, TX 76106
T: (817) 226-2287
F: (817) 534-4620
www.fwcats.com
E: monty.clegg@fwcats.com
P: Marty Scott
GM: Monty Clegg

Jackson Senators
1200 Lakeland Drive
Jackson, MS 39205
T: (601) 362-2294
F: (601) 362-9577
www.jacksonsenators.com
P: Marty Scott
GM: Craig Brasfield

Ozark Mountain Ducks
PO Box 1472
5245 N. 17th Street
Ozark, MO 65721
T: (417) 581-2868
F: (417) 581-8342
www.mountainducksbaseball.com
E: info@ozarkducksbaseball.com
GM: Brad Eldridge
PR: Jim Metcalf

Rio Grande Valley WhiteWings
1216 Fair Park Blvd.
Harlingen, TX 78550
T: (956) 412-9464
F: (956) 412-9479
www.rgvwhitewings-com
E: homerun@rgvwhitewings-com
GM: Jason Driskell

San Angelo Colts
1600 University Avenue
San Angelo, TX 76904
T: (915) 94-COLTS (942-6587)
F: (915) 947-9480
www.sanangelocolts.com
E: colts@wcc.net
GM: Harlan Bruha

Shreveport Sports Baseball Club
2901 Pershing Blvd.
Shreveport, LA 71109
T: (318) 636-5555
F: (318) 636-5670
www.shreveportbaseballclub.com
E:
GM: Brian Viselli

The Central League, formerly the Tx-LA League began in 1994.

2002 Central League Championship
San Angelo d Jackson 3 Games to 2.

2003 Central League All-Star Game
July 14, 2003 Edinburg, TX

Frontier League
PO Box 2662
Zanesville, OH 43702
T: (740) 452-7400
F: (740) 452-2999
www.FrontierLeague.com
E: office@frontierleague.com
Commissioner: Bill Lee

The Frontier League was formed In 1993.

Chillicothe Paints
59 N. Paint Street
Chillicothe, OH 45601
T: (740) 773-8326
F: (740) 773-8338
www.chillicothepaints.com
E: paints@bright.net
GM: Bryan Wickline

Cook County Cheetahs
13152 S. Cicero Ave., Suite 281
Crestwood, IL 60445
T: (708) 489-2255
F: (708) 489-2999
www.cookcocheetahs.com
E: cheetahsbaseball@aol.com
GM: Chuck Heeman

Evansville Otters
PO Box 3565
1701 N. Main Street
Evansville, IN 47734
T: (812) 435-8686
F: (812) 435-8688
www.evansville.net/~ottersbb
E:Ottersbb@evansville.net
GM: Jim Miller

Florence Freedom
20 N. High Street
Hamilton, OH 45011
T: (513) 894-4487
F: (513) 894-5005
www.freedombaseball.com
E: freedombaseball@aol.com
GM: Jeff Hollis

Gateway Grizzlies
2301 Grizzlie Bear Blvd.
Sauget, IL 62206
T: (618) 337-3000
F: (618) 332-3625
www.gatewaygrizzlies.com
E: tfunderburg@gatewaygrizzlies.com
GM: Tony Funderburg

Kalamazoo Kings
252 Mills Street
Kalamazoo, MI 49001
T: (269) 388-8326
F: (269) 388-8333
www.kalamazookings.com
E: info@kalamazookings.com
GM: Joe Rosenhagen

Kenosha Mammoths
7817 Sheridan Road
Kenosha, WI 53143
T: (262) 925-8888
F: (262) 925-1254
www.
E:
GM: Bill Larsen

Mid Missouri Mavericks
810 E. Walnut
Columbia, MO 65201
T: (573) 256-4004
F: (573) 256-4003
www.midmissourimavericks.com
E: info@midmissourimavericks.com
GM: Pat Daly

Richmond Roosters
201 NW 13th Street
Richmond, IN 47374
T: (765) 935-7529
F: (765) 962-7047
www.richmondroosters.com
E: staff@richmondroosters.com
GM: Deanna Beaman

River City Rascals
PO Box 662
O'Fallon, MO 63366
T: (636) 240-2287
T: (888) 762-BATS
F: (636) 240-7313
www.rivercityrascals.com
E: info@rivercityrascals.com
GM:Matt Jones

Rockford RiverHawks
Marinelli Field
101 15th Avenue
Rockford, IL 61104
T: (815) 964-BALL (2255)
F: (815) 964-2462
www.rockfordriverhawks.com
E: playball@rockfordriverhawks.com
GM: Mike Babcock

Washington Wild Things
Washington Crown Center, Ste 666
1500 W. Chestnut Street
Washington, PA 15301
T: (724) 250-9555
F: (724) 250-2333
www.washingtonwildthings.com
E: cblaine@washingtonwildthings.com
GM: Ross Vecchio

2002 Frontier Championship
Richmond Roosters d *Washington Wild Things 3 Games to 1.*

2003 All Star Game
July 16, 2003 Gateway Grizzlies home park

Northern League
3220 North Freeway, Suite 100
Fort Worth, TX 76111
T: (817) 378-9898
F: (817) 378-9805
www.northernleague.com
E: sgates@northernleague.com
Commissioner: Mike Stone
P: Dan Moushon
PR: Stephen Gates
Oper: Mike Marshall

Fargo-Moorhead Redhawks
PO Box 5258
Fargo, ND 58105
T: (701) 235-6161
F: (701) 297-9245
www.fmredhawks.com
E: redhawks@fmredhawks.com
GM: Lee Schwartz

Gary Southshore Railcats
201 E. Fifth Avenue
Gary, IN 46402
T: (219) 882-2255
F: (219) 882-2259
www.railcatsbaseball.com
E: railcatsbaseball@aol.com
P: Mike Tatoian
VP/GM: Roger Wexelberg

Joliet Jackhammers
55 N. Ottawa Street
Joliet, IL 60432
T: (815) 726-2255
F: (815) 726-9223
www.jackhammerbaseball.com
E: info@jackhammerbaseball.com
GM: Steve Malliet

KC T-Bones
PO Box 12205
Kansas City, KS 66112
T: (913) 328-2255
F: (913) 685-3642
www.kctbones.com
E: batterup@kcnlbaseball.com
GM: Adam Ehlert

Lincoln Saltdogs
403 Line Drive
Lincoln, NE 68501
T: (402) 474-2255
F: (402) 474-2254
www.saltdogs.com
E: info@saltdogs.com
GM: Tim Utrup

St. Paul Saints
1771 Energy Park Drive
St. Paul, MN 55108
T: (651) 644-3517
F: (651) 644-1627
www.saintsbaseball.com
E: funsgood@saintsbaseball.com
GM: Bill Fanning

Schaumburg Flyers
1999 Springsinguth Road
Schaumburg, IL 60193
T: (847) 891-2255
F: (847) 891-6441
www.flyersbaseball.com
E: info@flyersbaseball.com
GM: Rick Rungnitis

Sioux City Explorers
3400 Line Drive
Sioux City, IA 51106
T: (712) 277-9467
F: (712) 277-9406
www.xsbaseball.com
E: siouxcityxs@yahoo.com
GM: George Stavrenos

Sioux Falls Canaries
PO Box 84412
Sioux Falls, SD 57118
T: (605) 333-0179
F: (605) 333-0139
www.canariesbaseball.com
E: canaries@canariesbaseball.com
GM: Brad Seymour

Winnipeg Goldeyes
1 Portage Avenue East
Winnipeg, Manitoba R3B 3N3, CAN
T: (204) 982-2273
F: (204) 982-2274
www.goldeyes.com
E: goldeyes@goldeyes.com
GM: Andrew Collier

The modern day Northern League began in 1993.

2002 Northern League Finals
New Jersey Jackals d Winnipeg Goldeyes 3 Games to 1.

2003 Northern Lg All Star Game
August , 2003 TBA

Northeast League
PO Box 1282
Durham, NC 27702
T: (919) 956-8150
F: (919) 683-2693
www.northeastleague.com
E: info@northeastleague.com
Commissioner: Miles Wolff
P: Dan Moushon

Allentown Ambassadors
1511 Hamilton Street
Allentown, PA 18102
T: (610) 437-6800
F: (610) 437-6804
www.ambassadorbaseball.com
E: info@ambassadorbaseball.com
GM: Tony Quagliata

Bangor Lumberjacks
663 Stillwater Avenue
Bangor, ME 04401
T: (207) 947-1900
F: (207) 947-9900
www.bangorlumberjacks.com
E: info@bangorlumberjacks.com
GM: Curt Jacey

Berkshire Black Bears
PO Box 646
Pittsfield, MA 01201
T: (413) 448-2255
F: (413) 445-5500
www.pittsfieldbaseball.com
E: frontoffice@pittsfieldbaseball.com
GM: Mike Kardamis

Brockton Rox
PO Box 7547
Brockton, MA 02301
T: (508) 587-1660
F: (508) 587-2802
www.brocktonrox.com
E: info@brocktonrox.com
P: Tom Whaley
GM: David Echols

Elmira Pioneers
546 Luce Street
Elmira, NY 14901
T: (607) 734-1270
F: (607) 734-0891
www.elmirapioneers.com
E: pioneers@elmirapioneers.com
GM: John Ervin

New Jersey Jackals
One Hall Drive
Little Falls, NJ 07424
T: (973) 746-7434
F: (973) 655-8021
www.jackals.com
E: njjackals@aol.com
GM: Larry Hall

North Shore Spirit
PO Box 8120
Lynn, MA 01904
T: (781) 592-0007
F: (781) 592-0004
www.northshorespirit.com
E: info@northshorespirit.com
GM: Ben Wittkowski

Quebec Les Capitales
100 rue du Cardinal Maurice Roy
Quebec, Quebec G1K 8Z1 Canada
T: (418) 521-2255
F: (418) 521-2266
www.capitalesdequebec.com
E: baseball@capitalesdequebec.com
GM: Nicholas Labbe

2003 NEL Championship Series

2003 NEL All Star Game
July 29, 2003 Quebec City, Que

Western Baseball League
2481 E. Palo Verde Street
Yuma, AZ 85365
T: (928) 344-7909
F: (928) 344-7912
www.westernbaseball.com
E: office@westernbaseball.com
P: Sam Pepper

As of presstime, the WBL may be inactive for the 2003 season.

Chico Heat
250 Vallombrosa, Suite 200
Chico, CA 95926
T: (530) 343-4328 (HEAT)
F: (530) 894-1799
www.chicoheat.com
GM: Brian Ceccon
PR: Rory Miller

Long Beach Breakers
4700 Deukmejian Drive
Long Beach, CA 90804
T: (562) 987-4487
F: (562) 570-1737
www.breakersbaseball.com
GM: Jerry Schoenfeld
PR: Kimberly Edds
Manager: Steve Yeager

Solano Steelheads
1691 E. Monte Vista Drive
Vacaville, CA 95688
T: (707) 452-7400
F: (707) 452-7410
www.steelheadsbaseball.com
GM: Scott Richardson
PR: Angie Louis

Sonoma County Crushers
5900 Labath Avenue
Rohnert Park, CA 94928
T: (707) 588-8300
F: (707) 588-8721
www.crushersbaseball.com
GM: Bob Fletcher
PR: Steve Wendt

Yuba-Sutter Gold Sox
904 B Street
Marysville, CA 95901
T: (530) 741-3600
F: (530) 741-6658
www.goldsox.com
P: Bob Bavasi
GM: Scott Blackwood

Yuma Bullfrogs
280 S. Main Street
Yuma, AZ 85364
T: (520) 782-3536
F: (520) 782-3911
www.yumafrogs.com
GM: Dave Mc Dowell
PR: Jim Howell

The WBL has folded prior to the 2003 season. The WBL began in 1995.

2002 WBL Championship Final
Chico Heat d Long Beach
3 Games to 1.

Southeastern League
227 Southeast Blvd., Suite 7
Morgan City, LA 70380
T: (985) 385-9195
F: (985) 385-9155
www.southeasternleague.com
E: jgamble@southeasternleague.com
E: ljdupuy_riverbats@cox.net
President: L.J. Dupuy
Commissioner: James Gamble

The SEL enters its 2nd season in 2003.

Baton Rouge Riverbats
PO Box 129
Addis, LA 70710
T: (225) 334-2287 (BATS)
F: (225)
www.brriverbats.com
E:
GM: L.J. Dupuy
PR: Damon Sunde
Mkt: Blake Andrews

Houma Hawks
1520 Division Avenue
Houma, LA 70360
T: (985) 991-9390
T: (866) 334-2957
F: (985) 223-1582
www.houmahawks.com
E: gbrown3@houmahawks.com
E: ncotten@houmahawks.com
Owner: Gus Brown, Jr.
GM: Gus Brown III
Asst GM: Nathan Cotton

Macon Peaches
225 Willie "Smoky" Glover Blvd.
Macon, GA 31202
T: (478) 742-1717
F: (478)
www.maconpeachesbaseball.com
E:
GM: Joe Terry
PR:

Montgomery Wings
120 Madison Avenue
Montgomery, AL 36107
T: (334) 834-2543
F: (334) 834-2544
www.montgomerywings.com
E: wings@montgomerywings.net
P: Charles Cuttone

Pensacola Pelicans
913 Gulf Breeze Pkwy, Suite 36
Gulf Breeze, FL 32561
T: (850) 934-8444
F: (850) 934-8744
www.pensacolapelicans.com
E: rishy@pensacolapelicans.com
GM: Rishy Studer
PR: Becca Smith

Selma Cloverleafs
410 Church Street, Suite A
Selma, AL 36701
T: (334) 875-6232
F: (334)
www.selmacloverleafs.com
E:stevenichols@selmacloverleafs.com
GM: Steven Nichols
PR: Mary Susan Rives

2002 SEL Champions
Baton Rouge Riverbats

Arizona-Mexico League

105 E. San Antonio, Suite 377
El Paso, TX 79901
T: (623) 826-0174
F: (623) 321-7837
www.arizonamexicoleague.com
E: indyproball@aol.com
President: Bob Lipp

The AZ-Mex League begins its inaugural season in 2003.

Bisbee-Douglas Copper Kings
PO Box 535
Bisbee, AZ 85603
T: (520) 432-3220
F: (520) 432-3488
www.copperkingsbaseball.com
E: copperkingsbaseball@msn.com
GM: John Guy
Asst GM: Mark Hebard

Cananea Mineros
T: (645) 340-1390
F: (645) 332-2017
F: (702) 548-8425
www.mineros.net
E: beisboldecannanea@hotmail.com
GM: Espiridion Miranda

Juarez Hawks
T: (915) 204-0693
F: (702) 548-8216
www.halconesbeisbol.com
E: halconesbeisbol@hotmail.com
GM: Alicia Barboza

Nogales Charros

Nogales, AZ
T: (520) 405-0409
F: (520)
www.nogalescharros.com
E: fsfolsom@nogalescharros.com
P: David Delk
GM: Shane Folsom

Women's Baseball League
13938A Cedar Road, Suite 375
Cleveland, OH 44118
T: (416) 788-4535
F: (416)
www.baseballglory.com
E: info@baseballglory.com
P: Justine Siegal
Media:

Winter Leagues

The following winter baseball leagues play an October to February schedule culminating with the Caribbean World Series.

Many past, present & future stars have played in these Caribbean leagues.

Caribbean Baseball Confederation
Frank Felix Miranda No. 1, Naco,
PO Box 21070 y 21416
Santo Domingo, Dom. Republic
T: (809) 562-4737
F: (809) 565-4654
P: Juan Fco. Puello Herrera

2003 Caribbean World Series
Champions
Aguilas de Cibao (Dominican Rep)

The Dominican League

Apartado postal 1246
Santo Domingo, Dom. Republic
T: (809) 567-6371
F: (809) 567-5720
www.beisboldominicano.com
info@beisboldominicano.com
P: Dr. Leonardo Matos

Aguilas Cibaenas
Estadio Cibao, Ave. Imbert
Santiago, Dominican Republic
Mail: EPS B-225, PO Box 02-5360
Miami, FL 33102
T: (809) 575-4310
F: (809) 575-0865
www.lasaguilas.com
P: Winston Lienas

Escogido Lions
Apartado 1287
Santiago, Dominican Republic
T: (809) 565-1910
F: (809) 567-7643
www.escogido.com.do
E: info@escogido.com
P: Daniel Aquino-Mendez

Estrellas Orientales
Av. Lopez de Vega
No. 45 Altos, Ens. Piantini,
San Pedro de Macoris, Dom. Rep.
T: (809) 529-3618
F: (809) 526-7658
E: estrellasdeoriente@hotmail.com
P: Carlos Juan Musa-Hazim

Licey Tigers
Estadio Quisqueya
Apartado postal 1321
Santo Domingo, Dominican Rep.
T: (809) 567-3090
F: (809) 542-7714
www.licey.com
E: licey.club@codetel.net.do
P: Miguel Hedded

Los Azucareros (La Romana)
Estadio Francisco Micheli
La Romana, Dominican Republic
T: (809) 556-4955
F: (809) 550-1550
E: arturo.miguel@codetel.net.do
P: Arturo Gil

Pollos del Cibao
Estadio Julian Javier
San Francisco de Macoris,
Dominican Republic
Mail: EPS No. F-1447
PO Box 02-5301
Miami, FL 33102
T: (809) 588-8882
F: (809) 588-8733
www.pollosbeisbolclub.com
P: Julio Hazim

The Dominican League was formed in 1951 and plays a October to January schedule.

2002 Dominican Champion
Aguilas Cibaenas d Escogido Lions
4 Games to 0.

Mexican Pacific League

Av. Insurgentes No. 847 Sur
Interior 402, Col. Centro
CP 80120 Culican, Sinaloa, Mexico
T/F: (52.667) 761.25.70
www.ligadelpacifico.com.mx
E: ligadelpacifico@imparcial.com.mx
P: Renato Vega Alvarado
GM: Oviel Dennis Gonzalez

The Mexican Pacific League was established in 1958, plays a October-December schedule.

Culiacan Tomatogrowers
Ave. Alvaro Obregon 348 Sur
CP 80200 Culiacan, Sinaloa, Mexico
T/F: (52.667) 713.39.69
www.tomateros.com.mx
E: administracion@tomateros.com.mx
P: Juan Manuel Ley Lopez
GM: Jaime Blancarte

Guasave Cottoneers
Ave. Obregon No. 43
Guasave, Sinaloa, Mexico
T: (52.687) 872.29.98
F: (52.687) 872.14.31
P: Carlos Chavez
GM: Leonardo Ovies

Hermosillo Naranjeros
Blvd. Solidaridad S/N
Col. Pimentel, CP 83188
Hermosillo, Sonora, Mexico
T: (52.662) 260.69.32
F: (52.662) 260.69.31
www.naranjeros.com
P: Enrique Mazon Rubio

Los Mochis Sugarcane Growers
Madero No. 116 Ote, CP 81200
Los Mochis, Sinaloa, Mexico
T: (52.668) 812.86.02
F: (52.668) 812.67.40
P: Mario Lopez Valdez

Mazatlan Deer
Av. Gutierrez Najera No. 821
Col Montuosa, Centro, CP 8200
Mazatlan, Sinaloa, Mexico
T: (52.669) 981.17.10
F: (52.669) 981.17.11
P: Jesus Ismael Barros Cebreros

Mexicali Eagles
Pesqueira No. 401 R, Sur Altos
CP 85800
Navojoa, Sonora, Mexico
T: (52.686) 567.0400
F: (52.686) 567.5129
P: Dio Alberto Murrillo

Navojoa Mayos
Rosales No. 102, Col Reforma
Navojoa, Sonora, Mexico
Mexico, CP 85830
T: (52.642) 422.1433
F: (52.642) 422.8997
P: Victor Cuevas Garibay

Obregon Yaquis
Calle Guerrero y Michoacan
Estadio de Beisbol Tomas Oroz
Gaytan
Ciudad Obregon, Sonora
Mexico, CP 85130
T: (52.644) 413.7766
F: (52.644) 414.1156
P: Jorge Torres

2002 Mexican Pacific Champions
Mochis Sugarcane Growers

Puerto Rican League
PO Box 191852
San Juan, Puerto Rico 00019
T: (787) 765-6285
F: (787) 767-3028
P: Enrique Cruz Colon
Adm: Benny Agosto

The Puerto Rican League plays a October to January schedule.

Bayamon Cowboys
PO Box 1667
Bayamon, Puerto Rico 00960
T: (787) 269-3531
F: (787) 269-3874
P: Carlos Baerga
GM: Candy Maldonado

Caguas Criollos
Apartado 1415
Caguas, Puerto Rico 00726
T: (787) 258-2222
F: (787) 743-0545
P: Jose Guillermo

Carolina Giants
Roberto Clemente Stadium
PO Box 366246
Carolina, PR 00630
T: (787) 643-4351
F: (787) 731-7051
P: Benjamin Rivera
GM: Johnny Ramos

Mayaguez Indians
Apartado 3089, Marina Station
Mayaguez, Puerto Rico 00681
T: (787) 834-6111
F: (787) 834-7480
P: Luis Ivan Mendez

Ponce Lions
Apartado 363148
San Juan, Puerto Rico 00936
T: (787) 848-8884
F: (787) 848-0050
P: Antonio Munoz, Jr.

Santurce Crabbers
Apartado 1077
Hato Rey, Puerto Rico 00919
T: (787) 772-9573
F: (787) 772-9574
P: Reinaldo Paniagua Diaz

The Puerto Rican League was founded in 1938 and has had many past MLB & Negro League stars as its alumni.

2002 Puerto Rican Champions Mayaguez Indians

The Venezuelan League
Avenida Casanova
Centro Commercial El Recreo
Torre Sur, Piso 3, Officinas 36-37
Caracas, Venezuela
T: (58.212) 761-4932
F: (58.212) 761-7661
www.lvbp.com
P: Ramon Guillermo Aveledo

Aragua Tigers
Estadio Jose Perez Colmenares
Calle Campio Elias
Barrio La Democracia
Maracay-Edo, Aragua, Venezuela
T: (58.243) 554-4134
F: (58.243) 253-8655
www.tigresdearagua.com.ve
E: tigres@telcel.net.ve
P: Rafael Rodriguez

Caracas Lions
Edif. Centro Seguros La Paz Mall:
Piso 4 La Pas, Officina N42-C
Caracas, Venezuela 1070
T: (58.212) 238-0691
www.leones.com
P: Ariel Prat

LaGuaira Tiburones
Primera Transversal
Urbanizacion Miramar
Detras del Periferico de Pariata
Maiquetia, Vargas, Venezuela
T: (58.212) 332-5579
F: (58.212) 332-3116
www.tiburones.com
P: Freddy Chacin

Lara Cardinals
Ave. Rotaria, Estadio Antonio Herrera Gutierez
Barquisimeto-Edo.,
Lara, Venezuela 3001
T: (58.251) 442-4543
F: (58.251) 442-8321
www.cardenalesdelara.com
E: cardenal@cardenales.org
P: Adolfo Alvarez

Magallanes Navigators
Centro Comercial Caribbean Plaza
Modulo 8, Piso 1, Local 173
Valencia, Carabobo, Venezuela
T: (58.241) 824-0321
F: (58.241) 824-0705
www.magallanes.com
E: magallanes@telcel.net.ve
P: Juan Jose Avila

Occidente Pastora
Estadio Bachiller Julio Hernandez Molina, Avda. Romulo Gallegos
Aruare, Venezuela
T: (58.255) 622-2945
F: (58.255) 621-8595
P: Enrique Finol

Oriente Caribbeans
Avda. Estadio Alfonso Carrasquel
Off. del Equipo Caribes de Oriente
Centro Comercial Novocentro
Piso 2, Local 2-4
Puerto la Cruz, Anzoategui, Venezuela
T: (58.281) 266-2536
F: (58.281) 266-7054
www.caribesbbc.com
P: Pablo Ruggeri

Zulia Eagles
Ave. 8 Antes, Urb. Santa Rita
Edificio Las Carolinas, Local M-3,
Maracaibo, Zulia Venezuela
T: (58.261) 798-0541
F: (58.261) 798-0579
www.aguilas.com
E: aguizuli@aguilas.com
P: Lucas Rincon

The Venezuelan League was founded in 1946.

2002 Venezuelan Champion

Amateur Baseball

The following summer collegiate leagues are sanctioned members of the NCAA. Most leagues play a June to August schedule with most league champions going to the NBC, AABC & NABF national tournaments.

National Alliance of Collegiate Summer Baseball
3649 Post Road
Warwick, RI 02887
T: (401) 732-2002
F: (401) 732-2025
Executive Director: Thomas Hutton

The NACSB comprises the following leagues: the AZ Summer, Atlantic Collegiate, Cape Cod, Central IL, Great Lakes, Jayhawk, New England, Northeastern, Northwest, San Diego Collegiate & the Shenandoah Valley.

Alaska Baseball League

207 E. Northern Lights Blvd., Ste 106
Anchorage, AK 99503
T: (907) 274-3627
F: (907) 2274-3628
www.goldpanners.com/abl
P: Chuck Shelton
VP/Mkt: Dennis Mattingly

The Alaska League formed in 1974.

Alaska Goldpanners
PO Box 71154
Fairbanks, AK 99707
T: (907) 451-0095
F: (907) 456-6429
www.goldpanners.com
E: todd@goldpanners.com
GM: Don Dennis

Anchorage Bucs
PO Box 240061
Anchorage, AK 99524
T: (907) 561-2827
F: (907) 561-2920
www.anchoragebucs.com
E: admin@anchoragebucs.com
GM: Dennis Mattingly

Anchorage Glacier Pilots
207 E. Northern Lights, Suite 105
Anchorage, AK 99503
T: (907) 274-3627
F: (907) 274-3628
www.glacierpilots.com
E: gpilots@alaska.net
GM: Chuck Shelton

Kenai Peninsula Oilers
PO Box 318, 601 S. Main St.
Kenai, AK 99611
T: (907) 283-7133
F: (907) 283-3390
www.oilersbaseball.com
E: penoilbb@kenai.net
GM: Mike Baxter

Mat-Su Miners
PO Box 113
Sutton, AK 99645
T: (907) 746-2580
F: (907) 746-2579
www.matanuska.com/miners
E: moosewood@alaska.net
P: Bill Bartholomew

Athletes In Action Alaska
777 Columbus Ave., Suite 8M
Lebanon, OH 45036
T: (513) 934-1587
F: (513) 934-1589
www.aia.com
E: aiachris@juno.com
GM: Chris Beck
Will share Goldpanners facility in Fairbanks, Alaska

2002 Alaska League Champion
Alaska Goldpanners

Arizona Collegiate League

995 E. Baseline Rd., Ste. 1024
Tempe, AZ 85283
T/F: (480) 949-4225
President: Jeff Antoon

AZ League founded in 1989.

Atlantic Collegiate League
401 Timber Drive
Berkeley Heights, NJ 07922
T: (908) 464-8042 (Smookler)
F: (908) 234-7036
www.acbl-online.com
E: acbl@vs-inc.com
Commissioner: Bob Pertsas
Sec: Ben Smookler

Delaware Valley Gulls
3223 Saw Mill Road
Newtown Square, PA 19073
T: (215) 662-2089
F: (215) 614-0953
GM: Jim Mullen

Jersey Pilots
401 Timber Drive
Berkeley Heights, NJ 07922
T: (908) 464-8042
F: (908) 234-7036
GM: Ben Smookler

Metro NY Cadets
158-50 90th Street
Howard Beach, NY 11414
T: (718) 978-1000
F: (718) 323-2535
P: Gus Antico

Nassau Collegians
431 Centre Island Road
Oyster Bay, NY 11771
T: (516) 686-7513
F: (516) 626-0750
GM: Bob Hirschfield

Newburgh Generals
625 Shore Acres Drive
Mamaroneck, NY 10543
T: (845) 855-1738
F: (845) 855-1058
P: Ralph Vasami

New Jersey Colts
8 Millbrook Drive
Middletown, NJ 07748
T: (732) 671-0616
E: njcolts@home.com
GM: Bob Hoffman

Quakertown Blazers
105 Mews Drive
Sellersville, PA 18960
T: (215) 258-1175
GM: Todd Zartman

Scranton Red Soxx
RR #6, Box 6403
Moscow, PA 18444
T: (570) 422-3263
F: (570) 422-3586
P: Roger Barren

2002 Atlantic League Champions
New Jersey Colts

Cape Cod League
449 Braggs Lane
Barnstable Village, MA 02630
T: (508) 362-3036
F: (508) 362-4467
www.capecodbaseball.org
E: info@capecodbaseball.org
P: Judy Scarafile
Commissioner: Bob Stead

Bourne Braves
PO Box 822
West Wareham, MA 02576
T: (508) 224-9312
F: (508) 224-7628
www.bournebraves.org
E: braves@capecodbaseball.com
GM: Randy Vacchi

Brewster Whitecaps
PO Box 2349
Brewster, MA 02631
T: (781) 740-0800
E: dpmf@aol.com
GM: Dave Porter

Chatham A's
PO Box 428
West Chatham, MA 02633
T: (508) 945-3841
F: (508) 945-4787
www.chathamas.com
E: cthoms@capecod.net
GM: Charles Thoms

Cotuit Kettleers
PO Box 411
Cotuit, MA 02635
T: (508) 428-3358
F: (508) 420-5584
www.kettleers.com
E: kettleers@hotmail.com
GM: Bruce Murphy

Falmouth Commodores
33 Wintergreen Road
Mashpee, MA 02649
T: (508) 477-5724
F: (508) 561-7643
www.falcommodores.org
E: chuckhs@mediaone.net
GM: Chuck Sturtevant

Harwich Mariners
PO Box 201
Harwich Port, MA 02646
T: (508) 236-2000
F: (508) 432-5357
www.harwichmariners.org
GM: Mike De Anzeris

Hyannis Mets
PO Box 852
Hyannis, MA 02601
T: (508) 420-0962
F: (508) 428-8199
www.hyannismets,org
GM: John Howitt

Orleans Cardinals
PO Box 504
Orleans, MA 02653
T: (508) 255-2237
F: (508) 240-2467
GM: Sue Horton & Margo Beaudy

Wareham Gatemen
71 Towhee Road
Wareham, MA 02571
T: (508) 295-3956
F: (508) 295-8821
www.gatemen.org
GM: John Wylde

Yarmouth-Dennis Red Sox
PO Box 814
South Yarmouth, MA 02664
T: (508) 394-9387
F: (508) 398-2239
E: ydredsox@mediaone.net
GM: Jim Martin

Cape Cod League founded in 1885.

2002 Cape Cod Championship
Wareham Gatemen d Orleans
Cardinals 2 Games to 0.

2003 Cape Cod All Star Game
July 26, 2003 Falmouth, MA

Central Illinois Collegiate League
200 Glasgow Street
Springfield, IL 62702
T: (217) 793-6538
F: (217) 786-2788
www.ciclbaseball.com
E: ron.riggle@llcc.cc.il.us
Commissioner: Ron Riggle

Bluff City Bombers
PO Box 141
Alton, IL 62010
T: (618) 377-7789
F: (618) 377-8040
www.altonweb.com/bombers
E: actjac@hotmail.com
GM: Jack Tracz

Danville Dans
138 E Raymond
Danville, IL 61832
T: (217) 446-5521
F: (217) 442-2137
www.soltec.net/dansbaseball
GM: Rick Kurth

Decatur Blues
3619 Northhaven Ct., #2B
Decatur, IL 62526
T: (217) 424-3608
F: (217) 362-6414
GM: Josh Manning

Quincy Gems
300 Civic Center Plaza, Suite 237
Quincy, IL 62301
T: (217) 223-1000
F: (217) 223-1330
www.quincygems.com
GM: Jeff Jansen

Springfield Rifles
7501 Southport Lane
Springfield, IL 62707
T: (217) 786-2425
F: (217) 786-2788
GM: Claude Kracik

Twin City Stars
907 N. School Street
Normal, IL 61761
T: (309) 452-3317
F: (309) 452-0377
E: duffybass@aol.com
GM: Duffy Bass

The CICL was founded in 1963

2002 CICL Tournament Champion
Decatur Blues

Clark C. Griffith College Baseball League
8010 Crescent Drive, 3 FL
Vienna, VA 22182
T: (703) 760-1684
F: (703) 821-8949
www.clarkgriffithbaseball.org
E: cglbaseball@aol.com
P: Bill Dolan

Arlington Senators
3298 Wilson Blvd.
Arlington, VA 22201
T: (703) 247-3065
F: (703) 247-3070
www.arlingtonsenators.org
GM: Bob Menefee

Baltimore Steam
9716 Red Branch Rd., Suite M
Columbia, MD 21045
T: (800) 641-4487
F: (410) 715-1975
www.baseballfactory.com
E: dana@baseballfactory.com
GM: Dana Burton

Bethesda Big Train
PO Box 30306
Bethesda, MD 20824
T: (301) 652-4019
F: (301) 652-0691
www.bigtrain.com
GM: Elda Hacopian

Fauquier Gators
345 Winchester Street
Warrenton, VA 20189
T: (540) 347-0194
F: (540) 341-3478
www.fauquiergators.com
P: Steve Athey

Germantown Black Rox
841-J Quince Orchard Blvd.
Gaithersburg, MD 20878
T: (301) 527-0640
F: (301) 963-2426
P: Buddy Gibson

Reston Hawks
12606 Magna Carta Road
Herndon, VA 22071
T: (703) 860-4780
F: (703) 860-0143
GM: Frank Fannan

Silver Spring-Takoma Thunderbolts
7110 Maple Avenue
Takoma Park, MD 20912
T: (301) 270-6595
F: (301) 762-3382
www.tbolts.org
P: Dick O'Connor

Vienna Mustangs
2800 Chariton Street
Oakton, VA 22124
(703) 255-6198
F: (703) 519-7208
www.viennamustangs.com
P: Fred Haden

2002 Griffith Champions
Arlington Senators

2003 Griffith All Star Game
July 1, 2003 Bethesda, MD
Shirley Povich Field

Coastal Plain League
4900 Waters Edge Drive, Suite 201
Raleigh, NC 27606
T: (919) 852-1960
F: (919) 852-1973
www.coastalplain.com
E: info@coastalplain.com
P: Pete Bock
Oper: Mark Cryan
Media: Jay Snead

Asheboro Copperheads
PO Box 4425
Asheboro, NC 27204
T: (336) 636-5796
F: (336) 636-5400
E: baseball@asheboro.com
GM: Pat Brown

Durham Americans
PO Box 126
Durham, NC 27702-0126
T/F: (919) 956-9555
P: Jim Nelson
GM: Dan Karlsberg

Edenton Steamers
PO Box 86
Edenton, NC 27932
T: (252) 482-4080
F: (252) 482-2337
www.edentonsteamers.com
GM: Todd Hunter

Fayetteville Swampdogs
PO Box 64691
Fayetteville, NC 28306
T: (910) 426-5900
F: (910) 426-3544
www.fayettevilleswampdogs.com
GM: Curt VanDerzee

Florence Redwolves
PO Box 809
Florence, SC 29503
T: (843) 629-0700
F: (843) 629-0703
GM: Jay Baldacci

Gastonia Grizzlies
PO Box 177
Gastonia, NC 28053
T: (704) 866-8622
F: (704) 864-6122
GM: Clay Batlin

Outer Banks Daredevils
PO Box 1747
Nags Head, NC 27959
T: (252) 441-4889
F: (252) 441-3722
P: Warren Spivey

Peninsula Pilots
1889 W. Pembroke Avenue
Hampton, VA 23661
T: (757) 245-2222
F: (757) 245-8032
www.peninsulapilots.com
GM: Jason Matlock

Petersburg Generals
1981 Midway Avenue
Petersburg, VA 23803
T: (804) 722-0141
F: (804) 722-0142
GM: Mike Germain

Spartanburg Stingers
PO Box 5493
Spartanburg, SC 29304
T: (864) 591-2250
F: (864) 591-2131
GM: Lenny Mathis

Thomasville Hi-Toms
PO Box 3035
Thomasville, NC 27360
T: (336) 472-TOMS
F: (336) 472-7198
GM: Roman Stout

Wilmington Sharks
PO Box 15233
Wilmington, NC 28412
T: (910) 343-5621
F: (910) 343-8932
www.wilmingtonsharks.com
GM: Joe Harrington
Asst GM: John Wilson

Wilson Tobs
PO Box 633
Wilson, NC 27894
T: (252) 291-TOBS (8627)
F: (252) 291-1224
www.tobs.bbnpr.com
GM: Chris Allen
Asst GM: Michael Daniels

The Coastal Plains League was founded in 1997. The original Coastal Plain League was founded in 1937, as a Class D minor league.

The CPL operated until 1941 before a wartime hiatus, returning in 1946, with its final season in 1952.

**2002 Coastal Plain League
Playoff Champions
Outer Banks Daredevils**

*2003 Coastal Plain All Star Game
July 22, 2003 Gastonia, NC*

Cranberry Baseball League
10 Woodlawn Avenue
Holbrook, MA 02343
T: (781) 767-0164
www.cranberryleague.com
E: cranberry.league@worldnet.att.net
Commissioner: Louie Di Tullio

The Cranberry League began in 1960

Braintree Whitesox
48 Cochato Park
Randolph, MA 02368
T: (781) 963-2326
GM: John Mariani

Brockton Tigers
58 N. Bassett Road
Brockton, MA 03401
T: (508) 583-1008
GM: Bob Bonnette

Canton A's
42 Trayer Road
Canton, MA 02021
T: (718) 828-6112
E: canton@cranberryleague.com
GM: Jerry Holtzman

East Bridgewater Royals
492 Central Street
East Bridgewater, MA 02333
T: (508) 378-2738
GM: Bob DeChristopher

Easton Huskies
39 Roundtable Road
North Easton, MA 02356
T: (508) 580-0711
E: huskies@cranberryleague.com
GM: Bob Wooster

Hingham Phillies
10 Liberty Road
Hingham, MA 02043
T: (781) 749-8775
GM: Joe Sullivan, Jr.

Mansfield Red Sox
PO Box 293
Wrentham, MA 02093
T: (508) 384-8763
E: redsox@cranberryleague.com

Norton Knights
7 John F. Kennedy Drive
Norton, MA 02766
T: (508) 222-9021
E: knights@cranberryleague.com
GM: Dan Dennis

Norwood-Canton Reds
12-B Billings Street
Sharon, MA 02067
T: (781) 784-5937
GM: Richard "Red" Conley

Rockland Cardinals
11 Everett Street
Rockland, MA 02370
T: (781) 871-5381
E: crancard@aol.com
GM: Myles Angeley

Sandwich Braves
72 John Ewer Road
Sandwich, MA 02563
T: (508) 830-8466
GM: Bob Coolidge

Wrentham Wrens
842 Upper Union Street
Franklin, MA 02038
T: (508) 520-4500
E: wrens@cranberryleague.com
GM: Ted Novio

*2002 Cranberry League Champion
Rockland Cardinals*

Great Lakes Summer Collegiate League
690 Bunty Station Road
Delaware, OH 43015
T: (740) 368-3738
F: (740) 368-3799
www.greatlakesleague.com
E: rdingles@ccowu.edu
Commissioner: Roger Ingles

Columbus All-Americans
50 Broad Street, Suite 700
Columbus, OH 43215
T: (614) 876-7361
F: (614) 459-1806
GM: Rodney Garnett

Delaware Cows
3800 Criswell Drive
Columbus, OH 43220
T: (614) 451-9863
F: (614) 771-7078
GM: Bruce Heine

Grand Lake Mariners
717 W. Walnut Street
Coldwater, OH 45828
T: (419) 678-3607
F: (419) 586-4735
GM: Wayne Miller

Lake Erie Monarchs
2059 18th Street
Wyandotte, MI 48192
T: (734) 284-6045
F: (734) 285-8193
GM: Ron Cameron

Lima Locos
3700 S. Dixie Hwy.
Lima, OH 45806
T: (419) 991-4296
F: (419) 999-4586
GM: Barry Ruben

Motor City Marauders
4976 Spring Meadow Drive
Clarkston, MI 48348
T: (248) 393-0381
F: (248) 371-0850
GM: Rob Hilliard

Murrysville Mighty Eagles
709 Stonehaven Drive
Greensburg, PA 15601
T: (412) 759-4444
F: (412) 366-2064
GM: Bob Bozzuto

Northern Ohio Baseball Club
14675 Foltz Industrial Pkwy.
Strongsville, OH 44136
T: (440) 871-6638
F: (440) 846-0606
GM: Don Mills

Pittsburgh Pandas
118 Hetherton Drive
Pittsburgh, PA 15237
T: (412) 364-5889
GM: Frank Gilbert

Southern Ohio Baseball Club
Grove E 146, Ohio University
Athens, OH 45701
T: (740) 593-4666
F: (740) 593-0539
GM: Andrew Kreutzer
GM: Brad Kimmel

Stark County Terriers
1019 35th Street NW
Canton, OH 44709
T: (330) 492-9220
F: (330) 492-9236
GM: Greg Trbovich

Youngstown Express
945 Windham Court
Boardman, OH 44512
T: (330) 726-8028
F: (330) 726-6384
GM: Jack Kucek

The Great Lakes League was founded in 1986.

2002 Great Lakes Champions
Northern Oho

2003 Great Lakes All Star Game
July , 2003 TBA

Jayhawk League
5 Adams Place
Halstead, KS 67056
T: (316) 755-1285
T: (417) 667-8308 (PR)
F: (316) 755-1285
Commissioner: Bob Considine
PR: Pat Chambers

Eldorado Broncos
865 Fabrique
Wichita, KS 67218
T: (316) 687-2309
www.eldoradobroncos.com
GM: J.D. Schneider

Elkhart Dusters
PO Box 793
Elkhart, KS 67950
T: (620) 697-2095
www.elkhart.com/dusters
GM: Brian Elsen

Hays Larks
3409 Summer Lane
Hays, KS 67601
T: (785) 628-6703
GM: Frank Leo

Liberal Bee Jays
PO Box 352
Liberal, KS 67901
T: (316) 624-1904
GM: Kim Snell

Nevada Griffons
PO Box 601
Nevada, MO 64772
T: (417) 667-8308
www.ardenteagle.com/nevadagriffons
GM: Pat Chambers

Topeka Capitols
2005 SW Sims Street
Topeka, KS 66604
T: (785) 271-3196
GM: Don Carlile

The Jayhawk League began in 1976.

2002 Jayhawk League Champs
Hays Larks

Mink Baseball League
PO Box 1363
St. Joseph, MO 64502
T: (816) 279-6777
www.MINKbaseball.com
P: Noel Bogdanski
Commissioner: Linden Black
Sec: Jim Hamlin

AIA Baseball
777 Columbus Avenue, Ste 10B
Lebanon, OH 45036
T: (513) 934-1587
GM: Jason Lester
Home Games-Lee Summit, MO

Beatrice Bruins
Box 2
Beatrice, NE 68310
T: (402) 223-3081
GM: Bob Steinkamp

Chillicothe Mudcats
1503 Walnut Street
Chillicothe, MO 64601
T: (660) 646-4424
www.chillicothemudcats.com
GM: GM: Ed Crawford

Clarinda A's
225 E. Lincoln
Clarinda, IA 51632
T: (712) 542-4272
www.clarindaiowa-as-baseball.org
GM: Merle Eberly

Kansas City Sluggers
4108 Wimbledon Drive
Lawrence, KS 66047
T/F: (785) 749-0078
E: BBFreak@msn.com
GM: Dave Bingham

Kearney River Bandits
1809 Regency Drive
Kearney, MO 64060
T: (816) 628-6148
GM: Dan Snyder I

St. Joseph Saints
2219 Agency Road
St. Joseph, MO 64503
T: (816) 232-7964
F: (816) 279-9025
P: Jim Hamlin
GM: Greg Kastner

MINK League (MO, IA, NE, KS) established in 1996.

2002 MINK League Champion St. Joseph Saints

New England Collegiate Baseball League
3649 Post Road
Warwick, RI 02888
T: (401) 732-2002
F: (401) 739-9789
www.necbl.org
E: thutton@ix.netcom.com
P: Fay Vincent
Commissioner: Thomas Hutton

Concord Quarry Dogs
48 Palmer Road
Candia, NH 03034
T/F: (603) 483-0241
www.quarrydogs.org
E: cbarry@dupontgroup.com
GM: Pete Dupuis

Danbury Westerners
37 Grammar School Drive
Danbury, CT 06811
T/F: (203) 744-5874
www.danburywesterners.com
E: mtiani@snet.com
GM: Mario Tiani

Keene Swamp Bats
31 W. Surry Road
Keene, NH 03431
T: (603) 352-5120
F: (603) 352-1860
www.swampbats.com
GM: Vicki Bacon

Manchester Silkworms
16 West Street
Manchester, CT 06040
T: (860) 559-3126
F: (860) 649-8487
www.manchestersilkworms.org
E: slegeski@harthosp.org
GM: Ed Slegeski

Middletown Giants
115 Azalea Drive
Middletown, CT 06457
T: (877) MID-GIANTS
F: (203) 688-3264
www.middletowngiants.com
P: Ronald Lucia
GM: Jeff Clark

Mill City All-Americans
PO Box 218
Chelmsford, MA 01863
T: (978) 251-8852
F: (978) 251-1211
E: mcallamericans@hotmail.com
GM: Harry Ayotte

Newport Gulls
PO Box 777
Newport, RI 02840
T: (877) 774-8557
www.newportgulls.com
P: Dave Dittman

North Adams SteepleCats
PO Box 812
North Adams, MA 01247
T: (413) 664-7227
www.steeplecats.com
GM: Jon Watterson

Riverpoint Royals
PO Box 226
West Warwick, RI 02893
T: (401) 828-6798
F: (401) 823-1119
GM: Dan Sylvester

Sanford Mainers
924 Main Street
Sanford, ME 04073
T: (207) 324-0010
F: (207) 324-2227
E: niles300z@hotmail.com
GM: Tom Niles

Thread City Tides
902 east Street
Andover, CT 06232
T: (860) 463-9530
F: (860) 649-1272
www.tctides.com
E: mona.s.monograms@snet.net
GM: Al Garray

Torrington Twisters
4 Blinkoff Court
Torrington, CT 06790
T/F: (860) 482-0450
www.torringtontwisters.org
P: Pat Power
GM: Kirk Fredriksson

NECBL was founded in 1993.

2002 NECBL Championship
Newport Gulls d *Keene Swamp Bats*
2 Games to 0.

2003 NECBL-Cape Cod League
All-Star Game
July , 2003, TBA

New York Collegiate Baseball League
(After May 15-September)
28 Dunbridge Heights
Fairport, NY 14450
T/F: (585) 223-2328
T/F: (727) 942-9120 (Winter)
www.NYCBL.com
E: ncbl@angelfire.com
Commissioner: Dave Chamberlain
P: Tom Kenney
VP: Jeff DeLutis

The NYL was established in 1978.

Cortland Apples
15 Bellrose Avenue
Cortland, NY 13045
T: (607) 753-4312
F: (607) 753-5979
GM: John Ryder

Geneva Lakers
151 Widmere Road
Rochester, NY 14617
T: (585) 342-6322
P: Sam Rutkowski

Hornell Dodgers
952 Almond Road
Hornell, NY 14843
T: (607) 587-4369
F: (607) 587-4331
GM: Tom Kenney

Newark Raptors
1024 Plain Street
Newark, NY 14513
T: (315) 331-0888
F: (315) 926-1005
www.nraptors.com
P: Nancy Visingard
GM: Amanda Mitchell

Plattsburgh Thunder
17 Carlton Drive
Plattsburgh, NY 12901
T: (518) 561-0046
GM: Terry Meran

Rome Indians
PO Box 4337
Rome, NY 13440
T: (315) 339-0079
F: (315) 793-0498
www.rome-indians.org
GM: Jeff Delutis

Schenectady Mohawks
99 Longmeadow Drive
Delmar, NY 12054
T: (518) 475-1005
F: (518) 458-5457
GM: Bob Bellizzi

Watertown Wizards
645 Ferry Street
Easton, PA 18042
T: (610) 252-7050
F: (610) 252-7607
GM: George Daniels

Wellsville Nitros
398 E. Dyke Street
Wellsville, NY 148955
T: (585) 593-1512
www.wellsvillenitros.com
GM: Dan Russo

2002 NYL Championship
Hornell Dodgers d *Schenectady Mohawks 2 Games to 1.*

Northwoods League
PO Box 482
Rochester, MN 55903
T: (507) 536-4579
F: (507) 289-1866
www.northwoodsleague.com
P: Dick Radatz, Jr.
Exec VP: Jon Olson

Alexandria Beetles
418 3rd Avenue E., Suite 111
Alexandria, MN 56308
T: (320) 763-8151
www.alexandriabeetles.com
E: beetles@alexandriabeetles.com
GM: Ryan Voz

Brainerd Mighty Gulls
PO Box 122, 2011 S. 6th Street
Brainerd, MN 56401
T: (218) 828-8901
F: (218) 828-8902
www.mightygulls.com
GM: John Brabbit

Madison Mallards
The Duck Pond
2920 N. Sherman Avenue
Madison, WI 53704
T: (608) 246-4277
F: (608) 246-4163
www.mallardsbaseball.com
P: Steve Schmitt
GM: Vern Stenman

Mankato Moondogs
310 Belle Street, Suite L10
Mankato, MN 56001
T: (507) 344-8877
F: (507) 344-0871
www.moondogs.com
E: moondogs@moondogs.com
GM: Joe Schwei

Rochester Honkers
PO Box 482
Rochester, MN 55903
T: (507) 289-1170
F: (507) 289-1866
www.rochesterhonkers.com
E: honkers@rconnect.com
GM: Dan Litzinger

St. Cloud River Bats
PO Box 5059, 5001 8th Street N.
St. Cloud, MN 56303
T: (320) 240-9798
F: (320) 255-5228
www.riverbats.com
GM: Scott Schreiner

Waterloo Bucks
PO Box 4124
Waterloo, IA 50704
T: (319) 232-0500
F: (319) 232-0700
www.waterloobucks.com
E: garyrima@cloudnet.com
GM: Gary Rima

Wisconsin Woodchucks
Washington Squ., 300 Third St., L4
Wausau, WI 54402
T: (715) 845-5055
F: (715) 845-5015
www.woodchucks.com
E: info@woodchucks.com
GM: Clark Eckhoff

2002 Northwoods Championship
Waterloo d Brainerd 2 Games to 0.

2003 Northwoods All Star Game
July , 2003 TBA

The Northwoods League was founded in 1994.

Shenandoah Valley Baseball League
58 Bethel Green Road
Staunton, VA 24401
T: (540) 885-8901 (W)
F: (540) 885-2068
www.valleyleaguebaseball.com
E: dmbiery@cfw.com
P: Dave Biery

Covington Lumberjacks
315 W. Main Street
Covington, VA 24426
T/F: (540) 962-7867
www.covingtonlumberjacks.com
E: covjacks@intelos.net
P: Allen Howard

Front Royal Cardinals
PO Box 995
Front Royal, VA 22630
T/F: (540) 635-6498
www.frcardinals.com
E: sminkeen@shentel.net
P: Linda Keen

Harrisonburg Turks
1489 S. Main Street
Harrisonburg, VA 22801
T: (540) 434-5919
www.harrisonburgturks.com
E: hbg-turks@rica.net
GM: Bob Wease

Luray Wranglers
1203 W. Main Street
Luray, VA 22835
T: (540) 743-3338
www.lurraywranglers.com
E: bturner@shentel.net
P: Bill Turner

New Market Rebels
PO Box 902
New Market, VA 22844
T: (540) 740-3173
F: (540) 740-4186
www.shentel.net/nmrebels
E: nmrebels@shentel.net
GM: Bruce Alger

Staunton Braves
14 Shannon Place
Staunton, VA 24401
T: (540) 886-0987
F: (540) 886-0905
www.stauntonbraves.com
E: sbraves@hotmail.com
GM: Steve Cox

Waynesboro Generals
PO Box 615
Waynesboro, VA 22980
T: (540) 942-2474
F: (540) 949-0653
www.waynesborogenerals.com
P: Jim Critzer

Winchester Royals
PO Box 2485
Winchester, VA 22604
T: (540) 667-9227
F: (540) 662-3299
www.winchesterroyals.com
GM: Todd G. Thompson

Valley League established in 1962

2002 Valley League Champion
New Market Rebels d Covington
Lumberjacks 3 Games to 1.

2002 Amateur National Champions (Open Division)

National Baseball Congress
Alaska Goldpanners of Fairbanks

All-American Amateur BB Assn.
Arlington (VA) Senators

AABC Stan Musial (Open)
NW Houston Wildcats

National Amat. Baseball Assn.
Springfield (OH) Giants

Amateur Leagues

Adray Collegiate Baseball League
30432 Glenmuer
Farmington Hills, MI 48018
T: (248) 626-1479
Director: Bob Atkins

Alleghany Mountain Coll. League
151 Beimel Lane
Kersey, PA 15846
T: (814) 885-8480
E: aaaba@key-net.net
P: Roger Beimel

Big State League
PO Box 128, Hwy. 109 S.
New Ulm, TX 78950
T: (409) 992-3351
P: Ray Dungen

California Baseball League
275 Greenlea Place
Thousand Oaks, CA 91360
T: (805) 375-2929
www.eteamz.com/cbl
E: calbseballleague@aol.com

California Coastal Coll. League
4299 Carpinteria Ave., Suite 201
Carpinteria, CA 93013
T: (805) 684-0657
F: (805) 684-8596
E: whc1@mindspring.com
P: Bill Pintard
Director: Christine Wilson

Coal Belt League
8388 Kingston Drive
Newburgh, IN 47630
T: (812) 858-5496
P: Tim Turpin

Colonial Diamond Baseball Assn.
2803 Boving Road
Lancaster, OH 43130
T: (740) 654-3505
P: Eric L. Nelson

Colorado Semi-Pro BB League
10033 W. 30th Street
Lakewood, CO 80215
T: (303) 233-9525
P: Dick Orcutt

Dallas Amateur Baseball Association
2828 Forest Lane, Suite 1147
Dallas, TX 75234
T: (214) 243-2288
P: Jerold Prager

Demopolis Baseball League
Rte. 2, Box 144
Falkville, AL 35622
T: (256) 796-7159
P: Phillip Hill

Eastern Missouri League
2001 Perryville
Cape Girardeau, MO 63701
T: (573) 334-7327
P: Jess Bolen

Federal Baseball League
4655 Rothschild Drive
Coral Springs, FL 33067
T: (954) 344-9026
Commissioner: Jamie Siragusa

Florida Collegiate League
Bollettieri Campus
5500 34th Street West
Bradenton, FL 34210
T: (941) 727-0303
F: (941) 727-2962
P: Tom Pluto

Fort Worth Collegiate Baseball Association
3220 Jane Lane
Fort Worth, TX 76117
T: (817) 838-7190
P: Trae Fowler

Georgia Interstate League
506 N. Patterson Street
Valdosta, GA 31603
T: (912) 242-4649
P: Miles Hannan

Indiana Amateur Baseball League
518 Sunset Drive
Noblesville, IN 46060
T: (317) 773-2769
P: Don Jellison

Long Island Baseball League
1973 Lake End Road
Merrick, NY 11566
T: (516) 379-5453
P: Mike Leiderman

Middle Alabama Baseball League
910 Simmons Circle
Talladega, AL 35160
T: (256) 362-1744
P: George Dye

Mountains Collegiate League Of Vermont
PO Box 206
North Hero, VT 05474
T: (802) 372-4812
P: Walter Page

Northern Baseball League of Vermont
PO Box 424
Saxtons River, VT 05154
T: (802) 869-2020
Commissioner: Dave Moore

North Shore Baseball League
13 Pine Road
Lynn, MA 01904
T: (781) 596-9588
www.nsbl.org
E: fess_22@yahoo.com

Northwest Collegiate BB Lg.
16077 Bales Way
Sherwood, OR 97140
T: (503) 725-5634
F: (503) 725-5610
Commissioner: Reed Rainey
NWCBL founded in 1992.

Puerto Rico Baseball League
Via 64 3-EN 7, Villa Fontana
Carolina, Puerto Rico 00983
P: Angel Delgado

Red River League
1011 Locust Lane
Edmond, OK 73034
T: (405) 348-3733
P: Mark Craft

San Diego Collegiate BB Lg.
948 Jasmine Court
Carlsbad, CA 92009
T: (760) 438-0347
Commissioner: Gerald Clements
SDCBL established in 1984.

South Central Texas League
PO Box 864
Weimar, TX 78962
T: (409) 725-6244
P: Tom Strickland

Southern Collegiate BB League
8429 Castlebay Drive
Charlotte, NC 28277
T: (704) 540-9397
F: (704) 540-9395
www.southerncollegiatebb.com
E: WSScout@aol.com
P: Freddie Davis
Commissioner: H. William Capps, II

Southern Illinois League
505 Country Acres Lane
Eldorado, IL 62930
T: (618) 273-2773
P: David Gilley

Southern Indiana Semi-Pro League
844 19th Street
Jasper, IN 47546
T: (812) 367-1155
P: Rock Emmert

Southwest Collegiate Baseball League
901 N. McDonald, Suite 502
Mc Kinney, TX 75069
T: (972) 562-1334
F: (972) 562-5281
www.scbl.com

Spring-Klein Collegiate Baseball League
6146 Northway Drive
Spring, TX 77389
T: (281) 370-1641
P: Tyrone Caruso

Walter Johnson Kansas League
1324 New York Street
Lawrence, KS 66044
T: (785) 749-3072
P: Richard Todd

Zaragosa Baseball League
6613 Wolfcreek Pass
Austin, TX 78749
T: (512) 288-6561
P: Wayne Elliott

Unlimited Amateur Baseball

The following leagues are considered open amateur leagues. Players who are former professionals, semi-pro, amateurs or collegians are allowed to play in these leagues without jeopardizing their amateur status.

National Semi-Pro BB Assn.
Double I Semi-Pro BB League
13 B Yorkshire
Newburgh, IN 47630
T: (812) 490-3399
www.eteamz.com/NSPBA
www.eteamz.com/DISBL
E: timturp15@aol.com
P/Commissioner: Tim Turp

Pacific International League
504 Yale Avenue N.
Seattle, WA 98109
T: (206) 623-8844
T: (206) 324-8365 (PR)
F: (206) 623-8361
www.pacificinternationalleague.com
E: potter@seanet.com
P: Mickie Schmith
Treasurer: Beth Schmith
Sec: Steve Potter

The PIL was founded in 1992.

Aloha Knights
PO Box 40212
Portland, OR 97240
T: (503) 219-9919
F: (503) 371-0599
www.alohaknights.com
GM: Dan Segal

Bellingham Bells
1732 Iowa Street
Bellingham, WA 98226
T: (360) 527-1035
F: (360) 671-3934
www.bellinghambells.com
GM: Tony Larson

Bend Elks
PO Box 9009
Bend, OR 97708
T: (541) 312-9259
F: (541) 388-8837
www.bendelks.com
E: info@bendelks.com
GM: Jim Richards

Everett Merchants
7504 Heather Way
Everett, WA 98203
T: (425) 353-8053
F: (425) 258-2045
www.everettmerchantsbaseball.com
GM: Harold Pyatte

Gresham Kings
T: (503) 252-7640
P: Mick Ellett

Kelowna Falcons
1130 Richter Street
Kelowna, B.C., Canada V1Y 2K7
T: (250) 862-1506
F: (250) 763-0501
P: Dan Nonis
GM: Bill Featherstone

Kirkland Kodiaks
T: (425) 350-2232
P: Arnie Anderson

Seattle Studs Baseball Club
1405 132nd Ave. NE, Suite 4
Bellevue, WA 98005
T: (425) 451-1165
F: (425) 451-1032
P: Mike Carr
GM: Mark Dow

Spokane RiverHawks
PO Box 3888
Spokane, WA 99220
T: (509) 747-4991
F: (509) 838-5153
www.spokaneriverhawks.com
E: mccoy@spokaneriverhawks.com
P: Bill Hogeboom
Bus Mgr: Matt McCoy

Wenatchee Apple Sox
PO Box 5100
Wenatchee, WA 98807
T: (509) 665-6900
F: (509) 663-4599
www.applesox.com
E: sales@applesox.com
GM: Jim Corcoran

Yakima Paladin Knights
732 Summitview, #528
Yakima, WA 98902
T: (509) 965-2810
www.yakimaknights.tk
GM: Rusty Mc Ewen

2002 PIL Champions
Seattle Studs

Western Semi Pro Baseball Assn.
7848 Silverton Ave., Suite C
San Diego, CA 92126
T: (858) 689-6810
F: (858) 689-0432
www.woodbatbaseball.org
E: onbase@woodbatbaseball.org
P: Jeff Sewell

Independent Amateur Clubs for 2003

Hollywood Legends
909 E Yorba Linda Blvd.
Placentia, CA 92670
T: (310) 281-7354
F: (323) 469-3301
GM: John Greene
Barnstorming club made up of former major leaguers.

Humboldt Crabs
PO Box 4422
Arcata, CA 95518
T: (707) 826-2333
www.crabsbaseball.org
The Crabs have been active since the 1950's.

Senior Leagues

Men's Adult Baseball League
Men's Senior Baseball League
One Huntington Quad., Suite 3N07
Mellville, NY 11747
T: (516) 753-6725
F: (516) 753-4031
www.msblnational.com
E: info@msblnational.com
P: Steve Sigler

National Adult Baseball Assn.
3900 E. Mexico Ave., Suite GL-8
Denver, CO 80210
T: (800) 621-6479
T: (303) 639-9955
www.dugout.org
F: (303) 753-6804
E: nabanatl@aol.com
P: Shane Fugita

Roy Hobbs Baseball Assn.
2224 Akron Peninsula Road
Akron, OH 44313
T: (888) 484-7422
T: (330) 923-3400
F: (330) 923-1967
www.royhobbs.com
E: tom@royhobbs.com
P: Tom Giffen

National Tournaments

Amateur Athletic Union
The Walt Disney World Resort
PO Box 10000
Lake Buena Vista, FL 32830
T: (800) 228-4872
F: (407) 934-7242
www.aaubaseball.org
BB Oper: Sheldon Walker

American Amateur
Baseball Congress
118-119 Redfield Plaza, PO Box 467
Marshall, MI 49068
T: (616) 781-2002
F: (616) 781-2060
Exec. Director: Joe Cooper
Stan Musual World Series for
Unlimited Division, Battle Creek, MI

National Baseball Congress
PO Box 1420
Wichita, KS 67201
T: (316) 267-3372
F: (316) 267-3382
www.wichitaeagle.com/NBC
P: Bob Rich
VP: Steve Shaad
GM: Derik Dukes
2003 NBC Tournament
Wichita, KS

Grand Forks International
Tournament
PO Box 221
Danville, WA 99121
T: (604) 442-2238
F: (604) 442-3788
Director: Larry Seminoff
Grand Forks, B.C., Canada.
Labor Day Weekend in September

Listed in this next section are the provin(
associations for Canada.

Baseball Canada

2212 Gladwin Crescent
Ottawa, Ontario K1B 5N1
T: (613) 748-5606
F: (613) 748-5767
www.baseball.ca
E: info@baseball.ca
Director General: Jim Baba

Alberta Baseball
Percy Page Centre
11759 Groat Road
Edmonton, Alberta T5J 3K6
T: (780) 453-8601
F: (780) 453-8603
Exec. Director: Randy Strocki

British Columbia Baseball
200-1367 W. Broadway
Vancouver, B.C. V6H 4A9
T: (604) 737-3037
F: (604) 737-6043
Exec. Director: Rob Arnold

British Columbia Senior Baseball
PO Box 1214
Grand Forks, B.C. V0H 1H0
T: (604) 442-2238
Commissioner: Larry Seminoff

Manitoba Baseball
200 Main Street
Winnipeg, Manitoba R3C 4M2
T: (204) 985-4121
F: (204) 985-4028
Exec. Director: Lorne Korol

Baseball New Brunswick
80 Saint Roach Street
Fredericton, NB E3C 1A9
T: (506) 450-1891
F: (506) 444-9889
Exec. Director: Donna Whalen

Newfoundland Baseball
83 Ashford Drive
Mount Pearl, NF A1N 3N7
T: (709) 368-2819
F: (709) 368-6080
Exec. Director: Ken Dawe

Baseball Nova Scotia
PO Box 3010 South
Halifax, NS B3J 3G6
T: (902) 425-5450
F: (902) 425-5606
Exec. Director: Grand MacDonald

Ontario Baseball
1425 Bishop Street, Unit 16
Cambridge, Ontario N1R 6J9
T: (519) 740-3900
F: (519) 740-6311
Exec. Director: Jillian Graves

Prince Edward Island Baseball
PO Box 92
Morell, PEI C0A 1S0
T: (902) 961-2021
F: (902) 961-3040
Exec. Director: George Morrison

Baseball Quebec
4545 Pierre de Coubertin
Montreal, Quebec H1V 3R2
T: (514) 252-3000
F: (514) 252-3134
Exec. Director: Leonard Pelland

Saskatchewan Baseball
1870 Lorne Street
Regina, Saskatchewan S4P 2L7
T: (306) 780-9200
F: (306) 352-3669
Exec. Director: Sharon Bergerman

Yukon Baseball
7 Wren Place
Whitehorse, Yukon Y1A 5X5
T: (403) 633-7026
Exec. Director: Mark Dyrbye

Canadian Leagues

Intercounty Major Baseball League
9 Delamere Avenue
Stratford, Ontario, Canada N5A 4Z6
T: (519) 271-3269
F: (519) 271-5088
www.ICbaseball.com
Commissioner: Jim Rooney
PR/Media: Lee Griffi
T: (519) 655-3250
E: Lgriffi@Icbaseball.com

Barrie Bay Cats
21 Callaghan Drive
Barrie, Ontario L4N 6E8
T: (705) 737-2590
F: (705) 739-4244
www.barriebaycats.com
E: gcalvert@city.barrie.on.ca
GM: Gary Calvert

Brantford Red Sox
320 N. Park Street
Brantford, Ontario, CAN N3R 4L3
T: (519) 756-8100
F: (519) 756-8102
www.brantfordredsox.com
GM: Mike Calbeck

Guelph Royals
62 Arnold Street
Guelph, Ontario, CAN N1H 5G9
T: (519) 745-3411
F: (519) 745-5772
www.guelphroyals.com
P: Terry Churchill

Hamilton Cardinals
PO Box 20394, 856 Upper James St.
Hamilton, Ontario L9C 7M8
T/F: (905) 562-1894
www.hamiltoncardinals.com
P: Brian Hanson

Kitchener Panthers
18 Roehampton Court
Kitchener, Ontario N2A 3K8
T: (519) 742-5961
F: (519) 742-2889
www.panthersbaseball.com
GM: Max Rausch

London Majors
1328 Base Line Road W.
London, Ontario N6K 2E3
T: (519) 641-2137
F: (519) 641-7033
www.londonmajors.com
P: Arden Eddie

Oshawa Dodgers
1288 Ritson Road N., Suite 356
Oshawa, Ontario L1G 8B2 Canada
T: (905) 576-1099
F: (905) 428-7769
www.oshawadodgers.com
E: info@oshawadodgers.com
GM: Rod Holinaty

St. Thomas Storm
755 Lenore Street
London, Ontario N6J 4A7
T: (519) 679-9593
F: (519) 679-8846
www.thestorm.org
P: Geoff Cain

Toronto Maple Leafs
42 Chestnut Hills Pkwy.
Etobicoke, Ontario M9A 3P6
T: (416) 631-2600
F: (416) 239-9898
www.mapleleafsbaseball.com
P: Jack Dominico

Waterloo Tigers
464 Redfox Road
Waterloo, Ontario N2K 2T1
T: (519) 539-9831
F: (519) 746-2119
www.waterlootigers.com
GM: Roger Dupuis

The Intercounty League was established in 1919, played until 1941, returning 1946 after WWII.

2002 Intercounty Championship
Toronto Maple Leafs d Hamilton Cardinals 4 Games to 1.

Manitoba Senior League
219-11th Street E.
Brandon, Manitoba R7A 5W6, Canada
T: (204) 729-2783
F: (204) 728-2886
www.MSBL.mb.ca
E: wowkb@westman.wave.ca
P: Barry Wowk

2002 MSBL Champions
Birtle Blue Jays

Central Ontario Senior Baseball League
70 Wildercroft Avenue
Brampton, Ontario L6V 4G5
T: (905) 846-8656
www.eteamz.com/coba-senior
E: frankf@worldwise.ca

Western Major League
Box 700
Melville, Sask. S0A 2P0
T: (306) 728-5435
P: Brian Hicke

Lethbridge Bulls
2425 N. Parkside Drive
Lethbridge, Alberta T1J 4W3
T: (403) 320-2025
GM: Kevin Kvame

Melville Millionaires
Box 2698
Melville, Sask. S0A 2P0
T: (306) 728-2038
www.spreda.sk.ca/melvillemillionaires
GM: Edwin Miller

Moose Jaw Millers
712 Hochelaga Street
Moose Jaw, Sask. S6H 2H6
T: (306) 693-4490
GM: Kris Ireland

Regina Maroons
203-438 Victoria Avenue East
Regina, Sask. S3N 0N7
T: (306) 584-1859
GM: Darrell Baker

Swift Current Indians
1137 Bothwell Drive
Swift Current, Sask. S9H 1Z8
T: (306) 773-1887
GM: Harv Martinez

New teams are Saskatoon Yellow Jackets, Weyburn Beavers & Yorkton Cardinals.

2002 WMBL Champions
Swift Current Indians

The league was formerly known as the Saskatchewan Major Baseball League.

Baseball Organizations

International Baseball Association
Ave. de Mon-Repos 24, C.P. 131
1000 Lausanne 5, Switzerland
T: (41.21) 318 82 40
F: (41.21) 318 82 41
www.baseball.ch
E: ibaf@baseball.ch
P: Aldo Notari
Sec. Gen: John Ostermeyer

All American Amateur
Baseball Association
331 Parkway Drive
Zanesville, OH 43701
T: (740) 453-8531
F: (740) 453-3978
P: David Niro

Amateur Athletic Union
The Walt Disney World Resort
PO Box 10000
Lake Buena Vista, FL 32830
T: (800) 228-4872
T: (407) 934-7200
F: (407) 934-7242
www.aaubaseball.org
BB Oper: Sheldon Walker

Amer. Amateur Baseball Congress
PO Box 467, 118-119 Redfield Plaza
Marshall, MI 49068
T: (616) 781-2002
F: (616) 781-2060
www.voyager.net/aabc
P: Joe Cooper

American Amateur Youth
Baseball Alliance
12919 Four Winds Farm
St. Louis, MO 63131
T: (573) 518-0319
www.aayba.com
Exec. Dir: Carroll Wood

American Legion Baseball
PO Box 1055
Indianapolis, IN 46206
T: (317) 630-1213
F: (317) 630-1369
www.legion.org
Program Coord: Jim Quinlan

Association of Professional
Baseball Players of America
12062 Valley View St., Suite 211
Garden Grove, CA 92645
T: (714) 882-9900
F: (714) 897-0233
P: John McHale

Babe Ruth Baseball
1770 Brunswick Pike, PO Box 5000
Trenton, NJ 08638
T: (609) 695-1434
F: (609) 695-2505
www.baberuthleague.org
P: Ronald Tellefsen

Baseball Assistance Team (BAT)
245 Park Avenue
New York, NY 10167
T: (212) 949-5652
P: Joe Garagiola

Baseball Chapel
21755 W. Ravine Rd.
Forest Lake, IL 60047
T: (847) 438-0978
F: (847) 438-6554
E: baseballchapel@juno.com
P: Gary Carter
Exec. Dir: Vince Nauss

Baseball Writers Association
of America
78 Olive Street
Lake Grove, NY 11755
T: (631) 981-7938
F: (631) 585-4669
E: bbwaa@aol.com
P: Ian McDonald

Continental Amateur Baseball Association
82 University Strreet
Westerville, OH 43081
T/F: (614) 899-2103
www.caba.baseball.com
P: Carl Williams
Exec. Dir: Roger Tremaine

Dixie Baseball, Inc.
PO Box 231536
Montgomery, AL 36123
T: (334) 241-2300
F: (334) 241-2301
Exec. Dir: P.L. Corley

Dizzy Dean Baseball, Inc.
PO Box 856
Hernando, MS 38632
T: (662) 429-4365
Comm: Danny Phillips

Elias Sports Bureau, Inc.
500 Fifth Avenue
New York, NY 10110
T: (212) 869-1530
F: (212) 354-0980
GM: Seymour Siwoff

Hap Dumont Youth Baseball
1325 N. Westlink
Wichita, KS 67227
T: (316) 721-1779
F: (316) 721-8054
Exec Dir: Jerry Crowell

Howe Sportsdata International
Boston Fish Pier
West Bldg. 1, Suite 302
Boston, MA 02210
T: (617) 951-0070
F: (617) 737-9960
P: Jay Virshbo

International Baseball Foundation
1313 13th Street S.
Birmingham, AL 35205
T: (205) 558-4235
F: (205) 918-0800
Exec. Dir: David Osinski

Junior Pan Am & World Baseball Program
PO Box 72711
Roselle, IL 60172
T: (630) 893-6273
F: (630) 893-5549
P: Peter Caliendo

Little League Baseball, Inc.
PO Box 3485, Rte. 15 S.
Williamsport, PA 17701
T: (570) 326-1921
F: (570) 326-1074
www.littleleague.org
P/CEO: Steve Keener
Media: Lance Van Auken

Major League Baseball Players Alumni Association
33 6th Street S.
St. Petersburg, FL 33701
T: (727) 892-6744
F: (727) 892-6771
P: Brooks Robinson

Major League Baseball Players Association
12 E. 49th Street, 24th FL
New York, NY 10017
T: (212) 826-0808
F: (212) 752-3649
www.bigleaguers.com
Exec Dir: Donald Fehr
Communications: Greg Bouris

Major League Baseball Player Relations
245 Park Avenue
New York, NY 10167
T: (212) 931-7800
Exec. Dir: Randy Levine

Major League Baseball Productions
3 Empire Blvd.
South Hackensack, NJ 07606
T: (201) 807-0888
F: (201) 807-0272
P: James Holland

Major League Baseball Umpire Development Program
PO Box A
St. Petersburg, FL 33731
T: (727) 823-1286
F: (727) 823-7212
Exec Dir: Edwin Lawrence

Major League Scouting Bureau
23712 Birtcher Drive, Suite A
Lake Forest, CA 92630
T: (949) 458-7600
F: (949) 458-9454
P: Don Pries

National Amateur Baseball Federation
PO Box 705
Bowie, MD 20718
T/F: (301) 262-5005
www.nabf.com
E: nabf1914@aol.com
P: Charles Blackburn

National Association of Police Athletic Leagues
618 U.S. Hwy. 1, Suite 201
North Palm Beach, FL 33408
T: (561) 844-1823
F: (561) 863-6120
www.nationalpal.org
Exec Dir: Brad Hart

National Baseball Coaches Association
PO Box 12354
Omaha, NE 68112
T: (402) 457-1962
P: Jerry Miles

National Baseball Congress
PO Box 1420
Wichita, KS 67201
T: (316) 267-3372
F: (316) 267-3382
www.wichitaeagle.com/NBC
P: Bob Rich, Jr.
GM: Derik Duke
PR: Justin Givens

National Baseball Hall of Fame
PO Box 590, 25 Main Street
Cooperstown, NY 13326
T: (607) 547-7200
F: (607) 547-2044
www.baseballhalloffame.org
Chmn: Ed Stack
Curator: Ted Spencer
Librarian: Jim Gates

National Junior Baseball League
PO Box 1021
East Northport, NY 11731
T: (516) 757-6675
P: Nick Nappy

Negro League Baseball Museum
mail: PO Box 414847, 64141
1616 E. 18th Street
Kansas City, MO 64108
T: (816) 221-1920
F: (816) 221-8424
www.nlbm.com
Cmnn.: Buck O'Neil
Exec. Dir: Don Motley

Negro Baseball Players Assn.
PO Box 244
Manassas, VA 22110
T: (703) 368-2571
P: Wilmer Fields, Sr.

Pony Baseball, Inc.
PO Box 225
Washington, PA 15301
T: (724) 225-1060
F: (724) 225-9852
www.pony.org
E: pony@pulsenet.com
P: Abraham Key

Reviving Baseball in Innercities
245 Park Avenue
New York, NY 10167
T: (212) 931-7800
F: (212) 949-5695
National Dir: Tom Brausell

Society of American Baseball Research (SABR)
PO Box 93183
Cleveland, OH 44101
T: (216) 575-0500
F: (216) 575-0502
www.sabr.org
P: Larry Gerlach
Exec. Dir.: Morris Eckhouse

Stats, Inc.
8131 N. Monticello
Skokie, IL 60076
T: (847) 676-3322
F: (847) 676-0821
www.stats.com
P: John Dewan

T-Ball USA Association
2499 Main Street
Stratford, CT 06615
T: (203) 381-1449
F: (202) 381-1440
www.teeballusa.org
E: teeballusa@aol.com
P: Bing Broido

USA Baseball
3400 E. Camino Campestre
Tuscon, AZ 85716
T: (520) 327-9700
F: (520) 327-9221
www.usabaseball.com
E: usabaseball@aol.com
P: Mark Marquess

**U.S. Amateur
Baseball Association**
7101 Lake Ballinger Way
Edmonds, WA 98026
T/F: (425) 776-7130
www.usaba.com
E: usaba@usaba.com
P: Al Rutledge

U.S. Amateur Baseball Federation
7355 Peter Pan Avenue
San Diego, CA 92114
T/F: (619) 527-9205
www.usabf.com
E: halbig@msn.com

Baseball Publications

Amateur Baseball News
PO Box 467
Marshall, MI 49068
T: (616) 781-2002
F: (616) 781-2060

Athlon's Baseball
220 25th Ave. N., Suite 200
Nashville, TN 37203
T: (615) 327-0747
F: (615) 327-1149
Mng Editor: Charlie Miller

Baseball America
PO Box 2089
Durham, NC 27702
T: (800) 845-2726
F: (919) 682-2880
www.baseballamerica.com
Editor: Allan Simpson

Baseball Digest
990 Grove Street
Evanston, IL 60201
T: (847) 491-6440
F: (847) 491-0459
Publisher: Norman Jacobs

Collegiate Baseball
PO Box 50566
Tucson, AZ 85703
T: (520) 623-4530
F: (520) 624-5501
Editor: Lou Pavlovich

International Baseball Rundown
PO Box 608
Glen Ellyn, IL 60138
T: (630) 790-3087
F: (630) 790-3182
Editor: Jeff Elijah

Junior League Baseball
PO Box 9099
Canoga Park, CA 91309
T: (818) 710-1234
F: (818) 710-1877
www.jlbmag.com
Editor: Dave Destler

SABR Bulletin
PO Box 93183
Cleveland, OH 44101
T: (216) 575-0500
www.sabr.org

Street & Smith's Baseball
342 Madison Avenue
New York, NY 10017
T: (212) 880-8698
F: (212) 880-4347
Editor: Gerald Kavanaugh

Total Baseball
445 Park Avenue
New York, NY 10022
T: (212) 319-6611
F: (212) 319-3820
www.totalbaseball.com
Editor: Mike Gershman

Basketball

National Basketball Association
Olympic Tower
645 Fifth Avenue
New York, NY 10022
T: (212) 407-8000
F: (212) 826-0579
www.nba.com
Commissioner: David Stern
CommDir:: Brian McIntyre
Sports Media: Tim frank

All NBA team websites are accessed through www.nba.com

NBA Entertainment, Inc.
450 Harmon Meadow Blvd.
Secaucus, NJ 07094
T: (201) 865-1500
VP/CEO: Adam Silver

NBA Players Association
1775 Broadway, Suite 2401
New York, NY 10019
T: (212) 333-7510
F: (212) 956-5687
Exec. Dir: Charles Grantham

NBA Properties, Inc.
Olympic Tower
645 Fifth Avenue
New York, NY 10022
T: (212) 407-8000
: Rick Welts

Atlanta Hawks
One CNN Center
South Tower, Suite 405
Atlanta, GA 30303
T: (404) 827-3800
F: (404) 827-4229
www.hawks.com
GM: Pete Babcock
PR: Arthur Triche

Boston Celtics
151 Merrimac Street
Boston, MA 02114
T: (617) 523-6050
F: (617) 523-5949
www.celtics.com
GM: Chris Wallace
PR: Jeff Twiss

Chicago Bulls
1901 W. Madison Street
Chicago, IL 60612
T: (312) 455-4000
F: (312) 455-4198
www.bulls.com
GM: Jerry Krause
PR: Tim Hallam

Cleveland Cavaliers
Gund Arena, One Center Court.
Cleveland, OH 44115
T: (216) 420-2000
F: (216) 420-2298
www.cavs.com
GM: Jim Paxon
PR: Bob Price

Dallas Mavericks
2500 Victory Avenue
Dallas, TX 75201
T: (214) 665-4660
F: (214) 752-3860
www.dallasmavericks.com
GM: Don Nelson
PR: Gregg Elkin

Denver Nuggets
Pepsi Arena
1000 Chopper Place
Denver, CO 80204
T: (303) 405-1100
F: (303) 405-1326
GM: Kiki Vandeweghe
PR: Tommy Sheppard

Detroit Pistons
The Palace
Two Championship Dr.
Auburn Hills, MI 48057
T: (248) 377-0100
F: (248) 377-3260
www.pistons.com
GM: John Hammond
PR: Kevin Grigg

Golden State Warriors
1011 Broadway
Oakland, CA 94607
T: (510) 986-2200
F: (510) 452-0142
www.warriors.com
GM: Garry St. Jean
PR: Raymond Ridder

Houston Rockets
Two Greenway Plaza
Suite 400
Houston, TX 77046
T: (713) 627-3865
F: (713) 963-7339
www.rockets.com
GM: Carroll Dawson
PR: Nelson Luis

Indiana Pacers
One Conseco Court
125 S. Pennsylvania Street
Indianapolis, IN 46204
T: (317) 917-2500
F: (317) 917-2599
www.pacers.com
GM: Donnie Walsh
PR: Kathryn Jordan

Los Angeles Clippers
1111 S. Figueroa, Suite 1100
Los Angeles, CA 90015
T: (213) 742-7500
F: (213) 742-7569
www.clippers.com
GM: Elgin Baylor
PR: Joe Safety

Los Angeles Lakers
Staples Center
1111 S Figueroa Street
Los Angeles, CA 90015
T: (310) 426-6000
F: (310) 426-6105
www.lakers.com
GM: Mitch Kupchak
PR: John Black

Memphis Grizzlies
175 Toyota Plaza, Suite 150
Memphis, TN 38103
T: (901) 205-1234
F: (901) 205-1499
www.grizzlies.com
GM: Dick versace
PR: Kirk Clayborn

Miami Heat
American Airlines Arena
601 Biscayne Blvd.
Miami. FL 33132
T: (786) 777-1000
F: (786) 777-4087
www.heat.com
GM: Randy Pfund
PR: Tim Donovan

Milwaukee Bucks
1001 N. Fourth Street
Milwaukee, WI 53203
T: (414) 227-0500
F: (414) 227-0543
www.bucks.com
GM: Ernie Grunfeld
PR: Cheri Hanson

Minnesota Timberwolves
Taget Center
600 First Avenue N.
Minneapolis, MN 55403
T: (612) 673-1600
F: (612) 673-1699
www.timberwolves.com
GM: Kevin McHale
PR: Kent Wipf

New Jersey Nets
390 Murray Hill Parkway
East Rutherford, NJ 07073
T: (201) 935-8888
F: (201) 935-1088
www.njnets.com
GM: Rod Thorn
PR: Gary Sussman

New Orleans Hornets
1501 Girod Street
New Orleans, LA 70113
T: (504) 301-4000
F: (504) 301-4001
www.hornets.com
GM: Jeff Bower
PR: Harold Kaufman

New York Knickerbockers
Two Pennsylvania Plaza
New York, NY 10121
T: (212) 465-6000
F: (212) 465-6498
www.nyknicks.com
GM: Scott Layden
PR: Jonathan Supranowitz

Orlando Magic
Two Magic Place
8701 Maitland Summit Blvd.
Orlando, FL 32810
T: (407) 916-2400
F: (407) 916-2810
www.orlandomagic.com
GM: John Gabriel
PR: Joel Glass

Philadelphia 76ers
3601 S. Broad Street
Philadelphia, PA 19148
T: (215) 339-7600
F: (215) 339-7632
www.sixers.com
GM: Billy King
PR: Karen Frascona

Phoenix Suns
201 E. Jefferson
Phoenix, AZ 85004
T: (602) 379-7900
F: (602) 379-7922
www.suns.com
CEO: Jerry Colangelo
PR: Julie Fie

Portland Trail Blazers
One Center Court, Suite 200
Portland, OR 97227
T: (503) 234-9291
F: (503) 236-4906
www.blazers.com
GM: Bob Whitsitt
PR: Mike Hanson

Sacramento Kings
One Sports Parkway
Sacramento, CA 95834
T: (916) 455-4647
F: (916) 928-6912
www.kings.com
Pres: Geoff Petrie
PR: Troy Hanson

San Antonio Spurs
100 Montana Street
San Antonio, TX 78203
T: (210) 554-7700
F: (210) 554-0992
www.spurs.nba.com
GM: R.C. Buford
PR: Tom James

Seattle Supersonics
351 Elliott Ave. West, Suite 500
Seattle, WA 98119
T: (206) 281-5800
F: (206) 281-5877
www.sonics.com
GM: Rick Sund
PR: Valerie O'Neil

Toronto Raptors
Air Canada Centre
40 Bay Street, Suite 400
Toronto, Ontario M5J 2X2
T: (416) 815-5600
F: (416) 359-9205
www.raptors.com
GM: Glen Grunwald
PR: Jim LaBumbard

Utah Jazz
Delta Center
301 W. South Temple
Salt Lake City, UT 84101
T: (801) 325-2500
F: (801) 325-2578
www.utahjazz.com
GM: Kevin O'Connor
PR: Kim Turner

Washington Wizards
MCI Center
601 F Street NW
Washington, DC 20001
T: (202) 661-5000
F: (202) 661-5113
www.washingtonwizards.com
GM: Wes Unseld
PR: Matt Williams

The NBA began in the 1946-47 season with the merger of the Basketball Association of America (BAA) and the NBL. The first NBA champions were the Philadelphia Warriors who defeated Chicago Stags 4 games to 1.

2002 NBA Finals
Los Angeles Lakers d New Jersey Nets 4 Games to 0.

Women's Professional Basketball

With the success of the USA's Gold medal women's basketball team in the 1996 Atlanta Summer Olympics, the re-birth of women's professional basketball began in the Fall of 1996 with the ABL and the Summer of 1997 with the NBA-sponsored WNBA.

The ABL's inaugural season began in March '97, ending on a sad note with the demise of the league, only to cease operations during the Christmas holiday of 1998.

The ABL was the fifth women's pro basketball league in the U.S. to fold since the 1970's.

Women's National Basketball Association

Olympic Tower
645 Fifth Avenue
New York, NY 10022
T: (212) 688-WNBA (9622)
F: (212) 750-WNBA (9622)
www.wnba.com
P: Val Ackerman
Media Relations: John Maxwell
Corp. Comm.: Traci Cook

All team websites can be accessed through www.wnba.com

Charlotte Sting
3308 Oak Lake Blvd., Suite B
Charlotte, NC 28208
T: (704) 357-0252
F: (704) 329-4970
www.wnba.com/sting/
GM: Sam Russo
PR: Suzanne Werdann

Cleveland Rockers
One Center Court
Cleveland, OH 44115
T: (216) 420-2000
F: (216) 420-2101
www.clevelandrockers.com
GM: Jim Paxon
PR: Amanda Ludwig

Connecticut Sun
1 Mohegan Sun Blvd.
Uncasville, CT 06382
T: (877) 786-8499
F: (860) 862-4010
www.connecticutsun.com
GM: Chris Sienko
Mkt: Stacey Dengler
PR: TBA

Detroit Shock
The Palace of Auburn Hills
Two Championship Drive
Auburn Hills, MI 48326
T: (248) 377-0100
F: (248) 377-3260
www.wnba.com/shock
P: Tom Wilson
PR: Dennis Sampier

Houston Comets
Two Greenway Plaza
Suite 400
Houston, TX 77046
T: (713) 627-9622
F: (713) 963-7339
www.wnba.com/comets/
GM: Van Chancellor
PR: Bub Schranz

Indiana Fever
125 S. Pennsylvania St
Indianapolis, IN 46204
T: (317) 917-2500
F: (317) 917-2899
CEO: Kelly Krauskopf
PR: Tom Savage

Los Angeles Sparks
555 E. Nash Street
El Segundo, CA 90245
T: (310) 330-2434
F: (310) 330-2437
www.lasparks.com
GM: Penny Toler
PR: Kristal Shipp

Minnesota Lynx
Target Center
600 First Avenue North
Minneapolis, MN 55403
T: (617) 673-1600
F: (617) 673-8367
GM: Brian Agler
PR: Mike Cristaldi

New York Liberty
2 Pennsylvania Plaza
New York, NY 10121
T: (212) 564-9622
F: (212) 465-6250
www.nyliberty.com
GM: Carol Blazejowski
PR: Amy Scheer

Phoenix Mercury
201 E. Jefferson Street
Phoenix, AZ 85004
T: (602) 514-8333
F: (602) 514-8303
www.wnba.com/mercury/
GM: Seth Sulka
PR: Tami Scott

Sacramento Monarchs
One Sports Parkway
Sacramento, CA 95834
T: (916) 928-0000
F: (916) 928-8109
www.sacramentomonarchs.com
GM: Jerry Reynolds
PR: Kimberly Williams

San Antonio Silver Stars
One SBC Center
San Antonio, TX 78219
T: (210) 444-5050
F: (210) 554-0992
www.sasilverstars.com
GM: Clarissa Davis-Wrightsil
PR: Chris Davis

Seattle Storm
351 Elliott Ave. W., Suite 500
Seattle, WA 98119
T: (206) 281-5800
F: (206) 281-5839
GM: Lin Dunn
PR: Valerie O' Neil

Washington Mystics
601 F St NW
Washington, DC 20004
T: (202) 661-5000
F: (202) 661-5113
www.washingtonmystics.com
P: Susan O'Malley
PR: Matt Williams

2002 WNBA Championship
LA Sparks d New York 2-0 Games

Minor Leagues

Continental Basketball Association
1412 W. Idaho St., Suite 235
Boise, ID 83702
T: (208) 429-0101
F: (208) 429-0303
www.cbahoopsonline.com
E: info@cbahoopsonline.com
Commissioner: Gary Hunter
Deputy Comm: Wade Morehead
Dir of Operations: Scott Johnson
Media: Bryant Kuechle

The CBA is the minor league that began in 1946 as the Eastern Basketball League and later as the EBA and for a brief period, the United Basketball Assn, being born just a few months prior to the birth of the NBA.

www.sportsbooksempire.com

Dakota Wizards
PO Box 4066
Bismarck, ND 58504
T: (701) 258-2255
F: (701) 255-7967
www.dakotawizards.com
E: wizards@btigate.com
GM: Alex Geche

Gary Steelheads
One Genesis Center Plaza
Gary, IN 46402
T: (219) 882-4222
F: (219) 882-4667
www.steelheadshoops.com
GM: Todd DeMoss
PR: Michael Nieto

Grand Rapids Hoops
2500 Turner NW
Grand Rapids, MI 49544
T: (616) 559-7936
F: (616) 559-7935
www.grandrapidshoops.com
GM: Pete Rusticus
PR: Dena DeMarais

Great Lakes Storm
11660 N. Beyer Road
Birch Run, MI 48415
T: (989) 624-4665
F: (989) 624-5424
www.greatlakesstorm.com
E: tgiles@greatlakesstorm.com
GM: Larry Kiernan
PR: Tabitha Giles

Idaho Stampede
PO Box 6525
Boise, ID 83707
T: (208) 388-4667
F: (208) 388-3845
www.388hoop.com
E: todd@388hoop.com
GM: John Brunelle
PR: Todd Anderson

Rockford Lightning
3660 Publishers Drive
Rockford, IL 61109
T: (815) 874-4232
F: (815) 874-3421
www.rockfordlightning.com
E:rockfordlightning@hotmail.com
P: Wayne Timpe
PR: Mike Garrigan

Sioux Falls Sky Force
2101 W. 41st St., Suite 39
Sioux Falls, SD 57105
T: (605) 332-0605
F: (605) 332-2305
www.skyforceonline.com
E: info@skyforceonline.com
P: Greg Heineman
Asst GM: Jeremy DeCurtins
PR: Mark Campbell

Yakima Sun Kings
1301 S. Fair Avenue
Yakima, WA 98901
T: (509) 248-1222
F: (509) 248-4662
www.sunkings.com
E: sunkings@nwinfo.net
GM: Darren Uceny

2003 CBA Finals
Yakima 117 Grand Rapids 107

National Basketball Development League
24 Vardry Street, Suite 201
Greenville, SC 29601
T: (864) 248-1100
F: (864) 248-1102
www.NBDL.com
P: Phillip Evans
Exec Dir: Karl Hicks
Media: Kent Partridge

Asheville Attitude
87 Haywood Street
Asheville, NC 28801
T: (828) 782-1000
F: (828) 782-1002
P: Alfred White
PR: Patricia Harvey

Columbus Riverdragons
18 East 11th Street
Columbus, GA 31902
T: (706) 225-1100
F: (706) 225-1102
P: Tim Murphy
PR: Drew Ohlmeyer

Fayetteville Patriots
1960 Coliseum Drive
Fayetteville, NC 28306
T: (910) 213-1000
F: (910) 213-1002
P: Amy Privette Perko
PR: Brian Holloway

Greenville Groove
650 N. Academy Drive
Greenville, SC 29601
T: (864) 241-3831
F: (864) 241-3872
GM: Bryan Rucker
PR: Marsha Byers

Huntsville Flight
700 Monroe Street
Huntsville, AL 35801
T: (256) 429-1000
F: (256) 429-1002
P: Kellie Elliott
PR: Chris Rooks

Mobile Revelers
401 Civic Center Drive
Mobile, AL 36602
T: (251) 370-2000
F: (251) 370-2002
P: Rudolph Bourg
PR: Tonita Perry

North Charleston Lowgators
5001 Coliseum Drive, Suite B
North Charleston, SC 29418
T: (843) 460-1000
F: (843) 460-1002
GM: Stephannie Harvey
PR: Jeff Cataffa

Roanoke Dazzle
711 Fifth Street NE, Suite B
Roanoke, VA 24016
T: (540) 266-1000
F: (540) 266-1002
P: Joe Preseren
PR: Jack Bogaczyk

2003 NBDL Championships
Mobile Revelers d Fayetteville Patriots 2 Games to 1 in finals.

United States Basketball League

46 Quirk Road
Milford, CT 06460
T: (203) 877-9508
F: (203) 878-8109
www.usbl.com
E: USBL96@aol.com
Comm: Dan Meisenheimer
PR: Dennis Truax

Adirondack Wildcats
136 Glen Street
Glens Falls, NY 12801
T: (518) 743-9901
F: (518) 798-6793
www.adirondackwildcats.com
GM: Mike Sweet

Brevard Blue Ducks
PO Box 410064
Melbourne, FL 32941
T: (321) 751-2583
F: (321) 254-5970
www.brevardblueducks.com
GM: Michael Hawkins

Brooklyn Kings
621 Putnam Avenue, Suite 3
Brooklyn, NY 11221
T: (718) 453-3088
F: (718) 453-2442
www.brooklynkings.com
GM: Kenny Charles

Dodge City Legend
311 W. Spruce Street
Dodge City, KS 67801
T: (316) 227-2222
F: (316) 227-2571
www.dodgecitylegend.com
GM: Tom Nelson

Kansas Cagerz
215 S. Santa Fe, Suite 203
Salina, KS 67401
T: (785) 820-8585
F: (785) 820-8543
www.kansascagerz.com
GM: Francis Flaxson

Oklahoma Storm
PO Box 1873
Enid, OK 73701
T: (580) 237-8676
F: (580) 234-8460
www.theoklahomastorm.com
GM: Sean Voskuhl

Pennsylvania Valleydawgs
91 Larry Holmes Drive, Suite 210
Easton, PA 18042
T: (610) 250-9800
F: (610) 250-9970
www.valleydawgs.com
P: John E. Walson

Texas Rim Rockers
PMB 298, 6387 B Camp Bowie
Fort Worth, TX 85535
T: (888) 316) 9679
F: (512) 857-0956
www.texasrimrockers.com
GM: Donald Wesley

Westchester Wildfire
198 Central Avenue
White Plains, NY 10606
T: (877) 287-6488
F: (914) 470-3555
www.westchesterwildfire.com
P: Gary Lieberman

The USBL operates during the Summer. The USBL began play in May 1985.

2002 USBL Championship
Oklahoma Storm *d Kansas Cagerz 122-109 in one game championship.*

Eastern Basketball Alliance

4751 Lindle Road, #101-102
Harrisburg, PA 17111
T: (888) 322-7526
T: (717) 986-0720
F: (717) 986-0495
www.easternbasketballalliance.com
P: Dick Anzolut
Commissioner: Julius Mc Coy
PR: Becky Swabb-Hudson

Delaware Express
320 W. 9th Street Plaza
Wilmington, DE 19801
T: (302) 529-0761
F: (302) 529-7203
www.delawareexpresshoops.com
E: expresshoops2003@yahoo.com
P: Kyle Myers

Harrisburg Horizon
4751 Lindle Road, Suite 101-102
Harrisburg, PA 17111
T: (717) 986-0499
F: (717) 986-0495
www.harrisburghorizon.com
E: tsi_horizon@yahoo.com
GM: Cynthia Anzolut
PR: Brian Merrill

New Jersey Bullets
3 Thornwood Drive
Vorhees, NJ 08043
T: (856) 435-0486
F: (856) 435-3652
P: Norman Butch Ingram

New Philadelphia Firedogs
15 Alliance Street, Suite 212
New Philadelphia, PA 17958
T: (570) 624-7576
F: (435) 508-5305
www.geocities.com/the-firedogs
P: Dr. David Moylan
GM: Jeff Zemenchik

New York Blast
645 Ferry Street
Easton, PA 18042
T: (212) 714-8255
F: (610) 252-7607
GM: Maynard Melhem

2003 EBA Champions
Harrisburg Horizon

National Women's Basketball League

PO Box 1361
La Jolla, CA 98038
T: (619) 692-4447
F: (707) 248-2248
www.NWBL.com
E: leagueoffice@wnbl.com
CEO: Patrick Alexander

NWBL is a amateur league with a professional division.

NWBL Pro League

Exec Dir: Jeanine Michealsen
Commissioner: Jolynn Schneider
Media: Brian Lembo
E: brian@nwbl.com

Birmingham Power
2331 Bessemer Road
Birmingham, AL 35208
T: (205) 781-1212
F: (205) 781-0977
E: powerbball4770@aol.com
GM: Gerard Johnson

Chicago Blaze
E: rgraham@chicagoblaze.com
No other info as of presstime

Grand Rapids Blizzard
4616 44th Street SE
Grand Rapids, MI 49512
T: (616) 464-5604
F: (616) 956-1379
E: grndrpdsblizzard@aol.com
GM: Murat Bates

Houston Stealth
2600 Southwest Fwy.
Houston, TX 77098
T: (713) 862-7940
E: kgardner@nwbl.com
GM: John Chancellor
PR: Kristopher Gardner

Kansas City Legacy
2324 N. 88th Drive
Kansas City, KS 66109
T: (913) 621-1111
E: lallyc@usa.net
GM: Carrie Lally

Springfield Spirit
PO Box 1121
West Springfield, MA 01090
T: (413) 746-BALL (2255)
F: (413) 734-3876
www.springfieldspirit.com
E: steve@springfieldspirit.com
P/GM: Stephen Fox

Tennessee Fury
700 Hall of Fame Drive
Koxville, TN 37915
T: (865) 405-1175
www.nwbl.com/fury
E: nwblknox@yahoo.com
GM: Ryan McCallan
PR: Brian Gagnon

2003 NWBL Pro Champions
Houston Stealth 95 TN Fury 76

Women's American Basketball Association

PO Box 621
Dunmore, PA 18512
T: (570) 969-0368
F: (570)
www.womensaba.com
E: info@womensaba.com
CEO: J. David Evans
Commissioner: Owen Hannah

Southwest Basketball League

PO Box 771272
Houston, TX 77215
T: (713) 981-1409
www.spbl.com
E: leagueoffice@spbl.com
Commissioner: Charles Johnson

United Pro Basketball League

34900 Chardon Road, Suite 209
Willoughby Hills, OH 44094
T: (440) 975-0906
F: (440) 975-0613
www.unitedprobasketball.com
Commissioner: Ted Stepien
Asst Comm: George Baka
Office Mgr: Laura Robinson

Louisville Eagles
911 Brooks Street
Spectrum Bldg.
Louisville, KY 40203
T: (859) 805-0757
F: (502) 568-DUNK
www.louisvilleeagles.com
E: louisvilleeagles@aol.com
GM: Greg Ezel

Other UPBL teams are the Frankfort Statesman, Kentucky Coyotes & Mansfield Hawks.

Midwest Basketball Assn.

Buffalo City Thunder
T: (701) 252-3282
www.BuffaloCitythunder.com
E: info@buffalocitythunder.com

Dakota City Lightning Boltz
www.boltzbasketball.com

Frontier City River Dogz
T: (515) 576-8652
GM: Mark Miller

Magic City Snowbears
T: (701) 852-BEARS
www.snowbears.net
E: snowbears@srt.com
GM: Kirk Roos

No other information on MBA.

National Rookie League
444 N. Frederick Avenue
Bethesda, MD 20877
T: (301) 897-1596
F: (707) 220-4715
www.rookie.com
E: bstern@rookie.com
P: Bruce Stern

Summer Pro-Am Leagues

Atlanta Pro-Am League
2945 Burdette Road
College Park, GA 30349
T: (404) 766-0908
Director: Al Outlaw

Boston Pro-Am League
5 Brookbridge Road
West. Peabody, MA 01960
T: (978) 535-1284
F: (781) 937-6932
Director: Vernon Christopher

Charlotte Pro-Am League
9001 Bremerton Court, Ste. A
Charlotte, NC 28227
T: (704) 567-9511
F: (704) 567-9511
Exec. Dir: Bill Shelton

Chicago Pro-Am League
Garfield Park
100 N. Central Park
Chicago, IL 60624
T: (312) 326-2339
Director: Rubin Norris

Cleveland Pro-Am League
4041 Ascot Lane
Warrensville Heights, OH 44122
T: (216) 321-6211
Director: Joe Wise

Dallas Pro-Am League
5601 Lemon Avenue
PO Box 7066
Dallas, TX 75209
T: (214) 526-8811
Commissioner: Bill Patterson

Denver Pro-Am League
2701 Race Street
Denver, CO 80205
T: (303) 296-8705
Director: John Bailey

Detroit Pro-Am League
St. Cecilia High School
6327 Burlingame Street
Detroit, MI 48204
T: (313) 862-5409
Director: Sammy Washington

Houston Pro-Am League
Houston Parks & Recreation
2999 S. Wayside
Houston, TX 77023
T: (713) 641-5051
F: (713) 845-1188
Director: Johnny Weaner

Indianapolis Pro-Am League
1502 W. 16th Street
Indianapolis, IN 46202
T: (317) 327-7193
F: (317) 924-7203
Director: Thomas E. Davis

**Pro-Am League of
Los Angeles**
3230 Durham Drive
Riverside, CA 92503
T: (909) 359-4637
Director: Jim Bertolero

Nellie's Pro-Am City League
3000 N. Sherman Blvd.
Milwaukee, WI 53210
T: (414) 374-3174
Director: Nellie Weddle

**Greater New York
Pro-Am League**
71 Lincoln Avenue
Rockville Center, NY 11570
T: (516) 374-4576
F: (516) 974-6641
Director: Dr. Harvey Lustig

Portland Pro-Am League
700 NE Multnomah Street
Suite 950
Portland, OR 97232
T: (503) 234-9291

**Rucker Professional
Basketball League**
2340 Third Avenue
New York, NY 10037
T: (212) 410-3240
Commissioner: Bob McCullough

Salt Lake City Pro-Am
301 West S. Temple
Salt Lake City, UT 84101
T: (801) 325-2500
F: (801) 325-2599
www.deltacenter.com
Director: David Allred

San Antonio Pro-Am
814 Arkansas
San Antonio, TX 78210
T: (210) 534-6331
F: (210) 534-7299
Director: Charles James

**San Francisco Bay Area
Pro-Am League**
801 Arkansas
San Francisco, CA 94142
T: (415) 695-5009
F: (415) 668-3330
Director: Jon Greenberg

Sonny Hill Basketball League
429 S. 50th Street
Philadelphia. PA 19143
T: (215) 474-2801
F: (215) 474-2931
www.sonnyhillleague.com
Exec Dir: Sonny Hill

**Southern California Summer
Pro Basketball League**
11150 W. Olympic Blvd., Suite 1120
Los Angeles, CA 90064
T: (310) 445-4646
F: (310) 445-4665
www.summerproleague.com
E: summerproleague@aol.com
Dir of Operations: Marni Colbert
PR: Clay Czelusniak
T: (323) 651-9300 (PR)
F: (323) 651-5944 (PR)

Organizations

**Federation Internationale
de Basketball (FIBA)**
PO Box 700607
81306 Munich, Germany
T: (49.89) 74 81 58/0
F: (49.89) 74 81 58 33
www.fiba.com
E: secretariat@office.fiba.com
P: Abdoulaye Seye Moreau

USA Basketball
5465 Mark Dabling Blvd.
Colorado Springs, CO 80918
T: (719) 590-4800
F: (719) 590-4811
www.usabasketball.com
E: camiller@usabasketball.com
Exec Dir: Warren Brown
PR: Craig Miller

Basketball Canada
557 Dixon Road, Suite 102
Etobicoke, Ontario M9W 1H7, CAN
T: (416) 614-8037
F: (416) 614-9570
www.basketball.ca
E: basketball.canada@cdnsport.ca
Exec Dir: Rick Traer
Media: Sandra Gage

All American Red Heads
PO Box 100
Caraway, AR 72419
T: (870) 482-3922
P: Orwell Moore

Association for Professional Basketball Research
PO Box 35771
Phoenix, AZ 85069-5771
T: (602) 995-2365
http://members.aol.com/bradleyrd/apbr.html
E: bradleyrd13@hotmail.com

Athletes in Action
9815 Mason-Montgomery Rd.
Mason, OH 45040
T: (513) 459-9507
F: (513) 459-9690
Director: Scott Opplinger
PR: Lillie Nye

Biddy Basketball
4711 Bancroft Drive
New Orleans, LA 70122
T: (504) 283-5917
F: (504) 283-8225
National Director: Henry Beter

Club Basketball USA
215 North Ave., Suite 205
Westfield, NJ 07090
T: (908) 756-4502
F: (908) 654-0222
Executive Director: Bill Clancy

Harlem Globetrotters
Walt Disney World Sports Complex
PO Box 10000
Lake Buena Vista, FL 32830
T: (407) 363-6100
F: (407) 363-6601
Chmn: Mannie Jackson

Harlem Wizards
Harmon Cove Towers, Suite 9
Meadowlands Parkway
Secaucus, NJ 07094
T: (201) 271-3600
F: (201) 271-3604
www.harlemwizards.com
E: twiz@erols.com
P: Todd Davis

Naismith Memorial Basketball Hall of Fame
1150 W. Columbus Ave.
PO Box 179
Springfield, MA 01101
T: (413) 781-6500
F: (413) 781-1939
www.hoophall.com
P: Joe O'Brien

National Amateur Basketball Association
6832 W. North, Suite 4A
Chicago, IL 60635
T: (773) 637-0811
F: (773) 637-6304
P: Robert Lucenti

National Association of Basketball Coaches
9300 W. 110th St., Suite 640
Overland Park, KS 66210
T: (913) 469-1001
F: (913) 469-1390
Exec. Director: James Haney

National Wheelchair Basketball Association
711 Queensbury Loop
Winter Gardens, FL 32787
T: (407) 654-4315
F: (407) 654-4315
www.nwba.org
P: David Kiley

NBA Players Association
1700 Broadway, Suite 1400
New York, NY 10019
T: (212) 655-0880
F: (212) 956-5687
www.nbpa.org
Exec. Director: G. William Hunter

Streetball Partners International
4006 Belt Line Rd., Suite 230
Dallas, TX 75244
T: (214) 991-1110
F: (214) 991-1135
CEO: Terry Murphy
PR: Pam Silvestri

Women's Basketball Coaches Association
4646 B Lawrenceville Hwy
Lilburn, GA 30247
T: (770) 279-8027
F: (770) 279-8473
www.wbca.org
Exec. Director: Betty Jaynes

Women's Basketball Hall of Fame
700 Hall of Fame Drive
Knoxville, TN 37915
T: (865) 633-9000
F: (865) 633-9294
www.wbhof.com
Exec. Dir: Mr. Robin Hamilton

Youth Basketball of America, Inc.
10325 Orangewood Blvd.
Orlando, FL 32821
T: (407) 363-YBOA
F: (407) 363-0599
P: Donald Ruedlinger

Basketball Publications

Basketball America
PO Box 2982
Durham, NC 27715
T: (919) 477-4588
F: (919) 477-6368
Editor: John Roth

Basketball Digest
990 Grove Street
Evanston, IL 60201
T: (847) 491-6440
F: (847) 491-0459
Publisher: Norman Jacobs

Basketball News
2525 Waukegan Rd., Suite 270
Bannockburn, IL 60015
T: (847) 940-1100
F: (847) 940-1108
Publisher: Hub Arkush

Basketball Red Book
1950 First Ave. N., Ste. 225
St. Petersburg, FL 33713
T: (727) 826-9775
F: (727) 826-9534
Publisher: Larry Halstead

Basketball Times
Eastern Basketball Magazine
PO Box 865
Hull, MA 02045
T: (781) 925-5214
F: (781) 925-4466
www.basketballtimes.com
Editor: David Scott

Basketball Weekly
8033 NW 36th Street
Miami, FL 33166
T: (305) 594-0508
F: (305) 594-0518
www.basketballweekly.com
Publisher: Tom Curtis

Beckett Basketball Monthly
15850 Dallas Parkway
Dallas, TX 75248
T: (972) 991-6657
F: (972) 991-8930
www.beckett.com
Publisher: Dr James Beckett III

Coaching Women's Basketball
4646 B Lawrenceville Hwy.
Lilburn, GA 30247
T: (770) 279-8027
F: (770) 279-8473
Publisher: Betty Jaynes

College Hoops Illustrated
355 Lexington Avenue
New York, NY 10017
T: (212) 697-1460
F: (212) 286-8154
Editor: Kieran O' Dwyer

Dick Vitale's Collegiate Basketball Yearbook
Rte 22E, One Salem Square
Suite 201E
Whitehouse Station, NJ 08889
T: (908) 534-5390
F: (908) 534-5308

FIBA Basketball Monthly
Unicorn House, 3 FL
3 Plough Yard
London EC2A 3LP, England
T: (44.171) 375 37 73
F: (44.171) 892 20 58

Inside Basketball
7002 W. Butler Pike
Ambler, PA 19002
T: (215) 643-6385
F: (215) 628-3571

Slam
1115 Broadway
New York, NY 10010
T: (212) 807-7100
F: (212) 627-4678
Editor: Cory Johnson

**Sporting News College &
Pro Basketball Yearbooks**
10176 Corporate Square Drive
Suite 200
St. Louis, MO 63132
T: (314) 997-7111
F: (314) 993-7726
www.sportingnews.com
Publisher: Francis X. Farrell

**Street & Smith's College &
Pro Basketball Yearbooks**
342 Madison Street
New York, NY 10017
T: (212) 880-8698
F: (212) 880-4347
Publisher: Sal M. Schiliro

www.sportsbooksempire.com

www.usedbookempire.com

Football

National Football League
280 Park Avenue
New York, NY 10017
T: (212) 450-2000
F: (212) 681-7573
Commissioner: Paul Tagliabue
P: Neil Austrian
PR: Greg Aiello
www.nfl.com
www.superbowl.com
www.nflmedia.com

National Football League Players Association
2021 L Street, NW, Suite 600
Washington, D.C. 20036
T: (202) 463-2200
F: (202) 835-9725
Exec. Director: Gene Upshaw
Gen. Councel: Richard Berthelsen
PR: Frank Woschitz

American Football Conference

Baltimore Ravens
11001 Owings Mills Road
Owings Mills, MD 21117
T: (410) 654-6200
F: (410) 654-6249
www.baltimoreravens.com
P: Art Modell
PR: Kevin Byrne

Buffalo Bills
One Bills Drive
Orchard Park, NY 14127
T: (716) 648-1800
F: (716) 648-3202
www.buffalobills.com
GM: Tom Donahoe
PR: Scott Bechtold

Cincinnati Bengals
One Paul Brown Stadium
Cincinnati, OH 45202
T: (513) 621-3550
F: (513) 621-3570
www.bengals.com
GM: Michael Brown
PR: Jack Brennan

Cleveland Browns
76 Lou Groza Blvd.
Berea, OH 44017
T: (440) 891-5000
F: (440) 891-5009
www.clevelandbrowns.com
P: Carmen Policy
PR: Todd Stewart

Denver Broncos
13655 Broncos Parkway
Englewood, CO 80112
T: (303) 649-9000
F: (303) 649-9354
www.denverbroncos.com
GM: Neal Dahlen
PR: Jim Saccomano

Houston Texans
711 Louisiana, Suite 3300
Houston, TX 77002
T: (832) 200-2002
F: (713) 660-7248
www.houstontexans.com
feedback@fans.houstontexans.com
CEO: Robert McNair
GM: Charley Casserly
PR: Tony Wyllie

Indianapolis Colts
7001 W. 56th Street
Indianapolis, IN 46254
T: (317) 297-2658
F: (317) 297-8971
www.colts.com
GM: James Irsay
PR: Craig Kelley

Jacksonville Jaguars
One Stadium Place
Jacksonville, FL 32202
T: (904) 633-6000
F: (904) 633-6050
www.jaguarsnfl.com
GM: Mike Huyghue
PR: Dan Edwards

Kansas City Chiefs
One Arrowhead Drive
Kansas City, MO 64129
T: (816) 924-9300
F: (816) 923-4719
www.kcchiefs.com
P: Carl Peterson
PR: Bob Moore

Miami Dolphins
7500 SW 30th Street
Davie, FL 33314
T: (954) 452-7000
F: (954) 452-7055
www.dolphinsendzone.com
GM: Bryan Wiedmeier
PR: Harvey Greene

New England Patriots
60 Washington Street
Foxboro Stadium
Foxboro, MA 02035
T: (508) 543-8200
F: (508) 543-0285
www.patriots.com
GM: Andrew Wasynczuk
PR: Stacey James

New York Jets
1000 Fulton Avenue
Hempstead, NY 11550
T: (516) 560-8100
F: (516) 560-8197
www.newyorkjets.com
GM: Terry Bradway
PR: Frank Ramos

Oakland Raiders
1220 Harbor Bay Pkwy.
Alameda, CA 94501
T: (510) 864-5000
F: (510) 864-5134
www.raiders.com
P: Al Davis
PR: Mike Taylor

Pittsburgh Steelers
3400 S Water Street
Pittsburgh, PA 15202
T: (412) 432-7800
F: (412) 432-7878
www.pittsburghsteelers.com
P: Dan Rooney
PR: Ron Wahl

San Diego Chargers
4020 Murphy Canyon Road
San Diego, CA 92123
T: (858) 874-5400
F: (858) 292-2760
www.chargerspower.com
P: Alex Spanos
GM: John Butler
PR: Bill Johnston

Tennessee Titans
460 Great Circle Road
Nashville, TN 37221
T: (615) 565-4000
F: (615) 565-4105
www.nfl.com/titans
P: K.S. (Bud) Adams, Jr.
GM: Floyd Reese
PR: Robbie Bohren

National Football Conference

Arizona Cardinals
PO Box 888
Phoenix, AZ 85001
T: (602) 379-0101
F: (480) 379-1819
www.azcardinals.com
GM: Bob Ferguson
PR: Paul Jensen

Atlanta Falcons
4400 Falcon Parkway
Flowery Branch, GA 30542
T: (770) 965-3115
F: (770) 965-2766
www.atlantafalcons.com
P: Taylor Smith
PR: Aaron Salkin

Carolina Panthers
800 S. Mint Street
Charlotte, NC 28202
T: (704) 358-7000
F: (704) 358-7615
www.nfl.com/panthers
GM: Mark Richardson
PR: Charlie Dayton

Chicago Bears
Halas Hall, 1000 Football Drive
Lake Forest, IL 60045
T: (847) 295-6600
F: (847) 615-2387
www.bears.nfl.com
P: Mike McCaskey
PR: Scott Hagel

Dallas Cowboys
Cowboys Center
One Cowboys Parkway
Irving, TX 75063
T: (972) 556-9900
F: (972) 556-9918
www.dallascowboys.com
P: Jerry Jones
PR: Rich Dalrymple

Detroit Lions
1200 Featherstone Road
Pontiac, MI 48342
T: (248) 335-4131
F: (248) 335-0764
www.detroitlions.com
P/CEO: Matt Millen
PR: Matt Barnhart

Green Bay Packers
1265 Lombardi Avenue
Green Bay, WI 54304
T: (920) 496-5700
F: (920) 496-5712
www.packers.com
P: Bob Harlan
PR: Lee Remmel

Minnesota Vikings
9520 Viking Drive
Eden Prairie, MN 55344
T: (612) 828-6500
F: (612) 828-6541
www.vikings.com
Exec VP: Mike Kelly
PR: Bob Hagan

New Orleans Saints
5800 Airline Highway
Metairie, LA 70003
T: (504) 731-1799
F: (504) 731-1888
www.nfl.com/saints
P: Tom Benson
PR: Greg Bensel

New York Giants
Giants Stadium
East Rutherford, NJ 07073
T: (201) 935-8111
F: (201) 935-8493
www.giants.com
GM: Ernie Accorsi
PR: Pat Hanlon

Philadelphia Eagles
One NovaCare Way
Philadelphia, PA 19145
T: (215) 463-2500
F: (215) 339-5464
www.eaglesnet.com
P: Jeffrey Lurie
PR: Derek Boyko

St. Louis Rams
One Rams Way
St. Louis, MO 63045
T: (314) 982-7267
F: (314) 770-9261
www.stlouisrams.com
GM: Charley Armey
PR: Rick Smith

San Francisco 49ers
4949 Centennial Blvd.
Santa Clara, CA 95054
T: (408) 562-4949
F: (408) 727-4937
www.sf49ers.com
GM: Terry Donahue
PR: Kirk Reynolds

Seattle Seahawks
11220 NE 53rd Street
Kirkland, WA 98033
T: (425) 827-9777
F: (425) 827-9008
www.seahawks.com
Chmn: Paul Allen
PR: Dave Pearson

Tampa Bay Buccaneers
One Buccaneer Place
Tampa, FL 33607
T: (813) 870-2700
F: (813) 878-0813
www.nfl.com/buccaneers
GM: Rich McKay
PR: Reggie Roberts

Washington Redskins
21300 Redskin Park Drive
Ashburn, VA 20147
T: (703) 478-8900
F: (703) 877-2086
www.redskins.com
P: Steve Baldacci
PR: Michelle Tessier

The NFL began as the American Professional Football Assn. (APFA) in 1920. The league changed its name to the NFL in 1922.

2003 Super Bowl Championship
Tampa Bay Buccaneers 48
Oakland Raiders 21
at San Diego, CA

Canadian Football League
50 Wellington Street East, 3rd FL
Toronto, Ontario, Canada M5E 1C8
T: (416) 322-9650
F: (416) 322-9651
www.cfl.ca
Commissioner: Michael R. Lysko
Media: Shawn Lackie

In 1909 Albert Henry George, the fourth Earl of Grey and Governor General of Canada donated a trophy to be awarded for the Rugby Football Championship of Canada.

The CFL was formed in 1956 as the Canadian Football Council, in 1958 changing name to CFL.

Canadian Football League Players Association
603 Argus Road, Suite 207
Oakville, Ontario, Canada L6J 6G6
T: (905) 844-7852
F: (905) 844-5127
www.cflpa.com
E: cflpa@on.aibn.com
P: Stu Laird
Admin: Kathy McMullen

British Columbia Lions
10605 135th Street
Surrey, B.C., Canada V3T 4C8
T: (604) 930-5466
F: (604) 583-7882
www.bclions.com
E: info@palo.com
P: David Braley
GM: Adam Rita
PR: Debbie Butt

Calgary Stampeders
1817 Crowchild Trail NW
Calgary, Alberta, Canada T2M 4R6
T: (403) 289-0205
F: (403) 289-7850
www.stampeders.com
E: ronrooke@home.com
GM: Wally Buono
PR: Ron Rooke

Edmonton Eskimos
9023-111 Avenue
Edmonton, Alberta, Canada T5B 0C3
T: (780) 448-1525
F: (780) 429-3452
www.esks.com
E: davej@esks.com
P: Hugh Campbell
PR: Dave Jamieson

Hamilton Tiger-Cats
75 Balsam Avenue N.
Hamilton, Ontario, Canada L8L 8C1
T: (905) 547-2418
F: (905) 547-8423
www.tigercats.on.ca
E: mknack@tigercats.on.ca
GM: Ron Lancaster
PR: Bob Hooper

Montreal Alouettes
1255 rue University, bureau 120
Montreal, Quebec, Canada H3B 3A9
T: (514) 871-2266
F: (514) 871-2277
www.alouettes.net
E: lpdorais@alouettes.net
GM: Jim Popp
PR: Louis-Philippe Dorais

Ottawa Renegades
1015 Bank Street
Ottawa, Ontario K1S 3W7
T: (613) 231-5608
F: (613) 231-7677
www.ottawarenegades.net
E: mjulien@ottawacfl.com
GM: Eric Tillman
PR: Max Julien

Saskatchewan Roughriders
2940-10th Ave., PO Box 1277
Regina, Saskatchewan S4P 3B8
T: (306) 569-2323
F: (306) 566-4280
www.saskriders.com
E: ryanw@saskriders.com
GM: Roy Shivers
PR: Ryan Whippler

Toronto Argonauts
110 Eglinton Ave. W., Suite 303
Toronto, Ontario M4R 1A3
T: (416) 489-ARGO (2746)
F: (416) 489-5651
www.argonauts.on.ca
E: argos@argonauts.on.ca
P: Michael Pinball Clemons
PR: Dave Haggith

Winnipeg Blue Bombers
1465 Maroons Road
Winnipeg, Manitoba R3G 0L6
T: (204) 784-2583
F: (204) 783-5222
www.bluebombers.com
E: bbombers@bluebombers.com
P: Lyle Bauer
PR: Shawn Coates

2002 Grey Cup Championship
Montreal Alouettes 27
Edmonton Eskimos 19
Calgary, Alberta

NFL Europe
(New York Office)
280 Park Avenue
New York, NY 10017
T: (212) 450-2107
F: (212) 681-7557
www.nfleurope.com
E: nfleurope@sports.com
PR: Pete Abitante

London
99 Kings Road, First Floor
London SW3 4PA, England
T: (44.171) 355.1995
F: (44.171) 499.8098
E: response@nflp.co.uk
Director: Lisa Barber
PR: David Tossell

Amsterdam Admirals
Wibautstraat 137-C2
1097 DN Amsterdam, Netherlands
T: (31.20) 465.0550
F: (31.20) 465.0555
www.admirals.nl
E: info@admirals.nl
GM: Ronald Buys
PR: Perry Hendriks

Barcelona Dragons
Estadi Olimpic de Montjuic
Passeig Olimpic 17-19
Barcelona 08038, Spain
T: (34.93) 425.4949
F: (34.93) 426.9618
www.dragons.es
E: carmev@dragons.es
GM: Rafa Cervera
PR: Oriol Bonsoms

Berlin Thunder
Hanns-Braun-Str., Friesenhof 1
14053 Berlin, Germany
T: (49.30) 300.644.00
F: (49.30) 300.644.77
GM: Michael Lang
PR: Frank Weiss

Frankfurt Galaxy
Westerbachstrasse 47
60489 Frankfurt, Germany
T: (49.69) 978.279.10
F: (49.69) 978.2799.9
www.galaxy-online.com
E: pr@frankfurt-galaxy.de
GM: Tilman Engel
PR: Stephanie Bowe

Rhein Fire
Rather Strasse 49 A
40476 Dusseldorf, Germany
T: (49.211) 478.730
F: (49.211) 478.7329
www.rheinfire.de
GM: Alexander Leibkind
PR: Markus Muller

Scottish Claymores
205 St. Vincent Street
Glasgow G2 5QD, Scotland
T: (44.141) 222.3800
F: (44.141) 222.3828
www.claymores.co.uk
E: info@claymores.co.uk
GM: Steve Livingstone
PR: Gary Ralston

Formerly known as the World League, began in 1991, playing through the 1992 season before taking a two year hiatus, returning in 1995.

2003 World Bowl Championship
Frankfurt Galaxy   35
Rhein Fire   16

Indoor Football

Arena Football League
20 N. Wacker Drive, Suite 1231
Chicago, IL 60606
T: (312) 621-7000
F: (312) 621-7070
www.arenafootball.com
E: tgoodhines@arenafootball.com
Commissioner: C. David Baker
Media: Thomas H. Goodhines

AFL Properties
AFL Commissioners Office
AFL Business Development
330 Madison Avenue, 9 FL
New York, NY 10017
T: (646) 495-5558
F: (646) 495-5136

Arizona Rattlers
201 East Jefferson
Phoenix, AZ 85004
T: (602) 514-8300
F: (602) 514-8303
www.azrattlers.com
P: Bryan Colangelo
PR: Tami Scott

Buffalo Destroyers
661 Delaware Avenue
Buffalo, NY 14202
T: (716) 881-5676
F: (716) 881-4516
www.buffalodestroyers.com
CEO: Mark Hamister
PR: Brendan McDaniels

Carolina Cobras
4222 Emperor Blvd., Suite 335
Durham, NC 27703
T: (919) 281-0400
F: (919) 281-0410
www.cobrasfootball.com
P: Roddy Jones
GM: Bo Hussey

Chicago Rush
8735 W. Higgins Road, Suite 160
Chicago, IL 60631
T: (773) 243-3434
F: (773) 243-3435
www.rushfootball.com
GM: Mike Polisky
PR: Mike Alzamora

Colorado Crush
1701 Bryant St., Suite 900
Denver, CO 80204
T: (303) 777-7717
F: (303) 258-3108
www.coloradocrush.com
P: John Elway
PR: Michael Maciszewski

Dallas Desperados
One Cowboys Parkway
Irving, TX 75063
T: (972) 556-9333
F: (972) 556-9910
www.dallasdesperados.com
GM: Jerry Jones
PR: Doug Hood

Detroit Fury
2 Championship Drive
Auburn Hills, MI 48326
T: (248) 377-0100
F: (248) 377-3260
www.palacenet.com/fury
P: William Clay Ford, Jr.
PR: Jason Miller

Georgia Force
1269 Barclay Circle, Suite 338
Marietta, GA 30060
T: (404) 878-3825
F: (678) 581-9193
www.georgiaforce.com
GM: P/CEO: Jim Thomas
GM: Darin Kellett
PR: Jason Gilham

Grand Rapids Rampage
130 W. Fulton
Grand Rapids, MI 49503
T: (616) 559-1871
F: (616) 336-5464
www.grrampage.com
P/GM: Dan DeVos
PR: Leon Goner

Indiana Firebirds
One Conseco Court
125 Pennsylvania Street
Indianapolis, IN 46204
T: (317) 917-3090
F: (317) 917-3099
www.firebirds.com
P: Glenn Mazula
PR: Tim Farrell

Las Vegas Gladiators
4505 Maryland Pkwy
Las Vegas, NV 89154
T: (702) 731-4977
www.lvgladiators.com
E: lvgladiators.info@lvgladiators.com
GM: Mary Ellen Garling
PR: Adam Grant

Los Angeles Avengers
9975 Santa Monica Blvd.
Beverly Hills, CA 90212
T: (310) 788-7744
F: (310) 788-7747
www.laavengers.com
E: Info@laavengers.com
P: Casey Wasserman
PR: John Tamanaha

New York Dragons
1535 Old Country Road
Plainview, NY 11803
T: (516) 501-6700
F: (516) 501-6741
www.newyorkdragons.com
P: Charles B. Wang
PR: Howie Wirtheim

Orlando Predators
4901 Vineland Rd., Suite 150
Orlando, FL 32811
T: (407) 447-7337
F: (407) 648-8101
www.orlandopredators.com
E: opredators@aol.com
P: Dave Berryman
PR: Dan Pearson

San Jose SaberCats
600 E. Brokaw Road
San Jose, CA 95112
T: (408) 573-5577
F: (408) 573-5588
www.sanjosesabercats.com
E: sabercatpr@aol.com
GM: Terry Malley
PR: Phil Simon

Tampa Bay Storm
401 Channelside Drive
Tampa, FL 33602
T: (813) 272-7300
F: (813) 276-7301
www.tampastorm.com
E: stormshell@aol.com
GM: Tim Marcum
PR: Stephen Evans

The Arena Football League began in 1987.

2003 Arena Bowl Championship
Tampa Bay Storm   00
Arizona Rattlers   00
Game scores TBA

Arena Football League2
20 N. Wacker Drive, Suite 1231
Chicago, IL 60606
T: (312) 621-7800
F: (312) 621-7870
www.AF2.com
E: office@arenafootball.com
Commissioner: C. David Baker
Exec. Dir: Mary Ellen Garling
Oper: Robert Banks
PR: Ron Deuter

AFL2 will begin their fourth season in 2003.

Albany Conquest
51 S. Pearl Street
Albany, NY 12207
T: (518) 487-2245
F: (518) 487-2228
www.albanyconquest.com
P: Glenn Mazula

Arkansas Twisters
425 N. Broadway, Suite A
North Little Rock, AR 72114
T: (501) 975-KICK
F: (501) 907-2327
www.arkansastwisters.com
P: Dave Berryman

Bakersfield Blitz
4600 Ash Road, Suite 319
Bakersfield, CA 93313
T: (661) 634-9132
F: (661) 397-0820
www.bakersfieldblitz.com
GM: Brad Hoffman

Birmingham Steeldogs
2100 Richard Arrington Jr. Dr.
North Birmingham, AL 35203
T: (205) 458-8648
F: (205) 458-8489
www.steeldogs.com
P: Charles Felix

Bossier City Battle Wings
2000 CenturyTel Center Drive
Bossier City, LA 71112
T: (318) 752-2847
F: (318) 752-2878
www.battlewings.com
GM: Jason Rent

Cape Fear Wildcats
PO Box 198
Fayetteville, NC 28302
T: (910) 222-9453
F: (910) 222-2874
www.catsfootball.com
GM: Wilbur Christy

Charleston Swamp Foxes
3107 Firestone Road
Charleston, SC 29418
T: (843) 554-4321
F: (843) 554-4323
www.swampfoxes.net
P: Bobby Pearce

Cincinnati Swarm
100 Broadway
Cincinnati, OH 45202
T: (513) 421-4111
F: (513) 333-3040
www.
GM:

Columbus Wardogs
400 4th Street
Columbus, GA 31901
T: (706) 653-7789
F: (706) 653-7793
www.columbuswardogs.com
GM: Mike Sammond

Florida Firecats
11000 Everblades Parkway
Estero, FL 33928
T: (941) 390-2287
F: (941) 390-2286
www.firecatsfootball.com
GM: Kimberly Eckel

Green Bay Blizzard
1901 S. Oneida Street
Green Bay, WI 54304
T: (920) 405-1264
F: (920) 405-1221
www.greenbayblizzard.com
GM:

Greensboro Prowlers
1921 W. Lee Street
Greensboro, NC 27403
T: (336) 218-5428
F: (336) 218-5423
www.greensboroprowlers.com
P: Art Donaldson

Hawaiian Islanders
733 Bishop Street, Suite 2500
Honolulu, HI 96813
T: (808) 532-7362
F: (808) 537-9165
www.hawaiianislanders.com
GM: Jerry Kurz

Louisville Fire
937 Phillips Lane
Louisville, KY 40221
T: (502) 368-0009
F: (502) 368-4006
www.firefootball.com
GM: Tamer Afr

Macon Knights
170 Starcadia Circle
Macon, GA 31210
T: (478) 314-3000
F: (478) 314-3001
www.maconknights.com
GM: Bryan Watson
PR: Christa Timms

Memphis Xplorers
4560 Venture Drive
South Haven, MS 38671
T: (662) 342-1755
F: (662) 342-1156
www.xplorersaf2.com
E: info@riverkings.com
GM: Greg Griffith

Mohegan Wolves
311 State Street
New London, CT 06320
T: (860) 443-1900
F: (860) 443-2900
www.moheganwolves.com
GM: Jim Odle

Norfolk Nighthawks
201 E. Brambleton Avenue
Norfolk, VA 23501
T: (757) 626-0500
F: (757) 626-1855
www.norfolknighthawks.com
P: Ken Easley

Peoria Pirates
456 Fulton Street, Suite 398
Peoria, IL 61602
T: (309) 637-7777
F: (309) 637-7778
www.peoriapirates.net
GM: Greg Griffith

Quad City Steam Wheelers
207 E. Second Street
Davenport, IA 52801
T: (319) 324-4888
F: (319) 324-4777
www.steamwheelers.com
P: Jim Foster

Richmond Speed
1809 E. Broad Street
Richmond, VA 23223
T: (804) 780-2352
F: (804) 780-2446
www.richspeed.com
P: Harry Feuerstein

Rochester Brigade
2700 Brighton Henrietta Townline Rd.
Rochester, NY 14623
T: (585) 292-1530
F: (585) 292-6263
www.rochesterbrigade.com
E: clarge@rochesterbrigade.com
GM: Tim Peloza
PR: Jeff Roncone

San Diego Riptide
5465 Morehouse Dr., Suite 160
San Diego, CA 92121
T: (858) 404-0232
F: (858) 455-8379
www.sandiegoriptide.com
P: Gil Saidy

Tennessee Valley Vipers
Von Braun Center
700 Monroe Street
Huntsville, AL 35801
T: (256) 551-3240
F: (256) 551-3242
www.vipersaf2.com
P: Art Clarkson

Tulsa Talons
9128 E. 46th Street
Tulsa, OK 74145
T: (918) 664-4453
F: (918) 632-0006
www.bestoftulsa.com/talons
P: Jeff Lund

Wichita Stealth
Kansas Coliseum
1229 E. 85th Street N.
Valley Center, KS 67147
T: (316) 755-3307
F: (316) 755-3670
www.wichitastealth.com
GM: Mike McCoy
PR: Leon Goner

Wilkes-Barre/Scranton Pioneers
275 Mundy Street, Suite 203
Wilkes-Barre, PA 18702
T: (570) 208-5422
F: (570) 208-9233
www.wbspioneers.com
GM: Rick Sneed

2002 Arena Cup Championship
Peoria Pirates   65
Florida Firecats   47

National Indoor Football League
600 Loire Avenue
Lafayette, LA 70507
T: (888) 422-9682
T: (337) 896-4456
F: (337) 896-7652
www.nationalindoorfootballleague.net
E: NIFL1@aol.com
P: Carolyn Shiver
Oper: Tina Johnson

Austin Rockers
6901 N. Lamar Blvd., Suite 126
Austin, TX 78752
T: (512) 302-5656
F: (512) 302-5670
www.austinknights.com
GM: Hugh Lewis

Bayou Bucks
346 Civic Center Blvd.
Houma, LA 70360
T: (985) 851-3600
F: (985) 850-4663
www.bayoubucks.com
GM: Travis Carrell

Beaumont Drillers
2355 I-10 South, Suite 806
Beaumont, TX 77705
T: (409) 840-9229
F: (409) 840-9219
GM: Roy Reap

Billings Outlaws
303 N. Broadway, Suite 616
Billings, MT 59101
T: (406) 259-2226
F: (406) 259-2227
www.billingsoutlaws.com
GM: Duane Anderson

Bismarck Roughriders
601 E. Sweet Avenue
Box 2652
Bismarck, ND 58504
T: (701) 250-8900
F: (701) 250-8911
www.bismarckroughriders.com
GM: Chris Geiss

Evansville Blue Cats
18 S. Congress Avenue
Evansville, IN 47714
T: (812) 491-9401
F: (812) 491-9403
GM: Mike Arnold

Fort Wayne Freedom
535 W. Wayne Street
Fort Wayne, IN 46802
T: (260) 422-2293
F: (260) 422-3664
www.fwfreedom.com
E: info@fwfreedom.com
GM: Rich Coffee

La Crosse Night Train
110 Causeway Blvd., Suite A
La Crosse, WI 54601
T: (608) 782-1212
F: (608) 782-1206
www.nighttrainfootball.com
GM: Michael Grego

Lake Charles LandSharks
900 Lakeshore Drive
Lake Charles, LA 70602
T: (337) 477-3467
F: (337) 436-6222
www.landsharksfootball.com
E: lcindoorfootball@aol.com
GM: Carolyn Shiver

Lexington Horsemen
410 W. Vine Street, Suite 103
Lexington, KY 40507
T: (859) 422-7277
F: (859) 422-7276
www.lexingtonhorsemen.com
GM: Ron Borkowski

Lincoln Capitals
1610 N Street, Suite 100
Lincoln, NE 68508
T: (402) 477-8888
F: (402) 477-8998
www.lincolncapitals.com
GM: Michael Ryan

Myrtle Beach Stingrays
11943 Grand Haven, Suite A
Murrels Inlet, SC 27958
T: (843) 357-8498
F:
E: mbindoorfootball@aol.com
GM: April Coble

Ohio Valley Greyhounds
1310 Market Street
Wheeling, WV 26003
T: (304) 232-4101
F: (304) 232-1320
www.ovgreyhounds.com
GM: John Blackmore

Oklahoma Crude
1909 S. Van Buren
Enid, OK 73701
T: (580) 233-2704
F: (580) 233-9601
www.chisholmtrailexpo.com/crude
E: sales@enidok.com
GM: Jamie Lumuyan

Omaha Beef
1905 Harney Street, Suite 540
Omaha, NE 68102
T: (402) 346-2333
F: (402) 344-2333
www.beeffootball.com
E: omaha@beeffootball.com
GM: John Bostick

Rapid City Red Dogs
201 Main Street, Suite G
Rapid City, SD 57701
T: (606) 343-3535
F: (605) 343-3565
www.reddogsfootball.com
E: reddogs@enetis.net
GM: Dan Maciejczak

Show Me Believers
1000 Country Club Road
Suite 100
Saint Charles, MO 63303
T: (636) 916-0132
F: (636) 916-0137
www.showmebelievers.com
GM: Alexander Wright

Sioux City Bandits
401 Gordon Drive
PO Box 3183
Sioux City, IA 51104
T: (712) 224-3900
F: (712) 224-3901
www.scbandits.com
GM: Bob Scott

Sioux Falls Storm
200 N. Phillips Ave., Suite 202
Sioux Falls, SD 57104
T: (605) 332-4225
F: (605) 332-4051
www.siouxfallsstorm.com
GM: Dan Boyum

Tennessee River Hawks
109 Central Street
Knoxville, TN 37902
T: (865) 637-2000
F: (865) 633-8830
www.riverhawksfootball.com
GM: John Camblish

Tri-City Diesel
609 Platte Road
Kearney, NE 68845
T: (308) 338-8180
F: (308) 338-8175
www.dieselfootball.com
E: info@dieselfootball.com
P: Bruce D. Baily
GM: Mike Skeen

Tupelo Fire Ants
PO Box 2303
375 E Main Street
Tupelo, MS 38804
T: (662) 620-7543
F: (662) 620-7540
www.fireantsfootball.com
E: info@fireantsfootball.com
GM: Juliana Nykolaiszyn

Utah Warriors
1842 W. 2770 South
Suite 60
West Valley, UT 84119
T: (801) 973-7311
F: (801) 973-6194
www.utahwarriors.com
GM: Lee Leslie

Wyoming Cavalry
800 Werner Court, Suite 125
Casper, WY 82604
T: (307) 472-5030
F: (307) 472-5040
www.wyomingcavalry.com
GM: Brian Fleisher

2002 NIFL Championship Game
Ohio Valley Greyhounds   54
Billings Outlaws   51

Women's Pro Football

Women's Professional Football League
5631 Dorbrandt Street
Houston, TX 77023
T: (713) 926-7677
F: (713) 921-1881
www.womensprofootball.com
E: info@womensprofootball.com
Exec Dir: Robin Howington
Commissioner: Lisa Vesse
Operations: Dee Kennemar
Expansion Dir: Dawn Berndt

Arizona Knighthawks
5334 E. Thomas Road
Phoenix, AZ 85018
T: (602) 957-5441
F: (602) 934-2435
www.arizonaknighthawks.com
E: azknighthawksgm@aol.com
P: Rufino Uribe

Austin Rage
8760-A Research, #417
Austin, TX 78758
T: (888) 787-1313
F: (713) 880-3849
www.austinragefootball.net
E: gm@austinragefootball.net
GM: Donna Roebuck

Dallas Diamonds
232 Belmont Street
Hurst, TX 76053
T: (817) 690-3126
F: (817) 595-3126
www.dallasdiamondsfootball.com
P: Dawn Berndt

Florida Stingrays
6005 NW 67th Avenue
Tamarac, FL 33321
T: (954) 444-5783
F: (561) 391-8102
www.floridastingrays.com
E: angela@floridastingrays.com
P: Angela Belden

Hawaii Pacific Blast
PO Box 29568
Honolulu, HI 96820
T: (808) 286-5150
www.pacificblast.com
GM: Nicole Wylie

Houston Energy
5631 Dorbrandt Street
Houston, TX 770234
T: (713) 926-7677
F: (713) 921-1881
www.houstonenergyfootball.com
E: info@houstonenergyfootball.com
GM: Robin Howington

Indiana Speed
PO Box 781411
Indianapolis, IN 46278
T: (317) 293-2780
F: (317) 293-1113
www.indianaspeed.com
E: inspeed4@yahoo.com
GM: Charlene Daniels

Los Angeles Amazons
1992 Juanita Avenue
Pasadena, CA 91104
T: (626) 798-8105
www.losangelesamazonsfootball.com
P: Aubrey Duncan

Minnesota Vixens
300 Fifth Street NE
Mayer, MN 55360
T: (952) 657-2380
www.vixens.00sports.com
GM: Jan Peterson

Missouri Prowlers
Rte 1, Box 222-D
Sunrise Beach, MO 65079
T: (573) 317-2600
F: (573) 348-8297
www.missouriprowlers.com
E: info@missouriprowlers.com
GM: Joe Eldridge

New England Storm
PO Box 808
Medford, MA 02155
T: (781) 395-TEAM
F: (781) 306-1133
www.newenglandstorm.com
E: info@newenglandstorm.com
P: Melissa Korpacz

Orlando Fire
2090 Arbor way Drive
Apopka, FL 32703
T: (407) 758-7414
F: (407) 388-2827
www.orlandofirefootball.com
E: gm@orlandofirefootball.com
GM: Cyndi Long

San Diego Sunfire
2635 Camino Del Rio S., Suite 111
San Diego, CA 92108
T: (619) 295-8649
F: (619) 295-9285
www.sandiegosunfire.com
E: info@sandiegosunfire.com
GM: Donna Fox

Syracuse Sting
PO Box 17
Honeoye Falls, NY 14472
T: (315) 418-0905
www.syracusesting.com
E: stingfootball@aol.com
GM: Beth Markell

Wisconsin Riveters
1430 Sheridan Road
Kenosha, WI 53140
T: (262) 551-0322
www.wisconsinriveters.com
E: info@wisconsinriveters.com
GM: Holly Barrett

2002 WPFL Championship
Houston Energy 56
Wisconsin Riveters 7

The WPFL enters its fourth season in 2003.

National Womens Football Association
608 Vantrease Road
PO Box 286
Madison, TN 37115
T: (615) 860-4084
F: (615) 865-6256
www.NWFLcentral.com
E: footballmedia@cs.com
P: Catherine Masters
VP Media: Debby Lening

Women's Football League
3640 Dickerson Pike, Suite 1
Nashville, TN 37207
T: (615) 612-0061
www.wfleague.com
E: wfleague@aol.com
Commissioner:

Minor League/Semi-Pro Football

American Football Assocation/USFF
PO Box 1257
Sarasota, FL 34230
T: (941) 388-3510
F: (941) 388-2224
www.americanfootballassociation.com
E: usafoot.@aol.com
PR: David Burch
T: (607) 748-7140
E: Americanfoot@aol.com

The AFA is now in its 20th year as a national association & info centre on semi-pro football.

2002 AFA Champions
Kane County Eagles

2002 USFA Champions
Racine Raiders

Semi-Pro Leagues

Listed here are semi-pro leagues for a reference source. Please keep in mind that most of these leagues are very "grass roots", while only a few are truely organized, thus many changes occur without notice.

Atlantic Football League
8599 Oak Chase Circle
Fairfax, VA 22039
T: (703) 690-1930
T: (703) 931-8700
E: tdelaney@ecgcom.com
Commissioner: Tom Delaney

Eastern Football League
153 Cornell Street
Roslindale, MA 02131
T: (617) 327-0475
F: (781) 344-7784
www.efl-football.com
P: Fred Rihbany

Empire Football League
HC 65, Box 40-C
Honesdale, PA 18431
T: (570) 253-5226
F: (570) 251-3674
www.empire-football-league.com
E: empirefoot@aol.com
Commissioner: Allen Keller

Federal Football League
6608 Paradise Lane
Indianapolis, IN 46236
T: (317) 485-5482
E: tornado@indy.net
Commissioner: Kevin Johnson

Garden State Football league
475 Parker Avenue
Hackensack, NJ 07601
T: (201) 996-1965
www.eteamz.com/GSFL
E: michael.harris@allfun.com
Commissioner: Michael G. Harris

Maine State Football League
48 E. Grand Avenue
Old Orchard, ME 04064
T: (207) 934-2286
P: Peter Vorias

Mason-Dixon Football League
311 Country Lane
Petersburg, VA 23805
T: (804) 732-3806 (Lockhart)
F: (804) 733-0914
www.eteamz.com/masondixonfb
P: Travis Parker
T: (757) 654-9491
E: MDFootball@aol.com
Sec: Mary Lockhart
The MDFL was established in 1978

Mid-American Football League
574 Prairie Center Dr., Ste 135/118
Eden Prairie, MN 55346
T: (952) 451-2104
F: (612) 833-0916
www.mid-americanfootball.com
E: wwsports@hotmail.com
Exec Dir: Terry Sullivan
Comm: Al Howard

Mid-Continental Football League
1986 N. Telegraph Road
Monroe, MI 48162
T: (734) 241-0259
F: (734) 241-2335
www.mcfl.org
E: tclake@foxberry.com
Commissioner: Tim Lake
The MCFL began in 1991.

Mid-Ohio Football League
723 4th Street NW
New Philadelphia, OH 44663
T/F: (330) 602-4742
www.eteamz.com/mofl
E: rudyrudynd@aol.com

Midwest Football League
17011 Oketo Avenue
Tinley Park, IL 60477
T: (708) 532-3285
Commissioner: James H. Jones

National Football Events
PO Box 2175
Darien, IL 60561
T: (630) 916-5115
F: (630) 515-1885
www.nationalfootballevents.com
E:info@nationalfootballevents.com
CEO: Jim Nugent
Organizes semi-pro football tournaments in the midwest.

National Minor Pro FB League
100 Highland Pines #332
Pittsburgh, PA 15237
T: (412) 366-2973
www.swmich.simplenet.com/nmpfl
Commissioner: Tom Averell

New England Football League
505 S. Broadway
Lawrence, MA 01841
T: (978) 794-9256
P: Thomas Torrisi

NY Amateur Football League
PO Box 3571
Syracuse, NY 13220
T: (315) 382-1333
F: (315) 779-8432
Commissioner: Greg Portzline

New York Football League
7239 Winbert Drive
N. Tonowanda, NY 14120
T: (716) 693-8225
F: (716) 693-0650
www.nyfl.com
P: Pat Annunziata

North American Football League
208 Carriage Drive
Wernersville, PA 19565
T: (605) 987-5020
F: (605) 987-4184
www.nafl.net
E: sniles@@nafl.net
E: mricker@nafl.net
CEO: Robert Licopoli
Comm: Steven Niles
PR: Mark Ricker

Northwest Football League
PO Box 5361
Kent, WA 98064
T: (253) 472-0969
F: (253) 472-6081
www.nwfootball.net
E: commissioner@nwfootball.net
Commissioner: Ron Baines

Southern Football League
PO Box 160045
Atlanta, GA 30316
T: (404) 373-5295
F: (770) 360-0309
www.southernfootballleague.net
E: pmfrazier2002@yahoo.com
P: P.M. Frazier

Southern Plains Football League
610 W. State Street
Cannon Falls, MN 55009
T: (507) 263-7320
F: (507) 263-4177
www.eteamz.com/spfl
www.safe-usa.com/spfl
E: josh@safe-usa.com

Southwest Football League
PO Box 3892
Ontario, CA 91761
T: (909) 940-0275
F: (909) 657-9925
www.eteamz.com/swfl
P: Clyde Penland

Texas International Football League
1126 Alametos Street
San Antonio, TX 78201
T: (210) 734-6189
www.eteamz.com/TIFL
E: TIFL@football.com
P: Robert Romo

Utah Football League
PO Box 9401
Ogden, UT 84409
T: (801) 509-8899
www.eteamz.com/rhino-raiders
E: uflfootball@aol.com
P: Dave Stireman

United Football League of NY
334 Eastern Pkwy., Suite 5B
Brooklyn, NY 11225
T: (718) 953-7843
www.uflonline.com
E: ufl95@email.msn.com
Commissioner: Steven Ellis

Semi-pro/Minor League Publication

Minor League Football News
2522 N. Proctor Ave., PMB 183
Tacoma, WA 98404
T: (253) 272-7631
www.minorleaguefootballnews.com
E: PIFL98@aol.com
Editor/Publisher: Dick Suess

Football Canada

Canadian Amateur Football Association
Lansdowne Park Center
1015 Bank Street
Ottawa, Ontario K1S 3W7
T: (613) 564-2675
F: (613) 564-6309
www.footballcanada.com
E: dsprott@footballcanada.com
Executive Director: Jack Jordan
Coordinator: Deborah Sprott

Canadian Major Football League
Football Manitoba
200 Main Street
Winnipeg, Manitoba R3C 4M2 CAN
T: (204) 925-5769
F: (204) 925-5792
www.CSFL.net
E: bwall@shaw.ca
Exec. Dir: Barry Wall

The CSFL comprises the Alberta & Northern Ontario conferences.

Canadian Junior Football League
9611 No. 1 Road
Richmond, B.C V7E 1R8
T: (604) 277-8133
F: (604) 277-8136
www.CJFL.ca
E: ronald_white@telus.net
Commissioner: Ron White
PR: Jason Sperling
T: (780) 975-8424
F: (780) 473-3023
E: sperling@edmc.net

The CJFL is the developmental system to the CFL, and is a member of the CAFA, the governing body of football in Canada.

The CJFL comprises the B.C., Ontario, Prairie & Quebec FB Conferences.

2002 Canadian Bowl National Title
Saskatoon Hilltops 45 Okanagan 11

British Columbia Jr. Football Conference
1588 Rowan Street
Victoria, B.C., Canada V8P 1X3
T: (250) 592-1623
F: (250) 592-1603
E: paul_shortt@telus.net
P: Paul Shortt
PR: Chris Swartz
E: bcfcmedia@telus.net

Abbotsforce Air Force FB
Box 2322
Abbotsford, B.C. V2T 4X2
T: (604) 854-1254
F: (604) 775-6888
E: abbotsfordairforce@hotmail.com
P: George Sigaty

Kamloops Cowboys
#2-726 A Sydney Avenue
Kamloops, BC V2B 1M9
T: (250) 572-5510
F: (250) 376-3753
P: Dave Gracey
PR: Joe Liberatore
E: dgracey@city.kamloops.bc.ca

Okanagan Sun
PO Box 1660, Station A
Kelowna, B.C. V1Y 8M3
T: (250) 860-5850
F: (250) 860-4148
www.okanagansun.org
E: info@okanagansun.org
P: Bob Lindsay

South Fraser Rams
27012 28th Avenue
Aldergrove, BC V4W 3A3
T: (604) 856-3186
F: (604) 857-0131
www.playfootballbc.ca/rams
E: southfrasierrams@hotmail.com
P: Peter McCullough

Tri-City Meraloma Bulldogs
PO Box 612
34A-2755 Lougheed Hwy
Port Coquitlam, B.C. V3B 5Y9
T: (604) 464-1262
F: (604) 941-8199
www.tricitybulldogs.com
E: dawgs@tricitybulldogs
P: Keith Klements

Valley Huskers
#1-9360 Mill Street
Chilliwack, B.C. V2P 4N2
T: (604) 795-5657
F: (250) 795-3360
www.valleyhuskers.com
E: sunrise@dowco.com
P: Wayne Reimer

Vancouver Trojans
2929 E. 22nd Avenue
Vancouver, B.C. V6L 1M9
T: (604) 434-7176
F: (604) 681-9134
E: hfoster@home.com
P: Heather Foster

Victoria Rebels
PO Box 6012, Depot 1
3410 Shelbourne St.
Victoria, B.C. V8P 5L4
T: (250) 479-1590
www3.bc.sympatico.ca/rebels
E: rebels@telus.net
P: Joe Frenette

Ontario Football Conference
237 Marlborough Street
Brantford, Ontario N3S 4T4
T: (519) 758-0888
F: (519) 758-8013
E: kak@execulink.com
P: Paul Bartle
PR: Jack Low

Burlington Braves
New St. PO Box 62012
Burlington Mall
Burlington, Ontario
T: (905) 681-1126
F: (905) 691-8771
P: Peter Pebbles

London Beefeaters
PO Box 27086, Masonville RPO
London, Ontario N5X 3X5
T: (519) 850-7469
F: (519) 850-7544
www.londonbeefeaters.org
E: nbishop@sympatico.ca
P: Doug Dittmer
GM: Neil Bishop

Ottawa Jr. Riders
28 Canbury Crescent
Nepean, Ontario K2G 4L4
T: (613) 723-1302
F: (613) 226-2360
www.JrRiders.com
P: Sandy Ruckstuhl

St. Leonard Cougars
PO Box 574
Postal Sta "Jean-Talon"
Montreal, Quebec H1S 2Z4
T/F: (514) 727-2899
www.stleonardcougars.com
E: rachedj@sympatico.ca
P: Tony ladeluca, Sr.

Windsor AKO
PO Box 1027
Windsor, Ontario N9A 6P4
T: (519) 737-1444
F: (519) 737-1286
www.windsorakofratmen.com
E: ccarter@windsorakofratmen.com
P: Don Wiley

Prairie Jr. Football Conference
820, 10055-106 Street
Edmonton, Alberta T5J 2Y2
T: (780) 975-8424
F: (780) 472-3023
E: jimrea@canada.com
P: John Pyra
Registrar: Colleen Connelly
PR: Jim Rea

Calgary Colts
Box 6060, Sta D
Calgary, Alberta T2P 2C7
T: (403) 240-1340
F: (403) 249-4249
www.calgarycolts.com
E: calcolts@home.com
P: Gary Lehew

Edmonton Huskies
12317-128th Street
Edmonton, Alberta T5L 1C6
T: (780) 433-0906
F: (780) 448-0765
www.edmc.net/huskies
P: Curtis Craig
GM: Mike Assaly

Edmonton Wildcats
Box 1139, Main PO
Edmonton, Alberta T5J 2M1
T: (780) 448-0717
F: (780) 463-0871
www.edmontonwildcats.com
P: Barry Kowalski

Regina Prairie Thunder
300 McDonald Street
Regina, Saskatchewan S4N 6P6
T: (306) 721-0000
F: (306) 359-3828
www.prairiethunder.sk.ca
E: r.gaebel.rfm@sk.sympatico.ca
P: Kevin Holmes
GM: Royce Gaebel

Saskatoon Hilltops
1530 Kilburn Avenue
Saskatoon, Saskatchewan S7M 0K1
T: (306) 665-2911
F: (306) 653-2751
www.3.sk.sympatico.ca/garrett/hiltops
P: Rick Hopkinsi

Winnipeg Rifles
400-777 Portage Avenue
Winnipeg, Manitoba R3G 0N3
T: (204) 489-9534
F: (204)
www.winnipegrifles.com
E: info@winnipegrifles.com
P: Jim Ladd
Director: Lisa Lewis

Quebec Major Jr. Football League
1064 Ave. des Pines
Rockland, Ontario K4K 1N2 Canada
T/F: (613) 446-7999
www.QMJFL.ca
P: Joe Pistilli
PR: John Saint-Martin
T: (450) 671-0415

Chateauquay Raiders
117 St. George
Chateauguay, Quebec J6K 2S4
T: (450) 692-8212
F: (450) 692-1166
www.qmjfl.ca/raiders
E: moul@sympatico.ca
P: John Mouland
Governor: Bruce Bennett

North Shore Broncos
16722 boul. Gouin
St Genevieve, Quebec H9H 1E4
www.qmjfl.ca/broncos
T: (514) 683-1463
GM: Joe Dawson

Ottawa Sooners
PO Box 5162
Ottawa, Ontario K2C 3H4
T: (613) 730-4435
F: (613) 833-4185
www.ottawasooners.com
P: Rick Sowieta
GM: Micky Green

South Shore Packers
789 Madel
Greenfield Park, Quebec
T: (450) 466-8181
www.qmjfl.ca/packers
GM: Steve Britton

2002 QMJFL Manson Cup Final
Ottawa Sooners 18 Ottawa Jr Riders 17

The following league is part of the Canadian Senior football system.

Northern Football Conference

283 Wilson Street E., Suite 167
Ancaster, Ontario L9G 2B8
T: (905) 648-6915 (Metcalfe)
F: (905) 648-5477
www.cybersudbury.com/sports/spartans/NFC
P: Steve Harrington
E: ttsharrington@hotmail.com
Sec/Media Rel: John Metcalfe
E: jdmzeus@sympatico.ca

Belleville Panthers
33 Tracey Street
Belleville, Ontario K8P 2R7
T: (613) 967-4594
F: (905) 281-4278
E: cboyd@landcanada.ca
GM/Coach: Craig Boyd

Markham Raiders
818 Broadview, Unite #24
Toronto, Ontario M4K 2P7
T: (416) 598-3731
F: (416) 598-0513
E: VolkX@aol.com
GM: Logan Lubera

Mega-City Maddogs
217 Cass Avenue
Scarborough, Ontario M1T 2C3
T: (416) 716-1001
E: megacitymaddogs@hotmail.com
Oper: Michelle McBride

Milton Marauders
54 Dawson Crescent
Milton, Ontario L9T 5H9
T: (905) 818-1255
F: (905) 693-9608
E: atodd@cogeco.com
Oper: Andrew Todd

Mississauga Wolverines
1504-200 Burnhamthorpe Rd. E.
Mississauga, Ontario L5A 4L4
T: (905) 277-5529
F: (905) 277-4065
E: madsen5529@aol.com
GM: Finn Madsen

North Bay Bulldogs
848 Elizabeth Street
North Bay, Ontario P1B 3T7
T: (705) 476-3019
F: (705) 744-0104
E: timbertom68@hotmail.com
Oper: Tom Graham

Oakville Longhorns
115 Kenilworth Avenue N.
Hamilton, Ontario L8H 4R6
T: (905) 549-5050
F: (905) 549-5056
E: karlauto@execulink.com
Oper: Karl Kustor

Oshawa Hawkeyes
915 Dublin Street
Whitby, Ontario L1N 1Y9
T: (905) 668-4862
F: (905) 886-3608
E: oshawahawkeyes@hotmail.com
GM: Frazer Grosse

Sault Ste. Marie Storm
500 Bay Street, 2 FL
Sault Ste. Marie, Ontario P6A 1X5
T: (705) 946-1742
F: (705) 256-1664
E: oahs.on@aibn.com
GM: Don McBain

Sudbury Spartans
2-492 Montague Street
Sudbury, Ontario P3C 4G8
T: (705) 673-8074
E: pwalsh@sympatico.ca
GM/Coach: Paddy Walsh

2002 Northern Conf. Championship
Oakville Longhorns   36
Mississauga Wolverines 34

The OVFL is 19 & under junior football

Ontario Varsity Football League

10 Borland Drive
Guelph, Ontario N1G 5B6, Canada
T: (519) 836-4364
F: (519) 837-3573
www.ovfootball.com
E: ovfladam@home.com
CEO/Commissioner: Mike Adam
Sec: Rita Sauvage
E: rsavauge@home.com

Organizations

American Football Association
PO Box 43885
Las Vegas, NV 89116
T: (702) 431-2100
F: (702) 641-3432
P: M.J. Cuzdey

American Football Coaches Association
5900 Old McGregor Road
Waco, TX 76712
T: (817) 776-5900
Exec Dir: Grant Teaff

Arena Football Hall of Fame
319 7th St. @ Locust
Des Moines, IA 50318
T: (515) 362-5955

Blesto Pro Football Scouting Combine
428 Forbes Avenue
Lawyers Building
Pittsburgh, PA 15219
T: (412) 391-0770
F: (412) 391-2358
Director: Jack Butler

Canadian Football Hall of Fame and Museum
58 Jackson Street West
Hamilton, Ontario L8P 1L4
www.footballhof.com
T: (905) 528-7566
F: (905) 528-9781

Football Writer's Association of America
PO Box 909
Bloomington, IN 47402
T: (812) 332-4401
F: (812) 331-4383
Exec Dir: Bob Hammel

Green Bay Packer Hall of Fame
855 Lombardi Avenue
Green Bay, WI 54307
T: (920) 499-4281
F: (920) 494-9229

Indiana Football Hall of Fame
815 North A Street
Richmond, IN 47374
T: (765) 966-2235

National Collegiate Football Assn.
15 Tulipwood Drive
Commack, NY 11725
T: (516) 543-0730
Commissioner: Stan Gural

National Football Foundation & College Football Hall of Fame
111 South St. Joseph Street
PO Box 11146
South Bend, IN 44634
T: (219) 235-5581
F: (219) 235-9185
www.collegefootball.org/info

National Football League Alumni, Inc.
6550 N. Federal Hwy. Suite 400
Fort Lauderdale, FL 33308
T: (954) 492-1220
F: (954) 492-8297
P: Frank W. Krauser
PR: Remy Mackowski

National Football League Official's Association
609 Brainerd Place
Exton, PA 19341
T: (610) 363-1733

National Football Scouting Combine
4870 S. Lewis Ave., Suite 100
Tulsa, OK 74105
T: (918) 743-8874
F: (918) 743-8804
Director: Duke Babb

Pop Warner Football
920 Town Center Dr., Suite I-25
Langhorne, PA 19047
T: (215) 752-2691
F: (215) 752-2879
www.dickbutkus.com/popwarner
E: PWLSREG@aol.com

Pro Football Athletic Trainer Soc.
400 Colony Square, Suite 1750
1201 Peachtree Street
Atlanta, GA 30361
T: (404) 875-4000
F: (404) 892-8560
P: Ronnie Barnes

Pro Football Hall of Fame
2121 George Halas Drive NW
Canton, OH 44708
T: (330) 456-8207
F: (330) 456-8175
www.profootballhof.com
Exec. Dir: John Bankert
PR: Joe Horrigan
Mkt: Dave Motts

Pro Football Researcher's Assn.
12870 Route 30
North Huntingdon, PA 15642
T: (412) 863-6345
Exec. Director: Robert Carroll

Senior Football League
5200 Main St., Suite 210
Skokie, IL 60077
T: (847) 679-2700
F: (847) 679-2709
P: John H. Childers

U.S. Flag Football League
9861 Mainsail Court
Fort Myers, FL 33919
T: (941) 466-0166
P: John D. Carrigan

**U.S. Flag & Touch
Football League**
7709 Ohio Street
Mentor, OH 44060
T: (440) 974-8735
F: (440) 974-8441
www.E-sports.com/usftl
E: usftl@interax.com
Exec. Director: Mike Cihon

Publications

American Football Quarterly
840 U.S. Hwy 1, Suite 330
North Palm Beach, FL 33408
T: (561) 627-3393
F: (561) 627-5275
Publisher: Barry Terranova

Athlon's Football Publications
220 25th Avenue N., Suite 200
Nashville, TN 37203
T: (615) 327-0747
T: (800) 284-5668
F: (615) 327-1149
Editor: Charlie Miller

Beckett Football Card Monthly
15850 Dallas Parkway
Dallas, TX 75248
T: (972) 991-6657
F: (972) 991-8930
www.beckett.com
Publisher: Dr. James Beckett III

Coffin Corner
12870 Route 30
North Huntingdon, PA 15642
T: (412) 863-6345
Editor: Bob Carroll

**College & Pro Football News
Football Action**
18 Industrial Park Drive
Port Washington, NY 11050
T: (516) 484-3300
Publisher: Jack Cohen

Football Digest
990 Grove Street
Evanston, IL 60201
T: (847) 491-6440
F: (847) 491-0459
www.centurysports.net
Publisher: Norman Jacobs

The Football News
8033 NW 36th Street
Miami, FL 33166
T: (305) 594-0508
F: (305) 594-0518
www.footballnews.com
E: info@footballnews.com
Publisher: Tom Curtis

Football Times Newsletter
PO Box 133
Wallingford, CT 06492
T: (203) 269-8224

**Game Plan College Preview
Game Plan Pro Preview**
PO Box 3169
Syracuse, NY 13220
T: (315) 458-1287
Publisher: Joseph Del Popolo

Gridiron Coach Magazine
PO Box 69
Wabasha, MN 55981
T: (320) 734-4940
F: (320) 734-4462
www.gridironcoach.com
E: rstock@gridironcoach.com
Publisher: Ron Stock

**Don Hansen's
Football Gazette**
PO Box 514
Brookfield, IL 60513
T: (708) 485-2268
F: (708) 485-2269
Publisher: Don Hansen

Heinrich's Pro/College Previews
17962 Midvale Ave. N., Ste. 204
Seattle, WA 98133
T: (206) 546-2461
F: (206) 546-6015

International Football News
PO Box 1257
Sarasota, FL 34230
T: (941) 388-3510
F: (941) 388-4060

Minor League Football News
2522 N. Proctor Ave., PMB 183
Tacoma, WA 98404
T: (253) 272-7631
www.minorleaguefootballnews.com
Publisher/Editor: Dick Suess

Petersen's Pro Football Annual
6420 Wilshire Blvd.
Los Angeles, CA 90048
T: (213) 782-2828
F: (213) 782-2835
www.petersenco.com
Publisher: Lee Kelley

Pro Football Weekly
2525 Waukegan Rd., Ste. 270
Bannockburn, IL 60015
T: (847) 940-1100
F: (847) 940-1108
www.profootballweekly.com
Publisher: Hub Arkush

The Rouge Magazine
PO Box 71105, Northtown Mall
Edmonton, Alberta T5E 6J8 Canada
T: (780) 975-8424
F: (780) 473-3023
www.Rouge.ca
E: info@rouge.ca
CEO: Jason Sperling
*Covering football above the
49th parallel. An on-line magazine.*

**Sporting News College
& Pro Football Yearbooks**
10176 Corporate Sq. Dr., Suite 200
St. Louis, MO 63132
T: (314) 997-7111
F: (314) 993-7726
www.sportingnews.com
Publisher: Francis X. Farrell

**Street & Smith's College
& Pro Football Yearbooks**
342 Madison Avenue
New York, NY 10017
T: (212) 880-8698
F: (212) 880-4347
www.streetandsmiths.com
Publisher: Sal Schiliro

Superprep
PO Box 487
Laguna Beach, CA 92652
T: (949) 494-7866
F: (949) 497-3173
www.superprep.com
Publisher: Allen Wallace

Touchdown Illustrated
355 Lexington Avenue
New York, NY 10017
T: (212) 697-1460
F: (212) 949-6109

Ice Hockey

National Hockey League
1251 Avenue of the Americas
New York, NY 10020
T: (212) 789-2000
F: (212) 789-2020
F: (212) 789-2080 (PR)
www.NHL.com
Commissioner: Gary Bettman
VP Oper: Colin Campbell
VP/Media: Bernadette Mansur

National Hockey League Player's Association
777 Bay Street
Suite 2400
Toronto, Ontario M5G 2C8, Canada
T: (416) 408-4040
F: (416) 408-3685
www.nhlpa.com
Exec. Dir: Robert Goodenow
PR: Devin Smith

Anaheim Mighty Ducks
2695 E. Katella Avenue
PO Box 61077
Anaheim, CA 92806
T: (714) 940-2900
F: (714) 940-2953
www.mightyducks.com
GM: Bryan Murray
PR: Merit Tully

Atlanta Thrashers
One CNN Center, 12th South Tower
Box 105366
Atlanta, GA 30303
T: (404) 827-5300
F: (404) 827-5909
www.atlantathrashers.com
E: atlanta.thrashers@turner.com
GM: Don Waddell
Media: Tom Hughes

Boston Bruins
One Fleet Center
Suite 250
Boston, MA 02114
T: (617) 624-1900
F: (617) 523-7184
www.bostonbruins.com
GM: Mike O'Connell
PR: Heidi Holland

Buffalo Sabres
HSBC Arena
One Seymour H. Knox III Plaza
Buffalo, NY 14203
T: (716) 855-4100
F: (716) 855-4110
www.sabres.com
GM: Darcy Reiger
PR: Mike Gilbert

Calgary Flames
The Saddledome
PO Box 1540, Station M
Calgary, Alberta T2P 3B9
Canada
T: (403) 777-4636
F: (403) 777-2171
www.calgaryflames.com
E: flamesinfo@calgaryflames.com
GM: Craig Button
PR: Peter Hanlon

Carolina Hurricanes
1400 Edwards Mill Road
Raleigh, NC 27607
T: (919) 467-7825
F: (919) 462-7030
www.carolinahurricanes.com
GM: Jim Rutherford
PR: Jerry Higgins

Chicago Black Hawks
United Center
1901 W. Madison Street
Chicago, IL 60612
T: (312) 455-7000
F: (312) 455-7041
www.chicagoblackhawks.com
GM: Mike Smith
PR: Jim DeMaria

Colorado Avalanche
Pepsi Center
1000 Chopper Place
Denver, CO 80204
T: (303) 405-1000
F: (303) 893-0614
www.coloradoavalanche.com
GM: Pierre Lacroix
PR: Jean Martineau

Columbus Blue Jackets
200 W. Nationwide Blvd.
Columbus, OH 43215
T: (614) 246-4625
F: (614) 246-4007
www.columbusbluejackets.com
GM: Doug MacLean
Media: Todd Sharrock

Dallas Stars
Dr. Pepper StarCenter
211 Cowboys Parkway
Irving, TX 75063
T: (972) 831-2401
F: (972) 868-2860
www.dallasstars.com
GM: Doug Armstrong
PR: Rob Schich

Detroit Red Wings
Joe Louis Arena
600 Civic Center Drive
Detroit, MI 48226
T: (313) 396-7544
F: (313) 567-0296
www.detroitredwings.com
GM: Ken Holland
PR: John Hahn

Edmonton Oilers
Edmonton Coliseum
11230-110th Street
Edmonton, Alberta T5G 3H7
Canada
T: (780) 414-4000
F: (780) 414-4659
www.edmontonoilers.com
GM: Kevin Lowe
PR: Bill Tuele

Florida Panthers
Office Depot Centre
One Panthers Parkway
Sunrise, FL 33323
T: (954) 835-7000
F: (954) 835-7700
www.floridapanthers.com
GM: Rick Dudley
PR: Randy Simenski

Los Angeles Kings
555 Nash Street
El Segundo, CA 90245
T: (213) 742-7100 (Staples)
T: (310) 535-4500
F: (310) 535-4540 (PR)
www.lakings.com
GM: Dave Taylor
PR: Mike Altieri

Minnesota Wild
Piper Jaffrey Plaza
444 Cedar St., Suite 900
St. Paul, MN 55101
T: (651) 602-6000
F: (651) 222-1055
www.wild.com
CEO: Jac K. Sperling
GM: Doug Risebrough
Media: Bill Robertson

Montreal Canadiens
Molson Centre
1260 rue de la Gauchetiere Ouest
Montreal, Quebec H3B 5E8, Canada
T: (514) 932-2582
F: (514) 932-8285
www.canadiens.com
E: dsaillant@centre-molson.ca
GM: Andre Savard
PR: Donald Beauchamp

Nashville Predators
501 Broadway
Nashville, TN 37203
T: (615) 770-2300
F: (615) 770-2309
www.nashvillepredators.com
GM: David Poile
PR: Ken Anderson

New Jersey Devils
Continental Airlines Arena
PO Box 504, 50 Rte 120 N.
East Rutherford, NJ 07073
T: (201) 935-6050
F: (201) 935-2127
www.newjerseydevils.com
GM: Lou Lamoriello
PR: Mike Levine

New York Islanders
Nassau Coliseum
Uniondale, NY 11553
T: (516) 501-6700
F: (516) 501-6746
www.newyorkislanders.com
GM: Mike Milbury
PR: Chris Botta

New York Rangers
Madison Square Gardens
Two Pennsylvania Plaza
New York, NY 10121
T: (212) 465-6486
F: (212) 465-6494
www.newyorkrangers.com
GM: Glen Sather
PR: John Rosasco

Ottawa Senators
Corel Centre
1000 Paladium Drive
Kanata, Ontario K2V 1A5
Canada
T: (613) 599-0250
F: (613) 599-5562
www.ottawasenators.com
GM: John Muckler
PR: Phil Legault

Philadelphia Flyers
First Union Center
3601 S. Broad Street
Philadelphia, PA 19148
T: (215) 465-4500
F: (215) 389-9403
www.philadelphiaflyers.com
GM: Bobby Clarke
PR: Zack Hill

Phoenix Coyotes
9375 E. Bell Road
Scottsdale, AZ 85260
T: (480) 473-5600
F: (480) 473-5640
www.phoenixcoyotes.com
GM: Mike Barnett
PR: Rich Nairn

Pittsburgh Penguins
Mellon Arena, Gate 9
Pittsburgh, PA 15219
T: (412) 642-1300
F: (412) 642-1322
www.pittsburghpenguins.com
GM: Craig Patrick
PR: Steve Bovino

St. Louis Blues
Savvis Center
1401 Clark Avenue
St. Louis, MO 63103
T: (314) 622-2500
F: (314) 622-2582
www.stlouisblues.com
GM: Larry Pleau
PR: Frank Buonomo

San Jose Sharks
525 W. Santa Clara Street
San Jose, CA 95113
T: (408) 287-7070
F: (408) 999-5707
www.sjsharks.com
GM: Dean Lombardi
PR: Ken Arnold

Tampa Bay Lightning
Ice Palace
401 Channelside Drive
Tampa, FL 33602
T: (813) 301-6500
F: (813) 301-1680
www.tampabaylightning.com
GM: Jay Feaster
PR: Bill Wickett

Toronto Maple Leafs
Air Canada Centre
40 Bay Street, Suite 500
Toronto, Ontario M5J 2X2, Canada
T: (416) 815-5500
F: (416) 359-9331
www.torontomapleleafs.com
GM: Pat Quinn
PR: Pat Park

Vancouver Canucks
GM Place, 800 Griffiths Way
Vancouver, B.C. V6B 6G1, Canada
T: (604) 899-4600
F: (604) 899-4640
www.canucks.com
GM: Brian Burke
PR: Chris Brumwell

Washington Capitals
MCI Center
601 F Street NW
Washington, DC 20001
T: (202) 266-2200
F: (202) 266-2210
www.washingtoncaps.com
GM: George McPhee
PR: Brian Potter

The NHL organized in 1917, upon the ceased operation of the NHA.

2003 Stanley Cup Finals
New Jersey d Anaheim 4 Games to 3

Minor League Hockey

American Hockey League
One Monarch Place, Suite 2400
Springfield, MA 01144
T: (413) 781-2030
F: (413) 746-8409
www.theAHL.com
P: Dave Andrews
Media: Bret Stothart

Albany River Rats
51 S. Pearl Street
Albany, NY 12207
T: (518) 487-2244
F: (518) 487-2248
www.albanyriverrats.com
GM: Garen Szablewski
PR: Jonathan Scherzer

Binghamton Senators
49 Court Street
Binghamton, NY 13901
T: (607) 722-7367
F: (607) 722-7424
www.binghamtonsenators.com
GM: Tom Mitchell
PR: Grady Whittenburg

Bridgeport Sound Tigers
600 Main Street
Bridgeport, CT 06604
T: (203) 334-GOAL
F: (203) 333-1719
www.Soundtigers.com
P: Roy Boe
PR: Bill McLaughlin

Chicago Wolves
2301 Ravine Way
Glenview, IL 60025
T: (847) 724-4625
F: (847) 724-1652
www.chicagowolves.com
GM: Kevin Cheveldayoff
PR: Judd Sirott

Cincinnati Mighty Ducks
2250 Seymour Avenue
Cincinnati, OH 45212
T: (513) 351-3999
F: (513) 351-5898
www.cincinnatimightyducks.com
GM: Chuck Fletcher
PR: Don Helbig

Cleveland Barons
Gund Arena, 200 Huron Road
Cleveland, OH 44115
T: (216) 420-0000
F: (216) 420-2500
www.clevelandbarons.com
GM: Wayne Thomas
PR: Jamie Smock

Grand Rapids Griffins
Van Andel Arena
130 W. Fulton
Grand Rapids, MI 49503
T: (616) 774-4585
F: (616) 336-5464
www.griffinshockey.com
GM: Bob McNamara
PR: Randy Cleves

Hamilton Bulldogs
85 York Blvd.
Hamilton, Ontario L8R 3L4
T: (905) 529-8500
F: (905) 529-1188
www.hamiltonbulldogs.com
GM: Scott Howson
PR: Craig Downey

Hartford Wolf Pack
196 Trumbull Street, Third Floor
Hartford, CT 06103
T: (860) 246-7825
F: (860) 240-7618
www.hartfordwolfpack.com
GM: Al Coates
PR: Kevin Kavanaugh

Hershey Bears
PO Box 866
100 W. Hersheypark Drive
Hershey, PA 17033
T: (717) 534-3380
F: (717) 534-3383
www.hersheybears.com
GM: Doug Yingst
PR: David Mishkin

Houston Aeros
3100 Wilcrest Drive, Suite 260
Houston, TX 77042
T: (713) 974-7825
F: (713) 361-7900
www.aeros.com
GM: Dave Barr
PR: Sandy Kirk

Lowell Lock Monsters
Tsongas Arena
300 Arcand Drive
Lowell, MA 01852
T: (978) 458-7825
F: (978) 453-8452
www.lockmonsters.com
GM: Jim Leahy
PR: Danielle Clermont

Manchester Monarchs
555 Elm Street
Manchester, NH 03101
T: (603) 626-7825
F: (603) 626-7022
www.monarchshockey.com
GM: Kevin Gilmore
PR: Katie McDonald

Manitoba Moose
1430 Maroons Road
Winnipeg, Manitoba R3G OL5
T: (204) 987-7825
F: (204) 896-6673
www.moosehockey.com
GM: Craig Heisinger
PR: Chris Zuk

Milwaukee Admirals
1001 N. Fourth Street
Milwaukee, WI 53203
T: (414) 227-0550
F: (414) 227-0568
www.milwaukeeadmirals.com
GM: Phil Wittliff
PR: Brian Manthey

Norfolk Admirals
1300 Diamond Springs Rd., Suite 101
Virginia Beach, VA 23455
T: (757) 363-1900
F: (757) 363-9166
www.norfolkadmirals.com
GM: Al MacIsaac
PR: Mary Garrett

Philadelphia Phantoms
First Union Spectrum
3601 S. Broad Street
Philadelphia, PA 19148
T: (215) 465-4522
F: (215) 952-5245
www.phantomshockey.com
GM: Bob Clarke
PR: Al Cohen

Portland Pirates
531 Congress Street
Portland, ME 04101
T: (207) 828-4665
F: (207) 773-3278
www.portlandpirates.com
GM: Shawn Simpson
PR: Dave Ahlers

Providence Bruins
1 LaSalle Square
Providence, RI 02903
T: (401) 273-5000
F: (401) 273-5004
www.providencebruins.com
GM: Mike O'Connell
PR: Adam Alper

Rochester Americans
1 War Memorial Square
Rochester, NY 14614
T: (716) 454-5335
F: (716) 454-3954
www.amerks.com
GM: Jody Gage
PR: Steve Rossi

St. John's Maple Leafs
50 New Gower Street
St. John's, Newfoundland A1C 1J3
T: (709) 726-1010
F: (709) 726-1511
www.sjmapleleafs.ca
GM: Glenn Stanford
PR: Chris Schwartz

San Antonio Rampage
100 Montana Street
San Antonio, TX 78203
T: (210) 554-7700
F: (210) 554-7701
www.sarampage.com
GM: Brent Flahr
PR: Justin Cupertino

Springfield Falcons
PO Box 3190
Springfield, MA 01101
T: (413) 739-3344
F: (413) 739-3389
www.falconsAHL.com
E: hockey@falconsahl.com
GM: Bruce Landon
PR: Damon Markiewicz

Syracuse Crunch
800 S. State Street
Syracuse, NY 13203
T: (315) 473-4444
F: (315) 473-4449
www.syracusecrunch.com
E: info@syracusecrunch.com
GM: Vance Lederman
PR: Jim Sarosy

Toronto Roadrunners
Exhibition Place
100 Princes Blvd.
Toronto, Ontario M6K 3C3 Canada
T: (416) 263-3900
F: (416) 263-3901
www.torontoroadrunners.com
Oper: David Garrick

Utah Grizzlies
The "E" Center
3200 S. Decker Lake Drive
West Valley City, UT 84119
T: (801) 988-8000
F: (801) 988-7000
www.utahgrizz.com
GM: David Gasaway
PR: Bob Hoffman

Wilkes-Barre/Scranton Penguins
415 Arena Hub Plaza
Wilkes-Barre, PA 18702
T: (570) 208-7367
F: (570) 208-5432
www.wbspenguins.com
GM: Craig Patrick
PR: Jim Morlock

Worcester IceCats
105 Commercial Street
Worcester, MA 01608
T: (508) 798-5400
F: (508) 799-5267
www.worcestericecats.com
E: icecats@worcestericecats.com
GM: John Ferguson, Jr.
PR: Michael Thornton

The AHL was born in 1936-37, with eight franchises.

2003 Calder Cup Finals
Houston Aeros d Hamilton Bulldogs 4 Games to 3 in finals.

ECHL
103 Main Street, Suite 300
Princeton, NJ 08540
T: (609) 452-0770
F: (609) 452-7147
www.echl.com
E: echl@echl.com
P: Brian McKenna
VP Oper: Bryan Graham
VP Mkt: Glen Thornborough
Media: Jack Carnefix

The East Coast Hockey League merged with the WCHL at end of the 2003 season and became the ECHL, with the WCHL dissolving its name.

Anchorage Aces
3838 W. 50th, Suite #1
Anchorage, AK 99501
T: (907) 258-2237
F: (907) 278-4297
www.anchorageaces.com
E: office@anchorageaces.com
GM: Derek Donald
PR: Jack Michaels

Arkansas Riverblades
425 W. Broadway, Suite A
North Little Rock, AR 72114
T: (501) 975-2327
F: (501) 907-2327
www.riverblades.com
P: Ron Calcagni
PR: Chris Cichocki

Atlantic City Boardwalk Bullies
2301 Boardwalk
Atlantic City, NJ 08401
T: (609) 348-7825
F: (609) 348-7828
www.boardwalkbullies.com
GM: Matt Loughran
PR: Mary Rose Faustman

Augusta Lynx
712 Telfair Street
Augusta, GA 30901
T: (706) 724-4423
F: (706) 724-2423
www.augustalynx.com
GM: Derek Bundy
PR: Kyle Shultz

Bakersfield Condors
PO Box 1806
1001 Truxton Avenue
Bakersfield, CA 93303
T: (661) 324-7825
F: (661) 324-6929
www.bakersfieldcondors.com
E: condors@bakersfieldcondors.com
GM: Matthew Riley
PR: Kevin Bartl

Baton Rouge Kingfish
PO Box 2142
Baton Rouge, LA 70821
T: (225) 336-4625
F: (225) 336-4011
www.kingfishhockey.com
P: Scott Bolduc
PR: TBA

Charlotte Checkers
2700 E. Independence Blvd.
Charlotte, NC 28205
T: (704) 342-4423
F: (704) 377-4595
www.gocheckers.com
GM: Doug MacAdam
PR: Marilynn Bowler

Cincinnati Cyclones
100 Broadway
Cincinnati, OH 45202
T: (513) 421-7825
F: (513) 421-1210
www.cycloneshockey.com
P: Pat Pylypuik
PR: Gregg DeVitto

Columbia Inferno
701 Assembly Street
Columbia, SC 29201
T: (803) 256-7825
F: (803) 256-7866
www.columbiainferno.com
GM: Rick Woodard
PR: Wendy Hennessy

Columbus Cottonmouths
Columbus Civic Center
400 Fourth Street
Columbus, GA 31901
T: (706) 571-0086
F: (706) 571-0080
www.cottonmouths.com
E: cottonmouths@mindspring.com
GM: Phil Roberto
PR: Billy Carter

Dayton Bombers
3640 Colonial Glenn Hwy.
Suite 417
Dayton, OH 45435
T: (937) 775-4747
F: (937) 775-4749
www.daytonbombers.com
GM: Ed Gingher
PR: Matt Gorsky

Florida Everblades
11000 Everblades Parkway
Estero, FL 33928
T: (941) 948-7825
F: (941) 948-2248
www.floridaeverblades.com
P: Craig Brush
PR: Dan Guenther

Fresno Falcons
PO Box 232
2300 Tulare St., Suite 150
Fresno, CA 93708
T: (559) 485-7825
F: (559) 497-6077
www.fresnofalcons.com
E: bclark@fresnofalcons.com
P: Charles Davenport
PR: Brian Clark

Greensboro Generals
PO Box 3387
Greensboro, NC 27402
T: (336) 218-5428
F: (336) 218-5498
www.greensborogenerals.com
P: Rocco Scarfone
PR: Arley Johnson

Greenville Grrrowl
650 Academy Street
Greenville, SC 29601
T: (864) 467-4777
F: (864) 241-3872
www.grrrowl.com
P: Carl Scheer
PR: David Miller

Gwinnett Gladiators
PO Box 957238
Duluth, GA 30095
T: (770) 497-5100
F: (770) 497-5101
www.gwinnettgladiators.com
GM: Steve Chapman
PR: Dustin Bixby

Idaho Steelheads
251 S. Capitol Blvd.
Boise, ID 83702
T: (208) 383-0080
F: (208) 383-0194
www.idahosteelheads.com
P: William Waller
PR: Bonnie Way

Jackson Bandits
800 Carlisle Street
Jackson, MS 39205
T: (601) 352-7825
F: (601) 352-2715
www.thebandits.com
GM: Chris Bates
Oper: Lisa Strong

Johnstown Chiefs
326 Napolean Street
Johnstown, PA 15901
T: (814) 539-1799
F: (814) 536-1316
www.johnstownchiefs.com
GM: Jim Brazill
PR: Kevin McGeehan

Las Vegas Wranglers
4500 W. Tropicana Avenue
Las Vegas, NV 89103
T: (702) 471-PUCK
F: (702) 471-0234
www.lasvegaswranglers.com
E: info@lasvegaswranglers.com
P: Charles Davenport
Oper: Jim McKinnon

Lexington Man O War
410 W. Vine Street, Suite 230
Lexington, KY 40507
T: (859) 455-9900
F: (859) 455-9905
www.lexingtonmanowar.com
GM: Tim Woodburn
PR: Kristin Klingsturn

Long Beach Ice Dogs
300 E. Ocean Blvd.
Long Beach, CA 90802
T: (562) 423-3647
F: (562) 437-5116
www.icedogs.com
E: ternst@icedogs.com
P: Paul Solby
PR: Tobin Ernst

Louisiana IceGators
444 Cajundome Blvd.
Lafayette, LA 70506
T: (318) 234-4423
F: (318) 232-1254
www.IceGators.com
GM: Brian Kelly
PR: Andy Davis

Mississippi Sea Wolves
2350 Beach Blvd.
Biloxi, MS 39531
T: (228) 388-6151
F: (228) 388-5848
www.msseawolves.com
GM: Mike Fitzpatrick
PR: Mike Kelly

Pee Dee Pride
One Civic Center Plaza
3300 W. Radio Drive
Florence, SC 29501
T: (843) 669-7825
F: (843) 669-7149
www.peedeepride.com
GM: Jack Capuano, Jr.
PR: Joe Babik

Pensacola Ice Pilots
201 E. Gregory Street
Pensacola, FL 32501
T: (850) 432-7825
F: (850) 432-1929
www.icepilots.com
GM: Neil Hoyt
PR: Paul Chestnutt

Peoria Rivermen
201 SW Jefferson
Peoria, IL 61602
T: (309) 676-1040
F: (309) 676-2488
www.rivermen.net
P: John Butler
PR: Norm Ulrich

Reading Royals
35 N. Sixth Street, 1F
Reading, PA 19601
T: (610) 898-7825
F: (610) 898-4625
www.royalshockey.com
GM: Ray Delia
PR: John Curtis

Roanoke Express
2740 Franklin Rd., Suite 3
Roanoke, VA 24014
T: (540) 343-4500
F: (540) 343-4523
www.roanokeExpress.com
GM: Perry Florio
PR: Kevin Reiter

San Diego Gulls
3500 Sports Arena Blvd.
San Diego, CA 92110
T: (619) 224-4625
F: (619) 224-3010
www.sandiegogulls.com
E: tblack@sandiegogulls.com
GM: Steve Martinson
PR: Tera Black

South Carolina Stingrays
3107 Firestone Road
North Charleston, SC 29418
T: (843) 744-2248
F: (843) 744-2898
www.stingrayshockey.com
P: Sean O'Connell
PR: Darren Abbott

Texas Wildcatters
Jefferson County Courthouse
1149 Pearl Street, 4F
Beaumont, TX 77701
T: (409) 839-2344
F: (409) 839-2383
www.wildcattershockey.com
GM: Jenna Armando
PR: Stacy Thompson

Toledo Storm
One Main Street
Toledo, OH 43605
T: (419) 691-0200
F: (419) 698-8998
www.toledostorm.com
GM: Mike Miller
PR: Mark Thompson

Trenton Titans
650 S. Broad Street
Trenton, NJ 08611
T: (609) 599-9500
F: (609) 599-3600
www.trentontitans.com
GM: Richard Lisk
PR: Joe Zydlo

Wheeling Nailers
1144 Market St., Ste. 202
Wheeling, WV 26003
T: (304) 234-4625
F: (304) 233-4846
www.wheelingnailers.com
GM: Fred Traynor
PR: Ned Bowdern

Founder Henry Brabham started the ECHL in 1988-89 with Bill Coffey. Both men owned 3 clubs between them in the All-American Hockey League (AAHL) in 1987-88.

The ECHL began with five clubs its first season.

**2003 ECHL Kelly Cup Champions
Atlantic City Boardwalk Bullies**

Central Hockey League
14040 N. Cave Creek Rd., Suite 100
Phoenix, AZ 85022
T: (602) 485-9399
F: (602) 485-9449
www.centralhockeyleague.com
E: info@centralhockeyleague.com
P: Brad Treliving
PR: Steve Cherwonak
Oper: Duane Lewis

Amarillo Gorillas
720 S. Tyler, Suite B-134
Amarillo, TX 79101
T: (806) 242-7825
F: (806) 242-0079
www.amarillogorillas.com
GM: Grant Buckborough
PR: Dennis Puska

Austin Ice Bats
7311 Decker Lane
Austin, TX 78724
T: (512) 927-7825
F: (512) 927-7828
www.icebats.com
E: icebats@texas.net
GM: Charles Newman
PR: Glen Norman

Bossier-Shreveport Mudbugs
2000 CenturyTel Center Drive
Bossier City, LA 71112
T: (318) 752-2847
F: (318) 752-2878
www.mudbugshockey.com
E: info@mudbugshockey.com
GM: Jason Rent
PR: Steve Mears

Colorado Eagles
1625 Pelican Lakes Point, Suite 200
Windsor, CO 80550
T: (866) 679-PUCK
F: (970) 674-1743
www.coloradoeagles.com
E: info@coloradoeagles.com
GM:

Corpus Christi Ice Rays
500 N. Water Street, Suite 412
Corpus Christi, TX 78471
T: (361) 814-7825
F: (361) 980-0003
www.icerayshockey.com
E: info@icerayshockey.com
GM: Taylor Hall
PR: Dan Weiss

Fort Worth Brahmas
1314 Lake Street, Suite 200
Fort Worth, TX 76102
T: (817) 336-4423
F: (817) 336-3334
www.brahmas.com
E: info@brahmas.com
GM: Mike Barack
PR: Jeff Bowerman

Indianapolis Ice
1202 E. 38th Street
Indianapolis, IN 46205
T: (317) 925-4423
F: (317) 931-4511
www.indianapolisice.com
GM: Larry Linde
PR: Jason Burkman

Laredo Bucks
6700 Arena Blvd.
Laredo, TX 78041
T: (956) 791-9192
F: (956) 729-9393
www.laredobucks.com
GM: Marc Solis
PR: Jim Talamonti

Lubbock Cotton Kings
1309 University
Lubbock, TX 79401
T: (806) 747-7825
F: (806) 792-8396
www.cottonkings.com
E: info@lubbockcottonkings.com
GM: Mark Adams
PR: Chris Due

Memphis RiverKings
4560 Venture Drive
Southaven, MS 38671
T: (662) 342-1755
F: (662) 342-1156
www.riverkings.com
E: memphishockey@yahoo.com
GM: Robin Costa
PR: Bob DeCourcey

New Mexico Scorpions
5111 San Mateo NE
Albuquerque, NM 87109
T: (505) 881-7825
F: (505) 883-7829
www.scorpionshockey.com
E: scorpions@scorpionshockey.com
GM: Dan Burgess
PR: Mike Sheehan

Odessa Jackalopes
PO Box 9580
Midland, TX 79708
T: (915) 520-2255
F: (915) 520-8326
www.jackalopes.org
E: jackalopes@iglobal.net
GM: Monty Hoppel
PR: Bob Hards

Oklahoma City Blazers
119 N. Robinson, Suite 230
Oklahoma City, OK 73102
T: (405) 235-7825
F: (405) 272-9875
www.okcblazers.com
E: blazershockey@aol.com
GM: Chris Pressen
PR: Josh Evans

Rio Grande Valley Killer Bees
2600 State Hwy 336
Hidalgo, TX 78557
T: (956) 843-7825
F: (956) 843-6644
www.killerbeeshockey.com
GM: Trey Medlock

San Angelo Saints
3111 Knickerbocker Road
San Angelo, TX 76901
T: (915) 949-7825
F: (915) 223-0999
www.sanangelosaints.com
GM: Daniel Chaput
PR: Tom Nurre

Tulsa Oilers
9128 E. 46th Street
Tulsa, OK 74133
T: (918) 632-7825
F: (918) 632-0006
www.tulsaoilers.com
GM: Corey MacIntyre
PR: Brad Borror

Wichita Thunder
505 W. Maple, Suite 100
Wichita, KS 67213
T: (316) 264-4625
F: (316) 264-3037
www.wichitaThunder.com
E: wichitathunder@feist.com
GM: Bill Shuck
PR: Joel Lomurno

The current day CHL began in the 1992-93 season. The original CPHL, later CHL, was born with five clubs in the 1962-1963 season. The CHL merged with the WPHL following the 2001-02 season and the CHL name lives on.

2003 CHL Championship
(Wm."Bill" Levins Memorial Trophy)
Memphis Riverkings d *Austin Ice Bats* 4 Games to 1.

United Hockey League
1831 Lake St. Louis Blvd.
Lake St. Louis, MO 63367
T: (636) 625-6011
F: (636) 625-2009
www.theUHL.com
E: lpeppin@theuhl.com
Commissioner: Richard Brosal
Bus Oper: Ron Caron
VP Hky Oper: Mitch Lamoureux
Media: Lisa Peppin
Admin: Lori Kessel

Adirondack Icehawks
1 Civic Center Plaza
Glens Falls, NY 12801
T: (518) 926-7825
F: (518) 761-9112
www.adirondackicehawks.com
icehawks@adirondackicehawks.com
P: Art Shaver
PR: Kevin Crawley

Elmira Jackals
PO Box 669
Elmira, NY 14902
T: (607) 734-7825
F: (607) 733-2237
www.elmirajackals.com
E: jackalsinfo@jackalshockey.com
P: Tamer Afr
PR: Tom Callahan

Flint Generals
3501 Lapeer Road
Flint, MI 48503
T: (810) 742-9422
F: (810) 742-5892
www.flintgenerals.com
E: info@flintgenerals.com
GM: Robb King
PR: Brian Smith

Fort Wayne Komets
1010 Memorial Way, Suite 100
Fort Wayne, IN 46805
T: (260) 483-0011
F: (260) 483-3899
www.komets.com
E: office@komets.com
GM: David Franke
PR: Chuck Bailey

Kalamazoo Wings
3620 Van Rick Drive
Kalamazoo, MI 49001
T: (616) 349-9772
F: (616) 345-6584
www.kwings.com
E: info@kwings.com
GM: Paul Pickard
PR: Mike Modugno

Lehigh Valley Extreme
PO Box 4441
Allentown, PA 18105
T: (610) 439-3400
F: (610) 439-7330
www.lvxtreme.com
P: Terry Bender
GM: Dave Schultz
PR: Mark Thompson

Missouri River Otters
2071 Exchange Drive
St. Charles, MO 63303
T: (636) 946-0003
F: (636) 946-3844
www.riverotters.com
E: info@riverotters.com
GM: Kevin Fitzpatrick
PR: David Rak

Muskegon Fury
470 W. Western Ave.
Muskegon, MI 49440
T: (231) 726-3879
F: (231) 728-0428
www.furyhockey.com
E: furyhockey@webshore.com
GM: Tony Lisman
PR: Terry Ficorelli

Port Huron Beacons
222 Huron Avenue
Port Huron, MI 48060
T: (810) 989-9701
F: (810) 989-9708
www.beaconshockey.com
E: svickeryl@comcast.net
GM: Kevin Carr
PR: Stephanie Vickery

Quad City Mallards
1509 3rd Avenue A
Moline, IL 61265
T: (309) 764-7825
F: (309) 764-7858
www.qcmallards.com
E: info@qcmallards.com
GM: Howard Cornfield
PR: Ken Jacoby

Richmond UHL Club
601 E. Leigh Street
Richmond, VA 23219
T: (804) 780-4970 (Arena)
F: (804) 780-4606
www.
E: TBA
GM: TBA
PR: TBA

www.sportsbooksempire.com

Rockford Icehogs
PO Box 5984
Rockford, IL 61125
T: (815) 986-6465
F: (815) 963-0974
www.icehogs.com
E: icehogs@icehogs.com
GM: Ryan Washatka
PR: Mike Peck

Columbus, OH 2003-04 expansion.

The UHL was formed in 1991, playing in 1991-92 as the Colonial Hockey League.

2003 UHL Cup Finals
Fort Wayne Komets d Quad Cities Mallards 4 Games to 2.

West Coast Hockey League

At end of 2003 season the WCHL merged with the ECHL and will now cease operations as the WCHL. The WCHL began its inaugural season in 1995-96.

2003 WCHL Taylor Cup Finals
San Diego Gulls d Fresno Falcons 4 Games to 3 in the last WCHL finals.

Atlantic Coast Hockey League

1021 Sea Mountain Hwy., Suite B-2
North Myrtle Beach, SC 29582
T: (843) 280-2840
F: (843) 281-1268
www.achl2.net
E: achl@atmc.net
P: William B. Coffey
Commissioner: Jim Riggs

Cape Fear FireAntz
1960 Coliseum Drive
Fayetteville, NC 28306
T: (910) 321-0123
F: (910) 321-0200
www.fireantzhockey.com
E: galen@fireantzhockey.com
GM: Kevin MacNaught
PR: Galen Clavio

Knoxville Ice Bears
500 Howard Baker Jr. Drive
Knoxville, TN 37915
T: (865) 521-9991
F: (865)
www.knoxvilleicebears.com
E: tbenizio@knoxvilleicebears.com
GM: Tommy Benizio
PR: Tom Sye

Winston-Salem Parrots
414 Deacon Blvd.
Winston-Salem, NC 27105
T: (336) 722-7445
F: (336) 722-7502
www.wsparrots.com
E: info@wsparrots.com
GM: Darryl Noren
PR/Mkt: Kevin Hohl

Several ACHL clubs split to form the new WHA2 and the ACHL is expanding with new teams for 2003-2004 season.

2003 ACHL Inaugural Finals
Orlando Seals d Knoxville 3-0 games

WHA2

215 Celebration Place, Suite 500
Celebration, FL 34747
T: (321) 559-1200
F: (321) 559-1201
www.wha2.com
E: info@wha2.com
P: David Waronker
Hky Oper: Peter Young

Several ACHL clubs split to form the new WHA2. More clubs are proposed.

Alabama Slammers
www.alabamaslammers.com

Jacksonville Barracudas
5740-1 Spring Park Road
Jacksonville, FL 32216
T: (904) 367-1ICE
F: (904) 367-1424
www.jacksonvillebarracudas.com
bwells@jacksonvillebarracudas.com
GM: Bryan Wells
PR: Howard Brigance

Lakeland Loggerheads
www.lakelandloggerheads.com

Macon Trax
433 Cherry Street, Suite A
Macon, GA 31201
T: (478) 743-6010
F: (478) 743-0639
www.macontrax.com
E: smccall@macontrax.com
P: Dave Adams
PR: Steve McCall

Miami Manatees
www.miamimanatees.com

Orlando Seals
33 E. Robinson Street, Suite 101
Orlando, FL 32801
T: (407) 999-7887
F: (407) 423-2374
www.orlandoseals.com
E: info@orlandoseals.com
GM: Stan Drulia
VP Mkt: Sammy Wallace

Canadian Hockey
Father David Bauer Arena
2424 University Drive NW
Calgary, Alberta T2N 3Y9, Canada
T: (403) 777-3636
F: (403) 777-3635
www.canadianhockey.ca
E: info@canadianhockey.ca
P: Bob Nicholson
VP Oper: Scott Smith
Communication: Brad Pascall

Canadian Hockey
801 King Edward Avenue, Suite N204
Ottawa, Ontario K1N 6N5, Canada
T: (613) 562-5677
F: (613) 562-5676
www.canadianhockey.ca
E: info@canadianhockey.ca
Dir. Member Svcs: Glenn McCurdie
Merch/Lic: Dale Ptycia

Canadian National Team
Olympic Saddledome, PO Box 1060
Calgary, Alberta T2P 2K8, Canada
T: (403) 777-3633
F: (403) 777-3635
E: danmoro@agt.net
Manager: Dan Moro
Men GM/Coach: Wayne Fleming
Women's Coach: Melody Davidson
Junior Coach: Claude Julien

Canadian Hockey Assn.
Provincial Associations

Hockey Alberta
1-7875 48th Avenue
Red Deer, Alberta T4P 2K1
T: (403) 342-6777
F: (403) 346-4277
E: hockeyab@telusplanet.net
Exec. Dir: Howard Wurban

British Columbia AHA
6671 Oldfield Road
Saanichton, B.C. V8M 2A1
T: (250) 652-2978
F: (250) 652-4536
www.bcaha.org
E: info@bcaha.org
Exec. Dir: Barry Petrachenko

Hockey Manitoba
200 Main Street
Winnipeg, Manitoba R3C 4M2
T: (204) 925-5757
F: (204) 925-5761
www.hockeymanitoba.mb.ca
E: pkirby@hockeymanitoba.mb.ca
Exec. Dir: Pat Kirby

New Brunswick AHA
165 Regent Street
Suite 4, PO Box 456
Fredericton, NB E3B 4Z9
T: (506) 453-0862
F: (506) 453-0868
E: nbahabrw@nbnet.nb.ca
Exec. Dir: Brian Whitehead

Newfoundland & Labrador AHA
15 A High St., Box 176
Grand Falls Windsor, Newfoundland
A2A 2J4
T: (709) 489-5512
F: (709) 489-2273
E: ctulk@thezone.net
Exec. Dir: Craig Tulk

Hockey Northwestern Ontario
516 E. Victoria Ave., PO Box 27085
Thunder Bay, Ontario P7C 1A7
T: (807) 622-4792
F: (807) 623-0037
E: hkynwo@air.on.ca
P: Joe Tookenay
Exec. Dir: Joseph Ward

North West Territories
Hockey North
Sport North Federation
PO Box 223
Yellowknife, NWT X1A 2N2
T: (867) 873-3032
F: (867) 920-4047
P: Jim Ramsay

Nova Scotia-NSHA
6080 Young St., Suite 910
Halifax, Nova Scotia B3K 2A2
T: (902) 454-9300
F: (902) 454-3883
www.Nshockey.org
E: tomk@nshockey.org
Exec. Dir: Tom Krzyski

Ontario Hockey Association
1425 Bishop St., Unit 6
Cambridge, Ontario N1R 6J9
T: (800) 463-7962
T: (519) 622-2402
F: (519) 622-3550
www.ohahockey.org
E: oha@in.on.ca
Exec. Dir: Brent Ladds

Ontario Hockey Federation
1185 Eglinton Ave. E., Suite 202
North York, Ontario M3C 3C6
T: (416) 426-7249
F: (416) 426-7347
www.ohf.on.ca
E: sfarley@ohf.on.ca
P: Alan Morris
E: almorris@bmts.com
GM: Scott Farley

Ottawa District Hockey Assn.
1900 Merivale Rd., Suite 204
Nepean, Ontario K2G 4N4
T: (613) 224-7686
F: (613) 224-6079
www.odha.com
E: rts-ed@odha.com
Exec. Dir: Richard Sennott

Prince Edward Island-PEIHA
PO Box 302
Charlottetown, PEI C1A 7K7
T: (902) 368-4334
F: (902) 368-4337
E: peiha@pei.sympatico.ca
Exec. Dir: Mike Whelan

Hockey Quebec
4545 av. Pierre de Coubertin
C.P. 1000, Succ. M
Montreal, Quebec H1V 3R2
T: (514) 252-3079
F: (514) 252-3158
www.hockeyqc.ca
E: guy.blondeau@hockey.qc.ca
Exec. Dir: Guy Blondeau

Saskatchewan Hockey Assn.
#2-575 Park Street
Regina, Saskatchewan S4N 5B2
T: (306) 789-5101
F: (306) 789-6112
E: kellym.sha@sk.sympatico.ca
Exec. Dir: Kelly McClintock

Ontario Hockey Offices

Greater Toronto Hockey League
60 Carl Hall Road, Bldg. 39
Toronto, Ontario M3K 2B6
T: (416) 636-6845
F: (416) 636-2035
P: John Gardner

Hockey Development Centre of Ontario
1185 Eglinton Ave. E., Suite 301
North York, Ontario M3C 3C6
T: (416) 426-7252
F: (416) 426-7348
www.hdco.on.ca
E: hdco@orsc.com
P: Wayne Dillon

Minor Hockey Alliance of Ontario
150 Huron Street
Stratford, Ontario N5A 5S8
T: (519) 273-7209
F: (519) 273-2114
www.alliancehockey.com
E: alliance@alliancehockey.com
Exec Dir: Jason Bonnyman

Northern Ontario AHA
108 Lakeshore Drive
North Bay, Ontario P1B 2A8
T: (705) 474-8851
F: (705) 474-6019
www.noha.on.ca
E: cmay@onlink.net
Exec Dir: Chris May

Ontario Minor Hockey Assn.
40 Vogell Rd., Unit 43
Richmond Hill, Ontario L4B 3N6
T: (905) 780-6642
F: (905) 780-0344
P: Graham Brown

Ontario Women's Hockey Association
5515 Spectrum Way, Unit 3
Mississauga, Ontario L4W 5A1
T: (905) 282-9980
F: (905) 282-9982
www.owha.on.ca
E: Fran@owha.on.ca
P: Sue Rawson
Exec Dir: Fran Rider

Major Junior Hockey

Canadian Hockey League
305 Milner Avenue, Suite 201
Scarborough, Ontario M1B 3V4
T: (416) 332-9711
F: (416) 332-1477
www.chl.ca
E: chl@chl.ca
P: David E. Branch
Mkt Dir: Norm Webb
Information: Dave Lord
PR: Chris McCarthy

The CHL acts as the governing body to the three Major Junior Leagues.

Ontario Hockey League
305 Milner Ave., Suite 200
Scarborough, Ontario M1B 3V4
T: (416) 299-8700
F: (416) 299-8787
www.ontariohockeyleague.com
E: ohl@chl.ca
Commissioner: David E. Branch
PR: Aaron Bell

Barrie Colts
555 Bayview Drive
Barrie, Ontario L4N 8Y2
T: (705) 722-6587
F: (705) 721-9709
www.barriecolts.com
E: operations@barriecolts.com
Governor: Jamie Massie
GM: Mike McCann
PR: Jason Fordch

Belleville Bulls
265 Cannifton Road
Belleville, Ontario K8N 4V8
T: (613) 966-8338
F: (613) 966-8761
www.bellevillebulls.com
E: hockey@bellevillebulls.com
GM: Brad Vaughan
PR: Nancy Sommerville

Brampton Battalion
7575 Kennedy Road S.
Brampton, Ontario L6W 4T2
T: (905) 874-2393
F: (905) 874-2394
www.battalionhockey.com
E: info@batallionhockey.com
P: Michael Griffin
PR: Darryl Bricknell

Erie Otters
809 French Street
Erie, PA 16501
T: (814) 455-7779
F: (814) 455-0911
www.ottershockey.com
E: puck@ottershockey.com
GM: Sherwood Bassin
Oper: Ron Sertz
PR: Mark Jeanneret

Guelph Storm
55 Wyndham Street N.
Guelph, Ontario N1H 7T8
T: (519) 837-9690
F: (519) 837-9692
www.guelphstorm.com
E: storm@sentex.net
GM: Alan Millar
PR: Matt Newby

Kingston Frontenacs
PO Box 665
303 York Street
Kingston, Ontario K7L 4X1
T: (613) 542-4042
F: (613) 542-2834
www.kingstonfrontenacs.com
E: kgnfront@kos.net
P: Doug Springer
Mkt/PR: Jeff Stilwell

Kitchener Rangers
PO Box 43013, Eastwood Squ.
Kitchener, Ontario N2H 6S9
T: (519) 576-3700
F: (519) 576-7571
www.kitchenerrangers.com
E: info@kitchenerrangers.com
P: Steve Bienkowski
PR: Jeff Young

London Knights
99 Dundas Street
London, Ontario N6A 6K1
T: (519) 681-0800
F: (519) 668-7291
www.londonknights.com
E: info@londonknights.com
Governor: Dale Hunter
Asst GM/PR: Jim McKellar
Mkt: Stefanie Turnbull

Mississauga Ice Dogs
5500 Rose Cherry Place
Mississauga, Ontario L5Z 4B6
T: (905) 502-7788
F: (905) 502-0169
www.mississaugaicedogs.com
E: icedogs@mississaugaicedogs.com
P: Michael Ricci
PR: Jerome Dupont

Oshawa Generals
99 Thornton Road S.
Oshawa, Ontario L1J 5Y1
T: (905) 433-0900
F: (905) 433-0868
www.oshawagenerals.com
E: admin@oshawagenerals.com
P: John Humphreys
GM: Mike Dahle
PR: Jason Hickman

Ottawa 67's
Ottawa Cicic Centre
1015 Bank Street
Ottawa, Ontario K1S 3W7
T: (613) 232-6767
F: (613) 232-5582
www.ottawa67s.com
E: ott67s@ottawa67s.com
GM: Brian Kilrea
Mkt/PR: Jason O'Connor

Owen Sound Attack
PO Box 1420
1900 Third Ave. East
Owen Sound, Ontario N4K 6T5
T: (519) 371-7452
F: (519) 371-7990
www.attackhockey.com
E: attack@bmts.com
GM: Michael Futa
PR: Dave Middleton

Peterborough Petes
121 Lansdowne St. West
Peterborough, Ontario K9J 1Y4
T: (705) 743-3681
F: (705) 743-5497
www.gopetesgo.com
E: pbopetes@accel.net
Governor: Ed Rowe
GM: Jeff Twohey
Mkt/PR: Aaron Garfat

Plymouth Whalers
14900 Beck Road
Plymouth Township, MI 48170
T: (734) 453-8400
F: (734) 453-4201
www.plymouthwhalers.com
E: frontoffice@plymouthwhalers.com
P: Mike Vellucci
PR: Scott Kelley

Saginaw Spirit
PO Box 6157
6200 State Street
Saginaw, MI 48608
T: (989) 497-7747
F: (989) 497-9426
www.saginawspirit.com
E: info@saginawspirit.com
GM: Costa Papista
PR: Cameron Knowles

Sarnia Sting
1455 London Road
Sarnia, Ontario N7S 6K7
T: (519) 542-4494
F: (519) 542-2388
www.sarniasting.com
E: buzz@ebtech.net
P: Robert Ciccarelli
GM: Terry Doran
Oper: Joe Bronzi
PR: Mark Glavin

Sault Ste. Marie Greyhounds
269 Queen Street E.
Sault Ste. Marie, Ontario P6A 1Y9
T: (705) 253-5976
F: (705) 945-9458
www.soogreyhounds.com
E: info@soogreyhounds.com
GM: John Vanbiesbrouck
Mkt/PR: Gino Cavallo

Sudbury Wolves
240 Elgin Street S.
Sudbury, Ontario P3E 3N6
T: (705) 675-3941
F: (705) 675-7951
www.sudburywolves.com
E: wolves@isys.ca
P: Mark Burgess
PR/Mkt: Curtis Hall

Toronto St. Michael's Majors
1515 Bathurst Street
Toronto, Ontario M5P 3H4
T: (416) 653-3180
F: (416) 653-8010
www.stmichaelsmajors.com
E: majors@chl.ca
GM: Dave Cameron
Mkt/PR: Tammy Carlson

Windsor Spitfires
Windsor Arena
334 Wyandotte Street E.
Windsor, Ontario N9A 3H6
T: (519) 254-9256
F: (519) 254-9257
www.windsorspitfires.com
frontoffice@windsorspitfires.com
GM: Mike Kelly
Mkt/PR: Steve Horne

2003 OHL Champions
Kitchener Rangers

Quebec Major Junior Hockey League

255 Boul. Roland-Therrien, Ste 101
Longueuil, Quebec J4H 4A6, CAN
T: (450) 442-3590
F: (450) 442-3593
www.lhjmq.qc.ca
E: hockey@lhjmq.qc.ca
P: Gilles Courteau
PR: Claude Rompre

Baie-Comeau Drakkar
70 Michel Hemon Avenue
Baie-Comeau, Quebec G4Z 2A5
T: (418) 296-8484
F: (418) 296-0011
www.le-drakkar.com
E: drakkar@globetrotter.net
Governor: Jacques Tremblay
Mkt/PR: Sylvie Fortier

Bathurst Acadie Titan
850 rue Sainte-Anne
Bathurst, NB E2A 6X2
T: (506) 549-3300
F: (506) 549-3355
www.letitan.com
E: letitan@nbnet.nb.ca
GM: Pierre Roux
Mkt: Earl Dimitroff

Cape Breton Screaming Eagles
PO Box 8
479 George Street
Sydney, Nova Scotia B1P 6G9
T: (902) 567-6378
F: (902) 567-6303
www.capebretoneagles.com
E: admin@capebretoneagles.com
P: Greg Lynch
GM: Pascal Vincent
PR/Mkt: Paul MacDonald

Chicoutimi Sagueneens
C.P. 323
643 rue begin Street
Chicoutimi, Quebec G7H 5C2
T: (418) 549-9489
F: (418) 549-1645
www.sagueneens.com
E: sagueneens@videotron.ca
P: Guy Carbonneau
GM: Marc Desforges
PR: Gaston Senechal

Drummondville Voltigeurs
300, rue Cockburn
Drummondville, Quebec J2C 4L6
T: (819) 477-9400
F: (819) 477-0561
www.voltigeurs.ca
E: info@voltigeurs.ca
GM: Michel Georges
PR: Raynald Forcier

Halifax Mooseheads
5284 Duke Street
Halifax, Nova Scotia B3J 3L2
T: (902) 496-5993
F: (902) 423-6413
www.halifaxmooseheads.ca
E: jill@halifaxmooseheads.ca
Governor: Joe Richard
PR: Terry Waterfield

Hull Olympiques
C.P. 251, Succ. A
125 Carillon Street
Hull, Quebec J8Y 6M8
T: (819) 777-0661
F: (819) 777-6933
www.olympiquesdehull.com
E: hockey@olympiquesdehull.com
Governor: Charles Henry
Mkt: Daniel Brunet

Moncton Wildcats
100 Midland Drive
Dieppe, N.B. E1A 6X4
T: (506) 382-5555
F: (506) 858-2222
www.moncton-wildcats.com
E: wildcats@moncton-wildcats.com
Gov: Jean Brousseau
PR: Joey Parent

Montreal Rocket
2800 rue Viau
Montreal, Quebec H1V 3J3
T: (514) 868-3829
F: (514) 868-3831
www.rocket.qc.ca
E: hockey@rocket.qc.ca
GM: Serge Savard, Jr.
PR: Gary Connelly

Quebec Remparts
Colisee de Quebec
250 Wilfred Hamel Blvd.
Quebec City, Quebec G1L 5A7
T: (418) 525-1212
F: (418) 525-2242
www.remparts.qc.ca
E: info@remparts.qc.ca
Governor: Julien Gagnon
PR/Mkt: Lucie Cloutier

Rimouski Oceanic
111, 2ieme Rue Ouest
Rimouski, Quebec G5L 7C9
T: (418) 723-4444
F: (418) 725-0944
www.oceanic.qu.ca
E: hockey@oceanic.qc.ca
GM: Doris Labonte
PR: Eric Forest

Rouyn-Noranda Huskies
218 rue Murdoch
Rouyn-Noranda, Quebec J9X 1E6
T: (819) 797-6222
F: (819) 797-4311
www.huskies.qc.ca
E: secreta@huskies.qc.ca
GM: Sylvain Danis
PR: Nicole Heroux

Shawinigan Cataractes
855 rue Broadway
Shawinigan, Quebec G9N 8B8
T: (819) 537-6237
F: (819) 537-3538
www.cataractes.qc.ca
E: shcats@cgobable.ca
Governor: Gilles Guay
PR: Michel Boisvert

Les Castors de Sherbrooke
Le Palais Des Sports
360 rue Parc
Sherbrooke, Quebec J1E 2J9
T: (819) 346-8789
F: (819) 346-6505
www.castors.net
E: castors@castors.net
GM: Normand Gosselin
PR/Mkt: Pierre Sasseville

Les Foreurs de Val-D'Or
810, Sierne, 6th Avenue
Val D'Or, Quebec J6P 1B4
T: (819) 824-0093
F: (819) 824-7602
www.lino.com/foreurs
E: foreurs@lino.com
GM: Stephane Pilotte
PR: Serge Trudel

Victoriaville Tigres
C.P. 857, 400 boul Jutras Est
Victoriaville, Quebec G6P 7W7
T: (819) 752-6353
F: (819) 758-2846
www.ivic.qc.ca/tigre
E: tigres@ivic.qc.ca
GM: John Greene
PR: Sylvie Yockell

2003 QMJHL Champions
Hull Olympiques

Western Hockey League
#1-3030 Sunridge Way NE
Calgary, Alberta T1Y 7K4
T: (403) 693-3030
F: (403) 693-3031
www.whl.ca
E: info@whl.ca
Commissioner: Ron Robison
VP Hockey: Richard Doerksen
Operations: Yvonne Bergmann
Information: Leroy McKinnon
Admin Asst: Dallas Kitt
E: mckinnonl@whl.ca

Brandon Wheat Kings
#2, 1175-18th Street
Brandon, Manitoba R7A 7C5
T: (204) 726-3535
F: (204) 726-3540
www.wheatkings.com
E: office@wheatkings.com
GM: Kelly McCrimmon
Mkt: Rick Dillabough

Calgary Hitmen
PO Box 1540, Station M
555 Sadledome Rise SE
Calgary, Alberta T2P 3B9
T: (403) 571-2200
F: (403) 571-2211
www.hitmenhockey.com
E: info@hitmen.com
Governor: Michael Holditch
GM: Kelly Kisio
PR: Charla Odgers

Everett Hockey Club (2003-04)
2733 Colby Avenue
Everett, WA 98201
T: (425) 252-5100
F: (425) 257-0700
www.everetthockeyteam.com
E: info@everetthockeyteam.com
GM: Doug Soetaert
Mkt/PR: Mike MacCulloch
Admin Asst: Mary Brown

Kamloops Blazers
300 Lorne Street
Kamloops, B.C. V2C 1W3
T: (250) 828-1144
F: (250) 828-7822
www.kamloopsblazers.bc.ca
E: hockey@kamloopsblazers.bc.ca
Governor: Colin Day
GM: Mike Moore
Mkt/PR: Kirk Fraser

Kelowna Rockets
101-1223 Water Street
Kelowna, B.C. V1Y 9V1
T: (250) 860-7825
F: (250) 860-7880
www.kelownarockets.com
E: info@kelownarockets.com
Governor: Bruce Hamilton
PR: Anne-Marie Hamilton

Kootenay Ice
#2-1777-2nd Street North
Cranbrook, B.C. V1C 7G9
T: (250) 417-0322
F: (250) 417-0323
www.kootenayice.net
E: info@kootenayice.net
P: Ed Chynoweth
PR: Sara Jerke

Lethbridge Hurricanes
PO Box 2143
2510 Scenic Drive S.
Lethbridge, Alberta T1J 4K7
T: (403) 328-1986
F: (403) 329-1622
www.lethbridgehurricanes.com
E: info@lethbridgehurricanes.com
Governor: Herman Elfring
Oper: Darren Stocker
PR/Mkt: Doug Campbell

Medicine Hat Tigers
PO Box 507
155 Ash Ave. SE
Medicine Hat, Alberta T1A 7G2
T: (403) 526-2666
F: (403) 526-3072
www.tigershockey.com
E: admin@tigershockey.com
Governor: Darrell Maser
Mkt/PR: Dave Andjelic

Moose Jaw Warriors
PO Box 74
1251 Main Street North
Moose Jaw, Sask. S6H 4N7
T: (306) 694-5711
F: (306) 692-7833
www.mjwarriors.com
E: warriors1@mjwarriors.com
Governor: John LaBuick
GM: Barry Webster
Mkt: Brad Delorey

Portland Winter Hawks
PO Box 3009
300 N. Winning
Portland, OR 97208
T: (503) 238-6366
F: (503) 238-7629
www.winterhawks.com
E: hockey@winterhawks.com
Governor: Ken Hodge
Oper: Mark Miller
PR: Dean Vrooman

Prince Albert Raiders
690-32nd Street E.
Prince Albert, Sask. S6V 2W8
T: (306) 764-5348
F: (306) 764-5454
www.raiderhockey.com
E: info@raiderhockey.com
Governor: Marty Popeseul
Mkt: Bruce Vance

Prince George Cougars
102-2817 Ospika Blvd. South
Prince George, B.C. V2N 6Z1
T: (250) 561-0783
F: (250) 561-0743
www.pgcougars.com
E: cougars@mag-net.com
Governor: Rick Brodsky
GM: Daryl Lubiniecki
PR: Frank Peebler

Red Deer Rebels
4847-19th Street, Unit C
Red Deer, Alberta T4R 2N7
T: (403) 341-6000
F: (403) 341-6009
www.reddeerrebels.com
E: rebels@telusplanet.net
Governor: Brent Sutter
Mkt/PR: Dean Williams

Regina Pats
PO Box 104
Regina Agridome, Exhibition Park
Regina, Saskatchewan S4P 2Z5
T: (306) 522-5604
F: (306) 569-1021
www.reginapats.com
E: pats@reginapats.com
GM: Brent Parker
PR: Nathan Morrison

Saskatoon Blades
201-3515 Thatcher Avenue
Saskatoon, Saskatchewan S7R 1C4
T: (306) 975-8844
F: (306) 934-1097
www.saskatoonblades.com
E: info@saskatoonblades.com
Governor: Jack Brodsky
GM: Brent McEwan
PR: Sean Gilchrist

Seattle Thunderbirds
1813-130th Avenue NE
Suite 210
Bellevue, WA 98005
T: (425) 869-7825
F: (425) 497-0812
www.seattle-thunderbirds.com
E: stbirds@seattle-thunderbirds.com
GM: Russ Farwell
Mkt: Colin Campbell

Spokane Chiefs
PO Box 5371, 700 W. Mallon
Spokane, WA 99205
T: (509) 328-0450
F: (509) 328-7608
www.spokanechiefs.com
E: fanmail@spokanechiefs.com
Governor: Bobby Brett
GM: Tim Speltz
PR: Jay Stewart

Swift Current Broncos
PO Box 2345
2001 Chaplin
Swift Current, Sask. S9H 4X6
T: (306) 773-1509
F: (306) 773-5406
www.scbroncos.com
E: s.c.broncos@sasktel.net
Governor: Ben Wiebe
Asst. GM: Elden Moberg

Tri-City Americans
7100 W. Quinault Street
Kennewick, WA 99336
T: (509) 736-0606
F: (509) 783-4591
www.amshockey.com
E: admin@amshockey.com
Gov: Darryl Porter
GM: Bob Tory

Vancouver Giants
100 N. Renfrew Street
Vancouver, BC V5K 3N7, Canada
T: (604) 444-2687
F: (604) 254-2687
www.vancouvergiants.com
E: rlemire@vancouvergiants.com
P: Ron Toigo
GM: Scott Bonner
Mkt: Roger Lemire

2003 WHL Champions
Kelowna Rockets

The three Major Junior League champions compete for the Memorial Cup National Championship with the host team.

2003 Memorial Cup Champions
Kitchener Rangers

Canadian Junior A

The following eleven Junior A hockey leagues are part of the Canadian Jr. A Hockey League. Junior A leagues compete for the Centennial Cup. Junior A players are drafted by the Major Junior Leagues.

Many former & current NHL players have played in these Junior A leagues.

Canadian Jr. A Hockey League
404 Hermitage Road
Edmonton, Alberta T5A 3K9 Canada
T: (780) 406-1935
F: (780) 406-7447
www.cjahl.com
E: knaxfax@connect.ab.ca
P: Marty Knack

Alberta Junior A Hockey League
PO Box 72
Red Deer, Alberta T4N 5E7
T: (403) 347-7410
F: (403) 342-1389
www.ajhl.ab.ca
E: ajhloffice@ajhl.ab.ca
P: Kim Marsh

Bonnyville Pontiacs
PO Box 5554
Bonnyville, Alberta T9N 2G6
T: (780) 826-2893
F: (780) 826-5486
www.telusplanet.net/public/pontiac
E: pontaics@ajhl.ab.ca
P: Fred Farrell
GM/Coach: Brett Cox

Brooks Bandits
PO Box 196
Brooks, Alberta T1R 1B3
T: (403) 501-0122
F: (403) 501-0162
www.brooksbandits.ca
E: bbhockey@telusplanet.net
P: Byron Smith
GM/Coach: Randy Wong

Calgary Canucks
1001 Barlow Trail SE
Calgary, Alberta T2E 6S2
T: (403) 272-7211
F: (403) 272-1791
www.calgarycanucks.com
E: canucks@ajhl.ab.ca
P: Ken Bracko
GM: Carl Archibald

Calgary Royals
Box 72108, 1600-90 Ave SW
Calgary, Alberta T2V 5H9
T: (403) 640-7333
F: (403) 640-7343
E: royals@mail.com
P: Ted Grisdale
GM: Don Allan

Camrose Kodiaks
PO Box 1175
Camrose, Alberta T4V 1X2
T: (780) 679-2603
F: (780) 679-2608
www.net-works.ab.ca/kodiaks
E: kodiaks@net-works.ab.ca
P: Lorne Broen
GM: Boris Rybalka

Canmore Eagles
PO Box 8131
Canmore, Alberta T1W 2T9
T: (403) 678-1855
F: (403) 678-0057
www.eagles.ab.ca
E: eagles@ajhl.ab.ca
GM: Bob Miller

Crowsnest Pass Timberwolves
Box 1562
Blairmore, Alberta T0K 0E0
T: (403) 562-2455
F: (403) 562-2691
E: timberwolves@ajhl.ab.ca
P: Stacy Ewen
GM/Coach: George Cochrane

Drayton Valley Thunder
Box 6242
Drayton Valley, Alberta T7A 1R7
T: (780) 542-7846
F: (780) 542-7045
www.mccauley-tech.ab.ca/dvthunder
E: dvthunder@telusplanet.net
P: Bill Ballas
GM/Coach: Milan Dragicevic

Fort McMurray Oil Barons
PO Box 5689
Fort McMurray, Alberta T9H 4V9
T: (780) 743-5509
F: (780) 743-2602
www.oilbarons.com
E: oilbarons@ajhl.ab.ca
P: Nick DeHoog
GM/Coach: Fran Gow

Fort Saskatchewan Traders
PO Box 3333
Fort Saskatchewan, AB T8L 2T3
T/F: (780) 998-7170
www.tradershockey.com
E: fttrader@icrossroads.com
P: Ron Gauf
GM: Mac Danyluk

Grand Prairie Storm
PO Box 625
Grand Prairie, Alberta T8V 3A8
T: (780) 538-4919
F: (780) 513-2232
www.gpstorm.com
E: gpstorm@ccinet.ab.ca
P: Brian Nash
GM/Coach: Kevin Mackay

Lloydminster Blazers
PO Box 1122
Lloydminster, Sask. S9V 1E9
T: (306) 825-0788
F: (306) 825-8939
www.blazers.ab.ca
E: jblazers@telusplanet.net
P: John Kelly
GM: Vern Belsheim

Olds Grizzlys
5133-52 Street
Olds, Alberta T4H 1G9
T: (403) 556-2600
F: (403) 556-1230
www.airenet.com/grizzlys
E: grizzlys@ccinet.ab.ca
P: Garrett Funkhouser

St. Albert Saints
PO Box 91
St. Albert, Alberta T8N 1N2
T: (780) 459-6052
F: (780) 459-7006
www.stalbertsaints.com
E: saints1@telusplanet.net
P: Glen Staheli

Sherwood Park Crusaders
PO Box 57152, Eastgate PO
2010 Sherwood Drive
Sherwood Park, Alberta T8A 0Z1
T: (780) 417-1175
F: (780) 417-3767
www.crusaders.ab.ca
E: crusaders@telusplanet.net
P: Tom Maxwell

The AJHL was established in 1964-65. Some former alumni included Mark Messier, Lanny McDonald, Mike Vernon, Brent Sutter John Davidson & Troy Murray.

**2003 AJHL Champion
Camrose Kodiaks**

British Columbia Jr. A Hockey League
220 Lower Bench Road
Penticton, BC V2A 1A8 Canada
T: (250) 490-4600
F: (250) 490-4012
www.bchl.bc.ca
E: rboileau@bchl.bc.ca
P: Ron Boileau

Burnaby Bulldogs
3676 Kensington Avenue
Burnaby, BC V5B 4Z6
T: (604) 205-7591
F: (604) 205-7581
www.burnabybulldogs.com
E: info@burnabybulldogs.com
Gov: Darcy Taylor
GM/Coach: Darcy Rota

Chilliwack Chiefs
9291 Corbould Street
Chilliwack, B.C. V2P 4A6
T: (604) 795-7300
F: (604) 795-6588
www.chilliwackchiefs.com
E: chilliwackchiefs@ntonline.com
P: Al Brew
Gm/Coach: Harvey Smyl

Coquitlam Express
633 Poirier Street
Coquitlam, BC V3J 6A9
T: (604) 939-7468
F: (604) 939-7465
www.coquitlamexpress.com
E: info@coquitlamexpress.com
P/GM: Darcy Rota
Admin: Tod Dean

Cowichan Valley Capitals
2687 James Street
Duncan, B.C. V9L 2X5
T: (250) 748-9930
F: (250) 748-9938
www.cowichan.com/rec/capitals
E: capitals@cowichan.com
P: Dr. Ron Smith
GM: Clayton Wright

Langley Hornets
20699-42 Avenue
Langley, B.C. V3A 3B1
T: (604) 514-1253
F: (604) 514-1257
www.langleyhornets.com
E: admin@langleyhornets.com
P: Gary Bailey
GM/Coach: Rick Lanz

Merritt Centennials
PO Box 1730
Merritt, B.C. V0K 2B0
T: (250) 378-3607
F: (250) 378-3609
www.merrittcentennials.com
Gov: Bruce Tisdale
Mkt: Charlie Baxter

Nanaimo Clippers
#20-1925 Bowen Road
Nanaimo, B.C. V9S 1H1
T: (250) 751-0593
F: (250) 751-0598
www.nanaimoclippers.com
P: Dieter Peter
GM/Coach: Bill Bestwick

Penticton Panthers
399 Power Street
Penticton, B.C. V2A 7K9
T: (250) 493-4312
F: (250) 493-1722
www.pentictonpanthers.com
E: panthers@vip.net
P: Wes Reinheller
GM/Coach: Bryant Perrier

Powell River Paper Kings
PO Box 342
Powell River, B.C. V8A 5C2
T: (604) 485-7550
F: (604) 485-7530
www.powellriverkings.com
E: prkings@armourtech.com
GM: Dave Sales
PR: Terry Dyer

Prince George Spruce Kings
PO Box 2174
Prince George, B.C. V2N 2J6
T: (250) 564-1747
F: (250) 563-3239
www.sprucekings.bc.ca
E: sprucekings@yjdproductions.com
Governor: Adrian Vander-Velden

Quesnel Millionaires
PO Box 4478
Quesnel, B.C. V2J 3J4
T: (250) 992-7181
F: (250) 992-7148
www.quesnel-millionaires.com
E: mills@goldcity.net
P: Kit Collins
GM: Dale Marquette

Salmon Arm Silverbacks
2600-10 Avenue NE
Salmon Arm, BC V1E 2S4
T: (250) 832-3856
F: (250) 832-3812
www.salmonarmsilverbacks.com
E: gdavidson@sunwave.net
GM: Garry Davidson

South Surrey Eagles
#130-1711-152nd Street
Surrey, B.C. V4A 4N3
T: (604) 531-4625
F: (604) 535-6710
www.surreyeagles.com
E: Eagles98@netcom.ca
P: Audrey Bakewell

Trail Smoke Eaters
#204-1199 Bay Avenue
Trail, B.C. V1R 4A4
T: (250) 364-9994
F: (250) 364-9920
www.trailsmokeeaters.com
E: smokin@direct.ca
P: Dean Civitarese
GM/Coach: Bruno Campese

Vernon Vipers
#209-2411 Highway 6
Vernon, B.C. V1T 5G4
T: (250) 542-6022
F: (250) 545-7360
www.vipers.bc.ca
E: vipers@junction.net
P: Dr. Duncan Wray

Victoria Salsa
1925A Blanshard Street
Victoria, B.C. V8T 4J2
T: (250) 385-1555
F: (250) 385-1550
www.salsa.ampsc.com
E: salsa@ampsc.com
P: Mark Wagstaff
Mkt: Barry Rankin

The BCJHL was established in 1961-62. Notable alumni include Brett Hull, Dallas Drake, Andy Moog, Joe Murphy, Paul Kariya.

2003 BCJHL Champions
Vernon Vipers

Central Junior A Hockey League
PO Box 850
Kemptville, Ontario K0G 1J0
T: (613) 258-3475
F: (613) 258-4826
www.cjhl.on.ca
Commissioner: Don Valcour

Brockville Braves
1275 Kensington Pkwy.
Suite 110
Brockville, Ontario K6V 7E6
T: (613) 342-7881
F: (613) 342-9035
www.brockvillebraves.com
E: braves@recorder.ca
P: Jack Dornan

Cornwall Colts
PO Box 10
Martintown, Ontario K0C 1S0
T: (613) 930-9300
F: (613) 930-9497
www.colts.on.ca
E: colts@colts.on.ca
P: Allan Wagar

Cumberland Grads
1329 Colonial Road
Navan, Ontario K4B 1N1
T/F: (613) 835-4297
www.cumberlandgrads.bizland.com
E: cumberlandgrads@hotmail.com
P: Arnold Dashney

Gloucester Rangers
2020 Ogilvie Road
Gloucester, Ontario K1J 7N8
T: (613) 749-9472
F: (613) 749-8378
www.rangers-hockey.com
E: team@rangers-hockey.com
P: Denis Lacroix

Hawkesbury Hawks
PO Box 514, 425 Blvd. Cartier
Hawkesbury, Ontario K6A 2Y2
T: (613) 632-7219
F: (613) 632-1993
www.hawkesbury-hawks.com
E: hawks@hawks.igs.net
P: Jean Pierre Piche

Kanata Valley Lasers
10 McKitrick Drive
Kanata, Ontario K2L 1M7
T/F: (613) 831-0445
www.kvlasers.on.ca
E: kvlasers@capitalnet.com
P: Guy Latraverse

Lanark Thunder
63 Princess St., PO Box 93
Lanark, Ontario K0G 1K0
T: (613) 741-8080
F: (613) 741-8034
E: lanarkthunder@videotron.ca
P: Daniel Labine

Nepean Raiders
PO Box 5695, Merivale Depot
Nepean, Ontario K2C 3M1
T: (613) 228-3500
F: (613) 228-1706
www.nepeanraiders.on.ca
E: headcoach@nepeanraiders.on.ca
P: Gord Black

Ottawa Jr. Senators
1265 Walkey Road
Ottawa, Ontario K1V 6P9
T: (613) 248-1575
F: (613) 248-1576
www.comnet.ca/~jrsens
E: jrsens@comnet.ca
P: Louis Riopelle

Pembroke Lumber Kings
PO Box 92
Pembroke, Ontario K8A 6X1
T: (613) 732-8146
F: (613) 732-4036
www.pembrokelumberkings.com
coaches@pembrokelumberkings.com
P: Terry Olsheski

Smith Falls Bears
PO Box 1046
Smith Falls, Ontario K7A 5A5
T: (613) 283-3131
F: (613) 283-3331
E: bears@perth.igs.net
P: Michael McLean
VP: Richard Green

The Central Junior was established in 1967. Notable alumni were Larry Robinson, Steve Yzerman, Darren Pang, Garry Galley, Ray Sheppard.

2003 CJHL Champion
Nepean Raiders

Manitoba Junior A Hockey League
14 Shorecrest Drive
Winnipeg, Manitoba R3P 1N2
T: (204) 488-1227
F: (204) 488-1119
www.MJHLhockey.ca
E: MJHL@shaw.ca
Commissioner: Kim Davis

Dauphin Kings
Box 509
Dauphin, Manitoba R7N 2V3
T: (204) 638-7117
F: (204) 638-6038
www.dauphinkings.com
E: dauphinkings@mb.sympatico.ca
GM: Mike Sauter

Neepawa Natives
Box 446
Neepawa, Manitoba R0J 1H0
T/F: (204) 476-5308
www.neepawanatives.com
E: nnatives@mb.sympatico.ca
GM: Mike Stinchcombe

Opaskwayak OCN Blizzard
Box 838
The Pas, Manitoba R9A 1K8
T: (204) 627-7077
F: (204) 623-1007
www.ocnblizzard.com
E: ocnblizzard@yahoo.com
GM: Glen Watson

Portage Terriers
Box 33
Portage la Prairie, MB R1N 3B2
T: (204) 857-7380
F: (204) 261-3564
GM: Don MacGillivray

St. Boniface Saints
4185 St. Mary's Road
Winnipeg, Manitoba R2N 4K6
T: (204) 992-8871
F: (204) 256-1933
www.sportsmanitoba.com/saints
GM: Dwayne Joseph

St. James Canadians
Box 42205, 1881 Portage Ave.
Winnipeg, Manitoba R3J 3X8
T: (204) 837-3004
F: (204) 832-1157
Governor: Diane Woods

Selkirk Steelers
1011 Manitoba Avenue
Selkirk, Manitoba R1A 2B1
T: (204) 482-7020
F: (204) 482-7106
www.selkirksteelers.com
E: ken@selkirksteelers.com
GM: Ken Petrash

Swan Valley Stampeders
Box 2818
Swan River, Manitoba R0L 1Z0
T: (204) 734-7825
F: (204) 734-3282
www.stampeders.mb.ca
E: stamps@mb.sympatico.ca
GM: Mark Johnston

Waywayseecappo Wolverines
Box 315
Waywayseecappo, MB R0J 1S0
T: (204) 859-3377
F: (204) 859-3388
www.waywaywolverines.mb.ca
E: pedricks@escape.ca
GM: Barry Butler

Winkler Flyers
Box 2531
Winkler, Manitoba R6W 4C2
T: (204) 325-9411
F: (204) 325-9438
www.wdd.cx/flyers
E: flyers@mb.sympatico.ca
GM: Ken Pearson

Winnipeg South Blues
5 Donald Street, Suite 200
Winnipeg, Manitoba R3L 2T4
T: (204) 478-1900
F: (204) 284-6211
E: deanipc@aol.com
Governor: Ken Kronson
GM: Dean Cockell

Winnipeg Southeast Blades
314 Arnold Avenue
Winnipeg, Manitoba R3L 0W7
T: (204) 984-0094
F: (204) 983-5365
www.southeastblades.mb.ca
E: southeast_blades@hotmail.com
Governor: Mike Fontain

The MJHL was established in 1919. Notable alumni include Ed Belfour, Reg Leach, Andy Van Hellemond, Bobby Clarke, Butch Goring, Sheldon Kennedy & Kevin Hodson.

2003 MJHL Champions
Opaskwayak OCN Blizzard

Maritime Junior A Hockey League

6725 Peter Lowe Avenue
Halifax, Nova Scotia
Canada B2L 1Y7
T: (902) 455-3747
F: (902) 492-1697
E: qtr@istar.ca
P: Eric Thomson
Sec/Treas: Al Hollingsworth

Amherst Ramblers
PO Box 868
Amherst, Nova Scotia B4H 4B9
T: (902) 664-8523
F: (902) 667-2522
E: sgibson@ns.sympatico.ca
P: George Baker
GM/Coach: Steve Gibson

Antigonish Bulldogs
50 Whidden Street
Antigonish, N.S. B2G 2V7
T: (902) 863-2014
F: (902) 863-2017
E: dberry@aehs.ednet.ns.ca
Gov: Gordon MacMillan
GM: Danny Berry

Campbellton Tigers
PO Box 175
Campbellton, New Brunswick
Canada E2N 3H2
T: (506) 826-3277
F: (506) 826-1994
E: ahier@nbnet.nb.ca
P: Lionel Ahier
GM: Gilles LeClair

Charlottetown A&S Abbies
46 Kensington Road
Charlottetown, PEI C1A 5H7
T: (902) 894-9996
F: (902) 628-8033
www.abbies.com
E: abbies@abbies.com
Gov: Ivan Noonan

Dartmouth Blizzard
110 Wyse Road
Dartmouth, NS B3A 1M2
T: (902) 463-6517
F: (902) 463-8817
homestead.com/dartmouthblizzard
E: dartmouthblizzard@yahoo.com
P: Gary Fox
GM: Paul Currie

Halifax Oland Exports
Halifax Forum
2901 Windsor Street
Halifax, Nova Scotia B3K 5E5
T: (902) 453-9606
F: (902) 435-3043
www.halifaxorlandexports.com
GM: Ralph Matheson

Miramichi Timberwolves
PO Box 153
Miramichi, NB E1V 3M3
T: (506) 622-5075
F: (506) 622-4660
www.miramichitimberwolves.com
E: timber00@nbnet.nb.ca
Gov: Kevin Dunn

Moncton Gagnon Beavers
PO Box 224
Moncton, New Brunswick E1C 8K9
T: (506) 382-7154
F: (506) 861-1817
www.monctonbeavers.com
E: lovat@nbnet.nb.ca
P: Al Bowness
GM: Jack Cameron

Summerside Western Capitals
116 Gaudet Crescent
Summerside, PEI C1N 5E1
T: (902) 888-2277
F: (902) 888-2244
www.gocapsgo.com
E: phil.bridges@pei.sympatico.ca
GM: Phil Bridges

Truro Bearcats
PO Box 1456
Truro, Nova Scotia B2N 5V2
T: (902) 897-0059
F: (902) 897-2457
E: bearcats@tru.eastlink.ca
Gov: Stu Rath

The Maritime League was born in 1967. Notable Alumni include Bill Riley, Wendel Young, Rick Vaive, Rick Bowness & Gerard Gallant.

**2003 Maritime Champion
Charlottetown Abbies**

Northern Ontario Junior A Hockey
Suite 10, 109 Elm Street
Sudbury, Ontario P3C 1T4
T: (705) 688-8651
F: (705) 688-8652
www.nojha.com
E: nojhl@cyberbeach.net
Commissioner: Oscar Clouthier

Blind River Barons
PO Box 1859
Blind River, Ontario P0R 1B0
T: (705) 356-4461
F: (705) 356-4462
P: Ian Mills

Espanola Screaming Eagles
207 Watson Street
Espanola, Ontario P3E 1A4
T: (705) 869-4949
F: (705) 869-5582
GM: Mark Seidel

Iroquois Falls Eskis
PO Box 1131
Iroquois Falls, Ontario P0K 1G0
T: (705) 258-3183
F: (705) 232-4241
P: Scott Marshall

Northern Wolves
910 Windemere Crescent
Sudbury, Ontario P3A 5A5
T: (705) 682-0909
F: (705) 682-4774
www.northernwolves.net
E: coach@northernwolves.net
GM: Chris Flick

Rayside Balfour Sabrecats
9 Prevost Street N.
Azilda, Ontario P0M 1B0
T: (705) 669-1112
F: (705) 669-1123
GM: Mitch Tetreault
GM/Coach: Ken MacKenzie

Soo Thunderbirds
47 Birshire Place
Sault Ste. Marie, Ontario P6A 6J8
T: (705) 942-5540
F: (705) 942-1130
Capyj@soonet.ca
GM: Sam Biasucci
Coach: Jim Capy

Sturgeon Falls Lynx
395 Elmwood
North Bay, Ontario P1B 9N4
T: (705) 497-9034
F: (705) 497-1666
P: Guy Blanchard

Notable alumni include Dave Taylor, Bill Barber, Brian Savage, Tony Esposito, Sheldon Kannegeiser, Randy Carlyle & Ivan Boldirev.

**2003 NOJHA Champion
North Bay Skyhawks**

Ontario Provincial Jr. A Hockey League
115 Main Street North
Georgetown, Ontario L7G 3H5
T: (905) 877-6867
F: (416) 252-2544
E: rhoop@aztec-net.ca
Commissioner: Bob Hooper

Ajax Axemen
97 Pittmann Crescent
Ajax, Ontario L1S 3G6
T: (905) 686-1223
F: (905) 686-1250
GM: Larry Labelle

Auburn Jr. Crunch
60 Edgewood Drive
Baldwinsville, NY 13027
T/F: (315) 635-7345
P: Jon Ames

Aurora Tigers
4 Avondale Crescent
Aurora, Ontario L4G 3P6
T: (905) 833-2961
P: Diane Kipp

Bancroft Hawks
Box 321
Bancroft, Ontario K0L 1C0
T: (613) 332-5385
F: (613) 332-1942
GM: George Eastman

Bowmanville Eagles
4215 Tooley Road
Courtice, Ontario L1E 1Z4
T: (905) 579-6245
F: (905) 579-7667
E: mlaing@1direct.ca
GM: Michael Laing

Bramalea Blues
102 Eagleridge Drive
Brampton, Ontario L6R 1E3
T: (905) 772-0298
GM: Bob Taylor

Brampton Capitals
14 Cashel Street
Brampton, Ontario L6Z 2X5
T: (905) 781-6247
F: (905) 840-4862
GM: David Brown

Buffalo Lightning
12108 Anne Drive
Alden, NY 14004
T: (716) 652-0439
F: (716) 652-0214
GM: Chuck Giambra

Burlington Cougars
5230 S. Service Road
Burlington, Ontario L7L 5K2
T: (905) 639-0100
F: (905) 639-0090
GM: Ron Sedlbauer

Cobourg Cougars
569 Shirley Street
Cobourg, Ontario K9A 2A8
T: (905) 738-0066
F: (905) 377-9537
E: gdrush@netrover.com
GM: Gary Rush

Collingwood Blues
88 Irwin Road
Barrie, Ontario L4N 7A8
T: (705) 735-9094
F: (705) 735-9095
GM: Peter Artemchuk

Couchiching Terriers
2 Charles Road
Orillia, Ontario L3V 3H4
T: (705) 326-6427
F: (705) 326-1819
E: cdunn@bconnex.net
P: Dave Dunn

Durham Huskies
PO Box 272
Durham, Ontario N0G 1R0
T: (519) 369-3244
F: (519) 369-2640
P: Dennis Graham

Georgetown Raiders
168 Delrex Blvd.
Georgetown, Ontario L7G 4E2
T: (905) 453-2639
F: (905) 453-9391
P: Hal Pells

Hamilton Kilty Bees
137 E. 8th Street
Hamilton, Ontario L9A 4Y7
T: (905) 428-3413
F: (905) 428-6086
GM: Robert Turnbull

Huntsville Wildcats
RR #1
Dwight, Ontario P0A 1H0
T: (705) 635-8732
F: (705) 635-8734
P: Bob Sillick

Kingston Voyageurs
18 Limeridge Drive
Kingston, Ontario K7K 6M3
T/F: (613) 546-2363
P: Rob Blaskon

Lindsay Muskies
24 Madill Crescent
Lindsay, Ontario K9V 5X1
T: (705) 324-2267
F: (705) 878-9083
P: Mathew Bondaruk

Markham Waxers
70 Petman Avenue
Toronto, Ontario M4S 2S8
T: (416) 361-0737
F: (416) 361-0923
P: Al Ringler

Milton Merchants
381 Valleyview Crescent
Milton, Ontario L9T 3H9
T: (905) 878-8389
F: (905) 878-7137
P: Brad Grant

Mississauga Chargers
3796 Wyewood Road
Mississauga, Ontario L4T 2A2
T: (905) 677-8470
E: stockley@yesic.com
P: Lloyd Stockley

Newmarket 87's Hurricanes
158 Park Avenue
Newmarket, Ontario L3Y 1V1
T/F: (905) 895-6921
GM: Charles Macoun

North York Rangers
9 Lloydminster Crescent
Willowdale, Ontario M2M 2R9
T/F: (416) 250-1735
P: Jim McGowan

Oakville Blades
1408 Thistledown Road
Oakville, Ontario L6L 2H5
T: (905) 813-8308
F: (905) 813-8309
E: brian.hodge@ftctoys.com
P: Brian Hodge

Oshawa Legionaires
597 Adelaide Ave. W.
Oshawa, Ontario L1J 2S5
T/F: (905) 723-4019
P: Cliff Maddock

Parry Sound Shamrocks
36 Virginia Heights
Parry Sound, Ontario P2A 3A8
T: (705) 746-8033
F: (705) 746-4919
P: Doug Renwick

Peterborough Bees
1003 Baker
Peterborough, Ontario K9H 7P7
T: (705) 876-1282
F: (705) 741-8845
P: Ed Lacey

Pickering Panthers
715 Kingston Road
Pickering, Ontario L1V 1A9
T: (905) 831-2693
F: (905) 420-0299
P: Michael Boyer

Port Hope Buzzards
685 Ansley Court
Oshawa, Ontario L1G 4E8
T: (905) 619-2004
F: (905) 721-8845
P: Edward Sullivan

St. Michael's Buzzers
1515 Bathurst Street
Toronto, Ontario M9R 2H3
T: (416) 653-3180 x 231
P: Giancarlo Mazzanti

Stouffville Spirit
113 Nelson Street
Bradford, Ontario L3Z 1E4
T: (416) 586-2948
F: (416) 586-2939
P: Dieter Schmidt

Streetsville Derbys
PO Box 133
Campbellville, Ontario L0P 1B0
T: (905) 858-5046
GM: Stan Kalapaca

Thornhill Rattlers
198 Blackwell Drive
Kitchener, Ontario N2N 2S2
T: (905) 771-0362
F: (519) 579-9580
P: Bob Turow

Trenton Sting
8 Couch Crescent
Trenton, Ontario K8V 1G8
T: (613) 394-5114
F: (613) 394-3572
GM: Jon Gibbons

Vaughan Vipers
113 Kilmuire Gate
Woodbridge, Ontario L4L 3L8
T: (905) 660-4077
F: (905) 660-4078
P: Al Doria

Wellington Dukes
292 Noxon Avenue
Wellington, Ontario K0K 3L0
T: (613) 399-3177
F: (613) 399-1706
P: Garry Lavender

Wexford Raiders
364 Calvert Road
Markham, Ontario L6C 1Y1
T: (905) 475-0200
F: (905) 475-0907
P: Andrew Darbyson

2003 OHA Provincial Champion
Wellington Dukes

Ligue de Hockey Jr. 'AAA' du Quebec

1966 de Boulogne
Bellefeuille, Quebec J2S 5H9
T: (514) 946-7376
F: (450) 438-0056
www.lhjaaaq.interlinx.qc.ca
E: admin@lhjaaaq.qc.ca
P: Richard Morency
VP: Jean Hebert

Les Frontaliers de Coaticook
161, rue Maple
Coaticook, Quebec J1A 1C5
T: (819) 849-6617
F: (819) 822-105?
E: coatic@interlinx.qc.ca
P: Renald Boisvert

Le Eperviers de Contrecoeur
C.P. 841
Contrecoeur, Quebec J0L 1C0
T/F: (450) 587-5726
E: contre@interlinx.qc.ca
GM: Gilles Lacroix

Les Husky Cowansville
C.P. 275
Cowansville, QC J2K 3S7
T/F: (450) 266-0555
E: cowans@interlinx.qc.ca
GM: Gilles McCann

Le National de Joliet
C.P. 615
Joliette, Quebec J6E 7N3
T: (450) 755-6888
F: (450) 755-6868
E: joliet@interlinx.qc.ca
GM: Alain Primeau

Les Condors de Kahnawake
90, avenue de la Mennais
La Prairie, Quebec J5R 2E7
T: (450) 659-9181
F: (450) 672-1255
E: laprai@interlinx.qc.ca
GM: Pierre Mouton

Les Maroons de Lachine
C.P. 34084
Lachine, Quebec H8S 4H4
T: (514) 634-8814
F: (514) 334-5724
E: lachine@interlinx.qc.ca
GM: Pierre Bernier

Les Cobras de La Plaine
1045, des Escoumains
Lachenaie, Quebec J6W 5H2
T: (450) 581-1143
F: (450) 585-6090
E: laplai@interlinx.qc.ca
Gov: Michel Leveille

Colleges Francais de Longueuil
, des Recollets
Longueuil, Quebec J4L 3E1
T: (450) 674-8738
F: (450) 443-4507
E-mail: longue@interlinx.qc.ca
P: Gilles Houle

Le Junior de Montreal
1010, De la Gauchetiere ouest
Suite 1325
Montreal, Quebec H3B 2N2
T: (514) 875-5666
F: (514) 875-8666
E: montre@interlinx.qc.ca
P: Robert L. Racker

Saint-Hyacinthe Dragons
5825, Desjardins
Saint-Hyacinthe, Quebec J2S 1A4
T: (450) 261-1679
F: (514) 261-1783
E: st-hya@interlinx.qc.ca
Governor: Jean-Guy Brillon

Les Chevaliers de St-Jean
390, 3e Rang Nord
Iberville, Quebec J2X 4H9
T: (450) 346-5254
E: st-jea@interlinx.qc.ca
Gov: Louise Leduc

Saint-Jerome Pantheres
1966 De Boulogne
Bellefeuille, Quebec J0R 1A0
T: (450) 431-7580
F: (450) 438-0056
E: st-jer@interlinx.qc.ca
P: Paul Pilon

Les Braves de Valleyfield
24 Pauline
Les Coteaux, Quebec J7X 1M5
T: (450) 370-0876
F: (450) 267-8528
www.braves.qc.ca
E: valley@interlinx.qc.ca
Governor: Robert Richer

Kingsey de Warwick
C.P. 731
Warwick, Quebec J0A 1M0
T: (819) 358-3487
F: (819) 358-3459
E: warwic@interlinx.qc.ca
Governor: Jean-Pierre Gregoire

The Quebec Junior Ligue was established in 1988-89.

2003 Quebec Tier II Champion
Lennoxville Cougars

Saskatchewan Junior 'A' Hockey League
152 McDougall Crescent
Regina, Saskatchewan S4S 5M7
T: (306) 586-2615
F: (306) 585-0005
www.sjhl.sk.ca
E: sjhl.league@fillthenet.com
P: Wayne Kartusch
PR: Penny McEwen

Estevan Bruins
Box 146
Estevan, Sask. S4A 2A2
T: (306) 634-7730
F: (306) 634-9398
www.cap.estevanbruins.com
E: estevan.bruins@fillthenet.com
P: Andy Schroeder
GM/Coach: Nick Serregela

Flin Flon Bombers
Box 762
Flin Flon, Manitoba R8A 1N6
T: (204) 687-4404
F: (204) 687-4704
www.flinflonjrbombers.com
E: flinflon.bombers@fillthenet.com
Governor: Dan Reagan

Humboldt Broncos
PO Box 1414
Humboldt, Sask. S0K 2A0
T: (306) 682-5575
F: (306) 682-4205
www.humboldtbroncos.com
E: humboldt.broncos@fillthenet.com
GM: Len Hergott

Kindersley Klippers
Box 2398
Kindersley, Sask. S0L 1S0
T: (306) 463-2927
F: (306) 463-1028
www.klippershockey.com
E: kindersley.klippers@fillthenet.com
Governor: Larry Stevens

La Ronge Ice Wolves
Box 869
La Ronge, Sask. S0J 1L0
T: (306) 425-4141
F: (306) 425-4146
www.icewolves.com
E: laronge.icewolves@fillthenet.com
P: Rick Schultz
GM: Bob Robson

Melfort Mustangs
Box 3640
Melfort, Sask. S0E 1A0
T: (306) 752-2799
F: (306) 752-3899
www.melfortmustangs.com
E: melfort.mustangs@fillthenet.com
Governor: Leonard Strandberg

Melville Millionaires
Box 2197
Melville, Sask. S0A 2P0
T: (306) 728-2363
F: (306) 728-4513
www.melvillemillionaires.com
E: melville.millionaires@fillthenet.com
Gov: Ernie Iluk

Nipawin Hawks
Box 2678
Nipawin, Sask. S0E 1E0
T: (306) 862-4878
F: (306) 862-2557
www.cybervillage.com/nipawinhawks
E: nipawin.hawks@fillthenet.com
Governor: Ian Rushmer

North Battleford North Stars
Box 1247
North Battleford, Sask. S9A 3K2
T: (306) 446-0166
F: (306) 445-8406
www.battlefordsnorthstars.com
battlefords.northstars@fillthenet.com
Governor: Keith Strawford

Notre Dame Hounds
Box 100
Wilcox, Saskatchewan S0G 5E0
T: (306) 732-2080
F: (306) 732-2115
www.notredame.sk.ca
E: notredame.hounds@fillthenet.com
Governor: Bill Gibson

Weyburn Red Wings
Box 1112
Weyburn, Sask. S4H 2L3
T: (306) 842-2212
F: (306) 842-3717
www.weyburnredwings.com
weyburn.redwings@fillthenet.com
P: Winston Bailey
GM: Ron Rumball

Yorkton Terriers
Box 277
Yorkton, Sask. S3N 2V7
T: (306) 783-4077
F: (306) 782-4633
www.yorktonterriers.com
E: yorkton.terriers@fillthenet.com
P: Glen Kozak

The SJHL was established in 1968.
Notable alumni are Al MacInnis, Chris Chelios, Curtis Joseph, Tim Cheveldae, Ron Hextall, Brian Skrudland, Brian Propp, Esa Tikkanen, Rod Brind'Amour, Joey Kocur, Blaine Lacher, Brad McCrimmon

2003 SJHL Hanbidge Cup Champ
Humboldt Broncos

Superior Int'l Junior Hockey League
235 Hinton Avenue
Thunder Bay, Ontario P7A 7E5
T: (807) 767-5335
F: (807) 767-6381
www.sijhl.org
E: jblazino@tbaytel.net
P: Jerry Blazino
Commissioner: Harvey Fedell
T: (807) 623-6239
The league began in 2001-02. Teams are Borderland Thunder, Dryden Ice Dogs, Lake Nipigon Hawks, NW WI Knights, Thunder Bay KC Bulldogs & Thunder Bay Wolves.

2003 SIJHL Champions
Borderland Thunder

2003 Royal Bank Cup Jr. A Canada National Champions
Humboldt Broncos d *Camrose Kodiaks 3-1 in the Final game.*

USA Hockey
1775 Bob Johnson Drive
Colorado Springs, CO 80906
T: (719) 576-USAH (8724)
F: (719) 538-1160
www.usahockey.com
E: raeb@usahockey.org
P: Walter J. Bush, Jr.
Exec. Director: Dave Ogrean
Director, Member Svc: Rae Briggle
Media: Heather Ahearn

USA Hockey Junior Council
531 Commercial St., Suite 300
Waterloo, IA 50701
T: (319) 291-7202
F: (319) 291-6787
E: usavpjr@mcleodusa.net
Chairman: W. David Tyler

U.S. Junior A Leagues

American West Hockey League
2104 E. 5th Street
Superior, WI 54880
T: (715) 392-1862
F: (715) 392-1863
www.AWHL.com
E: steve@awhl.com
Commissioner: Steven Nelson
Hky Oper: Scott Brand
PR: Juliana Nykolaiszyn
E: juliana@awhl.com

The America West League was established in 1994.

Billings Bulls
13970 Mountain View Road
Molt, MT 59057
T: (406) 669-3855
F: (406) 669-3165
www.billingsbulls.com
E: atb@ttc-cmc.net
GM: Al Bloomer

Bismarck Bobcats
1200 N Washington Street
Bismarck, ND 58501
T: (701) 222-3300
F: (701) 222-3335
www.bismarckbobcats.com
E: BisBobcats@aol.com
P: Chad Johnson

Bozeman IceDogs
269 Jackrabbit Lane
Bozeman, MT 59718
T: (406) 585-1415
F: (406) 585-1416
www.bozemanicedogs.com
E: jlafontaine@bozemanicedogs.com
GM: John LaFontaine

Central Texas Blackhawks
PO Box 1836
Belton, TX 76513
T: (254) 933-3600
F: (406) 933-1888
www.blackhawkshockey.com
GM: Rikard Gronborg
PR: Penny Kinn

Fairbanks Ice Dogs
PO Box 74786
Fairbanks, AK 99707
T: (907) 452-2111
F: (907) 452-1643
www.fairbanksicedogs.com
coachproffitt@fairbanksicedogs.com
P: Jack Tragis

Fargo-Moorhead Jets
807 17th Avenue North
Fargo, ND 58102
T: (701) 235-2354
F: 701) 235-2692
www.fmjuniorhockey.com
E: fmjuniorahockey@cableone.net
GM: Randy Nielsen

Fernie Ghostriders
PO Box 178
Fernie, B.C. V0B 1M0, Canada
T: (250) 423-4153
F: (250) 423-3214
www.fernieghostriders.com
E: info@fernieghostriders.com
P: Phil Iddon

Great Falls Americans
PO Box 2652
Great Falls, MT 59403
T: (406) 452-8911
F: (406) 452-8914
www.greatfallsamericans.com
E: gfa@mcn.net
GM: Eric Ray

Helena Bighorns
400 Lola Street
Helena, MT 59601
T: (406) 457-2817
F: (406) 457-2818
www.helenabighorns.com
E: sknicker@helenabighorns.com
GM: Scott Knickerbocker

Lone Star Cavalry
8851 Ice House Drive
North Richland Hills, TX 76180
T: (817) 788-5400
F: (817) 665-0433
www.lonestarcavalry.com
GM: Trevor Converse

Phoenix Polar Bears
2001 W. Alameda Drive
Temple, AZ 85282
T: (480) 337-0224
F: (480) 337-0231
www.phoenixpolarbears.com
E: info@phoenixpolarbears.com
GM: Harry Mahood

Tupelo T-Rex
PO Box 2303
Tupelo, MS 38803
T: (662) 844-7825
F: (662) 620-7540
www.t-rexhockey.com
E: info@t-rexhockey.com
P: Monty Fletcher
PR: Juliana Nykolaiszyn

Wichita Falls Rustlers
PO Box 599
Wichita Falls, TX 76307
T: (940) 723-7825
F: (940) 767-4423
www.wfrustlers.com
GM: Bill Yeakel
PR: Tim Best

2003 AWHL Borne Cup Finals
Bismarck Bobcats d Billings Bulls
4 Games to 2.

North American Hockey League
23995 Freeway Park Dr., Suite 101
Farmington Hills, MI 48335
T: (248) 427-8100
F: (248) 427-8114
www.nahl.com
E: pedrie@aol.com
Commissioner: Larry Pedrie
PR/Mkt: Kelly M. Skinner

Capital Centre Pride
The Summit at Capital Centre
9410 Davis Hwy.
Dimondale, MI 49315
T: (517) 319-1000
F: (517) 319-1004
www.capitalcentre.com
E: thesummit@capitalcentre.com
GM: Larry Clark

Chicago Freeze
1996 S. Kirk Road
Geneva, IL 60134
T: (630) 262-0010
F: (630) 262-1388
www.chicagofreeze.com
E: info@chicagofreeze.com
GM: Jim Cain

Cleveland Barons
PO Box 81172
Cleveland, OH 44181
T: (216) 225-0582
F: (216)
E: BaronsJra@aol.com
GM: Barry Butler

Compuware Ambassadors
14900 Beck Road
Plymouth, MI 48170
T: (734) 453-6400
F: (734) 453-3427
www.compuwareambassadors.com
Ambassadors@plymouthwhalers.com
GM: Todd Watson

Dayton Gems Jr. A
Gem City Arena
10561 Success Lane
Dayton, OH 45458
T: (937) 885-4364
F: (937)
www.daytongemshockey.com
E: info@daytongemshockey.com
P: Jeff Walker

Mahoning Valley Phantom Rockets
360 McClurg Road
Boardman, OH 44512
T: (330) 965-7500
F:
www.phantomrockets.com
P: Bruce Zoldan

Soo Kewadin Indians
2 Ice Circle Drive
Sault St. Marie, MI 49783
T: (906) 635-4956
F: (906) 635-4916
www.sooindians.com
E: qhockey@northernway.net
P: Bernard Bouschor

Springfield Jr. Blues
1601 N. 5th Street
Springfield, IL 62702
T: (217) 525-2589
F: (217) 525-6528
www.jrblues.com
E: jrblues@cityscape.net
GM: Peter Crawford

Springfield Spirit
635 E. Trafficway
Springfield, MO 63806
T: (417) 866-7444
F: (417) 866-4888
www.springfieldspirit.com
P: Anthony Sansone

Texarkana Bandits
222 W. Broad Street
Texarkana, TX 75501
T: (903) 794-7825
www.txkbandits.com
E: info@txkbandits.com

Texas Tornado
9289 Huntington Square, Suite 100
North Richland Hills, TX 76180
T: (817) 498-5002
F: (817) 498-5058
www.tornadohockey.com
E: info@tornadohockey.com
GM: Quentin Bourjeaurd

Toledo Ice Diggers
1258 W. Alexis Road
Toledo, OH 43612
T: (419) 476-4690
F: (419) 476-4863
www.icediggers.com
E: icediggershockey@aol.com

USA NAHL National Under 18
2121 Oak Valley Road
Ann Arbor, MI 48103
T: (734) 327-9251
F: (734) 327-9256
www.usahockey.com
GM: Scott Monaghan

The NAHL was founded in 1975 when the Michigan Jr. & Wolverine Jr. Leagues formed the Great Lakes Jr. Hockey League. In 1984, the name was changed to NAJHL, and since, modified to NAHL.

NAHL notable alumni include Eric Lindros, Doug Weight, Todd Marchant, Brian Rolston and Ken Morrow & Mark Wells of the 1980 Lake Placid Gold Medal USA Team.

2003 NAHL Chuck Robertson Championship Finals
Pittsburgh Forge

2003 USA Hockey Junior A Gold Cup National Champions
Pittsburgh Forge

United States Hockey League

300 N. 5th Street, Suite 2
Grand Forks, ND 58203
T: (701) 775-7334
F: (701) 775-2684
www.USHL.com
E: USHL@ushl.com
P: Ellis Moose
Commissioner: Gino Gasparini
Media: Jason Hron

Cedar Rapids Roughriders
228 3rd Avenue SE
Cedar Rapids, IA 52401
T: (319) 247-0340
F: (319) 247-0343
www.roughridershockey.com
E: info@roughridershockey.com
P: Butch Johnson

Chicago Steel
735 E Jefferson Street
Bensenville, IL 60106
T: (630) 594-1111
F: (630) 521-1112
www.chicagosteelhockey.com
E: info@chicagosteelhockey.com
GM: Bruce Liimatainen

Danville Wings
3295 E. Main St., Suite A
Danville, IL 61832
T: (217) 477-9295
F: (217) 477-9273
www.danvillewings.com
E: wings@soltec.net
GM: Joshua Mervis

Des Moines Buccaneers
7201 Hickman Road
Des Moines, IA 50322
T: (515) 278-9757
F: (515) 278-5401
www.bucshockey.org
E: bucsushl@aol.com
P: Ellis Moose

Green Bay Gamblers
1901 S. Oneida Street
Green Bay, WI 54304
T: (920) 405-1150
F: (920) 494-6868
www.Gamblershockey.com
P: Ken Wachter

Lincoln Stars
PO Box 80327
1800 State Fair Drive
Lincoln, NE 68501
T: (402) 474-7827
F: (402) 474-7831
www.lincolnstars.com
E: info@lincolnstars.com
P: Steve Zoucha

River City Lancers
5015 Underwood Avenue
Omaha, NE 68132
T: (402) 556-7825
F: (402) 556-0969
www.lancers.com
E: lancers@novia.net
P: Ted Baer
GM: Mike Hastings

Sioux City Musketeers
PO Box 3313
Sioux City, IA 51102
T: (712) 252-2116
F: (712) 252-2117
www.musketeershockey.com
E: muskies@pionet.net
GM: Shawn Teal

Sioux Falls Stampede
1600 W. 51st Street
Sioux Falls, SD 57105
T: (605) 977-4737
F: (605) 977-4738
www.sfstampede.com
E: hockey@sfstampede.com
GM: Jim Loria

St. Louis Heartland Eagles
U.S. Ice Sports Complex
St. Louis, MO
T: (636) 227-7275
F:
www.eagleshockey.us
E: sandyemuncy@yahoo.com
P: Mark Stephens

Tri-City Storm
4009 6th Avenue, Suite 32
Kearney, NE 68845
T: (308) 338-8809
F: (308) 338-9098
www.stormhockey.com
E: info@stormhockey.com
P: Ted Baer

USA Hockey-USHL
2121 Oak Valley Drive
Ann Arbor, MI 48103
T: (734) 327-9251
F: (734) 327-9256
www.usahockey.com
E: ntdppr@ix.netcom.com
GM: Scott Monaghan

Waterloo Blackhawks
PO Box 2222
Waterloo, IA 50704
T: (319) 232-3444
F: (319) 232-6140
www.waterlooblackhawks.com
E: wlobkhwk@sbtek.net
P: Butch Johnson
GM: Scott Koberinski

The present day USHL was formed in 1972 as the Midwest Jr. Hockey League and merged with the USHL in 1977, becoming an all-junior league. The professional USHL was a minor league that operated in the 1950's & early 1960's.

2003 USHL Clark Cup Champions
Lincoln Stars

Continental Elite Hockey League
34400 Utica Road, Suite A
Fraser, MI 48026
T: (586) 296-7278
F: (586) 296-7291
www.cehlonline.com
E: kbelletire@aol.com
Commissioner: Kevin Shanahan

The CEHL is a Junior A league. Teams are the Brownstown Bombers, Detroit Lightning, Traverse City Enforcers. More expansion TBA.

2003 CEHL Champions
Detroit Lightning

We will return to U.S. & Canada Tier II Junior B & C hockey leagues after the following Women's Hockey & Senior/Semi-professional section.

Women's Pro Hockey

National Women's Hockey League
7575 Kennedy Road South
Brampton, Ontario L6W 4T2, Canada
T: (905) 453-5218
F: (905) 453-2698
www.NWHLhockey.com
E: president@nwhlhockey.com
P: Susan Fennell
VP: Barb Fisher
E: bfisher@bmts.com

The NWHL is classified as the elite women's league in Canada & the world"s premier women's league.

Beatrice North York Aeros
402 Highland Drive
Kincardine, Ontario N2Z 1X3 Canada
T: (519) 396-2936
www.beatrice.aeros.com
E: info@beatriceaeros.com
GM: Barb Fisher

Brampton Thunder
742 Hillside Drive
Brampton, Ontario L6S 1A3
T: (905) 820-4562
F: (905) 820-7976
www.bramptonthunder.com
E: thunder@whockey.com
GM: Terry Richardson

Calgary Oval X-Treme
2500 University Dr. NW
Calgary, Alberta T2N 1N4
T: (403) 220-8923
F: (403) 284-4815
www.oval.ucalgary.ca
E: kberg@ucalgary.ca
GM: Kathy Berg

Durham Telus Lightning
256 Randall Crescent
Scarborough, Ontario M1M 3K4
T: (416) 267-9581
F: (416) 264-8205
E: lightning@whockey.com
GM: Bill Williamson

Edmonton Chimos
#205, 8908-99th Street
Edmonton, Alberta T6E 3V4 Canada
T: (780) 442-4466
F: (780) 439-2893
www.edmontonchimos.com
E: dbateman@edmontonchimos.com
P: Dee Bateman

Montreal Wingstar
8801 Chateaubriand
Montreal, Quebec H4M 1Y4
T: (514) 381-8541
F: (514) 384-0966
www.montrealwingstar.com
E: france.st@attcanada.net
E: joseefortier@hotmail.com
P: Josee Fortier
GM: France St. Louis

Oakville Ice
Box 304
Oakville, Ontario L6S 5A2
T: (416) 720-2536
www.icebears.net
E: bmmetcalfe@meraymotors.com
GM: Bill Metcalfe

Ottawa Raiders
80 Melanie Crescent
Kanata, Ontario K2l 2J8
T: (613) 831-2569
F: (613) 763-4149
E: ottawaraiders@hotmail.com
GM: Mel L. Avery

Quebec Avalanche
11-800 Pasteur
Montreal, Quebec H3M 2P7
T: (514) 335-1105
F: (514) 335-0199
www.quebecavalanche.com
E: avalanche@nwhlhockey.com
P: Vinnie Matteo
GM: Mario Limperis

Vancouver Griffins
14-3980 Canada Way
Vancouver, BC V5G 1G7 Canada
T: (604) 786-3575
F: (604) 980-5290
www.vancouvergriffins.com
E: pd@vancouvergriffins.com
P: Diane Nelson
GM: Phillip DeGrandpre

2003 NWHL Cup Champions
Calgary Oval X-Treme

2003 Esso National Champions
Calgary Oval X-Treme

Canadian Senior Hockey

OHA Southwest Senior Hockey League
PO Box 2
Belmont, Ontario N0B 1B0 Canada
T: (519) 640-5197
F: (519) 644-5166
Chairman: Donald Yeck
PR: Bill Stobbs
T: (519) 380-9474
E: wmstobbs@netrover.com

Brantford Prowl
57 Clench Avenue
Brantford, Ontario N3T 1B7
T: (519) 759-5603
E: hamsportsinc@sympatico.ca
P: Lindsay Ham

Cambridge Hornets
240 Elm Avenue N.
Listowell, Ontario N4W 3E8
T: (519) 291-2130
E: mhodgkinson@preceptgroup.net
P: Marc Hodgkinson

Dundas Real McCoys
1677 Hwy 5 E.
Troy, Ontario L0R 2B0
T: (905) 627-4880
E: donrobertson@on.aibn.com
GM: Don Robertson

Petrolia Chippewa Squires
4925 Egremont Road, RR #1
Camlachie, Ontario N0N 1E0
T: (519) 845-0743
F: (519) 899-2832
E: kimandkent@hotmail.com
P: Kent Helps

Tillsonburg Vipers
565 N. Broadway
Tillsonburg, Ontario N4G 3S8
T: (519) 842-7351
F: (519) 842-3082
E: dan@tillsonburghomes.com
GM: Dan Sanders

Highway Hockey League
Box 668
Lumsden, Saskatchewan S0G 3C0
T: (306) 536-5652
F: (306) 247-7377
www.Highwayhockey.ca
E: info@highwayhockey.ca
P: Gerry Tomkins

The HHL is a 9 team league

2003 HHL Champions
Raymore Rockets

Qu'Apelle Valley Hockey League
#23-41 Munroe Place
Regina, Saskatchewan S4S 6A7
T: (306) 569-4646
F: (306) 569-4628
www.QVHL.com
E: qvhl@hotmail.com
P: Don Mc Ewen

Ligue Semi-Pro Quebec LHSPQ

9, rue St-Marc
Pont-Rouge, Quebec G3H 1Y4
T: (418) 873-4234
F: (418) 873-1360
www.LHSPQ.com
E: mike.god@sympatico.ca
P: Michel Gaudette
Media: Martin Lavoie
E: martinlavoie@ca.inter.net

Le Dube d' Asbestos
321 rue Du Roi
Asbestos, Quebec J1T 1S7
T: (819) 879-6318
F: (819) 879-0136
www.angelfire.com/home/dubeasbestos
E: beaudoin@dube.qc.ca
P: Raynald Dodier
PR: Anick Beaudoin

Le Blitz de Granby
*01 rue Leon-Hamel
Granby, Quebec
T: (450) 777-2444
F: (450) 375-4960
www.visioweb.qc.ca/leblitz
E: modcoton@endirect.qc.ca
GM: Gilles Larochelle

Le Mission de Joliette
205 rue Lajoie Sud
Joliette, Quebec J6E 5L5
T: (514) 755-5225
F: (514) 525-5442
www.intermonde.net/cbess/webmission/menup.html
E: missionjoliette@videotron.ca
P: Stephan Brien

Jonquiere Condors
4240 rue Des Ormes
Jonquiere, Quebec G8A 1S1
T: (418) 542-3917
F: (418) 668-7975
http://pages.infinit.net/condors
E: robin026@sympatico.ca
GM: Marc Robitaille
Sec: Lisa Tremblay

Les Rapides de La Salle
C.P. 171, Succursale Champlain
La Salle, Quebec H8P 3J1
T: (514) 367-1062
F: (514) 367-1054
www.lesrapides.ca
GM: Jean-Paul Lariviere

Les Chiefs de Laval
301 St-Isidore
St-Lin-Laurentides, Que. J0R 1C0
T: (514) 953-8080
F: (450) 439-8726
www.chez.com/vochiefs
E: nicosoul@total.net
P: Richard Savaria
Sec: Nicole Souligny

Le Caron et Guay de Pont-Rouge
9 rue St-Marc
Pont-Rouge, Quebec G3H 1Y4
T: (418) 873-5009
F: (418) 873-1360
www.caronetguay.ca.tc
GM: Michel Godin

Les As de Quebec
25, rue des Erables
L'Ange-Gardien, Quebec G0A 2K0
T: (418) 822-1912
F: (418) 822-2137
GM: Frank Lefrancois
www.angelfire.com/dc/asquebec/
E: frank.cfl@videotron.ca
GM: Frank Lefrancois

Le Promutuel de Riviere-du-Loup
C.P. 1225
Riviere-du-Loup, Quebec G5R 4C3
T: (418) 862-9520
F: (418) 862-2205
Membres.tripod.fr/promutuelRDL
P: Paul Thibault
GM: Gilles Lortie

La Garaga de St-Georges-de-Beauce
C.P. 252
St-Georges de Beauce, Que G5Y 5C7
T: (418) 228-3949
F: (418) 228-7011
www.garaga.com/hockey
E: hockey@garaga.com
P: Roger Doyon
Mkt: Pierre Jacob

Le Cousin de Saint-Hyacinthe
800 rue Turcot
Saint-Hyacinthe, Quebec J2S 1M2
T: (450) 546-5654
F: (450) 546-0888
www.lecousin.ca
E: pierre@champigny.ca
P: Pierre Champigny
GM: Guy St-Amand

Les Royaux de Sorel
1222 rue Filiatrault
Sorel-Tracy, Quebec J3R 3T5
T: (450) 743-2484
F: (450) 743-0293
www.LesRoyaux.com
E: cjso@cjso.qc.ca
GM: Yanick Levesque

Les Prolab de Thetford Mines
841, 13e Avenue
Thetford Mines, Quebec G6G 1W4
T: (418) 338-8316
F: (418) 338-6697
www.prolab-lub.com/plt/index.htm
E: nfecteau@megantic.net
P: Gaston Gagne
GM: Nelson Fecteau

Les Dragons de Verdun
1527 Autoroute 440 ouest, Suite 200
Laval, Quebec J7L 3W3
T: (450) 971-4114
F: (450) 681-3374
www.lesdragons.org
E: defoy@vroum.com
E: dragonsverdun@hotmail.com
P: Alban Gauthier
GM: Michel Laurendeau
PR: Michel Poirier-Defoy

Le Lacroix de Windsor
84, 5ieme Avenue
Windsor, Quebec J1S 1V7
T: (819) 845-5635
F: (819) 845-5917
www.geocities.com/le_lacroix
E: gaetanpelissier@sympatico.ca
P: Martial Frappier
GM: Gaetan Pelissier

This is the LHSPQ sixth season.

2003 LHSPQ Champions
Chiefs de Laval

Ligue Centrale de Hockey Senior AA
No address available
T: (418) 293-2558
F: (418) 289-2558
www.lch.qc.ca
E: valcle@globetrotter.net
P: Clement Vallieres
PR: Rene Morin
E: lchpub@globetrotter.net

Le Caron et Guay de Montagnards de Charlevoix
31 Ave. Larouche
Clermont, Quebec G4A 1K1
T: (418) 439-3773
F: (418) 665-0013
http://caronguay.tripod.ca/page1.htm
E: harveysylvain@hotmail.com
P: Andre Fortin
PR: Georges Dallaire

Le Metro Gagnon
300 route de l'Eglise
Donnacona, Quebec
T: (418) 285-3284
www.geocities.com/hockey/agagnon
E: loisipr@globetrotter.net
E: dannygenois@sympatico.ca
GM: Danny Genois

Les Seigneurs La Pocatiere
604, 9ieme rue
La Pocatiere, Quebec G0R 1Z0
T: (418) 856-1346
F: (418) 856-5415
www.siegneurs.qc.ca
E: fdude@globetrotter.net
P: Jacques Caron

Les Sentinelles Montmagny
21, Ste-Brigitte Nord
Montmagny, Quebec G5V 4E8
T: (418) 248-5995
F: (418) 248-3855
www.montmagny.com/sentinelles
E: poirstepr@ldcotesud.qc.ca
GM: Pierre Bouffard

P.G. Lotbiniere St-Gilles
1530 rue de l'Arena
St-Gilles, Quebec G0S 2P0
T: (418) 888-3863
F: (418) 888-4145
E: pglotbiniere@hotmail.com
P: Guy Lessard
PR: Alain Aubert

Les Piliers de St-Jean-Port-Joli
392 rue Jean-Leclerc
St-Jean-Port-Joli, Quebec G0R 3G0
T: (418) 598-3144
F: (418) 598-3165
P: Marc-Andre Dufour
GM: Gaetan Dube

Les Predateur St-Marc-des-Carrieres
1650 boul. Bona Dussault
St-Marc-des-Carrieres, Quebec
G0A 4B0 Canada
T: (418) 268-8060
F: (418) 268-3462
www.predateurs.ca.tc
E: guyluc@globetrotter.qc.ca
P: Jean-Luc Moisan
GM: Maryon Leclerc

L'Express St-Pierre-les Becquets
185, Rte. 218
St-Pierre-les-Becquets, Que. G0X 2Z0
T: (819) 263-2466
F: (819) 263-2373
www.multimania.com/leexpress
E: express@moncourrier.com
P: Yvon Crochetiere
GM: Yves Dumoulin

The LCH began its inaugural Season In 1990-91.

2003 LCH Champions
Les Eperviers Black Lake

Independent Senior Club

Les Eperviers Black Lake
1155, 12e Avenue
Thetford Mines, Quebec G6G 1X6
T: (418) 423-4843
F: (418) 335-2178
P: Claude Binet
PR: Jean-Francois Morissette

Ligue Promutuel Senior AA
579 des Jonquilles
Pointe-au-Pere, Quebec G5M 1G2
T/F: (418) 724-6528
Cell: (418) 725-8675
www.LHSBSL.com
E: infini@ri.cgocable.ca
P: Jean-Real Couture

2003 LHSBSL Champion
Le Castors de Mantane

U.S. Senior Hockey

Great Lakes Hockey League
PO Box 1021
Rhinelander, WI 54501
T: (715) 369-3265
F: (715) 369-1951
Commissioner: Peter Krueger
Secretary: Warner Stebbeds
T/F: (715) 479-1033
www.eteamz.com/GLHL
E: jrjlstebbeds@hotmail.com

Calumet Wolverines
1747 Isle Royale Street
Laurium, MI 49913
T: (906) 337-4808
F: (906) 337-1611
www.eteamz.com/calwolverines
GM: Ray Pomroy

Eagle River Falcons
7416 Birch Tree Drive
Eagle River, WI 54521
T: (715) 272-1984
F: (715) 479-8717
E: don@waha-hockey.com
P: Dan Schmidt
GM: Don Kohlman

Fond Du Lac Bears
307 Gillett Street
Fond Du Lac, WI 54935
T: (920) 926-0640
F: (920) 929-8958
www.eteamz.com/fondybears
E: familyonice@yahoo.com
GM/Coach: Todd Larson

Green Bay Deacons
2623 Oakwood Drive
Green Bay, WI 54304
T: (920) 499-7478
http://home.new.rr.com/deaconhockey
GM: Carl Magnuson

Milwaukee Flyers
8735 W Orchard Street
West Allis, WI 53214
T: (414) 771-6388
F: (414) 325-7898
semandel.skip@towerautomotive.com
GM/Coach: Skip Semandel

Mosinee Papermakers
303 Birch Street
Mosinee, WI 54455
T: (715) 693-6256
GM: Mike Kennedy

Portage Lake Pioneers
506 W. Baraga
Houghton, MI 49931
T: (906) 482-9402
F: (906) 482-5130
www.eteamz.com/pioneers
E: clucches@up.net
GM: Cathy Lucchesi

Waupun Wolves
662 Cochrane Street
Waupun, WI 53963
T: (920) 324-9501
www.eteamz.com/wolves
E: randpshaw@powerweb.net
GM: Roger Shaw

The GLHL was formerly known as the Badger State League and is the only full-check Senior hockey league in the U.S.A.

**2003 Great Lakes Lg. Champion
Mosinee Papermakers**

U.S. Junior B Hockey

Central States Hockey League
#1 Villawood
Webster Groves, MO 63119
T: (314) 961-3558
F: (314) 961-5620
www.cshlhockey.com
E: fferrara@ralston.com
P: Frank Ferrara

Cincinnati Cobras
6112 Chappelfield Drive
West Chester, OH 45069
T: (513) 563-0008
F: (513) 563-0141
www.cincinnaticobras.com
E: rinkman333@aol.com
GM: Bob Nydick

Cleveland Jr. Lumberjacks
1616 9th Blvd.
Lorain, OH 44052
T: (440) 246-1075
F: (440) 246-3113
www.clevelandjrlumberjacks.org
E: jimrufo@adelphia.net
GM: Jim Rufo

Columbus Crush
5196 Red Oak Lane
Dublin, OH 43016
T: (800) 233-5700
F: (614) 379-4506
www.columbuscrush.com
E: rparkcrush@aol.com
GM: Bobb Park

Flint Jr. Generals
13316 N. Horrell Road
Fenton, MI 48430
T: (810) 629-2161
F: (810) 629-0776
www.jrgenerals.com
E: dj7255@aol.com
GM: Daniel Jewell

Grand Rapids Jr. Owls
3010 Byron Center Rd SW, #203
Wyoming, MI 49509
T: (616) 249-0208
F: (616) 878-3746
www.gr-jrb-owls.com
E: flags@cdhphockey.com
GM: Mike Flanagan

Metro Jets
8717 Buffalo Drive
Commerce Township, MI 48382
T: (248) 363-1516
F: (248) 363-5887
www.metrojetshockey.com
E: hwolfe@teleweb.net
GM: Butch Wolfe

Motor City Chiefs
4176 Hill Dr., Bldg 10, #107
Shelby Twp., MI 48317
T: (810) 254-0348
F: (810) 364-2469
www.chiefsjrhockeyclub.com
E: dmajkowski@us.tiauto.com
GM: Doug Majkowski

Peoria Mustangs
1086 Spring Bay Road
East Peoria, IL 61611
T: (309) 698-0265
F: (309) 698-1782
www.peoriamustangs.com
E: jmolaughlin@worldnet.att.net
GM: John O'Laughlin

St. Louis Junior Blues
5428 Hollow Oak Court
St. Louis, MO 63129
T: (314) 481-7171
F: (314) 481-9271
www.STLjrblues.org
E: ssmwi@mindspring.com
GM: Jim Jost

Toledo Cherokee
5702 Angola Rd., #135
Toledo. OH 43615
T: (419) 861-4967
F: (419) 861-6113
www.cherokeehockey.com
E: cherokeegm@westbrookvillage.tv
GM: Mike Robertson

Wayne Wheels
3601 Hannan #210
Wayne, MI 48184
T: (734) 722-8223
F: (313) 647-0041
www.waynewheels.com
E: coachcip@aol.com
GM: Matthew Cipriani

Empire Junior Hockey League
306 S. Salina Street
Syracuse, NY 13202
T: (305) 472-6359
F: (305) 471-3629
www.empirehockey.com
E: info@empirehockey.com
P: Don Kirnan

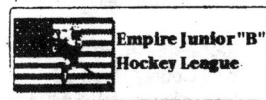

Binghamton Tornadoes
547 Maple Street
Big Flats, NY 14814
T: (607) 562-3609
E: tornadoJrB@aol.com
GM: Chuck Annis

Bucks-Mont Jr. Bandits
3204 Gurley Road
Philadelphia, PA 19154
T: (215) 824-0842
GM: Art Stevenson

Elmira Jackals
815 W. Water Street
Elmira, NY 14905
T/F: (607) 733-9169
www.elmirajrbhockey.com
E: GM: Allan
Charlapallanc@stny.rr.com

Johnstown Jr. Chiefs
326 Napoleon Street
Johnstown, PA 15901
T: (814) 539-1799
E: info@johnstownchiefs.com
GM: Toby O'Brien

Mass. Maple Leafs
PO Box 30314
Acushnet, MA 02743
T: (508) 999-4908
E: mass@empirehockey.com
GM: Anthony DeSilva

Metro Falcons
3 Downing Street
Carlisle, PA 17013
T/F: (717) 243-0763
www.metrofalcons.org
E: deelwags@aol.com
GM: Dee Wagner

Pittsburgh Jr. Penguins
135 Mc Kee Road
North Versailles, PA 15137
T: (412) 394-3059
F: (412) 281-0677
E: gkelly@buckconsultants.com
GM: George Kelly

Rochester Jr. Americans
7675 County Road 32
Canandiagua, NY 14424
T: (716) 229-4836
F: (716) 229-5260
E: rochester@empirehockey.com
E: jdorak@starband.net
GM: John Dorak

Syracuse Stars
306 S. Salina St.
Syracuse, NY 13202
T: (315) 472-6359
F: (315) 471-3629
E: syracuse@empirehockey.com
E: DIkirnan@aol.com
GM: Don Kirnan

Wheatfield Jr. Blades
82 Irving Terrace
Buffalo, NY 14223
T: (716) 874-2849
F: (716) 871-8958
www.wheatfieldbladesjrb.com
E: wheatfield@empirehockey.com
GM: Greg Desantis

Interstate Junior Hockey League
PO Box 480
Stoneham, MA 02180
T: (781) 279-0859
F: (781) 397-0847
www.IJHL.org
E: Goalies@tiac.net
P: Bob Rotondo

Boston Jr. Blackhawks
18 Harding Road
Wakefield, MA 01880
T: (781) 245-9330
F: (781) 245-9256
GM: Rich Salsman

Canton Rangers
PO Box 1229
N. Falmouth, MA 02556
T: (508) 265-5492
E: cantonrangers@yahoo.com
GM: Mark Jones

Connecticut Whalers
300 Alumni Road
Newton, CT 06111
T: (860) 665-7825
F: (860) 665-7824
E:ck@ciscusa.com
GM: Chris Kiene

Laconia Leafs
444 Route 107
Laconia, NH 03246
T: (603) 528-0789
F: (603) 527-0333
www.laconialeafs.com
GM: Will Fay

Salem Ice Dogs
1 Maude Street, Unit 4
Malden, MA 02148
T: (781) 397-2773
F: (781) 397-6334
GM: Marc Salsman

Springfield Jr. Pic's
485 Rogers Avenuet
West Springfield, MA 01089
T: (860) 688-4884
F: (860) 769-2905
GM: Charlie Nielen

Twin City SaberCats
1000 John Fitch Hwy.
Fitchburg, MA 01420
T: (978) 345-7593
F: (978) 343-8217
E: mounty@mindspring.com
GM: Bradley Mount

West River Wolves
PO Box 1021
Londonderry, NH 03053
T: (603) 621-0452
F: (603) 621-0451
www.westriverwolves.com
E: rjbrousseau@mediaone.net
GM: Ron Brouseau

Metropolitan Junior Hockey League
251 E. Glen Avenue
Ridgewood, NJ 07450
T: (201) 670-9370
F: (201) 445-0761
www.atlantic-district.org/MJHL
E: mhgh@aol.com
P: Glenn Hefferan

Central Penn Panthers
1105 Valley Road
Lancaster, PA 17603
T: (717) 295-9527
F: (717) 295-9501
E: rayferry1@aol.com
GM: Ray Ferry

Connecticut Clippers
6 Progress Drive
Cromwell, CT 06416
T: (860) 632-0323
F: (860) 632-2088
E: rcraw1959@aol.com
GM: Bob Crawford

Connecticut Wolves
1346 Wolf Hill Road
Cheshire, CT 06410
T: (203) 272-8428
E: dmccar1238@aol.com
GM: Dan McCarthy

New Jersey Jr. Titans
PO Box 428
Old Bridge, NJ 08857
T: (732) 919-1110
F: (732) 919-7732
E: kashockey@aol.com
GM: Ken Seltzer

New York Bobcats
34 Lexington Street
Westbury, NY 11590
T: (516) 333-2372
F: (516) 334-5087
www.nybobcats.com
E: wenlex@aol.com
GM: Wendy Liotti

Philadelphia Little Flyers
827 Hunters Drive
Deptford, NJ 08096
T: (856) 228-1082
F: (856) 227-1114
E: jsgflyers@aol.com
GM: John Giacobbo

Suffolk PAL Silver Shields
4 Strathmore Village Drive
South Setauket, NY 11720
T: (631) 736-0201
F: (631) 716-0536
E: rkinnear@mindspring.com
GM: Ron Kinnear

Washington Junior Capitals
42 Brinkwood Road
Brookville, MD 20833
T: (301) 774-8568
F: (301) 774-5372
E: jrcaps@aol.com
GM: Linda Clifford

Minnesota Junior Hockey League
16660 Mankato Street NE
Ham Lake, MN 55304
T/F: (612) 434-7440
www.MJHL.com
E: MJHL@concentric.net
P: Phil Pascuzzi

Coon Rapids Jr. Owls
10221 Olive Street NW
Coon Rapids, MN 55433
T/F: (612) 757-9734
E: starkuz@baldeagle.com
GM: Cindy Kuznia

Dubuque Thunderbirds
PO Box 1083
Dubuque, IA 52004
T: (563) 557-1228
F: (563) 583-1649
E: dbqhocinc@aol.com
GM: Ken Gaber

Iron Range Yellowjackets
PO Box 268
Coleraine, MN 55722
T/F: (218) 245-2181
E: yjackets@uslink.net
GM: Eric Ballard

Minnesota Ice Hawks
10 Lakewood Knoll
Cleveland, MN 56017
T: (507) 931-3797
F: (507) 931-0257
E: icehawks@prairie.lakes.com
GM: Michael Fatis

Northwest Wisconsin Knights
16507 W. State Road 77
Hayward, WI 54843
T: (715) 634-1606
F: (715) 635-6688
www.nwknights.com
E: dan.foss@nestechemicals.com
GM: Dan Foss

Shattuck St. Mary's Sabres
1000 Shumway, PO Box 218
Fairbault, MN 55021
T: (507) 333-1615
F: (507) 333-1603
E: bbreau@11.net
GM: Bob Breau

South Suburban Steers
901 Cheri Lane
Mendota Heights, MN 55120
T: (651) 454-1018
F: (800) 451-9195
E: sssteers@aol.com
GM: Jim Martin

White Bear Lake Lakers
5214 E. Bald Eagle Blvd.
White Bear Lake, MN 55110
T: (651) 426-4147
F: (651) 426-7276
E: lakersjrhky@baldeagle.com
http://lakersjrhockey.tripod.com/lakers
GM: Ralph Hayne

Northern Pacific Junior Hockey League
1137 Joyce Drive
Fairbanks, AK 99701
T: (907) 452-7246
www.nor-pachockey.com
E: tragis@ptialaska.net
Commissioner: Jack Tragis

Eugene Thunder
PO Box 24951
Eugene, OR 97402
T: (541) 682-7301
F: (541) 682-7372
www.eugenethunder.com
E: bigguy@eugenethunder.com
GM: Mike Ankney

Kootenai Colts
E 26910 Eastland Drive
Spokane, WA 99025
T: (509) 226-0550
www.kootenaicolts.com
GM: Dean Gorman

Liberty Lake Lumberjacks
18015 N. Mt. Spokane Park Dr.
Mead, WA 99021
T: (509) 238-3017
www.lllumberjacks.com
E: lumberjill123@aol.com
GM: Izzy Knudsen

Portland Pioneers
5325 NW Ponderosa Drive
Portland, OR 97229
T: (503) 297-2521
F: (503) 291-1104
www.portland-pioneers.com
E: robert@valleyicearena.com
GM: John McBride

Puget Sound Kings
3610 Ray Nash Drive NW
Gig Harbor, WA 98335
T: (253) 973-1574
F: (253) 265-3102
www.pugetsoundkings.com
E: info@pugetsoundkings.com
GM: Rob Kaufman

Tri-City Titans
PO Box 3229
Pasco, WA 99302
T: (509) 545-9977
www.Tctitans.com
E: gm@Tctitans.com
GM: Gary Hoffer

Western States Junior Hockey League
4675 MacArthur Court, Suite 1590
Newport Beach, CA 92660
T: (949) 474-5915
F: (949) 474-5917
E: wshlhky@aol.com
P: Don R. Thorne

Bay City Bombers
1000 E. Cerritos Ave.
Anaheim, CA 92805
T: (714) 502-9185
F: (714) 502-9375
www.jrbombers.com
E: rrwglacial@aol.com
GM: Ron White

Nevada Rattlers
2887 Green Valley Pkwy #348
Henderson, NV 89014
T/F: (702) 568-1325
E: nevrattlers@yahoo.com
GM: Phil Dean

Phoenix Polar Bears
2001 W. Alameda Drive
Phoenix, AZ 85282
T: (480) 337-0224
www.phoenixpolarbears.com
E: hoody@primenet.com
GM: Harry Mahood

Salt Lake Maple Leafs
2375 S. Tennessee Ave.
Provo, UT 84606
T: (801) 812-0739
E: karlkuhnen@hotmail.com
GM: Karl Kuhnen

San Diego Surf
2226 Puesta Del Sol
Escondido, CA 92027
T: (619) 990-3812
F: (760) 745-8427
www.eteamz.com/sandiegojrsurf
E: mfschurman@cs.com
GM: M.F. Schurman

Utah Valley Golden Eagles
433 West 870 S.
Orem, UT 84058
T: (801) 235-9190
F: (801) 235-9192
E: golden_eagles_2@yahoo.com
GM: Stan Weiss

Valencia Flyers
27745 N. Smyth Drive
Valencia, CA 91355
T: (661) 775-8686 x 204
F: (661) 775-8681
www.valenciaflyers.com
E: larry@icestation.net
GM: Larry Bruyere

2003 National Junior B Silver Cup Champions
Phoenix Polar Bears

Junior C Hockey

Continental Hockey League
5259 Geddes Way
Pipersville, PA 18947
T: (215) 766-2255
P: Andy Richards

Apple Core Jr. Selects
35 Seacoast Terr., # 6U
Brooklyn, NY 11235
T/F: (718) 332-4555
www.applecorejunior.com
E: lizard77@prodigy.net
GM: Henry Lazar

Belleville Jr. Blackhawks
433 Weatherstone Drive
Belleville, IL 62221
T: (618) 650-2159
F: (618) 650-2696
E: wmisiak@siue.edu
P: Bill Misiak

Bucks County Generals
5259 Geddes Way
Pipersville, PA 18947
T: (215) 677-2255
E: ihockey@bellatlantic.net
P: Andrew Richards

Indiana Thunder
497 East Pike
Indiana, PA 15701
T: (724) 465-2665
F: (724) 465-4710
E: ron@indianaicecenter.com
GM: Ron Hellen

Mass. Maple Leafs Jr C
23 Fairfield Street
Acushnet, MA 02743
T: (508) 999-4908
P: Anthony DeSilva

Norwich Ice Breakers
641 New London Turnpike
Norwich, CT 06360
T: (860) 892-2559
P: Michael Goldblatt

Oklahoma Bazooka Blues
415 E. Third Street
Tulsa, OK 74120
T: (918) 587-2300
F: (918) 587-0428
www.bazookablues.com
E: fswign@ionet.net
GM: Randy Frederick

Pittsburgh Amateur Penguins
1302 William Flynn Hwy.
Glenshaw, PA 15116
T: (412) 487-5655
F: (412) 487-6999
www.penaltybox.net
E: hockey5655@home.com
GM: Kevin Morrison

Ramapo Jr. Rangers
10 Academy Avenue
Sloatsburg, NJ 10974
T/F: (914) 753-2128
E: ramaporang@aol.com
P: Ron Skibin

Eastern Junior Hockey League

PO Box 1023
East Arlington, MA 02474
T: (617) 268-9811
F: (617) 464-0227
www.easternjunior.com
E: ejhl@net1plus.com
Commissioner: Daniel Esdale
PR: Jim Prior

Apple Core Jr. C
35 Seacoast Terr., # 6U
Brooklyn, NY 11235
T/F: (718) 332-4555
www.applecorejunior.com
E: lizard77@prodigy.net
GM: Henry Lazar

Bay State Breakers
PO Box 1178
Marshfield, MA 02050
T: (781) 834-2346
F: (781) 792-2950
www.baystatebreakers.com
E: Baystate_breakers@msn.com
GM: David McCauley

Boston Harbor Wolves
8 Lawrence Street
Charlestown, MA 02129
T: (617) 242-3006
F: (617) 241-5321
GM: Phil Coleman

Bridgewater Bandits
20 Bedford Park
Bridgewater, MA 02324
T: (508) 878-5009
F: (508) 697-6804
E: banditsjrs@aol.com
GM: Daniel Crockett

Capital District Selects
19 Oakwood Blvd.
Clifton Park, NY 12065
T: (518) 371-3795
F: (518) 458-7017
E: jodygbs@aol.com
GM: Jim Salfi

Green Mountain Glades
38 Bayberry Lane
South Burlington, VT 05403
T: (802) 865-6811
F: (802) 863-6985
P: Brad Holt

Lawrence Jr. Warriors
654 S. Union Street
Lawrence, MA 01842
T: (978) 557-9018
F: (978) 557-5519
E: aheinze@valley-association.com
GM: Andy Heinze

Lexington Junior Bruins
PO Box 460
Lexington, MA 02173
T: (781) 862-4033
F: (781) 861-8274
www.bostonjuniorbruins.com
E: peter_masters@hotmail.com
GM: Peter Masters, Jr.

Lowell Jr. Lock Monsters
PO Box 405, Middlesex Rd.
Middlesex, MA 01879
T: (781) 862-9387
F: (781) 674-2203
GM: Jack Callahan

New England Coyotes
177 Sawmill Road
West Springfield, MA 01089
T: (413) 734-6860
F: (860) 741-6235
www.necoyotes.com
E: GDHS7@aol.com
P: Gary Dineen

New Hampshire Jr. Monarchs
348 Grove Street
Needham, MA 02492
T: (781) 431-8689
F: (781) 431-1627
E: welane@mediaone.net
GM: Fred Lane

Walpole Jr. Stars
PO Box 227, 2130 Providence Hwy.
Walpole, MA 02081
T: (508) 660-2005
F: (508) 660-2043
GM: Dave LaCouture

Florida Junior Hockey League

2650 N. Military Trail, #125
Boca Raton, FL 33431
T: (561) 997-4002
F: (561) 997-4003
www.fjhl.com
E: rgoldstein@fjhl.com
P: Robert N. Goldstein

Daytona Riptide
PO Box 290627
Import Orange, FL 32129
T/F: (904) 756-5916
E: skateman@bellsouth.net
P: Terry Crowder

Ellenton Eels
5309 29th Street E.
Ellenton, FL 34222
T: (941) 723-3663
F: (941) 722-1121
E: jpigloo@aol.com
GM: Jimmy Perez

Kendall Hurricanes
8235 SW 102nd Avenue
Miami, FL 33173
T: (305) 595-5018
F: (305) 594-9162
E: xxgocanesx@aol.com
GM: Carlos Santa Cruz, Jr.

Miami Jr. Matadors
PO Box 451083
Sunrise, FL 33345
T: (954) 749-4543
F: (954) 749-0472
E: presmjm@aol.com
P: Harvey Kline

Little Caesar's Hockey League
45093 Lemont
Canton, MI 48187
T: (734) 981-1665
E: mcrocket@mediaone.netr
P: Mike Crocket

Flint Icelanders
1338 Farnsworth
Lapeer, MI 48446
T: (810) 350-8771
F: (810) 667-9694
GM: Bob Lawson

St. Clair Shores Saints
24612 Regal Place
Harrison Township, MI 48045
T: (810) 468-0380
GM: Jim Rini

USA Eagles
1369 Greenleaf Drive
Rochester Hills, MI 48309
T: (248) 650-0128
GM: John White

White Lake Wolverine
3059 Towering Oaks
White Lake, MI 48383
T: (248) 684-0694
GM: Joe Dziurman

Canadian Junior B

Capital Junior Hockey League
#202, 15520-96 Avenue
Edmonton, Alberta T5P 0G6
T: (780) 484-7592
F: (780) 444-6150
E: gbruce@planet.eon.net
P: Gary Bruce

Eastern Ontario Jr. B Hockey League
PO Box 908
Richmond, Ontario K0A 2Z0
T: (613) 838-5065
F: (613) 838-3782
www.odha.com
Commissioner: Dwaine Barkley

Empire B Hockey Lg.
19 Johnson St., PO Box 2406
Picton, Ontario K0K 2T0
T: (613) 476-4775
E: hezlep@reach.net
Chmn: Dick Woods

Amherstview Jets
63 Mortensen Drive
Amherstview, Ontario K7N 1W2
T: (613) 546-2661
F: (613) 544-8935
GM: Mason Budarick

Campbellford Rebels
231 Russet Road
Campbellford, Ontario K0L 1L0
T/F: (705) 653-2542
E: rebels@accel.net
GM: Larry Metcalfe

Napanee Raiders
131 West Street
Napanee, Ontario K7R 2P3
T: (613) 388-2276
F: (613) 354-6276
E: hartj@ihorizons.net
P: Morris Hart

North Frontenac Flyers
RR #3
Harrowsmith, Ontario K0H 1V0
T: (613) 376-3143
P: Gerald Irwin

Picton Pirates
Box 2284, RR #8
Picton, Ontario K0K 2T0
T: (613) 476-0033
F: (613) 476-0091
P: Larry Hicks

Golden Horseshoe Lg.
143 Sutherland St. W.
Caledonia, Ontario N3W 1B4
T/F: (905) 765-6648
E: jrichardson@mountaincable.net
Chmn: Rick Richardson

Fort Erie Meteors
225 Gilmore Rd.
Fort Erie, Ontario L2A 2M2
T: (905) 871-1878
F: (905) 871-8117
P: Tony Passero

Niagara Falls Canucks
5652 Main Street
Niagara Falls, Ontario L2G 5Z4
T: (905) 356-6646
F: (905) 356-6706
P: Kevin Maves

Port Colborne Sailors
32 Terrace Avenue
Welland, Ontario L3C 2C4
T: (905) 735-3771
E: ddagazio@iaw.on.ca
P: Dan Degazio

St. Catharines Falcons
4389 John Street
Beamsville, Ontario L0R 1B1
T: (905) 468-3321
F: (905) 684-2237
P: Howard Culp

Stoney Creek Spirit
440 Melvin Avenue
Hamitlon, Ontario L8H 2L5
T: (905) 516-9882
F: (905) 547-2908
E: angelca@sprint.ca
P: Cathy Anger

Thorold Blackhawks
16 Sentence Ave.
Thorold, Ontario L2V 4W9
T: (905) 227-3434
F: (905) 227-1586
P: Dan Timmins

Welland Cougars
127 St. Lawrence Drive
Weland, Ontario L3C 7H3
T: (905) 374-3666
F: (905) 735-8367
E: macnevin@iaw.on.ca
P: Al MacNevin

Heritage Junior B Hockey League
47 Warwick Drive
Red Deer, Alberta T4N 6L4
T: (403) 342-6978
F: (403) 340-6978
P: Gerry Arnusch
Gov: Gary Wournell
T: (403) 948-5840
www.heritagejuniorb.com
E: wournell@home.com

Kootenay Inter. Jr. B Hockey League
PO Box 9160, RPO 3
Revelstoke, B.C V0E 3K0
T: (250) 837-5097
F: (250) 837-5098
www.kijhl.com
P: Len Dergousoff

Beaver Valley Nite Hawks
Box 568
Fruitvale, B.C. V0G 1L0
T: (250) 367-6201
F: (250) 367-0120
P: George Robbins

Castlegar Rebels
Box 3621
Castlegar, B.C. V1N 3W3
T: (250) 365-0653
F: (250) 365-6885
P: Debbie La Hue

Columbia Valley Rockies
Box 2799
Invermere, B.C. V0A 1K0
T: (250) 354-0060
F: (250) 342-7263
P: Harold Hazelaar

Golden Rockets
Box 2584
Golden, B.C. V0A 1H0
T: (250) 344-5615
F: (250) 344-2841
P: Marko Shehovac

Grand Forks Border Bruins
Box 1433
Grand Forks, B.C. V0H 1H0
T: (250) 442-0215
F: (250) 442-2154
P: Art Kelley

Nelson Leafs
PO Box 311
Nelson, B.C. V1L 5R3
T: (250) 352-1624
F: (250) 354-6250
P: Larry Price

North Okanagan Kings
Box 33
Enderby, B.C. V0E 1V0
T: (250) 838-9584
F: (250) 838-9504
P: Eric Borhaven

Osoyoos Heat
Box 260
Osoyoos, B.C. V0H 1V0
T: (250) 495-5128
F: (250) 495-3525
P: Mike Doherty

Revelstoke Grizzlies
Box 2512
Revelstoke, B.C. V0E 2S0
T: (250) 837-4838
F: (250) 837-5859
P: Roy Williams

Sicamous Eagles
RR #1 Site 5 Comp 3
Sicamous, B.C. V0E 2V0
T: (250) 836-4721
P: Arnis Veideman

Spokane Braves
N 13529 E. Newman Lake Rd.
Newman Lake, WA 99025
T: (509) 226-0875
F: (509) 325-5584
P: Bob Tobiason

Ligue de Hockey Junior de Montreal

7501, rue Francois-Perrault
Montreal, Quebec H2A 1M1
T: (514) 872-6799
F: (514) 872-1882
www.lhjm.qc.ca
E: stephrose@sympatico.ca
P: Roger Pepin
VP: Bruno Lepore
PR/Stats: Stephane Rose

Braves d' Ahuntsic
10 442, boul. Saint-Laurent
Montreal, Quebec H3L 2P3
T: (514) 384-2771
F: (514) 333-7861
GM: Louis Hadsipantelis

Dragons d' Anjou
61, rue Longueuil
Repentigny, Quebec J6A 3X6
T: (450) 585-1727
P: Michel Miscioscia

Broncos de Brossard
2640, rue Anjou
Brossard, Quebec J4Z 3B6
T/F: (450) 676-4334
P: Andre Madore

Etoiles de l' Est
602, rue Cadillac
Montreal, Quebec H1N 2T1
T: (514) 251-8141
P: Marcel Labrecque

Predateurs d' Iberville
125, rue Hamel
Iberville, Quebec J2X 2P3
T: (450) 347-6773
F: (450) 347-7954
E: mike433@netc.net
P: Mike Miclette

Express de Laval
3860, rue Duhamel
Laval, Quebec H7R 1K7
T: (514) 350-7280
F: (514) 350-7282
GM: Michel Emard

Jets de Notre Dame de l' Assomption
2570, rue Nicolet
Montreal, Quebec H1W 3L5
T: (514) 527-8297
P: Rejean Legace

National de Rosemere
187, boul. Arthur-Sauve #101
Saint-Eustache, Quebec J7P 2A6
T: (450) 491-1311
P: Edmond Lavallee

The LHJM is a Junior B league.

Mid-Western Jr. B League

RR #1
Fullarton, Ontario N0K 1H0
T: (519) 348-9865
F: (519) 348-4100
Chmn: Paul Lake

Brant County Golden Eagles
50 Terrace Park Drive
Hamilton, Ontario L9G 1C2
T: (905) 575-1212
F: (905) 575-2294
P: Rick Knowles

Cambridge Winterhawks
20 Rosevelt Avenue
Waterloo, Ontario N2L 1N1
T: (519) 886-5266
F: (519) 886-0429
P: Peter Brill

Elmira Sugar Kings
117 St. Andrew St.
Fergus, Ontario N1M 1P9
T: (519) 669-2454
F: (519) 669-1744

Guelph Fire
110 Delhi street
Guelph, Ontario N1H 4J8
T: (519) 824-1060
F: (519) 837-1254
P: Barry Martin

Kitchener Dutchmen
5 Forwell Rd. #7
Kitchener, Ontario N2B 1W3
T: (519) 653-1111
F: (519) 571-0132

Listowel Cyclones
PO Box 143
Listowel, Ontario N4W 3H2
T: (519) 887-6365
F: (519) 887-6381
P: Steve Coulter

Orangeville Crushers
95 Dawson Road
Orangeville, Ontario L9W 2W7
T: (519) 942-9547
F: (519) 942-8681
P: Neil Anderson

Owen Sound Greys
PO Box 324
Owen Sound, Ontario N4K 5P5
T: (519) 376-8691
F: (519) 376-0483
P: Carl Fairman

Stratford Cullitans
148 Strachen Street
Stratford, Ontario N5A 2B3
T: (519) 271-9193
F: (519) 273-3354
E: moorhead@orc.ca
P: Roger Moorehead

Waterloo Siskins
374 Bing Crescent
Waterloo, Ontario N2K 2A6
T: (519) 579-3310
F: (519) 884-9123
P: Greg Beaupre

Northeast Alberta Jr. B Hockey League
Box 3376
Vermilion, Alberta T9X 2B3
T: (780) 875-8160
F: (780) 875-1625
P: John D. Kelley

Northern Ontario Hockey Assn. Jr. B
109 Elm Street, Suite 10
Sudbury, Ontario P3C 1T4
T: (705) 688-8651
Commissioner: Joe Drago

Hearst Elans
Box 2006
Hearst, Ontario P0L 1N0
T: (705) 362-5699
P: Martin Lanoix

Wawa Travellers
77 McKinley
Wawa, Ontario P0S 1K0
T: (807) 856-2561
P: Allen Cresswell

Northwest Jr. B Hockey League
Box 1047
Dawson Creek, B.C. V1G 4H9
T/F: (250) 782-2575
http://nwjhl.hypermart.net/
E: n-w-j-h-l@telesplanet.net
P: Gordon Reid

Beaverlodge Blades
PO Box 8
Valhalla, Alberta T0H 3M0
T: (780) 356-2117
F: (780) 356-2119
P: Randy Moe

Dawson Creek Canucks
1100-100 Avenue
Dawson Creek, B.C. V1G 1W5
T: (250) 782-8693
P: Richard Frank

Fort St. John Huskies Jr. B
PO Box 6483
Fort St. John, B.C. V1J 4H9
T: (250) 785-3195
F: (250) 785-2624
P: Carolyn Krauss

Grand Prairie Wheelers
RR #1
Grand Prairie, Alberta T8V 2Z8
T: (780) 532-6686
F: (780) 513-0322
P: Sharon Kimble

Sexsmith Vipers
Box 272
Sexsmith, Alberta T0H 3C0
T: (780) 568-2512
F: (780) 539-3530
P: Duane Haakstad

Slave Lake Wolves
Box 1002
Slave Lake, Alberta T0G 2A0
T: (780) 849-5282
F: (780) 849-9603
P: Rachel Dunlap

Tumbler Ridge Icemen
Box 1145
Tumbler Ridge, B.C. V0C 2W0
T: (250) 242-3458
F: (250) 242-3044
P: Doug Cameron

2002 NWJHL Championships
Fort St. John Huskies d Dawson Creek Canucks 4 Games to 3.

Pacific International Jr. Hockey League
8711 Camden Crescent
Richmond, B.C. V7C 3G5
T: (604) 277-0151
F: (604) 277-0156
www.2ptshockey.com/pijhl
P: Harold Brittain

Abbotsford Pilots
34816 Orchard Dr., RR #6
Abbotsford, B.C. V3G 2B4
T/F: (604) 853-5258
P: Jack Goeson

Delta Ice Hawks
7187 Vantage Way
Delta, B.C. V4G 1K7
T: (604) 940-4448
F: (604) 940-4454
www.deltaicehawks.com
P: Gerry Metheral

Grandview Steelers
1569 E. 19th Street
Vancouver, B.C. V5N 2T8
T: (604) 874-5912
F: (604) 874-5914
P: Louie Szendrei

Port Coquitlam Buckeroos
PO Box 133
Port Coquitlam, B.C. V3C 3V5
T: (604) 465-9263
F: (604) 465-1339
P: Ken Williamson

Queen's Park Pirates
#1-8560 Roseberry Avenue
Burnaby, B.C. V5J 3N3
T/F: (604) 272-3414
P: Ken Kirby

Richmond Sockeyes Jr. Hockey
8660 Camden Crescent
Richmond, B.C. V7C 3G4
T: (604) 277-4369
F: (604) 266-4369
P: Romeo Bon

Ridge Meadows Flames
#138-2721 Atlin Place
Coquitlam, B.C. V3C 5B1
T: (604) 469-2522
F: (604) 469-8924
P: Ray Stonehouse

Vancouver Island Jr. B Hockey League
PO Box 4, RR #1
Cowichan Valley, B.C. V0R 1N0
T: (250) 748-9143
F: (250) 748-8065
P: Jim Williams

Campbell River Storm
PO Box 528
Campbell River, B.C. V9W 5C1
T/F: (250) 334-9537
P: Ed Kingston

Comox Valley Glacier Kings
321 Panorama Crescent
Courtenay, B.C. V9N 6Y7
T: (250) 334-4709
F: (250) 334-0499
P: Marsha Webb

Kerry Park Islanders
Box 4, RR #1
Cowichan Valley, B.C. V0R 1N0
T: (250) 748-9143
F: (250) 748-8065
P: R.J. Williams

Parksville Generals
Box 149
Parksville, B.C. V9P 2G3
T: (250) 248-2351
F: (250) 758-4660
P: Gordon Ireland

Peninsula Panthers
#514-10 Paul Kane Place
Victoria, B.C. V9A 7J8
T: (250) 361-4989
F: (250) 385-1550
P: Mark Wagstaff

Port Alberni Bandits
Box 151
Port Alberni, B.C. V9Y 7M7
T: (250) 723-4658
F: (250) 724-6611
P: Gerald Trees

Saanich Braves
Box 48025, 3575 Douglas St.
Victoria, B.C. V8Z 7H5
T: (250) 385-9924
F: (250) 385-5542
P: Tom Sims

Victoria Cougars
626 Normanton Court
Victoria, B.C. V8C 5H7
T: (250) 598-3792
F: (250) 598-9024

Western Jr. B Hockey League
310 Braemar Place
Corunna, Ontario N0G 1G0
T: (519) 383-3629
E: Bhaley@suncor.com
Chmn: Bob Haley

Aylmer Aces
PO Box 416
Aylmer, Ontario N5H 3E8
T: (519) 268-0286
E: aylmeraces@hotmail.com
P: Robert Wise

Chatham Maroons
RR 1
Chatham, Ontario N7M 5J1
T/F: (519) 352-7171
P: Dave Torrie

Leamington Flyers
1021 Oak Street East
Leamington, Ontario N8H 3V7
T: (519) 326-0937
F: (519) 326-7886
P: Rob Williams

London Nationals
PO Box 122, Lambeth Sta.
London, Ontario N6P 1P9
T: (519) 681-1980
F: (519) 681-1926
E: jsimmons@lweb.net
P: John Simmons

Petrolia Jets
332 Walnut Court, Box 557
Corunna, Ontario N0N 1G0
T: (519) 481-1233
F: (519) 481-1521
P: Bruce Helps

Sarnia Steeplejacks
2195 Stoney Creek Dr.
Brights Grove, Ont. N0N 1C0
T/F: (519) 869-6328
P: Steve McKichan

St. Marys lincolns
22 Cobourg Ave.
Stratford, Ontario N5A 1E7
T: (519) 271-2161
F: (519) 284-2563
P: Angie Nigro

St. Thomas Stars
108 Hazelwood Crescent
Belmont, Ontario N0L 1B0
T: (519) 644-4121
F: (519) 644-5144
E: ve3sme@goldennet.com
P: Rick Smith

Strathroy Rockets
23 Rickingham Court
London, Ontario N6C 4L7
T: (519) 686-5552
F: (519) 686-9018

Tecumseh Bulldogs
355 E. Lawn Blvd.
Windsor, Ontario N8S 3H3
T: (519) 979-1607
F: (519) 979-0968
P: Pete Slijivic

There are no National Championships for Junior B hockey in Canada.

Canadian Junior C Hockey

Central Ontario Jr C League
14 Truman Road
Willowdale, Ontario M2L 2L5
T: (416) 593-4385
F: (416) 449-0402
Chmn: Bill Markle

Eastern Ontario Jr C League
213 Carillon Street
Ottawa, Ontario K1L 5X7
T: (613) 749-2046
F: (613) 742-8127
E: glatour@cyberus.ca
www.odha.com
Commissioner: Roger Latour

Georgian Bay Mid-Ontario Junior C League
Box 5230
Huntsville, Ontario P1H 2K6
T: (705) 788-3188
F: (705) 788-3144
Convenor: Bob Adams

Great Lakes Junior C Hockey League
310 Braemar Place
Corunna, Ontario N0N 1G0
T/F: (519) 862-3777
E: bhaley@suncor.com
Chmn: Bob Haley

Junior Rive Sud Ligue Quebec
43 Chateaubriand
Levis, Quebec G6V 4Z9
T: (418) 835-0072
www.juniorqc.com
E: plantelacroix@juniorqc.com
P: Ghislaine Plante

Niagara District Jr. C
143 Sutherland Street W.
Caledonia, Ontario N3W 1B4
T/F: (905) 765-6648
E: jrichardson@mountaincable.net
Chmn: Rick Richardson

Western Junior C Hockey League
PO Box 712
Port Elgin, Ontario N0H 2C0
T: (519) 361-4158
F: (519) 361-4697
Chmn: Gord Gottscheu

Junior Development League
139 Main Street S.
Belmont, Ontario N0L 1B0
T: (519) 537-3311
F: (519) 644-0006
Convenor: Wayne Smith

Hockey Organizations

American Hearing Impaired Hockey Association
1143 W. Lake Street
Chicago, IL 60607
T: (312) 226-5880
F: (312) 829-2098
P: Stan Mikita

American Hockey Coaches Association
7 Concord Street
Gloucester, MA 01930
T: (978) 283-2662
F: (978) 281-8021
Exec. Director: Joe Bertagna

Canadian Adult Recreation Hockey Association
1600 James Naismith Dr., Suite 301
Gloucester, Ontario K1B 5N4
T: (613) 748-5646
F: (613) 748-5714
www.carha.ca
E: hockey@carha
Exec. Dir: Mike Peski

Hockey Hall of Fame & Museum
BCE Place, 30 Yonge Street
Toronto, Ontario M5E 1X8
T: (416) 360-7735
F: (416) 360-1501
www.hhof.com
Chmn: William C. Hay
Mgr. Resource Ctr: Philip Pritchard

International Hockey Hall of Fame
York & Alfred Streets, Box 82
Kingston, Ontario K7L 4V6
T: (613) 544-2355
F: (613) 544-2355
Exec. Dir: Doug Nichols

Professional Hockey Player's Association
1 St. Paul St., Suite 701
St. Catharines, Ontario L2R 7L2
T: (905) 682-4800
F: (905) 682-4822
www.phpa.com
E: phpa@vaxxine.com
Exec. Director: Larry Landon
Mkt: Dino Fazio

Professional Hockey Writer's Association
Buffalo News
1 News Plaza
Buffalo, NY 14240
T: (716) 849-4462
F: (716) 856-5150
P: Jim Kelley

USA Hockey
1775 Bob Johnson Drive
Colorado Springs, CO 80906
T: (719) 576-8724
F: (719) 538-1160
www.usahockey.com
E: usah@usahockey.org
P: Walter L. Bush, Jr.
Media: Darryl Seibel

U.S. Hockey Hall of Fame
801 Hat Trick Ave., PO Box 657
Eveleth, MN 55734
T: (800) 443-PUCK
T: (218) 744-5167
F: (218) 744-2590
www.ushockyhall.com
P: Janes Findley
Exec Dir: Ted Brill

Hockey Publications

American Hockey Magazine
1775 Bob Johnson Drive
Colorado Springs, CO 80906
T: (719) 576-8724
F: (719) 538-1160
Editor-in-Chief: Darryl Seibel

Beckett Hockey Card Monthly
15850 Dallas Parkway
Dallas, TX 75248
T: (972) 448-9035
F: (972) 991-8930
www.beckett.com
Pub: Dr. James Beckett III
Editor: Mike McAllister

Hockey Business News
12327 Santa Monica Blvd.
Suite 202
Los Angeles, CA 90025
T: (310) 442-6660
F: (310) 442-6663
E: hbn@artnet.net
Pub: Mark Brown
Editor: Michael Scarr

Hockey Digest
990 Grove Street
Evanston, IL 60201
T: (847) 491-6440
F: (847) 491-0667
Pub: Norman Jacobs
Editor: Ken Keiker

Hockey Illustrated
233 Park Ave. S., 6th FL
New York, NY 10003
T: (212) 780-3500
F: (212) 780-3555
P: John Plunkett
Editor: Steve Ciacciarelli

The Hockey News
777 Bay St., Ste 2700, Box 148
Toronto, Ontario M5G 2C8
T: (416) 340-8000
T: (800) 268-7793
F: (416) 340-1641
www.thn.com
Pub: Lance Neal
Editor-in-Chief: Steve Dryden

Hockey Stars
7002 W. Butler Pike
Ambler, PA 19002
T:(215) 643-6385
F: (215) 628-3571
Editor: Stuart M. Saks

Hockey Times
185 Frobisher Drive
Waterloo, Ontario N2V 2E6
T: (519) 746-1171

Hockey USA
33 Erin Road
Stoughton, MA 02072
T/F: (617) 341-3971

Hockey Weekly
25042 W. Warren Rd.
Dearborn Heights, MI 48127
T: (734) 563-9130
F: (734) 563-9538

Inside Hockey Monthly
18030 Brookhurst Street #11
Fountain Valley, CA 92708
T: (949) 593-0350
F: (949) 593-0341
Editor: Tim Meyer

In The Crease
www.lnthecrease.com

The Junior Hockey News
PO Box 963
145 Temple Street
Duxbury, MA 02331
T: (781) 934-5888
F: (781) 934-5878
www.tjhn.com
E: tjhn@adelphia.net
Pub: Richard De Lisle
Editor: Brian McDonough

Just Hockey
3671 S. Livernois
Rochester Hills, MI 48307
T: (248) 853-9515
F: (248) 852-0076
www.come.to/justhockey
E: ReadHockey@aol.com
Editor: Terry Elkins

Let's Play Hockey
2721 E. 42nd Street
Minneapolis, MN 55406
T: (612) 729-0023
F: (612) 729-0259
www.letsplayhockey.com
E: letsplay@letsplayhockey.com
Pub: Doug Johnson
Editor: Shane Frederick

Michigan Hockey Weekly
25042 W. Warren Road
Dearborn Heights, MI 48127
T: (313) 563-9130
F: (313) 563-9538
Pub: Johanna Mullin

Power Play Magazine
888 W. Big Beaver Rd., Suite 600
Troy, MI 48084
T: (248) 362-7400
F: (248) 362-7425
Editor: Vince Aversano

U.S. College Hockey Magazine
PO Box 1050
Flagler Beach, FL 32136-1050
T: (800) 255-1050
T: (904) 439-2250
F: (904) 439-6224

Western Hockey League News
#1-3030 Sunridge Way NE
Calgary, Alberta T1Y 7K4 Canada
T: (403) 693-3030
F: (403) 693-3031
www.whl.ca
E: whl@chl.ca
Editor: Leroy McKinnon
E: mckinnonl@whl.ca

Late Additions

World Hockey Association
6150 Valleyway Drive
Niagara Falls, Ontario L2E 1Y3
Canada
T: (905) 357-9723
F: (905)
www.worldhockeyassociation.net
Exec Dir: Tim Keighan
Hky Oper: Peter Young

Proposed pro league for 2004-05.

Federal Hockey League
1006 Ogden Street
Coquitlam, BC V3C 1P6
T: (604) 464-3579
F: (604) 464-3519
www.federalhockeyleague.ca
E: fhl@federalhockeyleague.ca
P: John Larsen

Proposed Canadian pro league for 2003-04

www.sportsbooksempire.com   www.sportsbooksempire.com

Lacrosse

U.S. Lacrosse
The Lacrosse Hall of Fame
113 W. University Parkway
Baltimore, MD 21210
T: (410) 235-6882
F: (410) 366-6735
www.lacrosse.org
E: info@lacrosse.org
Exec Dir: Steve Stenersen

National Lacrosse League
1212 Ave. of the Americas, 5 FL
New York, NY 10036
T: (917) 510-9200
F: (917) 510-9890
www.NLL.com
Commissioner: Jim Jennings
VP Oper: Barry Powless
PR: Doug Fritts
Mkt: Jan Yelenock

Buffalo Bandits
HSBC Arena
One Seymour H. Knox III Plaza
Buffalo, NY 14203
T: (716) 855-4100
F: (716) 855-4110
www.bandits.com
GM: Kurt Silcott
PR: Garry Dunlap

Calgary Roughnecks
PO Box 1540, Station M
Calgary, Alberta T2P 3B9 Canada
T: (403) 294-9244
F: (403) 206-4888
www.calgaryroughnecks.com
P: Brad Banister

Colorado Mammoth
Pepsi Center
1000 Chopper Place
Denver, CO 80204
T: (303) 405-1100
F: (303) 893-0614
www.coloradomammoth.com
GM: Steve Govett
PR: Alexandra Santiago

Columbus Land Sharks
200 W. Nationwide Blvd.
Columbus, OH 43215
T: (614) 246-5297
F: (614) 246-5295
www.columbuslandsharks.com
GM: Chris Bandura
PR: Molly Schirner

New Jersey Storm
1099 Wall Street W., Suite 355
Lyndhurst, NJ 07071
T: (201) 939-8374
F: (201) 939-0676
www.NJstorm.com
GM: Jim Rogers
PR/Mkt: Dave Popkin

New York Saints
1675 Roosevelt Avenue
Bohemia, NY 11716
T: (631) 567-9114
F: (631) 567-4570
www.Nysaints.com
P: Michael Gongas
PR: Shawn Field

Ottawa Rebel
1000 Palladium Dr., Box 107
Kanata, Ontario K2V 1A5 Canada
T: (613) 599-0183
F: (613) 599-0210
www.ottawarebel.com
GM: Johnny Mouradian
VP Oper: Michael Campbell
PR: Greg Hotte

Philadelphia Wings
3601 S. Broad Street
Philadelphia, PA 19148
T: (215) 389-9464
F: (215) 389-9403
www.philadelphiawings.com
GM: Marty O'Neill
PR: Ike Richman

Rochester Knighthawks
One War Memorial Square
Rochester, NY 14614
T: (716) 454-5335
F: (716) 454-3954
www.knighthawks.com
GM: Jody Gage
PR: Steve Rossi

San Jose NLL Club
HP Pavillion
525 W. Santa Clara Street
San Jose, CA 95113
T: (408) 999-5782
F: (408) 999-5707
www.bayarealacrosse.com
GM: Dean Lombardi
PR: Ken Arnold

Toronto Rock
634 Yonge Street, 2 FL
Toronto, Ontario M4Y 1Z9 Canada
T: (416) 596-3075
F: (416) 977-3475
www.torontorock.com
GM: Les Bartley

Vancouver Ravens
800 Griffiths Way
Vancouver, BC V6B 6B1 Canada
T: (604) 899-5300
F: (604) 899-5301
www.vancouverravens.com
GM: Tom Mayenknecht

2003 NLL Championship Final
Toronto Rock d Rochester Knighthawks 8-6 in champ. game

While the NLL is an indoor league, the MLL is an outdoor league.

Major League Lacrosse

One Harmon Plaza, 3 FL
Secaucus, NJ 07094
T: (201) 325-0800
F: (201) 325-8788
www.majorleaguelacrosse.com
E: info@majorleaguelacrosse.com
P:/Founder: Jake Steinfeld
Exec Dir: Gabby Roe
League Oper: Dave Klewan
Lacrosse Oper: Tim Shea
Dir of Mkt: Brian Cawley
Mkt Mgr: Jill Haber
Media: Jaye Cavallo

logo

Baltimore Bayhawks
100 W. Padonia Road, Suite 2A
Timonium, MD 21093
T: (410) 560-3511
F: (410) 666-2666
www.baltimorebayhawks.com
GM: Gordon Boone
PR: Mike Hardisky

Boston Cannons
15 Kane Industrial Drive
Hudson, MA 01749
T: (978) 568-3677
F: (978) 568-8715
www.bostoncannons.com
GM: Dave Gross
PR: Jason Chandler

Bridgeport Barrage
500 Main Street
Bridgeport, CT 06604
T: (203) 345-4800
F: (203) 345-1655
www.bridgeportbarrage.com
GM: Ken Paul
PR: Chris Romano

Long Island Lizards
373 Nesconset Hwy, Suite 198
Hauppauge, NY 11788
T: (866) Lizard 1
F: (366-2372
www.longislandlizards.com
GM: Kevin Fox
PR: Janine Stange

New Jersey Pride
1235 Route 23 South
Wayne, NJ 07470
T: (212) 499-2300
F: (212) 499-2301
www.newjerseypride.com
GM: Bob Turco

Rochester Rattlers
333 N. Plymouth Avenue
Rochester, NY 14608
T: (716) 454-5425
F: (716) 454-5453
www.rochesterrattlers.com
GM: Chris Economides

2002 MLL Championship Game
Baltimore Bayhawks d Long Island Lizards 21-13

Canadian Lacrosse

Canadian Lacrosse
211 Riverside Drive, Suite B-4
Ottawa, Ontario K1H 7X5
T: (613) 260-2028
F: (613) 260-2029
www.lacrosse.ca
E: info@lacrosse.ca
P: Jim Burke
GM: David Minguay

**Canadian Lacrosse
Hall of Fame**
Civic Center Complex
66 E. 6th Ave., PO Box 308
New Westminster, B.C. V3L 4Y6
T: (604) 521-7656
F: (604) 525-5133
Chmn: Rick Richards

Provincial Associations

Alberta Lacrosse Association
68 Butterfield Crescent
St. Albert, Alberta T8N 2W7
T: (780) 458-1534
F: (780)
www.lacrosse.ab.ca
E: Mclennan_b@hotmail.com
P: Brian McLennan

British Columbia Lacrosse Assn.
4041 B Remi Place
Burnaby, B.C. V5A 4J8
T: (604) 421-9755
F: (604) 421-9775
www.bclacrosse.com
E: rochelle@bclacrosse.com
Exec. Dir: Rochelle Winterton

Can-Am Lacrosse
13764 Four Mile Level Road
Gowanda, NY 14070
T: (716) 532-4548
F: (716)
P: Butch Jimerson

Iroquois Lacrosse Association
North American Travelling College
RR #3
Cornwall Island, Ontario K6H 5R7
T: (613) 932-9452
F: (613) 932-0092
www.iroquoisnationals.com
E: nnatc@glen-net.ca
Exec. Dir: Barbara Barnes

Manitoba Lacrosse Association
200 Main Street
Winnipeg, Manitoba R3C 4M2
T: (204) 925-5684
F: (204) 925-5703
www.manitobalacrosse.mb.ca
E: mblax@mts.net
Exec. Director: Laralie Higginson

New Brunswick Lacrosse
Box 698, Station A
Fredericton, N.B. E3B 5B4
T: (506) 457-0158
F: (506) 446-5097
E: mallet@fundy.net
Exec. Dir: Wayne Mallet

Lacrosse Nova Scotia
PO Box 3010 South
Halifax, Nova Scotia B3J 3G6
T: (902) 435-2057
F: (902) 424-5735
E: hami@ns.sympatico.ca
P: Bruce Hamilton

Ontario Lacrosse Association
1185 Eglinton Avenue East, 6 FL
North York, Ontario M3C 3C6
T: (416) 426-7066
F: (416) 426-7382
www.ontariolacrosse.com
E: info@ontariolacrosse.com
Exec. Director: Stan Cockerton

Quebec Lacrosse Association
4545 Pierre de Coubertin
CP 1000, Station M
Montreal, Quebec H1V 3R2
T: (514) 252-3058
F: (514) 252-5658
www.lacrosse.qc.ca
E: pierre.filion@crosse.qc.ca
Exec. Dir: Pierre Filion

Saskatchewan Lacrosse
2205 Victoria Avenue
Regina, Saskatchewan S4P 0S4
T: (306) 780-9216
F: (306) 525-4009
www.accesscomm.ca/nonprofits/lacrosse
E: sask.lacrosse@sasktel.net
Exec. Dir: Curt Keil

The Can-Am, OLA Major Series & the WLA play indoor box lacrosse.

OLA Major Lacrosse Series
33 Robertson Place
St. Catharines, Ontario L2P 3E9
T: (905) 988-5489
F: (905) 988-9933
Commissioner: Jim Brady

Ahewsaswe Thunder
RR #3 Kawenoke
Cornwall Island, Ont. K6H 5R7
T: (613) 936-1583

Brampton Excelsiors
7575 Kennedy Road South
Brampton, Ontario L6W 4T2
T: (905) 459-1850
www.bramptonexcelsiors.com
E: info@bramptonexcelsiors.com
GM: Shane Sanderson

Brooklin Redmen
PO Box 146
Brooklin, Ontario L1M 1B5
T: (905) 433-4267
F: (905) 668-5933
www.brooklinredmen.org
P: Mark Stehlin

Ohsweken Wolves
25 Hester Street
Hamilton, Ontario
T: (905) 546-4938

Peterborough Lakers
1050 Airport Road, R.R. #5
Peterborough, Ontario K9J 8H1
T: (705) 745-8887
F: (705) 745-1430
www.ptbolakerslacrosse.net
E: lakerlax@nexicom.net
GM: Ted Higgins

St. Catharines Athletics
16 Division Street
St. Catharines, Ontario
T: (905) 937-7210

Six Nations Chiefs
RR #2
Ohsweken, Ontario N0A 1M0
T: (905) 765-1228
F: (519) 445-2501
GM: Cap Bomberry

Can-Am Lacrosse League
Niagara Regional Native Center
RR #4, Taylor Road
Niagara-on-the-Lake, Ontario
Canada L0S 1J0
T: (905) 688-6484
F: (905) 688-4033
P: Butch Jimerson

Hagersville Warriors Lacrosse
PO Box 114
Ohsweken, Ontario N0A 1M0
T: (519) 445-4542
GM: Lelsey Isaacs

Newton Golden Eagles
PO Box 28
Lawtons, NY 14091
T: (716) 337-4524
F: (716) 827-0133 (Arena)
GM: Darwin John

Ohsweken Wolves
RR #2
Ohsweken, Ontario N0A 1M0
T: (519) 445-4804
F: (519) 445-0440
GM: Dawn Smith

Pinewoods Athletic Club Lacrosse
PO Box 244
Versailles, NY 14168
T: (716) 532-5228
GM: Barbara Kennedy

Tuscarora Thunderhawks
5704 Walmore Road
Lewiston, NY 14092
T: (716) 297-2590
GM: Kenny Vanevery

Western Lacrosse Assn.
4041 B Remi Place
Burnaby, BC V5A 4J8 Canada
T/F (604) 421-9755
www.theboxrocks.com
E: sgill@theboxrocks.com
Exec Dir: Toby Baker
Commissioner: Sohen Gill

Burnaby Lakers
#12-5901 E. Broadway
Burnaby, B.C. V5B 2Y1
T: (604) 298-9613
F: (604) 298-3841
Governor: Jack Crosby

Coquitlam Adanacs
1430 Sandstone Crescent
Coquitlam, B.C. V3C 4X4
T/F: (604) 944-2646
P: Don Daunais

Maple Ridge Burrards
#201-20050 Stewart Crescent
Maple Ridge, B.C. V2X 0T4
T: (604) 465-6047
F: (604) 463-9192
P: Wayne Funk

New Westminster Salmonbellies
424 Glen Brook Drive
New Westminster, B.C. V3L 5J5
T: (604) 522-7338
F: (604) 540-0138
www.salmonbellies.com
P: K.C. Cook

North Shore Thunder
325 Furry Creek Dr., Box 1400
Lions Bay, B.C. V0N 2E0
T: (604) 298-4678
GM: Buchan Jr.

Victoria Shamrocks
2538 Margate Avenue
Victoria, B.C. V8S 3A4
T: (250) 544-4301
F: (250) 544-4371
www.rockslax.com
E: shamrocks@pacificcoast.net
GM: John Vickers

2002 WLA Champions
Victoria Shamrocks

2002 Mann Cup Senior A
National Champions
Brampton Excelsiors

West Coast Senior Lacrosse Association
#128-2721 Atlin
Coquitlam, B.C. V3C 5B1
T: (604) 945-7550
Chmn: Mike Petrie

Burnaby Lakers
#69-1240 Falcon Drive
Coquitlam, B.C. V3E 2B4
T: (604) 944-7530
F: (604) 944-6530
E: mo@bc.sympatico.ca
GM: Maurizio Cecchetto

Ladner Pioneers
5413-64th Street
Delta, B.C. V4K 3M5
T: (604) 946-8891
F: (604) 946-0159
GM: John Burr

Langley Knights
19941-44B Avenue
Langley, B.C. V3A 4V9
T/F: (604) 530-1331
GM: Kim Billon

Nanaimo Timbermen
60 Porter Road
Nanaimo, B.C. V9X 1B6
T: (250) 741-1230
F: (250) 390-3235
E: brykar@hotmail.com
GM: Bryan Baxter

North Shore Indians
239 Mathias Road
West Vancouver, B.C. V7P 1P6
T: (604) 986-5426
GM: Kevin Rivers

Port Coquitlam Saints
8263-19th Street
Burnaby, B.C. V3N 1G7
T: (604) 525-1992
GM: George Edwards

Surrey Rebels
#128-2721 Atlin
Coquitlam, B.C. V3C 5B1
T: (604) 945-7550
GM: Mike Petrie

Vancouver Vipers
2375 East 37th Avenue
Vancouver, B.C. V5R 2T5
T/F:(604) 435-7534
GM: Mickey Meslo

The following are Canadian Junior A lacrosse leagues.

B.C. Major Junior Lacrosse League
449 Glenbrook Drive
New Westminster, B.C. V3L 5J3
T: (604) 525-5737
F: (604) 525-8301
P: Bernie Treasurer

Burnaby Lakers
#12-5901 East Broadway
Burnaby, B.C. V5B 2Y1
T: (604) 298-9613
F: (604) 298-3841
GM: Jack Crosby

Coquitlam Adanacs
1800 Grover Avenue
Coquitlam, B.C. V3J 3G6
T: (604) 936-6320
F: (604) 468-4491
GM: Phil McMillan

New Westminster Salmonbellies
1728 Dublin Street
New Westminster, B.C. V3M 3A1
T: (604) 522-2660
F: (604) 594-1887
GM: John Van Os

Port Coquitlam Saints
3880 Clematis Crescent
Port Coquitlam, B.C. V3B 4B1
T: (604) 942-9150
F: (604) 464-4218
GM: Reg Thompson

South Fraser Stickmen
13439-64A Avenue
Surrey, B.C. V3W 1Z4
T: (604) 596-3195
F: (604) 597-1890
GM: Walter Clark

Victoria Shamrocks
4040 Magdelin
Victoria, B.C. V8P 4X3
T/F: (250) 477-4916
GM: Dave Ward

OLA Junior A Series
39 Dorchester Drive
Bramalea, Ontario L6T 3C8
T: (416) 793-7547
F: (905) 790-6093
Commissioner: Dean McLeod

Brampton Excelsiors
6 Gregory Street
Brampton, Ontario L6Y 1G1
T: (905) 823-8222
F: (905) 823-9547
GM: Ziggy Musial

Burlington Chiefs
519 Hillfair Place
Burlington, Ontario L7N 2W8
T: (905) 333-7402
F: (905) 634-3047
GM: Dave Smith

Kitchener Waterloo Braves
79 Euclid
Waterloo, Ontario N2L 1Z5
T: (519) 888-4100
F: (519) 888-4269
GM: Lawrie Hallman

Mississauga Tomahawks
1073 West Avenue
Mississauga, Ontario L5E 1W1
T: (905) 828-6412
GM: Jack Wilson

Orangeville Northmen
32 Westdale Avenue
Orangeville, Ontario L9W 1B7
T: (519) 941-0330
F: (519) 941-1830
GM: John Lackey

Peterborough Traders
1005 Albany Court
Peterborough, Ontario K9J 1J3
T: (705) 745-6730
GM: Lee Vitarelli

Sarnia Cranes Pacers
476 Cromwell Street
Sarnia, Ontario N7T 3Z1
T: (519) 337-7805
F: (519) 337-1983
GM: Mike McGugan

Six Nation Arrows
PO Box 154
Ohsweken, Ontario N0A 1M0
T: (519) 445-4567
F: (519) 445-0798
GM: Lewis C. Staats

St. Catharines Athletics
469 Linwell Road
St. Catharines, Ontario L2M 2P6
T: (905) 688-9100
F: (905) 688-9989
GM: Bob Luey

Toronto Beaches
72 Osborne Avenue
Toronto, Ontario M4E 3B2
T: (416) 690-2355
GM: Norm Holman

Whitby Warriors
33 Robertson Place
St. Catharines, Ontario L2P 3E9
T: (905) 988-5489
F: (905) 988-9933
GM: Jim Brady

West Coast Junior Lacrosse Association
8083-112A Street
Delta, B.C. V4C 4Y7
T: (604) 591-4280
F: (604) 501-0211
Commissioner: Fraser MacDonald

B.C. Intermediate A Lacrosse League
11742-96A Avenue
Surrey, B.C. V3V 2A1
T: (604) 581-6602
F: (604) 951-0639
Chmn: Wayne Woolard

Burnaby Intermediate Lakers
#12-5901 E. Broadway
Burnaby, B.C. V5B 2Y1
T: (604) 298-9613
F: (604) 298-3841
P: Jack Crosby

Coquitlam Intermediate Adanacs
3758 Coast Meridian
Pt. Coquitlam, B.C. V3B 3P1
T: (604) 944-1859
F: (604) 944-0483
P: Ian Holloway

Fraser Valley Intermediate Lacrosse
2191 Ware Street
Abbotsford, B.C. V2S 3C4
T: (604) 852-0820
GM: Mark Graham

Nanaimo Intermediate A
388 Trinity Street
Nanaimo, B.C. V9R 5X3
T: (250) 753-2365
F: (250) 753-4603
GM: Deb Stocks

New Westminster Intermed. Salmonbellies
1105 Hamilton Street
New Westminster, B.C. V3M 2M8
T: (604) 525-7836
F: (604) 525-7896
GM: Julie Castagner

Poco Saints Intermediate A
3880 Clematis Crescent
Port Coquitlam, B.C. V3B 4B1
T: (604) 942-9150
GM: Reg Thompson

Richmond Intermediate A
8171 Seafair Drive
Richmond, B.C. V7C 1X3
T/F: (604) 275-2255
GM: Jenny Gilles

South Fraser Intermed. A
13439-64A Avenue
Surrey, B.C. V3W 1Z4
T: (604) 596-3195
GM: Walter Clark

Victoria Shamrocks Intermediate
1016 Brock Avenue
Victoria, B.C. V9B 3E1
T: (250) 478-2622
F: (250) 478-2629
P: Murray Muralt

Canada West Field Lacrosse Association
33341-13 Avenue
Mission, B.C. V2V 4X1
T: (604) 888-4322
F: (604) 888-1707
Commissioner: Randy West-Pratt

Pacific Coast Field Lacrosse Association
#309-15895-84 Avenue
Surrey, B.C. V3S 2N8
T: (604) 543-5161
Chmn: Dave Goulet

OLA Junior B Series
39 Connaught Avenue
Welland, Ontario L3C 1G4
T: (905) 735-5311
Commissioner: Dave Vernon

Akwesasne Lightning
R.R. #3
Cornwall Island, Ontario K6H 5T3
T: (519) 358-2272
GM: Brian Conners

Brantford Possee
77 Henry Street
Brantford, Ontario N3S 5C6
T: (905) 572-2200
GM: Ray Inder

Elora Mohawks
420 Hill Street E.
Fergus, Ontario N1M 2R4
T: (905) 602-1737
F: (905) 602-1744
GM: Jim Bomhof

Georgetown Bulldogs
31 Brock Street
Acton, Ontario L7J 1N3
T: (905) 857-2033
GM: Barry Trood

Gloucester Griffins
2140 Johnston Road
Ottawa, Ontario K1G 5K1
T: (613) 737-3476
GM: Dave Smith

Huntsville Hawks
34 Brunel Road
Huntsville, Ontario P1H 1P5
T: (705) 789-2644
GM: Geri Cain

Milton Mavericks
R.R. #3, Hwy. 25
Milton, Ontario L9T 2X7
T: (905) 878-1815
F: (905) 876-4033
GM: Jim Leworthy

Mimico Mountaineers
27 Hay Avenue
Etobicoke, Ontario M8Z 1G2
T: (416) 918-7966
F: (416) 255-8670
GM: Rob Michalsky

Nepean Knights
6 Woodwind Crescent
Stittsville, Ontario K2S 1G4
T: (613) 562-2112
GM: Ron Bois

Orillia Rodgers Kings
9 Lawson drive
Orillia, Ontario L3V 3V5
T: (705) 325-3310
F: (705) 327-5892
GM: Garry Balkwill

Oshawa Green Gaels
957 Sandcliff Drive
Oshawa, Ontario L1K 2E4
T: (416) 285-7044
F: (905) 576-9725
GM: Dieter Kirner

Owen Sound Flying Dutchmen
550 6th Avenue East
Owen Sound, Ontario N4K 2V2
T: (519) 376-6120
F: (519) 376-8303
GM: Lorne Ainsworth

Royal City Regals
69 Harvard Road
Guelph, Ontario N1G 2X9
T: (519) 822-5887
GM: Huck O' Connell

Scarborough Saints
17 Burgess Avenue
Toronto, Ontario M4E 1W8
T: (416) 690-7999
F: (416) 690-3431
GM: Doug Taylor

Six Nations Red Rebels
PO Box 246
Ohsweken, Ontario N0A 1N6
T: (519) 445-4640
GM: Tony Styres

Spartan Warriors
74 Margery Avenue
St. Catharines, Ontario L2R 6K1
T: (905) 357-0919
F: (905) 685-1740
GM: Al Welsh

Ontario Senior Field Lacrosse League
112 Upper Paradise Road
Hamilton, Ontario L9C 5B8
T: (416) 348-1431
Commissioner: Ed Comeau

Ontario Junior Field Lacrosse League
54 Aurora Heights Drive
Aurora, Ontario L4G 2W7
T: (905) 726-1083
F: (905) 579-6614
Commissioner: Jim Callaghan
Treasurer: Terry Lloyd

BCLA Women's Field Lacrosse Commission
130 Buckingham Drive
Pt. Moody, B.C. V3H 2T3
T: (604) 461-7166
E: susanjenner@bc.sympatico.ca
Chmn: Susan Jenner

OLA Women's Senior Field Lacrosse
108 Botany Hill Drive
Scarborough, Ontario M1G 3K7
T: (905) 477-7766
F: (416) 431-3606
Commissioner: Joanne Stanga

2002 CLA National Champions
Senior A Box, Mann Cup
Brampton Excelsiors (OLA)

Senior B Box President's Cup
Edmonton Outlaws

Minto Cup Junior A Box Champions
Burnaby B.C. Lakers

Founders Trophy Junior B Box
Clarington Ont. Green Gaels

P.D. Ross Senior Field Div I Cup
Victoria, BC (BCLA)

Victory Cup Senior Field Div II
Saskatchewan

First Nations Trophy Men's Field Junior Championship Cup
Saskatchewan

Organizations

Lacrosse USA, Inc.
PO Box 1116
Basalt, CO 81621
T: (970) 927-9338
F: (970) 927-9751
Exec. Dir: Michael J. Martin

U.S. Club Lacrosse Association
2600 Whitney Avenue
Baltimore, MD 21215
T: (410) 235-8532
Exec. Dir: Ray Little

Publications

Lacrosse Magazine
113 W. University Parkway
Baltimore, MD 21210
T: (410) 235-6882
F: (410) 366-6735

Face-Off 2003
8 Glen Hill Court
Shoreham, NY 11786
T: (516) 821-1816
F: (516) 821-4075
E: faceoff1@li.net

Soccer

Federation of International Football Association
Hitzigweg 11, Case postale 85
8030 Zurich, Switzerland
T: (41.1) 384 95 95
F: (41.1) 384 96 96
www.FIFA.com
E: media@fifa.com
P: Joseph S. Blatter
Sec Gen: Michel Zen-Ruffinen

The following is a list of professional outdoor & indoor leagues.

Division I Outdoor

Major League Soccer
110 E. 42nd Street, 10th Floor
New York, NY 10017
T: (212) 450-1200
F: (212) 450-1300
www.MLSnet.com
E: mls96@ix.netcom.com
Commissioner: Don Garber
PR: Trey Fitz-Gerald

The MLS begins its eighth season.

Chicago Fire
980 N. Michigan Ave.
Suite 1998
Chicago, IL 60611
T: (312) 705-7200
F: (312) 705-7393
www.chicago-fire.com
GM: Peter Wilt
PR: Diana Lopez

Colorado Rapids
555 17th Street, Suite 3350
Denver, CO 80202
T: (303) 299-1570
F: (303) 299-1580
www.coloradorapids.com
GM: Dan Counce
PR: Rich Schneider

Columbus Crew
One Black and Gold Blvd.
Columbus, OH 43211
T: (614) 447-2739
F: (614) 447-4109
GM: Jim Smith
PR: Jeff Wuerth

Dallas Burn
2602 McKinney, Suite 200
Dallas, TX 75204
T: (214) 979-0303
F: (214) 979-1118
GM: Andy Swift
PR: Chris Ward

D.C. United
14120 Newbrook Drive, Suite 170
Chantilly, VA 20151
T: (703) 478-6600
F: (703) 736-9451
GM: Stephen Zack
PR: Doug Hicks

Kansas City Wizards
2 Arrowhead Drive
Kansas City, MO 64129
T: (816) 920-9300
F: (816) 920-4773
GM: Curt Johnson
PR: Justin Gorman

Los Angeles Galaxy
18400 Avalon Blvd., Suite 200
Carson, CA 90746
T: (310) 630-2200
F: (310) 630-2250
www.lagalaxy.com
GM: Doug Hamilton
PR: Adam Sandler

New England Revolution
Foxboro Stadium, Route 1
Foxboro, MA 02035
T: (508) 543-0350
F: (508) 384-9129
www.nerevolution.com
GM: Todd Smith
PR: Jurgen Mainka

New York/New Jersey MetroStars
One Harmon Plaza, 3 FL
Secaucus, NJ 07094
T: (201) 583-7000
F: (201) 583-7055
www.metrostars.com
GM: Nick Sakiewicz
PR: John Neves

San Jose Earthquakes
3550 Stevens Creek Blvd., Ste. 100
Santa Clara, CA 95117
T: (408) 260-6300
F: (408) 554-8886
www.sjearthquakes.com
GM: Tom Neale
PR: Jed Mettee

The MLS began in 1996.

2002 MLS Championship Game
Los Angeles Galaxy 1
NE Revolution 0

2002 U.S. Open Cup Champion
Columbus Crew

Women's Professional Soccer

Women's United Soccer Association
The Palisades, Bldg A, Suite 460
5901 Peachtree Dunwoody Road
Atlanta, GA 30328
T: (404) 269-8800
F: (404) 269-3800
www.wusaleague.com
E: info@wusaleague.com
CEO: Lynn Morgan
Commissioner: Tony DiCicco
VP Comm: Dan Courtemanche

Atlanta Beat
5901 Peachtree Dunwoody Road
Bldg A, Suite 530
Atlanta, GA 30328
T: (877) 762-2371
F: (404) 847-6200
www.theatlantabeat.com
GM: Lynn Morgan
PR: Colleen Brannan

Boston Breakers
200 Highland Avenue, 4 FL
Needham, MA 02494
T: (781) 292-1016
F: (781) 292-1017
www.bostonbreakers.com
GM: Joe Cummings
PR: Marci Tyldesley

Carolina Courage
101 Innovation Ave., Suite 200
Morrisville, NC 27560
T: (919) 573-7626
F: (919) 573-7640
www.carolinacourage.com
P: Jerome Ramsey
PR: Michael Kaylor

New York Power
135 W. 50th Street, 3F
New York, NY 10020
T: (212) 372-0423
F: (212) 372-0440
www.newyorkpower.com
GM: Sue Morenoff
PR: Paul LeSueur

Philadelphia Charge
734 E. Lancaster Avenue, Suite 200
Villanova, PA 19085
T: (215) 952-2467
F: (215) 952-5490
www.wphiladelphiacharge.com
GM: Tim Murphy
PR: Al Cohen

San Diego Spirit
2650 Camino del Rio N., Suite 200
San Diego, CA 92108
T: (619) 692-9872
F: (619) 692-8144
www.sandiegospirit.com
GM: Kevin T. Crowe
PR: Jon Green

San Jose Cyberrays
1991 Park Avenue
San Jose, CA 95126
T: (408) 535-0980
F: (408) 535-0985
www.SJcyberrays.com
GM: Marlene Bjornsrud
PR: Jody Meacham

Washington Freedom
Robert F. Kennedy Mem. Stadium
2400 E. Capitol Street SE
Washington, DC 20003
T: (202) 547-8351
F: (202) 547-0176
www.washingtonfreedom.com
GM: Katy Button
PR: Hilary Jones

2002 WUSA Championship Game
Philadelphia 3 Washington 2

Indoor Pro Soccer

Major Indoor Soccer League
1175 Post Road East
Westport, CT 06880
T: (203) 222-4900
F: (203) 221-7300
www.MISL.net
E: gbibb@MISL.net
Commissioner: Steve Ryan
Operations: Brian Fleming
PR: Greg Bibb
Oper: Dave Grimaldi
Asst to Commish: Milly Caruso

Baltimore Blast
1301 S. Ellwood Avenue
Baltimore, MD 21224
T: (410) 732-5278
F: (410) 732-1737
www.baltimoreblast.com
E: akeller@baltimoreblast.com
GM: Kevin Healey
PR: Amy Keller

Cleveland Force
4400 Renaissance Pkwy, Suite A
Warrensville, OH 44128
T: (216) 896-1140
F: (216) 896-1141
www.clevelandforce.com
E: jmiller@clevelandforce.com
GM: Paul Garofolo
PR: Jeff Miller

Dallas Sidekicks
777 Sports Street
Dallas, TX 75207
T: (214) 653-0200
F: (214) 741-6731
www.dallassidekicks.com
E: herman.hudson@dallasmavs.com
GM: Jim Tolbert
PR: Herman Hudson

Harrisburg Heat
PO Box 60123
Harrisburg, PA 17106
T: (717) 652-4328
F: (717) 233-8297
www.heatsoccer.com
E: heatsoccerpr@aol.comom
GM: Gregg Cook
PR: Phil Yerger

Kansas City Comets
1800 Genessee, Suite 111
Kansas City, MO 64102
T: (816) 474-2255
F: (816) 474-8730
www.kccomets.com
E: kschultz@kccomets.com
GM: Zoran Savic
PR: Kevin Schultz

Milwaukee Wave
1040 N. Water Street
Milwaukee, WI 53202
T: (414) 224-9283
F: (414) 224-9290
www.milwaukeewave.com
E: twynn@milwaukeewave.com
GM: Keith Tozer
PR: Tom Wynn

Philadelphia Kixx
First Union Spectrum
3601 S. Broad Street
Philadelphia, PA 19148
T: (215) 952-5499
F: (215) 952-5488
www.kixxonline.com
E: davekixx2002@yahoo.com
GM: Omid Namazi
PR: David Deal

San Diego Sockers
9606 Aero Drive, Suite 1400
San Diego, CA 92123
T: (858) 836-4625
F: (858) 244-1166
www.sockers.com
E: billzi@sockers.com
GM: Brian Quinn
PR: Bill Zavestoski

The league was formed in 1984, as the American Indoor Soccer Association before changing to NPSL and now the MISL.

2003 MISL Championship Final
Baltimore Blast d *Milwaukee* 2 Games to 1 in finals.

Division 2 Outdoor

A-League/USL
14497 N. Dale Mabry, Suite 201
Tampa, FL 33618
T: (813) 963-3909
F: (813) 963-3807
www.USLsoccer.com
E: uslpr@unitedsoccerleagues.com
Comm.: Francisco Marcos
PR: Rui Farias

In 1997 the American Prof. Soccer League merged with the USISL to form a unified second division outdoor soccer league recognized by the USSF.
The A-League was born in 1989 with the merger of the WSL & the ASL.

Atlanta Silverbacks
5960 Crooked Creek Rd., Suite 10
Norcross, GA 30092
T: (770) 248-0492
F: (770) 248-0493
www.atlantasilverbacks.com
E: sb@atlantasilverbacks.com
GM: Stephen Pratten

Calgary Storm
203-1982 Kensington Road NW
Calgary, Alberta T2N 3R5 Canada
T: (403) 770-1183
F: (403) 770-1187
www.calgaryfc.com
E: info@calgaryfc.com
GM: Michael Vandale

Charleston Battery
1990 Daniel Island Drive
Mount Pleasant, SC 29492
T: (843) 971-4625
F: (843) 856-6958
www.charlestonbattery.com
E: nigel.cooper@charlestonbattery.com
GM: Nigel Cooper

Charlotte Eagles
2101 Sardis Rd. N., Suite 201
Charlotte, NC 28227
T: (704) 841-8644
F: (704) 841-8652
www.CharlotteEagles.com
E: charlotteeagles@compuserve.com
GM: Tom Engstrom

Cincinnati Riverhawks
11641 Chester Road
Cincinnati, OH 45246
T: (513) 326-4625
F: (513) 326-3700
www.riverhawks.com
E: jmacdonald@riverhawks.com
GM: Jenny MacDonald

El Paso Patriots
6941 Industrial
El Paso, TX 79915
T: (915) 771-6620
F: (915) 778-8802
www.elpasopatriots.com
E: patriots@htg.net
GM: Diana Cervantes

Indiana Blast
PO Box 50980
Indianapolis, IN 46250
T: (317) 585-9203
F: (317) 585-9205
www.indianablast.com
E: blastblaze@aol.com
GM: Kim Morris

Milwaukee Rampage
1040 N Water Street
Franklin, WI 53202
T: (414) 224-9283
F: (414) 224-9290
www.milwaukeerampage.com
E: info@milwaukeerampage.com
P: Rob Arent

Minnesota Thunder
1700 105th Ave. NE
Blaine, MN 55449
T: (763) 785-FOOT (3668)
F: (763) 785-5999
www.mnthunder.com
E: info@mnthunder.com
GM: Jim Froslid

Montreal Impact
8770 Langelier Blvd., Suite 224
St Leonard, Quebec H1P 3C6 Canada
T: (514) 328-3668
F: (514) 328-1287
www.montrealimpact.com
E: info@montrealimpact.com
GM: Nick Filippone

Pittsburgh Riverhounds
2425 Sidney Street
Pittsburgh, PA 15203
T: (412) 381-4625
F: (412) 481-2529
www.riverhounds.com
E: talarico@riverhounds.com
GM: Christina Heasley

Portland Timbers
1844 SW Morrison
Portland, OR 97205
T: (503) 553-5440
F: (503) 553-5445
www.portlandtimbers.com
E: jtaylor@pdxfe.com
GM: Jim Taylor

Richmond Kickers
2320 W. Main Street
Richmond, VA 23220
T: (804) 644-5425
F: (804) 359-5037
www.richmondkickers.com
E: bhakkock@richmondkickers.com
GM: Billy Hallock

Rochester Raging Rhinos
333 N. Plymouth Avenue
Rochester, NY 14608
T: (585) 454-KICK (5425)
F: (585) 454-5453
w.rhinossoccer.com
E: info@rhinossoccer.com
GM: Chris Economides

Seattle Sounders
1964 4th Avenue South
Seattle, WA 98134
T: (206) 622-3415
F: (425) 643-3515
www.seattlesounders.net
E: andreab@seattlesounders.net
GM: Adrian Hannauer

Syracuse Pro Soccer
PO Box 11716
Syracuse, NY 13218
T: (315) 635-3216
F: (315) 635-3218
www.syracuseprosoccer.com
GM: Tim Kuhl

Toronto Lynx
100 The East Mall, Suite 11
Toronto, Ontario M8Z 5X2 Canada
T: (416) 251-4625
F: (416) 251-7054
www.lynxsoccer.com
E: lynx@lynxsoccer.com
GM: Nicole Hartrell

Vancouver Whitecaps
4460 Ross Crescent
W. Vancouver, BC V7W 1B2 Canada
T: (604) 669-9283
F: (604) 925-3665
www.whitecapssoccer.com
E: info@whitecapssoccer.com
GM: Greg Kerfoot

Virginia Beach Mariners
2181 Landstown Road
Virginia Beach, VA 23456
T: (757) 430-9800
F: (757) 427-2850
www.marinerssoccer.com
GM: Mike Field

The A-League is the top level of play within the USL. The SISL started in 1986 as the SW Indoor Soccer League, later changing name to SW Indep. SL, before becoming the current day USL.

2002 A-League Championship
Milwaukee Rampage d *Richmond Kickers* 2-1

Division Three Outdoor Soccer

USL D3 Pro League

Arizona Sahuaros
PO Box 2748
Carefree, AZ 85377
T: (623) 516-2133
F: (623) 492-0602
www.azsahuaros.com
GM: Ali Alexander

California Gold
PO Box 579227
Modesto, CA 95357
T: (209) 652-7925
F: (209) 524-7132
www.cruiserssoccer.com
E: brokerluciano@att.net
GM: Luciano Silveira

Carolina Dynamo
9D Dundas Circle
Greensboro, NC 27407
T: (336) 316-1266
F: (336) 316-1276
www.carolinadynamo.com
E: cwilliams@carolinadynamo.com
GM: Joe Brown

Connecticut Wolves
635 S, Main Street
New Britain, CT 06051
T: (860) 223-5425
F: (860) 223-2759
www.ct-wolves.com
E: recnpark@aol.com
GM: Dan Gaspar

Greenville Lions
1200 Woodruff Road A9
Greenville, SC 29607
T: (864) 675-6609
F: (864) 675-0370
www.greenvillelions.com
E: scotthalkett@greenvillelions.com
GM: Scott Halkett

Long Island Rough Riders
3 Courthouse Drive
Central Islip, NY 11722
T: (631) 940-3825
F: (631) 940-3800
www.rough-riders.com
E: info@rough-riders.com

New Hampshire Phantoms
One Park Avenue
Hudson, NH 03051
T: (603) 578-5588
F: (603) 882-7747
www.nhphantoms.com
phantomssoccerschool@hotmail.com
GM: Jim DeDeus

New Jersey Stallions
3 Mt. Prospect Avenue
Clifton, NJ 07013
T: (973) 773-4562
F: (973) 773-9672
www.njstallions.com
E: prosocr@aol.com
GM: Maryanne DeFranco

New York Freedoms
223-05 56th Road, 2 FL
Bayside, NY 11364
T: (516) 487-7306
F: (718) 631-8944
GM: Arias Alpian

Northern Nevada Aces
937 W. Moana Lane
Reno, NV 89509
T: (775) 826-2770
F: (775) 786-8281
GM: Mo Mandagary

Northern Virginia Royals
PO Box 1447
Centreville, VA 20120
T: (703) 680-6562
F: (703) 492-9944
www.northernvirginiasoccer.com
E: nvroyals@aol.com
GM: Mo Sheta

Reading Rage
2201 Ridgewood Rd., Suite 375
Wyomissing, PA 19610
T: (610) 375-4405
F: (610) 375-6839
www.readingrage.com
E: rdgrage@ptd.net
GM: Jerry Wojton

San Diego Gauchos
2835 Highland Avenue
National City, CA 91950
T: (619) 336-9861
F: (619) 336-9864
www.sandiegogauchos.com
E: bmaruca@aol.com
GM: Bob Maruca

South Jersey Barons
427 Jackson Rd., Suite B
Atco, NJ 08004
T: (856) 753-7608
F: (856) 753-7351
www.sjbarons.com
E: mdriver@sjbarons.com
GM: Matt Driver

Utah Blitzz
PO Box 635
Centerville, UT 84014
T: (801) 298-4194
F: (801) 298-7190
www.utahblitzz.com
E: cagnello@utahblitzz.com
GM: Dell Nichols
PR: Chris Agnello

Westchester Flames
10 Jason Lane
Mamaroneck, NY 10543
T: (914) 833-2024
F: (914) 833-3064
www.westchesterflames.com
E: guscons@aol.com
GM: Gus Skoufis

Western MA Pioneers
PO Box 457
Ludlow, MA 01056
T: (413) 583-4814
F: (413) 583-8192
www.wmpioneers.com
E: wmpioneers@yahoo.com
GM: Rick Andre

Wilmington Hammerheads
420 Raleigh St., Suite E
Wilmington, NC 28412
T: (910) 796-0076
F: (910) 796-0502
www.wilmingtonhammerheads.com
E: staff@wilmingtonhammerheads.com
GM: Bill Rudisill

2002 D-3 Champions
Long Island Roughriders

Women's Outdoor USL League

W-1 Women's USL

The Women's Leagues are a Part of the USL System

Albuquerque Crush
PO Box 16038
Albuquerque, NM 87191
T/F: (505) 255-5535
www.soccerinalbuquerque.com
E: albuquerquecrush@yahoo.com
GM: Chris Horner

Arizona Heatwave
13211 W Granada Rd.
Goodyear, AZ 85338
T: (602) 207-8435
F: (623) 535-5630
www.arizonaheatwave.com
E: thomas.p.mcconkey@irs.gov
GM: Tom McConkey

Asheville Splash
One Holiday Inn Dr., Bldg E
Asheville, NC 28806
T: (828) 255-7774
F: (828) 255-7754
www.splash-n-slide.com
E: bob@habitatforsoccer.com
GM: Steve Woody

Boston Renegades
12 Irving Street
Framingham, MA 01702
T: (508) 872-8998
F: (508) 872-8822
www.bostonrenegades.com
E: pbradley@mpbsr.com
GM: Pete Bradley

Charlotte Lady Eagles
2101 Sardis Rd. N., Suite 201
Charlotte, NC 28227
T: (704) 841-8644
F: (704) 841-8652
www.charlotteeagles.com
E: gwest@charlotteeagles.com
GM: Graham West

Chicago Cobras
35 W. 945 Fieldcrest Drive
St Charles, IL 60175
T: (630) 377-3545
F: (630) 377-0933
www.camptonsoccer.com
GM: Mike Nesci

Cincinnati Lady Hawks
260 Northland Blvd.
Suite 216
Cincinnati, OH 45246
T: (513) 772-5425
F: (513) 772-5430
www.ladyhawks.com
E: hawks@riverhawks.com
GM: Tom Westfall

Denver Lady Cougars
10920 Jay Street
Westminster, CO 80020
T: (303) 778-6093
F: (303) 715-9726
www.ladycougars.com
E: jcrun2win@aol.com
GM: Theresa Echtermeyer

Fort Collins Force
3930 Automation
Fort Collins, CO 80522
T: (970) 223-6644
F: (970) 223-3636
www.forcesoccer.org
E: info@forcesoccer.org
GM: Amy Snider

Greensboro Twisters
9 D Dundas Circle
Greensboro, NC 27407
T: (336) 316-1266
F: (336) 316-1276
www.carolinadynamo.com
GM: Joe Brown

Hampton Roads Piranhas
2181 Landstown Road
Virginia Beach, VA 23456
T: (757) 430-9800
F: (757) 427-2850
www.hrpiranhas.com
E: hrpiranhas@mindspring.com
GM: Marcie Laumann

Jacksonville Jade
4404 Post Street
Jacksonville, FL 32205
T: (904) 269-7449
F: (904) 269-3693
www.jaxjade.com
E: jmccarth@fccj.org
GM: J.J. McCarthy

Kansas City Mystics
4604 Wedd Street
Overland Park, KS 66204
T: (913) 268-5425
F: (913) 962-6886
www.kcmystics.com
E: denniss@kcmystics.com
GM: Dennis Strickland

Kentucky Fillies
2134 Nicholasville Road #12
Lexington, KY 40503
T: (859) 983-2010
F: (208) 263-3889
www.kyfillies.com
E: kyfillies@yahoo.com
GM: Sam Wooten

Long Island Lady Riders
96 Clearmeadow Drive
East Meadow, NY 11554
T: (516) 735-2277
F: (516) 735-2288
www.ladyriders.com
E: ridersmail@aol.com
GM: Kim Wyant

Maryland Pride
303 Najoles Road, Ste. 112
Millersville, MD 21108
T: (410) 729-1100
F: (410) 729-1604
www.mdpride.com
E: info@mdpride.com
GM: Jack Wetherson

Memphis Mercury
2176 West Street
Germantown, TN 38138
T: (901) 755-668878
F: (901) 755-9464
www.soccermemphis.com
E: klong@midsouth.T.com
GM: Karen Long

Mile High Mustangs
PO Box 265
Arvada, CO 80001
T: (303) 403-0902
F: (303) 403-0903
www.milehighmustangs.com
E: brian@arvadasoccer.com
GM: Brian Barkley

New Hampshire Lady Phantoms
One Park Avenue
Hudson, NH 03051
T: (603) 578-5588
F: (603) 882-7747
www.nhphantoms.com
E: cleary5@hotmail.com
GM: Paul Cleary

New Jersey Lady Stallions
3 Mt. Prospect Avenue
Clifton, NJ 07013
T: (732) 797-0693
F: (732) 797-0695
www.njstallions.com
E: prosccr@aol.com
GM: Rich Gentile

New Jersey Wildcats
PO Box 393
Cranbury, NJ 085120
T/F: (609) 860-2995
E: edgeofthebox@home.com
GM: Peter Wilson

New York Magic
165 E. 32nd Street, Suite 4-E
New York, NY 10016
T/F: (212) 447-0932
E: magicus1@aol.com
GM: Lyndelle Phillips

North Kentucky TC Stars
1018 Town Drive
Wilder, KY 41076
T: (859) 442-5800
F: (859) 442-9003
E: info@towncountrysports.com
GM: John Toebben

North VA Majestics
PO Box 229
Woodbridge, VA 22194
T: (703) 680-6562
F: (703) 590-6202
www.northernvirginiasoccer.com
E: nvmagestic@aol.com
GM: Tim Schweitzer

Oklahoma Outrage
4200 E. Skelly Drive #770
Tulsa, OK 74135
T: (918) 488-9665
F: (918) 488-6178
www.okoutrage.com
GM: Herman Luette

Ottawa Fury
1 Eleanor Drive
Nepean, Ontario K2E 6A3
T: (613) 224-3000
F: (613) 248-4859
GM: Kim Gamble

Rhode Island Rays
44 Border Drive
Wakefield, RI 02879
T: (401) 789-7477
F: (401) 782-1652
GM: James Kelly

Rochester Ravens
172 Shelbourne Road
Rochester, NY 14620
T: (716) 461-4813
F: (716) 442-9527
www.rochesterravevs.com
GM: Jill McCabe

Seattle Sounders Select
10838 Main Street
Bellevue, WA 98804
T: (425) 747-3546
F: (425) 643-3515
www.soundersselect.net
E: davidu@seattlesounders.com
GM: David Uchida

South Jersey Banshees
427 Jackson Rd., Suite B
Atco, NJ 08004
T: (856) 753-7608
F: (856) 753-7351
www.sjbarons.com
E: klittle@sjbarons.com
GM: Karen Little

Springfield Sirens
15 Warriner Avenue, Suite 1
Springfield, MA 01108
T: (413) 599-4774
F: (413) 599-1905
www.springfieldsirens.com
E: spfldsiren@aol.com
GM: Dianne Kopec

Tampa Bay Extreme
13355 Park Blvd.
Seminole, FL 33776
T: (727) 393-5182
F: (727) 393-6137
www.tampabayextreme.com
E: mjsousa54@aol.comm
GM: Steve Putnam

Texas Odyssey
14902 Preston Rd, #404-504
Dallas, TX 75240
T: (972) 661-8806
F: (469) 372-9935
www.texasrattlers.com
E: admin@crusadersoccer.com
GM: Courtney Linex

Toronto Inferno
6 Emeline Crescent
Markham, Ontario, L3P 4G3 CAN
T: (905) 294-6199
F: (905) 294-4969
www.torontoinferno.com
E: tonymarmo@para.com
GM: Tony Marmo

Vancouver Breakers
856 Homer Street, Suite 100
Vancouver, BC V6B 2W5 Canada
T: (604) 899-9283
F: (604) 684-6949
www.breakerssoccer.com
E: tcrawford@breakerssoccer.com
GM: Tammy Crawford

Windy City Bluez
12023 Aer Drive
Plainfield, IL 60544
T: (815) 254-1390
F: (815) 254-1392
E: kojon2@aol.com
GM: Ko Thanababouth

2002 Women's League Finals
Baltimore Renegades d Charlotte
Lady Eagles 3-0

Men's PDSL League

Austin Lightning
4304 Endcliffe Drive
Austin, TX 78731
T/F: (512) 345-4034
E: chrisveselka@hotmail.com
GM: Chris Veselka

Boulder Rapids Reserve
PO Box 17202
Boulder, CO 80308
T: (720) 841-8911
F: (303) 938-9986
www.bouldernova.com
E: bouldernova@soccer.com
GM: Dave Nesbit

Bradenton Academics
5500 34th Street W
Bradenton, FL 34210
T: (941) 758-4760
F: (941) 753-2747
www.bolletieri.com
E: ashobe@imgworld.com
GM: Amanda Gatchel

Brooklyn Knights
7620 18th Ave., Suite 2F
Brooklyn, NY 11214
T: (718) 621-1900
F: (718) 621-1332
www.brooklynknights.com
E: knightssocr@aol.com
GM: Chuck Jacob

Calgary Storm
203-1982 Kensington Rd NW
Calgary, Alberta T2N 3R5 Canada
T: (403) 770-1183
F: (403) 770-1187
www.calgaryfc.com
E: mgebraad@calgaryfc.com
GM: Mike Vandale

Cape Cod Crusaders
143 Station Avenue
S. Yarmouth, MA 02664
T: (508) 394-1171
F: (508) 398-1354
www.capecodcrusaders.com
E: kgamble@mpsbr.com
GM: Kim Gamble

Cascade Surge
PO Box 2689
Salem, OR 97308
T: (503) 362-7308
F: (503) 371-3639
www.cascadesurge.com
E: info@cascadesurge.com
GM: Dave Irby

Central Coast Roadrunners
21 Santa Rosa St., Ste. 100
San Louis Obispo, CA 93405
T: (805) 543-2172
F: (805) 543-4801
www.ccroadrunners.com
E: ccroadrunners@cs.com
GM: Larry Smyth

Central Florida Kraze
5627 Elmhurst Circle #113
Oviedo, FL 32765
T: (407) 696-2640
F: (407) 696-8630
www.orlandosoccer.org
E: mediamom1@aol.com
GM: Jeffrey Gay

Chesapeake Dragons
2152 Cedar Barn Way
Baltimore, MD 21244
T: (410) 419-5364
F: (410) 997-4898
www.dragonsoccer.org
E: futbolr@excite.com
GM: Sheldon Phillips

Chicago Eagles Select
PO Box 793
Wheaton, IL 60189
T: (630) 462-9420
F: (630) 462-9422
www.eaglesfc.com
E: info@eaglesfc.com
GM: Rick McKinley

Chicago Fire Reserves
9924 Walden Pkwy #100
Chicago, IL 60643
T: (773) 238-5881
F: (773) 238-9377
www.firereserve.com
E: amadansoccer@cs.com
GM: Mark Boyle

Chico Rooks
901 Dayton Road
Chico, CA 95928
T: (530) 343-7665
F: (530) 345-9434
www.chicorooks.com
E: cmstahl@jps.net

Cocoa Expos
500 Friday Road
Cocoa, FL 32926
T: (407) 639-3976
F: (407) 504-3716
www.cocoaexpo.com
E: soccer@cocoaexpo.com
GM: Giles Malone

Dayton Gems
1341 Highview Drive
Fairborn, OH 45324
T: (937) 878-2416
F: (937) 878-2854
www.daytongemini.com
E: netkicker3@aol.com
P: John Tackis

Denver Cougars
10920 Jay Street
Westminster, CO 80020
T: (303) 474-0817
F: (303) 474-0859
www.denvercougars.com
E: jrcrun2win@aol.com
GM: Jim Copeland

Des Moines Menace
6400 W Westown Pkwy.
Des Moines, IA 50266
T: (515) 226-9890
F: (515) 226-1595
www.dmmenace.com
E: soccer@dmmenace.com
GM: Jim McMahon

Greenville Lions Premier
503 Tiger Terrace Dr.
Seneca, SC 29678
T: (864) 654-0878
F: (864) 654-5473
www.greenvillelions.com
E: khbranan@aol.com
GM: Kaye Branan

Houston Toros
11414 Richmond Ave., #B232
Houston, TX 77082
T: (832) 715-8330
F: (713) 278-1890
E: mariaperez23@hotmail.com
GM: Gina Spivey

Indiana Invaders
50929 Mullholland Drive
South Bend, IN 46628
T: (219) 272-1525
F: (219) 272-2383
www.indianainvadersfc.com
E: inindvaders@aol.com
GM: Mario Manta

Jersey Falcons
33 Station Road
Lincoln Park, NJ 07035
T: (973) 686-9404
F: (973) 686-9405
www.njfalcons.com
E: BajekG@msn.com
GM: Greg Bajek

Kalamazoo Kingdom
6833 Welbury
Portage, MI 49024
T: (616) 226-2000
F: (616) 226-9078
www.kalamazookingdom.com
E: kingdom@lserv.com
GM: Chris Keenan

Kansas City Brass
12326 Walmer
Overland Park, KS 66209
T: (913) 491-0372
F: (913) 451-9607
E: ablinzl@swbell.net
GM: Dr. Emilio John

Los Angeles Heroes
7955 San Fernando Rd
Sun Valley, CA 91352
T: (818) 768-0965
F: (818) 768-5213
E: rmardirosian@msn.com
GM: Roubik Mardirosian

Louisiana Outlaws
211 Republic Ave., #323
Lafayette, LA 70508
T/F: (337) 989-1703
www.laoutlaws.com
E: kmmooney1@cs.com
GM: Kevin Mooney

Memphis Express
2176 West Street #300
Memphis, TN 38138
T: (901) 755-6688
F: (901) 753-2380
www.soccermemphis.com
E: klong@midsouth.rr.com
GM: Kim Long

Mid Michigan Bucks
2795 Clear Lake Drive
Saginaw, MI 48609
T: (517) 781-6888
F: (517) 781-6623
www.mmbucks.com
E: mmbucks@worldnet.att.net
GM: Jim Duggan

Nashville Metros
PO Box 17207
Nashville, TN 37217
T: (615) 832-5678
F: (615) 832-5632
www.nashvillemetrossoccer.com
E: nashvillemetros@aol.com
GM: Devinder Sandhu

Orange County Blue Star
2418 Santiago Drive
Newport Beach, CA 92660
T: (949) 645-8777
F: (949) 645-8425
www.bluestarsoccer.com
E: bluestarsoccer@socal.rr.com
GM: Nick Theslof

Palm Beach Pumas
108 Pacer Lane
West Palm Beach, FL 33413
T: (561) 588-8852
F: (561) 649-0377
www.palmbeachpumas.com
E: pumasfc@aol.com
GM: Cookie Ketcham

Raleigh Elite
3344 Hillsborough St
Raleigh, NC 27607
T: (919) 834-3951
F: (919) 834-4369
www.caslnc.com
E: sspink@casl.ncfast.com
GM: Sue Spink

Rhode Island Stingrays
501 Waterman Ave.
E. Providence, RI 02914
T: (401) 438-9700
F: (401) 438-9702
www.stingrayssoccer.com
E: frontoffice@stingrayssoccer.com
GM: Mario Pereira

Richmond Kickers Future
2320 W Main St
Richmond, VA 23220
T: (804) 644-5425
F: (804) 359-5037
www.richmondkickers.com
E: psterbenz@richmondkickers.com
GM: Paul Sterbenz

Santa Barbara Sharks
945 Ward Dr #12
Santa Barbara, CA 93111
T: (805) 896-7815
F: (805) 683-1839
E: airgeek67@aol.com
GM: Rick Barker

Seattle Sounders Select
10838 Main Street
Bellevue, WA 98004
T: (206) 622-3415
F: (425) 643-3515
www.seattlesounders.net
E: paul_hurme@hotmail.com
GM: David Uchida

Sioux Falls Spitfire
401 West 39th Street
Sioux Falls, SD 57105
T: (605) 339-4923
F: (801) 729-4519
www.sfspitfire.com
E: gery.baar@home.com
P: Gery Baar

Southern CA Seahorses
14752 Beach Blvd., Suite 244
La Mirada, CA 90638
T: (714) 739-8375
F: (714) 739-8377
www.seahorsesoccer.com
E: info@seahorsesoccer.com
GM: Paul Gizzi

Spokane Shadow
West 4918 Everett
Spokane, WA 99205
T: (509) 326-4625
F: (509) 326-0636
www.spokaneshadow.com
E: robbinsjb@aol.com
GM: Jeff Robins

Tampa Bay Hawks
13355 Park Blvd.
Seminole, FL 33776
T: (727) 393-5182
F: (727) 393-6137
www.tampabayhawks.com
E: mjsousa54@aol.com
GM: Al Sousa

Texas Spurs
PO Box 560161
The Colony, TX 75056
T: (972) 738-9090
F: (469) 384-8437
www.txspurs.com
E: snssoccer@aol.com
GM: Peggy Prior

Thunder Bay Chill
191 Hazelwood Dr., RR #15
Thunder Bay, Ontario P7B 5N1
T: (807) 623-5911
F: (807) 344-7171
www.thunderbaychill.com
E: tbchill@home.com
P: Tony Colistro

Vermont Voltage
890 Fairfax Road
St. Albans, VT 05478
T/F: (802) 527-2499
www.vermontvoltage.com
E: isa@together.net
GM: Bo Vuckovic

West Michigan Edge
154 E Main Avenue
Zeeland, MI 49464
T: (616) 931-9905
F: (616) 931-9908
www.edgesoccer.com
E: bob@edgesoccer.com
P: Bob Dykstra

Williamsburg Legacy
PO Box 296
Williamsburg, VA 23187
T: (757) 220-3794
F: (757) 220-0489
www.williamsburglegacy.com
E: legacy@williamsburgsoccer.com
P: Richard Butler

Wisconsin Rebels
PO Box 471
Appleton, WI 54913
T: (920) 730-1605
F: (920) 725-3027
www.wisconsinrebels.org
E: info@wisconsinrebels.org
GM: Steve Rakita

Worcester Kings
PO Box 10
Auburn, MA 01501
T: (508) 922-7880
F: (508) 757-5126
E: vampata@gis.net
GM: Luigi Romeo

Yakima Reds
PO Box 9187
Yakima, WA 98903
T: (509) 453-2086
F: (509) 453-2298
www.yakimareds.com
E: reds@irwinresearch.com
GM: Hector Vega

2002 PDSL Championship
Cape Cod Crusaders d Boulder Rapids reserve 2-1 (OT) in final game.

Canadian Professional Soccer League

7601 Martingrove Road
Vaughan, Ontario L4L 9E4
T: (905) 856-5439
F: (905) 856-9325
www.canadakicks.com/cpsl
E: directorofmediapr@cpsl.org
P: Vincent Ursini
Dir of Oper: Chris Bellamy
PR: Stan Adamson

The premier amateur league in Canada operating in Ontario & Quebec. Canada does not have a national professional soccer league.

Brampton Hitmen
T: (416) 677-0237
www.bramptonhitmen.com
P: Steve Nijjar

Glen Shields Sun Devils
1441 Clark Avenue
Thornhill, Ontario L4J 7R4
T: (905) 738-6744
F: (905) 738-7196
GM: John Knox

London City SC
PO Box 125, Station B
London. Ontario N6A 4V6
T: (519) 432-2489
F: (519) 438-4625
GM: Harry Paul Gauss

Montreal Dynamites
400 St-Hubert
Pont-Viau Laval, Quebec H7G 2Y7
T: (514) 366-1280
F: (514) 336-2701
www.dynamitesdelaval.com
E: soccerlaval@hotmail.com
GM: Tony Incollingo

North York Astros
1589 Weston Road
Toronto, Ontario M9N 1T4
T: (416) 240-1718
F: (416) 240-1648
www.northyorksoccer.com
E: nyastros@northyorksoccer.com
GM: Bruno Ierullo

Oshawa Flames
1255 Terwillegar Ave., Unit 1
Oshawa. Ontario L1J 7A4
T: (905) 579-3008
F: (905) 738-7196
P: Steve Kralj

Ottawa Wizards
221 Westbrook Road
Carp, Ontario K0A 1L0
T: (613) 831-3121
F: (613) 831-1880
www.ottawawizards.com
P: Omur Sezerman
GM: Jim Lianos

St. Catharines Roma Wolves
22 Rampart Drive
St. Catharines, Ontario L2P 1T4
T: (905) 682-3291
F: (905) 682-8811
P: Joe Colonna
PR: Armand Di Fruscio

Toronto Croatia SC
89 Queen Street
South Mississauga, Ontario L5M 1K7
T: (905) 812-7868
F: (905) 276-9957
P: Mario Skara

Toronto Olympians SC
477 Ellesmere Road
Scarborough, Ontario M1R 4E5
T: (416) 288-8515
F: (416) 288-8895
GM: Tony Lupinacci

York Region Shooters
12930 Yonge Street
Richmond Hill, Ontario L4E 1A5
T/F: (905) 773-1454
GM: Ralph Aquino

No info on the Durham Flames & the Toronto Supra.

Pacific Coast Soccer League
#31-15860 82nd Avenue
Surrey, BC V3S 8M4 Canada
T: (604) 572-9028
F: (604) 572-9029
www.PCSL.bc.ca
E: pcsl@telus.net
P: Len McAdams

The PCSL is the premier league for B.C. and Pacific Northwest.

Soccer Organizations

American Youth Soccer Organization
12501 S. Isis Avenue
Hawthorne, CA 90250
T: (310) 643-6455
F: (310) 643-5310
www.soccer.org
E: webmaster@ayso.org
Exec. Dir: Dick Wilson
Oper: Cheri Tucker

Canadian Soccer Association
237 Metcalfe Street
Ottawa, Ontario K2P 1R2
T: (613) 237-7678
F: (613) 237-1516
www.canoe.ca/soccercan
E: info@soccercan.ca
P: Terry Quinn
COO: Kevan Pipe
Media: Mehrdad Masoudi

**Intercollegiate Soccer
Assn. of America**
1821 Sunny Drive
St. Louis, MO 63122
T: (314) 822-2814
F: (314) 984-0314
Exec. Dir: Bob Albus

**National Intercollegiate
Soccer Officials Assn.**
541 Woodview Drive
Longwood, FL 32779
T: (407) 862-3305
F: (407) 862-8545
Exec. Dir: Dr. Raymond Bernabei

**National Soccer Coaches
Association**
6700 Squibb Road, Suite 215
Mission, KS 66202
T: (913) 362-1747
T: (800) 458-0678
F: (913) 362-3439
www.nsaa.com
Exec. Dir: Jim Sheldon
PR: Michael McFarland

National Soccer Hall of Fame
5-11 Ford Avenue
Oneonta, NY 13820
T: (607) 432-3351
F: (607) 432-8429
www.wpe.com/~nshof/
Exec. Dir: Albert Colone

Pro Beach Soccer Tour
Chesterbrook Corporate Center
1325 Morris Drive, Suite 207
Wayne, PA 19087
T: (610) 722-0500
F: (610) 722-0800
E: beachsoccer@aol.com
Director: Richard Graham
Mkt: Gabby Roe

Soccer Association for the Youth
4050 Executive Park Dr., Suite 100
Cincinnati, OH 45241
T: (513) 769-3800
F: (513) 769-0500
E: sayusa@aol.com
P: Burt McIntyre
PR: Roland Bedard

**Soccer Industry Council
of America**
200 Castlewood Drive
North Palm Beach, FL 33408
T: (561) 840-1171
F: (561) 863-8984
www.sportlink.com/soccer
E: sbsgma@aol.com
Exec. Dir: John Briggs, Jr.

**United States Amateur
Soccer Association**
7800 River Road
N. Bergen, NJ 07047
T: (201) 861-6277
F: (201) 861-6341
Chmn: Mike Edwards

United States Soccer Federation
1801-1811 S. Prairie Avenue
Chicago, IL 60616
T: (312) 808-1300
F: (312) 808-1301
www.us-soccer.com
E: socfed@aol.com
Exec. Dir: Hank Steinbrecher
Communications: Jim Trecker

U.S. Indoor Soccer Association
PO Box 6569
Arlington, VA 22206
T: (703) 820-2810
F: (509) 357-7096
www.usindoor.com
E: info@usindoor.com
P: Don Shapero

U.S. Youth Soccer Association
899 Presidential Drive, Suite 117
Richardson, TX 75081
T: (800) 4-SOCCER
T: (972) 235-4499
F: (972) 235-4480
www.youthsoccer.org
Chmn: Virgil Lewis
Exec. Dir: Kit Simeone

Soccer Publications

In-Play
12501 S. Isis Ave.
Hawthorne, CA 90250
T: (310) 643-6455
F: (310) 643-5310
Editor: Sean Hilferty

Sidekicks International
200 Willard St., Suite 2C
Cocoa, FL 32922
T: (407) 638-0202
F: (407) 638-0206

Soccer America
PO Box 23704
Oakland, CA 94623
T: (510) 528-5000
F: (510) 528-5177
Editor: Lynn Berling-Manuel

Soccer Business International
PO Box 218
Atlantic, VA 23303
T: (757) 824-3942
F: (757) 824-4480
E: Sportsvue@aol.com
Editor: Charles Cuttone

Soccer Digest
990 Grove Street
Evanston, IL 60201
T: (847) 491-6440
F: (847) 491-0459
Publisher: Norman Jacobs
Sr. Editor: Ken Leiker

Soccer International
PO Box 246
Artesia, CA 90702
T: (310) 860-2831

Soccer Jr.
27 Unquowa Road
Fairfield, CT 06430
T: (203) 259-5766
F: (203) 256-1119
E: soccerJrol@aol.com
Editor: Joe Provey

Soccer Magazine
5211 S. Washington Avenue
Titusville, FL 32780
T: (407) 268-5010
F: (407) 269-2025
Publisher: Don Welk
Editor: Michael Lewis

Soccer Match
302 S. Brand Blvd., Suite 1
Glendale, CA 91204
T: (818) 242-9970
Publisher: Almir Santre

Soccer News
1207 Brittany Point Court
Apex, NC 27502
T: (800) 551-9721
T: (919) 303-6611
F: (919) 303-7111
www.soccernews.com
Editor: Tim Nash

Soccer Now
PO Box 5045
Hawthorne, CA 90251
T: (310) 643-6455
F: (310) 643-5310
www.soccer.org
Editor: Sean Hilferty

World Soccer
Central House, 27 Park Street
Croydon CRO 1YD, England
T: (44.81) 686.97.77

Late Arrival

American Indoor Soccer League
PO Box 505
Feeding Hills, MA 01030
T: (413) 569-1920
F: (413) 569-6188

Long Distance Rates For Less!

Looking for Low Long distance Rates?

These rates apply to business & residential service

Most States

4.9 cents per minute on interstate calls

Calling Card/Travel Cards
14.9 cents per minute

Key Elements of Program
* Good for 1+ and inbound 800 service
* No Monthly Fees

* Six (6) Second increment Billing (unlike AT&T and others)

These rates apply to 1+ Direct Dial and 800 toll-free number calls (without changing your 800 #)

Call us at (800) 576-1144

Pro Softball

U.S. Pro Softball League
777 S. Flagler Drive
8th Floor, West Tower
West Palm Beach, FL 33401
T: (561) 515-6179
F: (561)
www.uspl.com
E: uspl7@aol.com
P: Chase W. Hays
Commissioner: Mike Schmidt

Women's Professional Softball League
90 Madison Street, Suite 200
Denver, CO 80206
T: (303) 316-7800
F: (303) 316-2779
www.prosoftball.com
CEO: John Carroll
PR: Drew Russell
Mkt: Rich Levinen

The WPSL will play a tour schedule this year.

Softball organizations & publications are listed in the Sport-by-Sport Softball section.

Pro Team Tennis

World Team Tennis
250 Park Avenue South, 9 FL
New York, NY 10003
T: (212) 979-0202
F: (212) 477-2797
www.worldteamtennis.com
E: Maltby@imgworld.com
P/CEO: Billie Jean King
Exec Dir: Ilana Kloss
PR: Tracey Maltby

Delaware Smash
C/o Dupont Dacron
Barley Mill Plaza
Bldg. 22-1373
Wilmington, DE 19880
T: (302) 992-3680
F: (302) 992-41748
www.delawaresmash.com
GM: Crystal Freeman

Hartford Foxforce
21 Waterville Road
Avon, CA 06001
T: (860) 678-0014
F: (860) 677-4232
www.foxforce.com
P: Brian Foley
GM: Deidre Baker

Kansas City Explorers
PO Box 1521
Mission, KS 66222
T: (913) 362-9944
F: (913) 362-9953
www.kcexplorers.com
GM: Jeff Launius

Newport Beach Breakers
27662 Aliso Creek Rd., Suite 4304
Aliso Viejo, CA 92656
T: (949) 916-6682
F:
www.newportbeachbreakers.com
GM: Lisa Forman
PR: TBA

New York Buzz
Park/Tennis Dept.
City Hall, Jay Street
Schenectady, NY 12305
T: (518) 377-5250
F: (518) 382-5108
www.nybuzzwtt.com
E: info@nybuzz.com
GM: Nitty Singh

New York Hamptons
320 Abrahams Path
Amagansett, NY 11930
T: (631) 267-1039
F: (631) 267-1082
P: Patrick McEnroe
GM: Claude Okin

Philadelphia Freedoms
Same info as DE Smash

Sacramento Capitals
2483 Sunrise Blvd., Suite C
Gold River, CA 95670
T: (916) 638-4001
F: (916) 635-3315
www.saccapitals.com
E: sacramentocapitals@earthlink.net
GM: Lonnie Nielson

St. Louis Aces
7730 Carondelet Ave., Suite 404
St. Louis, MO 63105
T: (314) 726-2237
F: (314) 726-2362
www.stlouisaces.com
P: Jack Levitt
PR: Kristy Reed

Springfield Lasers
1923 N. Weller
Springfield, MO 65803
T: (417) 864-1049
F: (417) 864-5019
www.springfieldlasers.com
GM: Tom Adams
PR: David Taylor

The original WTT was formed in 1974 with players like Bjorn Borg, Jimmy Conors, Chris Evert, Billy Jean King and other top pros.
The original WTT folded after the 1978 season. World Team Tennis under the present structure began in 1981.

2002 WTT Championship Final
Hartford Foxforce

Pro Volleyball

U.S. Pro Volleyball League
One Lincoln Center, Suite 400
18W140 Butterfield Road
Oakbrook Terrace, IL 60181
T: (630) 575-USPV (8778)
F: (630) 575-8777
www.uspv.com
E: mmiazga@uspv.net
P: William Hawkins
VP Oper: Sue Nucci-Ward
PR: Michael Miazga

The USPV suspended operations for the 2003 season but plans to reorganize.

Roller Derby Roller Games

American Roller Derby League
PO Box 5072
Richmond, CA 94805
T: (510)
www.baycitybombers.com
E: press@baycitybombers.com

Roller Games
10923 Ruffner Avenue
Granada hills, CA 91344
T:
www.rollergames.com
E: rgimail@rollergames.com

Roller Derby Preservation Association
250 Starlight Avenue
London, Ontario N5W 4X9 Canada
T:
www.RDPA.com
www.skategrrl.com/rollerderby
P: Mike Yohnicki

Roller Hockey

Major League Roller Hockey
228 S. Washington St., Suite 115
Alexandria, VA 22314
T: (703) 535-5996
F: (703) 519-9316
www.MLRH.com
E: mlrh@MLRH.com
P: Bill Raue

Sport by Sport Organizations

Listed in this section are traditional individual sports that are usually considered non-professional team sports or non-team sports.

Air Sports

American Air Show Network
6385-A Rose Lane
Carpinteria, CA 93013
T: (805) 684-0155
F: (805) 684-0990
P: James Breen

Balloon Federation of America
112 E. Salem, PO Box 400
Indianola, IA 50125
T: (515) 961-8809
F: (515) 961-3537
Exec Dir: Wally Miller

Canadian Sport Parachuting Association
4185 Dunning Road
Navan, Ontario K4B 1J1
T/F: (613) 835-3731
E: cspa@travel~net.com
P: Mary Watson

National Aeronautic Association
1815 N. Ft. Myer Dr., Suite 700
Arlington, VA 22209
T: (703) 527-0226
F: (703) 527-0229
E: naa@ids2.idsonline.com
P: Stev Brown

Soaring Society of America
PO Box E
Hobbs, NM 88241
T: (505) 392-1177
F: (505) 392-8154
Exec Dir: Larry Sanderson

U.S. Base Association
BASE Federation
12619 Manor Drive
Hawthorne, CA 90250
T: (213) 678-0163
Director: Jean Boenisch .
Base Jumping

U.S. Hang Gliding Association
559 E. Pikes Peak Blvd., Ste 101
Colorado Springs, CO 80903
T: (719) 632-8300
F: (719) 632-6417
www.ushga.org
E: ushga@ushga.org
Exec Dir: Phil Bachman

U.S. Parachuting Association
1440 Duke Street
Alexandria, VA 22314
T: (703) 836-3495
F: (703) 836-2843
www.uspa.org
E: uspa@uspa.org
Exec Dir: Christopher Needles

Air Sports Publications

Baloon Life
2336 47th St. SW
Seattle, WA 98116
T: (206) 935-3649
F: (206) 935-3326
www.baloonlife.com
E: tom@baloonlife.com
Publisher: Tom Hamilton

Flying
500 W. Putnam Avenue
Greenwich, CT 06830
T: (203) 622-2701
F: (203) 622-2725
Publisher: Dick Koenig

General Aviation News & Flyer
PO Box 39099
Tacoma, WA 98439
T: (253) 471-9888
F: (253) 471-9911
www.ganflyer.com
E: comments@ganflyer.com
Publisher: Dave Sclair

Parachutist
1440 Duke Street
Alexandria, VA 22314
T: (703) 836-3495
F: (703) 836-2843
E: uspa@uspa.org
Editor: Emily Bump

Paragliding Magazine
559 E. Pikes Peak Blvd., Ste. 101
Colorado Springs, CO 80903
T: (719) 632-8300
F: (719) 632-6417
E: ushga@ushga.org
Editor: Gil Dodgen

Skydiving Magazine
1725 N. Lexington Ave.
DeLand, FL 32724
T: (904) 736-4793
F: (904) 736-9786
www.skydivingmagazine.com
E: admin@skydivingmagazine.com
Editor: Sue Clifton

Soaring Magazine
PO Box E
Hobbs, NM 88241
T: (505) 392-1177
F: (505) 392-8154
Editor: Mark Kennedy

Sport Pilot
7950 Deering Avenue
Canoga Park, CA 91304
T: (818) 887-0550
F: (818) 883-3019
Editor: Jum Campbell

Archery

Association of Professional Archers
2156 N. Oak Road
Plymouth, IN 46563
T: (219) 935-6666
F: (219) 936-4882

Bowhunters of America
725 Memorial Hwy.
Bismarck, ND 58504
T: (701) 255-1631
F: (701) 222-0103
Chmn: Scott Lang

Federation of Canadian Archers
1600 James Naismith Drive
Gloucester, Ontario K1B 5N4
T: (613) 748-5604
F: (613) 748-5785
Tech Dir: Pascal Colmaire

International Bowhunting Organization
3409 Liberty Ave., Suite 201
Vermillion, OH 44089
T: (216) 967-2137
F: (216) 967-2052
P: Ken Watkins

National Archery Association
One Olympic Plaza
Colorado Springs, CO 80909
T: (719) 578-4576
F: (719) 632-4733
Exec Dir: Robert Balink:

National Field Archery Assn.
31407 Outer I-10
Redlands, CA 92373
T: (909) 794-2133
F: (909) 794-8512
www.narcheryas.com
P: Charles Crowell

Archery Publications

Bow & Arrow Hunting
242 S. Anita, Suite 120
Orange, CA 92868
T: (714) 939-9991
F: (714) 939-9909
Editor: Bob Torres

Bowhunting
6420 Wilshire Blvd.
Los Angeles, CA 90048
T: (213) 782-2836
F: (213) 782-2867
Editor: Jay Strengis

Bowhunting World
3D & Target Archery
601 Carlson Pkwy., Suite 600
Minnetonka, MN 55305
T: (612) 476-2200
F: (612) 476-8065
Publisher: Kevin Horrocks

Arm Wrestling

American Arm Wrestling Assn.
PO Box 79
Scranton, PA 18504
T: (570) 342-4984
F: (570) 342-1368
www.eclipse2000.com/arm
Exec Dir: Bob O'Leary

**International Federation
Of Arm Wrestling**
4219 Burbank Blvd.
Burbank, CA 91505
T: (818) 953-2222
F: (818) 953-2220
Director: Joe Weider

Arm Wrestling Pubs.

A Call to Arms
200-14 45th Drive
Bayside, NY 11361
T: (718) 544-4592
F: (718) 261-8111
Publisher: Gene Camp

Bicycling

Adventure Cycling Association
PO Box 8308
Missoula, MT 59807
T: (406) 721-1776
F: (406) 721-8754
www.adv-cycling.org
E: acabike@aol.com
Exec Dir: Gary MacFadden

American Bicycle Association
9831 S. 51st Street, Suite D135
Phoenix, AZ 85044
T: (602) 961-1903
F: (602) 961-1842
www.abamx.com
P: Clayton John

**Bicycling Federation &
Institute of America**
1506 21st Street NW, Suite 200
Washington, D.C. 20036
T: (202) 463-6622
F: (202) 463-6625
Exec. Dir: William Wilkinson III

**Bicycle Manufacturer's
Association of America**
3050 K Street, Suite 400
Washington, D.C. 20007
T: (202) 944-9297
Exec. Dir: Thomas Shannon

Canadian Cycling Association
1600 James Naismith Drive
Gloucester, Ontario K1B 5N4
T: (613) 748-5629
F: (613) 748-5692
Exec. Dir: Patrick Healy

Union Cycliste Internationale
Case Postale
1000 Lausanne 23, Switzerland
T: (41.21) 622 05 80
F: (41.21) 622 05 88
www.uci.ch
E: Admin@uci.ch
P: Hein Verbruggen

**International Bicycle
Touring Society**
7964 Lowry Terrace
La Jolla, CA 92037
T: (619) 454-6428
P: Catharina Graves

**League of American
Wheelman**
190 W. Ostend Street
Suite 120
Baltimore, MD 21230
T: (410) 539-3399
F: (410) 539-3496
E: bikeleague@aol.com
Director: Erin O'Brien

**National Bicycle Dealers
Association**
2240 University Drive, Suite 130
Newport Beach, CA 92660
T: (949) 722-6909
F: (949) 722-6975
Exec. Dir: Fred Clements

National Bicycle League, Inc.
3958 Brown Park Drive, Suite D
Hilliard, OH 43026
T: (614) 777-1625
F: (614) 777-1680
www.nbl.org
CEO: Bob Tedesco

**National Off-Road Bicycling
Association (NORBA)**
One Olympic Plaza
Colorado Springs, CO 80909
T: (719) 578-4581
F: (719) 578-4596
E: Norba@aol.com
Mng Dir: Leslie Kleim

Professional Bicycle League
835 Broadway, Suite 1516
New York, NY 10003
T: (212) 539-6785
E: probikelg@aol.com
P: Pete O'Neil

**Ultra Marathon
Cycling Association**
2761 N. Marengo Avenue
Altadena, CA 91001
T/F: (806) 499-3210
P: Michael Shermer

U.S. Bicycling Hall of Fame
166 W. Main Street
Somerville, NJ 08876
T: (800) BICYCLE
T: (908) 722-3620
F: (908) 704-1494
P: Frank Torpey

U.S. Cycling, Inc.
One Olympic Plaza
Colorado Springs, CO
T: (719) 578-4581
F: (719) 578-4596
www.usacycling.com
E: usacycling@aol.com
P: Mike Plant

**U.S. Professional Cycling
Federation**
7733 Brobst Hill Road
New Tripoli, PA 18066
T: (215) 298-3262
F: (215) 298-3199

Bicycle Publications

Adventure Cyclist
PO Box 8308
150 E. Pine Street
Missoula, MT 59807
T: (406) 721-1776
F: (406) 721-8754
E: jhvg.@ saf.org

Bicycle Business Journal
1904 Wenneca Street
Fort Worth, TX 76102
T: (817) 870-0341
F: (817) 332-1619
Publisher: Rix Quinn

**Bicycle Guide
MTB Magazine**
6420 Sunset Blvd.
Los Angeles, CA 90048
T: (213) 782-2201
F: (213) 782-2372
Publisher: Joe Kensil

**Bicycle Retailer &
Industry News**
502 S. Cordova Road
Santa Fe, NM 87501
T: (505) 988-5099
F: (505) 988-7224
E: brin2@aol.com
Publisher: Terry Moyes

Bicycle USA
190 W. Ostend St., Suite 120
Baltimore, MD 21230
T: (410) 539-3399
F: (410) 539-3496
www.bikeleague.org
E: bikeleague@aol.com
Editor: Donald Tighe

**Bicycling Magazine
Mountain Bike**
33 E. Minor Street
Emmaus, PA 18098
T: (610) 967-5171
F: (610) 967-8960
E: bicmagdm@aol.com
Editor: Geoff Drake

Bike Magazine
33046 Calle Aviador
San Juan Capistrano, CA 92675
T: (949) 496-5922
F: (949) 496-7849
Editor: Steve Casimiro

**Bike Pulse
Mountain & City Biking
Super BMX Freestyle**
7950 Deering Avenue
Canoga Park, CA 91304
T: (818) 887-0550
F: (818) 884-1343
Publisher: Edwin Schnepf

**Bike Trade Canada
Pedal Magazine**
2 Pardee Avenue, Suite 204
Toronto, Ontario M6K 3H5
T: (416) 530-1350
F: (416) 530-4155

**BMX Plus
Mountain Bike Action**
25233 Anza Drive
Valencia, CA 91355
T: (661) 295-1910
F: (661) 295-1278
Editor: Jody Weisel

Cycling USA
One Olympic Plaza
Colorado Springs, CO 80909
T: (719) 578-4581
F: (719) 578-4596
E: usacycling @ aol.com

Dirt Rag
181 Saxonburg Road
Pittsburgh, PA 15238
T: (412) 767-9910
F: (412) 767-9920
E: dirtrag1@aol.com

Pro Bike News
1506 21st Street NW
Suite 200
Washington, D.C. 20036
T: (202) 463-6622
F: (202) 463-6625
Editor: Andy Clarke

Tandem Magazine
26895 Petzold Road
Eugene, OR 97402
T: (541) 485-5262
F: (541) 341-0788
E: tandem@efn.org

VeloNews
1830 N. 55th Street
Boulder, CO 80301
T: (303) 440-0601
F: (303) 444-6788
E: velonews@aol.com
Publisher: Felix Magowan

Winning: Bicycling Illustrated
121 Second Street
San Francisco, CA 94105
T: (415) 777-6939
F: (415) 777-6935
Publisher: Thierry Deketelaere

Billiards

American Pool Players Assn.
1905 Corbridge Lane
Monkton, MD 21111
T: (410) 472-9092
F: (410) 472-3364
P: Peter Bell

Billiards & Bowling Institute
200 Castlewood Drive
North Palm Beach, FL 33408
T: (561) 840-1120
F: (561) 863-8984
Exec. Dir: Sebastian DiCasoli

Billiard Congress of America
910 23rd Avenue
Coralville, IA 52241
T: (319) 351-2112
F: (319) 351-7767
www.bca-pool.com
Exec. Dir: Bruce Cottew

Pro Billiards Tour Association
4412 Commercial Way
Spring Hill, FL 34606
T: (352) 596-7808
F: (352) 596-7441
Commissioner: Don Mackey

U.S. Billiard Association
2238 W. Carmen Street
Chicago, IL 60625
T: (773) 561-3723
Exec. Dir: Michael Melloy

**Women's Professional
Billiard Tour**
1411 Pierce Street
Sioux City, IA 51105
T: (712) 252-4789
F: (712) 252-4799
www.wpba.com
Exec. Dir: Mark Cord

Billiard Publications

Billiards Digest
200 S. Michigan, Suite 1420
Chicago, IL 60604
T: (312) 341-1110
F: (312) 341-1469
Publisher: Michael Panozzo

Pool & Billiard Magazine
1701 Bloomingdale Road
Glendale Heights, IL 60139
T: (630) 260-8500
F: (630) 260-8566
Publisher: Harold Simonsen

Boating/Sailing

**American Power
Boat Association**
17640 E. Nine Mile Road
Eastpointe, MI 48021
T: (810) 773-9700
F: (810) 773-6490
E: apbahq@aol.com
P: Steven David

BOAT
40 Sunset Drive, Unit 6
Basalt, CO 81621
T: (970) 927-4123
F: (970) 927-3568
P: Bill Seebold

Canadian Yachting Association
1600 James Naismith Drive
Gloucester, Ontario K1B 5N4
T: (613) 748-5687
F: (613) 748-5688
Exec. Dir: France A. Martin

**International Jet Sports
Boating Association**
27412 Burbank
Foothill Ranch, CA 92610
T: (949) 598-5560
F: (949) 598-5872
Mgr: Kirk Holland

**International Motor
Boating Union**
Union Internationale Motonautique
Stade Louis II
Monte Carlo, Monaco 98000
T: (33.93) 50 12 60
F: (33.93) 50 22 94
P: Ralf Froehling
Sec Gen: Jose Mawet

**International Outboard
Grand Prix**
4545 S. Mingo Road
Tulsa, OK 74146
T: (918) 663-7776
F: (918) 663-5343
Exec. Dir: Terry Phipps

International Sailing Federation
27 Broadwall
Waterloo
London SE1 9PL, England
T: (44.171) 928 66 11
F: (44.171) 401 83 04
www.sailing.org
P: Paul Henderson
Sec Gen: Arve Sundheim

**Marine Retailer's Assn.
of America**
150 E. Huron Street
Suite 802
Chicago, IL 60611
T: (312) 944-5080
F: (312) 944-2716
P: Phil Keeter

Museum of Yachting
PO Box 129
Fort Adams State Park
Newport, RI 02840
T: (401) 847-1018
Exec. Dir: Bruce Coursoa

**National Marine
Manufacturers Association**
200 E. Randolph Dr., Suite 5100
Chicago, IL 60601
T: (312) 946-6200
F: (312) 946-0388
Chmn: Lew Haeck

Prosail
301 East Blvd.
Charlotte, NC 28203
T: (704) 376-0736
F: (704) 376-2003

Super Boat Racing
1323 20th Terrace
Key West, FL 33040
T: (305) 296-8963
F: (305) 296-9770
P: John Carbonnell

**Unlimited Hydroplane Racing
Association**
19530 Pacific Hwy. S., Suite 200
Seattle, WA 98188
T: (206) 870-8888
F: (206) 878-0866
www.uhra.com
E: Thunder@uhra.com
Commissioner: Bill Doner
PR: J. Michael Kenyon

U.S. Offshore Racing Association
18 N. Franklin Blvd.
Pleasantville, NJ 08232
T: (609) 383-3700
F: (609) 383-9501
CEO: Bill Gifford

U.S. Sailing Association
15 Maritime Drive
Portsmouth, RI 02871
T: (401) 683-0800
F: (401) 683-0840
Exec Dir: Terry Harper

Women's Ocean Racing Sailing Association
PO Box 2403
Newport Beach, CA 92663
T: (949) 840-1869
F: (949) 846-1481
P: Marti Parker

The World Match Racing Conference, Inc.
46 Cummings Point Road
Stamford, CT 06902
T: (203) 324-5407
F: (203) 324-5417

Publications

American Sailor
15 Maritime Drive
Portsmouth, RI 02871
T: (401) 683-0800
F: (401) 683-0840

Boating
1633 Broadway
New York, NY 10019
T: (212) 767-5525
F: (212) 767-5618
Editor: John Owens

Cruising World/Sailing World
5 John Clarke Rd., PO Box 3400
Newport, RI 02840
T: (401) 847-1588
F: (401) 848-5048
Editor: Bernadette Brennan

Motor Boat & Sailing
250 W. 55th Street
New York, NY 10019
T: (212) 649-4092
F: (212) 489-9258
Publisher: Peter Janssen

Power & Motoryacht
249 W. 17th Street
New York, NY 10011
T: (212) 462-3300
F: (212) 367-8330
Publisher: John Bean

Powerboat
1691 Spinnaker Drive
Suite 206
Ventura, CA 930016
T: (805) 639-2222
Editor: Lisa Nordskog

Sail
84 State Street
Boston, MA 02109
T: (617) 720-8600
F: (617) 723-0911
Editor: Patience Wales

Sailing Magazine
125 E. Main Street
Port Washington, WI 53074
T: (414) 284-3494
F: (414) 284-7764
Editor: Micca Hutchins

Watercraft World
601 Lakeshore Pkwy.
Suite 600
Minnetonka, MN 55305
T: (612) 476-2200
F: (612) 476-8065
Editor: Bruce Hampson

Yachting
Two Park Avenue
New York, NY 10016
T: (212) 779-5300
F: (212) 725-1035
www.yachtingmag.com
Editor: Charles Barthold

Bocce

International Bocce Association
400 Rutger Street
PO Box 170
Utica, NY 13503
T: (315) 733-9611
P: Paul Vitagiano

Bowling

**American Blind
Bowling Association**
411 Sheriff Street
Mercer, PA 16137
T: (412) 662-5748
P: Wayne Keeney

American Bowling Congress
5301 S. 76th Street
Greendale, WI 53129
T: (414) 421-6400
F: (414) 421-1194
Exec. Dir.: Roger Dalkin

Billiards & Bowling Institute
200 Castlewood Drive
North Palm Beach, FL 33408
T: (561) 840-1120
F: (561) 863-8984
Exec. Dir: Sebastian DiCasoli

Bowling Proprietors Association
PO Box 5802
615 Six Flags Drive
Arlington, TX 76011
T: (817) 649-5105
F: (817) 633-2940
www.bpaa.com
Exec. Dir: Don Harris

**Federation of International
Bowling (FIQ)**
1631 Mesa Avenue, Suite A
Colorado Springs, CO 80906
T: (719) 636-2695
F: (719) 636-3300
E: fiq@mindspring.com
P: Gerald L. Koenig

Ladies Pro Bowler's Tour
7171 Cherryvale Blvd.
Rockford, IL 61112
T: (815) 332-5657
F: (815) 332-9636
Commissioner: John Falzone

National Bowling Association
377 Park Avenue South, 7th FL
New York, NY 10016
T: (212) 689-8308
F: (212) 725-5063
P: Perry Daniels

National Bowling Council
2300 Clarendon Blvd., Suite 1107
Arlington, VA 22201
T: (703) 841-1660
F: (703) 841-1822
Exec. Dir: Lance Elliott

National Bowling Hall of Fame
111 Stadium Plaza
St. Louis, MO 63102
T: (314) 231-6340
F: (314) 231-4054
Exec. Dir: Gerald Baltz

**National Deaf
Bowling Association**
9244 E. Mansfield Avenue
Denver, CO 80237
TDD: (303) 771-9018
P: Van Scheppach

**National Duckpin
Bowling Congress**
4991 Fairview Avenue
Lithicum, MD 21090
T: (800) 221-3564
F: (410) 636-3256

**Professional Bowler's
Association (PBA)**
1720 Merriman Road
Akron, OH 44313
T: (330) 836-5568
F: (330) 836-2107
www.pba.org
Commissioner: Mark Gerberich
PR: Dave Schroder

**Women's International
Bowling Congress (WIBC)**
5301 S. 76th Street
Greendale, WI 53129
T: (414) 421-9000
F: (414) 421-4420
Exec. Dir: Roseann Kuhn

Young American Bowling Alliance
5301 S. 76th Street
Greendale, WI 53129
T: (414) 421-4700
F: (414) 421-1301
P: Jo Smith

Bowling Publications

Bowler's Journal
200 S. Michigan Ave.
Suite 1430
Chicago, IL 60604
T: (312) 341-1110
F: (312) 341-1469
Editor: Jim Dressell

Bowling Digest
990 Grove Street
Evanston, IL 60201
T: (847) 491-6440
F: (847) 491-0459
Publisher: Norman Jacobs

Bowling Business News
Bowling Magazine
Woman Bowler
5301 S. 76th Street
Greendale, WI 53129
T: (414) 421-6400
F: (414) 421-7977
Editor: Bill Vint

The Bowling Review
427 Chez Paree
Hazelwood, MO 63042
T: (314) 831-4000
F: (314) 831-3610
Publisher: Bill Winders

Boxing

Association International de Boxing Amateur
PO Box 0141
10321 Berlin, Germany
T: (49.30) 423-6766
F: (49.30) 423-5943
P: Prof. Anwar Chowdhry

USA Boxing
One Olympic Plaza
Colorado Springs, CO 80909
T: (719) 578-4506
F: (719) 632-3426
E: USAboxing@aol.com
P: Gary Toney
PR: Steve Ross

Boxing Canada
1600 James Naismith Drive
Gloucester, Ontario K1B 5N4
T: (613) 748-5611
Exec Dir: Stuart Charbula

Golden Gloves Association of America, Inc.
8801 Princess Jeanne NE
Albuquerque, NM 87112
T: (505) 298-8042
F: (505) 298-1191
Exec. Dir: Stan Gallup

International Boxing Federation
United States Boxing Association
134 Evergreen Place, Ninth Floor
East Orange, NJ 07018
T: (201) 414-0300
F: (201) 414-0307
P: Robert W. Lee

International Boxing Hall of Fame
PO Box 425
Canastota, NY 13032
T: (315) 697-7095
Exec Dir: Edward P. Brophy

International Veteran Boxer's Association
35 Brady Avenue
New Rochelle, NY 10805
T: (914) 235-6820
P: Scoop Gallello

North American Boxing Federation
5307 E. Mockingbird Lane
Suite 411
Dallas, TX 75206
T: (214) 823-3787
Vice President: Dick Cole

Women's International Boxing Federation
PO Box 398123
Miami Beach, FL 33139
T: (305) 922-6494
F: (305) 923-1199

World Boxing Association (WBA)
Centro Comercial Ciudad Turmero
Local No. 21, piso no. 2
Calle Petion Cruce Con Urdaneta
Tumero, 2115 Estado Aragua
Venezuela
T: (58) 44 61 645
P: Gilbert Mendoza

World Boxing Board/Penta
233 Belvidere Street
El Paso, TX 79912
T: (915) 581-2409
P: Thomas J. Hoggan

World Boxing Council
Genova 33, Desp. 503
Col. Juarez
Cuahtemoc, 06600, Mexico DF, Mex.
T: (52-5) 533-6547
P: Jose Sulaiman

World Boxing Organization
57 Boriquena, Santa Rita
San Juan, Puerto Rico 00925
T: (787) 751-6861
P: Francisco Valcarcel

World Boxing Union, Ltd.
328 Minorca Avenue
Coral Gables, FL 33134
T: (305) 446-0684
F: (305) 446-1480
Chmn: Ed Levin

Boxing Publications

Boxing USA
One Olympic Plaza
Colorado Springs, CO 80909
T: (719) 578-4506
F: (719) 632-3426

Boxing Record Book
PO Box 896
Sicklerville, NJ 08081
T: (609) 782-8868
F: (609) 782-8483

International Boxing Digest
530 Fifth Avenue, 4th Floor
New York, NY 10036
T: (212) 730-1374
F: (212) 840-7246
Publisher: John Ledes

Boxing 2000/Knockout
KO Magazine/Ring Magazine
World Boxing Magazine
London Publishing Co.
7002 W. Butler Pike
Ambler, PA 19002
T: (215) 643-6385
F: (215) 540-0146
Editor: Stuart Saks

Broomball

U.S. Broomball Association
PO Box 13369
Salem, OR 97309
T: (503) 390-6023
F: (503) 390-5506
P: Marc Hunter

Canoe/Kayak

American Canoe Association
7432 Alban Station Blvd.
Suite B-226
Springfield, VA 22150
T: (703) 451-0141
F: (703) 451-2245
Exec. Dir: Jeffrey Yeager

Canadian Canoe Association
1600 James Naismith Drive
Gloucester, Ontario K1B 5N4
T: (613) 748-5623
F: (613) 748-5700
Exec. Dir: Anne Merklinger

International Canoe Federation
Dozsa Gyorgy ut 1-3
H-1143 Budapest, Hungary
T: (36.1) 163 48 32
F: (36.1) 157 56 43
P: Sergio Orsi

North American Paddle Sports Assn./Trade Association of Sea Kayaking
12455 N. Wauwatosa Road
Mequon, WI 53097
T: (414) 242-5228
F: (414) 242-4428
Exec. Dir: Neil Weisner-Hanks

U.S. Canoe & Kayak Team
Pan American Plaza, Suite 610
Indianapolis, IN 46225
T: (317) 237-5690
F: (317) 237-5694
www.usacanoekayak.org
E: usckt@aol.com
Exec. Dir: Terry Kent
PR: Lisa Fish

Canoe/Kayak Publications

Canoe Magazine
Canoe & Kayak Racing News
PO Box 3146
Kirkland, WA 98083
T: (425) 827-6363
F: (425) 827-1893
www.canoekayak.com
Publisher: David Harrison

Paddler
Paddle Dealer
PO Box 775450
Steamboat Springs, CO 80477
T: (970) 879-1450
F: (970) 870-1404
www.aca/paddler.com
Publisher: Eugene Buchanon

Sea Kayaker
PO Box 17170
Seattle, WA 98107
T: (206) 789-6413
F: (206) 781-1141
www.seakayakermag.com
E: mail@seakayaker.com
Publisher: Michael Collins

Climbing/Alpine

Alpine Club of Canada
PO Box 1026
Banff, Alberta, Canada T0L 0C0
T: (403) 762-4481

American Alpine Club
710 10th Street, Suite 100
Golden, CO 80401
T: (303) 384-0110
F: (303) 384-0111
www.americanalpineclub.org
E: getinfo@americanalpineclub.org
Exec. Dir: Charles Shimanski

American Sport Climbers Federation
35 Greenfield Drive
Moraga, CA 94556
T: (888) 272-3769
www.climbnet.com/ascf
Exec. Dir: Hans Florine
Admn: Heather Jenesky

Cricket

International Cricket Council
The Clock-Tower, Lord's Cricket Ground, St. John's Wood
London, NW8 8QN England
T: (44.171) 266 18 18
F: (44.171) 266 17 77
Chief Exec: David L. Richards

Australian Cricket Board
90 Jolimont Street
Jolimont, Victoria 3002, Australia
T: (61.3) 654 39 77
F: (61.3) 654 81 03
Chief Exec: Graham Halbish

Canadian Cricket Association
1650 Abbey Road
Ottawa, Ontario, Canada K1G 0H3
T: (613) 526-0173
P: James Siew

United States Cricket Assn.
PO Box 2355
Westfield, NJ 07091
T: (908) 272-1711
F: (908) 233-4805
P: Jim Heaning

World Cricket League
301 W. 57th Street, Suite 5D
New York, NY 10019
T: (212) 582-8556
F: (212) 582-8531
www.worldcricketleague.com
P: Max Shaukat
Proposed professional league in the United States.

Croquet

Croquet Foundation of America
U.S. Croquet Association
11585-B Polo Club Road
Wellington, FL 33414
T: (561) 753-9080
F: (561) 753-8201
P: W. Ellery McClatchy

Croquet Publications

The Croquet Annual
USCA Croquet Bulletin
11558 Polo Club Road
West Palm Beach, FL 33414
T: (561) 753-9141
F: (561) 753-8801
Editor: Bert Myer

Equestrian/Horse Racing

Amateur Riders Club of America
716 Kingston Road
Princeton, NJ 08543
T: (609) 924-6446
F: (609) 683-8313
P: Pierre Bellocq

American Association of Equine Practitioners
4075 Iron Works Pike
Lexington, KY 40511
T: (606) 233-0147
F: (606) 233-1968
www.aaep.org
Exec. Dir: Gary Carpenter

American Grand Prix Association
840 National City Bank Bldg.
Cleveland, OH 44114
T: (216) 781-2050
F: (216) 781-5333
Exec. Dir: Leonard King, Jr.

American Horse Council/American Horse Racing Federation
1700 K Street NW, Suite 300
Washington, D.C. 20006
T: (202) 296-4031
F: (202) 296-1970
www.horsecouncil.org
E: Ahorse@aol.com
P: James Hickey, Jr.

American Horse Shows Association
220 E. 42nd Street
New York, NY 10017
T: (212) 972-2472
F: (212) 983-7286
www.ahsa.org
P: Alan Balch

American Minature Horse Association
5601 S. Interstate Hwy. 35 W.
Alvarado, TX 76009
T: (817) 783-5600
F: (817) 783-6403
www.minihorses.com/amha/
P: William King

American Morgan Horse Association
PO Box 960
Shelburne, VT 05482
T: (802) 985-4944
F: (802) 985-8897
E: info@morganhorse.com
Exec. Dir: Jesse Smith

American Paint Horse Association
PO Box 961023
10405 N. I-35 W.
Fort Worth, TX 76131
T: (817) 439-3400
F: (817) 439-3484
Exec. Sec: Ed Roberts

American Quarter Horse Association
1600 Quarter Horse Drive
Amarillo, TX 79104
T: (806) 376-4811
F: (806) 349-6409
www.aqha.com
P: Ginger Hyland

American Saddlebred Horse Association
4093 Iron Works Pike
Lexington, KY 40511
T: (606) 259-2742
F: (606) 259-1628
Exec Sec: Patricia Nichols

American Vaulting Association
642 Alford Place
Bainbridge Island, WA 98110
T: (206) 780-9353
F: (206) 780-9355
www.horsenet.com/ava
E: avaulta@aol.com
P: Charles Bittenbring

Association of Racing Commissioners International
2343 Alexandria Drive, Suite 200
Lexington, KY 40504
T: (606) 224-7070
F: (606) 224-7071

Breeders' Cup Limited
2525 Harrodsburg Road
Lexington, KY 40504
T: (606) 223-5444
F: (606) 223-3945
www.breederscup.com
E: breederscup@breederscup.com
P: D.G. Van Clief, Jr.

Canadian Equestrian Federation
1600 James Naismith Drive
Gloucester, Ontario K1B 5N4
T: (613) 748-5632
F: (613) 747-2920
P: Don Martz

Canadian Trotting Association
2150 Meadowvale Blvd.
Mississauga, Ontario L5N 6R6
T: (905) 858-3060
F: (905) 858-3111
P: Paula Burchell

Federation Equestre Internationale
C.P. 157
Avenue Mon-Repos 24
1000 Lausanne 5, Switzerland
T: (41.21) 312 56 56
F: (41.21) 312 86 77
Telex 454802 FEI CH

Harness Racing Hall of Fame & Museum
240 Main Street
Goshen, NY 10924
T: (914) 294-6330
F: (914) 294-3463
Director: Gail Cunard

Hambletonian Society
1200 Tices Lane
East Brunswick, NJ 08816
T: (908) 249-8500
F: (908) 249-3170
www.hambletonian.org
P: Hugh Grant, Jr.

Harness Horsemen International
14 Main Street
Robbinsville, NJ 08698
T: (609) 259-3717
F: (609) 259-3778
Exec. Dir: Michael Izzo

Harness Tracks of America
4640 E. Sunrise Drive, Suite 200
Tucson, AZ 85718
T: (520) 529-2525
F: (520) 529-3235
E: harness@azstarnet.com
P: Bruce Garland

Horsemen's Benevolent & Protective Association
20801 Biscayne Blvd., Suite 442
Aventura, FL 33180
T: (305) 935-4700
F: (305) 933-2299
Exec. Dir: Scott Savin

International Arabian Horse Association
10805 E. Bethany Drive
Aurora, CO 80014
T: (303) 696-4500
F: (303) 696-4599
Exec. VP: Carol Alm

The Jockey Club
40 East 52nd Street
New York, NY 10022
T: (212) 371-5970
F: (212) 371-6123
Exec. Dir: Nick Nicholson

The Jockeys' Guild, Inc.
250 West Main Street
Lexington, KY 40507
T: (606) 259-3211
F: (606) 259-0938
P: J.D. Bailey

Kentucky Derby Museum
704 Central Avenue
Louisville, KY 40208
T: (502) 637-1111
F: (502) 636-5855
www.derbymuseum.org
Exec. Dir: Lynn Ashton

National Museum of Racing Hall of Fame
Union Avenue
Saratoga, NY 12866
T: (518) 584-0400
F: (518) 584-4574
Director: Peter Hammell

National Steeplechase Association
400 Fair Hill Drive
Elkton, MD 21921
T: (410) 392-0700
F: (410) 392-0706
P: William Pape

Racetrack Chaplaincy of America
3607 Hillcrest Drive
Belmont, CA 94002
T: (415) 598-0139
F: (415) 594-1932

Racetracks of Canada
2150 Meadowvale Blvd.
Mississauga, Ontario L5N 6R6
T: (905) 821-7795
F: (905) 858-3111

Thoroughbred Owners & Breeders Association
PO Box 4367
Lexington, KY 40544
T: (606) 276-2291
F: (606) 276-2462
Exec. Dir: John Hamilton

Thoroughbred Racing Associations of North America
420 Fair Hill Drive, Suite 1
Elkton, MD 21921
T: (410) 392-9200
F: (410) 398-1366
P: Harold Handel

Thoroughbred Racing Communications
40 East 52nd Street
New York, NY 10022
T: (212) 371-5910
F: (212) 371-5917
Exec. Dir: Tom Merritt

Triple Crown Productions, Inc.
700 Central Avenue
Louisville, KY 40208
T: (502) 635-2494
F: (502) 636-4430

U.S. Equestrian Team
Pottersville Road
Gladstone, NJ 07934
T: (908) 234-1251
F: (908) 234-9417
www.uset.com
Exec. Dir: Bob Standish

U.S. Trotting Association
750 Michigan Avenue
Columbus, OH 43215
T: (614) 224-2291
F: (614) 224-4575
www.ustrotting.com
P: Corwin Nixon

Publications

American Turf Monthly
306 Broadway
Lynbrook, NY 11563
T: (800) 645-2240
F: (516) 599-0451
Publisher: Diane Karron

Daily Racing Form
2231 E. Cammelback Road
Suite 100
Phoenix, AZ 85016
T: (602) 468-6500
F: (602) 468-6505
Publisher: Jack Farnsworth

Equus Magazine
656 Quince Orchard Road
Gaithersburg, MD 20878
T: (301) 977-3900
F: (301) 990-9015
Publisher: Ami Shinitzky

Horse & Horsemen
34249 Camino Capistrano
Capistrano Beach, CA 92624
T: (949) 493-2101
F: (949) 240-8680

Horse Illustrated
PO Box 6050
Mission Viejo, CA 92690
T: (949) 855-8822
F: (949) 855-3045
Editor: Audrey Pavion

Horse & Rider
12265 W. Bayaud
Suite 300
Lakewood, CO 80228
T: (303) 445-4700
F: (303) 914-3017
Publisher: Pat Eskew

Practical Horseman
1288 Doe Run Road
Coatesville, PA 19320
T: (610) 380-8977
F: (610) 380-8304
Publisher: Lua Southard

Thoroughbred Times
496 Southland Drive
Lexington, KY 40533
T: (606) 260-9800
F: (606) 260-9812
Editor: Mark Simon

Western Horseman
PO Box 7980
Colorado Springs, CO 80933
T: (719) 633-5524
F: (719) 633-1392
Publisher: Randy Witte

Exercise/Fitness

Aerobics & Fitness Association of America
15250 Ventura Blvd., Suite 200
Sherman Oaks, CA 91403
T: (818) 905-0040
F: (818) 990-5468
www.afaa.com
P: Linda Pfeffer

Amateur Bodybuilders Assn.
Golds Gym
1307 W. 6th Street
Corona, CA 91720
T: (909) 734-3900
P: Denny Kakos

American Alliance for Health, Physical Education, Recreation & Dance (AAHPERD)
1900 Association Drive
Reston, VA 22091
T: (703) 476-3400
F: (703) 476-9527
www.aahperd.com
P: Keith Henshcen

Association of National Aerobic Championships
9000 Sunset Blvd., Suite 1408
Los Angeles, CA 90069
T: (310) 278-9700
F: (310) 278-2148
E: nacusa@aol.com
P: Howard Schwartz

Assn. of Oldetime Barbell & Strongmen
4959 Viceroy Street, Ste 203
Cape Coral, FL 33904
T: (941) 549-8407
Director: Vic Boff

Body Builders International
2875 Bates Road
Montreal, Quebec H3S 1B7
T: (514) 731-3053
F: (514) 731-9026
P: Ben Weider

Canadian Association for Health, Phys. Education & Recreation
1600 James Naismith Drive
Gloucester, Ontario K1B 5N4
T: (613) 748-5622
F: (613) 748-5737
Exec. Dir: Sue Cousineau

The International Assn. of Fitness Professionals
6190 Cornerstone Court E.
Suite 204
San Diego, CA 92121
T: (619) 535-8979
F: (619) 535-8234
www.ideafit.com
Exec. Dir: Kathie Davis

International Health, Racquet & Sports Club Association
263 Summer Street
Boston, MA 02210
T: (617) 951-0055
F: (617) 951-0056
www.ihrsa.org
Exec. Dir: John McCarthy

International Fitness Sanctioning Body
PO Box 2378
Corona, CA 91718
T: (909) 371-0606
F: (909) 371-0608
E: MSFitness@aol.com
P: Michelle Boyko

National Assn. for Sport and Physical Education
1900 Association Drive
Reston, VA 20191
T: (703) 476-3410
F: (703) 476-8316
Exec Dir: Dr. Judith Young

National Association of Governor's Councils on Physical Fitness & Sports
201 S. Capitol Ave., Suite 560
Indianapolis, IN 46225
T: (317) 237-5630
F: (317) 237-5632
E: Govcouncil@aol.com
Exec. Dir: Cindy Porteous

National Athletic Trainers Assn.
2952 Stemmons Fwy.
Dallas, TX 75247
T: (214) 637-6282
F: (214) 637-2206
www.nata.org
Exec. Dir: Eve Beckler-Doyle

National Institute for Fitness & Sport
250 N. University Blvd.
Indianapolis, IN 46202
T: (317) 274-3432
F: (317) 274-7408
P: Jerry Taylor

National Strength & Conditioning Association
530 Communication Circle
Suite 204
Colorado Springs, CO 80905
T: (719) 632-NSCA
F: (719) 632-6367
E: NSCA@usa.net
P: Donald Chu

The President's Council on Physical Fitness & Sports
200 Independence Ave. SW
HHH Bldg., Rm. 738-H
Washington, DC 20201
T: (202) 690-9000
F: (202) 690-5211
Exec. Dir: Sandra Perlmutter

Sport Development-YMCA
101 N. Wacker Drive
Chicago, IL 60606
T: (312) 977-0031
F: (312) 977-9063
Chmn: Daniel Emerson

U.S. Powerlifting Federation
PO Box 650
Roy, UT 84067
T: (801) 776-3628
P: Don Haley

World Natural Bodybuilding Federation
350 Fifth Ave., Suite 8216
New York, NY 10118
T: 9212) 947-4322
Chmn: Steve Downs

YMCA of the USA
350 Fifth Ave., 3 FL
New York, NY 10118
T: (212) 273-7800
F: (212) 465-2281
Ex. Dir: Dr. Prema Mathai-Davis

Exercise Publications

Journal of Athletic Training
2952 Stemmons Fwy.
Dallas, TX 75247
T: (214) 637-6282
F: (214) 637-2206

Journal of Physical Education, Recreation & Dance
1900 Association Drive
Reston, VA 22091
T: (703) 476-3477
F: (703) 476-9527
Editor: Frances Rowan

Men's Exercise
350 5th Ave., Suite 3323
New York, NY 10118
T: (212) 273-7800
F: (212) 465-2281

Men's Fitness/ Prime Health & Fitness/ Muscle & Fitness/ Shape Magazine
21100 Erwin Street
Woodland Hills, CA 91367
T: (818) 884-6800
Publisher: Joe Weider

Fishing

American Sportfishing Assn.
1033 N. Fairfax St., Suite 200
Alexandria, VA 22314
T: (703) 519-9691
F: (703) 519-1872
www.asafishing.org
P: Mike Hayden

Bass Anglers Sportsmen Society (BASS)
PO Box 17116
5845 Carmichael Road
Montgomery, AL 36117
T: (334) 272-9530
F: (334) 279-7148
www.bassmaster.com
CEO: Helen Sevier

Catskill Fly Fishing Center & Museum
Old Route 17, PO Box 1295
Livingston Manor, NY 12758
T: (914) 439-4810

Federation of Fly Fishers
502 S. 19th Street
Bozeman, MT 59771
T: (406) 585-7592
F: (406) 585-7596
www.fedflyfishers.org
P: Jim Watkins

International Bass Fishing Hall of Fame
290 S. Main Street
PO Box 295
Lakeport, CA 95453
T: (707) 263-6911

International Game Fish Association/ International Reference Library of Fishes & Museum
1301 E. Atlantic Blvd.
Pompano Beach, FL 33060
T: (954) 941-3474
F: (954) 941-5868
www.igfa.org
P: Mike Leech

Izaak Walton League of America
707 Conservation Lane
Gaithersburg, MD 20878
T: (301) 548-0150
F: (301) 548-0146
Exec. Dir: Paul Hansen

National Fresh Water Fishing Hall of Fame
One Hall of Fame Drive
Hayward, WI 54843
T: (715) 634-4440

Sport Fishing Institute
1010 Massachusetts Ave. NW
Suite 320
Washington, D.C. 20001
T: (202) 898-0770
F: (202) 371-2085

Trout Unlimited
1500 Wilson Blvd., Suite 310
Arlington, VA 22209
T: (703) 522-0200
F: (703) 284-9400
www.tu.org
E: troutu@aol.com
P: Charles Gauvin

Fishing Publications

American Angler
PO Box 4100
Bennington, VT 05201
T: (802) 447-1518
F: (802) 447-2471

Bass Fishing
Route 2, Box 74B
Gilbertsville, KY 42044
T: (502) 362-4880
Publisher: Mike Whitaker

Bassmaster
Bass Times
5845 Carmichael Road
Montgomery, AL 36117
T: (334) 272-9530
F: (334) 279-7148
www.ono.com/bass
Editor: Dave Precht

Fishing Tackle Trade News
PO Box 370
Camden, ME 04843
T: (800) 776-1670
F: (207) 544-5144
Editor: Silvio Calabi

Fishing World Magazine
51 Atlantic Avenue
Floral Park, NY 11001
T: (516) 352-9700
F: (516) 437-6841

Fly Fisherman
PO Box 8200, 6405 Flank Dr.
Harrisburg, PA 17112
T: (717) 657-9555
F: (717) 657-9526
Editor: John Randolph

North American Fisherman
PO Box 3403
12301 Whitewater Drive
Minnetonka, MN 55343
T: (800) 843-6323
F: (612) 936-9755
Publisher: Rich Sandberg

Salt Water Sportsman
77 Franklin St., 10th Floor
Boston, MA 02210
T: (617) 338-2300
F: (617) 338-2309
Editor: Rip Cunningham

Frisbee

Ultimate Players Association
3595 E. Fountain Blvd, Suite J-2
Colorado Springs, CO 80910
T: (719) 591-1168
F: (719) 591-2461
www.upa.org
E: upa_hq@upa.org
Exec. Dir: Bob Byrne

U.S. Disc Sports Association
855 Tujunga Valley Road
Sunland, CA 91040
T: (818) 353-6339
Director: Beth Verish

World Flying Disc Federation
200 Linden
Ft. Collins, CO 80524
T: (970) 484-6932
F: (970) 490-2714
P: Bill Wright

Golf

American Junior
Golf Association
2415 Steeplechase Lane
Roswell, GA 30076
T: (770) 998-4653
F: (770) 992-9763
www.ajga.org
E: ajga@ajga.org
Exec. Dir: Steve Hamblin

American Society of
Golf Course Architects
221 N. LaSalle Street
Chicago, IL 60601
T: (312) 372-7090
F: (312) 372-6160
www.golfdesign.org
E: asgca@selz.com
P: Robert Lohmann

Canadian Ladies Golf Assn.
Golf House
1333 Dorval Drive
Oakville, Ontario L6J 4Z3
T: (800) 455-2542
T: (905) 849-9700
F: (905) 849-0188
Exec Dir: Peggy Grimsteed

Futures Golf Tour
1300 Eaglebrooke Blvd.
Lakeland, FL 338135
T: (941) 709-9100
F: (941) 709-9200
www.futurestour.com
E: golf@futurestour.com
P: Eloise Trainor

Golf Course Builders Assn.
920 Airport Road, Suite 210
Chapel Hill, NC 27514
T: (919) 942-8922
F: (919) 942-6955
www.gcbaa.org
Exec. Dir: Phil Arnold

Golf Course Superintendents Association of America
1421 Research Park Drive
Lawrence, KS 66049
T: (785) 841-2240
F: (785) 832-4433
www.gcsaa.org
CEO: Stephen Mona

Golf Writers Assn. of America
25882 Orchard Lake Road
Farmington Hills, MI 48336
T: (810) 442-1481
P: Tim Rosaforte

Ladies' Professional Golf Association (LPGA)
100 International Golf Drive
Daytona Beach, FL 32124
T: (904) 274-6200
F: (904) 274-1099
www.lpga.com
Commissioner: Jim Ritts

Minigolf Sport Association
PO Box 32353
Jacksonville, FL 32237
T: (904) 781-4653
F: (904) 781-4843
www.minigolf.com
E: minigolf@minigolf.com
Exec Dir: Skip Laun

National Golf Foundation
1150 U.S. Highway 1
Jupiter, FL 33477
T: (561) 744-6006
F: (561) 744-6107
www.ngf.org
P: Joseph Beditz

Professional Golf Association Men's & Seniors PGA Tour Nike Tour
Sawgrass
112 PGA Tour Blvd.
Ponte Vedra Beach, FL 32082
T: (904) 285-3700
F: (904) 285-7913
www.pgatour.com
Comm: Tim Finchem

Professional Golfer's Association of America & Hall of Fame
100 Avenue of Champions
Palm Beach Gardens, FL 33410
T: (561) 624-8400
F: (561) 624-8448
www.pgaonline.com
CEO: Jim Awtrey
Museum Director: Peter Stillwell

Professional Putters Association
PO Box 35237
Fayetteville, NC 28303
T: (910) 485-7131
F: (910) 485-1122
www.putt-putt.com
P: Bobby Owens

Royal Canadian Golf Association
Golf House
1333 Dorval Drive
Oakville, Ontario L6J 4Z3
T: (905) 849-9700
F: (905) 845-7040
www.rcga.org
E: golfhouse@rcga.org
Exec Dir: Stephen D. Ross

United States Golf Association & Museum/ World Amateur Golf Council
Golf House
PO Box 708
Liberty Corner Road
Far Hills, NJ 07931
T: (908) 234-2300
F: (908) 234-9687
www.usga.org
Exec Dir: David Fay

U.S. Blind Golfers Assn.
160 Lago Vista Blvd.
Casselberry, FL 32707
T: (407) 332-0700
P: Bob Andrews
VP: Worth Dalton

World Golf Hall of Fame
One World Golf Place
St. Augustine, FL 32092
T: (904) 940-4000
F: (904) 940-4194
Director: Karen Bednarski

Golf Publications

Fairway
Golf Magazine
Tour
Two Park Avenue
New York, NY 10016
T: (212) 779-5000
F: (212) 481-8085
Publisher: James Kahn

Golf Digest
Golf World
5520 Park Avenue
Trumbull, CT 06611
T: (203) 373-7000
F: (203) 373-7033
Publisher: James Fitzgerald

The Golfer
21 E. 40th Street
New York, NY 10016
T: (212) 696-2484
F: (212) 696-1678
Editor: Matthew Tolan

Golf Journal
USGA
Liberty Corner Road
Far Hills, NJ 07931
T: (908) 234-2300
F: (908) 234-9687
E: golfjournal@usga.org
Editor: Brett Avery

National Golfer
57 N. Washington Street
Plainville, CT 06062
T: (860) 747-4404
F: (860) 747-4226
Editor: David Gould

PGA Magazine
888 W. Big Beaver Rd.
Suite 600
Troy, MI 48084
T: (810) 362-7400
F: (810) 362-7426
Editor: Vince Aversano

Senior Golfer
1 Park Ave., 10th Floor
New York, NY 10016
T: (212) 545-4800
F: (212) 685-9644
Editor: Larry Dennis

Greyhound Racing

American Greyhound Council/
American Greyhound Track
Operators Association
PO Box 100279
Birmingham, AL 35210
T: (205) 838-1574
F: (205) 838-1575
P: Ron Sultemeier

Greyhound Hall of Fame
407 S. Buckeye
Abilene, KS 67410
T: (913) 263-3000
Director: Edward Scheele

National Greyhound Association
PO Box 543
Abilene, KS 67410
T: (913) 263-4660
P: Herb Koerner

Greyhound Publications

Greyhound USA
12 Michael Road
Watefield, MA 01880
T: (617) 742-7575
Publisher: Greg Farley

Gymnastics/Trampoline

International Gymnastics Fed.
Rue des Oeuches 10, C.P. 359
2740 Moutier 1, Switzerland
T: (41.32) 494.64.10
F: (41.32) 494.64.19
www.worldsport.com/gymnastics
P: Bruno Grandi

International Gymnastics Hall of Fame & Museum
120 N. Robinson-East Concourse
Oklahoma City, OK 73102
T: (405) 235-5600
F: (405) 235-5678
Director: Frank Bare
Historian: A. Bruce Frederick

USA Gymnastics
Pan American Plaza
201 S. Capitol Ave., Suite 300
Indianapolis, IN 46225
T: (317) 237-5050
F: (317) 237-5069
www.usa-gymnastics.org/usga
Exec. Dir: Kathy Scanlan

USA Trampoline & Tumbling
PO Box 306
Brownfield, TX 79316
T: (806) 637-8670
F: (806) 637-9046
www.usa-t.org
Exec. Dir: Ann Sims

U.S. Sports Acrobatics
PO Box 41356
Sacramento, CA 95841
T: (916) 488-9499
F: (916) 488-9497
Rmcfarla@lasierra.edu
P: Tonya Case-Patterson

Gymnastics Publications

International Gymnast
PO Box 721020
Norman, OK 73070
T: (405) 447-9988
F: (405) 447-5810
Publisher: Paul Ziert

USA Gymnastics Magazine
Pan American Plaza
201 S. Capitol Ave., Suite 300
Indianapolis, IN 46225
T: (317) 237-5050
F: (317) 237-5069
www.usa-gymnastics.org/usga
Editor: Luan Peszek

Health & Sports Medicine

American Academy of Podiatric Sports Medicine
1729 Glastonberry Road
Potomac, MD 20854
T: (800) 438-3355
Exec. Dir: Larry Shane

American Athletic Trainers Association
660 W. Duarte Road
Arcadia, CA 91007
T: (626) 845-1978

American College Health Association
780 Elkridge Landing Road
Linthicum, MD 21090
T: (410) 859-1500
F: (410) 859-1510
Exec. Dir: Dr. Charles Hartman

American College of Sports Medicine
401 W. Michigan Street
Indianapolis, IN 46202
T: (317) 637-9200
F: (317) 634-7817
www.acsm.org/sportsmed
P: Charlotte A. Tate

American Orthopaedic Society for Sports Medicine
6300 N. River Road, Suite 200
Rosemont, IL 60018
T: (847) 292-4900
F: (847) 292-4905
www.sportsmed.org
P: Duane Messner

American Osteopathic Academy of Sports Medicine
7611 Elmwood Ave., Suite 201
Middleton, WI 53562
T: (608) 831-4400
F: (608) 831-5122
Exec. Dir: Sheila Endicott

American Physical Therapy Association
Sports PTA Section
505 King St., Suite 345
La Crosse, WI 54601
T: (608) 784-0112
F: (608) 784-5800
www.spts.org
P: George Davies

Canadian Association for Health, Phys. Education & Recreation
1600 James Naismith Drive
Gloucester, Ontario K1B 5N4
T: (613) 748-5622
F: (613) 748-5737
Exec. Dir: Sue Cousineau

International Sports Medicine Federation
Center for Sports Medicine
Pennsylvania State University
146 REC Bldg.
University Park, PA 16802
T: (814) 865-7107
F: (814) 865-7077
P: Dr. Eduardo Henrique De Rose
Sec Gen: Prof. Howard G. Knuttgen

The National Academy of Sports Medicine
2434 N. Greenview Avenue
Suite 205
Chicago, IL 60614
T: (773) 929-5101
F: (773) 929-5733
Director: Dr. Mark Slavin

National Youth Sport Safety Foundation
333 Longwood Ave., Suite 202
Boston, MA 02115
T: (617) 277-1171
F: (617) 277-2278
E: nyss@aol.com
Exec. Dir: Michelle Glassman

Sports Medicine Council of Canada
1600 James Naismith Drive
Gloucester, Ontario K1B 5N4
T: (613) 748-5671
F: (613) 748-5729
P: Chuck Armstrong

Health Publications

American Journal of Sports Medicine
230 Calvary Street
Waltham, MA 02154
T: (781) 736-0707
F: (781) 736-0607
Editor: Robert Leach

Journal of Health Education
1900 Association Drive
Reston, VA 22091
T: (703) 476-3468
F: (703) 476-9527
Editor: Patricia Lyle

Journal of Orthopaedic & Sports Physical Therapy
100 Oakdale Campus, #38 PRL
Iowa City, IA 52242
T: (319) 335-4650
F: (319) 335-4470
Editor: Gary Schmidt

Journal of Sports Exercise Phychology/ Rehabilitation Journal
PO Box 5076
Champaign, IL 61825
T: (800) 747-4457
F: (217) 351-2674
www.humankinetics.com
Publisher: Human Kinetics

Medicine & Science Sports & Exercise
351 W. Camden Street
Baltimore, MD 21201
T: (410) 528-4000
F: (410) 361-8040
www.wwilkins.com
Publisher: John Ewers

The Physician & Sportsmedicine
4530 W. 77th Street
Edina, MN 55435
T: (612) 835-3222
F: (612) 835-3460
www.physsportsmed.com
Editor: Susan Hawthorne

Sports Medicine Digest
7100 Hayvenhurst, Suite 107
Van Nuys, CA 91406
T: (800) 365-2468
F: (818) 997-1316

Ice Racing

International Ice Racing Assn.
PO Box 8105
St. Paul, MN 55108
T: (651) 538-8012
P: Steve Beddor

Ice Skating/Speed Skating

American Speedskating Union of the U.S.
1033 Shady Lane
Glen Ellyn, IL 60137
T: (630) 790-3230
P: James Chapin

Ice Skating Institute of America
355 W. Dundee Road
Buffalo Grove, IL 60089
T: (847) 808-7528
F: (847) 808-8329
Exec Dir: Justine Smith

International Skating Union
Chemin de Primerose 2
Lausanne, Switzerland
T: (41.21) 612.66.66
F: (41.21) 612.66.77
www.isu.org
E: info@isu.org
P: Ottavio Cinquanta
Sec Gen: Fredi Schmid

Professional Skaters Assn. of America
1821 2nd Street SW
Rochester, MN 55902
T: (507) 281-5122
F: (507) 281-5491
E: skatepsa@aol.com
Exec. Dir: Carole Shulman

U.S. Figure Skating Association
20 First Street
Colorado Springs, CO 80906
T: (719) 635-5200
F: (719) 635-9548
E: usfsa1@aol.com
Exec. Dir: Jerry Lace

U.S. Speedskating
2074 122nd Ave. NW
Coon Rapids, MN 55448
T: (612) 767-4277
F: (612) 767-4279
www.usspeedskating.org
E: info@roller-dome.com
P: Mike Cofrin

The World Figure Skating Hall of Fame & Museum
20 First Street
Colorado Springs, CO 80906
T: (719) 635-5200
F: (719) 635-9548
Curator: Beth Davis

Skating Publications

American Skating world
1816 Brownsville Road
Pittsburgh, PA 15210
T: (800) 245-6280
F: (412) 885-7617

Skating
20 First Street
Colorado Springs, CO 80906
T: (719) 635-5200
F: (719) 635-9548
E: Skatemag@aol.com
Exec. Editor: H. Kermit Jackson

In Line/Roller Hockey

American In Line Roller Hockey Series
109 Chestnut Avenue
W. Berlin, NJ 08091
T: (609) 428-9393
F: (609) 428-0455
www.airhs.aol.com
P: Todd Melton

Buffalo Wings
49 Illinois Street, Suite 201
Buffalo, NY 14203
T: (716) 856-0102
F: (716) 856-0214
www.buffalowings.net
P: Frances Ann Edmonston
PR: John Hopkins
Independent club for 2000 that was part of ill-fated RHI in 1999.

International In-Line Skating Assn.
105 S. 7th Street
Wilmington, NC 28401
T: (910) 762-7004
F: (910) 762-9477
www.iisa.org
E: director@iisa.org
Exec. Dir: Gilbert Clark

Major League Roller Hockey
PO Box 25621
Alexandria, VA 22304
T: (703) 519-8672
T: (703) 535-5996
F: (703) 549-2611
www.MLRH.com
P: Bill Raue
The MLRH is operating AAA regional pro leagues in the mid-atlantic, mid-west, southwest & a Women's pro league for 2000.

USA Hockey In-Line
1775 Bob Johnson Drive
Colorado Springs, CO 80906
T: (800) 888-4656
F: (719) 538-7838
E: usahockeyinline@usahockey.org

Publications

Box
In-Line
In-Line Hockey News
2025 Pearl Street
Boulder, CO 80302
T: (303) 440-5111
F: (303) 440-3313
Editor: Neil Feineman

Inline Skater
13645 Beta Road
Dallas, TX 75244
T: (972) 851-1700
F: (972) 851-1753
Editor: Paula Caballero

Roller Hockey Magazine
12327 Santa Monica Blvd.
Suite 202
Los Angeles, CA 90025
T: (310) 442-6600
F: (310) 442-6663
www.rhockey.com
Publisher: Mark Brown

USA Hockey Inline Magazine
1200 N. 7th Street
Minneapolis, MN 55411
T: (612) 522-1200
F: (612) 522-1182
Editor: Darryl Seibel

Kiting

American kitefliers Association
1559 Rockville Pike
Rockville, MD 20852
T: (800) AKA-2550
F: (312) 642-8693
Exec. Dir: Mel Hickman

Publications

American Kite
PO Box 699
Cedar Ridge, CA 95924
T: (916) 273-3855
F: (916) 273-3319
Publisher: Daniel Prentice

Martial Arts

American Amateur Karate Federation
1930 Wilshire Blvd., Suite 1208
Los Angeles, CA 90057
T: (213) 483-8261
P: Hidetaka Nishiyama
Gen Sec: William Bottger, Jr.

International Judo Federation
33 FL, Doosan Tower
18-12. Ulchi-ro, 6 ka
Chung-Ku, Seoul, South Korea
T: (82.2) 759.69.36
F: (82.2) 754.10.75
www.ijf.org
E: yspark@ijf.org
P: Yong Sung Park

U.S. Judo, Inc.
One Olympic Plaza
Colorado Springs, CO 80909
T: (719) 578-4730
F: (719) 578-4733
www.usjudo.org
Exec. Dir: William Rosenberg

USA Karate Federation
1300 Kenmore Blvd.
Akron, OH 44314
T: (330) 753-3114
F: (330) 753-6967
P: George Anderson

U.S. Taekwondo Union
One Olympic Plaza
Colorado Springs, CO 80909
T: (719) 578-4632
F: (719) 578-4642
www.ustu.com/taekwondo
P: Dr. Sang Lee

World Karate Federation
Princesa 22, 4o Izqda
28008 Madrid, Spain
T: (349.1) 542.46.25
F: (349.1) 542.49.13
www.wkf.net
P: Antonio Espinos

The World Taekwondo Federation
635 Yuksam-dong, Kangnam-ku
Seoul 135-080, South Korea
T: (82-2) 566 25 05
F: (82-2) 553 47 28
www.worldsport.com/wtf
E: wtf@unitel.co.kr
P: Un Yong Kim

Publications

Black Belt
Karate/Kung-Fu Illustrated
Martial Arts Training
PO Box 918
Santa Clarita, CA 91380
T: (661) 257-4066
F: (661) 257-3028
Publisher: Michael James

Inside Karate
Inside Kung-Fu
4201 Vanowen Place
Burbank, CA 91505
T: (818) 845-2656
F: (818) 845-7761
Publisher: Mark Komuro

Tae Kwon Do Times
1423 18th Street
Bettendorf, IA 52722
T: (319) 359-7202
F: (319) 355-7299
Publisher: Chung Kim

Motor Sports

Listed in this section are organizations for auto racing, drag racing, hot rods, motorcycles, truck & off-road racing.

American Hot Rod Association
111 N. Hayford Road
Spokane, WA 99204
T: (509) 244-2372
F: (509) 244-2472

American Motorcycle Association
33 Collegeview Road
Westerville, OH 43081
T: (614) 856-1900
F: (614) 856-1920
www.ama-cycling.org
P: Ed Youngblood

American Speed Association
202 S. Main Street
Pendleton, IN 46064
T: (765) 778-8088
F: (765) 778-4006
P: Rex Robbins

**Automobile Racing Club
of America (ARCA)**
PO Box 5217
Toledo, OH 43611
T: (734) 847-6726
F: (734) 847-3137
P: Ron Drager
PR: Don Radebaugh

**Championship Auto Racing
Teams (CART)**
5350 W. Lakeview Pkwy South Drive
Indianapolis, IN 46268
T: (317) 715-4100
F: (317) 715-4110
www.Champcarworldseries.com
E: emauk@cart.com
P: Christopher Pook
VP Comm: Adam Saal

**Driver's Independent Race
Tracks (DIRT) & Hall of Fame**
1 Speedway Drive
Weedsport, NY 13166
T: (315) 834-6667
F: (315) 834-9734
www.dirtmotorsports.com
P: Glenn Donnelly
PR: Gary Spaid

**Federation of International
De l' Automobiles (FIA)**
8 Place de la Concorde
75008 Paris, France
T: (33.1) 43.12.44.55
F: (33.1) 43.12.44.66
P: Max Mosley

**Formula One Contractors
Association**
Roebuck House
Cox Lane, Surrey
Chessington, England K1T 1DG
T: (44) 391.01.21

**Formula One Driver's
Association**
2 rue Jean Jaures
L-1836 Luxembourg
T: (45) 0045

**Formula One Spectators
Association**
8033 Sunset Blvd., Suite 60
Los Angeles, CA 90046
T: (213) 658-5884
Exec. Dir: Pam Louesen

**Don Garlits International
Drag Racing Hall of Fame**
13700 SW 16th Avenue
Ocala, FL 34473
T: (352) 245-8661
F: (352) 245-6895
www.garlits.com
GM: Greg Capitano
Location: I-75, Exit 67

**Indianapolis Motor Speedway
Hall of Fame & Museum**
4790 W 16th Street
Indianapolis, IN 46224
T: (317) 484-6747
F: (317) 484-6449
www.brickyard.com
Director: Ralph Kramer

Indy Racing League (IRL)
4790 W. 16th Street
Indianapolis, IN 46224
T: (317) 484-6526
F: (317) 484-6525
www.indyracingleague.com
Exec. Dir: Leo Mehl

International Drag Bike Assn.
3936 Raceway Park Road
Mt. Olive, AL 35117
T: (800) 553-IDBA
T: (205) 849-7886
F: (205) 841-0553
www.idbapix.netcom.com
P: Leigh Ann Min

**International Hot Rod
Association (IHRA)**
9½ E. Main Street
Norwalk, OH 44857
T: (419) 663-6666
F: (419) 663-4472
www.ihra.com
GM: Bill Bader, Sr.
PR: Jim Marchyshyn

International Kart Federation
4650 Arrow Hwy, Suite C-7
Montclair, CA 91763
T: (909) 625-5497
F: (909) 621-6019
COO: Kristy Hellman

International Motorsports Hall of Fame
PO Box 1018
3198 Speedway Blvd.
Talladega, AL 35161
T: (205) 362-5002
F: (205) 362-3717
Exec. Dir: Don Naman

International Race of Champions (IROC)
45 Park Road
Tinton Falls, NJ 07724
T: (732) 542-4762
F: (732) 542-2122
P: Jay Signore

Motorsports Museum & Hall Of Fame of America
43700 Expo Center Drive
Novi, MI 48375
T: (248) 349-RACE
F: (248) 349-2113
Exec Dir: Ronald Watson
I-96 & Novi Road

National Association of Stock Car Racing (NASCAR)
1801 W. Int'l. Speedway Blvd.
Daytona Beach, FL 32114
T: (904) 253-0611
F: (904) 252-8804
www.nascar.com
P: William France, Jr.
Mkt: George Pyne

NASCAR Craftsman Truck Series
PO Box 66518
Scotts Valley, CA 95067
T: (408) 438-3392
F: (408) 438-7173
Media: Owen Kearns, Jr.

National Hot Rod Association (NHRA)
2035 Financial Way
PO Box 5555
Glendora, CA 91741
T: (626) 914-4761
F: (626) 914-1491
www.nhra.com
P: Dallas Gardner
PR: Jim Edmunds

National Sprint Car Hall of Fame & Museum
PO Box 542
One Sprint Capital Place
Knoxville, IA 50138
T: (515) 842-6176
F: (515) 842-6177
www.knoxvilleiowa.com
Exec. Dir: Thomas Schmeh

National Street Rod Association (NSRA)
4030 Park Avenue
Memphis, TN 38111
T: (901) 452-4030
P: Vernon Walker

National Tractor Pullers Association/
6969 Worthington-Galena Rd.
Suite J
Worthington, OH 43085
T: (614) 436-1761
F: (614) 436-0964
P: David Schreier

North American Swamp Racing Association
100 Mesa Park Blvd.
Fellsmere, FL 32948
T: (877) 466-2772
F: (561) 571-1008
www.nasra.com
Oper: Matthew Graney

Pikes Peak Auto Hill Climb Museum
135 Manitou Avenue
Manitou Springs, CO 80829
T: (719) 685-5996
F: (719) 685-5885
www.motorcity.com/pphc
E: ppihc@ppihc.com
Exec Dir: Nick Sanborn

Professional Sportscar Racing, Inc.
3502 Henderson Blvd.
Tampa, FL 33679
T: (813) 877-4672
F: (813) 876-4604
www.professionalsportscar.com
P: Mike Gue
Mkt: Bob Holland

Race Car Club of America
166 Elm Street
New Rochelle, NY 10805
T: (914) 576-RCCA
F: (914) 235-0081
E: rccahdq@aol.com
P: A.J. Pugliese

**SCORE International
Off-Road Racing Association**
23961 Craftsman Rd., Suite A
Calabasas, CA 91302
T: (818) 225-8402
F: (818) 225-8102
www.score-international.com
P: Sal Fish

**Short Course Off-Road
Drivers Association (SODA)**
7839 W. North Avenue
Wauwatosa, WI 53213
T: (414) 453-SODA
P: Terry Wolfe

Sports Car Club of America
9033 E. Easter Place
Englewood, CO 80112
T: (303) 694-7222
F: (303) 694-7391
www.scca.org
P: Nicholas Craw

**Sportscar Vintage
Racing Association**
1 Maple Street
Hanover, NH 03755
T: (603) 640-6161
F: (603) 640-6130
P: Frank Rupp

United Dirt Track Racing Assn.
PO Box 2300
Woodstock, GA 30188
T: (770) 516-6717
F: (770) 924-1340
www.havatamparacing.com
P: Mike Swims

**United Drag Racers
Association**
7601 Hamilton Avenue
Burr Ridge, IL 60521
T: (630) 887-0442
F: (630) 887-0443
P: Jack Thomas

United States Auto Club
4910 W. 16th Street
Speedway, IN 46224
T: (317) 247-5151
F: (317) 247-0123
P: John Capels
PR: Dick Jordan

U.S. Hot Rod Association
477 E. Butterfield Rd., Suite 400
Lombard, IL 60148
T: (630) 963-4810
F: (630) 963-5649
P: Charley Mancuso
*Monster Trucks, Mud racing &
Tractor pulling Events*

World Karting Association
5725D Hwy 29 N.
Harrisburg, NC 28075
T: (704) 455-1606
F: (704) 455-1609
P: Randy Kugler

World of Outlaws
624 Krona Drive
Suite 115
Plano, TX 75074
T: (972) 424-2202
F: (972) 423-3930
www.goracing.com/outlaws/
P: Ted Johnson
PR: Richard Day

World Pulling International
6969 Worthington-Galena Rd.
Suite J
Worthington, OH 43085
T: (614) 436-1761
F: (614) 436-0964
P: David Schreier

Motorsports Publications

American Rider
601 Carlson Pkwy., Suite 600
Minnetonka, MN 55305
T: (612) 476-2200
F: (612) 476-8065
Editor: Buzz Buzzelli

Automobile Magazine
120 E. Liberty Street
Ann Arbor, MI 48104
T: (313) 994-3500
F: (313) 994-1153
www.automobilemag.com
Editor: David Davis, Jr.

Auto Racing Business
PO Box 218
Atlantic, VA 23303
T: (757) 824-3942
F: (757) 824-4480
Editor: Charles Cuttone

Autoweek
1400 Woodbridge
Detroit, MI 48207
T: (313) 446-6000
F: (313) 446-0347
www.autoweek.com
Publisher: Leon Mandel

Auto Racing Digest
990 Grove Street
Evanston, IL 60201
T: (847) 491-6440
F: (847) 491-0867
Publisher: Norm Jacobs

Beckett Racing Monthly
15850 Dallas Parkway
Dallas, TX 75248
T: (972) 991-6657
F: (972) 233-6488
www.beckett.com

Car & Driver
2002 Hogback Road
Ann Arbor, MI 48106
T: (313) 971-3600
F: (313) 971-9188
Publisher: William Jeanes

Circle Track & Racing Tech.
4 Wheel & Off-Road
Hot Rod
Inside Racing
Motor Trend Magazine
Mustang & Fords
Sport Truck
Motorcyclist
Dirt Rider
Petersen Publishing Company
6420 Wilshire Blvd.
Los Angeles, CA 90048
T: (213) 782-2000
F: (213) 782-2263

Cycle World
Road & Track
1499 Monrovia Avenue
Newport Beach, CA 92663
T: (949) 720-5300
F: (949) 631-2757
Editor: Tom Bryant

Indy Car Racing Magazine
1933 Southwest Ave.
Waukesha, WI 53186
T: (414) 896-9229
F: (414) 896-9203
www.icr.com
Publisher: Debbie Wicker

NASCAR News
1801 W. Int'l. Speedway Blvd.
Daytona Beach, FL 32114
T: (904) 253-0611
F: (904) 252-8804

NASCAR Yearbook
PO Box 30036
Charlotte, NC 28230
T: (800) 357-6584
T: (704) 374-0420
F: (704) 374-0729
Publisher: Ivan Motherhead

National Dragster
PO Box 5555
Glendora, CA 91740
T: (626) 963-8475
F: (626) 335-4307
E: ndrag@ix.netcom.com

National Speed Sport News
6508 Hudspeth Road
Harrisburg, NC 28075
T: (704) 455-2531
F: (704) 455-2605
Editor: Chris Economaki

Off-Road Advertiser
PO Box 1154
Arcata, CA 95518
T: (707) 822-8508

Off-Road Magazine
Popular Hot Rodding
Street Rodder
774 S. Placentia Avenue
Placentia, CA 92670
T: (714) 572-2255
F: (714) 572-1864
Editor: Tom Vogele

Old Cars Weekly News & Marketplace
700 E. State Street
Iola, WI 54990
T: (715) 445-2214
F: (715) 445-3087

Open Road
PO Box 1757
Newport Beach, CA 92663
T: (949) 720-5394
F: (949) 631-2757

Open Wheel Magazine
Stock Car Racing
Drag Racing
65 Parker Street, Suite 2
Newburyport, MA 01950
T: (978) 463-3787
F: (978) 463-3250
Publisher: James Martise

Racer
Sports Car
1371 E. Warner Ave., Suite E
Tustin, CA 92780
T: (800) 999-9718
T: (714) 259-8240
F: (714) 259-8556
Publisher: Bill Sparks

Short Track Racing
PO Box 1058
Acworth, GA 30101
T: (770) 917-1660
Publisher: Mark Lutes

Winston Cup Scene
Winston Cup Illustrated
128 S. Tryon St., Suite 2275
Charlotte, NC 28202
T: (800) 883-7323
T: (704) 371-3966
F: (704) 371-3990
Publisher: Steve Waid

Speedways

The following is a list of speedways that are part of the CART, NASCAR (Winston Cup & Busch series) & IRL.

Atlanta Motor Speedway
PO Box 500
Hampton, GA 30228
T: (770) 946-3950
F: (770) 946-3939
GM: Ed Clark
Location: Hwy 19 & 41

Bristol International Raceway
PO Box 3966
Bristol, TN 37625
T: (423) 764-1161
F: (423) 764-1646
GM: Jeff Byrd
Location: Hwy 11 East

California Speedway
9300 Cherry Avenue
Fontana, CA 92335
T: (909) 428-9300
F: (909) 429-5500

Charlotte Motor Speedway
PO Box 600
Concord, NC 28026
T: (704) 455-3200
F: (704) 455-2547
www.charlottemotorspeedway.com
GM: H.A. Wheeler
Location: U.S. Hwy 29 North

Darlington Raceway
PO Box 500
1301 Harry Byrd Hwy.
Darlington, SC 29532
T: (803) 395-8499
F: (803) 393-3911
www.daytonausa.com/dr
P: Jim Hunter
Location: Bobo Newsome Hwy.

Daytona International Speedway
PO Box 2801
1801 W. Int'l Speedway Blvd.
Daytona Beach, FL 32114
T: (904) 254-2700
F: (904) 254-6791
www.daytonausa.com
P: John Graham
Location: International Speedway Blvd.

Dover Downs International Speedway
PO Box 843
Dover, DE 19903
T: (302) 674-4600
F: (302) 734-3124
GM: John Dawson
Location: 1131 N. Dupont Hwy.

Hickory Motor Speedway
1234 S. Center Street
Hickory, NC 28602
T: (704) 464-3655
F: (704) 465-5017
GM: Bob Friedman

Homestead-Miami Speedway
One Speedway Blvd.
Homestead, FL 33035
T: (305) 230-5000
F: (305) 230-5223
Oper: Al Garcia

Indianapolis Motor Speedway
4790 W. 16th Street
Speedway, IN 46222
T: (317) 481-8500
F: (317) 248-6759
www.brickyard.com
P: Anton George

Martinsville Speedway
PO Box 3311
Martinsville, VA 24115
T: (540) 956-3151
F: (540) 956-2820
www.martinsvillespeedway.com
GM: W. Clay Campbell
Location: U.S. 220 South

Michigan International Speedway
12626 U.S. 12
Brooklyn, MI 49230
T: (517) 592-6666
F: (517) 592-3848
P: Gene Haskett

Milwaukee Mile
7722 W. Greenfield Ave.
West Allis, WI 53214
T: (414) 453-8277
F: (414) 453-9920
www.milmile.com/races
GM: James Melvin
Location: WI State Fair Speedway

Myrtle Beach Speedway
4300 Highway 501
Myrtle Beach, SC 29577
T: (803) 236-0500
F: (803) 236-0525
GM: Roy Gore

Nashville Speedway USA
PO Box 101585
Nashville, TN 37224
T: (615) 726-1818

Nazareth Speedway
PO Drawer F
Route 191
Nazareth, PA 18064
T: (610) 759-8000
F: (610) 759-9055
GM: Scott Atherton

New Hampshire International Speedway
PO Box 7888
Loudon, NH 03301
T: (603) 783-4744
F: (603) 783-9691
www.nhis.com
P: Gary Bahre
Location: Route 106 North

North Carolina Motor Speedway
PO Box 500
Rockingham, NC 28379
T: (910) 582-2861
F: (910) 582-3324
www.penske.com
GM: Chris Browning
Location: 2152 U.S. Hwy 1 North

North Wilkesboro Speedway
PO Box 500
Winston-Salem, NC 27102
T: (910) 724-7932
F: (910) 722-3757
Location: Speedway Road

Phoenix International Raceway
PO Box 13088
Phoenix, AZ 85002
T: (602) 252-3833
F: (602) 254-4622
P: Emmett Jobe
Location: 7602 S. 115th Ave.
Tolleson, AZ

Pocono International Raceway
PO Box 500
Long Pond, PA 18334
T: (717) 646-2300
F: (717) 646-2010
CEO: Dr. Joseph Mattioli
Location: Long Pond Road

Richmond International Raceway
PO Box 9257
Richmond, VA 23227
T: (804) 329-6811
F: (804) 329-5029
GM: Paul Sawyer
Location: 602 E. Laburnum Ave.

Road Atlanta
5300 Winder Highway
Braselton, GA 30517
T: (770) 967-6143
F: (770) 967-2668
www.roadatlanta.com
P: James Kandy

Sanair International Raceway
669 Petit Rang St. Francois
St. Pie, Quebec J0H 1W0
T: (514) 772-2426
F: (514) 772-2236
GM: Jacques Guertin

Sears Point Raceway
Highways 37 & 121
Sonoma, CA 95476
T: (800) 870-RACE
T: (707) 938-8448
F: (707) 938-8430
www.searspoint.com
GM: Steve Page

Sebring International Raceway
113 Midway Drive
Sebring, FL 33870
T: (941) 655-1442
F: (941) 655-1777
Director: Tres Stephenson

South Boston Speedway
PO Box 759
South Boston, VA 24592
T: (804) 572-4947
F: (804) 572-2203
Location: Hwy 360 East

Talladega Superspeedway
PO Box 777
Talladega, AL 35161
T: (256) 362-2261
F: (256) 761-4777
www.daytonausa.com
P: Grant Lynch
Location: 3366 Speedway Blvd.

Texas Motor Speedway
PO Box 500
Fort Worth, TX 76101
T: (817) 215-8500
F: (817) 491-3749
GM: Eddie Gossage
Location: 3601 Hwy 114, Fort Worth

Watkins Glen International
PO Box 500
Watkins Glen, NY 14891
T: (607) 535-2486
F: (607) 535-7508
www.theglen.com
E: racing@theglen.com
GM: Tim Coleman
Location: 500 County Road 16

Race Circuits

The following is a list of race circuits.

Autodromo Internacional Nelson Piquet
Av. Embaixador Abelardo Bueno S/N
Jacarepagua, Rio de Janiero, Brasil
T: (55.2) 441-1493
F: (55.2) 441-1338
Event: CART Rio 400

Grand Prix of Cleveland
One Erieview Plaza
Suite 1300
Cleveland, OH 44114
T: (216) 781-3500
F: (216) 522-1145
Location: Burke Lakefront Airport
Event: CART Fed Ex Series

Detroit Grand Prix
300 River Place, Suite 2600
Detroit, MI 48207
T: (313) 393-7749
F: (313) 393-9454
www.grandprix.com
P: H. Kent Stanner
Location: Raceway on Belle Isle Park, temporary road course.
Event: CART Fed Ex Series

Laguna Seca Raceway
PO Box 2078
Monterey, CA 93942
T: (800) 327-SECA
T: (831) 648-5111
F: (831) 373-0533
www.laguna-secca.com
GM: John Stornetta
Event: CART Grand Prix of Monterey

Las Vegas Motor Speedway
7000 Las Vegas Blvd. South
Las Vegas, NV 89109
T: (702) 644-4444
F: (702) 644-7774
P: Ritchie Clyne
www.lvmss.com
E: *media@lvms.com*
Event: IRL Vegas 500 km, NASCAR

Lime Rock Park
497 Lime Rock Road
Lakeville, CT 06039
T: (860) 435-2571
F: (860) 435-4010
GM: Michael Rand

Long Beach Grand Prix
3000 Pacific Avenue
Long Beach, CA 90806
T: (562) 981-2600
F: (562) 981-2616
P: Chris Pook
Event: CART Long Beach Grand Prix

Mid-Ohio Sports Car Course
PO Box 3108
Steam Corners Road
Lexington, OH 44904
T: (419) 884-4000
F: (419) 884-0042
P: Michelle Trueman-Gajoch

Mosport
3233 Concession Rd., #10
RR #5
Bowmanville, Ontario L1C 3K6
T: (905) 983-9141
F: (905) 983-5195
P: Jim Selwa

Pikes Peak International Raceway
16650 Midway Ranch Road
Fountain, CO 80817
T: (719) 382-7223
F: (719) 382-9180
Event: IRL

Portland International Raceway
1940 N. Victory Blvd.
Portland, OR 97217
T: (503) 285-6635
F: (503) 285-0363
GM: Dale La Follette
Event: CART 200

Road America
N7390 Hwy 67
Elkhart Lake, WI 53020
T: (414) 892-4576
F: (414) 892-4550
www.roadamerica.com
E: info@roadamerica.com
GM: Jim Haynes
Event: CART 200

Surfers Paradise
Level 5
64 Marine Parade
Southport, Queensland
4217 Australia
T: (61.7) 5588.6800
F: (61.7) 5588.6899

Texas Motor Raceway
2421 Westport Pkwy., Suite 500
Fort Worth, TX 76177
T: (817) 226-7223
F: (817) 224-9093
P: Bruton Smith

**Molson Indy Toronto
Grand Prix**
175 Bloor Street East
North Tower, Suite 1500
Toronto, Ontario M4W 3R8
T: (416) 975-8000
F: (416) 975-1678
Event: CART Toronto Grand Prix

Molson Indy Vancouver
765 Pacific Blvd. South
Vancouver, B.C. V6B 4Y9
T: (604) 684-4639
F: (604) 684-1482
Event: CART Indy Vancouver

Walt Disney Speedway
PO Box 10000
Lake Buena Vista, FL 32830
T: (407) 363-6158
F: (407) 363-6160
Motorsprts Mgr.: Michael Waggoner
Events: IRL, NASCAR Truck Series

**Willow Springs International
Motorsports Park**
PO Box X
3500 75th Street West
Rosamond, CA 93560
T: (661) 256-2471
F: (661) 256-9140
GM: Stephanie Huth

NHRA Raceways

Atlanta Dragway
500 E. Ridgeway Road
Commerce, GA 30529
T: (706) 335-2301
F: (706) 335-7135
GM: Dennis Robarge

Bandimere Speedway
3051 S. Rooney Road
Morrison, CO 80465
T: (303) 697-6001

**Brainerd International
Raceway**
4343 Highway 371
Brainerd, MN 56401
T: (612) 475-1500
F: (612) 475-2149
GM: Richard Roe

**Firebird International
Raceway**
20000 Maricopa Road
Chandler, AZ 85224
T: (602) 268-0200
GM: Charles Allen

Gainesville Raceway
11211 N. CountyRoad 225
Gainesville, FL 32601
T: (352) 337-0046

Heartland Park Topeka
750 SW Topeka Blvd.
Topeka, KS 66603
T: (785) 862-4781
F: (785) 862-2016
P: Bill Kentling

Houston Raceway Park
2525 FM 565 South
Baytown, TX 77520
T: (281) 383-2666
F: (281) 383-3777
GM: Gerald Critchfield

Indianapolis Raceway Park
9901 Crawfordsville Road
Clermont, IN 46119
T: (317) 293-RACE
F: (317) 291-4220
GM: Mike Lewis

Maple Grove Raceway
R.D. 3, Box 3420
Mohnton, PA 19540
T: (610) 856-7200

**Memphis International
Motorsports Park**
5500 Taylor-Forge Drive
Millington, TN 38053
T: (901) 358-7223

National Trail Raceway
2650 National Blvd. SW
Hebron, OH 43025
T: (614) 928-5706
F: (614) 928-2922
GM: Aaron Polburn

**Old Bridge Township
Raceway Park**
230 Pension Road
Englishtown, NJ 07726
T: (732) 446-7800

Pomona Raceway
2780 Fairplex Drive
Pomona, CA 91766
T: (909) 623-9222

Rockingham Dragway
U.S. Highway 1 North
Rockingham, NC 28379
T: (910) 582-3400

Seattle International Raceway
31001 144th Avenue NE
Kent, WA 98042
T: (253) 631-1550
F: (253) 630-0888
GM: Jim Rockstad

Texas Motorplex
7500 W. Highway 287
Ennis, TX 75119
T: (972) 878-2641
F: (972) 878-1848
GM: Ryan Haas

Virginia Motorsports Park
8018 Boydton Plank Road
Petersburg, VA 23803
T: (804) 862-3174

Orienteering

U.S. Orienteering Federation
PO Box 1444
Forest Park, GA 30051
T/F: (404) 363-2110
E: jonnash@juno.com
P: Rick Worner
PR: Jon Nash

Paddle/Racquet Sports

American Paddle Association
PO Box 132049
Houston, TX 77219
T/F: (713) 680-1082
www.paddleamerica.com
P: Ed Thompson

U.S. Paddle Tennis
PO Box 49882
Los Angeles, CA 90049
T: (310) 826-3240
F: (310) 826-1615
P: Erin Henenway

American Platform Tennis
26 Park Street
Montclair, NJ 07042
T: (973) 744-1190
F: (973) 744-3290
Exec. Dir: Gina Ohlmuller

U.S. Racquetball Association
1685 W. Uintah
Colorado Springs, CO 80904
T: (719) 635-5396
F: (719) 635-0685
www.usra.org
Exec. Dir: Luke St. Onge

U.S. Squash Racquets Association
PO Box 1216
Bala Cynwyd, PA 19004
T: (610) 667-4006
F: (610) 667-6539
www.us-squash.org/squash
E: ussquash@us-squash.org
P: Andre Naniche

USA Table Tennis
One Olympic Plaza
Colorado Springs, CO 80909
T: (719) 578-4583
F: (719) 632-6071
www.usatt.org
E: usatt@usa.net
P: Terry Timmins

Polo

National Museum of Polo & Hall of Fame
9011 Lake Worth Road
Lake Worth, FL 33467
T: (407) 969-3210
F: (407) 964-8299
Exec. Dir: George DuPont, Jr.

United States Polo Association
4059 Iron Works Pike
Lexington, KY 40511
T: (606) 255-0593
F: (606) 231-9738
E: uspalexky@aol.com
Exec Dir: George Alexander, Jr.

U.S. Arena Polo League
Los Angeles Equestrian Center
480 Riverside Drive at Main
Burbank, CA 91503
T: (818) 840-9063

Polo Publications

Polo Magazine
3500 Fairlane Farms road
Suite 9
Wellington, FL 33414
T: (407) 793-9524
F: (407) 793-9576
Editor: Peter Rizzo

Rodeo

International Pro Rodeo Assn.
2304 Exchange Avenue
Oklahoma City, OK 73148
T: (405) 235-6540
F: (405) 235-6577
www.intprorodeo.com
Exec. Dir: Ronnie Williams

**National High School
Rodeo Association**
11178 N. Huron Street
Suite 7
Denver, CO 80234
T: (303) 452-0820
F: (303) 452-0912
P: Ken Norris

**National Intercollegiate
Rodeo Association**
2316 Eastgate N., Suite 160
Walla Walla, WA 99362
T: (509) 529-4402
F: (509) 525-1090
www.nira@tsln.com
E: nira@erni.net
Exec. Dir: Tim Corfield

**National Little Britches
Rodeo Association**
1045 W. Rio Grande
Colorado Springs, CO 80906
T: (719) 389-0333
F: (719) 578-1367
www.nlbra.org
GM: Bob Simpson

Pro Rodeo Cowboys Assn.
101 Pro Rodeo Drive
Colorado Springs, CO 80919
T: (719) 593-8840
F: (719) 548-4876
www.prorodeo.com
P: Lewis Cryer
Comm: Steven Hatchell
PR: Steve Fleming

Rodeo Publications

Pro Rodeo News
101 Pro Rodeo Drive
Colorado Springs, CO 80919
T: (719) 593-8840
F: (719) 548-4876
www.prorodeo.com
Editor: Steve Fleming

Roller Skating

**Federation of International
Roller-Skating**
Rambla Catalunya 121
piso 6, Puerta 7
Barcelona, Spain
T: (34.93) 237.70.55
F: 34.93) 237.27.33
www.firs.org
E: firs@idgrup.ibernet.com
P: Isidro Oliveras

USA Roller Skating
PO Box 6579
4730 South Street
Lincoln, NE 68506
T: (402) 483-7551
F: (402) 483-1465
www.usacrs.com
E: sk8SID@aol.com
P: Betty Ann Danna

Roller Skating Assn. Int'l.
6905 Corporate Drive
Indianapolis, IN 46278
T: (317) 347-2626
F: (317) 347-2636
www.rollerskating.org
Exec. Dir: Katherine McDonnell

Rowing

National Rowing Foundation
67 Mystic Road
North Stonington, CT 06359
T: (860) 535-0634
F: (860) 535-0637
www.rowing.org
P: Michael Meahan

U.S. Rowing
Pan American Plaza, Suite 400
201 S. Capitol Avenue
Indianapolis, IN 46225
T: (317) 237-5656
F: (317) 237-5646
www.coxing.com/usrowing/html
E: usrowing@aol.com
Exec. Dir: Frank Coyle
Publication: U.S. Rowing
Editor: Maureen Merchoff

Rugby

Federation of International Amateur Rugby
9 Rue de Liege
75009 Paris, France
T: (33.1) 42 81 00 04
F: (33.1) 45 26 19 19
P: Albert Ferrasse

International Rugby Football Board
Huguenot House
35/38 St. Stephen's Green
Dublin 2, Ireland
T: (353.1) 662 54 44
F: (353.1) 676 93 34
www.irfb.com
P: Vernon Pugh

USA Rugby Union
3595 E. Fountain Blvd.
Colorado Springs, CO 80910
T: (719) 637-1022
F: (719) 637-1315
www.usarugby.org
P: Ann Barry

Canadian Rugby Union
1600 James Naismith Drive
Gloucester, Ontario K1B 5N4
T: (613) 748-5657
Exec. Dir: John Billingsley

Midwest Rugby Football Union
814 N. Beatty Street
Pittsburgh, PA 15205
T: (412) 362-3655
F: (412) 256-1348
P: Tom manion

Pacific Coast Rugby Football Union
2601 E. Kleindale
Tucson, AZ 85716
T: (520) 621-8301
F: (520) 621-9030
P: Titus Purdin

USA Rugby-East
2312 Hillbeck
Columbia, SC 29210
T: (803) 798-2137
P: Jim Cross

U.S. Rugby Football Foundation
One Beacon Street
Boston, MA 02108
T: (617) 742-1510
F: (617) 431-0233
Exec. Dir: Alex von Lichtenberg

Rugby Publications

Rugby
2350 Broadway, Suite 220
New York, NY 10024
T: (212) 787-1160
F: (212) 595-0934
E: rugbymag@aol.com
Publisher: Ed Hagerty

Running

**Association of International
Marathon & Road Races (AIMS)**
Silver Screen House
4 Elliot Place
Glasgow G3 8EP, Scotland
T: (44.141) 221 03 42
F: (44.141) 221 54 59

**All American Trail Running
Association**
PO Box 9175
Colorado Springs, CO 80932
T: (719) 633-9740
F: (719) 633-3397
www.trailrunner.com
Exec. Dir: Nancy Hobbs

**American Running & Fitness
Association**
4405 E. West Hwy., Suite 405
Bethesda, MD 20814
T: (301) 913-9517
Exec. Dir: Susan Kalish

**Association of Road Racing
Athletes**
PO Box 21021
Spokane, WA 99201
T: (509) 838-8784
P: Don Kardong

**Road Runners Club
of America**
1150 S. Washington St.
Suite 250
Alexandria, VA 22314
T: (703) 836-0558
F: (703) 836-4430
www.rrca.org
Exec. Dir: Henley Gabeau

Major Marathons

B.A.A. Boston Marathon
131 Clarendon Street
Boston, MA 02116
T: (617) 236-1652
F: (617) 236-4505
www.bostonmarathon.org
E: mile27@baa.org
Director: Guy Morse

Chicago Marathon
900 W. Jackson, Suite 8W
Chicago, IL 60607
T: (312) 243-0003
F: (312) 243-5652
P: Carey Pinkowski

Los Angeles Marathon, Inc.
11110 W. Ohio Avenue
Suite 100
Los Angeles, CA 90025
T: (310) 444-5544
F: (310) 473-8105
www.LAMarathon.com
E: raceinfo@lamarathon.com
P: Dr. William Burke

New York City Marathon
NY Roadrunners Club
9 E. 89th Street
New York, NY 10128
T: (212) 860-4455
F: (212) 860-9754
www.NYrrc.org
P: Allan Steinfield

Running Publications

American Runner
137 Clinton Avenue
New Rochelle, NY 10801
T: (914) 576-6715
F: (914) 576-0971

BAA Boston Marathon Magazine
126 Brookline Avenue
Boston, MA 02215
T: (617) 859-3217
F: (617) 536-1463

Runner's World
33 E. Minor Street
Emmaus. PA 18098
T: (610) 967-5171
F: (610) 967-7725
www.runnersworld.com
E: rwedit@rodalepress.com
Publisher: George Hirsch
*Click on calendars for daily
updates for marathon dates.*

Running & Fitness
4405 E. West Hwy., Suite 405
Bethesda, MD 20814
T: (301) 913-9517
F: (301) 913-9520
Editor: Susan Kalish

The Running Network
833 Eastwind Drive
Westerville, OH 43081
T: (614) 823-7150
F: (614) 823-7152
www.runningnetwork.com

Running Times
98 N. Washington Street
Boston, MA 02114
T: (617) 367-2228
F: (617) 367-2350
Publisher: Carol Lasseter

The Walking Magazine
9-11 Harcourt Street
Boston, MA 02116
T: (617) 266-3322
F: (617) 266-7373
E: walknet@aol.com
Publisher: Kevin Weafer

Scuba Diving/ Underwater Swim

Confederation Mondiale des Activites Subaquatiques (CMAS)
Viale Tiziano 74
00196 Rome, Italy
T: (39.6) 36 85 84 80
F: (39.6) 36 85 84 90
P: Achille Ferrero

National Association of Underwater Instructors
PO Box 14650
Montclair, CA 91763
T: (909) 621-5801
F: (909) 621-6405
www.naui.org
P: James Bram

Professional Association of Diving Instructors (PADI)
1251 E. Dyer Rd., Suite 100
Santa Ana, CA 92705
T: (714) 540-7234
F: (714) 540-2609
CEO: John Cronin

Underwater Society of America
164 N. Bascom Avenue
San Jose, CA 95128
T: (408) 286-8840
F: (408) 294-3496
E: usafin@aol.com
P: Michael Gower
PR: Carol Rose

Subaquatic Publications

Canadian Diver
Diver Magazine
10995 Shellbridge Way #295
Richmond, B.C. V6X 3C6
T: (604) 274-4333
F: (604) 274-4366

Dive Training
1200 S. Federal Hwy., #301
Boynton Beach, FL 33435
T: (407) 731-4321
F: (407) 369-5882

Rodale's Scuba Diving
6600 Abercorn St., Suite 208
Savannah, GA 31405
T: (912) 351-0855
F: (912) 351-0735
Publisher: David McAfee

Scuba Times
14110 Perdido Key Drive
Suite P-2
Pensacola, FL 32507
T: (850) 492-7805
F: (850) 492-7807
www.scubatimes.com
Publisher: Fred Garth

Skin Diver Magazine
6420 Wilshire Blvd.
Los Angeles, CA 90048
T: (213) 782-2960
F: (213) 782-2121
Publisher: Petersen Publishing
Editor: Bill Gleasen

Sport Diver Magazine
330 W. Canton
Winter Park, FL 32789
T: (407) 628-4802
F: (407) 628-7061
Publisher: Terry Snow

The Undersea Journal
1251 E. Dyer Rd., #100
Santa Ana, CA 92705
T: (714) 540-7234
F: (714) 540-2609

Shooting

National Rifle Association
11250 Waples Mill Road
Fairfax, VA 22030
T: (703) 267-1316
F: (703) 267-3800
www.nra.org
Exec Dir: Craig Sander

National Shooting Sport Foundation
11 Mile Hill Road
Newtown, CT 06470
T: (203) 426-1320
F: (203) 426-1087
www.nssf.org
E: nssfinfo@i84.net
P: Robert Delfay

National Skeet Shooting Association
National Sporting Clays Association
5931 Roft Road
San Antonio, TX 78253
T: (210) 688-3371
F: (210) 688-3014
nssa.nsca.hdqtrs@internetMCI.com
Exec Dir: Mike Hampton

Trapshooting Hall of Fame & Museum
601 W. National Road
Vandalia, OH 45377
T: (937) 898-1945
F: (937) 898-5472
Director: Majorie Smith
Curator: Millie Link

Shooting Publications

American Hunter
American Rifleman
11250 Waples Mill Road
Fairfax, VA 22030
T: (703) 267-1316
F: (703) 267-3971
Editor: John Zent

Skeet Shooting Review
5931 Roft Road
San Antonio, TX 78253
T: (210) 688-3371
F: (210) 688-3014
Editor: Susue Fluckiger

Sporting Clays
5211 S. Washington Avenue
Titusville, FL 32780
T: (407) 268-5010
F: (407) 269-2025
Editor: George Conrad

Trap & Field Magazine
1200 Waterway Blvd.
Indianapolis, IN 46202
T: (317) 633-8800
F: (317) 264-2192
Editor: Bonnie Nash

Softball

Amateur Softball Association
USA Softball & National Softball Hall of Fame & Museum
2801 NE 50th Street
Oklahoma City, OK 73111
T: (405) 424-5266
F: (405) 424-3855
www.softball.org
E: rbabb@softball.org
Exec. Dir: Ron Radigonola
PR: Ronald Babb

Cinderella Softball Association
PO Box 1411
Corning, NY 14830
T: (607) 937-5469
P: Sandie Celelli

International Softball Congress
6007 E. Hillcrest Circle
Anaheim Hills, CA 92807
T: (714) 998-5694
F: (714) 282-7902
www.fastpitch-softball.com
Exec. Dir: Milt Stark

International Softball Assn.
2801 NE 50th Street
Oklahoma City, OK 73111
T: (405) 879-2004
F: (405) 879-9801
www.softball.org
E: isfsoftball@aol.com
Exec. Dir: Don Porter

National Softball Assn.
PO Box 7
Nicholasville, KY 40356
T: (606) 887-4114
F: (606) 887-4874
E: nsahdqtrs@aol.com
Exec. Dir: Hugh Cantrell

Pro Beach Softball Assn.
821 Ensenada Court
San Diego, CA 92109
T: (619) 294-4685
Oper: Dale Olson

Softball Canada
1600 James Naismith Drive
Gloucester, Ontario K1B 5N4
T: (613) 748-5668
F: (613) 748-5760
www.softball.ca
E: softblca@sprynet.com
P: Dale McMann

U.S. Slo-Pitch Softball Assn.
& Hall of Fame Museum
PO Box 2047
3935 S. Crater Road
Petersburg, VA 23805
T: (804) 732-4099
F: (804) 732-1704
www.usssa.com
E: usssahq@aol.com
Exec. Dir: Al Ramsey

Softball Publications

Balls & Strikes Softball
2801 NE 50th Street
Oklahoma City, OK 73111
T: (405) 424-5266
F: (405) 424-3855
Editor: Ronald Babb

Beach Softball Magazine
821 Ensenada Court
San Diego, CA 92109
T: (619) 294-4685

Fastpitch World
318 North Avenue
St. Charles, IL 60174
T: (630) 377-7917
F: (630) 377-3681
Editor: Julie Olsen

Let's Play Softball
2721 E. 42nd Street
Minneapolis, MN 55406
T: (612) 729-0023
F: (612) 729-0259
Publisher: Doug Johnson

The Slo-Pitch Game
PO Box 2047
Petersburg, VA 23805
T: (804) 732-4099
F: (804) 732-1704

Slo-Pitch News
13540 Lake City Way NE
Suite 3
Seattle, WA 98125
T: (206) 367-2420
F: (206) 367-2636
Publisher: Ozzie Boyle

Softball World
PO Box 10151
Oakland, CA 94610
T: (510) 428-2000
Publisher: George Epstein

Sports Acrobatics

United States Sports Acrobatics Federation
PO Box 41356
Sacramento, CA 95841
T: (916) 488-9499
F: (916) 488-9497
P: Tonya Case-Patterson

**International Federation
of Sports Acrobatics (FISA)**
75 Blvd. Vassil Levski
1040 Sofia, Bulgaria
T: (359.2) 86 54 83
F: (359.2) 980 09 13
P: Stoil Sotirov

Squash

National Squash Tennis Assn.
Yale Club
50 Vanderbilt Avenue
New York, NY 10017
T: (212) 661-2070
P: Gary Squires

Squash Canada
1600 James Naismith Drive
Gloucester, Ontario K1B 5N4
T: (613) 748-5672
F: (613) 748-5861
www.squash.ca
E: squash.canada@bpg.ca
P: Jim McAuliffe

**U.S. Squash Racquets
Association**
PO Box 1216
Bala Cynwyd, PA 19004
T: (610) 667-4006
F: (610) 667-6539
www.us-squash.org/squash
P: Andre Naniche

**World Professional
Squash Association**
56 Spooner Road
Chestnut Hill, MA 02167
T: (617) 731-6874
F: (617) 277-1457
E: psjn@aol.com
Exec. Dir: John Nimick

World Squash Federation
6 Havelock Road
Hastings, East Sussex
TN34 1BP, England
T: (44.1424) 42 92 45
F: (44.1424) 42 92 50
www.squash.org
E: squash@wsf.cablenet.co.uk
P: Susie Simcock

Squash Publications

Squash News
186 Arcadia road
Hope Valley, RI 02832
T: (401) 539-2381
F: (401) 539-2490
Publisher: Tom Jones

Surfing

**Association of Surfing
Professionals**
17942 Sky Park Circle
Suite 4401
Irvine, CA 92611
T: (949) 851-2774
F: (949) 851-2773
www.aspworldtour.com
E: aspintl@earthlink.net
Exec. Dir: Graham Stapelberg

**International Surfing
Association**
5580 La Jolla Blvd., Suite 145
La Jolla, CA 92037
T: (619) 514-3606
F: (619) 514-3620
www.isasurf.org
E: surf@isasurf.org
P: Fernando Aguerre

**International Surfing
Hall of Fame**
5580 La Jolla Blvd., Suite 373
La Jolla, CA 92037
T: (619) 755-5339
Director: Bobby Thomas

**Professional Surfing
Association of America**
530 Sixth Street
Hermosa Beach, CA 90254
T: (310) 372-0414
F: (310) 372-7457
Director: Ron Meistrell

U.S. Surfing Federation
350 Jericho Street
Jericho, NY 11753
T: (516) 935-0400
F: (516) 935-0238
Exec. Dir: Michael Angiulo

**Women's International
Surfing Association**
3202 Silver Spur Road
San Juan Capistrano, CA 92675
T: (949) 493-2591
Exec. Dir: Mary Lou Drummy

Surfing Publications

Surfer Magazine
33046 Calle Aviador
San Juan Capistrano, CA 92675
T: (949) 496-5922
F: (949) 496-7849
www.surfer.com
Editor: Steve Hawk

Surfing
PO Box 3010
950 Calle Amanecer
San Clemente, CA 92672
T: (949) 492-7873
F: (949) 498-6485
Editor: Nick Carroll

Swimming/Diving

**Federation Internationale
de Natation Amateur (FINA)**
Ave. de Beaumont 9
Rez-de-Chaussee
1012 Lausanne, Switzerland
T: (41.21) 312 66 02
F: (41.21) 312 66 10
P: Mustapha Larfaoui
Sec. Gen: Gunnar Werner

United States Diving Inc.
Pan American Plaza, Ste 430
201 S. Capitol Avenue
Indianapolis, IN 46225
T: (317) 237-5252
F: (317) 237-5257
Exec. Dir: Todd Smith

U.S. Swimming Inc.
One Olympic Plaza
Colorado Springs, CO 80909
T: (719) 578-4578
F: (719) 578-4669
www.usswim.org
Exec. Dir: Chuck Wielgus

**U.S. Syncronized
Swimming, Inc.**
Pan American Plaza, Ste 510
201 S. Capitol Avenue
Indianapolis, IN 46225
T: (317) 237-5700
F: (317) 237-5705
www.synchro-usa.org
Exec. Dir: Debbie Hesse

**Aquatic Federation of Canada
& Hall of Fame & Museum**
25 Poseidon Bay
Winnipeg, Manitoba R3M 3E4
T: (204) 986-5894
F: (204) 947-3747
P: Vaughan Baird

Canada Amateur Diving
1600 James Naismith Drive
Gloucester, Ontario K1B 5N4
T: (613) 748-5631
F: (613) 748-5766

Canada Syncro-Swim
1600 James Naismith Drive
Gloucester, Ontario K1B 5N4
T: (613) 748-5674
F: (613) 748-5724
P: Joan Roberti

**International Life Saving
Federation**
Gemeenteplein 26aftsstelle
3010 Leuven, Belgium
T: (32.16) 35 35 00
F: (32.16) 35 01 02
P: Derrick Whitting

**International Swimming
Hall of Fame**
One Hall of Fame Drive
Fort Lauderdale, FL 33316
T: (954) 462-6536
F: (954) 525-4031
E: ishof@ishof.org
P: Dr. Sam Freas

Swimming/Natation Canada
1600 James Naismith Drive
Gloucester, Ontario K1B 5N4
T: (613) 748-5673
F: (613) 748-5715
E: natloffice@swimming.ca
P: Rob Campbell

U.S. Lifesaving Association
425 E. McFetridge Drive
Chicago, IL 60605
T: (312) 294-2333
Exec. Dir: Ray Colonna

Swim/Dive Publications

Aqua Magazine
1846 Hoffman Street
Madison, WI 53704
T: (608) 249-0186
F: (608) 249-1153
www.aquamagazine.com
Editor: Alan Sanderfoot

Aquatics Magazine
13th century Hill Drive
Latham, NY 12110
T: (518) 783-1281
F: (518) 783-1386
Publisher: Jean Rench

Rodale's Fitness Swimmer
733 Third Avenue
New York, NY 10017
T: (212) 573-0376
F: (212) 682-2237

Swim Magazine
Swimming Technique
Swimming World
90 Bell Rock Plaza, Suite 200
Sedona, AZ 86351
T: (520) 284-4005
F: (520) 284-2477
E: swimworld@aol.com
Editor: Phil Whitten

Tennis

American Tennis Association
William Fitzgerald Tennis Center
16th & Kennedy Streets NW
Washington, DC 20011
T: (202) 291-9893
F: (202) 291-4887
Exec. Dir: Albert Rucker

American Tennis Industry Federation
200 Castlewood Drive
North Palm Beach, FL 33408
T: (561) 848-1026
F: (561) 863-8981
Exec. Dir: Brad Patterson

Association of Tennis Professionals (ATP)
200 ATP Tour Road
Ponte Vedra Beach, FL 32082
T: (904) 285-8000
F: (904) 285-5966
www.atptour.com
CEO: Mark Miles
PR: Peter Alfano

Intercollegiate Tennis Association
PO Box 71
Princeton University
Princeton, NJ 08544
T: (609) 258-6332
F: (609) 258-2935
www.tennisonline.com/ita
E: ita@tennisonline.com
Exec. Dir: David Benjamin

International Tennis Federation
Palliser Road, Barons Court
London W14 9EN, England
T: (44.171) 381 80 60
F: (44.171) 386 52 57
www.itftennis.com
P: Brian Tobin

International Tennis Hall of Fame
194 Bellevue Avenue
Newport, RI 02840
T: (401) 849-3990
F: (401) 849-8780
P: Jane Brown

U.S. National Tennis Center
Flushing Meadow, Corona Park
Flushing, NY 11368
T: (718) 592-8000
F: (718) 592-9488

U.S. Professional Tennis Assn.
1 USPTA Centre
3535 Briarpark Drive
Houston, TX 77042
T: (713) 978-7782
F: (713) 978-7780
www.uspta.org
CEO: Tim Heckler

U.S. Professional Tennis Registry
PO Box 4739
Hilton Head Island, SC 29938
T: (843) 785-7244
F: (843) 686-2033
www.usptr.org
P: Dennis Van der Meer

U.S. Racquet Stringers Assn.
337 S. Cedros, Suite D
Solana Beach, CA 92075
T: (619) 481-3545
F: (619) 481-0624
www.tennisone.com
E: usrsa@aol.com
Exec. Dir: Jill Fonte

U.S. Tennis Association
70 W. Red Oak Lane
White Plains, NY 10604
T: (914) 696-7000
F: (914) 696-7167
Exec. Dir: Richard Ferman, Jr.
PR: Page Crosland

Women's International Professional Tennis Council
215 Park Ave. S., Suite 1715
New York, NY 10003
T: (212) 228-4400
F: (212) 228-4800

Women's Tennis Association
1266 E. Main Street, 4 Fl
Stamford, CT 06902
T: (203) 978-1740
F: (203) 978-1702
www.corelwtatour.com
CEO: Anne Person Worcester
PR: Joe Favorito

WTA Tour Players Assn.
1266 E. Main Street, 4 Fl
Stamford, CT 06902
T: (203) 978-1740
F: (203) 978-1702
CEO: Bart McGuire
PR: Joe Favorito

Tennis Publications

Advantage Magazine
One USPTA Centre
Houston, TX 77042
T: (713) 97-USPTA
F: (713) 978-7780
www.uspta.org
E: uspta@uspta.org

Bob Larson's Tennis
PO Box 24379
Edina, MN 55424
T: (952) 920-8947
F: (952) 927-7155
Publisher: Bob Larson

International Tennis
200 ATP Tour Blvd.
Ponte Vedra Beach, FL 32082
T: (904) 285-8000
F: (904) 285-8765
Editor: Steve Franke

Racquet
21 E. 40th Street
New York, NY 10016
T: (212) 696-2484
F: (212) 696-1678
Mng Editor: Matthew Tolan

Tennis
Tennis Buyer's Guide
Tennis USTA
5520 Park Avenue
Trumbull, CT 06611
T: (203) 373-7000
F: (203) 371-2127
www.tennismagazine.com
Editor: Donna Doherty

TennisMatch
230 W. 13th Street, Suite 1B
New York, NY 10011
T: (212) 242-3687
F: (203) 454-2438
Editor: Norman Zeitchick

Tennis Week
341 Madison Avenue
Suite 600
New York, NY 10017
T: (212) 808-4750
F: (212) 983-6302
www.tennisweek.com
Mng Editor: Kim Kodl

Track & Field

Intercollegiate Assn. of Amateur Athletics of America (IC4A)
PO Box 3
Centerville, MA 02632
T: (508) 771-5060
F: (508) 771-9481
P: Jack Kvancz

International Amateur Athletics Federation (IAAF)
17, rue Princesse Florestine
B.P. 359
98007 Monte-Carlo, Monaco
T: (377) 93 10 88 88
F: (377) 93 15 95 15
www.iaaf.org
P: Lamine Diack

National Track & Field Hall of Fame
One RCA Dome
Indianapolis, IN 46225
T: (317) 261-0500
F: (317) 261-0481
P: Ollan C. Cassell

USA Track & Field
One Hoosier Dome, Suite 140
Indianapolis, IN 46225
T: (317) 261-0500
F: (317) 261-0481
www.usatf.org
Exec. Dir: Craig Masback

Track Publications

American Track & Field
583 D'onofrio Dr., Suite 203
Madison, WI 53719
T: (608) 827-0806
F: (608) 827-0811
Editor: Christine Johnson

National Masters News
1675 Willamette Street
Eugene, OR 97401
T: (541) 343-7716
F: (541) 345-2436
E: natnanews@aol.com
Publisher: Al Sheahen

Track & Field News
2570 El Camino Real, Suite 606
Mountain View, CA 94040
T: (650) 948-8188
F: (650) 948-9445
www.trackandfieldnews.com
E: biz@trackandfieldnews.com
Editor: Garry Hill

Triathlon

Triathlon Federation USA
3595 E. Fountain Blvd., Suite F-1
Colorado Springs, CO 80910
T: (719) 597-9090
F: (719) 597-2121
www.usatriathalon.org
Exec. Dir: Steven Locke

International Triathlon Union
1154 W. 24th Street
North Vancouver, BC, CAN V7P 2J2
T: (604) 926-7250
F: (604) 608-3195
www.triathlon.org/tri_itu
P: Les McDonald

Triathlon Publications

Inside Triathlon
1830 N. 55th Street
Boulder, CO 80301
T: (303) 440-0601
F: (303) 444-6788
Publisher: Felix Magowan

Triathlete
121 Second Street, 2 FL
San Francisco, CA 94105
T: (415) 777-6939
F: (415) 777-6935
Editor: Michael Findeis

Volleyball

Federation of International Volleyball (FIVB)
Case postale
Ave. de la Gare 12
1001 Lausanne, Switzerland
T: (41.21) 320-8932
F: (41.21) 320-8865
www.fivb.ch
P: Ruben Acosta

Association of Volleyball Professionals (AVP)
330 Washington Blvd., Ste. 600
Marina Del Rey, CA 90292
T: (310) 577-0775
F: (310) 577-0776
www.avptour.com
CEO: Jerry Solomon
COO: Lon Monk
professional beach volleyball

Canadian Volleyball Association
1600 James Naismith Drive
Gloucester, Ontario K1B 5N4
T: (613) 748-5681
F: (613) 748-5727
www.volleyball.ca
P: Allan Ahac

National Volleyball Assn.
1001 Mission Street
South Pasadena, CA 91030
T: (800) 682-6820
F: (619) 669-1141
www.nva-volleyball.com
E: nvavolley@aol.com
P: Kimberly Coleman
VP/Mkt: Gary Wyma
A women's pro indoor league that began in 1995 and temporarily ceased operations.

USA Volleyball
715 S. Circle
Colorado Springs, CO 80910
T: (719) 228-6800
F: (719) 228-6899
www.usavolleyball.org
Exec. Dir: Kerry Klostermann

U.S. National Team
4510 Executive Drive, Plaza 1
San Diego, CA 92121
T: (619) 625-8200
Director: Doug Bealle

U.S. Pro Volleyball League
1555 Mittel Blvd., Ste. J
Woodale, IL 60191
T: (877) 843-8785
F: (630) 787-9951
www.uspv.com
E: uspv@uspv.com
Dir. of Oper: Susan Nucci-Ward
PR: Heather Kolusch

Volleyball Hall of Fame
444 Dwight Street
PO Box 1895
Holyoke, MA 01040
T: (413) 536-5720
P: Richard Lajoie

Women's Pro Volleyball Assn.
840 Apollo St., Suite 205
El Segundo, CA 90245
T: (310) 726-0700
F: (310) 726-0719
www.volleyball.org/
Exec. Di: Nancy Lengel
PR: Tim Simmons

Volleyball Publications

Volleyball
21700 Oxnard St., Suite 1600
Woodland Hills, CA 91367
T: (818) 593-3900

Volleyball USA
3595 E. Fountain Blvd.
Colorado Springs, CO 80910
T: (719) 637-8300

Volleyball World
Ave. de la Gare 12
1003 Lausanne, Switzerland
T: (41.21) 320.8932
F: (41.21) 320.8865
www.fivb.ch

Water Skiing

American Water Ski Association & Hall of Fame
799 Overlook Drive
Winter Haven, FL 33884
T: (941) 324-4341
F: (941) 325-8259
www.usawaterskiing.org
Exec. Dir: Steve McDermeit

International Water Ski Federation (IWSF)
PO Box 2038
Medellin, Colombia
T: (57.4) 281 57 72
F: (57.4) 230 28 33
E: iwsf@intic.net
P: Andres Botero

Canadian Water Ski Association
1600 James Naismith Drive
Gloucester, Ontario K1B 5N4
T: (613) 748-5683
F: (613) 748-5867
Exec. Dir: Hugh Mitchener

Professional Association of Water Skiers
6354 Masters Blvd.
Orlando, FL 32819
T: (407) 876-0754
F: (407) 876-1615

Water Ski Publications

The Water Skier
799 Overlook Drive
Winter Haven, FL 33884
T: (941) 324-4341
F: (941) 325-8259
Publisher: Don Cullimore

Wake Boarding Water Ski
330 W. Canton Avenue
Winter Park, FL 32789
T: (407) 628-4802
F: (407) 628-7061
E: wakeboard@worldzine
Publisher: John McEver

Wind Surfing

American Windsurfing Industries Association
1099 Snowden Road
White Salmon, WA 98672
T: (800) 963-7873
F: (509) 493-9464
www.awia.org
E: awia@gorge.net
Exec. Dir: Scott See

International Women's Boardsailing Association
PO Box 116
Hood River, OR 97031
T: (541) 427-8566
Exec. Dir: Rhonda Smith-Sanchez

Professional Boardsailing Association
1 Barn Cottages, Albany Park
Colnbrook Slough
SL3 0HS England
T: (44.1) 753.683.484
F: (44.1) 753.683.507
P: Christian Herles

U.S. Professional Windsurfing Association
Bayview Business Park #10
Guilford, NH 03246
T: (603) 293-2727
F: (603) 293-2723
Exec. Dir: Peter Thomas

U.S. Windsurfing Association
PO Box 978
Hood River, OR 97031
T: (541) 386-8708
F: (541) 386-2108
www.windsurfer.com/uswa
E: uswa@aol.com
P: Bill Collins

World Boardsailing Association
Feldafinger Platz 2
Munich 71,
D-8000 Germany
T: (48.89) 78 10 74
Exec. Dir: Susan Rowe

Windsurf Publications

American Windsurfer
Bayview Business Park
Suite 10
Guilford, NH 03246
T: (603) 293-2727
F: (603) 293-2723
Editor: John Chao

Windsurfing
330 W. Canton
Winter Park, FL 32789
T: (407) 628-4802
F: (407) 628-7061
Publisher: Terry Snow

Wrestling

Canadian Amateur Wrestling
1600 James Naismith Drive
Gloucester, Ontario K1B 5N4
T: (613) 748-5686
F: (613) 748-5756
www.wrestling.ca
Exec. Dir: Greg Mathieu

**Federation Internationale
de Luttes Associees (FILA)**
Avenue Juste-Olivier 17
1006 Lausanne, Switzerland
T: (41.21) 312 84 26
F: (41.21) 323 60 73
P: Milan Ercegan

**National Wrestling
Hall of Fame**
405 W. Hall of Fame Ave.
Stillwater, OK 74075
T: (405) 377-5243
Director: Bob Dellinger

USA Wrestling
6155 Lehman Drive
Colorado Springs, CO 80918
T: (719) 598-8181
F: (719) 598-9440
www.usawrestling.org
Exec. Dir: Jim Scherr

World Wrestling Federation
1241 E. Main Street
Stamford, CT 06902
T: (203) 352-8600
F: (203) 359-5109
www.wwf.com
CEO: Vince McMahon
P: Linda McMahon
*Entertainment promoters of
WWF pro events*

Wrestling Publications

Amateur Wrestling News
PO Box 60387
Oklahoma City, OK 73146
T: (405) 524-8550
F: (405) 524-8240
www.amateurwrestlingnews.com
E: awns@aol.com
Editor: Ron Good

Championship Wrestling
1115 Broadway
New York, NY 10010
T: (212) 807-7100
F: (212) 627-4678
Editor: Norman MacLean

**Inside Wrestling
Pro Wrestling Illustrated
Sports Review Wrestling
World Championship Wrestling
Wrestle America
The Wrestler**
London Publishing Co.
7002 W. Butler Pike
Ambler, PA 19002
T: (215) 643-6385
F: (215) 628-3571

USA Wrestler
6155 Lehman Drive
Colorado Springs, CO 80918
T: (719) 598-8181
F: (719) 598-9440
www.usawrestling.org

Wrestling USA
109 Applehouse Lane
Missoula, MT 59802
T: (406) 549-4448
F: (406) 549-4879
www.wrestlingusa.com
E: wrestling@montana.com
Editor: Lanny Bryant

WWF Magazine
1241 E. Main Street
Stamford, CT 06902
T: (203) 353-2819
F: (203) 353-2855

Winter Sports

Listed in this section are sports that are played during the winter other than ice hockey, figure & speed skating, which are listed earlier.

Biathlon

International Biathlon Union (IBU)
Airport Center- Kasernenstrasse 1
Postfach 1
5071 Wals Himmelreich, Austria
T: (43.662) 85.50.50
F: (43.662) 855.05.08
www.ibu.at
E: biathlon@ibu.at
P: Anders Besseberg

U.S. Biathlon Association
PO Box 297
Burlington, VT 05402
T: (802) 862-0338
F: (802) 862-0443
E-mail: USBiathlon@aol.com
Exec. Dir: Steve Sands

Biathlon Canada
1600 James Naismith Drive
Gloucester, Ontario K1B 5N4
T: (613) 748-5608
F: (613) 748-5762
Exec. Dir: Terrence Sheahan

Bobsledding

Federation Internationale de Bobsleigh et de Tobagganing
Via Piranesi 44B
20137 Milan, Italy
T: (39.2) 757.33.19
F: (39.2) 738.06.24
www.bobsleigh.com
E: egarde@tin.it
P: Robert Storey

Federation Internationale de Skibob
Lutherstrasse 27
4100 Duisburg, Germany
T: (49.203) 334.087
F: (49.203) 334.088
P: Wolfgang Hubner

U.S. Bobsled & Skeleton Federation
PO Box 828
421 Old Military Road
Lake Placid, NY 12946
T: (518) 523-1842
F: (518) 523-9491
E: info@usabobled.org
Exec. Dir: Matt Roy

Curling

Canada Curling Association
1600 James Naismith Drive
Gloucester, Ontario K1B 5N4
T: (613) 748-5628
F: (613) 748-5713
www.curling.ca
GM: Dave Parker

Curling Hall of Fame & Museum of Canada
122 Frederick Street
Kitchener, Ontario N2H 2L9
T/F: (519) 578-0094
Curator: Cheryl Reilly

USA Curling
PO Box 866
1100 Center Point Drive
Stevens Point, WI 54481
T: (715) 344-1199
F: (715) 344-6885
E: usacurl@coredes.com
Exec. Dir: David Garber

World Curling Federation
81 Great King Street
Edinburgh EH3 6RN, England
T: (44.131) 556.48.84
F: (44.131) 556.94.00
www.curling.org
E: wcf@dial.pipex.com
P: Gunther Hummelt
Sec Gen: Mike Thomson

Curling Publications

Curling News
1100 Centerpoint Drive
Stevens Point, WI 54481
T: (715) 344-1199
F: (719) 344-2279
www.usacurl.org
Editor: David Garber

Luge

**Federation Internationale
de Luge de Course (FIL)**
Rathausplatz 9
83471 Berchtesgaden, Germany
T: (49.8652) 669.60
F: (49.8652) 669.69
www.fil-luge.org
E: office@fil-luge.org
P: Josef Fendt

U.S. Luge Association
PO Box 651
35 Church Street
Lake Placid, NY 12946
T: (518) 523-2071
F: (518) 523-4164
www.usaluge.org
P: Dwight Bell

Skiing/Snowboard

**Federation Internationale
de Ski (FIS)**
Blochstrasse 2
3653 Oberhofen/Thunersee,
Swtzerland
T: (41.33) 244 61 61
F: (41.33) 243 53 53
www.fisski.org
E: lewis@fisski.ch
P: Marc Hodler
Dir: Sarah Lewis

U.S. Ski & Snowboard Assn.
PO Box 100
1500 Kearns Blvd.
Park City, UT 84060
T: (801) 649-9090
F: (801) 649-3613
www.usskiteam.com
P: Bill Marolt

Alpine Canada
1600 James Naismith Drive
Gloucester, Ontario K1B 5N4
T: (613) 748-5661
F: (613) 748-5704

Canadian Ski Association
1600 James Naismith Drive
Gloucester, Ontario K1B 5N4
T: (613) 748-5663
F: (613) 748-5710
Exec. Dir: Neil MacDonald

**Cross Country Ski
Areas Association**
259 Bolton Road
Winchester, NH 03470
T: (603) 239-4341
F: (603) 239-6387
www.xcski.org
E: ccsaa@xcski.org
P: Chris Frado

International Snowboard Assn.
108 A. Ave. Louis Casai
postfach 612
1215 Geneva, Switzerland
T: (41.29) 276.93
F: (41.22) 798.98.46
P: Eric Eberli

National Ski Areas Association
133 S. Van Gordon, Suite 300
Lakewood, CO 80228
T: (303) 987-1111
F: (303) 986-2345
P: Michael Berry

National Ski Hall of Fame
610 Palms Ave., PO Box 191
Ishpeming, MI 49849
T: (906) 485-6323
F: (906) 486-4570
www.portup.com/skihall
E: skihall@portup.com
P: Richard Goetzman

National Ski Patrol System
133 S. Van Gordon
Lakewood, CO 80228
T: (303) 988-1111
F: (303) 988-3005
Exec. Dir: Stephen Over

**Professional Ski Instructors
of America (PSIA)**
133 S. Van Gordon
Lakewood, CO 80228
T: (303) 987-9390
F: (303) 988-3005
Exec. Dir: Stephen Over

Snowsports Industries America
8377-B Greensboro Drive
McLean, VA 22102
T: (703) 556-9020
F: (703) 821-8276
www.snowlink.com
P: David Ingemie

U.S. Ski Writers Assn.
7 Kensington Road
Glens Falls, NY 12801
T: (518) 793-1201
F: (518) 792-0648
P: Don Metivier

World Loppet-Telemark Association
PO Box 911
Hayward, WI 54843
T: (715) 634-5025
F: (715) 634-5663
Exec. Dir: Marilyn Schutz
Long Distance X-C Skiing

World Pro Ski Tour
122 Front Street
Bath, ME 04530
T: (207) 443-4461
F: (207) 443-3847
www.zoro.com/wpst
E: wpskitour@aol.com
P: Ed Rogers
Men's & Women's pro ski Tours.

World Wide Ski Corp
402-D Aspen Airport Bus. Ctr.
Aspen, CO 81611
T: (970) 925-7864
F: (970) 925-7882
www.nastar.com
E: wwsc@csn.net
CEO: Bob Beattie
Sponsor of NASTAR events & other ski events

Ski/Board Publications

Cross Country Skier
1823 Fremont Avenue S.
Minneapolis, MN 55403
T: (612) 377-0312
Editor: Jim Chase

Nordic Network
259 Bolton Road
Winchester, NH 03470
T: (603) 239-4341
F: (603) 239-6387

Powder/Snowboarder
33046 Calle Aviador
San Juan Capistrano, CA 92675
T: (949) 496-5922
F: (949) 496-7849
E: powdrmag@aol.com
Editor: Steve Casimiro

Pro Skiing USA
122 Front Street
Bath, ME 04530
T: (207) 443-2743
F: (207) 443-3847
Editor: John Sousa

Ski America
PO Box 1140
370 Wahconah Street
Pittsfield, MA 01202
T: (413) 443-9200
F: (413) 443-3030

Ski Area Management
PO Box 644
45 N. Main Street
Woodbury, CT 06798
T: (203) 263-0888
F: (203) 266-0452
Editor: Janet Nelson

Ski Magazine/Skiing Magazine
929 Pearl Street
Boulder, CO 80302
T: (303) 448-7600
F: (303) 448-7676
Publisher: Andrew Clurman

Skiing Trade News
2 Park Avenue
New York, NY 10016
T: (212) 779-5000
F: (212) 779-5465
Publisher: Andrew Clurman

Ski Racing International
Ski Tech
PO Box 1125
Waitsfield, VT 05673
T: (802) 496-7700
F: (802) 496-7704
www.skiracing.com
Publisher: Gary Black, Jr.

SkiTrax
2 Pardee Ave., #204
Toronto, Ontario M6K 3H5
T: (416) 530-1350
F: (416) 530-4155
Editor: Ben Sadavy

Sno
PO Box 450
Bethel, ME 04217
T: (207) 824-3000
F: (207) 824-2111
Editor: Skip King

Snoboard Magazine
Three morgan Ave.
Norwalk, CT 06851
T: (203) 855-5766
F: (203) 855-0067
Editor: Chris McNeil

Snow Country
5520 Park Avenue
Trumbull, CT 06611
T: (203) 373-7059
F: (203) 373-7111
www.snowcountry.com
Editor: Perkins Miller

Transworld Snowboarding
353 Airport Road
Oceanside, CA 92054
T: (760) 722-7777
F: (760) 722-0653
E: transnow @ aol.com
Publisher: Larry Balma

Sled Dog Racing

Grand Portage Chippewa Beargrease Sled Dog Marathon
600 E. Superior St., Suite 305
Duluth, MN 55802
T: (218) 722-7631
F: (218) 722-2042
www.beargrease.com

Iditarod Trail Race Committee
PO Box 870800
Wasilla, AK 99687
T: (907) 376-5155
F: (907) 373-6998
www.alaska.net/iditarod
Exec. Dir: Stan Hooley

International Federation of Sled Dog Sports
HC 86, Box 3380
Merrifield, MN 56465
T: (218) 765-4297
Exec. Dir: Dave Steele

U.S. Sled Dog Sports Federation
1848-A Commercenter E.
San Bernardino, CA 92408
T: (760) 244-6592
F: (909) 884-0015
P: Sam Hlavaty

Snowmobiling

International Snowmobile Racing Hall of Fame & Museum
6035 Hwy 70 E.
St. Germain, WI 54558
T: (715) 359-9917
F: (715) 359-5447
P: Loren Anderson

Snowmobile Publications

American Snowmobiler
7582 Currell Blvd.
St. Paul, MN 55125
T: (612) 738-1953
F: (612) 738-2302
www.amsnow.com
Editor: Jerry Bassett

Michigan Snowmobiler
PO Box 417
East Jordan, MI 49727
T: (616) 536-2371
F: (616) 536-7691
Editor: Lyle Shipe

Snow Action
Snow West
520 Park Avenue
Idaho Falls, ID 83402
T: (208) 524-7000
F: (208) 522-5241
Editor: Lane Lindsrtom

Snow Goer
130 Spy Court, #310
Markham, Ontario L3R 0W5
T: (905) 475-8440
F: (905) 475-9246
Editor: Chris Knowles

Snow Goer Magazine
Snow Week
Snowmobile
Snowmobile Business
601 Lakeshore Pkwy, #600
Minnetonka, MN 55305
T: (612) 476-2200
F: (612) 476-8065
Editor: John Prusak

Snowmobiler's Race & Rally
PO Box 993
630 Hiawatha Circle NW
Alexandria, MN 56308
T: (612) 763-5411

Wisconsin Snowmobile News
PO Box 182
Rio, WI 53960
T: (920) 992-6370
F: (920) 992-6369
Editor: Cathy Hanson

Winter Swimming

Iceberg Athletic Club
4959 Viceroy Street, #203
Cape Coral, FL 33904
T: (941) 549-8407

Polar Bear Club-USA
376 Naughton Avenue
Staten Island, NY 10305
T: (708) 979-8370

Disabled Sports

International Organizations

International Paralympic Committee (IPC)
Abdijbekestraat 4B Box 6
8200 Sint-Andries, Belgium
T: (32.50) 38.93.40
F: (32.50) 39.01.19
P: Dr. Robert Steadward

International Organizations affiliated with the IPC

Cerebral Palsy International Sports & Recreation Association
PO Box 16 (CP-ISRA)
6666 ZG Heteren, Holland
T/F: (31.2647) 225.93
P: Elizabeth Dendy

International Blind Sports Association (IBSA)
42, rue Louis Lumiere
75020 Paris, France
T: (33.1) 40.31.45.00
F: (33.1) 40.31.45.42
P: Enrique Sanz Jiminez

International Committee of Sports for the Deaf
Langaavej 41
2650 Hvidovre, Denmark
T: (45.35) 36 15 88
F: (45.36) 78 99 39
P: John Lovett

International Sports Federation for Persons with Mental Handicap
Solecast House
13-27 Brunswick Place
London N1 6DX, England
T: (44.171) 250.11.00
F: (44.171) 250.01.10
P: Bernard Atha

International Sports Organization of the Disabled
353 Ontario Street
Newmarket, Ontario L3Y 2K2
T: (905) 898-3661
F: (905) 898-5527
P: Juan Palau Francas

International Stoke Mandeville Wheelchair Sports Federation
Guttman Sports Centre
Harvey Road, Aylesbury
Bucks HP21 8PP, England
T: (44.1296) 43 61 79
F: (44.1296) 43 64 84
P: Dr. Donald Royer

Special Olympics International
1325 G Street NW
Suite 500
Washington, D.C. 20005
T: (202) 628-3630
F: (202) 824-0200
www.specialolympics.com
E: specialolympics@msn.com
P: Timothy Shriver

North American Organizations

American Athletic Association of the Deaf, Inc.
3607 Washington Blvd., #4
Ogden, UT 84403
T: (801) 393-8710
TTY (801) 393-7916
F: (801) 393-2263
E: aaadeaf@aol.com
Exec. Dir: Shirley Platt

American Blind Bowling Association
41 Sheriff Street
Mercer, PA 16137
T: (412) 662-5748
P: Wayne Keeney

Canadian Blind Sports Association
1600 James Naismith Drive
Gloucester, Ontario K1B 5N4
T: (613) 748-5609
F: (613) 748-5899
P: Gerry York

Canadian Paralympic Committee
1600 James Naismith Drive
Gloucester, Ontario K1B 5N4
T: (613) 748-5630
F: (613) 748-5731
P: Helen Manning

Canadian Special Olympics
40 St. Clair Avenue West
Suite 209
Toronto, Ontario M4V 1M6
T: (416) 927-9050
F: (416) 927-8475
P: Jim Jordan

Disabled Sports USA
451 Hungerford Drive
Suite 100
Rockville, MD 20850
T: (301) 217-0960
TDD (301) 217-0963
F: (301) 217-0968
E-mail: dsusa@susa.org
Exec. Dir: Kirk Bauer

**Dwarf Athletic Association
of America**
418 Willow Way
Lewisville, TX 75067
T: (972) 317-8299
F: (972) 317-8299
P: Pamela Danberg

**National Deaf Bowling
Association**
9244 E. Mansfield Ave.
Denver, CO 80237
TDD: (303) 771-9018
P: Van Scheppach

**National Handicapped Sports
& Recreation Association**
1145 19th Street NW
Suite 717
Washington, D.C. 20036
T: (202) 652-7505

**National Wheelchair
Basketball Association**
Charlotte Institute of Rehabilitation
1100 Blythe Blvd.
Charlotte, NC 28217
T: (704) 355-1064
P: Marvin Lapicola

**U.S. Association for
Blind Athletes**
33 North Institute Street
Colorado Springs, CO 80903
T: (719) 630-0422
F: (719) 630-0616
www.usaba.org
Exec. Dir: Charles Huebner

**U.S. Cerebral Palsy
Athletic Association**
200 Harrison Avenue
Newport, RI 02840
T: (401) 848-2460
F: (401) 848-5280
www.uscpaa.org
E: uscpaa@mail.bbsnet.com
P: Jeff Jones

U.S. Deaf Skiers Association
130 Rosewood Place
Bridgeport, CT 06610
T: (203) 372-7248

Wheelchair Sports USA
3595 E. Fountain Blvd.
Suite L-1
Colorado Springs, CO 80910
T: (719) 574-1150
F: (719) 574-9840
E: wsusa@aol.com
Exec. Dir: Patricia Shepherd

Sports Organizations & Associations

All American Soap Box Derby
PO Box 7233
789 Derby Downs Drive
Akron, OH 44306
T: (330) 733-8723
F: (330) 733-1370
Exec Dir: Tony DeLuca

Amateur Athletic Foundation
2141 W. Adams Blvd.
Los Angeles, CA 90018
T: (323) 730-9600
F: (323) 730-9637
www.aafla.com
P: Anita DeFrantz
VP Research: Wayne Wilson

Amateur Athletic Union
The Walt Disney World Resort
PO Box 10000
Lake Buena Vista, FL 32830
T: (407) 363-6170
F: (407) 363-6171
www.aausports.org
P: Bobby Dodd
PR: Tim Neiman

America Outdoors
PO Box 10847
Knoxville, TN 37939
T: (423) 558-3595
F: (423) 558-3598
www.americaoutdoors.com
E: amoutdoors@aol.com
Exec Dir: David Brown

American Assn. of Museums
1575 I Street NW, Suite 400
Washington, DC 20005
T: (202) 289-1818
F: (202) 289-6578
Exec. Dir: Ed Abel

American Association for Leisure & Recreation
1900 Association Drive
Reston, VA 20191
T: (703) 476-3400
F: (703) 476-9527
www.aahperd.org/aalr
E: aalr@aahperd.org
P: Donna Thompson

American Association of School Administrators
1801 N. Moore Street
Arlington, VA 22209
T: (703) 528-0700
F: (703) 528-2146
www.aasa.org

American College Health Association
PO Box 28937
Baltimore, MD 21240
F: (410) 859-1500
F: (410) 859-1510
E: acha@access.digex.net

American College of Sports Medicine
PO Box 1440
Indianapolis, IN 46206
T: (317) 637-9200
F: (317) 637-7817
www.acsm.org

American Council on Excercise
5820 Oberlin Drive, Suite 102
San Diego, CA 92121
T: (800) 825-3636
T: (619) 535-8227
F: (619) 535-1778
www.acefitness.org
E: acemail@acefitness.org
Exec. Dir: Sheryl Marks Brown

American Council on International Sports
817 23rd Street NW
Washington, DC 20052
T: (703) 476-3462
Exec Dir: Dong Yang

American Hiking Society
1422 Fenwick Lane
Silver Springs, MD 20914
P: David Lillard
T: (301) 565-6704
F: (301) 565-6714
P: David Lillard

American Hospital Assn.
840 N. Lake Shore Drive
Chicago, IL 60611
T: (312) 280-6000

American Medical Association
515 North State Street
Chicago, IL 60610
T: (312) 464-5000

American Recreation Coalition
1225 New York Ave. NW, Suite 450
Washington, DC 20005
T: (202) 682-9530
F: (202) 682-9529
www.funoutdoors.com
E: arc@funoutdoors.com
P: Derrick Crandall

American Running & Fitness Association
4405 East-West Hwy., Suite 405
Bethesda, MD 20814
T: (800) 776-2732
T: (301) 913-9517
www.arfa.org.

American Society for Testing & Materials
100 Barr Harbor Drive
West Conshohocken, PA 19428
T: (610) 832-9500
F: (610) 832-9635
www.astm.org.

American Sports Education Institute
200 Castlewood Drive
North Palm Beach, FL 33408
T: (561) 842-4100
F: (561) 863-8984
www.sportlink.com/sport
Exec. Dir: Michael May

American Sports Institute
PO Box 1837
Mill Valley, CA 94942
T: (415) 383-5750
F: (415) 383-5785
www.amersports.org
Exec. Dir: Dr. Susan Kirsch

American Sportscasters Assn.
5 Beekman Street, Suite 814
New York, NY 10038
T: (212) 227-8080
F: (212) 571-0556
E: asassn@juno.com
P: Louis Schwartz
COB: Dick Enberg

American Sports Medicine Association
660 W. Duarte Road
Arcadia, CA 91007
T: (626) 445-1978

Association for the Advancement of Applied Sport Psychology
University of Colorado
Department of Kinesiology
Box 354
Boulder, CO 80309
T: (303) 492-8021
F: (303) 492-4009
P: Dr. Penny McCullough

Association for Convention Operations Management
1819 Peachtree St. NE, Ste. 620
Atlanta, GA 30309
T: (404) 351-3220
F: (404) 351-3348
P: Linda Johnson

Association for Women In Sports Media
PO Box 4205
Mililani, HI 96789
T: (808) 525-8040
P: Lynn Zinser
Exec Sec: Ann Miller

Association for Worksite Health Promotion
60 Revere Drive, Suite 500
Northbrook, IL 60062
T: (847) 480-9574
F: (847) 480-9282
www.awhp.com

Association of Black Sporting Goods Professionals
55 Marietta Street, Suite 2000
Atlanta, GA 30303
T: (888) 294-7020
T: (404) 588-1104
F: (404) 588-1601
Exec. Dir: Yolanda Allen

Association of Higher Education Facilities Officers
1643 Prince Street
Alexandria, VA 22314
T: (703) 684-1446
F: (703) 549-2772
www.appa.org

Association of Luxury Suite Directors
10017 McKelvy Road
Cincinnati, OH 45231
T: (513) 931-1101
F: (513) 522-2511
Exec. Dir: Bill Dorsey

Association of Physical Fitness Centers
600 Jefferson St. Suite 202
Rockville, MD 20852
T: (301) 424-7744

Association of Physical Plant Administrators or Universities & Colleges
1446 Duke Street
Alexandria, VA 22314
T: (703) 684-1446

Association of School Business Officials International
11401 North Shore Drive
Reston, VA 22090
T: (703) 478-0405

Athletes Against Drugs
180 N. LaSalle Street # 3800
Chicago, IL 60601
T: (312) 263-4618
F: (312) 263-4777
E: aad@enteract.com
Exec. Dir: Stedman Graham

Athletes In Action
5778 State Rte. 350
Oregonia, OH 45054
T: (513) 933-2421
F: (513) 933-2421
www.aiasports.org/aia
E: aiacom@aol.com
P: R. Wendell Deyo
PR: Lillie Nye

Athletic Equipment Managers Association
PO Box 2093
Ann Arbor, MI 48106
T: (734) 741-9447
F: (734) 741-0594
Exec Dir: Jon Falk
P: Terry Schlatter

Athletic Institute
200 Castlewood Drive
North Palm Beach, FL 33408
T: (561) 842-3600
F: (561) 863-8984
www.sportlink.com

Award & Recognition Association
35 E. Wacker Drive
Chicago, IL 60601
T: (312) 782-5252
F: (312) 236-1140
Exec. Dir: Ralph Bloch

Black Coaches Association
PO Box J
Des Moines, IA 50311
T: (515) 327-1248
www.bca.org
Exec. Dir: Rudy Washington

Black Entertainment & Sports Lawyers Association
1502 Fairlakes Place
Mitchellville, MD 20721
T: (301) 333-0003
F: (301) 333-0013
www.besla.org
Chmn: C. Lamont Smith

Booster Clubs of America
200 Castlewood Drive
North Palm Beach, FL 33406
T: (561) 842-3600
F: (561) 863-8984
www.sportlink.com

Boy Scouts of America
1325 W. Walnut Hill Lane
PO Box 152079
Irving, TX 75015
T: (972) 580-2423
F: (972) 580-2502

Boys & Girls Clubs of America
1230 W. Peachtree St. NW
Atlanta, GA 30909
T: (404) 815-5700
F: (404) 815-5757
P: Roxanne Spillett

Canadian Association for Health, Phys. Education, Rec. & Dance
1600 James Naismith Drive
Gloucester, Ontario K1B 5N4
T: (800) 663-8708
T: (613) 748-5622
F: (613) 748-5737
www.activeliving.ca/cahperd

Canadian Intramural Recreation Association
1600 James Naismith Drive
Gloucester, Ontario K1B 5N4
T: (613) 748-5639
F: (613) 742-5467
www.activeliving.ca/cira
P: Tim Rafter

Canadian Olympic Association
2380 avenue Pierre Dupuy
Montreal, Quebec H3C 3R4
T: (514) 861-2896
F: (514) 861-2896

Canadian Parks & Recreation Association
1600 James Naismith Drive
Gloucester, Ontario K1B 5N4
T: (613) 748-5651
F: (613) 748-5854
www.activeliving.ca/cpra
Exec Dir: Geraldine Hebert

Canadian Special Olympics
40 St. Clair Avenue West
Suite 209
Toronto, Ontario M4V 1M6
T: (416) 927-9050

Canadian Sport & Fitness Administration Centre
1600 James Naismith Drive
Gloucester, Ontario K1B 5N4
T: (613) 747-2900
F: (613) 748-5706

Canadian Sporting Goods Association
455, rue St. Antoine Ouest
Suite 510
Montreal, Quebec H2Z 1J1
T: (514) 393-1132
F: (514) 393-9513
www.globalsports.com/csga

Catholic Youth Organization
1011 First Avenue, Room 620
New York, NY 10022
T: (212) 371-1000
P: J. Peter Grace

Center for the Study of Sporting Society
716 Columbus Ave., Suite 161
Boston, MA 02120
T: (617) 373-4025
F: (617) 373-4566
Director: Richard Lapchick
PR: Adam Zand

Club Managers Association of America
1733 King Street
Alexandria, VA 22314
T: (703) 739-9500
F: (703) 739-0124
P: W.H. Kendall

Coaching Association of Canada
1600 James Naismith Drive
Gloucester, Ontario K1B 5N4
T: (613) 748-5624
F: (613) 748-5707
P: John Bales

Coalition of Americans To Protect Sports
200 Castlewood Drive
North Palm Beach, FL 33408
T: (561) 842-4100
F: (561) 863-8678
www.sportsafety.com
Exec. Dir: Sharon Lincoln

College Athletic Business Managers Association (CABMA)
19009-398 Laurel Park Road
Rancho Dominguez, CA 90220
T/F: (310) 637-0560
www.cabma.com

College Sports Information Directors of America
PO Box 5061, Rutgers University
New Brunswick, NJ 08903
T: (732) 932-4200
F: (732) 932-3063
www.cosida.org
P: Pete Kowalski

Collegiate Athletic Officials Association
411 Norman Road
Camp Hill, PA 17011
T: (717) 737-4435
F: (717) 730-9375
Exec. Dir: Leonard Czarnecki

Consolidated Athletic Commission
851 North Leavitt Street
Chicago, IL 60622
T: (773) 276-3762
Exec. Dir: Richard Wysznyski

Council of Parks & Recreation Association
1500 Lakeland Avenue
Bohemia, NY 11716
T: (516) 563-4800

European Assn for Sport Management (EASM)
Postfach 379
AJ, Groningen 9700, Netherlands
T/F: (31.50) 20 98 25
E: easm@rhg.hanze.nl

Fellowship of Christian Athletes
8701 Leeds Road
Kansas City, MO 64129
T: (816) 921-0909
P: Dal Shealy

Fish & Wildlife Service
Department of the Interior
Washington, DC 20240
T: (202) 343-5634

Fitness & Amateur Sport
365 Laurier Avenue West
Journal Tower South
Ottawa, Ontario K1A 0X6
T: (613) 992-9187

General Association of International Sports Federations
Villa Henri
7, Blvd. de Suise
Monte Carlo, Monaco
T: (33.93) 50 74 13
F: (33.93) 25 28 73
www.gaisf.org
Exec. Dir: Jean Claude Schupp
Sec. Gen: Peter Tallberg

Girl Scouts of the USA
420 Fifth Avenue
New York, NY 10018
T: (212) 852-8000

Healthcare Wellness & Fitness Association
233 E. Wacker Dr., 37th FL
Chicago, IL 60601
T: (312) 938-4407
F: (312) 938-4464

Institute for International Sport
2 Butterfield Rd., Suite 2
University of Rhode Island
Kingston, RI 02881
T: (401) 874-2375
F: (401) 874-2429
www.iis.davis.uri.edu
E: iis@uriacc.uri.edu
Exec. Dir: Daniel Doyle, Jr.

International Association for Sports Information (IASI)
1600 James Naismith Drive
Gloucester, Ontario K1B 5N4
T: (613) 748-5658
F: (613) 748-5701
www.sirc.ca/iasi
E: nclarke@ausport.gov.au
P: Nerida Clarke
Director: Gilles Chiasson

International Association for Sports and Leisure Facilities
Carl-Diem-Weg 3
D-50933 Koln, Germany
T: (49.221) 491 29 91
F: (49.221) 497 12 80
P: Eric Schumann
Sec. Gen: Frieder Roskam

International Association of Asembly Managers
4425 West Airport Freeway
Suite 590
Irving, TX 75062
T: (972) 255-8020
F: (972) 255-9582
www.iaam.org
E: iaam.info@iaam.org
Exec Dir: John Zimmer

International Association of Convention & Visitors Bureau
2000 L Street NW, Ste. 702
Washington, DC 20036
T: (202) 296-7888
F: (202) 296-7889
www.iacvb.org
P: Edward Nielsen
PR: Gina Barrett

International Association of Fairs & Expositions
PO Box 985
Springfield, MO 65801
T: (417) 862-5771

International Association of Sports Museums & Hall of Fame
4400-A Ambassador Caffrey Pkwy.
Suite 200
Lafayette, LA 70508
T/F: (318) 856-0643
P: Gerald Baltz

International Association of Sports Medicine Professionals
4411 N. 40th Street, Suite 33
Phoenix, AZ 85018
T: (602) 955-7669
F: (602) 955-3541

International City-County Management Association
777 N. Capitol Street NE
Suite 500
Washington, D.C. 20002
T: (202) 962-3652
F: (202) 962-3500
www.icma.org

International Health, Racquet & Sportsclub Association
263 Summer Street
Boston, MA 02210
T: (617) 951-0055
F: (617) 951-0056
www.ihrsa.org
E: info@ihrsa.org

International Schoolsport Federation
Minoritenplatz, Postfach 65
1014 Vienna, Austria
T: (43.1) 53 120 22 94
F: (43.1) 53 120 25 99
P: Norbert Bayer

International Shooting Coaches Association
17446 SW Granada Drive
Beaverton, OR 97007
T: (503) 642-5873
F: (503) 649-5182

International Special Events Society
9202 N. Meridien St., Suite 200
Indianapolis, IN 46260
T: (317) 571-5601
F: (317) 571-5603
www.ises.com
Exec. Dir: Sharon Gorup

International Sport Show Producers Association
1380 Lawrence Street
Suite 200
Denver, CO 80204
T: (303) 892-6800
F: (303) 892-6322

International Sports Exchange
5982 Mia Court
Plainfield, IN 46168
T: (317) 839-9257
P: Kelley Davis

International Sports Marketing Association
1080 Holcomb Bridge Road
Suite 300
Roswell, GA 30076
T: (770) 642-7595
F: (770) 998-9830

The International Sports Plaza
250 Spring Street NW
Suite 2W357
Atlanta, GA 30303
T: (404) 220-2816
F: (404) 220-2426
P: Jack Ryan

Irish American Sports Foundation
PO Box 1677
Kingston, RI 02881
T: (401) 792-2375
Exec. Dir: Daniel Doyle, Jr.

Japan-US Sports Federation
918 W. College Street
Suite 210
Los Angeles, CA 90012
T: (213) 481-2111
F: (213) 481-2900
Exec. Dir: Shuji Nakada

**Jewish Community
Centers Association**
15 East 26th Street
New York, NY 10010
T: (212) 532-4949
F: (212) 481-4174
P: Ann Kaufman

Jewish Sports Congress
134 Middle Neck Rdl, Suite 210
Great Neck, NY 10023
T: (516) 482-5550

**Licensing Industry
Merchandisers Association**
350 Fifth Avenue, Suite 2309
New York, NY 10118
T: (212) 244-1944
F: (212) 563-6552
www.licensing.org
Exec. Dir: Charles Riotto

**Maccabi USA / Sports
for Israel**
1926 Arch Street, 4th Floor
Philadelphia, PA 19103
T: (215) 561-6900
F: (215) 561-5470
www.maccabiusa.com
E: maccabi@dca.net
Exec. Dir: Barbara Lissy
PR: Joy Gordon

Maccabi World Union
Kfar Hamaccabiah
Rmat Gan 52 105, Israel
T: (972.3) 6715-733
F: (973.3) 6772-059
P: Marcos Arbaitman
Sec Gen: Mario Margulis

National Academy of Sports
220 East 63rd Street
New York, NY 10021
T: (212) 838-2980
P: Howard Hillman

**National Alliance of
African American Athletes**
PO Box 77433
Washington, DC 20013
T: (717) 234-6353
F: (717) 238-9979
Exec Dir: Glue Wilkins

National Alliance of Youth Sports
2050 Vista Parkway
West Palm Beach, FL 33411
T: (561) 684-1141
F: (561) 684-2546
www.nays.org
Director: Lisa Licata

National Amateur Sports Fed.
PO Box 24263, West Sta.
Gates, NY 14624
T: (800) 776-6719
F: (716) 247-3112
Exec. Dir: Donald Aselin

**National Association for
Girls & Women in Sports**
1900 Association Drive
Reston, VA 22091
T: (703) 476-3450
F: (703) 476-9527
www.aahperd.org/nagws.html
E: nagws@aahperd.org
Exec Dir: Diana Everett

**National Association for
Sport & Physical Education**
1900 Association Drive
Reston, VA 20191
T: (703) 476-3410
F: (703) 476-8316
www.aahperd.org/naspe
E: naspe@aahperd.org

**National Association of Club
Athletic Directors**
524 Post Street
San Francisco, CA 94102
T: (415) 775-4400
F: (415) 931-4383

**National Association of
Collegiate Directors of Athletics**
PO Box 16428
Cleveland, OH 44116
T: (440) 892-4000
F: (440) 892-4007
www.nacda.com

National Association of Concessionaires
35 East Wacker Dr., Suite 1849
Chicago, IL 60601
T: (312) 236-3858
F: (312) 236-7809
www.naconline.org
E: info@naconline.org

National Association of Education Buyers
450 Wireless Blvd.
Hauppauge, NY 11788
T: (516) 273-2600
F: (516) 273-2305

National Assn. Of Governor's Councils of Phys. Fitness & Sports
201 S. Capitol Ave., Suite 560
Indianapolis, IN 46225
T: (317) 237-5630
www.physicalfitness.org

National Association of Police Athletic Leagues
618 North U.S. 1, Suite 201
North Palm Beach, FL 33408
T: (561) 844-1823
F: (561) 863-6120
E: copnkid1@aol.com
P: Ralph Giardina

National Association of Sports Commissions
300 Main Street
Cincinnati, OH 45202
T: (513) 651-3999
F: (513) 651-1374
www.sportscommissions.com
E: nasc@fuse.net
Exec. Dir: Don Schumacher

National Association of Sports Officials (NASO)
2017 Lathrop Avenue
Racine, WI 53405
T: (414) 632-5448
F: (414) 632-5460
E: naso@execpc.com
P: Barry Mano

National Athletic Trainers Association (NATA)
2952 Stemmons Pkwy.
Dallas, TX 75247
T: (214) 637-6282
F: (214) 637-2206

National Board YWCA
726 Broadway, Fifth Floor
New York, NY 10003
T: (212) 614-2700
F: (212) 677-9716
Exec. Dir: Dr. Prema Mathai-Davis

National Club Association
One Lafayette Centre
1120 20th St. NW, Suite 725
Washington, DC 20036
T: (202) 822-9822
F: (202) 822-9808
Exec. Dir: Susanne Wegrzyn

National Coalition for Athletics Equity
1050 17th St. NW, Suite 600
Washington, DC 20036
T: (202) 496-1298
F: (202) 822-0987
E: teamsimple@sprintmail.com
Exec Dir: Michael Copperthite

National Congress of State Games
401 North 31st Street
Suite 620
Billings, MT 59103
T: (406) 254-7426
F: (406) 254-7439
www.stategames.org
E: tom@stategames.org
Exec. Dir: Thomas Osborn

National Council for Therapeutic Recreation Certification
PO Box 479
Thiells, NY 10984
T: (914) 947-4346

National Employee Services & Recreation Association
2211 York Rd., Suite 207
Oakbrook, IL 60521
T: (630) 368-1280
F: (630) 368-1286
www.nesra.com
Exec. Dir: Patrick Stinson

National Explorer Division, BSA
1325 W. Walnut Hill Lane
Irving, TX 75038
T: (972) 580-2423
F: (972) 580-2502
Assoc. Dir: Bill Evans

National Girls Athletic Association
1201 16th Street NW
Washington, DC 20036
T: (202) 833-5540

National Institute of Sports Camps
2920 W. St. Joseph St.
Lansing, MI 48917
T: (800) 878-5131
F: (517) 485-4178

**National Instirtute on Park
& Ground Management**
730 W. Frances Street
Appleton, WI 54914
T/F: (920) 733-2301

**National Interscholastic Athletic
Administrators Association**
PO Box 690
Indianapolis, IN 46206
T: (816) 464-5400
F: (816) 464-5571
www.nfhs.org/niaaa

**National Intramural Recreation
Sports Association**
4185 SW Research Way
Corvallis, OR 97333
T: (541) 766-8211
F: (541) 766-8284
www.nirsa.org
E: nirsa@nirsa.org
Exec. Dir: Kent Blumenthal

**National Law Enforcement
Sports Federation**
3000 34th Street S., Suite 17
St. Petersburg, FL 33711
T: (727) 864-0738
Exec. Dir: Chris McDonald

**National Recreation & Park
Association**
22377 Belmont Ridge Road
Ashburn, VA 20448
T: (800) 626-6772
T: (703) 858-0784
F: (703) 858-0707
www.nrpa.org
E: info@nrpa.org
Exec. Dir: Dean Tice

**National School Board
Association**
1680 Duke Street
Alexandria, VA 22314
T: (703) 838-6722

**National School Supply
& Equipment Association**
8300 Colesville Rd, Suite 250
Silver Spring, MD 20910
T: (800) 395-5550
T: (703) 495-0240
F: (703) 495-3330
www.nssea.org
E: nssea@aol.com

National Senior Games Assn.
3032 Old Forge Drive
Baton Rouge, LA 70802
T: (225) 925-5678
F: (225) 216-7552
www.nsga.com
E: dhull@nsga.com
Exec Dir: D. Hull

National Spa & Pool Institute
2111 Eisenhower Avenue
Alexandria, VA 22314
T: (703) 838-0083
F: (703) 549-0493
E: rgalvin@nspinat.com

**National Sporting Goods
Association**
1699 Wall Street
Mt. Prospect, IL 60056
T: (847) 439-4000
F: (847) 439-0111
www.nsga.org
P: James Faltinek

**National Sportscasters &
Sportwriters Association**
620 W. Innes Street
Salisbury, NC 28144
T: (704) 633-4275

National Sports Foundation
PO Box 888886
4923 Four Oaks Court
Atlanta, GA 30356
T: (770) 698-8600
F: (770) 698-0930
Exec. Dir: Ed Harris

National Sports Law Institute
Marquette University Law School
PO Box 1881
1103 W. Wisconsin Avenue
Milwaukee, WI 53201
T: (414) 288-5815
F: (414) 288-5818
www.marquette.edu/law/sports
Chmn: Charles Mentkowski

National Strength Professionals Association, Inc.
12623 Wisteria Dr., Suite M
Germantown, MD 20874
T: (301) 428-2879
F: (301) 428-9465
E: nspainc@aol.com

National Women's Coaches Association
333 Blue Hills Drive
Nashville, TN 37214
T: (800) 668-0108
T: (615) 885-7349
F: (615) 316-0711
www.nwcawebsite.org
E: agunders@bellsouth.net
P: Ann Gunderson
PR: Lisa Ray

National Youth Sports Coaches Association
2050 Vista Pkwy.
West Palm Beach, FL 33411
T: (561) 684-1141
F: (561) 684-2546
www.nays.com
Exec Dir; Michael Pfahl

Native American Sports Council
1765 S. 8th St., Suite T-6
Colorado Springs, CO 80906
T: (719) 527-8511
F: (719) 527-1649
Exec. Dir: John Eagle Day

North American Society for Sport Management
c/o Dr. Garth Paton
Univ. of New Brunswick
Physical Education & Recreation
Fredericton, N.B. E3B 5A3
T: (506) 453-5010
F: (506) 453-3511
www.unb.ca/sportmanagement
E: NASSM@unb.ca
P: Dr. Darlene Young

North American Society for Sport History
PO Box 1026
Lemont, PA 16851
T: (814) 238-1284
F: (814) 238-1288
www.nassh.uwo.ca
P: Patricia Vertinsky

North American Sport Library Network (NASLIN)
Univ. of Calgary Library
2500 University Drive NW
Calgary, Alberta T2N 1N4
T: (403) 220-6097
F: (403) 282-6837
E: gghent@acs.ucalgary.ca
Chair: Gretchen Ghent

North American Sports Federation
PO Box K
Drifton, PA 18221
T: (717) 454-1952
Exec. Dir: Jake Kislan

North American Youth Sport Institute
4985 Oak Garden Dr., Suite 91
Kernersville, NC 27284
T: (800) 767-4916
T: (336) 784-4926
F: (336) 784-5546
www.naysi.com
E: jack@naysi.com
Exec Dir: Jack Hutslar

Olympian International
Penn Center House
1900 John F. Kennedy Blvd
Philadelphia, PA 19103
T: (215) 563-1886

Outdoor Recreation Coalition of America
PO Box 1319
Boulder, CO 80306
T: (303) 444-3353
F: (303) 444-3284
Exec. Dir: David Secunda

Particip Action
40 Dundas St. W., Suite 220
Box 64
Toronto, Ontario M5G 2C2
T: (416) 954-1212
F: (416) 954-4949
E: fitness@participaction.com

**People to People
Sports Committee**
80 Cutler Mill Road
Great Neck, NY 11021
T: (516) 482-5158
F: (516) 482-6694
E: people@pipeline.com
Director: Ed Ryder

**President's Council on
Physical Fitness & Sports**
200 Independence Ave SW
Hubert H. Humphrey Bldg. #738H
Washington, DC 20201
T: (202) 690-9000
F: (202) 690-5211

**Professional Grounds
Management Society (PGMS)**
120 Cockeysville Rd., Suite 104
Hunt Valley, MD 21031
T: (800) 609-7467
T: (410) 584-9754
F: (410) 584-9756
www.pgms.org
E: ppgms@aol.com

Recreation Safety Institute
PO Box 392
Ronkonkoma, NY 11779
T: (516) 883-6399
F: (516) 563-4807
Exec. Dir: Dr. Arthur Mittelstaedt

**Resort & Commercial
Recreation Association**
PO Box 1998
Tarpon Springs, FL 34688
T: (727) 939-8811
E: rcraone@aol.com

**Senior Games
Development Council**
200 Castlewood Drive
North Palm Beach, FL 33408
T: (561) 842-3600

Special Olympics International
Joseph P. Kennedy Foundation
1325 G Street NW, Suite 500
Washington, DC 20005
T: (202) 628-3630
F: (202) 824-0200
www.specialolympics.org

Sport for Understanding
3501 Newark St. NW
Washington, DC 20016
T: (202) 966-6800
F: (202) 895-1104

**Sporting Goods Agents
Association**
PO Box 998
Morton Grove, IL 60053
T: (847) 296-3670
F: (847) 827-0196
Exec. Dir: Lois Halinton

**Sporting Goods
Manufacturers Association**
200 Castlewood Drive
North Palm Beach, FL 33408
T: (561) 842-4100
F: (561) 863-8984
www.sportlink.com/sport
E: paasgma@aol.com
P: John Riddle

Sports Ambassadors
25 Corning Avenue
Milpitas, CA 95035
T: (408) 249-7111

Sports Lawyers Association
11250 Roger Bacon Drive
Suite 8
Reston, VA 22090
T: (703) 437-4377
F: (703) 435-4390
Exec. Dir: William Drohan

**Sportsplex Operators &
Developers Association**
PO Box 24617, Westgate Sta.
Rochester, NY 14624
T: (716) 426-2215
F: (716) 247-3112
www.gnv.fdt.net/soda
E: SODAsite@netacc.net
Exec Dir: Don Aselin, Jr.

Sports Turf Managers Association
1375 Rolling Hills Loop
Council Bluffs, IA 51503
T: (800) 323-3875
T: (712) 366-2669
F: (712) 366-9119
www.aip.com/stma
Exec Dir: Steve Trusty

Stadium Managers Association
19 Mantua Road
Mt. Royal, NJ 08061
T: (609) 423-7222
F: (609) 423-3420
Exec. Dir: Robert Talley

United States Military Sports Association
909 North Washington St.
Suite 308
Alexandria, VA 22314
T: (703) 836-1288
F: (703) 836-7914

United States National Senior Sports Organization
12520 Olive Boulevard
St. Louis, MO 63141
T: (314) 621-5545
F: (314) 621-5536
Exec. Dir: Linda Heikkila

United States Water Fitness Association, Inc.
PO Box 3279
Boynton Beach, FL 33424
T: (561) 732-9908
F: (561) 732-0950

U.S. Armed Forces Sports
Hoffman Bldg. 1, Room 400
2461 Eisenhower Avenue
Alexandria, VA 22331
T: (703) 325-8871
F: (703) 325-2511
Sec: William G. Begel

U.S. Cultural Exchange & Sports Society
787 N. Woodlawn Drive
Thousand Oaks, CA 91360
T: (805) 495-3258
F: (805) 379-2951
P: John S. Brittan

Water Sports Industry Association
200 Castlewood Drive
North Palm Beach, FL 33408
T: (561) 842-4100
F: (561) 863-8984
Exec. Dir: Jim Hotchkiss

Women In Sports & Events
89 Middletown Road
Holmdel, NJ 07733
T: (732) 946-2711
F: (732) 946-8032
VP: Sylvia Allen

Women's Sports Foundation
Eisenhower Park
East Meadow, NY 11554
T: (516) 542-4700
F: (516) 542-4716
www.lifetimetv.com/WOsport
E: wosport@aol.com
Exec. Dir: Donna Lopiano
P: Nancy Lieberman Cline
PR: Lynnore Lawton

World T.E.A.M. Sports
2108 South Blvd., Suite 101
Charlotte, NC 28203
T: (704) 370-6070
F: (704) 370-7750
Exec Dir: Steve Whisnant

World Waterpark Association
PO Box 14826
Lenexa, KS 66285
T: (913) 599-0300
F: (913) 599-0520
www.waterparks.com
E: wwa@waterparks.com

YMCA of the USA
101 North Wacker Drive
Chicago, IL 60606
T: (800) 872-9622
T: (312) 977-0031
F: (312) 977-9063
Exec. Dir: Daniel Emerson

Youth Fitness Coalition Project ACES
PO Box 6452
Jersey City, NJ 07306
T: (201) 433-8993
F: (201) 332-3060

YWCA of the USA
726 Broadway, 5th Floor
New York, NY 10003
T: (212) 614-2700
F: (212) 677-9716
P: Ann Stallard

U.S. Olympic Family

The following sports federations are U.S. national governing bodies for amateur sports that are part of the Olympic family and make their home at the USOC sports complex or in other facilities around the U.S.

Those listed with the Olympic Complex with not have addresses.

United States Olympic Committee
One Olympic Plaza
Colorado Springs, CO 80909
T: (719) 632-5551
F: (719) 578-4654
www.olympic-usa.org
P: William J. Hybl
Exec. Dir: Richard D. Schultz
Media Relations: Mike Moran

National Archery Association
T: (719) 578-4576
F: (719) 632-4733
www.USArchery.org
Exec. Dir: Robert Balink

U.S. Badminton Association
T: (719) 578-4808
F: (719) 578-4507
P: Diane Cornell

USA Baseball
2160 Greenwood Ave.
Trenton, NJ 08609
T: (609) 586-2381
F: (609) 587-1818
www.usabaseball.org
P: Mark Marquess

USA Basketball
5465 Mark Dabling Blvd.
Colorado Springs, CO 80918
T: (719) 590-4800
F: (719) 590-4811
www.usabasketball.org
Exec. Dir: Warren Brown

U.S. Biathlon
PO Box 297
Burlington, VT 05402
T: (802) 862-0338
F: (802) 862-0443
Exec. Dir: Steve Sands

U.S. Bobsled & Skeleton
PO Box 828
Lake Placid, NY 12946
T: (518) 523-1842
F: (518) 523-9491
Exec. Dir: Matt Roy

USA Boxing
T: (719) 578-4506
F: (719) 632-3426
P: Gary Toney

American Canoe Assn.
7432 Alban Station Blvd.
Suite B-226
Springfield, VA 22150
T: (703) 451-0141
F: (703) 451-2245
Exec. Dir: Jeffrey Yeager

U.S. Canoe & Kayak Team
Pan-American Plaza, Suite 600
201 S. Capitol Ave.
Indianapolis, IN 46225
T: (317) 237-5690
F: (317) 237-5694
www.usacanoekayak.org
Exec. Dir: Terry Kent

USA Curling
PO Box 866
Stevens Point, WI 54481
T: (715) 344-1199
F: (715) 344-6885
www.coredes.com/~usacurl/
P: Tom Brooke

USA Cycling, Inc.
T: (719) 578-4581
F: (719) 578-4596
www.usacycling.org
Exec. Dir: Lisa Voight

U.S. Diving, Inc.
Pan American Plaza, Suite 430
201 S. Capitol Ave.
Indianapolis, IN 46225
T: (317) 237-5252
F: (317) 237-5257
Exec. Dir: Todd Smith

U.S. Equestrian Team
Pottersville Road
Gladstone, NJ 07934
T: (908) 234-1251
F: (908) 234-9417
www.uset.com
Exec. Dir: Bob Standish

U.S. Fencing Association
T: (719) 578-4511
F: (719) 632-5737
www.usfa.org
Exec. Dir: Michael Massik

U.S. Field Hockey Association
T: (719) 578-4567
F: (719) 632-0979
Exec. Dir: Jane Betts

U.S. Figure Skating Association
20 First Street
Colorado Springs, CO 80906
T: (719) 635-5200
F: (719) 635-9548
Exec. Dir: Jerry Lace

USA Gymnastics
Pan American Plaza, Suite 300
201 S. Capitol Ave.
Indianapolis, IN 46225
T: (317) 237-5050
F: (317) 237-5069
www.usa-gymnastics.org/usag
Exec. Dir: Kathy Scanlan

USA Hockey
1715 Bob Johnson Rd.
Colorado Springs, CO 80919
T: (719) 599-5500
F: (719) 599-5994
www.usahockey.com
Exec. Dir: Dave Ogrean

U.S. Judo, Inc.
T: (719) 578-4730
F: (719) 578-4733
www.usjudo.org
Exec. Dir: William Rosenberg

U.S. Luge
PO Box 651
Lake Placid, NY 12946
T: (518) 523-2071
F: (518) 523-4106
www.usaluge.org
Exec. Dir: Ron Rossi

U.S. Modern Pentathlon
530 McCullough, Suite 619
San Antonio, TX 78215
T: (210) 246-3000
F: (210) 246-3096
Exec. Dir: W. Dean Billick

U.S. Racquetball
1685 W. Uintah
Colorado Springs, CO 80904
T: (719) 635-5396
F: (719) 635-0685
www.usra.org
Exec. Dir: Luke St. Onge

U.S. Rowing
Pan American Plaza, Suite 400
Indianapolis, IN 46225
T: (317) 237-5656
F: (317) 237-5646
www.coxing.com/usrowing.html
Exec. Dir: Frank Coyle

U.S. Sailing
PO Box 1260
15 Maritime Drive
Portsmouth, RI 02871
T: (401) 683-0800
F: (401) 683-0840
Exec. Dir: Terry Harper

USA Shooting
T: (719) 578-4670
F: (719) 635-7989
www.usc.edu/dept/usashooting
Exec. Dir: Robert Jursnick

U.S. Ski & Snowboard
PO Box 100
1500 Kearns Blvd.
Park City, UT 84060
T: (801) 649-9090
F: (801) 649-3613
www.usskiteam.com
P: Bill Marolt

U.S. Soccer Federation
1801-1811 S. Prairie Ave.
Chicago, IL 60616
T: (312) 808-1300
F: (312) 808-1301
Exec. Dir: Hank Steinbrecher

U.S. Softball/ASA
2801 NE 50th Street
Oklahoma City, OK 73111
T: (405) 424-5266
F: (405) 424-3855
www.softball.org
Exec. Dir: Donald Porter

U.S. Speedskating
PO Box 16157
Rocky River, OH 44116
T: (216) 899-0128
F: (216) 899-0109
Exec. Dir: Katie Marquard

U.S. Swimming, Inc.
T: (719) 578-4578
F: (719) 578-4669
www.usswim.org
Exec. Dir: Chuck Wielgus

U.S. Synchronized Swimming
Pan American Plaza, Suite 901
201 Capitol Ave.
Indianapolis, IN 46225
T: (317) 237-5700
F: (317) 237-5705
www.synchro-usa.org
Exec. Dir: Debbie Hesse

USA Table Tennis
T: (719) 578-4583
F: (719) 632-6071
www.usatt.org
Exec. Dir: Paul Montville

U.S. Taekwondo Union
T: (719) 578-4632
F: (719) 578-4642
www.ustu.com/taekwondo
Exec. Dir: Michael Weintraub

U.S. Team Handball
1903 Powers Ferry Rd., Suite 230
Atlanta, GA 30339
T: (770) 956-7660
F: (770) 956-7976
www.sport.ussa.edu/handsplit.htm
Exec. Dir: Maureen Stone

U.S. Tennis
70 W. Red Oak Lane
White Plains, NY 10604
T: (914) 696-7000
F: (914) 696-7167
www.usta.com
Exec. Dir: Richard Ferman, Jr.

USA Track & Field
One RCA Dome, Suite 140
Indianapolis, IN 46206
T: (317) 261-0500
F: (317) 261-0481
www.usatf.org
P: Patricia Rico

USA Triathlon
3595 E. Fountain Blvd., Ste. F-1
Colorado Springs, CO 80910
T: (719) 597-9090
F: (719) 597-2121
www.usatriathlon.org
Exec. Dir: Steven Locke

USA Volleyball
3595 E. Fountain Blvd., Ste. I-2
Colorado Springs, CO 80910
T: (719) 637-8300
F: (719) 597-6307
www.volleyball.org/usav
P: Rebecca Howard

U.S. Water Polo
1685 W. Uintah
Colorado Springs, CO 80904
T: (719) 634-0699
F: (719) 634-0866
www.ewpra.org/uswp
Exec. Dir: Bruce Wigo

USA Weightlifting
T: (719) 578-4508
F: (719) 578-4741
www.usaw.org
Exec. Dir: George Greenway

USA Wrestling
6155 Lehman Drive
Colorado Springs, CO 80918
T: (719) 598-8181
F: (719) 598-9440
www.usawrestling.org
Exec. Dir: Jim Scherr

**United States
Olympic Congress**
T: (719) 578-4711
F: (719) 632-9802

U.S. Olympic Foundation
1631 Mesa Avenue, Suite E
Colorado Springs, CO 80906
T: (719) 577-7082
F: (719) 635-5590
Chmn: George Steinbrenner
P: George Gowan

**U.S. Olympic
Education Center**
Northern Michigan University
Marquette, MI 49855
T: (906) 227-2888
F: (906) 227-2848
Director: Jeff Kleinschmidt

U.S. Olympic Training Center
One Olympic Plaza
Colorado Springs, CO 80909
T: (719) 578-4644 (Tours & Events)
T: (888) OLY-TOUR (Tours)
T: (719) 578-4500
F: (719) 578-4645
Director: Patrice Mikovich

U.S. Olympic Training Center
421 Old Military Road
Lake Placid, NY 12946
T: (518) 523-2600
F: (518) 523-1570
Director: Jack Favro

U.S. Olympic Training Center
1750 Wueste Road
San Diego, CA 91915
T: (619) 656-1500
F: (619) 482-6200
Director: Benita Fitzgerald-Mosley

U.S. Olympic Visitor Center
T: (719) 578-4888
F: (719) 578-4728
GM: J. Michael Wilson

Olympian Magazine
T: (719) 578-4913

USOC Gift Shop
T: (719) 578-4792

Canadian Sports

Listed here is the National Sports & Fitness Centre. Most national sports governing bodies reside in the centre. Please contact the centre for the indivdual sports bodies.

**Canadian National Sports &
Fitness Administration Centre**
760 Belfast Road
Ottawa, Ontario K1G 6M8 Canada
T: (613) 235-1515
F: (613) 235-9773
www.cdnsport.ca

Sport Canada
15 Eddy Street, 8 FL
Hull, Quebec K1A 0M5
T: (819) 956-8003
F: (819) 956-8006
www.pch.qc.ca/sportcanada
E: Sportcanada@pch.qc.ca

Sports Publications

Listed in this section are multi-sport & international publications. Some may be duplicated from other sections of the book. Please send new listings or changes to the author.

Agent & Manager
650 First Avenue
New York, NY 10016
T: (212) 532-4150
F: (212) 213-6382

All Star Sports Report
PO Box 955
Lenoir, NC 28645
T: (704) 758-5827

American Cheerleader
250 W. 57th St., Suite 1701
New York, NY 10019
T: (212) 265-8890
F: (212) 265-8908
www.americancheerleader.com
Editor: Julie Davis

American Outdoors
1331 Pennsylvania Ave.
Suite 726
Washington, DC, 20004
T: (202) 662-7420

American Sports
PO Box 6100
Rosemead, CA 91770
T: (626) 292-2222
Editor: Sam Sadler

Amusement Business
49 Music Square West
Nashville, TN 37203
T: (615) 321-4250
F: (615) 327-1575
www.amusementbusiness.com
Editor: Karen Oertley

Athletic Administration
PO Box 16428
Cleveland, OH 44116
T: (440) 892-4000
F: (440) 892-4007
www.nacda.com
Editor: Laurie Garrison

Athletic Business
1846 Hoffman Street
Madison, WI 53704
T: (800) 722-8764
T: (608) 249-0186
F: (608) 249-1153
www.athleticbusiness.com
E: editors@athleticbusiness.com
Editor: Sue Schmid

Athletic Director and Coach
450 Lafayette Street
Salem, MA 01970
T: (978) 744-1793

Athletic/Coaching Management
438 W. State Street
Ithaca, NY 14850
T: (607) 272-0265
F: (607) 272-2015
Editor: Eleanor Frankel

Athion's Pro & College Publications
220 25th Avenue North
Nashville, TN 37203
T: (800) ATHLON-8
T: (615) 327-0747
F: (615) 327-1149

Backpacker
33 E. Minor Stareet
Emmaus, PA 18098
T: (610) 967-5171
F: (610) 967-8181
Editor: Tom Hogan

Black College Sports Review
617 N. Liberty Street
Winston-Salem, NC 27101
T: (336) 723-9026
F: (336) 723-9173
www.blacksports.com
Editor: Richard Williams

The Blue Chips
PO Box 20688
Oklahoma City, OK 73120
T: (405) 364-1050

Cablesports
647 U. S. Route 1
York, ME 03909
T: (207) 363-6222
F: (207) 363-6182

China Sports Magazine
8 Tiyuguan Road
Beijing, China
T: (86.10) 671 16 669
F: (86.10) 671 15n858

City Sports Magazine
214 S. Cedras
Solana Beach, CA 92075
T: (619) 793-2711
F: (619) 793-2710
www.competitor.com
Editor: Bob Babbitt

Club Industry
1300 Virginia Drive
Suite 400
Fort Washington, PA 19034
T: (215) 643-8081
F: (215) 643-4827
www.clubindustry.com
Publisher: Terry Moffatt

College Sports
13645 Beta Road
Dallas, TX 75244
T: (972) 851-1700
F: (972) 851-1753
Editor: Chris Greer

Competitor for Women
Competitor Magazine
214 S. Cedras
Solana Beach, CA 92075
T: (619) 793-2711
F: (619) 793-2710
www.competitor.com
Pub/Editor: Bob Babbit

Conde Nast Sports for Women
342 Madison Avenue, 21 FL
New York, NY 10017
T: (212) 880-8800
F: (212) 880-4656
Editor: Lucy Danziger

ESPN The Magazine
19 E. 34th Street
New York, NY 10016
T: (212) 515-1000
F: (212) 515-1285
www.espn.com
Editor: John Papeneck

European TV Sports
126 Clock Tower Place
Carmel, CA 93923
T: (831) 624-1536
F: (831) 625-3225
Publisher: Kagan World Media

Facilities Magazine
650 First Avenue, 7th FL
New York, NY 10016
T: (212) 532-4150
F: (212) 213-6382
Editor: Michael Coffin

Fantasy Sports
700 E. State Street
Iola, WI 54990
T: (715) 445-2214
F: (715) 445-4087
www.krause.com
Publisher: Hugh McAloon

Field & Stream
Two Park Avenue
New York, NY 10016
T: (212) 779-5000
F: (212) 686-6877
Editor: Duncan Barnes

Fitness Management
PO Box 1198
Solana Beach, CA 92075
T: (619) 481-4155
F: (619) 481-4228

Florida Sports Magazine
2875-A SW 69th Court
Miami, FL 33155
T: (305) 265-0060
F: (305) 265-0906
Pub/Editor: Jim Woodman, Jr.

Florida Sportsman
2700 S. Kanner Hwy
Stuart, FL 34994
T: (561) 219-7400
F: (561) 219-6900
www.Floridasportsman.com
E: Editor@flsportsman.com
Publisher: Karl Wickstrom

The Gold Sheet
9255 Sunset Blvd., Suite 523
Los Angeles, CA 90069
T: (310) 274-0848
F: (310) 273-5932
www.goldsheet.com
E: goldshee@goldsheet.com
Publisher: Mort Olshan

Gravity Magazine
2025 Pearl Street
Boulder, CO 80302
T: (303) 440-5111
F: (303) 440-3313
www.gravitymagazine.com
Editor: Neil Feineman

High School Sports for Women
2025 Pearl Street
Boulder, CO 80302
T: (303) 440-5111
F: (303) 440-3313
Editor: Heather Prouty

IEG Sponsorship Report
640 N. La Salle, Suite 600
Chicago, IL 60610
T: (312) 944-1727
F: (312) 944-1897
www.sponsorship.com
E: ieg@sponsorship.com
Editor: Lesa Ukman

Inside Sporting Goods
One Penn Plaza
New York, NY 10119
T: (212) 615-2314
F: (212) 279-4454
www.sgblink.com
Editor: Robert Carr

Inside Sports
990 Grove Street
Evanston, IL 60201
T: (847) 491-6440
F: (847) 491-0867
www.centurysports.com
Editor: Ken Leiker

Interscholastic Athletic Admin.
PO Box 690
Indianapolis, IN 46206
T: (317) 972-6900
F: (317) 822-5700
www.nfhs.org
Editor: Richard Fawcett

Jewish Sports & Fitness
PO Box 4549
Old Village Station
Great Neck, NY 11023
T: (516) 482-5550

Journal of Legal Aspects of Sport
5840 S. Ernest Street
Terre Haute, IN 47802
T: (812) 237-2186
F: (812) 237-4338
E: pmsawyer@scifac.indstate.edu
Editor: Tom Sayer

The Journal of Physical Education, Recreation & Dance
1900 Association Drive
Reston, VA 22091
T: (703) 476-3400

Journal of Sport History
Box 1026
Lemont, PA 16851
T/F: (814) 238-1288
Editor: David Wiggins

Journal of the Philosophy of Sport
Journal of Sport Management
PO Box 5076
Champaign, IL 61825
T: (800) 747-4457
T: (217) 351-5076
F: (217) 351-2674
www.kinetics.com
E: humank@hkusa.com
Pub: Human Kinetics
Editor: Joy Desensi

JUCO Review (Junior College)
1825 Austin Bluffs Pkwy.
Suite 100
Colorado Springs, CO 80918
T: (719) 590-9788
F: (719) 590-7324
www.njcaa.org
E: njcaa@ix.netcom.com
Editor: George Killian

Kidsports Magazine
9625 W. Sample Road
Coral Springs, FL 33065
T: (800) 938-5588
F: (305) 755-4725

Media Sports Business
126 Clock Tower Place
Carmel, CA 93923
T: (831) 624-1536
F: (831) 624-3225
Publisher: Paul Kagan Assoc.

Men's Journal
1290 Ave. of the Americas
New York, NY 10104
T: (212) 484-1616
F: (212) 767-8203
Publisher: Mark MacDonald

Metrosports Magazine
27 W. 24th Street
New York, NY 10010
T: (212) 627-7040
F: (212) 627-7446
www.metrosports.com
E: metrosport@aol.com
Editor: Miles Jaffe

MultiSport Facility News
1450 N.E. 123rd. Street
North Miami, FL 33161
T: (305) 893-8771

Mundo Deportivo
11111 Santa Monica Blvd.
Suite 210
Los Angeles, CA 90025
T: (310) 914-3007
F: (310) 914-0607
Publisher: Marcelino Miyares, Jr.

NAIA College News
6120 S. Yale Ave., Suite 1450
Tulsa, OK 74136
T: (918) 494-8828
F: (918) 494-8841
www.niai.org
E: khenry@naia.org
Editor: Kevin Henry

National Coach Magazine
PO Box 2569
Gig Harbor, WA 98335
T: (253) 853-6777
F: (253) 853-6788
Editor: Gary Brines

National High School Federation News
PO Box 690
Indianapolis, IN 46206
T: (816) 464-5400
F: (816) 464-5711
www.NFHS.com

National PAL CopsnKids Chronicles
618 N. U.S. Hwy 1, Suite 201
North Palm Beach, FL 33408
T: (561) 844-1823
F: (561) 863-6120
www.PAL.org
Editor: Shirley McCoy

NCAA News & Publications
PO Box 6222
Indianapolis, IN 46206
T: (317) 917-6222
F: (317) 917-6888
www.ncaa.org
Editor: P. David Pickle

The Olympian
One Olympic Plaza
Colorado Springs, CO 80909
T: (719) 578-4529
F: (719) 578-4677
www.olympic-usa.org
Editor: Bob Condron

Outdoor America Magazine
707 Conservation Lane
Gaithersburg, MD 20878
T: (301) 548-0150
F: (301) 548-0146
www.iwla.org
Editor: Zack Hoskins

Outdoor Life
Two Park Avenue
New York, NY 10016
T: (212) 779-5000
F: (212) 686-6877
www.outdoorlife.com
Editor: Todd Smith

Outside Magazine
400 Market Street
Santa Fe, NM 87501
T: (505) 989-7100
F: (505) 989-4700
www.outside.starwave.com
Editor: Mark Bryant

Parks & Recreation Magazine
22377 Belmont Ridge Road
Ashburn, VA 20148
T: (703) 820-4940
F: (703) 858-0794
Editor: Doug Vaira

Physical Education Digest
111 Kingsmount Boulevard
Sudbury, Ontario P3E 1K8
T: (705) 675-7055

The Physician and Sportsmedicine
4530 W. 77th Street
Suite 350
Minneapolis, MN 55435
T: (612) 835-3222

Recreation Resources
2101 S. Arlington Heights Rd.
Suite 150
Arlington Heights, IL 60005
T: (847) 427-9512
F: (847) 427-2006
www.rec-net.com
Editor: Miriam Wuonsch

Referee Magazine
PO Box 161
Franksville, WI 53126
T: (414) 632-8855
F: (414) 632-5460
www.referee.com
E: referee@referee.com
Editor: Bary Mano

Rocky Mountain Sports Magazine
1521 Central St., Suite 1C
Denver, CO 80211
T: (303) 477-9770
F: (303) 477-9747
www.rockymountainsports.com
E: Rockyedit@aol.com
Pub: Mary Thorne

Scholastic Coach & Athletic Director
555 Broadway
New York, NY 10012
T: (212) 343-6372
F: (212) 343-6376
E: coachad1@aol.com
Editor: Herman Masin

Sierra Magazine
85 Second St., 2 FL
San Francisco, CA 94105
T: (405) 977-5572
F: (415) 977-5794
www.sierraclub.org
E: sierra.letters@sierraclub.org
Editor: Joan Hamilton

Skybox Magazine
1328 Elm Street
Cincinnati, OH 45225
T: (513) 541-0269
F: (513) 541-0057
Editor: Bill Dorsey

Southern Outdoors
5845 Carmichael Road
Montgomery, AL 36117
T: (334) 272-9530
F: (334) 279-7148
www.bassmaster.com
Pub: Helen Sevier

Special Events Magazine
23815 Stuart Ranch Road
Malibu, CA 90265
T: (800) 543-4116
T: (310) 317-4522
F: (310) 317-9644
Editor: Liese Gardner

The Sponsorship Newsletter
89 Middletown Road
Holmdel, NJ 07733
T: (732) 946-2711
F: (732) 946-8032
Publisher: Sylvia Allen

Sportupdate
760 Belfast Road
Ottawa, Ontario K1G 6M8 Canada
T: (613) 235-1515
F: (613) 235-9773
www.sportquest.com
E: moreinfo@sirc.ca
Editor: Christine Lalande

Sport Business
4 Valentine Place
London SE1 8QH, England
T: (44.171) 928.93.93
F: (44.171) 928.94.66
www.sportbusiness.com
E: copydesk@sportbusiness.com
Editor: Kevin Roberts

Sport Intern
Postfach 710 420
Alescher Strasse 7
D-8154 Munich 71, Germany
T: (49.89) 79.61.77
F: (49.89) 79.00.626
Publisher: Karl-Heinz Huber

Sport Magazine
6420 Wilshire Blvd.
Los Angeles, CA 90048
T: (323) 782-2828
F: (323) 782-2835
www.petersenco.com
Editor: Norb Garrett

The Sport Psychologist
PO Box 5076
Champaign, IL 61825
T: (217) 351-5076
F: (217) 351-2674
Editor: Graham Jones

Sporting Goods Business
One Penn Plaza
New York, NY 10119
T: (212) 714-1300
F: (212) 279-4454
www.sgblink.com
Editor: Christopher McEvoy

Sporting Goods Dealer
445 Broad Hollow Road
Melville, NY 11747
T: (516) 845-2700
F: (516) 845-2797
Editor: Mike Reynolds

Sporting Goods Intelligence
442 Featherbed Lane
Glen Mills, PA 19342
T: (610) 558-1601
F: (610) 558-1650
www.sginews.com
E: sginews@sginews.com
Editor: Bob McGee

The Sporting News
10176 Corporate Square Drive
Suite 200
St. Louis, MO 63132
T: (314) 997-7111
F: (314) 993-7726
www.sportingnews.com
E: fans@sportingnews.com
Editor: John Rawlings

Sports Afield
250 W. 55th Street
New York, NY 10019
T: (212) 649-4300
F: (212) 581-3923
E: mwade@hearst.com
Publisher: Michael Wade

Sports & the Courts
PO Box 2836
Winston-Salem, NC 27102
T: (336) 725-7700
F: (336) 725-6777
Editor: C. Thomas Ross

Sports Business
3883 Hwy 7, Suite 214
Woodbridge, Ontario L4L 6C1
T: (905) 856-2600
F: (905) 856-2667
E: triscomm@istar.ca
Pub: Tony Muccilli

Sports Business Update
PO Box 218
Atlantic, VA 23303
T: (757) 824-3942
F: (757) 824-4480
www.sportsvueinc.com
E: sportsvue@aol.com
Editor: Charles Cuttone

Sports Collectors Digest
700 E. State Street
Iola, WI 54990
T: (715) 445-4612
F: (715) 445-4087
www.krause.com
Editor: Tom Mortenson

The Sports Daily
120 W. Morehead St., Suite 220
Charlotte, NC 28202
T: (704) 973-1500
F: (704) 973-1501
www.sportsbizdaily.com
Publisher: Sal Schiliro

Sports Focus
124 E. Diamond Ave., Suite 7
Gaithersburg, MD 20877
T: (301) 670-6717
F: (301) 670-9043
www.sportsfocusmagazine.com
E: spfocusmag@aol.com
Editor: Greg Greene

Sports Illustrated
1271 Avenue of the Americas
New York, NY 10020
T: (212) 522-1212
F: (212) 522-4543
www.timewarner.com
Editor: Mark Mulvoy

Sports Illustrated For Kids
1271 Avenue of the Americas
New York, NY 10020
T: (212) 522-1212
F: (212) 522-0120
www.sikids.com
Pub: Cleary Simpson

Sports Illustrated Women/Sport
1271 Avenue of the Americas
New York, NY 10020
T: (212) 522-2248
F: (212) 522-4543
Editor: Sandy Bailey

Sports Industry News
PO Box 946
Camden, ME 04843
T/F: (207) 236-8346
Editor: Ray Swan

Sports International
PO Box 10010
Ogden, UT 84409
T: (801) 394-9446
F: (801) 627-1453

The Sports Journal
3419 26th Ave. SW
Calgary, Alberta, T3E 0N4
T: (403) 240-3258
F: (403) 246-4464

Sports Map Magazine
38 Oliver Place
Ringwood, NJ 07456
T: (973) 962-4710
E: sportsmap@yahoo.com
www.sportsmap.com
Editor: Richard Lynch

The Sports Marketing Newsletter
PO Box 99
Southport, CT 06490
T: (203) 259-3890
F: (203) 255-1787
E: kdmurphy@worldnet.att.net
Publisher: Brian Murphy

Sports Marketing Quarterly
PO Box 4425, University Avenue
Morgantown, WV 26500
T: (800) 477-4348
F: (304) 599-3482
Publisher: Andrew Ostrow

Sports Parade
1720 Washington Blvd.
Ogden, UT 84409
T: (801) 394-9446

Sports Reporter
306 Broadway
Lynnbrook, NY 11563
T: (516) 599-2121
F: (516) 599-0451
www.winsports.com
Editor: Joe Lazzaro

Sports N Spokes
2111 E. Highland, Suite 180
Phoenix, AZ 85016
T: (602) 224-0500
F: (602) 224-0507
Publisher: Francis Farrell

Sports Travel
13274 Fiji Way, 4th FL
Marina del Rey, CA 90292
T: (310) 577-3700
F: (310) 577-3715
Publisher: Tim Schneider

Sports Traveler
110 5th Avenue, 5FL
New York, NY 10011
T: (212) 758-0881
F: (212) 685-6240
Editor: Carol Cooper Gary

Sports Trend
1115 Northmeadow Pkwy
Roswell, GA 30376
T: (770) 569-1540
F: (770) 569-5105
Editor: Darren Devik

Sportvision
Friars House, Suite 122
157-168 Blackfriars Road
London SE1 8EZ, England
T: (44.171) 401.99.88
F: (44.171) 401.71.91
E: sportvision@aol.com
Publisher: Paul Nicholson

Street & Smith's SportsBusiness Journal
120 W. Morehead St., 3FL
Charlotte, NC 28202
T: (704) 973-1400
F: (704) 973-1401
www.sportsbusinessjournal.com
Exec. Editor: Abraham Madkour

Super Outdoors
2695 Aiken Road
Shelbyville, KY 40065
T: (502) 722-9463
F: (502) 722-8093
www.ool.com/kids
Editor: John Vohn

Team Leader
7 W. 34th Street
New York, NY 10001
T: (212) 630-4000
F: (212) 630-4879

Team Licensing Business
3300 N. Central Ave., Suite 2500
Phoenix, AZ 85012
T: (602) 990-1101
T: (602) 990-0819
Pub: Mike Nichols

Team Marketing Report
660 W. Grand Ave.
Suite 100E
Chicago, IL 60610
T: (888) 616-1TMR
T: (312) 829-7060
F: (312) 733-4071
www.teammarketing.com
E: editor@teammarketingreport.com
Editor: Sean Brenner

Western Outdoors
PO Box 2027
Newport Beach, CA 92659
T: (949) 546-4370
F: (949) 662-3486
Editor: Jack Brown

Wintersport Business
502 W Cordova
Santa Fe, NM 87501
T: (505) 986-1257
F: (505) 988-7224
www.winterbiz.com
E: winterbiz@aol.com
Publisher: Terry Moyes

Women's Sports Channel
285 W. Broadway
New York, NY 10013
T: (212) 965-8500
F: (212) 965-8868
www.womenssportschannel.com
Editor: Michael Conniff

Women's Sports & Fitness
Women's Sports on Campus
2025 Pearl Street
Boulder, CO 80302
T: (303) 440-5111
F: (303) 440-3313
Editor: Jean Weiss

Women's Sports Market Report
5 Beeson Street, Suite 114
Marblehead, MA 01945
T: (781) 599-3314
F: (781) 593-0338
E: wmssports@aol.com
Publisher: Sharon Barbano

Women's Sports Job Wire
Women's Sports Wire
409 Utica, Suite D-36
Huntington Beach, CA 92648
T: (714) 960-0411
F: (714) 969-5881
www.womensportswire.com
E: wswire1@aol.com
Publisher: Becky Heidesch
Editor: Christin Crowley

Youth Sport Journal
2050 Vista Parkway
West Palm Beach, FL 33411
T: (561) 684-1141
F: (561) 684-2546
www.nays.org
E: nays@nays.com
Editor: Greg Bach

Sports Career Development

College Sports Administration & Management Studies

Listed in this section are colleges & universities that offer degree programs in sports & athletic management, sports administration, sports law, sports medicine, arena & event management, etc. for amateur & professional sports. This list is incomplete but will be expanded as more institutions announce programs.

Adelphi University
Woodruff Hall
Dept of PE & Hum. Perf.
Garden City, NY 11530
T: (516) 877-4260
F: (516) 877-4258
Dr. Ronald Feingold, Chmn
Dr. Mel Less, Dir Sport Mgt
Undergrad: BS, P.E.
Graduate: Sports Management

Alabama, University of
PO Box 1967
University, AL 35486
T: (205) 348-6075
Dr. Joseph Smith
Undergrad: Sports Fitness Mgt.

Alabama at Birmingham, University of
Dept. of Human Studies
207 Education Bldg.
UAB Station
Birmingham, AL 35294
T: (205) 934-2446
F: (205) 975-8040
Dr. David Macrina, Chmn.
Dr. Donna Hester, Grad. S.Adm.
Undergrad: Fitness Spec/Ed.
Graduate: Sports Adm.

Albertson College of Idaho
2112 Cleveland Blvd.
Caldwell, ID 83605
T: (208) 459-5866
F: (208) 459-5851
Jim Fennell, Chmn., P.E.
Undergrad: Sports Fitness Mgt.

Alcorn State University
Dept. of HPER
PO Box 510
Lorman, MS 39096
T: (601) 877-6506
F: (601) 877-3821
Dr. Robert Smith, Chr.
Undergraduate: BS Rec
Graduate: Athl. Adm., Coaching.

Allentown College
2755 Station Avenue
Center Valley, PA 18034
T: (610) 282-1335
F: (610) 282-2279
Dr. Joy M. Richman, Dir.
Undergraduate: B.S.Sports Administration, Athletic Adm.

Appalachian State University
Dept. HLES
Varsity Gym
Boone, NC 28608
T: (828) 262-3140
F: (828) 262-3138
Dr. Ed Turner, Coordinator
Graduate: M.A., Sport Mgt/PE, Athletic Administration

Arkansas, University of
Dept. of Health Science
Kinesiology, Rec. & Dance
306 HPER Bldg.
Fayetteville, AR 72701
T: (501) 575-2857
F: (501) 575-6401
Dr. Sharon Hunt, Dept. Head
Dr. Dean Gorman, Grad Coord
Graduate: M.E., PE/Sports Mgt.

Ashland University
Ashland, OH 44273
T: (419) 289-5443
Dr. Allan Hall
Undergraduate
Sports Communication

Averett College
420 W. Main Street
Danville, VA 24541
T: (804) 791-5759
Norma Roady, Director
Sports Mgt./PE

Baldwin-Wallace College
Sport/Dance/Arts Management Pgm
Berea, OH 44017
T: (440) 826-2306
F: (440) 826-2192
Coord: June Baughman
Undergrad: Degree in HPE with a concentration in Sport Mgt/fitness

Ball State University
Health & Phys. Activites Bldg. P
School of Physical Education
Muncie, IN 47306
T: (765) 285-1451
F: (765) 285-5610
E: jreno@wp.bsu.edu
Dr. John Reno, Director
Undergrad: B.A., Sports Adm.
Grad: M.A., P.E., Sports Mgt.

Baylor University
HPER, Box 7313
Waco, TX 76798
T: (254) 755-3505
F: (254) 755-1321
Dr. Nancy Goodloe, Dir. Grad. pgm.
Dr. Andy Pittman, Dir. of Sports
Graduate: M.S.-Education
Sports Mgt., Exer. Psychology

Bemidji State University
1500 Birchmont Dr. NE
Dept. of PE, Health & Sport
Bemidji, MN 56601
T: (218) 755-2940
F: (218) 755-3898
Dr. Karl Salscheider, Chr.
Dr. Murael Gilman, Grad Coord.
Undergrad:BA, Health, PE., Sport Mgt.
Grad: M.S., Sport Sudies

Bowling Green State Univ.
Sports Management Division
School of HMSLS
Bowling Green, OH 43403
T: (419) 372-2876
F: (419) 372-0383
E: jsidwel@bynet.bgsu.edu
Joy Sidwell, Chr. Sports Mgt.

Undergrad: B.S., Ath. Train., Sports Information, Sport Enterprise
Graduate: Sports Administration

California St. Univ.-Fullerton
Dept. of Kinesiology & Health
PO Box 34080
Fullerton, CA 92634
T: (714) 773-3316
F: (714) 449-5317
Dr. Anne Marie Bird, Chair.
Dr. Ian Bailey, Dir.
Graduate:M.S. in P.E., Corp. Fitness Mgt., Professional Sports Mgt.

California University of PA
Sport Management Studies
250 University Avenue
California, PA 15419
T: (724) 938-4562
F: (724) 938-4342
www.cup.edu
E: yarbrough@cup.edu
Dept/Pgm Dir: Dr. Roy E. Yarbrough
Undergrad: BS in Sport Mgt Studies

Campbell University
Dept. of Exercise Science
Box 414
Buies Creek, NC 27506
T: (910) 893-1360
F: (910) 893-1424
Dr. William Freeman, Chair
Undergrad: B.S., Sports Mgt., Fitness Mgt., Coaching, Sports Bus

Canisius College
Dept. of Phys Ed.
2001 Main St., KAC 169
Buffalo, NY 14208
T: (716) 888-3179
F: (716) 888-3219
Dr. James Sylvis, Chr. PE, Under.
Dr. Susan Denpf, Grad.
Jim Reardon, Sport Mgt. Dir.
Undergrad/Grad: BS/MS
Athletic Training, Sport Admin.

Capital University
2199 E. Main St.
Dept. of Health & Sport Sciences
Columbus, OH 43209
T: (614) 236-6911
F: (614) 236-6178
Don Charlton, Health & Sport Sci.
Undergrad: BA, Ath. Training, Health & Fitness

Central Michigan University
108 Rose Center
Dept. of PE & Sport
Mt. Pleasant, MI 48859
T: (517) 774-6661
F: (517) 774-5391
Dr. James Hornak, Chair
Dr. Walter Schneider, Dir. Spt. Adm.
Undergrad/Grad.: BA/MA Sport Stud.
Sports Adm./PE/Ath. Adm.

Central Missouri State University
Dept. of PE, Morrow 101
Warrensburg, MO 64093
T: (660) 543-4521
F: (660) 543-4167
Dr. Dan Gerdes, Sport Adm. Dir.
Undergrad: BS, Coaching
Grad: MS, Athletic Training, Ath. &
Bus. Admin., Exercise & Sport Sci.

Central Washington University
Dept. of PEHLS
Ellensburg, WA 98926
T: (509) 963-1919
F: (509) 963-1848
Jan Boyungs, Prog. Dir.
Finess & Sport Mgt.
Dr. John Gregor, Chm. PEHLS
Undergrad: BS, Fitness & Sport. Mgt.
Grad: MS in PEHLS., Leisure Serv.,
Ath. Adm, Exercise Sci., Coaching

Chadron State College
HPER
1000 Main Street
Chadron, NE 69337
T: (308) 432-6343
F: (308) 432-6464
Scott Ritson, Dept. Chr.
Grad: MA,Recreation Mgt.
Undergrad: BA, Leisure Mgt.

Cleveland State University
HPER Dept.
Euclid Ave. at E. 24th St.
Cleveland, OH 44115
T: (216) 687-4839
F: (216) 687-5410
Dr. Annie Clement, Dir. Sport Mgt.
Undergrad/Graduate
Sports Management

Columbus College
4225 University Avenue
Columbus, GA 31907
T: (706) 568-2046
F: (706) 569-2634
Dr. Michael Magnum, Dir.
Ungergrad: BS, Sport Fitness
Management

Concordia University
7141 rue Sherbrooke Ouest
Montreal, Quebec H4B 1R6
Canada
T: (514) 848-3334
George Short, Director
Sports Management

Connecticut, University of
2095 Hillside Road, U-110
Storrs, CT 06269
T: (860) 486-3623
F: (860) 486-1123
Dr. Carl Maresh, Dept. Head
Undergrad.: BS, Sport Medicine,
Athletic Training, Fitness Mgt.,
Park & Rec Mgt, Sports Mkt.
Grad: MA Phd., Sport Mgt.,
Recreation Mgt., Fitness Mgt.,
Leisure Mgt, Therapeutic Recreation.

Davis & Elkins College
Dept. of Health, PE
100 Campus Drive
Elkins, WV 26241
T: (304) 636-1993
F: (304) 637-1414
Dr. Jean Minnick, Chair.
Undergrad: BS, P.E., Ath.Training,
Sport Mgt, Health, Exercise Sci.

Dayton, University of
300 College Park
Dayton, OH 45469-1210
T: (937) 229-4225
F: (937) 229-4244
Lloyd Laubach, Director
Dr. Peter Tittlebaum, Pgm Coord.
Undergrad: BS, Sports Business,
Sports Marketing

Delta State University
Box B-2
Cleveland, MS 38733
T: (601) 846-4555
F: (601) 846-4571
Dr. Milton Wilder, Dir.
Undergrad: BS, P.E., Health, Recrea.,
Sports Mgt, Sports Information
Grad: MED, Phys. ED.

Denver, University of
Daniels College of Business
2020 S. Race Street
Denver, CO 80012
T: (303) 871-3736
F: (303) 871-4466
Dr. Gordon VonStroh, Prog Dir
Graduate: Masters in Science Mgt
With a concentration in Sport Mgt. &
Communication.

Durham College
2000 Simcoe St. N.
Oshawa, Ontario L1H 7L7, CAN
T: (416) 576-0210
Ramona Rickard, Director
Sports Administration

East Stroudsburg Univ.
Koehler Fieldhouse
E. Stroudsburg, PA 18301
T: (570) 422-3106
F: (570) 422-3586
Prof. Donald Cummings, Grad.
Prof. Robert Fleischman JD/MS,
Sport Mgt./Grad Dept.
Undergrad: BS, Sport Fitness Mgt.
Movement and Sports Studies
Grad: M.ED, Sport Mgt.

Eastern Illinois University
263 Lantz Gym
College of HPER
Charleston, IL 61920
T: (217) 581-2215
F: (217) 581-6434
Dr. Phoebe Church, Chr. PE
Dr. Kevin Lasley, Prof., P.E.
Undergrad & Grad. Studies
PE/Sports Adm. & Mgt. Studies
Corp. Fitness & Club Mgt.

Eastern Kentucky Univ.
EKU College of HPER & A
202 Weaver Health Bldg.
Richmond, KY 40475
T: (606) 622-1887
F: (606) 622-1254
Dr. Lonnie Davis, Chair.
Dr. Harold Holmes, Prof., Grad.
Dr. Paul Motley, Prof. Undergrad.
Undergrad: BS, HPER/ Sports Adm,
Athletic Training
Grad: MS, Sports Administration

Elon College
Campus Box 2500
Elon College, NC 27244
T: (336) 584-2420
F: (336) 584-2443
Dr. James P. Drummond, Dir.
Bill Ross, Sport Mgt.
Undergrad: B.S., Leisure/Sports Mgt.
Sports Medicine

Evansville University
Dept. of Physical Education
1800 Lincoln Ave.
Evansville, IN 47722
T: (812) 479-2360
F: (812) 479-2199
Cheryl Griffith, Chair, Phys. Ther.
Paul Jensen, Chair., H&PE
Undergrad: B.S., Spo Admin., Athl.
Training, Sport Comm, Sport Studies.
Grad: M.S., Physical Therapy

Florida, University of
100 Florida Gym
Gainesville, FL 32611
T: (352) 392-0584
F: (352) 392-3186
Dr. Sue Whidden, Grad Cord.
Undergrad: B.S., Athletic Adm.
Graduate: M.E.S.S., Sport Mgt.

Florida International University
University Park Campus
Dept. of HPER
Miami, FL 33199
T: (305) 348-3486
F: (305) 348-3571
Dr. Robert Wolff, Chr. HPER
Dr. Richard Lopez, Pgm. Dir.
Undergrad: BS, Sports Mgt.
Ex. Phys., Therapeutic Rec.
Grad: MS, Sports Mgt, Exercise
Physiology, Therapeutic Recreation

Florida State University
Dept. of PE, 200 Tully Gym
Tallahassee, FL 32306
T: (850) 644-4813
F: (850) 644-0975
Dr. Dewayne J. Johnson, Chr.
Undergrad: BS, PE/Sports Mgt.
Grad: MS, PhD, EdD, PE/Sport Adm.

George Washington University
Int'l. Institute of Tourism Studies
School of Business/Public Admin.
817 23rd St. NW, Bldg. K, Room 106
Washington, DC 20052
T: (202) 994-6280
F: (202) 994-1420
Lisa A Delpy, PhD, Director
Undergrad: BBA, BS, Sports Mgt.,
Exercise Science
Grad: MA, Exercise Science, Sport
Mkt., Sport Tourism, Intl. Sports Mkt.
Sport & Special Event Mgt., Sport
Tourism

Georgia, University of
Dept. of PE/Sport Studies
Athens, GA 30602
T: (706) 542-4379
F: (706) 542-4377
Dr. Stan Brassie, Dir.
Graduate: M.E., Sports Mgt/PE, Facility
& Event Mgt, Mgt. of Sports
Organizations

Georgia Southern University
Dept. of Sport Science/PE
LB 8076
Stattesboro, GA 30460
T: (912) 681-0200
F: (912) 681-0381
Dr. Larry Mc Carthy,Grad.Spt. Mgt.
Dr. Ming Li, Undergrad. Sport Mgt.
Undergrad/Grad: B.S./M.S., Athl.
Adm., Sport Promotion, Sport Comm

Georgia State University
Dept. of Kinesiology & Health
University Plaza
Atlanta, GA 30303
T: (404) 651-2536
F: (404) 651-4814
Dr. Jeff Rupp, Chmn.
Dr. G. Rankin Cooter, Coor. Spt. Adm.
Graduate: M.S., Athletic Admin.,
Facilities Mgt., Sports Club Mgt, Sport
Mkt & Promotion, Sports Information

Georgia Tech
Int'l Sports Business & Economics
Atlanta, GA 30332-0525
T: (404) 894-1039
F: (404) 894-8573
Dr. Malcolm MacKenzie,
Adm. Dir. of Intl Sports
Grad: MS, Business Mgt, Sports
Events & Proj. Mgt., Corp.Sponsor.

Gettysburg College
Dept. of Health, Educ. & Science
Bream/Wright/Hauser Ath. Comp.
W. Lincoln Avenue
Gettysburg, PA 17325-1486
T: (717) 337-6441
F: (717) 337-6528
E: gbiser@gettysburg.edu
Gareth Biser, Chmn., PE
Dr. Virginia Schein, Dir.Mgt.Prog.
Undergrad: BA, Sports Mgt

Grambling State University
Campus Box 4244
Grambling, LA 71245
T: (318) 274-2712
F: (318) 274-6053
Dr. Willie Daniel, Dept. Head
Dr. Dorothy Hardy,Coord. Sprt. Adm
Graduate: M.S., Sports Administration

Greenville College
315 E. College Ave.
Greenville, IL 62246
T: (618) 664-1840
F: (618) 664-1373
Dr. Rober Johnson, Director
Undergrad: B.S., Sports Adm,
Recreation, Adult Fitness

Guilford College
Dept. of Sport Studies
5800 Friendly Avenue
Greensboro, NC 27410
T: (336) 316-2329
F: (336) 316-2949
Todd Seidler, Dir. Sport Mgt Studies
Undergrad: B.S., Sports Studies/
Sport Mgt, Sports Medicine, PE

Harding University
900 East Center
Searcy, AR 72143
T: (501) 279-4360
Dr. Karyl Bailey, Director
Undergrad: B.A., HPE/Sports Mgt,
Club Mgt, Broadcast & Print
Journalism

Houston, University of
123 Melcher Gym
Houston, TX 77204
T: (713) 743-9840
F: (713) 743-9860
Dr. Dale G. Pease, Chr.
Dr. Dennis Smith, Dir. Sport Pgm.
Undergrad: B.S., Sport Adm,
Exercise Science
Grad: M.S., EdD, Med, PE,
Human Performance

Idaho, University of
Recreation Dept,
109 Memorial Gym
Moscow, ID 83844
T: (208) 885-6582
F: (208) 885-5929
E: call@udiaho.edu
Dr. Calvin Lathen, Dir.
Undergrad & Graduate: B.S./M.S.
Rec. & Sport Mgt, Sports Science

IIllinois at Chicago, Univ. of
Dept. of Kinesiology
901 W. Roosevelt Rd.
Chicago, IL 60608
T: (312) 996-9685
F: (312) 413-3699
Dr. Michael McGovern, Dir.
Grad: M.S., Sport Mgt, Fitness

IIllinois State University
Dept. of HPERD
Normal, IL 61761
T: (309) 438-8661
F: (309) 438-5559
Dr. Sandra Little, Cord. HPERD
Grad: M.S., Phys. Ed, Sports Adm,
Recreation Sport Mgt, Rec. Park
Admin., Sport Management

Illinois, University of
170 IMPE Bldg.
201 Peabody Drive
Champaign, IL 61820
T: (217) 333-9780
Dr. David Matthews
Graduate: PhD, Athletic & Recreation,
Communications

Indiana State University
HPER Bldg.
Terre Haute, IN 47809
T: (812) 237-2183
F: (812) 855-1158
Dr. Thomas Sawyer, Dir.
Grad: M.A., M.S., Sports Mgt/Adm.

Indiana Univ. of Pennsylvania
Indiana, PA 15705
T: (724) 357-2100
Undergrad: Sports Management

Indiana University
Dept. of Kinesiology
HPER 112 (Undergrad)
HPER 179 (Graduate)
Bloomington, IN 47405
T: (812) 855-1158
F: (812) 855-9417
Gary Sailes, Undergrad. Coord.
Larry Fielding, Graduate Coord.
Dr. Ronald Carlson, Internships
Undergrad: B.S.Sport Mkt. & Mgt.
Grad: M.S., Sport Mkt & Mgt, Spt Law

Iowa State University
Health & Human Perf. Dept.
Ames, IA 50011
T: (515) 294-8131
F: (515) 294-8740
Dr. Richard Engelhorn, Grad. Coord.
Undergrad/Grad.: BS/MS
PE/Sports Management

Ithaca College
953 Danby Road
School of Health Sci. & Hum. Per.
Dept. of Exer & Sport Science
Ithaca, NY 14850
T: (607) 274-3155
F: (607) 274-1943
Craig Fisher, Chmn

Wayne Blann, Cord. Sport Mgt.
Ellen Staurowsky, Coord. Sport Info/Communications
Grad: MS, Sport. Psyc, Sports Med.
Undergrad: BS, Sport Mgt, Sports Information & Communication

James Madison University
Godwin Hall
Dept. of Kinesiology
Harrisonburg, VA 22807
T: (540) 568-3954
Dr. Joel Vedelli, Prog. Dir.
Undergrad: B.S., Sport Mgt/Exercise Fitness

Johnson & Wales University
8 Abbot Park Place
Providence, RI 02903
T: (401) 598-1475
F: (401) 598-4764
Dr. Roberta Sebo, Chmn
Stephen Pyle, Prof
Undergrad: B.S., Sports/Facilities
Grad: M.A., Hospitality Admin.

Kansas, University of
HPER
104 Robinson Center
Lawrence, KS 66045
T: (785) 864-3371
F: (785) 864-3343
Dr. James LaPoint
Undergrad/Graduate: B.S./M.S., P.E./Sports Adm., Sport Science

Keene State University
229 Main St., PE Dept.
Keene, NH 03431
T: (603) 358-2817
Dr. Rebecca Brown
Undergraduate
Sports Mgt/Leisure Adm.

Kennesaw State University
1000 Chastain Road
HPER, PO Box 444
Kennesaw, GA 30144
T: (770) 423-6216
F: (770) 423-6561
Dr. Charles Ash, Chr. HPER
Dr. Bernie Goldfine, Director
Undergrad: BS in PE, Sports Mgt.

Kent State University
264 Memorial Annex
School of Exer. Leisure & Sports
Kent, OH 44242
T: (330) 672-2990
F: (330) 672-4106
Aaron Mulrooney, Director
Graduate: M.A., P.E./Sport Admin.

Laurentian University
School of Sports Administration.
Ramsey Lake Road
Sudbury, Ontario P3E 2C6, CAN
T: (705) 675-4834
F: (705) 675-4836
Greg Zorbas, Chmn.
Undergraduate: Honours Bachelor of Commerce Degree.
Sports Admin., Sports Business Mgt.

Le Tourneau University
PO Box 7001
Longview, TX 75607
T: (903) 753-0231
F: (903) 233-3377
Melba Burry, Dir. of PE
Undergrad: B.S., Sport Mgt.

Liberty University
Sports Adm. Studies
Box 20000
Lynchburg, VA 24506
T: (804) 582-2330
F: (804) 582-2554
Dr. Dale Gibson, Dir. of Sport Mgt.
Undergrad: BS, Sports Administration, Exercise Science

Long Beach State University
1250 Bellflower Blvd.
Long Beach, CA 90840
T: (562) 985-4051
F: (562) 985-8067
Dixie A. Grimmett, Chr. PE
Douglas Young, Grad Cord.
Undergrad: B.A., Graduate: M.A.
P.E., Sports Mgt.

Long Island University
Brooklyn Campus M-320
Brooklyn, NY 11201
T: (718) 834-6000
Dr. Milorad Stricevic
Undergraduate: B.A.
Sports Science/P.E.

Loras College
1450 Alta Vista Street
Dubuque, IA 52004
T: (319) 588-7053
F: (319) 588-4975
Dr. Robert Tucker, Chmn
Eric Johnson, Undergrad. Coord.
Undergrad/Grad: B.A./M.A.
Sport Mgt/Athletic Administration

Louisville, University of
HPES, HP Bldg.
Louisville, KY 40292
T: (502) 852-0547
F: (502) 852-6683
Dr. Dan Mahoney, Dir. Sport Mgt.
Undergrad/Graduate: BS/MS
Sport Adm. & Mgt, Sports Mkt;
Sports Medicine

Marshall University
HPER
College of Education
400 Hal Greer Blvd.
Huntington, WV 25755
T: (304) 696-6490
F: (304) 696-2928
Dr. C. Robert Barnett
Undergrad/Graduate: BS/MS
Ath. Adm/Sport Mgt & Mkt,
Arena Management

Maryland, University of
Dept. of Kinesiology
North Gym 2351
College Park, MD 20742
T: (301) 405-2451
F: (301) 314-9167
Dr. Jerry Wrenn, Director
Dr. Steve McDaniel, Pgm Coord.
Graduate: MA, Sports Management,
Professional Sport Mgt., Club Mgt.

Massachusetts, University of
16 Curry Hicks Bldg.
Amherst, MA 01003
T: (413) 545-0441
F: (413) 577-0642
www.umass.edu/sptmgt
Glenn M. Wong, Dept. Head
Laurie Gullian, Undergrad.
Dr. Harold Vanderzwang, Grad.
Howard Davis, Intership Coord.
Undergrad/Graduate: BS/MS
Sport Management

Medaille College
18 Agassiz Circle
Buffalo, NY 14214
T: (716) 884-3281
F: (716) 884-0291
Jerry Kissel, Director
Undergrad: B.S., Recreation,
Sport Mgt, Sports Communication

Memphis, University of
Sport & Leisure Commerce
204 Elma Roane Fieldhouse
Memphis, TN 38152
T: (901) 678-4556
F: (901) 678-5014
E: irwin.dickatcoe.memphis.edu
Dr. Richard Irwin, Director
Grad: M.S., Professional &
Commercial Sport & Leisure Mkt.

Miami, University of
Dept. of Exercise & Sport Science
School of Education
PO Box 248065
Coral Gable, FL 33124
T: (305) 284-3711
F: (305) 284-3003
Dr. Harry Mallios, Chmn.
Undergrad: Minor in Sport Mgt.,
Sport Medicine
Graduate: M.S., Sports Admin, Sports
Med., College/Pro Sports Mgt.

Michigan, University of
Dept. of Kinesiology
Central Campus Recreation Bldg.
Ann Arbor, MI 48109
T: (734) 747-2688
F: (734) 936-1925
Dee W. Edington, Director
Katarina Borer, Assoc Dir
Joyce Lindeman, Assoc Dir
Undergrad: BA, Sports Mgt & Comm.
Grad: MS, Facilities Mgt.

Michigan State University
134 1M Sports Circle
East Lansing, MI 48824
T: (517) 355-4741
Dr. John Haubenstricker, Director
Graduate: MS, Athletic Admin.

Minnesota, Univerity of
218 Cooke Hall
Minneapolis, MN 55455
T: (612) 625-0538
F: (612) 626-7700
March Krotee, Dir. Sport Mgt
Mary Jo Kane, Spo Mgt-Rec. Coord
Bruce Anderson, Spo Mgt-Educ.
Graduate: MA, PhD, Recreation &
Leisure Studies, Kinesiology

Minnesota State University-Mankato
Dept. of Human Performance
MSU Box 28
Mankato, MN 56002
T: (507) 389-5618
Gary Rushing, Dir. Sports Adm.
Undergrad: BS, Sports Admin.
Graduate: MA/MS, Sports Adm/P.E.

Mississippi, University of
HPER
Turner Complex
University, MS 38677
T: (601) 232-5521
Dr. Don Cheek, Chr.
Undergraduate: BS, Sports Mgt.

Missouri, University of
Health & Exercise Sciences
102 Rothwell Gym
Columbia, MO 65211
T: (573) 882-2121
F: (573) 884-4855
Linda Schoonmaker, Dir.
Graduate: M.Ed, Sport Mgt.,
Human Performance

Missouri Western State College
HPERD, 4525 Downs Drive
St. Joseph, MO 64507
T: (816) 271-4487
F: (816) 271-5940
Dr. Brenda Blessing, Chair.
Undergrad: BS, Sports Mkt & Mgt.

Montana State University
101 Hoseaus, P.E. Complex
Bozeman, MT 59717
T: (406) 994-4001
F: (406) 994-6314
Dr. Tim Dunnagan, Dir:
Dr. Peter Rehor, Asst. Dir.
Undergrad/Grad: BS/MS
Sports Management

Mount Union College
Sports Management Dept.
1972 Clark Avenue
Alliance, OH 44601
T: (330) 821-5320
F: (330) 823-2399
E: thomaje@muc.edu
Dr. James Thoma, Director
Undergrad: BA, Sports Mgt.

Neumann College
Sports Management Program
Div. of Business & Info. Mgt.
One Neumann Drive
Aston, PA 19014
T: (610) 558-5594
F: (610) 558-5574
Director: Sandra Slabik
Undergrad: Sports Management
Graduate: Sports Management

New Hampshire, Univ. of
Dept. of Kinesiology
New Hampshire Hall
Durham, NH 03824
T: (603) 862-2070
F: (603) 862-0154
Dr. Ronald Croce, Chmn.
Dr. Stephen Hardy, Sport Studies
Undergrad: BS, Kinesiology
Grad: MS, Outdoor Education,
Exercise Science

New Haven, University of
300 Orange Avenue
West Haven, CT 06516
T: (203) 932-7090
Dr. Allen L. Sack, Sports Mgt.
Undergrad: BS, Sports Ind. &
Sports Management, Communication

New Jersey City University
Athletic Recreation Fitness Ctr.
324-338 West Side Ave.
Jersey City, NJ 07305
T: (201) 547-3315
Eugene Bacha, Chair. Sport/Leisure Studies.
Undergrad: BS in Business with
a concentration in Sport Mgt.

New Mexico, University of
HPPELP
Johnson Center
Albuquerque, NM 87131
T: (505) 277-4726
F: (505) 277-0111
Dr. Bill De Groot, Chmn.
Graduate: M.S., Athletic Admin.,
Club Management, Coaching

New York University
Management Instiitute
48 Cooper Sq, Rm. 108
New York, NY 10003
T: (212) 998-7217
F: (212) 995-4138
Lynn Johnson, Director
Undergrad: Certificate in
Sports & Special Event Mkt.

New York University
239 Greene St, Suite 635
Washington Square
New York, NY 10003
T: (212) 998-5600
F: (212) 995-4138
Dr. Renee Harris, Director
Graduate: MS, Fitness Management,
Physical Educ. & Sport

North Carolina State University
Sports Management Dept.
Box 8004
Raleigh, NC 27695
T: (919) 515-3276
F: (919) 515-3687
Philip S. Rea, Chmn.
Dr. Beth Wilson, Grad. Admin.
Graduate: MS, Recr., Sports Adm.
Club Mgt, Facility Mgt., Spo Tourism

North Carolina, University of
209 Fetzer Gym, CB 8700
Chapel Hill, NC 27599
T: (919) 962-0017
F: (919) 962-0489
Dr. Frederick Mueller, Chmn.
Dr. John Billing, Coord. Spo Mgt
Graduate: MA, Sports Administration

Northeastern University
360 Huntington Ave.
100 Dockser Hall
Boston, MA 02115
T: (617) 373-4112
F: (617) 373-2968
Dr. Robert Curtin, Chmn.
Undergrad/Grad: BS, MS
Recreation, Sport & Fitness Mgt.,
Recreation Management

Northern Colorado, Univ. of
Sport Administration Program
School of Kinesiology/Phys. Educ.
Greeley, CO 80639
T: (970) 351-1722
F: (970) 351-1762
Dr. David K. Stotlar, Director
Graduate: MA, EdD, Facility Mgt,
Sport Promotion & Mkt, Sports Law

Northern Illinois University
Phys. ED Department
Anderson Hall
Dekalb, IL 60115
T: (815) 753-3907
F: (815) 753-1413
E: klambrecht@niu.edu
Dr. Keith W. Lambrecht, Director
Graduate: MS, Sport Mgt., Sports
Facilities, Sports Law

Northwestern State University
Dept of Health & Hum. Performance
Natchitoches, LA 71497
T: (318) 357-5126
F: (318) 357-5904
Dr. C. Newton Wilkes, Director
Graduate: MEd, Sports Adm/P.E.

Ohio Northern University
King Horn Ctr. - HPESS
Ada, OH 45810
T: (419) 772-2440
F: (419) 772-2470
E: r-beaschler@onu.edu
Ron Beaschler, Director
Undergrad: BS, HPE/Sports Mgt.

Ohio State University
Sports Management Program
HPER, 455 Larkins Hall
337 W. 17th Avenue
Columbus, OH 43210
T: (614) 292-7701
F: (614) 688-3432
Dr. Dennis Howard, Director
Graduate: MA, Arena/Facility Mgt,
Sports Mgt, Athletic Administration

Ohio University
Grover Center
Athens, OH 45701
T: (740) 593-4666
F: (740) 593-0539
E: sportsad@ohiou.edu
Dr. Andrew Kreutzer, Director
Graduate: MA in Sports Admin.,
Facility Management

Oklahoma State University
103 Colvin Center
School of HPEL
Stillwater, OK 74078
T: (405) 744-5493
F: (405) 744-6507
Dr. Jerry Jordan, Director
Undergrad/Grad: BS/MS, HPE,
Sports Administration

Oklahoma, University of
Dept. of Health & Sport Sciences
1401 Asp Ave, Room 104
Norman, OK 73019
T: (405) 325-5211
F: (405) 325-0594
Dr. Laurette Taylor, Chari.
Dr. David Wei Pan, Sport Mgt. Dir.
Undergrad: BS, Sports Sciences
Graduate: MS, Spo Mkt., Spo Mgt

Old Dominion University
Dept. of HPER
Room 140
Norfolk, VA 23529
T: (757) 683-4995
F: (757) 683-4270
Dr. Elizabeth Dowling, Grad. Pgm Dir.
Dr. Ladd Colston, RLS/Spo Mgt Pgm
Undergrad/Grad: BS/MS, Phys. Ed,
Sport Mgt, Recreation, Leisure Mgt.

Oregon, University of
James A Warsaw Sports
Marketing Center
Charles Lundquist College of Bus.
1208 University of Oregon
Eugene, OR 97403
T: (541) 346-3495
F: (541) 346-3341
Rick Burton, Director
Dr. Lynn Kahle, Prof. of Sport Mgt
Undergrad: BBA, Sports Mkt.
Graduate: MBA, Sports Mkt.

Pacific Christian University
Physical Ed Department
2500 E. Nutwood Ave.
Fullerton, CA 92631
T: (714) 879-3901
F: (714) 526-0231
Glenn Snyder, Director
Undergrad: BA, Physical Educ.,
Sports Management

Pacific, University of the
Sport Management Program
Sport Sciences Dept.
Stockton, CA 95211
T: (209) 946-2531
F: (209) 946-2731
Dr. Linda Koehler, Coord. Spo Mgt.
Undergrad/Grad: BA/MA, Sport
Sciences

Penn State University
105 White Bldg.
University Park, PA 16802
T: (814) 863-7367
Dr. Terry R. Haggerty, Director
Undergrad/Grad: BS, MS, PhD
Exercise & Sport Science,
Sport Management

Pfeiffer University
Highway 52 N.
Misenheimer, NC 28109
T: (704) 463-1360
F: (704) 463-5051
Jack Ingram, Director, Spo media/mgt
Undergrad: BA, Sports Mgt.

Quincy University
1800 College Avenue
Quincy, IL 62301
T: (217) 228-5475
F: (217) 228-5473
John Ortwerth, Director
Undergrad: BS, Sport Management

Rice University
HP & HS Dept.
6100 Main Street
Houston, TX 77005
T: (713) 527-4808
F: (713) 285-5329
Dr. Harmon Gallant, Spo Mgt.
Undergrad: BS, Sport Admin.,
Sport Mkt & Prom, Sport Law

Richmond, University of
Robins Center
Health & Sport Sciences Dept.
Richmond, VA 23173
T: (804) 289-8358
Dr. Donald W. Pate, Director
Graduate: Sport Management

Robert Morris College
881 Narrows Run Rd.
Moon Township, PA 15108
T: (412) 262-8416
F: (412) 262-8494
Dr. Susan Hofacre, Chair.
Undergrad/Graduate: BS, MS,
Sport Management

Rutgers, State University of NJ
Dept. of Exercise Science & Sport
Loree Gym, PO Box 270
New Brunswick, NJ 08903
T: (732) 932-9525
F: (732) 932-9151
David A. Feigley, Chmn.
Undergrad: BS, Sport Management,
Exercise Science

Saginaw Valley State University
Dept. of PE &Health Educ.
University Center, MI 48710
T: (517) 791-7307
F: (517) 790-0545
Dr. Douglas Hansen, Chmn.
Undergrad: BS, Fitness Mgt.

St. John's University
8000 Utopia Pkwy.
Jamaica, NY 11439
T: (718) 990-6415
F: (718) 990-1882
Anthony Missere, Director Ath. Adm.
Undergrad: BS, Athletic Admin.

St. Leo College
Div. of Professional Studies
MC 2067, PO Box 6665
St. Leo, FL 33574
T: (352) 588-8487
F: (352) 588-8289
Bill Foley, Dean
Tom Phillips, Dept Chair
Undergrad: BA, Sports Mgt/P.E.

St. Thomas University
16400 NW 32nd Avenue
Miami, FL 33054
T: (800) 367-9010
T: (305) 628-6634
F: (305) 628-6504
Dr. Janice A. Bell, Grad. Director
Dr. Ted Abernathy, Undergrad Dir.
Undergrad: BA, Sports Admin
Graduate: MS, MBA, Sports Adm.

San Francisco, University of
2130 Fulton Street
San Francisco, CA 94117
T: (415) 422-2678
F: (415) 422-6267
Lawrence Wenner, Director
Graduate: MA, Sports & Fitness
Management, Arena & Stad Mgt.

San Jose State University
Dept of Human Performance
San Jose, CA 95192
San Jose, CA 95192
T: (408) 924-3010
F: (408) 924-3053
E: jebryant@email.sjsu.edu
Dr. James E. Bryant, Chmn.
Dr. Richard Montgomery, Spo Mgt.
Undergrad/Graduate: BS, MA
Sport Management, Sport Mkt

Seattle Pacific University
Scvhool Of P.E./Athletic Admin.
3414 3rd West
Seattle, WA 98119
T: (206) 281-2896
F: (206) 281-2784
Grant Hill, Chmn.
Dr. Dan Tripps, Director
Undergrad: BA, BS Leisure & Rec.
Grad: MS, Athletic Administration

Slippery Rock University
Morrow Fieldhouse
Sport Management Program
Slippery Rock, PA 16057
T: (724) 738-2776
F: (724) 738-2921
E: robert.ammon@sru.edu
Dr. Rob Ammon, Spo Mgt. Director
Jean Hamilton, Internship Coord.
Undergrad: BS, PE, Sport Mgt.
Graduate: MS, MA Sports Adm.

South Carolina, University of
Dept of Sport Administration
College of Applied Spec. Sciences
Carolina Coliseum 2012
Columbia, SC 29208
T: (803) 777-4690
F: (803) 777-8788
E: regan@gwm.sc.edu
Tom Regan, Chr.
Guy Lewis, Prof
Undergrad: BS, Sport Administration

Southeastern Louiusiana Univ.
Dept. of Kinesiology
PO Box 845
Hammond, IA 70402
T: (504) 549-2129
F: (504) 549-3532
Dr. Betty S. Baker, Dept Head
Undergrad/Grad: BA, MA Health/
P.E./Sport Management

Southern Illinois University
Physical Education Dept.
106 Davies Gym
Carbondale, IL 62901
T: (618) 536-2431
F: (618) 453-3329
Dr. Ronald Knowton, Chmn.
Graduate: MS, PhD, Sport Mgt.

Southern Mississippi, Univ. of
School of Human Perf. & Recreation
Sports Administration Pgm.
Southern Sta. Box 5142
Hattiesburg, MS 39406
T: (601) 266-5386
F: (601) 266-5800
Dr. Sandra Gangstead, Chair.
Dr. C. Newton Wilkes, Spo Pgm Dir.
Undergrad/Graduate: BS, MS
Sports Adm., Fitness Management

Spring Arbor College
Dept. of Exer. & Sport Science
Spring Arbor, MI 49283
T: (517) 750-1200
F: (517) 750-2745
Dr. Ted Comden, Chmn.
Undergrad: BA, Sports Admin.,
Fitness Management

Springfield College
263 Alden Street
Springfield, MA 01109
T: (413) 748-3125
F: (413) 748-3745
E: bmann@spfldcol.edu
Dr. Betty Mann, Grad. Director
Dr. William Considine, Dir. Undergrad.
Undergraduate/Graduate: BS, MS
Sport Management/Athletic Adm.

SUNY-Brockport
B-304 Tuttle N.
Brockport, NY 14420
T: (716) 395-5331
F: (716) 395-2246
Dr. William Stier, Director
Undergrad/Grad: BS, MS
P.E., Athletic Administration

SUNY-Cortland
PO Box 2000
Cortland, NY 13045
T: (607) 753-4947
F: (607) 753-4929
Suzanne Wingate, Coord.
Undergrad: BS, Bus. Event,
Facility Mgt, Athletic Administration

Tampa, University of
401 Kennedy Blvd.
Tampa, FL 33606
T: (813) 253-6240
F: (813) 253-6288
Dr. Robert Birrenkott
Undergrad: BS, Sport Management

Temple University
Vivacqua Hall, Box 060-62
Philadelphia, PA 19122
T: (215) 204-8706
F: (215) 204-1455
Dr. Ira Shapiro, Chmn.
Dr. Betsy Barber, Grad. Prof.
Undergrad/Graduate: BA, MA
Athletic Adm, Facility Mgt, Sport Marketing, Recreation Mgt.

Tennessee State University
3500 John Merritt Blvd.
Nashville, TN 37209
T: (615) 963-5581
F: (615) 963-5594
Dr. Bernard Cromwell, Director
Undergrad/Grad: BS, MS
HPE & Recreation

Tennessee, University of
1914 Andy Holt Avenue
Knoxville, TN 37996
T: (423) 974-5111
F: (423) 974-8981
Dr. Dennie Ruth Kelley, Director
Undergrad/Graduate: BS, MS
Sport Studies, Spo Mgt., Sport Adm.

Texas A&M University
Dept. of Health & Kinesiology
158 Read Bldg.
College Station, TX 77843
T: (409) 845-2391
F: (409) 847-8987
Dr. Frank B. Ashley III, Dir. Spo Mgt.
Undergrad/ Graduate: BS, MS
Sport Management, Kinesiology

Texas, University of
Kinesiology & Health Educ.
Bellmont 222
Austin, TX 78712
T: (512) 471-1273
Dr. Dot Lovett, Chair.
Dr. Scott Watson, Spo Adm. Coord.
Undergrad: BS, Sports Mgt
Graduate: M.ed., Sports Adm.

Texas Wesleyan University
1201 Wesleyan Street
Fort Worth, TX 76105
T: (817) 531-4950
F: (817) 531-4229
Dr. Ed Olson, Chair. Exercise & Sport Studies
Rosie Stallman, Dir. of Sport Mgt
Undergrad: BS, Sports Mgt Teaching

Tiffin University
155 Miami Street
Tiffin, OH 44883
T: (419) 447-6444
F: (419) 443-5007
Bonnie Tiell, Sport Mgt. Director
Graduate: MBA, Sport Mgt.

Towson University
Dept. of Kinesiology
Towson Center, Rm. 200
Sport Studies Program
Towson, MD 21204
T: (410) 830-2376
F: (410) 830-3912
Vince Angotti, Spo Stud Pgm Dir.
Undergrad: BS, Sport Mgt, Sport Studies, Sport Communications

United States Sports Academy
One Academy Drive
Daphne, AL 36526
T: (334) 626-3303
F: (334) 621-2527
www.sport.ussa.edu
E: academy@ussa-sport.ussa.edu
Dr. Walter Cooper, VP Acad Affairs
Dr. Jerry Phillips, Chmn. Spo Mgt.
Graduate: Sport Management, Sport Medicine, Sport Research

Utah, University of
Dept. of Exercise & Sport Science
HPER 241 N.
Salt Lake City, UT 84112
T: (801) 581-7586
F: (801) 585-3992
Dr. Jim Ewers, Director
Graduate: MS, Sport Management

Valparaiso University
Dept. of Physical Ed
252 Ath-Rec Center
Valparaiso, IN 46383
T: (219) 464-5235
F: (219) 464-5154
Dr. Jerome Stieger, Chmn.
Undergrad: BS, Sport Mgt,
Athletic Adm., Facility Mgt, Sports
Information, Sports Promotion,
Fitness Management, Spo Bus Mgt.

Washburn University
Dept of HPED
Topeka, KS 66621
T: (785) 231-1010
F: (785) 231-1091
Dr. William Sparks, Chmn.
Undergrad: BS, BA, Athletic
Training, Sports Facility Mgt.

Washington State University
Dept. of Education Leadership
Pullman, WA 99164
T: (509) 335-6363
F: (509) 335-7977
Joanne Washburn, Coord. Sport Mgt.
Graduate: MA, Athletic Admin.

Wayne State University
Dept. of Sports Administration
260 Matthaei Bldg.
Detroit, MI 48202
T: (313) 577-4265
F: (313) 577-5999
Tim Domke, Director Spo Adm.
Roy Allen, Coord.
Graduate: MA, Sports Admin.,
Athletic Administration,
Pro Sports Administration

West Chester University
South New Street
S. Campus Athletic Complex
West Chester, PA 19383
T: (610) 436-2260
F: (610) 436-2860
E: ematejkovic@wcupa.edu
Dr. Monita Lank, Chair.
Dr. Edward Matejkovic, Dir.
Grad: MS, P.E./Sport Athletic Adm.

West Virginia University
PO Box 6116
265 Coliseum
Morgantown, WV 26506
T: (304) 293-3295
F: (304) 293-4641
Dr. Dallas Branch Jr., Director
Undergrad/Grad: BS, MS
Sport Management, Sports
Administration

Western Carolina University
Sport Management Program
Breese Gymnasium
Cullowhee, NC 28723
T: (704) 227-7332
F: (704) 227-7388
Dr. Susan C. Brown, Director
Undergrad: BS, Sport Management,
Athletic Training, Facility Mgt.,
Athletic Administration, Professional
Sport Mgt, Recreation Management,
Sports Information

Western Illinois University
Dept. of Physical Education
Brophy Hall
Macomb, IL 61455
T: (309) 298-1332
F: (309) 298-2641
Dr. Charles Spencer, Grad. Coord.
Dr. Darlene Young, Internship
Graduate: MS, Sport Management

Western State College of Colo.
Dept. of Kinesiology & Recreation
Gunnison, CO 81231
T: (970) 943-2115
Virginia Harris, Chair.
Undergrad: BA, Kinesiology with an
emphasis in Sports Management

Wichita State University
Kinesiology & Sport Studies Dept.
1845 Fairmount
Wichita, KS 67260
T: (316) 978-5440
F: (316) 978-5451
Lori Miller, Chairman
Greg Comfort, Undergrad Coord.
Clay Stoldt, Graduate Coord.
Graduate & Undergraduate Program
In Sports Administration

Wisconsin, University of
129/130 Mitchell Hall
La Crosse, WI 54601
T: (608) 785-8182
F: (608) 785-6520
Dr. Richard Mikat, Dir. of Undergrad.
Dr. Jane Meyers, Grad. Dir. Spo Adm
Undergrad/Grad: BS, MS
P.E./Sports Management, Athletic
Admin., Sports Administration

Wittenberg University
Dept. of Health/Sport Science
Box 720
Springfield, OH 45501
T: (937) 327-6457
Pat Holly, Chair. HPE
UIndergrad: BA, Sports Medicine,
Sport Mgt, Sport Psychology

Xavier University
3800 Victory Parkway
HPE, Sport Studies Dept.
Cincinnati, OH 45207
T: (513) 745-3653
F: (513) 745-4291
E: Quinn@xavier.xu.edu
Ronald W. Quinn, Coord Grad Pgm
C. Charlie Song, Coord. Undergrad.
Undergrad: BS, Sport Mkt, Spo Mgt
Graduate: MS, Sports Administration

Job Search/Job opportunity Services/Newsletters

The publisher of The Sports Address Bible does not offer recommendations or suggestions of the services listed here. We simply list some of the services that are available without being held liable. Some of these listings are paid services.

NCAA News Weekly Hotline
PO Box 6222
Indianapolis, IN 46206
T: (317) 917-6222
F: (317) 917-6888
www.ncaa.org/publications
This weekly publication offer job opportunities in its marketplace section.

Professional Baseball Employment Opportunities
PO Box 310
Old Fort, NC 28762
T: (800) 842-5618
F: (704) 668-4762
Director: Ann Perkins

Team Work
3645 Warrensville Ctr Rd., Ste 246
Shaker Heights, OH 44122
T: (216) 767-1790
F: (216) 767-1780
www.teamworkconsulting.com
E: infotwc@teamworkonline.com

Women's Sports Services
409 Utica Street, Suite D-36
Huntington Beach, CA 92648
T: (714) 960-0411
F: (714) 969-5881
www.womensportswire.com
E: WSwire1@aol.com
Dir./Publisher: Becky Heidesch
Publication: Women's Sports Wire

Work in Sports.com
7335 E. Acoma Drive, Suite 201
Scottsdale, AZ 85260
T: (480) 905-7221
F: (480) 905-7231
www.workinsports.com
E: info@workinsports.com

National Sports Employment Newsletter
www.on-linesports.com
www.sportsemploymentnews.com

Media

National Television Networks

ABC Sports
47 West 66th Street
New York, NY 10023
T: (212) 456-7777
F: (212) 456-2930
P: Steven Bornstein

Canadian Broadcasting Corporation (CBC)
PO Box 500, Station A
Toronto, Ontario M5W 1E6
T: (416) 205-7266
F: (416) 205-2400
GM: Peter Kretz
TV Sports Dir: Alan Clark

Canadian Television Network (CTV)
250 Yonge Street, Suite 1800
Toronto, Ontario M5B 2N8
T: (416) 595-4254
F: (416) 595-0559
El: sports@ctv.ca
P: John Cassaday
VP Sports: Doug Beeforth

Canwest Global System
81 Barber Greene Road
Don Mills, Ontario M3C 2A2
T: (416) 446-5311
F: (416) 446-5371

CBS Sports
51 West 52nd Street
30th Floor
New York, NY 10019
T: (212) 975-5230
F: (212) 975-8709
www.cbs.sportsline.com
P: Sean McManus

Fox Sports
Sunset Building
5746 Sunset Blvd., 2nd Floor
Los Angeles, CA 90028
T: (213) 856-1000
F: (213) 479-8856
www.foxsports.com
New York Office
1211 Ave. of the Americas
New York, NY 10036
T: (212) 556-2400
F: (212) 556-2490
P: David Hill
PR: Denise Seomin

Galavision
6701 Center Dr. W.
Los Angeles, CA 90045
T: (310) 348-3640
F: (310) 348-3643
P: Javier Saralegui
Oper: Alex Hadad

NBC Sports
30 Rockefeller Plaza
New York, NY 10112
T: (212) 664-4444
F: (212) 664-3930
www.nbc.com
P: Dick Ebersol

Public Broadcasting Service
1320 Braddock Place
Alexandria, VA 22314
T: (703) 739-5000
F: (703) 739-0775
www.pbs.org
P: Ervin Duggan

Telemundo
2470 W. 87th Avenue
Hialeah, FL 33010
T: (305) 882-8700
F: (305) 884-4704
P: Roland Hernandez
Sports Director: Rafael Torres

TVA
2600 Boul. de Maisonneuve est.
Montreal, Quebec H2L 4P2
T: (514) 526-9251

Univision
9405 NW 41st Street
Miami, FL 33178
T: (305) 471-3900
F: (305) 471-4236
P: Ray Rodriguez
Sports Dir: Jorge Hidalgo

National Cable Television Networks

Black Entertainment Television (BET)
1900 West Place NE
Washington, D.C. 20018
T: (202) 636-2400
F: (202) 608-2599
www.BET.org
VP Sports: Deborah Tang
PR: Michelle Moore

Cable News Network (CNN) Sports Division
One CNN Center
Atlanta, GA 30303
T: (404) 878-1600
F: (404) 878-0011
www.cnn.com/sports/index.html
VP/Exec. Prod: Jim Walton
CNN Sports: Jean McCormick

CNN/SI
One CNN Center
Atlanta, GA 30303
T: (404) 878-1600
F: (404) 878-0011
www.cnsi.com
Sr. VP: Jim Walton
Mng. Editor: Steve Robinson
PR: Andy Mitchell

Consumer News & Business Channel (CNBC)
2200 Fletcher Avenue
Fort Lee, NJ 07024
T: (201) 585-2622
F: (201) 585-6393
www.cnbc.com
P: Bill Bolster
PR: Philip Recchia

ESPN
ESPN Plaza
Bristol, CT 06010
T: (860) 585-2000
F: (860) 582-7699
www.espn.com
P: Steven Bornstein
Communications: Rob Tobias
This also includes the following:
ESPN 2, ESPN International & ESPN News

Fox Sports Net
1440 S. Sepulveda Blvd.
Los Angeles, CA 90024
T: (310) 444-8123
F: (310) 444-8101
PR: Dennis Johnson

FX Network
212 Fifth Avenue
New York, NY 10010
T: (212) 802-4000
F: (212) 802-4389
Exec. VP: Mark Sonnenberg
PR: John Solberg

The Golf Channel
7580 Commerce Center Dr.
Orlando, FL 32819
T: (407) 363-4653
F: (407) 363-4603
www.thegolfchannel.com
P/CEO: Joseph Gibbs
Mkt: Dave Manougian

Home Box Office (HBO)
1100 Ave. of the Americas
New York, NY 10036
T: (212) 512-1000
F: (212) 512-1751
www.hbo.com
VP Sports: Ross Greenburg
Media: Roy Stallone

Lifetime TV
309 W. 49th Street
New York, NY 10019
T: (212) 424-7000
F: (212) 957-4448
www.lifetimetv.com
Sports VP: Brian Donlon
PR: Meridith Wagner

MSNBC
1 MSNBC Plaza
Secaucus, NJ 07094
T: (201) 583-5000
F: (201) 583-5512
www.msnbc.com
P: Andrew Lack
VP/GM: Mark Harrington
Media: Lauren Leff

MTV Sports
1515 Broadway
New York, NY 10036
T: (212) 654-6177
F: (212) 654-4707
www.mtv.com
Exec. Prod: Patrick Byrnes
Host: Dan Cortese

The Nashville Network (TNN)
2806 Opryland Drive
Nashville, TN 37214
T: (615) 889-6840
F: (615) 871-6698
www.country.com
P: David Hall
Mkt: Nancy Neil

Newsport
3 Crossways Park N.
Woodbury, NY 11797
T: (516) 921-3764
F: (516) 364-1943
www.newsport-tv.com
EI: NewSportPR@aol.com
Exec. VP: Robert Pollichino
PR: Rod Mickler

Prime/Sportschannel Networks
3 Crossways Park West
Woodbury, NY 11797
T: (516) 921-3764
F: (516) 364-1943
www.sportschannel.com
Sr. VP: Robert Pollichino
PR: Craig Sanders

Showtime/TMC
1633 Broadway, 15th Floor
New York, NY 10019
T: (212) 708-1600
F: (212) 708-1530
Sports Sr. VP: Jay Larkin
Sports Dir: Robin Walker

Speedvision
2 Stamford Plaza
281 Tresser Blvd.
Stamford, CT 06901
T: (203) 406-2500
F: (203) 406-2534
www.speedvision.com
P: Roger Werner

The Sports Network (TSN)
2225 Sheppard Ave. East
Suite 100
North York, Ontario M2J 5C2
T: (416) 494-1212
F: (416) 490-7051
www.tsn.ca
P: Jim Thompson
GM: Rick Brace
VP Mkt: Paul Clark

Turner Sports
One CNN Center
Atlanta, GA 30303
T: (404) 827-1735
F: (404) 827-1339
www.tnt.turner.com
P: Harvey Schiller
Sr VP Sprts Prog: Kevin O'Malley
PR: Gregory Hughes
Includes TBS, TNT & Sports South Networks

USA Network
1230 Ave. of the Americas
New York, NY 10020
T: (212) 408-9100
F: (212) 408-2798
P: Kay Koplovitz
VP/Exec Prod: Gordon Beck
VP Sports Prog: Rob Correa
Sports PR: Dan Schoenberg

National Radio Networks

ABC Radio Sports
125 West End Avenue
6th Floor
New York, NY 10023
T: (212) 456-5185
F: (212) 456-5150
www.abcradionet.com
Sports Dir:: Shelby Whitfield

American Urban Radio Network
960 Penn Ave.
Pittsburgh, PA 15222
T: (800) 456-4211
T: (412) 456-4000
F: (412) 456-4040
Sports Director: Tony Girdano

AP Network Sports
1825 K Street, Suite 710
Washington, DC 20006
T: (202) 736-9540
F: (202) 736-1199
Sports Director: Dave Lubeski

Black Radio Network
166 Madison Ave., 4th Floor
New York, NY 10016
T: (212) 686-6850
F: (212) 686-7308
GM: Roy Thompson

Bloomberg Business News Radio
499 Park Avenue
New York, NY 10022
T: (212) 318-2351
F: (212) 940-1994
www.bloomberg.com
Sports Dir: John Kenelly

Business News Network
5025 Centennial Blvd.
Colorado Springs, CO 80919
T: (719) 528-7040
F: (719) 528-6544
E: bizradio@prodigy.com
Sports Dir: Jay Ritchie

CBS Radio Network
524 W. 57th Street
New York, NY 10019
T: (212) 379-9090
Fax (212) 975-6347
www.cbsradio.com
GM: Bob Kipperman
Sports Dir: David Kennin

CNN Radio Network
PO Box 105366
1050 Techwood Drive NW
Atlanta, GA 30348
T: (404) 827-2750
F: (404) 588-6539
www.cnn.com
GM: Robert Garcia

ESPN Radio Network
ESPN Plaza
Bristol, CT 06010
T: (860) 585-2000
F: (860) 589-5523
www.espnradio.com
GM: Drew Hayes

Motor Racing Network (MRN)
1801 International Speedway Blvd.
Daytona Beach, FL 32114
T: (904) 947-6400
F: (904) 947-6716
www.mrnnet.com
GM: Mark Williams

Motor Sports Radio Network
80 Zevan Road
Johnson City, NY 13790
T/F: (607) 770-9165
CEO: Paul Kaminski

Mutual Broadcasting News
1755 S. Jefferson Davis Hwy.
Arlington, VA 22202
T: (703) 413-8300
F: (703) 413-8445
News VP: Bart Tessler
Dir. of Sports: Larry Michael

NBC Radio Network
1755 S. Jefferson Davis Hwy.
Arlington, VA 22202
T: (703) 413-8300
F: (703) 413-8445
Director of Sports: Larry Michael

National Public Radio
635 Massachusetts Ave. NW
Washington, DC 20001
T: (202) 414-2000
F: (202) 414-3329
www.npr.org
E: nprnews@npr.org
Sports Dir: Mark Schramm

KNBR-AM 680 Sports Radio
KTCT-AM 1050 Sports Radio
55 Hawthorne St., Suite 1100
San Francisco, CA 94105
T: (415) 995-6800
F: (415) 995-6867
www.knbr.com
E: sports@knbr.com
Sports Dir: Pat Olson

Colorado

KRDO 1240 Sports Radio
PO Box 1457
3 S. 7th Street
Colorado Springs, CO 80901
T: (719) 632-1515
F: (719) 635-8455
Sports Dir: Mike Lewis

KKFN, The Fan AM 950 Sports Radio
1095 S. Monaco Parkway
Denver, CO 80224
T: (303) 321-0950
F: (303) 333-5313
www.sportsradio.com/fan
Sports Dir: Tim Spence

KOA-AM 850 Sports Radio
1380 Lawrence Street
Suite 1300
Denver, CO 80204
T: (303) 893-8500
F: (303) 892-4849
Sports Dir: Larry Zimmer

KYBG Sports Radio
5660 Greenwood Plaza
Suite 400
Englewood, CO 80111
T: (303) 721-9210
F: (303) 721-1435
GM: Ron Jamison

Connecticut

WPOP-AM Sports Radio
10 Columbus Blvd.
Hartford, CT 06106
T: (860) 249-9577
F: (860) 522-7567
Prog Dir: Steve Coates

Florida

WQAM 560 Sports Radio
9881 Sheridan Street
Hollywood, FL 33024
T: (800) 255-9956
T: (954) 621-4300
F: (954) 437-2466
www.wqam.com
GM: Greg Rees
Sports Dir: Duff Lindsey

WNZS-AM 930 Sports Radio
8386 Baymeadows Road, #107
Jacksonville, FL 32256
T: (904) 636-0507
F: (904) 448-3043
GM: Linda Byrd
Sports Dir: David Lamm

WQTM Sports Radio
2500 Maitland Center Pkwy.
Suite 401
Maitland, FL 32751
T: (407) 916-7800
F: (407) 660-0329
Sports Dir: Tom Morgan

WZTM Sports Radio
11300 4th St., Suite 318
St. Petersburg, FL 33716
T: (727) 577-7131
F: (727) 578-2477
Sports Dir: Al Dukes

WNLS Sports Radio
325 John Knox Rd., Bldg G
Tallahassee, FL 32303
T: (850) 422-3107
F: (850) 383-0747
www.wnls.com
E: wnls-am@cctall.com
GM: David Manning

Georgia

WCNN-AM 680 Sports Radio
209 CNN Center
Atlanta, GA 30303
T: (404) 898-0680
F: (404) 897-7363
GM: Rick Caffey

WQXI 790
3550 Peachtree Rd. NE
Atlanta, GA 30326
T: (404) 238-3431
F: (404) 365-9026
Sports Dir: Matt Edgar

WNML Sports Radio
7080 Industrial Hwy.
Macon, GA 31206
T: (912) 781-1063
F: (912) 781-6711
www.sports-animal.com
GM: Rick Humphrey

Hawaii

KGU Sports Radio
560 N. Nimitz Hwy.
Honolulu, HI 96817
T: (808) 533-0065
F: (808) 528-5467
Sports Dir: Russ Francis

Idaho

KTIK-AM 1340 Sports Radio
5257 Fairview Avenue
Boise, ID 83706
T: (208) 376-6666
F: (208) 375-9248
www.ktik.com
Sports Dir: Pat Metzger

KWIK Radio
PO Box 998
Pocatello, ID 83204
T: (208) 233-1133
F: (208) 232-1240
Sports Dir: Gary Shockley

Iowa

KJOC-AM 1170 Sports Radio
1229 Brady Street
Davenport, IA 52803
T: (319) 326-2541
F: (319) 326-1819
Sports Dir: Dan Burich

Illinois

WJBC Sports Radio
236 Greenwood
Bloomington, IL 61704
T: (309) 829-1221
F: (309) 827-8071
www.jbc.com
Sports Dir: Dick Luedke

WMVP-AM 1000 Sports Radio
875 N. Michigan Ave., Suite 3750
Chicago, IL 60611
T: (312) 980-1000
F: (312) 440-9397
www.am1000.com
E: wmvp@aol.com
Sports Dir: David Greenbaum
Prog Dir: Mitch Rosen

WSCR-AM 820 Sports Radio
4949 W. Belmont Ave.
Chicago, IL 60641
T: (773) 777-1700
F: (773) 777-5994
Sports/Prog Dir: Ron Gleason

WFMB Sports Radio
PO Box 2989
3055 S. Fourth St.
Springfield, IL 62708
T: (217) 528-3033
F: (217) 528-5348
www.fgi.net/wfmbam
E: wfmbam@fgi.net
Sports Dir: Sam Madonia

Indiana

WGAB Sports Radio
1180 Maple Lane
Newburgh, IN 47630
T: (812) 451-2422
F: (812) 853-3500
Sports Dir: Nick Patrick

Kansas

WIBW Sports Radio
PO Box 1818
Topeka, KS 66601
T: (785) 272-3456
F: (785) 272-3536
Sports Dir: Ed O'Donnell

KQAM Radio
2120 N. Woodlawn, Suite 352
Wichita, KS 67208
T: (316) 685-2121
F: (316) 685-3314
www.kqam.com
Sports Dir: Tony Duesing

Kentucky

WLGC Sports Radio
PO Box 685
Main & Harrison
Greenup, KY 41144
T: (606) 473-7377
F: (606) 473-5086
Sports Dir: Ron Meade

Louisiana

WIBR-AM 1300 Sports Radio
650 Woodale Road
Baton Rouge, LA 70806
T: (504) 926-1106
F: (504) 928-1606
www.team1300.com
Sports Dir: Charles Hanagriff

WQUE-AM 1280 Sports Radio
2228 Gravier Street
New Orleans, LA 70119
T: (504) 827-6000
F: (504) 827-6045

Maine

WLPZ-AM 1440 Sports Radio
PO Box 6713
Portland, ME 04104
T: (207) 775-6321
F: (207) 772-8087

WSKW Radio
PO Box 159, Middle Rd.
Showhegan, ME 04976
T: (207) 474-5171
F: (207) 474-3299
Sports Dir: Mike Estrada

Maryland

WTEM-AM 570 Sports Radio
11300 Rockville Pike
Rockville, MD 20852
T: (301) 770-5700
F: (301) 881-8030
www.wtem.com
E: lschreck@erols.com
GM: Lewis Schreck

WTGM-AM 960 Sports Radio
PO Box U
Salisbury, MD 21802
T: (410) 742-1923
F: (410) 742-2329
Sports Dir: Jim Whittemore

Massachusetts

WEEI-AM 850 Sports Radio
116 Huntington Avenue
Boston, MA 02116
T: (617) 375-8000
F: (617) 375-8905
Sports Dir: Sean Grande

Sports Final Radio Network
48 Fitchburg Street
Marlborough, MA 01752
T: (508) 460-0588
F: (508) 624-6496

WWTM Sports Radio
200 Friberg Pkwy., Suite 4000
Westborough, MA 01581
T: (508) 836-9223
F: (508) 366-0745
Sports Dir: Chuck Perks

Michigan

CKLW Radio
30100 Telegraph Rd., Ste 465
Bingham Farms, MI 48025
T: (313) 258-8888
F: (313) 258-0182
Dports Dir: Steve Bell

WDFN-AM 1130 Sports Radio
2930 E. Jefferson Avenue
Detroit, MI 48207
T: (313) 259-5440
F: (313) 259-0560
www.wdfn.com
Sports Dir: Jamie Samuelson

WVFN-AM 730 Sports Radio
3420 Pine Tree
Lansing, MI 48911
T: (517) 394-7272
F: (517) 394-3388
www.voyager/wvfnthefan.com
GM: Rod Krol

WSFN-AM 1600 Sports Radio
875 E. Summit Ave.
Muskegon, MI 49444
T: (616) 733-2126
F: (616) 739-9037
GM: Jill Gossett

WMAX-AM 1440 Sports Radio
3071 Bay Road, #100
Saginaw, MI 48603
T: (517) 799-1440
F: (517) 799-4680
www.sportstalkradio.com
Sports Dir: John Brock
Prog Dir: Gary Ratski

Minnesota

KBUN-AM 1450 Sports Radio
PO Box 1656
Bemidji, MN 56601
T: (218) 751-4120
F: (218) 751-8091
GM: Lou Biron

WDSM-710 Sports Radio
715 E. Central
Duluth, MN 55811
T: (218) 722-4321
F: (218) 722-5423
www.allsports710.com
E: sports@discover-net.net
Sports Dir: Mark Fleischer

KFAN-AM 1130 Sports Radio
7900 Xerxes Ave. S., Suite 102
Minneapolis, MN 55431
T: (612) 820-4300
F: (612) 820-4256
www.kfan.com
Sports Dir: Chad Hartman

WCCO Radio
625 2nd Ave. S.
Minneapolis, MN 55402
T: (612) 370-0611
F: (612) 370-0683
www.wcco.com
GM: Jim Gustafson

Mississippi

WFOR-AM 1400 Sports Radio
2414 W. 7th Street
Hattiesburg, MS 39401
T: (601) 544-1400
F: (601) 582-5481

Missouri

KFSB-AM 1310 Sports Radio
2620 Dogwood Road
Joplin, MO 64801
T: (417) 624-1310
F: (417) 624-1817

KFNS-AM 590 Sports Radio
1910 Pine Street
St. Louis, MO 63103
T: (314) 531-0000
F: (314) 531-5900
www.KFNS.com
Sports Dir: Mike Claiborne

Nebraska

KLIN Radio
Box 30181
Lincoln, NE 68503
T: (402) 475-4567
F: (402) 479-1411
Sports Dir: John Bishop

Nevada

KVEG-AM 840 Sports Radio
1455 E. Tropicana, #250
Las Vegas, NV 89119
T: (702) 262-6600
F: (702) 262-6601
GM: Jerry Kutner

KPLY Radio
255 W. Moana Lane, Ste. 208
Reno, NV 89509
T: (775) 829-1964
F: (775) 825-3183
GM: Kevin Mahek

New Hampshire

WCQL-AM 1380 Sports Radio
1555 Islington Street
Portsmouth, NH 03801
T: (603) 430-9500
F: (603) 430-9501
GM: Robert Knight

New Mexico

KDEF-AM 1150 Sports Radio
10424 Edith SE
Albuquerque, NM 87113
T: (505) 792-1150
F: (505) 899-4061
GM: Chip Lusko

KNML Radio
500 4th Street W.
Albuquerque, NM 87102
T: (505) 767-6700
F: (505) 767-6767
Sports Dir: Andrew Paul

New York

WFAN-AM 660 Sports Radio
34-12 36th Street
Astoria, NY 11106
T: (718) 706-7690
F: (718) 706-6481
www.wfan.com
VP/GM: Joel Hollander
Sports Dir: Eddie Scozzarel

WENE-AM 1430 sports Radio
3301 Country Club Rd., Suite 2218
Endwell, NY 13760
T: (607) 785-3131
F: (607) 786-3296
E: wene1430@aol.com
Sports Dir: Dave Clink

WCMF-AM 990 Sports Radio
3136 S. Winton Rd., Suite 300
Rochester, NY 14623
T: (716) 272-7260
F: (716) 272-7892

WHEN Sports Radio
500 Plum St., Suite 100
Syracuse, NY 13204
T: (315) 472-9797
F: (315) 472-2323
Sports Dir: Steve Hyder

North Carolina

WFNZ Sports Radio
PO Box 30247
4015 Stuart Andrew Blvd.
Charlotte, NC 28230
T: (704) 522-1103
F: (704) 523-9572
Sports Dir: Matt Pinto

WTCK Sports Radio
PO Box 5897
High Point, NC 27262
T: (336) 378-9825
F: (336) 887-0104
www.wtck.com
E: theticket@wtck.com
Sports Dir: Dennis Elliot

Ohio

WBOB-AM 1160 Sports Radio
WUBE-AM Sports Radio
625 Eden Park Dr., Suite 1050
Cincinnati, OH 45202
www.1160bob.com
E: bob@1160bob.com
T: (513) 721-1050
F: (513) 749-1160
Sports Dir: Jeff Piecoro

WKNR-AM 1220 Sports Radio
9446 Broadview Road
Cleveland, OH 44147
T: (800) 938-1333
T: (440) 838-1220
F: (440) 838-1119
Sports Dir: Marvin Durant

WBNS-AM 1460 Sports Radio
175 S. Third Street
Columbus, OH 43215
T: (614) 460-3850
F: (614) 460-2822
Sports Dir: Dwight Burgess

WRGM Sports Radio
2900 Park Avenue W.
Mansfield, OH 44906
T: (419) 529-5900
F: (419) 529-2319
Sports Dir: Jeff Alan

WTIG Sports Radio
PO Box 573
Massillon, OH 44648
T: (330) 837-9900
F: (330) 837-9844
Sports Dir: Bill Caples

WASN-AM 1330 Sports Radio
401 N. Blaine Avenue
Youngstown, OH 44505
T: (216) 746-1330
F: (216) 746-1311

Oklahoma

WWLS-AM 640 Sports Radio
4000 W. Indian Hills Road
Norman, OK 73072
T: (405) 360-7000
F: (405) 364-1557
GM: John Fox

KQLL-AM 1430 Sports Radio
5314 S. Yale Avenue
Tulsa, OK 74135
T: (918) 481-1061
F: (918) 481-1773
GM: Allen McGlaughlin

Oregon

KDUK-AM 1280 Sports Radio
75 Centennial Loop
Eugene, OR 97401
T: (541) 345-8888
F: (541) 686-0329

KFXX Sports Radio
4614 S. W. Kelly
Portland, OR 97201
T: (503) 223-1441
F: (503) 223-6909
Sports Dir: Scott Masteller

Pennsylvania

WTZK AM 1320 Sports Radio
961 Marcon Blvd., Ste. 400
Allentown, PA 18103
T: (610) 264-4040
F: (610) 266-6464
www.wtzk.com
E: 1320sports@n.n.l.com
Sports Dir: Tom Fallon

WIXZ All Sports Radio
400 Lincoln Hwy.
East McKeesport, PA 15035
T: (412) 343-3060
F: (412) 823-1166
GM: Alan Serena

WGMP-AM 1210 Sports Radio
City Line Avenue & Monument Rd.
Philadelphia, PA 19131
T: (610) 668-5900
F: (610) 668-5888

WIP-AM 610 Sports Radio
441 N. Fifth Street
Philadelphia, PA 19123
T: (215) 922-5000
F: (215) 922-2434
GM: Cecil R. Foster, Jr.
Prog Dir: Tom Bigby

South Carolina

WCOS Radio
PO Box 21567
Columbia, SC 29210
T: (803) 772-5600
F: (803) 798-5255
www.radiosports.com
Sports Dir: Kevin Cohen

Texas

The Game KGMM 1280 Sports
3911 S. First
Abilene, TX 79605
T: (915) 676-7711
F: (915) 676-3851
Sports Dir: Dave Harrison

KYYD-AM 1340 Sports Radio
4542 Loop 332, #102
Abilene, TX 79602
T: (915) 691-1022
F: (915) 691-1016

KLVI Radio
PO Box 5488
2885 I-10 E.
Beaumont, TX 77726
T: (409) 896-5555
F: (409) 896-5599
www.klvi.com
Sports Dir: Dave Hofferth

KTCK-AM 1310 Sports Radio
3500 Maple Ave.
Suite 1300
Dallas, TX 75219
T: (214) 526-7400
F: (214) 787-1310
www.theticket.com
Sports Dir: Mark Followill

KILT-AM 610 Sports Radio
24 E. Greenway Plaza
Suite 1900
Houston, TX 77046
T: (713) 881-5100
F: (713) 881-5450
GM: Dickie Rosenfeld

Prime Sports Radio
100 E. Royal Lane
Suite 100
Irving, TX 75039
T: (972) 402-4500
F: (972) 402-4505

KKAM Sports Radio
4413 83rd St., Suite 300
Lubbock, TX 79424
T: (806) 798-7078
F: (806) 798-7052
Sports Dir: Ryan Hyatt

KZEP Sports Radio
427 9th Street
San Antonio, TX 78215
T: (210) 226-6444
F: (210) 225-5736
GM: Jay Levine

KCMC Radio
3225 Summerhill Road
Texarkana, TX 75503
T: (903) 793-1137
F: (903) 792-5262
Sports Dir: Al Hanna

KKTK Sports Radio 1460
314 W. Hwy 6
Waco, TX 76712
T: (817) 776-3900
F: (817) 772-8708
GM: Mike Oppenheim

Utah

KFNZ Sports Radio
434 Bearcat Drive
Salt Lake City, UT 84115
T: (801) 485-6700
F: (801) 485-6611
GM: Peter Benedetti

KISN-AM 570 Sports Radio
4001 S. 700 East, #800
Salt Lake City, UT 84107
T: (801) 262-9797
F: (801) 262-9772

Virginia

WRVH-AM 910 Sports Radio
PO Box 1516
Richmond, VA 23212
T: (804) 780-3400
F: (804) 780-3427

WROV-AM 1240 Sports Radio
PO Box 4005
Roanoke, VA 24015
T: (540) 343-4444
F: (540) 343-0616

WGH-AM 1310 Sports Radio
5589 Greenwich Rd., Suite 200
Virginia Beach, VA 23462
T: (757) 497-1310
F: (757) 671-1010
Sports Dir: Tony Mercurio

Washington

KFLD Sports Radio
2621 W. A Street
Pasco, WA 99301
T: (509) 547-9791
F: (509) 547-8726
GM: Scott Souhrada

KJR-AM 950 Sports Radio
190 Queen Anne Av. N., Ste. 100
Seattle, WA 98109
T: (206) 285-2295
F: (206) 286-2376
www.sportsradio950.com
Sports Dir: Tom Lee

KTRW-AM 970 Sports Radio
500 W. Boone Avenue
Spokane, WA 99201
T: (509) 323-9393
F: (509) 325-0276
E: score970group@score970.com
Sports Dir: Paul Seebeck

KLAY
10025 Lakewood Drive SW
Tacoma, WA 98499
T: (253) 581-0324
F: (253) 581-0326
Sports Dir: Clay Huntington

West Virginia

WIRO Sports Radio
134 4th Avenue
Huntington, WV 25701
T: (304) 525-7788
F: (304) 525-3299
Sports Dir: Tom Roten

WKWK-AM 1400 Sports Radio
88 Waddlers Run Road
Wheeling, WV 26003
T: (304) 232-2250
F: (304) 232-9725

Wisconsin

WBIZ-AM 1400 SportsRadio
619 Cameron Street
Eau Claire, WI 54703
T: (715) 835-1007
F: (715) 835-9680
GM: Rick Hencley

WKBH-AM 1570 Sports Radio
PO Box 1624
La Crosse, WI 54602
T: (608) 779-9157
F: (608) 526-6813
GM: Tim Scott

WHIT-AM 1550 Sports Radio
PO Box 2058
2740 Ski Lane
Madison, WI 53744
T: (608) 273-1000
F: (608) 281-0005
www.whittheteam.com
Sports Dir: Mark Grantin

WDLB Radio
PO Box 630
1710 N. Central Ave.
Marshfield, WI 54449
T: (715) 384-2191
F: (715) 387-3588
Sports Dir: Gene DeLisio

Wauk All Sports Radio
1801 Coral Drive
Waukesha, WI 53186
T: (414) 544-6800
F: (414) 544-1705
www.doubleplay1510.com
GM: Kevin Heinlein

Canada

The Fan 590 Sports radio
40 Holly Street
Toronto, Ontario M4S 3C3
T: (416) 482-0590
F: (416) 486-2690
www.fan590.com
Sports Dir: Scott Metcalfe

Major Daily Newspapers

Listed in this section are the major daily newspapers in the U.S. and Canada.

Alabama

Athens News Courier
PO 670 Box
Athens, AL 35612
T: (256) 232:2720
F: (256) 233-7753
Sports Editor: Neil Chittam

Birmingham News
PO Box 2553
Brimingham, AL 35202
T: (205) 325-2431
F: (205) 325-2425
Sports Editor: Tom Arenberg

Birmingham Post-Herald
PO Box 2553
Birmingham, AL 35202
T: (205) 325-2222
F: (205) 325-2410
www.postherald.com
Sports Editor: Don Kauselor

Decatur Daily
PO Box 2213
201 First Ave, SE
Decatur, AL 35609
T: (256) 353-4612
F: (256) 340-2392
Sports Editor: Bruce Mc Lellan

Huntsville Times
PO Box 1487
2317 S. Mem. Pkwy.
Huntsville, AL 35807
T: (256) 532-4430
F: (256) 532-4420
www.htimes.com
Sports Editor: John Pruett

Mobile Register
PO Box 2488
304 Government St.
Mobile, AL 36630
T: (334) 433-1551
F: (334) 434-8662
www.mobileregister.com
Sports Editor: John Cameron

Montgomery Advertiser
PO Box 1000
200 Washington Ave.
Montgomery, AL 36101
T: (334) 262-1611
F: (334) 261-1505
www.accessmontgomery.com
Sports Editor: Ken Rogers

Tuscaloosa News
PO Box 20587
2001 6th Street
Tuscaloosa, AL 35402
T: (205) 345-0505
F: (205) 349-0845
Sports Editor: Harold Stout

Alaska

Anchorage Daily News
PO Box 149001
1001 Northway Dr.
Anchorage, AK 99514
T: (907) 257-4200
F: (907) 257-4342
www.and.com
Sports Editor: Beth Bragg

Fairbanks Daily News-Miner
PO Box 70710
200 N. Cushman
Fairbanks, AK 99707
T: (907) 456-6661
F: (907) 452-7917
Sports Editor: Bob Eley

Arizona

Mesa Tribune Newspapers
PO Box 1547
Mesa, AZ 85211
T: (480) 898-6500
F: (480) 898-6362
Sports Editor: Slim Smith

The Arizona Republic/ Phoenix Gazette
PO Box 2245
Phoenix, AZ 85002
T: (602) 444-8251
F: (602) 444-8295
www.azcentral.com
Sports Editor: Kathy Tulumello

Arizona Daily Star
PO Box 26807
Tucson, AZ 85726
T: (520) 573-4145
F: (520) 573-4149
Sports Editor: B. J. Bartlett

Tucson Citizen
PO Box 26767
Tucson, AZ 85726
T: (520) 573-4560
F: (520) 573-4569
www.tucsoncitizen.com
Sports Editor: Peter Madrid

Arkansas

Northwest Arkansas Times
PO Box 1607
Fayetteville, AR 72702
T: (501) 442-1700
F: (501) 442-1714
Sports Editor: Terry Wood

Southwest Times Record
PO Box 1359
920 Rogers Ave.
Ft. Smith, AR 72902
T: (501) 785-7700
F: (501) 784-0413
Sports Editor: Grant Tolley

Hot Springs Sentinel-Record
PO Box 580
Hot Springs, AR 71901
T: (501) 623-7711
F: (501) 623-2984
Sports Editor: Robert Wisener

Arkansas Democrat-Gazette
PO Box 2221
Little Rock, AR 72203
T: (501) 378-34563
F: (501) 375-4521
Sports Editor: Wally Hall

Pine Bluff Commercial
PO Box 6469, 300 Beech St.
Pine Bluff, AR 71611
T: (870) 543-1416
F: (870) 543-0113
Sports Editor: Trey Reed

California

Bakersfield Californian
PO Box, 440, 1707 Eye St.
Bakersfield, CA 93302
T: (661) 395-7500
F: (661) 395-7519
Sports Editor: John Millman

Fresno Bee
1626 E Street
Fresno, CA 93786
T: (559) 441-6340
F: (559) 441-6070
Sports Editor: John Rich

The Daily Review
PO Box 5050
Hayward, CA 94540
T: (510) 293-2455
F: (510) 293-2490
Sports Editor: Ken Silman

Press Telegram
PO Box 230, 604 Pine Ave.
Long Beach, CA 90844
T: (562) 499-1338
F: (562) 437-8914
Sports Editor: Jim Mc Cormack

Los Angeles Daily News
PO Box 4200
Woodland Hills, CA 91365
T: (818) 713-3608
F: (818) 713-3436
Sports Editor: Michael Anastasi

Los Angeles Times
Times-Mirror Square
Los Angeles, CA 90053
T: (323) 237-7145
F: (323) 237-7876
Sports Editor: Bill Dwyre

Modesto Bee
PO Box 5256
Modesto, CA 95352
T: (209) 578-2000
F: (209) 238-4551
Sports Editor: Tom Holliday

Oakland Tribune
66 Jack London Square
Oakland, CA 94607
T: (510) 208-6400
F: (510) 208-6477
Sports Editor: Pete Wevruski

Inland Valley Daily Bulletin
PO Box 4000, 2041 E. 4th St.
Ontario, CA 91761
T: (909) 987-6397
F: (909) 948-90387
Sports Editor: Keith St. Clair

Antelope Valley Press
PO Box 880, 37404 Sierra Hwy.
Palmdale, CA 93551
T: (661) 273-2700
F: (661) 947-4870
Sports Editor: Dan Dinsmore

The Desert Sun
PO Box 2734
Palm Springs, CA 92263
T: (760) 322-8889
F: (760) 778-4654
Sports Editor: Tom Gibbons

The Press-Enterprise
PO Box 792
Riverside, CA 92502
T: (909) 782-7595
F: (909) 782-6009
Sports Editor: John Garrett

Sacramento Bee
PO Box 15779
Sacramento, CA 95852
T: (916) 441-4100
F: (916) 326-5503
Sports Editor: Steve Blust

Salinas Californian
PO Box 81091
Salinas, CA 93912
T: (831) 424-2221
F: (831) 754-4293
Sports Editor: Jeremy Bonfiglio

The San Bernardino County Sun
399 North D Street
San Bernardino, CA 92401
T: (909) 889-9666
F: (909) 384-0327
Sports Editor: Paul Oberjuerge

San Diego Union-Tribune
PO Box 191
San Diego, CA 92112-4106
T: (619) 293-1431
F: (619) 293-2443
Sports Editor: Tom Cushman

San Francisco Chronicle
901 Mission Street
San Francisco, CA 94103
T: (415) 777-7750
F: (415) 957-0954
Sports Editor: John Curley

San Francisco Examiner
PO Box 7260
San Francisco, CA 94120
T: (415) 777-2424
F: (415) 777-2525
Sports Editor: Glenn Schwarz

San Jose Mercury-News
750 Ridder Park Drive
San Jose, CA 95190
T: (408) 920-5354
F: (408) 920-5244
Sports Editor: Reid Laymance

Orange County Register
PO Box 11626
625 N. Grand Avenue
Santa Ana, CA 92711
T: (714) 835-1234
F: (714) 543-3904
Sports Ed: MarkTomaszewski

Santa Barbara News-Press
PO Box 1359, 715 Anacapa St.
Santa Barbara, CA 93102
T: (805) 564-5200
F:: (805) 966-6258
Sports Editor: Mark Patton

Stockton Record
PO Box 900
Stockton, CA 95201
T: (209) 546-8282
F: (209) 943-8570
Sports Editor: Sam Smith

The Daily Breeze
PO Box 2982, 5215 Torrance Blvd.
Torrance, CA 90509
T: (310) 540-5511
F: (310) 540-3067
Sports Editor: Robert Whitley

Colorado

Boulder Daily Camera
PO Box 591
Boulder, CO 80306
T: (303) 442-1202
F: (303) 449-9358
Sports Editor: Dan Creedon

Colorado Springs Gazette-Telegraph
PO Box 1779
Colorado Springs, CO 80901
T: (719) 636-0250
F: (719) 636-0163
Sports Editor: Ralph Routon

Denver Post
PO Box 1709
Denver, CO 80201
T: (303) 820-1294
F: (303) 820-1703
Sports Editor: Neal Scarbrough

Rocky Mountain News
PO Box 719
Denver, CO 80201
T: (303) 892-5000
F: (303) 892-2841
Sports Editor: Barry Forbis

The Coloradoan
PO Box 1577
Fort Collins, CO 80522
T: (970) 493-6397
F: (970) 224-7899
Sports Editor: Sean Duff

Connecticut

Connecticut Post
410 State Street
Bridgeport, CT 06604
T: 203) 330-6210
F: (203) 367-8158
Sports Editor: Gary Rogo

Hartford Courant
285 Broad Street
Hartford, CT 06115
T: (860) 241-6435
F: (860) 520-3155
Sports Editor: Jeff Otterbein

New Haven Register
40 Sargent Drive
New Haven, CT 06511
T: (203) 789-5200
F: (203) 865-7894
Sports Editor: John Desanto

Waterbury Republican-American
PO Box 2090
Waterbury, CT 06722
T: (203) 574-3636
F: (203) 596-9277
Sports Editor: Lee Lewis

Delaware

Wilmington News Journal
PO Box 15505
Wilmington, DE 19850
T: (302) 324-2801
F: (302) 324-5509
Sports Editor: Richard Luna

District of Columbia

The Washington Post
1150 15th St. NW
Washington, DC 20071
T: (202) 334-7350
F: (202) 334-7345
Sports Editor: George Solomon

Washington Times
3600 New York Avenue NE
Washington, DC 20002
T: (202) 636-3000
F: (202) 529-7861
Sports Editor: Gary Hopkins

Florida

Boca Raton News
33 SE 3rd Street
Boca Raton, FL 33432
T: (561) 395-8300
F: (561) 338-4944
Sports Editor: Andy Kent

Bradenton Herald
PO Box 921
102 Manatee Avenue W.
Bradenton, FL 34206
T: (941) 745-7007
F: (941) 745-7097
Sports Editor: Michael Mersch

Daytona Beach News-Journal
PO Box 2831reet
Daytona Beach, FL 32120
T: (904) 252-1511
F: (904) 253-8433
Sports Editor: Dave Markowitz

Fort Lauderdale Sun-Sentinel
200 E. Las Olas Boulevard
Ft. Lauderdale, FL 33301
T: (954) 356-4635
F: (954) 356-4676
Sports Editor: Fred Turner

Fort Myers News-Press
PO Box 10
2442 Dr. Martin Luther King Blvd.
Fort Myers, FL 33902
T: (941) 335-0357
F: (941) 335-0265
Sports Editor: Tom Hayden

Gainesville Sun
PO Box 147147
2700 SW 13th Street
Gainesville, FL 32614
T: (352) 374-5000
F: (352) 374-5085
Sports Editor: Noel Nash

The Florida Times-Union
PO Box 1949
Jacksonville, FL 32231
T: (904) 359-4246
F: (904) 359-4478
Sports Editor: Jim Nasella

The Ledger
PO Box 408
Lakeland, FL 33802
T: (941) 802-7574
F: (941) 802-7812
Sports Editor: John Valerino

Florida Today
PO Box 419000
Melbourne, FL 32941
T: (407) 242-3500
F: (407) 242-6620
Sports Editor: Eric Girard

Diario Las Americas
PO Box 592698
Miami, FL 33159
T: (305) 633-3241
F (305) 625-7668
Sports Editor: Marino Martinez

El Nuevo Herald
1 Herald Square, 6th FL
Miami, FL 33132
T: (305) 376-3535
F: (305) 376-2170
Sports Editor: Javier Mota

Miami Herald
One Herald Plaza
Miami, FL 33132
T: (305) 376-3500
F: (305) 376-2295
Sports Editor: Dave Wilson

Orlando Sentinel
633 N. Orange Avenue
Orlando, FL 32801
T: (407) 420-5474
F: (407) 420-5350
Sports Editor: Donna Eyring

The Palm Beach Post
PO Box 24700
2751 South Dixie Hwy.
West Palm Beach, FL 33405
T: (561) 820- 4440
F: (561) 820 4481
Sports Editor: Tim Burke

Pensacola News Journal
PO Box 12710
Pensacola, FL 32574
T: (850) 435-8500
F: (850) 435-8633
Sports Editor: Gordon Paulus

St. Petersburg Times
PO Box 1121
St. Petersburg, FL 33731
T: (727) 893-8123
F: (727) 893-8782
Sports Editor: Kim Pendery

Sarasota Herald-Tribune
PO Box 1719
801 South Tamiami Trail
Sarasota, FL 34230
T: (941) 957-5172
F: (941) 957-5276
Sports Editor: Scott Peterson

Tallahassee Democrat
PO Box 990
Tallahassee, FL 32302
T: (850) 599-2100
F: (850) 599-2295
Sports Editor: Pete Reinwald

Tampa Tribune
PO Box 191
202 South Parker Street
Tampa, FL 33601
T: (813) 259-7655
F: (813) 259-8148
Sports Editor: Paul Smith

Vero Beach Press-Journal
PO Box 1268
1801 US Highway One
Vero Beach, FL 32961
T: (561) 562-2315
F: (561) 978-2364
Sports Editor: Bill Boeding

Winter Haven News-Chief
PO Box 1440
650 6th Street
Winter Haven, FL 33882
T: (941) 294-7731
F: (941) 294-2008
Sports Editor: Roy Fuoco

Georgia

Athens News / Banner-Herald
PO Box 912
Athens, GA 30603
T: (706) 549-0123
F: (706) 543-5234
Sports Editor: Brad Zimanek

The Atlanta Journal- Constitution
PO Box 4689
Atlanta, GA 30302
T: (404) 526-5331
F: (404) 526-5977
Sports Editor: Don Boykin

Augusta Chronicle
PO Box 1928
Augusta, GA 30903
T: (706) 724-0851
F: (706) 823-3408
Sports Editor: Ward Clayton

Columbus Ledger-Enquirer
PO Box 711
Columbus, GA 31902
T: (706) 324-5526
F: (706) 576-6290
Sports Editor: Kevin Price

Macon Telegraph
PO Box 4167
Macon, GA 31213
T: (912) 744-4200
F: (912) 744-4646
Sports Editor: Jemal Horton

Marietta Daily Journal
PO Box 449
Marietta, GA 30061
T: (770) 428-9411
F: (770) 422-9533
Sports Editor: Andy Johnston

**Savannah Evening Press /
Morning News**
PO Box 1088
111 W. Bay Street
Savannah, GA 31402
T: (912) 236-9511
F: (912) 234-6522
Sports Editor: Anthony Stastny

Hawaii

Honolulu Advertiser
PO Box 3110
Honolulu, HI 96802
T: (808) 525-8040
F: (808) 525-5491
Sports Editor: David Koga

Honolulu Star-Bulletin
PO Box 3080
Honolulu, HI 96802
T: (808) 525-8000
F: (808) 525-6711
Sports Editor: Joe Edwards

Idaho

The Idaho Statesman
PO Box 40
Boise, ID 83707
T: (208) 377-6200
F: (208) 377-6449
Sports Editor: Jennifer Swindell

Idaho Falls Post Register
PO Box 1800
Idaho Falls, ID 83403
T: (208) 522-1800
F: (208) 529-9683
Sports Editor: Jeff Pinkham

Idaho State Journal
PO Box 431
Pocatello, ID 83204
T: (208) 232-4161
F: (208) 233-8007
Sports Editor: Bob Brundage

Moscow Pullman Daily News
PO Box 8187
Moscow, ID 83843
T: (208) 882- 5661
F: (208) 883-8205
Sports Editor: Craig Staszkow

Twin Falls Times-News
PO Box 548
Twin Falls, ID 83303
T: (208) 733-0931
F: (208) 734-5548
Sports Editor: Damen Clow

Illinois

Paddock Publications
PO Box 280
Arlington Heights, IL 60006
T: (847) 427-4300
F: (847) 427-1301
Sports Editor: Tom Quinlan

The Pantagraph
PO Box 2907
Bloomington, IL 61702
T: (309) 829-9411
F: (309) 829-7000
Sports Editor: Bryan Bloodworth

Champaign News Gazette
PO Box 677
Champaign, IL 61824
T: (217) 351-5252
F: (217) 351-5374
Sports Editor: Jim Rossow

Daily Southtown
5959 South Harlem Avenue
Chicago, IL 60006
T: (312) 586-8800
F: (312) 229-2900
Sports Editor: Mike Walters

Chicago Sun-Times
401 N. Wabash Ave.
Chicago, IL 60611
T: (312) 321-2664
F: (312) 321-9404
Sports Editor: William Adee

Chicago Tribune
435 N. Michigan Avenue
Chicago, IL 60611
T: (312) 222-3474
F: (312) 828-9392
Sports Editor: Dan McGrath

Decatur Herald & Review
PO Box 311
Decatur, IL 62525
T: (217) 429-5151
F: (217) 421-7965
Sports Editor: Mark Tupper

Joliet Herald News
300 Caterpillar Drive
Joliet, IL 60436
T: (815) 729-6040
F: (815) 729-6059
Sports Editor: Richard Goss

The Daily Dispatch
1720 Fifth Avenue
Moline, IL 61265
T: (309) 764-4344
F: (309) 797-0317
Sports Editor: Marc Nesseler

Peoria Journal-Star
One News Plaza
Peoria, IL 61643
T: (309) 686-3216
F: (309) 686-3205
Sports Editor: Kirk Wessler

Rockford Register-Star
99 E. State Street
Rockford, IL 61104
T: (815) 987-1200
F: (815) 987-1365
Sports Editor: Randy Ruef

The State Journal-Register
PO Box 219
One Copley Plaza
Springfield, IL 62705
T: (217) 788-1300
F: (217) 788-1382
Sports Editor: Jim Ruppert

The News-Sun
100 W. Madison Street
Waukegan, IL 60085
T: (847) 249-7230
F: (847) 249-7202
Sports Editor: Jeff Bonato

Indiana

Bloomington Herald-Times
PO Box 909
Bloomington, IN 47402
T: (812) 332-4401
F: (812) 331-4383
Sports Editor: Gary McCann

Evansville Courier
PO Box 268
Evansville, IN 47702
T: (812) 424-7711
F: (812) 422-8196
Sports Editor: Chuck Fields

Evansville Press
PO Box 454
Evansville, IN 47703
T: (812) 464-7614
F: (812) 464-7641
Sports Editor: Jim Touvell

Fort Wayne Journal-Gazette
PO Box 88
Ft. Wayne, IN 46801
T: (219) 461-8222
F: (219) 461-8648
Sports Editor: Justice Hill

Fort Wayne News-Sentinel
PO Box 102
Fort Wayne, IN 46801
T: (219) 461-8346
F: (219) 461-8696
Sports Editor: Richard Griffis

Gary Post-Tribune
1065 Broadway
Gary, IN 46402
T: (219) 881-3100
F: (219) 881-3232
Sports Editor: Matt Dorney

Indianapolis Star News
PO Box 145
Indianapolis, IN 46206
T: (317) 633-9180
F: (317) 633-9209
Sports Editor: Nancy Winkley

Lafayette Journal & Courier
217 N. 6th Street
Lafayette, IN 47901
T: (765) 423-5511
F: (765) 420-5246
Sports Editor: Jim Lefko

South Bend Tribune
225 W Colfax Avenue
South Bend, IN 46626
T: (219) 235-6161
F: (219) 236-6091
Sports Editor: Bill Bilinski

Terre Haute Tribune-Star
PO Box 149
Terre Haute, IN 47808
T: (812) 231-4276
F: (812) 231-4321
Sports Editor: Mark Bennett

Valparaiso Vidette-Messenger
PO Box 2350
Valparaiso, IN 46384
T: (219) 462-5151
F: (219) 465-7298
Sports Editor: Paul Jankowski

Iowa

Ames Daily Tribune
PO Box 380
Ames, IA 50010
T: (515) 232-2160
F: (515) 232-2364
Sports Editor: Susan Harman

Cedar Rapids Gazette
PO Box 511
Cedar Rapids, IA 52406
T: (319) 398-8269
F: (319) 398-5861
Sports Editor: Mark Dukes

Quad-City Times
PO Box 3828
500 East 3rd Street
Davenport, IA 52808
T: (319) 383-2285
F: (319) 383-2370
Sports Editor: Brian Kollars

Des Moines Register
PO Box 957, 715 Locust St.
Des Moines, IA 50304
T: (515) 284-8130
F: (515) 284-2506
Sports Editor: Randy Brubaker

Dubuque Telegraph-Herald
PO Box 688
Dubuque, IA 52004
T: (319) 588-5611
F: (319) 588-5745
Sports Editor: Andy Piper

Iowa City Press-Citizen
PO Box 2480
Iowa City, IA 52244
T: (319) 337-3181
F: (319) 339-7342
Sports Editor: Teresa Thorpe

Sioux City Journal
PO Box 118
Sioux City, IA 51102
T: (712) 293-4250
F: (712) 279-5059
Sports Editor: Terry Hersom

Waterloo Daily Courier
PO Box 540
Waterloo, IA 50704
T: (319) 291-1400
F: (319) 291-2069
Sports Editor: Kevin Evans

Kansas

Kansas City Kansan
901 North 8th Street
Kansas City, KS 66101
T: (913) 371-4300
F: (913) 342-8620
Sports Editor: Marc McClure

Topeka Capital-Journal
616 SE Jefferson Street
Topeka, KS 66607
T: (785) 295-1188
F: (785) 295-1230
Sports Editor: Pete Goering

Wichita Eagle
PO Box 820
Wichita, KS 67201
T: (316) 268-6251
F: (316) 268-6536
Sports Editor: Sherry Johnson

Kentucky

Bowling Green Daily News
PO Box 90012
813 College Street
Bowling Green, KY 42102
T: (502) 783-3238
F: (502) 783-3237
Sports Editor: Les Dixon

Elizabethtown News-Enterprise
408 W. Dixie Avenue
Elizabethtown, KY 42701
T: (502) 769-2312
F: (502) 765-7318
Sports Editor: Jeff D'Alessio

Lexingtgon Herald-Leader
100 Midland Avenue
Lexington, KY 40508
T: (606) 231-3200
F: (606) 254-9738
Sports Editor: Gene Abell

The Courier-Journal
PO Box 740031
Louisville, KY 40201
T: (502) 582-4011
F: (502) 582-7186
Sports Editro: Harry Bryan

Louisiana

Alexandria Town Talk
PO Box 7558
Alexandria, LA 71306
T: (318) 487-6351
F: (318) 487-6488
Sports Editor: John Marcase

Baton Rouge Advocate
PO Box 588
525 Lafayette Street
Baton Rouge, LA 70821
T: (225) 383-1111
F: (225) 388-0318
Sports Editor: Butch Muir

Hammond Daily Star
Box 1149
Hammond, LA 70404
T: (504) 345-2333
F: (504) 542-0242
Sports Editor: John Lenz

The Daily Lafayette Advertiser
PO Box 3268
Lafayette, LA 70502
T: (318) 289-6300
F: (318) 289-6443
Sports Editor: Bruce Brown

Lake Charles American Press
PO Box 2893, 4900 Hwy. 90 E.
Lake Charles, LA 70602
T: (318) 433-3000
F: (318) 494-4070
Sports Editor: Scooter Hobbs

The News-Star
PO Box 1502
Monroe, LA 71210
T: (318) 322-5161
F: (318) 362-0279
Sports Editor: Barry Johnson

The Times-Picayune
3800 Howard Avenue
New Orleans, LA 70125
T: (504) 826-3405
F: (318) 826-3007
Sports Editor: Steve Rocca

Shreveport Times
PO Box 30222
222 Lake Stareet
Shreveport, LA 71130
T: (318) 459-3200
F: (318) 459-3301
Sports Editor: Dean Rock

Maine

Kennebec Journal
PO Box 1052
274 Western Avenue
Augusta, ME 04332
T: (207) 623-3811
F: (207) 623-2220
Sports Editor: Joe Halpern

Bangor Daily News
PO Box 1329, 491 Main Street
Bangor, ME 04402
T: (207) 990-8000
F: (207) 941-9476
Sports Editor: Joe McLaughlin

Portland Press-Herald
Maine Telegram
PO Box 1460
390 Congress St.
Portland, ME 04104
T: (207) 791-6650
F: (207) 791-6920
Sports Editor: Dave McNabb

Maryland

The Annapolis Capital
PO Box 911
2000 Capital Drive
Annapolis, MD 21404
T: (410) 268-5000
F: (410) 280-5953
Sports Editor: Joe Gross

The Baltimore Sun
PO Box 1377
501 N. Calvert Street
Baltimore, MD 21278
T: (410) 332-6419
F: (410) 783-2518
Editor: Molly Dunham

Frederick News-Post
PO Box 578
200 E. Patrick Street
Frederick, MD 21705
T: (301) 662-1177
F: (301) 662-8299
Sports Editor: Stan Goldberg

Hagerstown Herald-Mail
PO Box 439
100 Summit Ave.
Hagerstown, MD 21741
T: (301) 733-5131
F: (301) 714-0245
Sports Editor: Ron Somers

Montgomery Journal
1 Research Court
Rockville, MD 20850
T: (301) 670-1400
F: (301) 670-1421
Sports Editor: Dan Shepard

Salisbury Times
PO Box 937
115 E. Carroll Street
Salisbury, MD 21803
T: (410) 749-7171
F: (410) 749-7290
Sports Editor: John Evans

Massachusetts

The Boston Globe
PO Box 2378
135 Morrissey Blvd.
Boston, MA 02107
T: (617) 929-2000
F: (617) 929-2670
Sports Editor: Don Skwar

The Boston Herald
PO Box 2096
300 Harrison Avenue
Boston, MA 02106
T: (617) 426-3000
F: (617) 542-1314
Sports Editor: Mark Torpey

Cape Cod Times
PO Box 550
319 Main Street
Hyannis, MA 02601
T: (508) 775-1200
F: (508) 775-7337
Sports Editor: William Higgins

Lowell Sun
PO Box 1477
15 Kearney Square
Lowell, MA 01853
T: (978) 970-4628
F: (978) 970-4600
Sports Editor: Dennis Whitton

Springfield Union-News
PO Box 2350
1860 Main Street
Springfield, MA 01102
T: (413) 788-1000
F: (413) 788-1301
Sports Editor: Joe Deburro

Worcester Telegram & Gazette
PO Box 15012
Worcester, MA 01615
T: (508) 793-9350
F: (508) 793-9290
Sports Editor: David Nathan

Michigan

Ann Arbor News
PO Box 1147
340 E. Huron Street
Ann Arbor, MI 48106
T: (734) 994-6989
F: (734) 994-6879
Sports Editor: Geoff Larcom

Battle Creek Enquirer
PO Box 3093
155 W. Van Buren
Battle Creek, MI 49017
T: (616) 964-7161
F: (616) 964-0299
Sports Editor: Pat Sutherland

Bay City Times
311 5th Street
Bay City, MI 48708
T: (517) 894-9641
F: (517) 893-0649
Sports Editor: James Deland

Detroit Free Press
600 W. Fort Streetlvd.
Detroit, MI 48226
T: (313) 222-6400
F: (313) 222-5981
Sports Editor: Gene Myers

Detroit News
615 W. Lafayette Blvd.
Detroit, MI 48226
T: (313) 222-2300
F: (313) 222-2335
Sports Editor: Phil Laciura

Flint Journal
200 East First Street
Flint, MI 48502
T: (810) 766-6184
F: (810) 767-7518
Sports Editor: Dave Poniers

Grand Rapids Press
155 Michigan Street NW
Grand Rapids, MI 49503
T: (616) 222-5400
F: (616) 222-5224
Sports Editor: Robert Becker

Jackson Citizen Patriot
214 South Jackson Street
Jackson, MI 49201
T: (517) 787-2300
F: (517) 787-9710
Sports Editor: Jim Knight

Kalamazoo Gazette
PO Box 2007
401 South Burdick St.
Kalamazoo, MI 49003
T: (616) 345-3511
F: (616) 388-8447
Sports Editor: Jack Moss

Lansing State Journal
120 E. Lenawee Street
Lansing, MI 48919
T: (517) 377-1068
F: (517) 377-1298
Sports Editor: Gerry Ahern

Muskegon Chronicle
PO Box 59, 981 3rd Street
Muskegon, MI 49443
T: (616) 722-3161
F: (616) 722-2552
Sports Editor: Cindy Fairfield

Oakland Press
PO Box 436009
Pontiac, MI 48343
T: (248) 332-8181
F: (248) 253-9948
Sports Editor: James Walker

Port Huron Times Herald
PO Box 5009
911 Military Street
Port Huron, MI 48061
T: (810) 985-7171
F: (810) 989-6294
Sports Editor: Rick Jakacki

Saginaw News
203 S. Washington Avenue
Saginaw, MI 48607
T: (517) 752-7171
F: (517) 752-3115
Sports Editor: Paul Neumeyer

Minnesota

Duluth News-Tribune
PO Box 16900
424 W. First Street
Duluth, MN 55816
T: (218) 723-5315
F: (218) 723-5314
Sports Editor: Chris Miller

Mankato Free Press
PO Box 3287
Mankato, MN 56002
T: (507) 625-4451
F: (507) 388-4355
Sports Editor: Jim Rueda

Minneapolis Star Tribune
425 Portland Avenue
Minneapolis, MN 55488
T: (612) 673-4447
F: (612) 673-7774
Sports Editor: Tim Wheatley

Rochester Post Bulletin
PO Box 6118
Rochester, MI 55903
T: (507) 285-7600
F: (507) 285-7734
Sports Editor: Craig Swalboski

St. Paul Pioneer Press
345 Cedar Street
St. Paul, MN 55101
T: (651) 228-5518
F: (651) 228-5527
Sports Editor: Emilio Garcia-Ruiz

Mississippi

The Biloxi Sun Herald
PO Box 4567
Biloxi, MS 39535
T: (228) 896-2312
F: (228) 896-2104
Sports Editor: Kate Magandy

Hattiesburg American
PO Box 1111, 825 N. Main St.
Hattiesburg, MS 39403
T: (601) 582-4321
F: (601) 584-3130
Sports Editor: David Lanier

Jackson Clarion-Ledger
PO Box 40
Jackson, MS 39205
T: (601) 961-7000
F: (601) 961-7211
Sports Editor: Mike Knobler

The Northeast Mississippi Daily Journal
PO Box 909
1655 S. Green Street
Tupelo, MS 38802
T: (601) 842-2611
F: (601) 842-2233
Sports Editor: Gene Phelps

Missouri

Columbia Daily Tribune
PO Box 798, 101 N. 4th St.
Columbia, MO 65205
T: (573) 815-1500
F: (573) 815-1701
Sports Editor: Kent Heitholt

Independence Examiner
PO Box 459, 410 S.Liberty St.
Independence, MO 64050
T: (816) 254-8600
F: (816) 836-0211
Sports Editor: Karl Zinke

Joplin Globe
PO Box 7, 117 East 4th St.
Joplin, MO 64802
T: (417) 623-3480
F: (417) 623-8598
Sports Editor: James Fryar

Kansas City Star
1729 Grand Blvd.
Kansas City, MO 64108
T: (816) 234-4355
F: (816) 234-4360
Sports Editor: Rick Vacek

News-Press-Gazette
PO Box 29
825 Edmond St.
St. Joseph, MO 64502
T: (816) 271-8500
F: (816) 271-8692
Sports Editor: Paul Suellentrop

St. Louis Post-Dispatch
900 N. Tucker Blvd.
St. Louis, MO 63101
T: (314) 340-8170
F: (314) 340-3070
Sports Editor: Mike Smith

Springfield News-Leader
PO Box 798
651 Booneville Avenue
Springfield, MO 65801
T: (417) 836-1100
F: (417) 837-1381
Sports Editor: Jeff Majeske

Montana

Billings Gazette
PO Box 36300
401 N. Broadway
Billings, MT 59107
T: (406) 657-1200
F: (406) 657-1208
Sports Editor: Warren Rodgers

Bozeman Daily Chronicle
PO Box 1188
Bozeman, MT 59771
T: (406) 587-4491
F: (406) 587-7995
Sports Editor: Jeff Robinson

Butte Montana Standard
PO Box 627
25 W. Granite Street
Butte, MT 59703
T: (406) 496-5500
F: (406) 496-5551
Sports Editor: Bruce Saylor

Great Falls Tribune
PO Box 5468
205 S. River Drive
Great Falls, MT 59403
T: (406) 761-1268
F: (406) 791-1431
Sports Editor: George Geise

The Missoulian
PO Box 8029
500 S. Higgans
Missoula, MT 59807
T: (406) 523-5200
F: (406) 523-5294
Sports Editor: Bob Meseroll

Nebraska

Lincoln Journal Star
PO Box 81689
Lincoln, NE 68501
T: (402) 475-4200
F: (402) 473-7291
Sports Editor: John Mabry

Omaha World Herald
World Herald Square
1334 Dodge Street
Omaha, NE 68102
T: (402) 444-1000
F: (402) 345-0183
Sports Editor: Steve Sinclair

Nevada

Las Vegas Review-Journal
PO Box 70
1111 W. Bonanza Road
Las Vegas, NV 89125
T: (702) 383-0297
F: (702) 383-4676
Sports Editor: Jim Fossum

Las Vegas Sun
PO Box 4275
800 S. Valley View Blvd.
Las Vegas, NV 89127
T: (702) 385-3111
F: (702) 383-7264
Sports Editor: Ron Kantowski

Reno Gazette--Journal
Box 22000, 955 Kuenzli St.
Reno, NV 89520
T: (775) 788-6200
F: (775) 788-6458
Sports Editor: Ray Hager

New Hampshire

Concord Monitor
PO Box 1177, One Monitor Dr.
Concord, NH 03302
T: (603) 224-5301
F: (603) 224-8120
Sports Editor: Sandra Smith

The Union Leader
PO Box 9555
100 William Loeb Drive
Manchester, NH 03108
T: (603) 668-4321
F: (603) 668-0382
Sports Editor: Maureen Milliken

Nashua Telegraph
PO Box 1008
Nashua, NH 03061
T: (603) 882-2741
F: (603) 882-2681
Sports Editor: Alan Greenwood

New Jersey

Camden Courier-Post
PO Box 5300, 301 Cuthbert
Cherry Hill, NJ 08034
T: (609) 486-2424
F: (609) 663-2831
Sports Editor: Chuck Bausman

The Home News Tribune
PO Box 1049
35 Kennedy Boulevard
East Brunswick, NJ 08816
T: (732) 246-5500
F: (732) 937-6046
Sports Editor: Jack Genung

The Record
150 River Street
Hackensack, NJ 07601
T: (201) 646-4430
F: (201) 646-4428
Sports Editor: Gabe Buonauro

The Jersey Journal
30 Journal Square
Jersey City, NJ 07306
T: (201) 217-2490
F: (201) 653-1414
Sports Editor: Harvey Zucker

Asbury Park Press
PO Box 1550
3601 Hwy. 66
Neptune, NJ 07754
T: (732) 922-6000
F: (732) 922-5885
Sports Editor: John Quinn

Newark Star-Ledger
One Star Ledger Plaza
Newark, NJ 07102
T: (973) 877-4141
F: (973) 877-5948
Sports Editor: Kevin Whitmer

The Trentonian
600 Perry Street
Trenton, NJ 08618
T: (609) 989-7800
F: (609) 393-6072
Sports Editor: Storm Gifford

Trenton Times
PO Box 847, 500 Perry St.
Trenton, NJ 08605
T: (609) 989-5454
F: (609) 989-8368
Sports Editor: Jim Gauger

New Mexico

Albuquerque Journal
PO Box J, 7777 Jefferson NE
Albuquerque, NM 87103
T: (505) 823-3900
F: (505) 823-3998
Sports Editor: Mike Hall

Albuquerque Tribune
PO Box T, 7777 Jefferson NE
Albuquerque, NM 87103
T: (505) 823-3600
F: (505) 823-3689
Sports Editor: John O' Rourke

Las Cruces Sun-News
PO Box 1749, 256 W. Las Cruces
Las Cruces, NM 88004
T: (505) 541-5400
F: (505) 541-5498
Sports Editor: Sam Bradley

New York

Albany Times-Union
Box 15000, News Plaza
Albany, NY 12212
T: (518) 454-5413
F: (518) 454-5628
Sports Editor: Bill Callen

Auburn Citizen
25 Dill Street
Auburn, NY 13021
T: (315) 253-5311
F: (315) 253-6031
Sports Editor: Chris Sciria

Batavia Daily News
PO Box 870, 2 Apollo Drive
Batavia, NY 14021
T: (716) 343-8000
F: (716) 343-2623
Sports Editor: Bill Bruton

Binghamton Press & Sun Bulletin
PO Box 1270
Binghamton, NY 13902
T: (607) 798-1191
F: (607) 798-1113
Sports Editor: Charlie Jaworski

New York Daily Challenge
1195 Atlantic Avenue
Brooklyn, NY 11216
T: (718) 636-9500
F: (718) 857-9115
Sports Editor: Joe Bostick

Buffalo News
PO Box 100
One News Plaza
Buffalo, NY 14240
T: (716) 849-3434
F: (716) 849-4587
Sports Editor: Larry Felser

Elmira Star-Gazette
PO Box 285
201 Baldwin St.
Elmira, NY 14902
T: (607) 734-5151
F: (607) 733-4408
Sports Editor: Roger Neumann

The Glens Falls Post-Star
PO Box 2157
Glens Falls, NY 12801
T: (518) 792-3131
F: (518) 761-1255
Sports Editor: Ken Tingley

Ithaca Journal
PO Box 430
123 W. State Street
Ithaca, NY 14851
T: (607) 274-9215
F: (607) 272-4248
Sports Editor: Tom Fleischman

New York Daily News
450 W. 33rd Street
New York, NY 10001
T: (212) 210-1670
F: (212) 643-7845
Sports Editor: Barry Werner

New York Post
1211 Ave. of the Americas
New York, NY 10036
T: (212) 930-8700
F: (212) 930-8727
Exec. Editor: Greg Gallo

New York Times
229 W. 43rd Street
New York, NY 10036
T: (212) 556-7371
F: (212) 556-5848
Sports Editor: Neil Amdur

Newsday
235 Pinelawn Road
Melville, NY 11747
T: (516) 843-2020
F: (516) 454-6892
Sports Editor: Steve Ruinsky

Poughkeepsie Journal
PO Box 1231
85 Civic Center Plaza
Poughkeepsie, NY 12602
T: (914) 454-2000
F: (914) 437-4921
Sports Editor: Darren O'Sullivan

Rochester Democrat-Chronicle
Rochester Times Union
55 Exchange Boulevard
Rochester, NY 14614
T: (716) 258-2262
F: (716) 258-2776
Sports Editor: Tom Batzold

Schenectady Daily Gazette
PO Box 1090
2345 Maxon Road
Schenectady, NY 12301
T: (518) 395-3070
F: (518) 395-3089
Sports Editor: Cecil Walker

Staten Island Advance
950 Fingerboard Road
Staten Island, NY 10305
T: (718) 981-1234
F: (718) 981-5679
Sports Editor: Lou Bergonzi

Post-Standard & Herald Journal
PO Box 4915, 1 Clinton Square
Syracuse, NY 13221
T: (315) 470-0011
F: (315) 470-3019
Sports Editor: Steve Carlic

Troy Record
501 Broadway
Troy, NY 12180
T: (518) 270-1295
F: (518) 270-1202
Sports Editor: Kevin Moran

Utica Observer-Dispatch
221 Oriskany Plaza
Utica, NY 13501
T: (315) 792-5023
F: (315) 792-5033
Sports Editor: Craig Muder

North Carolina

Asheville Citizen-Times
PO Box 2090
14 O'Henry Ave.
Asheville, NC 28802
T: (828) 252-5611
F: (828) 251-0585
Sports Editor: Vince Ellis

Charlotte Observer
PO Box 30308
600 South Tryon Street
Charlotte, NC 28230
T: (704) 358-5125
F: (704) 358-5110
Sports Editor: Gary Schwab

Durham Herald-Sun
PO Box 2092
Durham, NC 27702
T: (919) 419-6670
F: (919) 419-6889
Sports Editor: Jimmy DuPree

Fayetteville Observer-Times
PO Box 849, 458 Whitfield St.
Fayetteville, NC 28302
T: (910) 486-3500
F: (910) 486-3545
Sports Editor: Doug Mead

Gaston Gazette
PO Box 1538
Gastonia, NC 28053
T: (704) 864-3293
F: (704) 867-5751
Sports Editor: Mark Anderson

Greensboro News & Record
PO Box 20848
Greensboro, NC 27420
T: (336) 373-7062
F: (336) 373-7067
Sports Editor: Allen Johnson

High Point Enterprise
PO Box 1009
High Point, NC 27261
T: (336) 888-3500
F: (336) 841-5582
Sports Editor: Benny Phillips

Raleigh News & Observer
PO Box 191
215 S. McDowell Street
Raleigh, NC 27602
T: (919) 829-4560
F: (919) 829-4888
Sports Editor: Steve Riley

Wilmington Morning Star
PO Box 840
Wilmington, NC 28402
T: (910) 343-2000
F: (910) 343-2227
Sports Editor: Paul Bowker

Winston-Salem Journal
PO Box 3159
418 N. Marshall Street
Winston-Salem, NC 27102
T: (336) 727-7310
F: (336) 727-4083
Sports Editor: Terry Oberle

North Dakota

Bismarck Tribune
PO Box 1498
707 E. Front Ave.
Bismarck, ND 58502
T: (701) 223-2500
F: (701) 224-2063
Sports Editor: Scooter Pursley

The Forum
PO Box 2020
101 Fifth Street
Fargo, ND 58107
T: (701) 225-7311
F: (701) 241-5487
Sports Editor: Kevin Schnepf

Grand Forks Herald
PO Box 6008
375 Second Ave. N.
Grand Forks, ND 58206
T: (701) 780-1125
F: (701) 780-1123
Sports Editor: Kevin Fee

Minot Daily News
PO Box 1150
301 Fourth St. NE
Minot, ND 58702
T: (701) 857-1900
F: (701) 857-1961
Sports Editor: Mike Zimmer

Ohio

Akron Beacon Journal
PO Box 640
44 E. Echange St.
Akron, OH 44309
T: (330) 996-3000
F: (330) 996-3629
Sports Editor: Larry Pantages

The Canton Repository
PO Box 9901
500 Market Avenue S.
Canton, OH 44711
T: (330) 580-8300
F: (330) 454-5745
Sports Editor: Robert Stewart

Cincinnati Enquirer
312 Elm Street
Cincinnati, OH 45202
T: (513) 768-8438
F: (513) 768-8589
Sports Editor: Julie Engebrecht

Cincinnati Post
125 East Court Street
Cincinnati, OH 45202
T: (513) 352-2767
F: (513) 621-3962
Sports Editor: Mike Bass

The Cleveland Plain Dealer
1801 Superior Ave NE
Cleveland, OH 44114
T: (216) 999-4370
F: (216) 999-6276
Sports Editor: Roy Hewitt

Columbus Dispatch
34 South Third Street
Columbus, OH 43215
T: (614) 469-9909
F: (614) 461-7571
Sports Editor: George Strode

Dayton Daily News
PO Box 1287
45 South Ludlow St.
Dayton, OH 45401
T: (937) 225-2250
F: (937) 225-7352
Sports Editor: Dwayne Bray

The Lima News
PO Box 690
Lima, OH 45802
T: (419) 223-1010
F: (419) 229-2926
Sports Editor: Paul Smith

Toledo Blade
541 N. Superior Street
Toledo, OH 43660
T: (419) 724-6000
F: (419) 724-6439
Sports Editor: Bob Kinney

The Youngstown Vindicator
PO Box 780
Youngstown, OH 44501
T: (330) 747-1471
F: (330) 747-6712
Sports Editor: Matt Arnold

Oklahoma

The Daily Oklahoman
PO Box 25125
Oklahoma City, OK 73125
T: (405) 475-3311
F: (405) 475-3183
Sports Editor: Bob Colon

Tulsa World
PO Box 1770
318 S. Main Mall
Tulsa, OK 74102
T: (918) 581-8300
F: (918) 581-8352
Sports Editor: Phil Parrish

Oregon

Bend Bulletin
1526 NW Hill Street
Bend, OR 97701
T: (541) 383-0352
F: (541) 385-5802
Sports Editor: Bill Bigelow

Corvallis Gazette-Times
PO Box 368, 600 SW Jefferson
Corvallis, OR 97339
T: (541) 753-2641
F: (541) 758-9505
Sports Editor: Jeff Welsch

The Register-Guard
PO Box 10188
Eugene, OR 97440
T: (541) 485-1234
F: (541) 687-6674
Sports Editor: John Conrad

Medford Mail Tribune
PO Box 1108, 111 N. Fir St.
Medford, OR 97501
T: (541) 776-4480
F: (541) 776-4376
Sports Editor: Tim Trower

The Oregonian
1320 SW Broadway
Portand, OR 97201
T: (503) 221-8160
F: (503) 221-8168
Sports Editor: Dennis Peck

Salem Statesman-Journal
PO Box 13009
280 Church St. NE
Salem, OR 97309
T: (503) 399-6723
F: (503) 399-6706
Sports Editor: Kathy Sheldon

Pennsylvania

Allentown Morning Call
PO Box 1260
101 N. 6tth St.
Allentown, PA 18105
T: (610) 820-6500
F: (610) 820-8654
Sports Editor: Paul Reinhard

Erie Daily Times
205 W. 12th Street
Erie, PA 16534
T: (814) 870-1600
F: (814) 870-1808
Sports Editor: Kevin Cuneo

Erie Morning News
205 W. 12th Street
Erie, PA 16534
T: (814) 870-1675
F: (814) 870-1808
Sports Editor: Jim Camp

Harrisburg Patriot-News
PO Box 2265
812 Market St.
Harrisburg, PA 17105
T: (717) 255-8100
F: (717) 255-8456
Sports Editor: Nick Horvath

Johnstown Tribune-Democrat
PO Box 340
425 Locust Street
Johnstown, PA 15907
T: (814) 532-5050
F: (814) 539-1409
Sports Editor: Sean Roane

Philadelphia Daily News
PO Box 7788
Philadelphia, PA 19101
T: (215) 854-4550
F: (215) 854-5524
Sports Editor: Pat McLoone

Philadelphis Inquirer
PO Box 8263
400 N. Broad Street
Philadelphia, PA 19101
T: (215) 854-4550
F: (215) 854-4564
Sports Editor: Tim Dwyer

Pittsburgh Post-Gazette
34 Blvd. of the Allies
Pittsburgh, PA 15222
T: (412) 263-1909
F: (412) 263-1926
Sports Editor: James Barger

Reading Eagle-Times
PO Box 582
Reading, PA 19603
T: (610) 371-5000
F: (610) 371-5098
Sports Editor: Michael Miorelli

Scranton Times-Tribune
PO Box 3311
149 Pennsylvania Avenue
Scranton, PA 18505
T: (570) 348-9100
F: (570) 348-9135
Sports Editor: Tom Robinson

Wilkes Barre Citizens Voice
75 N. Washington
Wilkes Barre, PA 18711
T: (570) 821-2000
F: (570) 821-2247
Sports Editor: Neil Corbett

Wilkes Barre Times-Leader
PO Box 730, 15 N. Main St.
Wilkes Barre, PA 18703
T: (570) 829-7100
F: (570) 829-5537
Sports Editor: Steve Sembrat

York Daily Record
PO Box 15122
122 S. George Street
York, PA 17405
T: (717) 771-2000
F: (717) 771-2009
Sports Editor: Paul Vigna

York Dispatch
205 N. George Street
York, PA 17401
T: (717) 854-1575
F: (717) 843-2958
Sports Editor: Greg Bowers

Puerto Rico

San Juan Star
PO Box 364187
San Juan, PR 00936
T: (809) 782-4200
F: (809) 783-5788

Rhode Island

Pawtucket Times
PO Box 307
23 Exchange Street
Pawtucket, RI 02860
T: (401) 722-4000
F: (401) 727-9252
Sports Editor: Terry Nau

Providence Journal-Bulletin
75 Fountain St.
Providence, RI 02902
T: (401) 277-7340
F: (401) 277-7444
Sports Editor: Dave Bloss

South Carolina

Charleston Post & Courier
134 Columbus St.
Charleston, SC 29403
T: (843) 937-5586
F: (843) 937-5579
Sports Editor: Malcolm DeWitt

The State
PO Box 1333
1401 Shop Road
Columbia, SC 29202
T: (803) 771-8470
F: (803) 771-8480
Sports Editor: Brian Tolley

The Greenville News
PO Box 1688
Greenville, SC 29602
T: (864) 298-4100
F: (864) 298-4137
Sports Editor: Ed Choate

Spartanburg Herald-Journal
PO Box 1657, Herald Square
Spartanburg, SC 29304
T: (864) 582-4511
F: (864) 594-6350
Sports Editor: Jim Fair

South Dakota

Rapid City Journal
PO Box 450
507 Main St.
Rapid City, SD 57709
T: (605) 394-8428
F: (605) 394-8463
Sports Editor: Ted Brockish

Sioux Falls Argus-Leader
PO Box 5034
200 S. Minnesota Ave.
Sioux Falls, SD 57117
T: (605) 331-2303
F: (605) 331-2294
Sports Editor: Jim Cheesman

Tennessee

Chattanooga Free Press
PO Box 1447
400 E. 11th Street
Chattanooga, TN 37401
T: (423) 756-6900
F: (423) 757-6383
Sports Editor: Sam Woolwine

Chattanooga Times
PO Box 951
100 E. 10th Street
Chattanooga, TN 37401
T: (423) 756-1234
F: (423) 752-3364
Sports Editor: Andy Daffron

The Jackson Sun
PO Box 1059
245 W. Lafayette
Jackson, TN 38302
T: (901) 427-3333
F: (901) 425-9639
Sports Editor: Charles Corder

Kingsport Times-News
PO Box 479
Kingsport, TN 37662
T: (423) 246-8121
F: (423) 392-1385
Sports Editor: Ron Bliss

Knoxville News-Sentinel
PO Box 59038
208 W. Church Ave.
Knoxville, TN 37950
T: (423) 521-8136
F: (423) 521-8127
Sports Editor: Steve Ahillen

The Commercial Appeal
PO Box 334
Memphis, TN 38101
T: (901) 529-2360
F: (901) 529-2362
Sports Editor: John Stamm

The Tennessean
PO Box 1387
1100 Broadway
Nashville, TN 37202
T: (615) 259-8010
F: (615) 259-8826
Sports Editor: John Gibson

Texas

Abilene Reporter-News
PO Box 30
101 Cypress St.
Abilene, TX 79604
T: (915) 673-4271
F: (915) 670-5242
Sports Editor: Al Pickett

Amarillo News & Globe-Times
PO Box 2091, 900 S. Harrison
Amarillo, Tx 79166
T: (806) 345-3307
F: (806) 373-0810
Sports Editor: Jon Mark Beilue

Austin American-Statesman
PO Box 670
305 S. Congress Ave.
Austin, TX 78767
T: (512) 445-3500
F: (512) 445-3868
Sports Editor: Tracy Dodds

Beaumont Enterprise
PO Box 3071, 380 Walnut St.
Beaumont, TX 77704
T: (409) 833-3311
F: (409) 838-2857
Sports Editor: Gerry Dickert

Corpus Christi Caller-Times
PO Box 9136
820 N. Lower Broadway St.
Corpus Christi, TX 78469
T: (512) 884-2011
F: (512) 886-3732
Sports Editor: Bart Wright

The Dallas Morning News
PO Box 655237
508 Young St.
Dallas, TX 75265
T: (214) 977-8444
F: (214) 651-0580
Sports Editor: David L. Smith

El Paso Herald-Post
PO Box 20
300 N. Campbell Street
El Paso, TX 79999
T: (915) 546-6381
F: (915) 546-6349
Sports Editor: Joe Muench

El Paso Times
PO Box 20
300 N. Campbell St.
El Paso, TX 79999
T: (915) 546-6100
F: (915) 546-6415
Sports Editor: Mark Jaworski

Fort Worth Star-Telegram
PO Box 1870, 400 W. 7th St.
Ft. Worth, TX 76101
T: (817) 390-7760
F: (817) 390-7210
Sports Editor: Scott Monserud

Houston Chronicle
PO Box 4260
801 Texas Ave.
Houston, TX 77210
T: (713) 220-7171
F: (713) 220-7866
Sports Editor: Dan Cunningham

Lubbock Avalanche-Journal
PO Box 491, 710 Ave. J
Lubbock, TX 79408
T: (806) 766-8844
F: (806) 744-9603
Sports Editor: Doug Hensley

Midland Reporter-Telegram
PO Box 1650
201 E. Illinois
Midland, TX 79702
T: (915) 682-5311
F: (915) 682-3793
Sports Editor: Terry Williamson

Odessa American
PO Box 2952
Odessa, TX 79760
T: (915) 337-4661
F: (915) 334-8641
Sports Editor: Cameron Holloway

San Antonio Express-News
PO Box 2171
San Antonio, TX 78297
T: (210) 250-3000
F: (210) 250-3105
Sports Editor: Brett Thacker

Tyler Morning-Telegraph
PO Box 2030
410 W. Erwin St.
Tyler, TX 75710
T: (903) 597-8111
F: (903) 595-0335
Sports Editor: Phil Hicks

Waco Tribune-Herald
PO Box 2588
900 Franklin Ave.
Waco, TX 76702
T: (254) 757-5757
F: (254) 757-0302
Sports Editor: Kim Gorum

The Times Record-News
PO Box 120
1301 Lamar St.
Wichita Falls, TX 76307
T: (940) 767-8341
F: (940) 767-1741
Sports Editor: Nick Gholson

Utah

Ogden Standard-Examiner
PO Box 951
Ogden, UT 84402
T: (801) 625-4200
F: (801) 625-4299
Sports Editor: Chris Miller

The Provo Daily Herald
PO Box 717
1555 N. Freedom Blvd.
Provo, UT 84603
T: (801) 373-5050
F: (801) 373-5489
Sports Editor: Steve Cameron

Deseret News
PO Box 1257
Salt Lake City, UT 84110
T: (801) 236-6000
F: (801) 236-2121
Sports Editor: Chuck Gates

The Salt Lake Tribune
PO Box 867
143 S. Main St.
Salt Lake City, UT 84110
T: (801) 237-2800
F: (801) 237-2316
Sports Editor: Tom Wharton

Vermont

Burlington Free Press
PO Box10
191 College Street
Burlington, VT 05402
T: (802) 863-3441
F: (802) 660-1802
Sports Editor: Steve Locklin

Rutland Herald
PO Box 668
27 Wales Street
Rutland, VT 05702
T: (802) 747-6121
F: (802) 775-2423
Sports Editor: Bob Fredette

Virginia

USA Today
1000 Wilson Blvd.
Arlington, VA 22209
T: (703) 276-3735
F: (703) 558-3988
www.usatoday.com
Managing Editor: Monte Lorell

Bristol Herald Courier
PO Box 609
Bristol, VA 24203
T: (540) 669-2181
F: (540) 645-2527
Sports Editor: George Stone

The Fairfax Journal Newspapers
6408 Edsall Road
Alexandria, VA 22312
T: (703) 560-4000
F: (703) 846-8366
Sports Editor: Paul Bergeron

The Freelance-Star
616 Amelia St.
Fredericksburg, VA 22401
T: (540) 374-5000
F: (540) 373-8450
Sports Editor: Lee Woolf

Lynchburg News & Advance
PO Box 10129, 101 Wyndale Dr.
Lynchburg, VA 24506
T: (804) 385-5555
F: (804) 385-5451
Sports Editor: Walt Moody

Newport News Daily Press
PO Box 746
7505 Warwick Blvd.
Newport News, VA 23607
T: (757) 247-4600
F: (757) 247-7899
Sports Editor: Skip Miller

The Virginian-Pilot
Box 449,150 W. Brambleton Ave.
Norfolk, VA 23501
T: (757) 446-2366
F: (757) 533-9004
Sports Editor: Chic Riebel

Richmond Times-Dispatch
PO Box 85333
333 Franklin Street
Richmond, VA 23293
T: (804) 649-6000
F: (804) 775-8059
Sports Editor: Jack Berninger

The Roanoke Times
PO Box 2491
201 Campbell Ave. SW
Richmond, VA 24010
T: (540) 981-3100
F: (540) 981-3346
Sports Editor: Bill Bern

Washington

Eastside Journal American
PO Box 90130
1705 132nd Ave. NE
Bellevue, WA 98009
T: (425) 455-2222
F: (425) 635-0603
Sports Editor: Mark McTyre

Bellingham Herald
PO Box 1277
Bellingham, WA 98227
T: (360) 676-2600
F: (360) 647-9260
Sports Editor: Bob Carter

The Everett Herald
PO Box 930
Everett, WA 98206
T: (425) 339-3470
F: (425) 339-3464
Sports Editor: Bob Bolerjack

Tri-City Herald
107 N. Cascade Street
Kennewick, WA 99336
T: (509) 582-1500
F: (509) 582-1510
Sports Editor: Jeff Morrow

Seattle Post-Intelligencer
PO Box 1909
101 Elliot Ave. W
Seattle, WA 98111
T: (206) 448-8370
F: (206) 448-8164
Sports Ed: Glenn Drosendahl

Seattle Times
PO Box 70, 1120 John St.
Seattle, WA 98111
T: (206) 464-2275
F: (206) 464-3255
Sports Editor: Cathy Henkel

Spokane Spokesman-Review
PO Box 2160
W. 999 Riverside
Spokane, WA 99210
T: (509) 459-5500
F: (509) 459-5098
Sports Editor: Jeff Jordan

The Tacoma News Tribune
PO Box 11000
1950 S. State St.
Tacoma, WA 98411
T: (253) 597-8511
F: (253) 597-8274
Sports Editor: Dale Phelps

The Vancouver Columbian
PO Box 180
701 W. 8th Street
Vancouver, WA 98666
T: (360) 696-1661
F: (360) 699-6031
Sports Editor: Don Chandler

Yakima Herald-Republic
PO Box 9668
Yakima, WA 98909
T: (509) 577-7687
F: (509) 577-7767
Sports Editor: Jim Scoggins

West Virginia

Charleston Daily Mail
PO Box 2993
1001 Virginia St. E.
Charleston, WV 25330
T: (304) 348-4807
F: (304) 348-4847
Sports Editor: Jody Jividen

Charleston Gazette
PO Box 2993
Charleston, WV 25330
T: (304) 348-5122
F: (304) 348-5133
Sports Editor: Mitchell Vingle

Huntington Herald-Dispatch
PO Box 2017, 946 Fifth Ave.
Huntington, WV 25720
T: (800) 333-6636
F: (304) 526-2857
Sports Editor: Brian Hofmann

The Dominion Post
1251 Earl Core Road
Morgantown, WV 26505
T: (304) 292-6301
F: (304) 291-2326
Sports Editor: Bob Hertzel

Wheeling News Register
1500 Main Street
Wheeling, WV 26003
T: (304) 233-0100
F: (304) 233-0327
Sports Editor: Nick Bedway

Wisconsin

Appleton Post Crescent
PO Box 59
306 W. Washington Street
Appleton, WI 54912
T: (920) 993-1000
F: (920) 954-1945
Sports Editor: Larry Gallup

Beloit Daily News
149 State Street
Beloit, WI 53511
T: (608) 365-8811
F: (608) 365-1420
Sports Editor: Jim Franz

Leader-Telegraph
PO Box 570
Eau Claire, WI 54702
T: (715) 833-9212
F: (715) 833-9201
Sports Editor: Tad Reeve

Green Bay Press-Gazette
PO Box 19430
Green Bay, WI 54307
T: (920) 435-4411
F: (920) 431-8379
Sports Editor: John Morton

La Crosse Tribune
401 N. Third Street
La Crosse, WI 54601
T: (608) 782-9710
F: (608) 782-9723
Sports Editor: Jon Masson

Wisconsin State Journal
PO Box 8058
Madison, WI 53708
T: (608) 252-6170
F: (608) 252-6119
Sports Editor: Greg Sprout

Milwaukee Journal Sentinel
PO Box 371
Milwaukee, WI 53201
T: (414) 224-2310
F: (414) 224-2049
Sports Editor: Garry Howard

Oshkosh Northwestern
PO Box 2926
Oshkosh, WI 54903
T: (920) 235-7700
F: (920) 235-1527
Sports Editor: Mike Sherry

The Journal Times
212 Fourth Street
Racine, WI 53403
T: (414) 634-3322
F: (414) 631-1702
Sports Editor: Susan Shemanski

The Sheboygan Press
PO Box 358, 632 Center Ave.
Sheboygan, WI 53081
T: (920) 457-7711
F: (920) 457-3573
Sports Editor: Mike Knuth

Wausau Daily Herald
PO Box 1286
800 Scott Street
Wausau, WI 54402
T: (715) 842-2101
F: (715) 848-9361
Sports Editor: Jay Lillge

Wyoming

Casper Star-Tribune
PO Box 80
170 Star Lane
Casper, WY 82602
T: (307) 266-0574
F: (307) 266-0568
Sports Editor: Ron Gullberg

Wyoming Tribune Eagle
702 W. Lincoln Way
Cheyenne, WY 82001
T: (307) 634-3361
F: (307) 778-7163
Sports Editor: Ken Pomponi

Canadian Newspapers

Alberta

Calgary Herald
PO Box 2400, Station M
Calgary, Alberta T2P 0W8
T: (403) 235-7373
F: (403) 235-7313
Sports Editor: Mark Tremblay

Calgary Sun
PO Box 4659, Station C
2615 12th Street NE
Calgary, Alberta T2T 5P1
T: (403) 250-4141
F: (403) 250-4180
Sports Editor: Martin Hudson

The Edmonton Journal
PO Box 2421
Edmonton, Alberta T4J 2S6
T: (780) 429-5300
F: (780) 498-5601
Sports Editor: Bob Remington

Edmonton Sun
4990 92nd Ave., #250
Edmonton, Alberta T6B 3A1
T: (780) 468-0100
F: (780) 468-0139
Sports Editor: Phil Rivers

The Lethbridge Herald
PO Box 670, 504 Seventh Street S.
Lethbridge, Alberta T1J 3Z7
T: (403) 328-4411
F: (403) 328-4536
Sports Editor: Randy Jensen

The Medicine Hat News
PO Box 10
Medicine Hat, Alberta T1A 7E6
T: (403) 527-1101
F: (403) 527-6029
Sports Editor: Todd Saelhof

The Advocate
Bag 5200
2950 Bremner Ave.
Red Deer, Alberta T4N 5G3
T: (403) 343-2400
F: (403) 341-6560
Sports Editor: John Stewart

British Columbia

Kamloops Daily News
393 Seymour St.
Kamloops, B. C. V2C 6P6
T: (250) 372-2331
F: (250) 372-0823
Sports Editor: Allen Cameron

The Prince George Citizen
PO Box 5700
Prince George, B.C. V2L 5K9
T: (250) 562-2441
F: (250) 562-9201
Sports Editor: Jim Swanson

The Daily News
801 W. 2nd Ave.
Prince Rupert, B.C. V8J 1H6
T: (250) 624-6781
F: (250) 624-2851
Sports Editor: Mitch Wright

The Province
200 Granville Street, # 1
Vancouver, B.C. V6C 3N3
T: (604) 605-2014
F: (604) 605-2223
Sports Editor: Mike Haddon

The Vancouver Sun
200 Granville Street, # 1
Vancouver, B.C. V6C 3N3
T: (604) 605-2395
F: (604) 605-2308
Sports Editor: Gary Mason

Times Colonist
PO Box 300
2621 Douglas St.
Victoria, B.C. V8W 2N4
T: (250) 380-5211
F: (250) 380-5353
Sports Editor: Dave Senick

Manitoba

The Brandon Sun
501 Rosser Ave.
Brandon, Manitoba R7A 5Z6
T: (204) 571-7442
F: (204) 727-0385
Sports Editor: Mike Jones

The Reminder
10 North Ave.
Flin Flon, Manitoba R8A 0T2
T: (204) 687-3454
F: (204) 687-4473
Sports Editor: Grant Elliot

Winnipeg Free Press
1355 Mountain Ave.
Winnipeg, Manitoba R2X 3B6
T: (204) 697-7300
F: (204) 697-7288
Sports Editor: Julian Rachey

Winnipeg Sun
PO Box 6900
1700 Church Ave.
Winnipeg, Manitoba R2X 3A2
T: (204) 694-2022
F: (204) 697-0759
Sports Editor: Dave Komosky

New Brunswick

The Daily Gleaner
PO Box 3370
Fredericton, N. B. E3B 5A2
T: (506) 452-6671
F: (506) 452-7405
Sports Editor: Dave Ritchie

Moncton Times-Transcript
PO Box 1001
939 Main Street
Moncton, N.B. E1C 8P3
T: (506) 859-4900
F: (506) 859-4904
Sports Editor: Dwayne Tingley

**The Times-Globe/
Telegraph-Journal**
PO Box 2350
210 Crown St.
St. John, N.B. E2L 3V8
T: (506) 632-8888
F: (506) 648-2654
Sports Editor: Peter McGuire

Newfoundland

The Western Star
PO Box 460
Corner Brook, Nfld A2H 6E7
T: (709) 634-4348
F: (709) 637-4675
Sports Editor: Don Bradshaw

The Evening Telegram
PO Box 5970
St. John's, Nfld A1C 5X7
T: (709) 748-0820
F: (709) 364-9333
Sports Editor: Robin Short

Nova Scotia

The Chronicle-Herald & Mail Star
PO Box 610
1650 Argyle Street
Halifax, Nova Scotia B3J 2T2
T: (902) 426-1187
F: (902) 426-1158
Sports Editor: Mike Flemming

Cape Breton Post
PO Box 1500
255 George St., Box 1500
Sydney, Nova Scotia B1P 6K6
T: (902) 564-5451
F: (902) 562-7077
Sports Editor: Russ Doyle

The Truro Daily News
PO Box 220
6 Louise Street
Truro, Nova Scotia B2N 5C3
T: (902) 893-9405
F: (902) 893-0518
Sports Editor: Joey Smith

Ontario

The Barrie Examiner
16 Bayfield St.
Barrie, Ontario L4M 4T6
T: (705) 726-6537
F: (705) 726-7706
Sports Editor: Steve Hardy

The Intelligencer
45 Bridge Street E.
Belleville, Ontario K8N 1L5
T: (613) 962-9171
F: (613) 962-9652
Sports Editor: Ady Vos

The Brantford Expositor
PO Box 965
53 Dalhousie St.
Brantford, Ontario N3T 5S8
T: (519) 756-2020
F: (519) 756-9470
Sports Editor: Ed O' Leary

Standard-Freeholder
44 Pitt Street
Cornwall, Ontario K6J 3P3
T: (613) 933-3160
F: (613) 933-7521
Sports Editor: Todd Hambleton

The Guelph Mercury
PO Box 3604
8-14 MacDonnell Street
Guelph, Ontario N1H 6P7
T: (519) 822-4310
F: (519) 767-1681
Sports Editor: Rob Massey

The Hamilton Spectator
PO Box 300
44 Frid Street
Hamilton, Ontario L8N 3G3
T: (905) 526-3333
F: (905) 521-8986
Sports Editor: Tim Doyle

The Whig-Standard
PO Box 2300
306 King Street E.
Kingston, Ontario K7L 4Z7
T: (613) 544-5000
F: (613) 530-4118
Sports Editor: Tim Gordanier

Kitchener-Waterloo Record
PO Box 938
225 Fairway Road
Kitchener, Ontario N2G 4E5
T: (519) 894-2231
F: (519) 894-3829
Sports Editor: Mickey Mowbray

The London Free Press
PO Box 2280
London, Ontario N6A 4G1
T: (519) 667- 4555
F: (519) 667-4528
Sports Editor: Dave Langford

Niagara Falls Review
PO Box 270
4801 Valley Way
Niagara Falls, Ontario L2E 6T6
T: (905) 358-5711
F: (905) 356-0785
Sports Editor: Bernie Puchalski

The North Bay Nugget
PO Box 570
North Bay, Ontario P1B 8J6
T: (705) 472-3200
F: (705) 472-5128
Sports Editor: Gerald Desormeau

Le Droit
PO Box 8860
47 Clarence St. #222
Ottawa, Ontario K1G 3J9
T: (613) 562-0111
F: (613) 562-7539
Sports Editor: Marandre Joanisse

The Ottawa Citizen
1101 Baxter Road
Ottawa, Ontario K2C 3M4
T: (613) 596-3750
F: (613) 596-8430
Sports Editor: Hugh Adami

Ottawa Sun
PO Box 9729, Station T
380 Hunt Club Road
Ottawa, Ontario K1G 5H7
T: (613) 739-7000
F: (613) 739-8041
Sports Editor: Tim Baines

The Sun Times
PO Box 200
290 Ninth Street E
Owen Sound, Ontario N4K 5P2
T: (519) 376-2250
F: (519) 376-7190
Sports Editor: Bill Walker

Peterborough Examiner
PO Box 3890
400 Water Street
Peterborough, Ontario K9J 8L4
T: (705) 745-4641
F: (705) 743-4581
Sports Editor: Bob Feaver

The Sarnia Observer
PO Box 3009
140 Front Street S.
Sarnia, Ontario N7T 7M8
T: (519) 344-3641
F: (519) 332-2951
Sports Editor: Dave Borody

The Sault Star
PO Box 460
145 Old Garden River Rd.
Sault Ste. Marie, Ontario
Canada P6A 5M5
T: (705) 759-3030
F: (705) 759-0102
Sports Editor: Alex Mitchell

The Standard
17 Queen Street
St. Catharines, Ontario L2R 5G5
T: (905) 684-7251
F: (905) 684-6032
Sports Editor: Peter Conradi

The Sudbury Star
33 MacKenzie Street
Sudbury, Ontario P3C 4Y1
T: (705) 674-5271
F: (705) 674-0624
Sports Editor: Norman Mayer

The Chronicle-Journal
75 S. Cumberland Street
Thunder Bay, Ontario P7B 1A3
T: (807) 343-6200
F: (807) 345-5991
Sports Editor: Gary Lawless

The Toronto Globe & Mail
444 Front Street West
Toronto, Ontario M5V 2S9
T: (416) 585-5333
F: (416) 585-5290
Sports Editor: Neil A. Campbell

Toronto Star
1 Yonge Street
Toronto, Ontario M5E 1E6
T: (416) 869-4385
F: (416) 865-3999
Sports Editor: Steve Tustin

The Toronto Sun
333 King Street East
Toronto, Ontario M5A 3X5
T: (416) 947-2266
F: (416) 947-2454
Sports Editor: Scott Morrison

The Tribune
PO Box 278
228 East Main Street
Welland, Ontario L3B 5P5
T: (905) 732-2411
F: (905) 732-4883
Sports Editor: Wayne Creighton

The Windsor Star
167 Ferry Street
Windsor, Ontario N9A 4M5
T: (519) 255-5711
F: (519) 255-5515
Sports Editor: Mark Falkner

Prince Edward Island

The Guardian
PO Box 760
165 Prince Street
Charlottetown, PEI C1A 7L8
T: (902) 629-6000
F: (902) 629-6044
Sports Editor: Garth Hurley

Journal-Pioneer
PO Box 2480
4 Queen Street
Summerside, PEI C1N 4K5
T: (902) 436-2121
F: (902) 436-0784
Sports Editor: Bill Semple

Quebec

Le Quotidien
1051 Talbot Boulevard
Chicoutimi, Quebec G7H 5C1
T: (418) 690-8800
F: (418) 690-8805
Sports Editor: Pierre Fellice

La Voix de L'Est
76 Dufferin
Granby, Quebec J2G 9L4
T: (514) 375-4555
F: (514) 777-4865
Sports Editor: Andre Bilodeau

The Gazette
250 St. Antoine Street Ouest
Montreal, Quebec H2Y 3R7
T: (514) 987-2522
F: (514) 987-2433
Sports Editor: Mark Tremblay

La Presse
7 Ouest Rue St. Jacques
Montreal, Quebec H2Y 1K9
T: (514) 350-4854
F: (514) 285-6808
Sports Editor: Michel Marois

Le Devoir
2050 de Bleury Street, 9 Fl.
Montreal, Quebec H3A 3M9
T: (514) 985-3333
F: (514) 985-3360
Sports Editor: Jean Diom

Le Journal de Montreal
4545 Frontenac
Montreal, Quebec H2H 2R7
T: (514) 521-4545
F: (514) 521-2173
Sports Editor: Yvon Pednault

Le Soleil
C.P. 1547, Succ. Terminus
925 Chemin St.-Louis
Quebec, Quebec G1K 7J6
T: (418) 686-3405
F: (418) 686-3373
Sports Editor: Maurice Dumas

La Tribune
1950 Roy Street
Sherbrooke, Quebec J1K 2X8
T: (819) 564-5450
F: (819) 564-8098
Sports Editor: Pierre Turgeon

The Sherbrooke Record
PO Box 1200
2850 Delorme Street
Sherbrooke, Quebec J1H 5L0
T: (819) 569-6345
F: (819) 569-3945
Sports Editor: Michael Innes

Le Nouvelliste
1920 Bellefeuille Street
Trois Rivieres, Quebec G9A 3Y2
T: (819) 376-2501
F: (819) 376-0946
Sports Editor: Stephan Frappier

Le Journal de Quebec
450 Rue Bechard
Ville Vanier, Quebec G1M 2E9
T: (418) 683-1573
F: (418) 688-8181
Sports Editor: Serge St. Hilaire

Saskatchewan

Times-Herald
PO Box 3000
44 Fairford Street West
Moose Jaw, Sask. S6H 1V1
T: (306) 692-6441
F: (306) 692-2101
Sports Editor: Rick Moore

Prince Albert Daily Herald
PO Box 550
30 Tenth St. East
Prince Albert, Sask. S6V 5R9
T: (306) 764-4276
F: (306) 763-3331
Sports Editor: Greg Nicholson

Regina Leader Post
PO Box 2020
1964 Park Street
Regina, Sask. S4P 3G4
T: (306) 565-8211
F: (306) 565-2588
Sports Editor: Gregg Drinnan

The Star Phoenix
204 Fifth Avenue North
Saskatoon, Sask. S7K 2P1
T: (306) 664-8298
F: (306) 664-8262
Sports Editor: Doug McConachie

Sports Museums & Hall of Fames

Listed in this section are many Museums & Hall of Fames for sports in North America and abroad.

American Assn. of Museums
1575 I St. NW, Suite 400
Washington, DC 20005
T: (202) 289-1818
F: (202) 289-6578
www.AAM-us.org
Exec. Dir: Ed Abel

Academy of Sports
4, rue de Teheran
75008 Paris, France
T: (33) 4562 9715

Afro-American Hall of Fame
550 E. Marshall Street
Richmond, VA 23219
T: (804) 649-2926
F: (804) 788-0454
www.sportshalls.com
Exec. Dir: Harrison Wilson III

Alabama Sports Hall of Fame
2150 Civic Center Blvd.
Birmingham, AL 35203
Location: Civic Center Plaza
T: (205) 323-6665
F: (205) 252-2212
Exec. Dir: William Ledd

Alberta Sports Hall of Fame and Museum
4920 51st. Street, Ste. 502
Red Deer, Alberta T4N 6K8
T: (403) 341-8614
F: (403) 341-8619
Coord: Marilyn Haley

Amateur Athletic Foundation of Los Angeles
2141 West Adams Blvd.
Los Angeles, CA 90018
T: (213) 730-9600
F: (213) 730-9637
www.aafla.org
P: Anita DeFrantz
Libr.: Wayne Wilson

American Indian Athletic Hall of Fame
155 Indian Avenue
Lawrence, KS 66044
T: (785) 749-8479
Located in Hiawatha Hall, Haskell Indian Nations University

American Museum of Fly Fishing
PO Box 42
Manchester, VT 05254
T: (802) 362-3300
Located On Rte. 7A, Seminary Avenue

Atlanta Olympic Museum
250 Williams St., PO Box 1995
Atlanta, GA 30301
T: (404) 224-1996
F: (404) 224-1997

Aquatic Hall of Fame and Museum of Canada
25 Poseidon Bay
Winnipeg, Manitoba R3M 3E4
T: (204) 986-5894
F: (204) 947-3647
P: Vaughan Baird

Australian Gallery of Sport
PO Box 175
East Melbourne, Australia 3002
T: (61.3) 654-8922
Dir: Tom McCullough

Australian Institute of Sport
National Sport Information Centre
Leverrier Crescent, Bruce ACT
(PO Box 176, Belconnen ACT 2616)
T: (61.6) 252 1369

Babe Ruth Birthplace Museum
216 Emory Street
Baltimore, MD 21230
T: (410) 727-1539
F: (410) 727-1652
www.baberuthmuseum.com
Exec. Dir: Michael Gibbons

Barcelona Museum & Sports Study Center
Buenos Aires Street 56-58 (Torre)
08036 Barcelona, Spain
T: (34.93) 230-61-18
Dir: Ricardo Sanchez

Barcelona Olympic Gallery
Olimpic Stadium
Passeig, Olimpic, s/n
08038 Barcelona, Spain
T: (34.93) 426 06 60

Yogi Berra Museum & Learning Ctr.
Montclair State University
Normal Avenue
Upper Montclair, NJ 07043
T: (973) 655-2377
www.yogiberramuseum.org

Braves Museum & Hall of Fame
Turner Field
Atlanta, GA 30302
T: (404) 614-2311
Artifacts from Boston, Milwaukee
& Atlanta Braves & Aaron exhibit

British Columbia Hockey
Hall of Fame
204 - 1475 Fairview Rd.
Penticton, B.C. Canada V2A 7W5
T: (250) 490-0711

British Columbia Sports
Hall of Fame & Museum
777 Pacific Blvd. S.
Vancouver, B. C. V6B 4Y8
T: (604) 687-5520
F: (604) 687-5510
E: sportsha@intergate.bc.ca
GM: Susan Lewis

Brooklyn History Museum
128 Pierrepont Street
Brooklyn, NY 11201
T: (718) 624-0890
Permanent exhibit of the
Brooklyn Dodgers

Paul W. (Bear) Bryant Museum
300 Paul W. Bryant Dr., Box 870385
Tuscaloosa, AL 35487
T: (205) 348-4668
F: (205) 348-8883
www.ua.edu/bryant.htm
Dir: Kenneth Gaddy

Canada Olympic Hall of Fame
8800 Canada Olympic Rd. SW
Calgary, Alberta T3B 5R5
T: (403) 286-2632
F: (403) 286-7213
Dir: J. Thomas West
Curator: Gladys Serafine

Canada's Sports Hall of Fame
Exhibition Place
Toronto, Ontario M6K 3C3
T: (416) 595-1046
F: (416) 595-1228
www.cshof.net
Exec. Dir: Allen Stewart

Canadian Baseball Hall of
Fame And Museum
386 Church Street, PO Box 1838
St. Marys, Ontario N4X 1C2
T: (519) 453-7857
www.baseballhof.ca
Curator: Carl McCoomb

Canadian Olympic Association
Information Center
2380 avenue Pierre Dupuy
Montreal, Quebec H3C 3R4
T: (514) 861-3371
F: (514) 861-2896

Canadian Figure Skating
Association Hall of Fame
1600 James Naismith Dr.
Gloucester, Ontario K1B 5N4
T: (613) 748-5635
F: (613) 748-5718
www.csfa.ca
Exec. Dir: Pamela Coburn

Canadian Football
Hall of Fame & Museum
58 Jackson Street West
Hamilton, Ontario L8P 1L4
T: (905) 528-7566
F: (905) 528-9781
Dir: Janice Smith

Canadian Lacrosse
Hall of Fame
PO Box 308
Centennial Community Ctr.
65 East 6th Avenue
New Westminster, BC V3L 4Y6
T: (604) 526-4281
F: (604) 324-4091
Sec.: Dorothy Robertson

Canadian Ski Museum
1960 Scott Street
Ottawa, Ontario K1Z 8L84
T: (613) 722-3584
F: (613) 722-2914
Chair: Keith Nesbitt
Curator: Andre Bedard

Catskill Fly Fishing Center
PO Box 1295. Old Rte. 17
Livingston Manor, NY 12758
T: (914) 439-4810
F: (914) 439-3387
www.cffcm.com
P: Paul Shultz

Ty Cobb Museum
461 Cook Street
Royston, GA 30262
T: (706) 245-1825
www.tycobbhealthcare.org

College Football Hall of Fame
111 S. St. Joseph Street
South Bend, IN 46601
T: (219) 235-5581
F: (219) 235-9185
http://collegefootball.org/info
Exec. Dir: Bernie Kish

Comiskey Park Hall of Fame
Comiskey Park
333 W. 35th Street
Chicago, IL 60016
T: (312) 674-1000

Curling Hall of Fame & Museum of Canada
122 Frederick Street
Kitchener, Ontario N2H 2L9
T: (519) 578-0094
Curator: Cheryl Reilly

Cyprus Olympic Museum
20 Ionos Street
PO Box 3931
Nicosin, Cypress
T: (357.2) 450875
www.olympic.org.cy
Curator: Andreas Hadjivassteiou

Delaware Sports Hall of Fame
1001 E. Matson Run Pkwy
Wilmington, DE 19802
T: (302) 762-2015
P: Sidney Balick

Dirt Motorsports Hall of Fame and Car Museum
PO Box 240
Weedsport, NY 13166
T: (315) 834-6667
F: (315) 834-9734
www.dirtmotorsports.com
Curator: Jack Speno

EAA Air Adventure Museum
Box 3086, 300 Poberezny
Oshkosh, WI 54903
T: (920) 426-4800
F: (920) 426-6560
Dir: Tom Barrett

Bob Feller Hometown Exhibit
310 Mill Street
Van Meter, IA 50261
T: (515) 996-2806
www.ioweb.com/feller

Florida Sports Hall of Fame
601 Hall of Fame Drive
Lake City, FL 32055
T: (904) 758-1310
F: (904) 752-9566
www.floridasports.org
P: Bert Lacey
Lacation: Intersection of
Interstate 75 & US 90

Georgia Sports Hall of Fame
PO Box 4644
301 Cherry Street
Macon, GA 31208
T: (912) 752-1585
F: (912) 752-1587
www.gshf.org
Exec. Dir: Joe Gerson

Green Bay Packers Hall of Fame
855 Lombardi Drive
PO Box 10567
Green Bay, WI 54307
T: (920) 499-4281
F: (920) 494-9229
Mgr: Kelly Schlitz

Greyhound Hall of Fame
407 South Buckeye
Abilene, KS 67410
T: (785) 263-3000
F: (785) 263-2604
E: gfon@access-one.com
Dir: Edward Scheele

Harness Racing Hall of Fame
240 Main Street
PO Box 590
Goshen, NY 10924
T: (914) 294-6330
F: (914) 294-3463
www.harnessmuseum.com
Dir: Gail Cunard

Harrah (William F.) Automobile Foundation and Museum
10 Lake Street S.
Reno, NV 89501
T: (775) 333-9300
F: (775) 333-9309
www.automuseum.org
Exec. Dir: Jackie Frady

Hellenic Sports Hall of Fame
180 Bolton Street
Marlboro, MA 01752
T: (508) 485-0736
Dir: Dr. Monthe Kofos

Hockey Hall of Fame & Museum
BCE Place, 30 Yonge Street
Toronto, Ontario M5E 1X8
T: (416) 360-7735
F: (416) 360-1501
Chair: Jan Morrison

Indiana Basketball Hall of Fame
One Hall of Fame Court
New Castle, IN 47362
T: (765) 529-1891
F: (765) 529-0273
www.hoopshall.com
Exec. Dir: J. Ronald Newlin

Indiana Football Hall of Fame
815 N. A Street
PO Box 1035
Richmond, IN 47374
T: (317) 966-2235
P: Earl Rodgers

Indiana Museum of Sport
202 N. Alabama Street
Indianapolis, IN 46204
T: (317) 232-1637
F: (317) 232-7090
www.state.in.us/ism
Exec. Dir: Richard Gantz

Indianapolis Motor Speedway Hall of Fame Museum
4790 West 16th Street
Indianapolis, IN 46224
T: (317) 484-6747
F: (317) 484-6449
www.brickyard.com
Dir: Ralph Kramer
Mgr: Ellen Birley

International Bass Fishing Hall of Fame
290 S. Main St., PO Box 295
Lakeport, CA 95453
T: (707) 263-6911
P: Byron Whipple

International Boxing Hall of Fame
PO Box 425
Canastota, NY 13032
T: (315) 697-7095
F: (315) 697-5356
www.ibhof.com
NY Thruway (Exit 34) on State Highway 13
Exec. Dir: Edward Brophy

International Gymnastics Hall of Fame & Museum
120 N Robinson - E. Concourse
Oklahoma City, OK 73102
T: (405) 235-5600
F: (405) 235-5678
www.ighof.com
Dir: Franke Bare

International Hockey Hall of Fame & Museum
PO Box 82
York & Alfred Streets
Kingston, Ontario K7L 4V6
T: (613) 544-2355
Exec. Dir: Doug Nichols
Historian/PR: William Fitsell

International Jewish Sports Hall of Fame
7922 Turncreat Drive
Potomac, MD 20854
T: (301) 229-3300
F: (301) 229-8345
www.jewishsports.net
Address in Israel:
Wingate Institute
Wingate Post Office
42902 Israel
Chair: Alan Sherman

International Motor Sports Hall of Fame
3198 Speedway Blvd.
Talladega, AL 35160
T: (256) 362-5002
www.historyonwheels.com
Exec. Dir: Don Naman

**International Museum and
Hall of Fame of Drag Racing /
Don Garlits Museum**
13700 SW 16th Avenue
Ocala, FL 34473
T: (352) 245-8661
F: (352) 245-6895
www.garlits.com
Dir: Greg Capitano
I-75, Exit 67

**International Reference Library
of Fishes and Museum**
300 Golf Stream Way
Dania Beach, FL 33004
T: (954) 927-2628
F: (954) 924-4299
www.igfa.org
P: Mike Leech
Librarian: Gail Morchower

**International Snowmobile
Racing Hall of Fame & Museum**
4302 Lakeshore Drive
Wausau, WI 54401
T: (715) 359-9917
F: (715) 359-5447
www.sportshalls.com
P: Loren Anderson

**International Surfing
Hall of Fame**
5580 La Jolla Blvd.
Suite 373
La Jolla, CA 92037
T: (760) 918-0763
Dir: Bobby Thomas

**International Swimming
Hall of Fame**
One Hall of Fame Drive
Fort Lauderdale, FL 33316
T: (954) 462-6536
F: (954) 525-4031
www.ishof.org
E-mail: ishof@ishof.org
P: Dr. Sam Freas

**International Tennis
Hall of Fame & Museum**
194 Bellevue Avenue
Newport, RI 62840
T: (401) 849-4567
F: (401) 849-8780
P: Jane Brown

**International Winter Sports
Hall of Fame**
130 Main Street, PO Box 1932
Lake Placid, NY 12946
T: (518) 523-4100

**International Women's
Sports Hall of Fame**
Eisenhower Park
East Meadow, NY 11554
T: (516) 542-4700
F: (516) 542-4716
E: wosport@aol.com

**Japanese Baseball
Hall of Fame**
1-3-61, Koraku-I-chome
Bunkyo-ku, Tokyo 112, Japan
T: (03) 811-3600
F: (03) 811-5369
P: Kiyoichi Ohata

Kentucky Derby Museum
704 Central Ave. PO Box 3513
Louisville, KY 40208
T: (502) 637-1111
F: (502) 635-5855
www.derbymuseum.org
Exec. Dir: Lynn Ashton

Klassix Auto Museum
2909 W. Int'l Speedway Blvd.
Daytona Beach, FL 32124
T: (904) 252-3800
F: (904) 252-3802
Dir: Jim Kelsey

**Lacrosse Hall of Fame
Foundation, Inc.**
113 W. University Pkwy.
Baltimore, MD 21210
T: (410) 235-6882
F: (410) 366-6735
www.lacrosse.org
Exec. Dir: Steven Stenersen

**Legends of the Game
Baseball Museum**
The Ballpark in Arlington
Arlington, TX 76004
T: (817) 273-5600
*Exhibits of Negro Leagues, Texas
League & old ballparks*

Little League Baseball Museum
PO Box 3485, Rte. 15 South
Williamsport, PA 17701
T: (570) 326-3607
F: (570) 326-1074
www.littleleague.org
Dir: Cynthia Stearns

Louisiana Sports Hall of Fame
Prather Coliseum
Northwestern State University
Natchitoches, LA 71497
T: (318) 357-6467
F: (318) 357-4515
www.lasportshof.com
Dir: Doug Ireland

Louisville Slugger Museum
800 W. Main Street
Louisville, KY 40201
T: (502) 588-7228
www.slugger.com/museum
*Rare artifacts & equipment
on sports, primarily baseball*

**Maine Sports Hall
of Fame & Museum**
3 Delano Park
Cape Elizabeth, ME 04107
T: (207) 799-4555
F: (207) 799-3861
P: Daniel Garetta

**Manitoba Sports Hall
of Fame & Museum**
The Bay Downtown, 5 FL
450 Portage Avenue
Winnipeg, Manitoba R3C 0E7
T: (204) 925-5735
F: (204) 925-5792
www.sports.mb.ca.mb
E: mansport@sport.mb.ca
Exec. Dir: Rick Brownell
Curator: Frank Jankac

Roger Maris Museum
West Acres Shopping Center
I-29 & 13th Avenue South
Fargo, ND 58102
T: (701) 282-2222
www.ndrogermaris.com/museum
Free exhibit in mall entrance

**Mexican Professional Baseball
& Soccer Hall of Fame**
Avenida Alfonso Reyes
2202 Norte, Col. Bellavista
Monterrey, NL, Mexico
T: (52-83) 757-583

**Metroplitan Detroit
Sports Museum**
PO Box 2532
Detroit, MI 48231
T: (313) 393-8618
Exec. Dir: George Witherspoon

**Michigan Jewish Sports
Hall of Fame**
6600 W. Maple
W. Bloomfield, MI 48322
T: (810) 661-7777
Exec. Dir: Harvey Frank

Michigan Sports Hall of Fame
Metro Detroit Convention &
Visitors Bureau
100 Renaissance Center
Suite 1950
Detroit, MI 48243
T: (313) 259-4333
F: (313) 259-7583
Chair: Ron Burton

**Ralph W. Miller Golf
Library & Museum**
One Industry Hills Parkway
City of Industry, CA 91744
T: (626) 854-2354
F: (626) 854-2305
Mgr: Marge Dewey
Librarian: Saundra Sheffer

**Dizzy Dean Museum & MS
Sports Hall of Fame**
1152 Lakeland Drive
Jackson, MS 39205
T: (601) 982-8264
www.msfame.com

Missouri Sports Hall of Fame
5051 Highland Springs Blvd.
Springfield, MO 65809
T: (417) 889-3100
F: (417) 889-2761
www.mosportshalloffame.com
E: info@mosportshalloffame.com
Exec. Dir: Jerald Andrews

Motorcycle Heritage Museum
33 Collegeville Rd.
Westerville, OH 43081
T: (614) 891-2425

**Motorsports Museum
& Hall of Fame**
43700 Expo Center Drive
Novi, MI 48375
T: (248) 349-7223 (Race)
F: (248) 347-7720
Exec. Dir: Ronald Watson

**Museum of Polo and
Hall of Fame**
9011 Lake Worth Road
Lake Worth, FL 33467
T: (407) 969-3210
F: (407) 964-8299
Exec. Dir: George DuPont, Jr.

The Museum of Sport
Tervuursevest 101
3030 Leuven, Belgium
T: (32) 1622-0405

**Museum of Western
Australia Sport**
Superdrome Sports Center
Stephenson Ave, PO Box 57
Claremont, W.A. 6010, Australia
T: (09) 387-8542

Museum of Yachting
Box 129, Fort Adams State Park
Newport, RI 02840
T: (401) 847-1018
F: (401) 847-8320
www.moy.org
Exec. Dir: Peter Marnane

**Naismith Memorial Basketball
Hall of Fame**
1150 West Columbus Avenue
PO Box 179
Springfield, MA 01101
T: (413) 781-6500
F: (413) 781-1939
www.hoophall.com
P: Joe O'Brien
PR: Kimberly Lee

National Art Museum of Sport
University Place
Indiana Univ.-Purdue University
850 W Michigan Street
Indianapolis, IN 46202-5198
T: (317) 274-3627
F: (317) 274-3878
www.namos.iupui.edu
E: arein@wpo.iupu.edu
Director: Ann Rein

**National Baseball Congress
Hall of Fame**
Lawrence-Dumont Stadium
Wichita, KS 67201
T: (316) 267-3372
*Amateur baseball exhibit of more
than 600 Major Leaguers who
played in NBC amateur tournament*

**National Baseball
Hall of Fame & Museum**
PO Box 590
25 Main Street
Cooperstown, NY 13326
T: (607) 547-7200
F: (607) 547-2844
www.baseballhalloffame.org

**National Bowling Museum &
Hall of Fame**
111 Stadium Plaza
St. Louis, MO 63102
T: (314) 231-6340
F: (314) 231-4054
Exec. Dir: Gerald Baltz
Curator: John Dalzell

**National Collegiate Athletic
Association Visitors Center**
700 W Washington Street
Indianapolis, IN 46206
T: (317) 917-6222
F: (317) 917-6888
www.ncaa.org

**National Cowboy Hall of Fame
& Western Heritage Center**
1700 NE 63rd Street
Oklahoma City, OK 73111
T: (405) 478-2250
F: (405) 478-4714
Dir: Ken Towsend

**National Football Foundation
& College Hall of Fame**
111 South St. Joseph Street
PO Box 11146
South Bend, IN 46634
T: (219) 235-5581
F: (219) 235-9185

**National Fresh Water Fishing
Hall of Fame**
PO Box 33, One Hall of Fame Dr.
Hayward, WI 54843
T/F: (715) 634-4440
Exec. Dir: Ted Dzialo

**National High School
Sports Hall of Fame**
11724 Plaza Circle, Box 20626
Kansas City, MO 64153
T: (816) 464-5400
F: (816) 464-5571
www.nfhs.org
Dir: Bruce Howard

**National Italian-American
Sports Hall of Fame**
187 Salem Court
Bloomingdale, IL 60108
T: (847) 952-9766
F: (847) 437-3078
P: George Randazzo

**National Museum of Racing
Hall of Fame**
191 Union Avenue
Saratoga Spring, NY 12866
T: (518) 584-0400
F: (518) 584-4574
www.racingmuseum.com
Dir: Peter Hammell

**National Polish-American
Sports Hall of Fame**
11445 Conant
Hamtramck, MI 48212
T: (313) 891-0340
F: (313) 891-6714
Chair: S. Nicholas Frontczak

**National Rivers Hall of
Fame & Riverboat Museum**
400 D. 3rd Street
Dubuque, IA 52001
T: (319) 557-9545
F: (319) 583-1241
Exec. Dir: Jerry Enzler
Port of Dubuque Ice Harbor

National Ski Hall of Fame
610 Palm Avenue
PO Box 191
Ishpeming, MI 49849
T: (906) 485-6323
F: (906) 486-4570
www.portup.com/skihall
P: John Pontti

National Soaring Museum
51 Soaring Hill Drive
Elmira, NY 14903
T: (607) 734-3128
F: (607) 732-6745
Dir: Jim Swinnich

**National Soccer Hall
of Fame**
5-11 Ford Avenue
Oneonta, NY 13820
T: (607) 432-3351
F: (607) 432-8429
www.wpe.com/~nshof/
Exec. Dir: Albert Colone

**National Softball Hall
of Fame & Museum**
2801 NE 50th Street
Oklahoma City, OK 73111
T: (405) 424-5266
F: (405) 424-3855
www.softball.org
Exec. Dir: Don Porter
HOF Mgr: Bill Plummer

National Sporting Library
102 Plains Road
Middleburg, VA 20117
T: (540) 687-6542
www.nsl.org
P: Ken Tomlinson
Librarian: Laura Rose
Horse, polo and field hunts sports.

**National Sportscasters &
Sportwriters Assn. Hall of Fame**
620 W. Innes Street
Salisbury, NC 28144
T/F: (704) 633-4275

**National Sports Gallery &
National Sportscasters Assn.
Hall of Fame**
MCI Center Complex
601 F Street NW
Washington, DC 20001
T: (202) 661-5133
F: (202) 661-5134
www.mcicenter.com
Curator: Frank Ceresi

**National Sprint Car Hall
of Fame & Museum**
PO Box 542
One Sprint Capital Place
Knoxville, IA 50138
T: (515) 842-6176
F: (515) 842-6177
www.knoxvilleiowa.com
E: sprintcarhof@lisco.net
Exec. Dir: Thomas Schmeh
Marion County Fairgrnds.

**National Track & Field
Hall of Fame**
One RCA Dome
Indianapolis, IN 46225
T: (317) 261-0500

National Wrestling Hall of Fame
405 West Hall of Fame Avenue
Stillwater, OK 74075
T: (405) 377-5243
F: (405) 377-5244
www.wrestlinghalloffaz.org
P: Myron Roderick

NCAA College Hall of Champions
700 W. Washington Street
Indianapolis, IN 46206
T: (317) 917-4255
F: (317) 917-6888
www.ncaa.org
Director: Jim Shaffer

**Negro League Baseball
Hall of Fame & Museum**
1616 East 18th Street
Kansas City, MO 64108
T: (816) 221-1920
F: (816) 221-8424
www.nlbm.com
Chair: Buck O'Neil
P: Randall Ferguson

**New Brunswick Sports
Hall of Fame**
PO Box 6000, 503 Queen Street
Fredericton, N. B.E3B 5H1
T: (506) 453-3747
F: (506) 459-0481
www.nbfhf.funday.ca
E: debbraw@gov.nb.ca
Exec. Dir: Kathy Meagher

New England Sports Museum
Fleet Center
Boston, MA 02114
T: (617) 787-7678
F: (617) 787-8152
Exec. Dir: Chris Stevens
Curator: Richard Johnson

**Newfoundland Sports
Hall of Fame**
Colonial Building, Room 18
Military Road
St. John's, Nfld. A1C 2C9
T: (709) 729-0591

New Jersey Sports Hall of Fame
Sports & Exposition Authority
East Rutherford, NJ 07073
T: (201) 507-8134
F: (201) 460-4035
www.njsea.com
Dir: Olga Betz

Newseum
1101 Wilson Blvd.
Arlington, VA 22209
T: (703) 284-3544
F: (703) 284-3777
www.newseum.org
Exec. Dir: Joe Urschel

**New South Wales Hall of
Champions**
State Sports Centre, PO Box 135
Flemington Market, NSW
2129 Australia
T: (02) 763-0111

**North Carolina Sports
Hall of Fame**
3316 Julian Drive
Raleigh, NC 27604
T: (919) 872-9289
P: Jack Murdock

Northern Indiana Historical Society
808 W. Washington Street
South Bend, IN 46556
T: (219) 235-9664
The national repository for the All-American Girls Professional Baseball League

Northwestern Ontario Sports Hall of Fame
219 May Street South
Thunder Bay, Ontario P7E 1B5
T: (807) 622-2852
F: (807) 622-2736
Exec. Dir: Diane Imrie
Curator: Kate Dwyer

University of Notre Dame Joyce Sports Research Collection
102 Theodore M. Hesburgh Library
Notre Dame, IN 46556
T: (219) 631-6506
F: (219) 631-6772
www.sports.nd.edu
E: george.k.rugg.1@nd.edu
Curator: George Rugg

Nova Scotia Sport Hall of Fame
1645 Granville St., Suite 101
Halifax, Nova Scotia B3J 1X3
T: (902) 421-1266
F: (902) 425-1148
Dir: Bill Robinson

Ohio Baseball Hall of Fame
Lucas County Recreation Center
2901 Key Street
Maumee, OH 43537
T: (216) 464-3049
Exec. Dir.: Thomas Eakin

Olympic Museum
Quai D' Ouchy 1, PO Box 100
1001 Lausanne, Switzerland
T: (41.21) 20.93.31
F: (41.21) 621.65.12
www.IOC.org
Director: Francoise Zweifel

Orange County Sports Hall of Fame
2000 Gene Autry Way
Anaheim, CA 92806
T: (714) 940-2356

Oregon Coast Sports Museum
110 NE Highway 101
PO Box 166
Depoe Bay, OR 97341
T: (541) 765-2923
F: (541) 765-3231
Exec. Dir: Eric Nash

Oregon Sports Hall of Fame & Museum
321 C SW Salmon
Portland, OR 97204
T: (503) 227-7466
F: (503) 227-6925
Exec. Dir: Kevin Toon
Museum Location:
Standard Insurance Center
900 SW Fifth Ave, Portland

Original Baseball Hall of Fame Museum of Minneapolis
910 S. Third Street
Minneapolis, MN 55415
T: (612) 375-1366 (Twins)
Across from the Metrodome.
Senators & Twins exhibit

Pennsylvania Sports Hall of Fame
937 Willow Street
PO Box 1140
Lebanon, PA 17042
T: (717) 274-3644
F: (717) 274-6782
www.pasportshalloffame.com
P: Thomas Harlan

PGA World Golf Hall of Fame
100 Ave. of the Champions
Palm Beach Gardens, FL 33410
T: (561) 624-8400
www.pgaonline.com
Dir: Peter Ross Stilwell

Planes of Fame Air Museum
WWII Cal-Aero Field
Chino Airport
7000 Merrill Avenue
Chino, CA 91710
T: (909) 597-3722
F: (909) 597-4755
Dir: Deborah Manning

**Prince Edward Island
Sports Hall of Fame**
120 Harbor Drive
Summerside, PEI C1N 5Y8
T: (902) 43600423
Chair: Claire Sudsbury

Pro Football Hall of Fame
2121 George Halas Drive NW
Canton, OH 44708
T: (330) 456-8207
F: (330) 456-8175
www.profootballhof.com

**Pro Rodeo Hall of Fame and
Museum of the Americn Cowboy**
101 Pro Rodeo Drive
Colorado Springs, CO 80919
T: (719) 528-4761
F: (719) 548-4874
Dir: Patricia Hildebrand

Cal Ripken Museum
Aberdeen City Hall Building
Aberdeen, MD 21001
T: (410) 273-2525
www.ripken.com
official repository for Ripken artifacts

**Rome Sports Hall of Fame
and Museum**
Erie Canal Village, Rte. 49W
Rome, NY 13440
T: (315) 337-3999
Exec. Dir: Ruth Demers

Rose Bowl Hall of Fame
391 S. Orange Grove Blvd.
Pasadena, CA 91184
T: (626) 449-4100
Chair: Fred Johnson

Nolan Ryan Center
Alvin Community College
Alvin, TX 77511
T: (281) 388-1134

**St. Louis Cardinals
Baseball Hall of Fame**
111 Stadium Plaza
St. Louis, MO 63102
T: (314) 421-FAME
F: (314) 982-7890
Dir: Kevin Kretzer
Curator: Paula Homan
*Exhibits on Cards, St. L Browns,
Negro BB & old Sportsman's Park*

San Diego Hall of Champions
2131 Pan American Plaza
Balboa Park
San Diego, CA 921901
T: (619) 234-2544
F: (619) 234-4543
www.sandiegosports.org
Exec. Dir: Ron Phillips

**Saskatchewan Sports
Hall of Fame**
2205 Victoria Avenue
Regina, Sask. S4P 0S4
T: (306) 780-9232
F: (306) 525-4009
www.dlcwest.com/~sshfm
Exec. Dir: Sheila Kelly
Curator: Jacqueline Campbell

Senior Athletes Hall of Fame
723 Oakview Drive
Bradenton, FL 34210
T: (941) 756-8808
Dir: Jack Fones

Singapore Sports Museum
Singapore Sports Council
National Stadium
Kallang, Singapore 1439
T: 345-7111 x 640

**South Dakota Amateur
Baseball Hall of Fame**
519 Main Street
Lake Norden, SD 57248
T: (605) 785-3553

Sport Australia Hall of Fame
Sports House Victoria
Level 1
120 Jolimont Street
Jolimont, Victoria 3002, Australia
T: (03) 9654 3755

Sport Information Resource Centre
1600 James Naismith Drive
Gloucester, Ontario K1B 5N4
T: (800) 665-6413
T: (613) 748-5658
F: (613) 748-5701
www.sportquest.com
P: Gilles Chiasson
Tech Dir: Christine Lalande
*Collects & organizes all information
about sports, sports books, etc.*

ACT Sports House
Maitland Street
Hackett, ACT 2602, Australia
T: (06) 247-0260

**Sports House
Western Australia**
PO Box 57
Sports Lotteries House
Stephens Avenue
Mt. Claremont, WA 6010
T: (09) 383-7344

Sports Immortals
6830 N Federal Hwy
Boca Raton, FL 33487
T: (561) 997-2575
F: (561) 997-6949
www.sportsimmortals.com

**State of Kansas Sports
Hall of Fame**
406 NW 3rd Sreet
Abilene, KS 67410
T: (913) 263-7403
Exec. Dir: Ted Hayes

Swiss Sports Museum
Postfach, Missionstrasse 28
CH-4003, Basel, Switzerland
T: (41) 061-25-12-21

Tasmania Sport House
GPO Box 442E
2 Wyralla Court
Austins Ferry, Tasmania 7011
Australia
T: (002) 49 1321

Texas Sports Hall of Fame
1108 S. University Parks Drive
Waco, TX 76706
T: (817) 756-1633
F: (817) 756-2384
www.halloffame.org
Exec. Dir: Steve Fallon

**Trapshooting Hall
of Fame & Museum**
601 W. National Road
Vandalia, OH 45377
T: (937) 898-1945
F: (937) 898-5472
www.shotata.com
Dir: Marjorie Smith

**United States Bicycling
Hall of Fame**
166 West Main Street
Somerville, NJ 08876
T: (800) BICYCLE
T: (908) 722-3620
F: (908) 722-3620
www.usbhof.com
P: Dottie Sailing

**United States Golf Association
Museum and Library**
Liberty Corner Road
Golf House
Far Hills, NJ 07931
T: (908) 234-2300
F: (908) 234-0319
www.usga.org
Exec. Dir: Amy Mutch

**United States Hockey
Hall of Fame**
801 Hat Trick Avenue
PO Box 657
Eveleth, MN 55734
T: (800) 443-7025
T: (218) 744-5167
F: (218) 744-2590
www.ushockeyhall.com
Exec. Dir: Michelle Kuitunen

**United States Olympic
Committee Hall of Fame**
One Olympic Plaza
Colorado Springs, CO 80909
T: (719) 632-5551

**United States Slo-Pitch
Softball Hall of Fame Museum**
3935 South Crater Rd.
Petersburg, VA 23804
T: (804) 732-4099
F: (804) 732-1705
www.usssa.com
Museum Dir: Robert Still

**United States World Figure
Skating Hall of Fame & Museum**
20 First Street
Colorado Springs, CO 80906
T: (719) 635-5200
F: (719) 635-9548
Chair: Ben Wright
Curator: Beth Davis

Victoria Institute of Sport
8th & 9th Floor
20-22 Albert Road
South Melbourne, Victoria 3205
T: (03) 9699 8055

Virginia Sports Hall of Fame
420 High Street
Portsmouth, VA 23704
T: (757) 393-8031
E: webbe@ci.portsmouth.va.us
Exec. Dir: J. Eddie Webb

Volleyball Hall of Fame
444 Dwight Street
PO Box 1895
Holyoke, MA 01040
T: (413) 536-0926
F: (413) 539-6673
www.volleyhall.org
E: info@volleyhall.org
P: Robert Kane

Water Ski Hall of Fame
799 Overlook Drive SE
Winter Haven, FL 33884
T: (941) 324-2472
F: (941) 324-3996
Exec. Dir: Carole Lowe

Ted Williams Museum & Hitters Hall of Fame
2455 N. Citrus Hills Blvd.
Hernando, FL 34442
T: (352) 527-6566
F: (352) 527-4163
Dir: Buzz Hamon

Windsor Hockey Heritage Centre
128 Gerrish Street
Windsor, Nova Scotia B0N 2T0
T: (902) 798-1800
Dir: Frank Gallager
Birthplace of Ice Hockey

Women's Basketball Hall of Fame
700 Hall of Fame Drive
Knoxville, TN 37915
T: (865) 633-9000
F: (865) 633-9294
www.wbhof.com
Exec. Dir: Mr. Robin Hamilton

World Golf Hall of Fame
World Golf Place
St. Augustine, FL 32092
T: (904) 940-4000
F: (904) 940-4394
www.wgv.com
Dir: Karen Bednarski

Ziffren Sports Resource Center
Amateur Athletic Foundation
2141 W. Adams Street
Los Angeles, CA 90018
T: (323) 730-9696
F: (323) 730-9637
www.aafla.com
Research Lib: Wayne Wilson
Largest sports library in North America

Designed For College Courses in Sports Media and Marketing

The Dream Job
$port$ Publicity, Promotio
and Marketing

The Most Acclaimed Book in Sports Marketing • Fourth Press Run and Over 25,000 i
Required Text at More Than 50 Colleges and Universities

Features Include:

- 25 SID responsibilities
- 16 basic press release rules
- 35 types of sports features
- 55 news conference checklist items
- 20 publicity formats that always work
- 150 different sports awards
- 26 major interview formats
- 11 rules for fund-raising banquets
- 12 most effective crisis solutions

How to Get:

- guests booked on radio & television
- publicity photos printed
- an effective press box
- a productive media tour
- a major event staged
- a star named All-American
- a coach's speech written

2nd Edition: Paperbound, 7"x10", 440 pages ISBN 0-9630-387-

" One of the most important books in our field. "
—*Journal of Sport Management*

Price $29.95 +
    3.50 shipping
    $33.45 Total

" A wealth of valuable information in sport mark
The chapter on *Event Planning* alone is worth the
—*Sport Marketing Quarterly*

Send payment to: Ed Kobak, Global Sports Productions
1223 Broadway, Suite 102, Santa Monica, CA 90404

Sports Commissions & Visitor's Bureaus

Listed in this section are sports commissions and convention & visitor bureaus that are responsible for their community's involvement in amateur & professional sports for scheduling of events, attracting sports franchises & organizations as well as convention site locations. Not all of the listings are NASC or IACVB members.

International Association of Convention & Visitor Bureaus
2000 L Street NW, Suite 702
Washington, D.C. 20036
T: (202) 296-7888
F: (202) 296-7889
www.iacvb.org
Exec. Director: Karen Jordan

National Association of Sports Commissions
300 Main Street, 1st Floor
Cincinnati, OH 45202
T: (513) 651-1330
F: (513) 651-1374
www.sportscommissions.com
E: nasc@fuse.net
Exec. Dir: Don Schumacher

Adirondack Sports Commission
PO Box 2022
Lake Placid, NY 12946
T: (518) 523-4875
F: (518) 523-4877
www.lakeplacid.com
E: adksport@northnet.org
Exec. Dir: Kris Bronander

Alabama Sports Foundation
PO Box 1996
Birmingham, AL 35201
T: (205) 967-8564
F: (205) 967-9940
Chmn: Lawrence Lemack

Albany Foundation for Sports & Special Events
51 S. Pearl
Albany, NY 12207
T: (518) 487-2022
F: (518) 487-2020
Exec. Dir: Lori Stachnik

Albuquerque Sports Council
PO Box 26866
20 First Plaza NW, Suite 601
Albuquerque, NM 87125
T: (800) 733-9918
F: (505) 247-9101
Exec. Dir: Marty Brown

Ames Area Sports Commission
213 Duff Avenue
Ames, IA 50010-6676
T: (515) 232-4032
F: (515) 232-6716
www.acvb.ames.ia.us
E: amescvb@netins.net
Exec. Dir: Rich Harter

Anaheim and Orange County Visitor & Convention Bureau
800 W. Katella Ave.
Anaheim, CA 92802
T: (714) 765-8888
F: (714) 991-8963
P: Charles Ahlers

Anchorage Convention Center & Visitors Bureau
524 W. 4th Avenue
Anchorage, AK 99501
T: (907) 276-4118
F: (907) 278-5559
www.anchorage.net
P: William Elander

Arkansas Major Sports Assn.
1 Spring Building
Little Rock, AR 72201
T: (501) 374-4871
F: (501) 374-6018
Exec. Dir: Suzie Marks

Atlanta Sports Council
235 International Blvd.
Atlanta, GA 30303
T: (404) 586-8510
F: (404) 586-8508
www.metroatlantachamber.com
Exec. Dir: Robert Kitzel

**Greater Augusta
Sports Council**
32 Eighth Street, Suite 200
Augusta, GA 30901
T: (706) 722-8326
F: (706) 823-6609
Exec. Dir: Tammy Stout

**Greater Austin
Sports Council**
111 Congress Ave, Plaza Level
Austin, TX 78701
T: (512) 322-5654
F: (512) 478-9615
www.hookem.com/gasc
Exec. Dir: Suzanne Hofmann

**Baton Rouge Area
Sports Foundation**
730 North Boulevard
Baton Rouge, LA 70821
T: (504) 382-3588
F: (504) 346-1253
P: Jerry Stovall

**City of Battle Creek Sports
Promotion**
Kellogg Arena
1 McCamly Square
Battle Creek, MI 49017
T: (616) 963-4800
F: (616) 968-8840
Dir: William Evans

**Bloomington Convention &
Visitors Bureau**
2855 N. Walnut Street
Bloomington, IN 47404
T: (800) 800-0037
T: (812) 334-8900
F: (812) 334-2344
Sports Dir: Rob DeCleene

**Greater Boston Convention &
Visitors Bureau /
Sports Marketing Division**
Prudential Towe, Suite 400
PO Box 990468
Boston, MA 02199
T: (800) 888-5515
T: (617) 536-4100
F: (617) 424-7664
Dir: Robert Mollica

Brooklyn Sports Foundation
7 Metrotech Center
Suite 2000
Brooklyn, NY 11201
T: (718) 875-7000
F: (718) 237-4274
Exec. Dir. Robert Zeig

Broward Alliance
350 SE 2nd St., Suite 400
Fort Lauderdale, FL 33301
T: (954) 524-3113
F: (954) 524-3167
Dir. Sports Dev: Bruce Douglas

**Greater Buffalo Convention &
Visitors Bureau**
617 Main Street, Ste. 400
Buffalo, NY 14203
T: (800) 283-3256
T: (716) 852-0511
F: (716) 852-0131
Dir. Sports Mktg: Mike Even

Central Florida Sports Authority
126 E. Lucerne Circle
Orlando. FL 32801
T: (407) 648-4900
F: (407) 649-2072
www.orlandosports.org
E: sportscommission@orlando.com
P: Randy Johnson

**Charleston Regional
Sports Council**
106 Capitol Street
Charleston, WV 25301
T: (304) 345-0777
F: (304) 345-0776
Director: Karl Gattlieb

Charlotte Regional Sports Commission
Two First Union Center
301 S. Tryon, Suite 2110
Charlotte, NC 28282
T: (704) 332-7717
F: (704) 332-1252
Exec. Dir: Chip Mark

Greater Chattanooga Sports Committee
2 Broad Street
Chattanooga, TN 37402
T: (423) 756-8689
F: (423) 267-6746
www.chattanoogasports.org
merrill@cvb.chattanooga.net
P: Merrill Eckstein

Chicago Metropolitan Organizing Committee
1177 N. Highland Ave., Suite 201
Aurora, IL 60506
T: (630) 897-5400
F: (630) 897-5029
E: cmoc1@aol.com
P/CEO: Akif B. Malik

Chicago Sports Development
121 N. LaSalle Street
Chicago, IL 60602
T: (312) 744-3315
F: (312) 744-8523
Director: David Kennedy

Greater Cincinnati Sports & Events Commission
300 Main Street, First Floor
Cincinnati, OH 45202
T: (513) 651-1330
F: (513) 651-1374
Exec. Dir: Don Schumacher

Greater Cleveland Sports Commission
1468 W 9th St., Suite 405
Cleveland, OH 44113
T: (800) 487-0446
T: (440) 363-0695
F: (440) 363-0698
E: GCSC@aol.com
Chmn: John Ferchill

Colorado Springs Sports Corporation
12 East Boulder
Colorado Springs, CO 80903
T: (800) 888-4718
T: (719) 634-7333
F: (719) 634-5198
Exec. Dir: Stephen D. Ducoff

Columbia Regional Sports Council
PO Box 1360
Columbia, SC 29202
T: (803) 733-1138
F: (803) 733-1149
Exec Dir: Alisha Bain

Columbus Convention & Visitors Bureau
90 N. High Street
Columbus, OH 43215
T: (800) 354-2657
T: (614) 222-6145
F: (614) 221-5618
www.columbuscvb.org
Sports Mkt. Mgr: Linda C. Logan

Corpus Christi Bay Area Sports Foundation
PO Box 2664
Corpus Christi, TX 78403
T: (512) 881-1816
F: (512) 887-9023
Director: Linda Peters

Dallas Convention Center
650 S. Griffin Street
Dallas, TX 75202
T: (214) 939-2750
F: (214) 939-2795
Director Events: Frank Poe

Dallas Convention & Visitors Bureau
1201 Elm St., Suite 2000
Dallas, TX 75270
T: (214) 746-6654
F: (214) 571-1008
Director: John Underwood

Sports Dekalb
750 Commerce Dr., Suite 200
Decatur, GA 30030
T: (404) 378-2525
F: (404) 378-0941
Sports Mgr: Tom Kamdul

Delaware County Sports Comittee
Delaware CVB
200 E. State Street, Suite 100
Media, PA 19063
T: (800) 343-3983
T: (610) 565-3679
F: (610) 565-0833
www.delcocvb.org
Dir: Charles Schweitzer

Denver Metro Convention & Visitors Bureau
1555 California St., Suite 300
Denver, CO 80202
T: (303) 892-1112
F: (303) 892-1636
Director: Andrea O'Reilly

Greater Des Moines Sports Authority, Inc.
4729 SW 9th Street
Des Moines, IA 50317
T: (515) 247-5955
F: (515) 287-2465
Exec Dir: Joyce Durlam

Detroit Convention & Visitors Bureau
211 W. Fort Street
Suite 1000
Detroit, MI 48226
T: (800) 94-METRO
F: (313) 202-1832
Sports Mkt: Dave Beachnau

D.C. Sports Commission
2400 E. Capitol Street SE
Washington, DC 20003
T: (202) 547-9077
F: (202) 547-7460
Exec. Dir: James Dalrymple

Fargo-Moorhead Convention & Visitors Bureau
2001 44th Street SW
Fargo, ND 58103
T: (701) 282-3653
F: (701) 282-4366
www.fargomoorhead.org
Mkt: Tim Bourdon

Florida Sports Foundation
2964 Wellington Circle N.
Tallahassee, FL 32308
T: (850) 488-8347
F: (850) 922-0482
www.flasports.com
E: fsf@flasports.com
Exec. Dir: Larry Pendleton

Ft. Wayne Convention & Visitors Bureau
1021 S. Calhoun Street
Ft. Wayne, IN 46835
T: (800) 767-7752
T: (219) 424-3700
F: (219) 424-3914
www.fwcvb.org
Sports Dir: Andrew Bengs

Fresno Convention & Visitors Bureau
808 M Street
Fresno, CA 93721
T: (559) 233-0836
F: (559) 445-0122
Exec. Dir: Lloyd Kennedy

Gainesville / Hall County Sports Council
830 Green Street
Gainesville, GA 30501
T: (770) 536-5209
F: (770) 503-1349
Exec. Dir: Lynda H. Hawkins
Sports Mkt: Vic Stephens

Gainesville Sports Organizing Committee
11 W. University Ave., Ste 1
Gainesville, FL 32601
T: (352) 338-9300
F: (352) 338-0600
www.gsoc.com
E: info@gsoc.com
Exec. Dir: Jack Hughes

Georgia Sports Alliance
PO Box 1776
Atlanta, GA 30301
T: (404) 657-6187
F: (404) 657-4309
Director: Kimberly Goff

Greater Grand Forks Convention & Visitor's Bureau
4251 Gateway Drive
Grand Forks, ND 58203
T: (701) 746-0444
F: (701) 746-0775
Director: Ben Hart

Greensboro Sports Commission
317 S. Greene Street
Greensboro, NC 27401
T: (336) 378-4499
F: (336) 378-1998
P: Tom Ward

Harris County-Houston Sports Authority
1200 Post Oak, Suite 416
Houston, TX 77056
T: (713) 355-2164
F: (713) 355-2427
Chmn: Billy Burge

Greater Hartford Sports Commission
Greater Hartford CVB
1 Civic Center Plaza
Hartford, CT 06103
T: (800) 446-7811
F: (860) 293-2365
www.grhartfordcvb.com
Sports Mkt: Curt Jensen

Greater Hartford Sports Foundation
250 Constitution Plaza
Hartford, CT 06103
T: (860) 525-4451
F: (860) 293-2592
Director: Scott Phelps

Hawaii Pacific Sports, Inc.
1493 Halekkoa Drive
Honolulu, HI 96821
T: (808) 732-8805
F: (808) 735-0188
P: Mark E. Zeug

Houston Sports Division / Greater Houston CVB
801 Congress
Houston, TX 77002
T: (713) 227-3100
F: (713) 227-6336
Dir. Sports Dev: Jim McConn

Huntsville-Madison County Convention & Visitors Bureau
700 Monroe Street
Huntsville, AL 35801
T: (256) 551-2230
F: (256) 551-2324
www.huntsville.org
E: info@huntsville.org
Exec Dir: Judy Ryals

Idaho Sports Authority
168 N. 9th Street, Suite 200
Boise, ID 83702
T: (800) 635-5240
T: (208) 344-7777
F: (208) 344-6236
www.boise.org
E: smartin@boisecvb.org
Director: Scott Martin

Indiana Sports Corporation
Pan American Plaza
201 S. Capitol Ave, Suite 1200
Indianapolis, IN 46225
T: (800) HI-FIVES
T: (317) 237-5000
F: (317) 237-5041
Chmn: John B. Swarbrick, Jr.

Irving Convention & Visitor Bureau
3333 N. Mc Arthur Blvd., Ste 200
Irving, TX 75062
T: (800) 2-IRVING
F: (972) 257-3153
Director: Dean Conwell

Jacksonville Sports Development Authority
220 W. Bay Street
Jacksonville, FL 32204
T: (904) 630-3600
F: (904) 630-3606
Exec. Dir: Michael R. Sullivan

**Greater Kansas Sports
Commission and Foundation**
1100 Pennsylvania Ave., Ste 1032
Kansas City, MO 64105
T: (816) 474-4652
F: (816) 474-7979
E: sportkc@aol.com
Exec. Dir: Kevin M. Gray

**Kissimmee-St. Cloud Convention
& Visitors Bureau**
1925 E. Bronson Memorial Hwy.
Kissimmee, FL 34744
T: (800) 831-1844
T: (407) 847-5000
F: (407) 847-0878
E: meet@florida.kiss.com
Sports Mktg. Mgr: Susan Bond

Knoxville Sports Corporation
Regency Business Park
900 E. Hill Ave., Ste 390
Knoxville, TN 37915
T: (865) 522-3777
F: (865) 522-3974
P/ CEO: Gloria S. Ray

**Las Vegas Convention &
Visitors Authority**
3150 Paradise Road
Las Vegas, NV 89109
T: (702) 892-0711
F: (702) 892-2903
Director: Rossi Ralenkotter

Lawrence Sports Corporation
734 Vermont, Suite 101
Lawrence, KS 66044
T: (785) 865-4490
F: (785) 865-4400
P: Kent Earl

**Lee County Convention &
Visitors Bureau**
2180 W. First Street, Suite 320
Ft. Myers, FL 33901
T: (800) 237-6444
T: (941) 338-3500
F: (941) 334-1106
Director of Sports: Buddy Martin

**Lincoln Sports Promotion
Commission**
PO Box 83737
1221 N Street, Suite 320
Lincoln, NE 68508
T: (800) 423-8212
T: (402) 434-5344
F: (402) 436-2360
www.lincoln.org/cvb/
Dir.of Op: Dan Quandt

Lisle Sports Commission
4746 Main Street
Lisle, IL 60532
T: (800) 733-9811
T: (630) 769-1006
F: (630) 769-1006
E-mail: lislecvb@lisle.net
www.lisle.net/lislecvb/
P: Larry Slade

**Long Island Sports Comm./
Long Island CVB**
330 Vanderbilt Motor Pkwy.
Suite 203
Hauppauge, NY 11788
T: (800) 441-4601
T: (516) 951-3440
F: (516) 951-3439
www.licvb.com
Co-Chmn: John Kiernan &
Gerard Toner

**Los Angeles Sports &
Entertainment Commission**
633 W. Fifth Street, Suite 6000
Los Angeles, CA 90071
T: (213) 624-7300
F: (213) 236-2368
P: Kathryn Schloessman

Los Angeles Sports Council
350 S. Bixel, Suite 250
Los Angeles, CA 90017
T: (213) 482-6333
F: (213) 482-6340
P: David Simm
Co-Chmn: John C. Argue &
Leonard H. Straus

**Greater Louisville
Sports Association**
400 S. First Street
Louisville, KY 40202
T: (502) 584-2121
F: (502) 584-6697
Dir: Ken Lindsey

Lubbock Sports Authority
1120 Avenue K
Lubbock, TX 79401
T: (806) 747-5232
F: (806) 747-1419
Sr. Dir: Gregg Fort

**Greater Lynchburg
Sports Capital of Virginia**
2015 Memorial Avenue
Lynchburg, VA 24501
T: (804) 845-5966
F: (804) 522-9592
Comm: Chris Ellis

**Greater Macon
Sports Commission**
200 Cherry Street
Macon, GA 32108
T: (912) 741-6030
F: (912) 745-2022
P: Billy Hester

**Maricopa County Sports
Commission**
One Renaissance Square
Two North Central, Ste. 2510
Phoenix, AZ 85004
T: (602) 258-MCSC
F: (602) 254-6773
www.mcsc.org
Exec. Dir: Michael J. Sculley

**Massachusetts Sports
Partnership**
200 Berkeley St., 16 FL
Boston, MA 02110
T: (617) 572-7115
F: (617) 572-7007
Pres: Robert Colarossi

**Memphis & Shelby County
Sports Authority**
47 Union Avenue
Memphis, TN 38103
T: (901) 543-5319
F: (901) 543-5350
Director: Ross Bartow

**Metropolitan Sports
Facilities Commission**
900 South Fifth Street
Minneapolis, MN 55415
T: (612) 332-0386
F: (612) 332-8334
Exec. Dir: William Lester

Metro Sports Council
PO Box 1360
Columbia, SC 29202
T: (803) 733-1125
F: (803) 733-1149
Exec. Dir: Jeffrey T. Turgeon

Metro Sports Foundation
PO Box 31536
Omaha, NE 68131
T: (402) 341-0866
F: (402) 341-0866
Exec. Dir: Sherman Poska

**Miami Sports & Exhibition
Authority**
444 SW 2nd Ave., Ste 920
Miami, FL 33130
T: (305) 416-1761
F: (305) 416-1764
Exec. Dir: Christina Abrams

**Greater Miami Chamber of
Commerce Sports Council**
Omni Complex
1601 Biscayne Blvd.
Miami, FL 33132-6902
T: (305) 577-5432
F: (305) 374-6902
VP/Comm.Dev: Cornelia Pereira

Great Minneapolis Convention & Visitors Association
33 South 6th Street
4000 Multi-Foods Tower
Minneapolis, MN 55402
T: (612) 661-4700
F: (612) 348-8359
www.Minneapolis.org
Dir: Kevin Lewis

Minnesota Amateur Sports Commission
1700 105th Ave. NE
Blaine, MN 55449
T: (612) 785-5699
F: (612) 785-5699
Exec Dir: Paul Erickson

Mobile Sports Commission
1 South Water Street
Mobile, AL 36602
T: (800) 566-2453
T: (334) 415-2060
F: (334) 415-2060
P: Brenda Scott

Monroe County Sports Commission
333 N. Plymouth Avenue
Rochester, NY 14608
T: (716) 262-3832
F:
P: Rocco DiGiovanni

Nashville Sports Council
211 Commerce Street
Nashville, TN 37201
T: (615) 743-3120
F: (615) 244-3540
www.nashvillesports.com
Exec. Dir: Scott Ramsey

Nassau County Sports Commission
1380 Northern Blvd., Ste A
Manhasset, NY 11030
T: (516) 365-9625
F: (516) 365-4427
www.nassausports.org
Chmn/P: Gary I. Wadler, M.D.

Greater New Haven Convention & Visitor Bureau
One Long Wharf Drive
New Haven, CT 06511
T: (800) 332-STAY
T: (203) 777-8550
F: (203) 782-7755
Sports Dir: Suzette Benitez

New Jersey Sports and Exposition Authority
50 State Highway 20
East Rutherford, NJ 07073
T: (201) 460-4011
Exec. Dir.: Robert Brennan

Greater New Orleans Sports Foundation
1400 Poydras St., Suite 918
New Orleans, LA 70112
T: (504) 525-5678
F: (504) 529-1622
www.gnosports.com
E: media@gnosports.com
CEO: Jay Cicero

Greater New Orleans Tourist and Convention Commission
1520 Sugar Bowl Drive
New Orleans, LA 70112
T: (504) 566-5061
F: (504) 566-5046
Mgr. Sports Mtngs: Lisa Browning

New York City Sports Commission
1 Centre Street, Rm. 2358
New York, NY 10007
T: (212) 788-8389
F: (212) 788-7154
Exec. Dir: Arlene Weltman

Sports Niagara
345 Third Street, Suite 470
Niagara Falls, NY 14307
T: (800) 953-2557
T: (716) 284-1197
F: (716) 285-8604
P: Peter Preteroti

North Carolina Amateur Sports
PO Box 12727
Research Triangle Park, NC 27709
T: (919) 361-1133
F: (919) 361-2559
www.ncsports.org
E: nca5@interpath.com
Exec. Dir: Barry Pennell

North Carolina Sports Development
301 N. Wilmington St.
PO Box 29571
Raleigh, NC 27626
T: (800) VISIT NC
T: (919) 733-4962
F: (919) 733-8356
www.commerce.state.nc.us/sports
Dir: Bill Dooley

North Little Rock Promotion Commission
#1 Eldor Johnson Drive
Burns Park
North Little Rock, AR 72118
T: (800) 643-4690
T: (501) 758-1424
F: (501) 758-5752
Exec. Dir: Mary Lou Davenport

Oklahoma City All Sports Association
100 W. Main, Suite 287
Oklahoma City, OK 73102
T: (800) 434-5000
T: (405) 236-5000
F: (405) 236-5008
Exec. Dir: Stanley Draper, Jr.

Oklahoma City Convention & Visitors Bureau
189 W. Sheridan Avenue
Oklahoma City, OK 73102
T: (800) 225-5652
www.okccvb.org
Exec. Dir:

Greater Omaha Sports Committee
666 Farnam Bldg.
1613 Farnam Street
Omaha, NE 68102
T: (800) 475-SHOW
T: (402) 346-8003
F: (402) 346-8003
P: Bob Mancuso

Oregon Sports Action
10514 NE Halsey
Portland, OR 97220
T: (503) 252-7755
F: (503) 252-7132
P/CEO: Jack Elder

Orlando Area Sports Commission
126 E. Lucerne Drive
Orlando, FL 32801
T: (407) 648-4900
F: (407) 649-2072
www.orlando.sports.org
Director: John Saboor

Palm Beach County Sports Authority, Inc.
1555 Palm Beach Lakes Blvd.
Suite 1410
West Palm Beach, FL 33401
T: (561) 233-1015
F: (561) 233-1012
Exec. Dir: Pam Gerig

Pensacola Sports Association
101 W. Main Street
PO Box 12463
Pensacola, FL 32582
T: (850) 434-2800
F: (850) 432-4237
Director: Shirley Cronley

Peoria Convention & Vis. Bureau
403 NE Jefferson
Peoria, IL 61603
T: (309) 676-0303
F: (309) 676-8470
P: Greg Edwards

Philadelphia Sports Congress
Convention & Visitors Bureau
1515 Market St., Suite 2020
Philadelphia, PA 19102
T: (215) 636-3417
F: (215) 636-3327
www.pcub.org
E: larryn@pcub.org
Dir: Larry Needle

Greater Phoenix Convention & Visitors Bureau
One Arizona Center
400 E. Van Buren, Suite 600
Phoenix, AZ 85004
T: (602) 254-6500
F: (602) 253-4415
P: David Radcliffe

Pima County Sports Authority
110 S. Church St., Suite 1160
Tucson, AZ 85701
T: (520) 629-9522
F: (520) 792-0668
Exec. Dir: Michael Brewer

Pittsburgh Sports & Festival Federation, Inc.
One Riverfront Center
20 Stanwix Street
Pittsburgh, PA 15222
T: (412) 434-6202
F: (412) 434-6208
P/Exec. Dir: James Richards

Polk County Sports Marketing
600 N. Broadway, Suite 300
Bartow, FL 33830
T: (941) 534-4370
F: (941) 534-0886
www.cfdc.org
Director: Mark jackson

Portland Metropolitan Sports Authority
700 NE Multnomah, Suite 920
Portland, OR 97232
T: (503) 234-4500
F: (503) 234-3853
Exec. Dir: Dave Mahalic

Quad Cities Sports Commission
2021 River Drive
Moline, IL 61265
T: (800) 747-7800
T: (309) 797-1733
F: (309) 788-7898
Exec. Dir: Jonathan White

Rhode Island Sports Council
30 Exchange Terrace
Providence, RI 02903
T: (401) 521-5000
F: (401) 751-2434
Exec. Dir: John T. Mousseau

Metropolitan Richmond Sports Backers
7275 Glen Forest Dr., Ste 204
Richmond, VA 23226
T: (804) 285-9495
F: (804) 285-3132
Exec. Dir: Jon Lugbill

Riverside Convention Bureau
3737 6th Street
Riverside, CA 92501
T: (909) 222-4700
F: (909) 222-4712
Sales Mgr: Laurie Mattson

Rockford Area Convention & Visitors Bureau
211 N. Main Street
Rockford, IL 61101
T: (800) 521-0849
F: (815) 963-4298
Sports Exec: Chris Davenport

Sacramento Sports Commission
106 K Street, Suite 630
Sacramento, CA 95814
T: (916) 264-7718
F: (916) 264-8273
Dir: John M. Mc Casey

St. Joseph Regional Sports Commission
109 S. 4th Street
St. Joseph, MO 64501
T: (800) 785-0360
F: (816) 233-9120
www.stjosports.com
Sports Dir: Kerry Strahm

St. Louis Sports Commission
211 N. Broadway, Suite 1000
St. Louis, MO 63102
T: (314) 992-0687
F: (314) 421-5727
Director: Frank Viverito

St. Petersburg / Clearwater Area Sports Foundation Committee
14450 46th St. N., Suite 108
St. Petersburg, FL 33731
T: (727) 464-7250
F: (727) 464-7255
E: spcsports@aol.com
P: Michael W. Davenport

Salem Convention & Visitor's Association
1313 Mill Street E.
Salem, OR 97301
T: (800) 874-7012
F: (503) 581-4540
www.oregonlink.com/~salem/scva/
E: convention@scva.org
Convention Mgr.: Peggy Crandall

San Antonio Sports Foundation
PO Box 830386
San Antonio, TX 78283
T: (210) 370-2158
F: (210) 370-2159
P: Susan Blackwood

San Bernardino Convention & Visitors Bureau
201 N. E Street, Suite 103
San Bernardino, CA 92401
T: (800) 867-8366
F: (909) 888-5998
www.san-bernardino.org
Sales Dir: David Patterson

San Diego International Sports Council
PO Box 880007
San Diego, CA 92168
T: (619) 682-3436
F: (619) 682-3440
www.sdisc.com
Exec. Dir: Sandy Purdon

San Jose Sports Authority
99 Almaden Blvd., Suite 975
San Jose, CA 95113
T: (408) 288-2930
F: (408) 288-7438
Exec. Dir: Dean Munro

Savannah Sports Council
222 W. Oglethorpe Avenue
Savannah, GA 31401
T: (912) 944-0444
F: (912) 944-0468
Exec. Dir: Dan Simmons

Seattle King County / Sports & Events Council
1301 5th Avenue, Suite 2400
Seattle, WA 98101
T: (206) 389-7229
F: (206) 389-7288
P: Michael Campbell

Seminole County Convention & Visitor's Bureau
105 International Parkway
Heathrow, FL 32746
T: (800) 800-7832
T: (407) 324-1217 (Sports)
F: (407) 324-4317
Sports Dir: John Giantonio

City of Shreveport Sports Commission
629 Spring Street
Shreveport, LA 71166
T: (318) 222-9391
F: (318) 222-0056
Exec. Dir: Andy Rosenbaum

Siouxland Sports & Cultural Events Congress
801 Fourth Street
Sioux City, IA 51101
T: (800) 593-2228
T: (712) 279-4800
F: (712) 279-4900
www.Siouxlan.com/ccat
P: Ron Wieck

Greater Spokane Sports Association
801 W. Riverside, Ste. 301
Spokane, WA 99201
T: (509) 456-5812
F: (509) 456-5837
www.spokanesports.org
Exec. Dir. Eric Sawyer

Syracuse Sports Corporation
572 South Salina Street
Syracuse, NY 13202
T: (800) 234-4797
T: (315) 470-1825
F: (315) 471-8545
Dir. Sports Dev: Kristen J. Wood

Tacoma / Pierce County Sports Commission
1001 Pacific Ave., Suite 400
Tacoma, WA 98402
T: (253) 627-2836
F: (253) 627-8783
www.tacomasports.com
E: info@tpctourism.org
Comm: Mike Shields

Tallahassee Sports Council
200 W. College Avenue
Tallahassee, FL 32302
T: (800) 628-2866
T: (850) 413-9200
F: (850) 487-4621
www.co.leon.fl.us/cvb/
Exec. Dir: Sheri Murphy

Tampa Sports Authority
4201 N. Dale Mabry
Tampa, FL 33607
T: (813) 673-4300
F: (813) 673-4308
Exec. Dir: Henry Saavedra

The Thunderbirds
7226 North 16th Street
Suite 100
Phoenix, AZ 85020
T: (602) 870-0163
F: (602) 870-4162
P: Tim Grant

Greater Toledo Sports Bureau
4142 Dunkirk Road
Toledo, OH 43606
T: (419) 535-9799
F: (419) 535-9799
Dir. Mark Tooman

The Sports Commission of Metropolitan Tulsa
616 South Boston
Suite 100
Tulsa, OK 74119
T: (800) 558-3311
T: (918) 585-1201
F: (918) 592-6244
P: Suzanne Stewart

SporTyler
Tyler Convention & Visitors Bureau
407 N. Broadway
Tyler, TX 75702
T: (800) 235-5712
F: (903) 593-2746
www.tylertexas.com
E: hbell@tylertexas.com
Exec. Dir: Henry M. Bell III (CVB)
Dir: Tory Hansen

Utah Sports Authority
2108 State Office Building
Salt Lake City, UT 84114
T: (801) 538-1118
F: (801) 538-9660
Exec. Dir: Randy Montgomery

Valdosta-Lowndes County Sports Commission
1703 Norman Drive, Suite F
Valdosta, GA 31603
T: (800) 569-8687
T: (912) 245-0513
T: (912) 245-5240
Sports Dir: Gena Kelly

Venue Saint John Commission
City Hall
15 Market Square
Saint John, NB E2L 4L1 Canada
T: (506) 658-2880
F: (506) 658-2879
GM: Robert Russell

Ventura Visitors & Convention Bureau
89 California St., Suite C
Ventura, CA 93001
T: (805) 648-2075
F: (805) 648-2150
Director: Debbie Giles

Vermont State Sports Council
60 Main Street, Suite 100
Burlington, VT 05401
T: (802) 863-3489
F: (802) 863-1538
Dir: Jim Thornton

Virginia Amateur Sports, Inc.
711-C Fifth Street
Roanoke, VA 24016
T: (540) 343-0987
F: (540) 343-7407
P: Peter Lampman

Sports Virginia, Inc.
3122 Clay Street, Suite 19
Richmond, VA 23230
T: (804) 353-9348
F: (804) 278-9555
P: Richard Hollander

Walt Disney Wide World of Sports
PO Box 10000
Lake Buena Vista, FL 32830
T: (407) 363-6100
Sr. VP: Phil Lengyel

Western New York Amateur Sports Commission
424 Main Street, Suite 300
Buffalo, NY 14202
T: (716) 842-0322
F: (716) 856-6754
Exec. Dir: Kenneth J. Vetter

Western Pennsylvania Sports Federation
Fifth Avenue Place, Suite 3026
Pittsburgh, PA 15222
T: (412) 255-7687
Dir: Mark Malick

Greater Wichita Sports Commission
100 S. Main St., Ste. 100
Wichita, KS 67202
T: (800) 288-9424
F: (316) 265-0162
Director: Robert Hanson

Wisconsin Sports Authority
901 North Fourth Street
Milwaukee, WI 53203
T: (414) 277-6787
F: (414) 277-6790
P: Brian Manthey

Worcester Sports Convention & Visitors Bureau
33 Waldo Street
Worcester, MA 06108
T: (508) 755-7400
F: (508) 754-2703
Dir. Sports Dept: Eleanor Vadenais

Late Additions

Gwinnett Convention & Visitors Bureau
6500 Sugarloaf Pkwy, Suite 200
Duluth, GA 30097
T: (888)-GWINNETT
T: (770) 623-3600
F: (770) 623-1667
www.gcvb.org
E: info@gcvb.org
Sports Sls Mgr: Shirley Corders

Be sure to send us your new address so we may keep you informed of new editions!

Thank you!

Edward T. Kobak, Jr.

Global Sports Productions, Ltd.
1223 Broadway, Suite 102
Santa Monica, California 90404

Sports Facilities

Listed in this section are sports facilities for the U.S. & Canada as well as foreign sports facilities. Included in these listings are arenas, ballparks & stadiums.

Alabama

Auburn

Auburn University
2047 Eaves-Memorial Coliseum
Auburn, AL 36849
T: (334) 844-4442
F: (334) 844-2399
Eaves Memorial Coliseum
Seating: 14,000
Sports Use: UA Basketball
Jordan-Hare Stadium
Seating: 85,000
Sports Use: UA Football

Birmingham

Birmingham-Jefferson Civic Center
1 Civic Center Plaza
Birmingham, AL 35203
T: (205) 328-8160
F: (205) 254-0320
Seating: 19,000
Sports Use: Bulls (ECHL), Steeldogs (AFL2)

Legion Field Stadium
400 Graymont Ave. W.
Birmingham, AL 35204
T: (205) 254-2556
F: (205) 254-2515
Seating: 80,000
Sports Use: Thunderbolts (XFL), UAB Football

UAB Arena
617 13th St. S.
Birmingham, AL 35294
T: (205) 934-7296
F: (205) 934-7505
Seating: 8,500
Sports Use: UAB Sports

Huntsville

Milton Frank Stadium
PO Box 1256
Huntsville, AL 35807
T: (205) 532-3090
Seating: 20,000
Sports Use: Univ. of Alabama

Von Braun Civic Center
700 Monroe St.
Huntsville, AL 35801
T: (205) 533-1953
F: (205) 551-2203
Seating: 8,738
Sports Use: UAB Sports, Flight (NBDL), TN Valley Vipers (AFL2)

Mobile

Mobile Civic Center
401 Civic Center Drive
Mobile, AL 36602
T: (334) 434-7261
F: (334) 434-7551
Seating: 10,676
Sports Use: Mysticks (ECHL), Univ. of South Alabama, Seagulls (NIFL), Revelers (NBDL)

Montgomery

Garret Coliseum
PO Box 70026
1555 Federal Drive
Montgomery, AL 36109
T: (334) 261-5597
F: (334) 240-3242
Seating: 11,500

Montgomery Civic Center
PO Box 4037
300 Bibb Street
Montgomery, AL 36103
T: (334) 241-2100
F: (334) 241-2117
Seating: 5,000 ice event

University

Memorial Coliseum
University of Alabama
PO Box 6689
University, AL 35486
T: (205) 348-7525
Seating: 15,547
Bryant Denny Stadium
Seating: 58,000
Sports Use: Univ. of Alabama
Crimson Tide

Alaska

Anchorage

George M. Sullivan Sports Arena
1600 Gambell St.
Anchorage, AK 95501
T: (907) 279-0618
F: (907) 274-0676
Seating: 8,935
Sports Use: U. of Alaska Seawolves
Anchorage Aces (WCHL)

Fairbanks

John A. Carlson Center Arena
2010 Second Ave.
Fairbanks, AK 99701
T: (907) 451-7800
F: (907) 451-1195
Seating: 6,500
Sports Use: Univ. AK- Fairbanks Nonooks

Arizona

Flagstaff

High Altitude Sports Training Complex
NAU Box 5769
Flagstaff, AZ 86011
T: (520) 523-4444
F: (520) 523-9401
www.nau.edu/nastc
multi-purpose training center

Phoenix

America West Arena
201 E Jefferson Street
Phoenix, AZ 85004
T: (602) 379-2000
F: (602) 379-2002
Seating: 19, 023
Sports Use: Coyotes (NHL),Suns (NBA), Rattlers (AFL), Mercury (WNBA)

Arizona Veterans Memorial Coliseum
PO Box 6728
1826 W. Mc Dowell
Phoenix, AZ 85005
T: (602) 252-6771
F: (602) 495-1302
Seating: 15, 681
13, 820 Hockey seating
Sports Use:

Bank One Ballpark
201 E. Jefferson Street
PO Box 433
Phoenix, AZ 85001
T: (602) 379-2000
F: (602) 379-2093
Seating: 48, 500
Sports Use: Diamondbacks(MLB)

Tempe

Sun Devil Stadium
ASU Public Events
Arizona State University
Tempe, AZ 85287
T: (602) 965-5062
F: (602) 965-7663
Seating: 73, 248
Sports Use: ASU Sun Devils, Arizona Cardinals (NFL)

Tucson

Hi Corbett Field
900 S. Randolph Way
Tucson, AZ 85716
T: (520) 791-4873
Seating: 10, 600
Sports Use: Tucson Toros (PCL)

Tucson Convention Center
PO Box 3053
Tucson, AZ 85702
T: (520) 791-2601
F: (520) 791-5572
Seating; 9, 700
Sports Use: Univ. of Arizona Ice Cats.

Arizona Stadium
University of Arizona
121 Sun Bldg.
2030 E. Speedway
Tucson, AZ 85721
T: (520) 621-1877
Seating: 57, 000
Sports Use: Wildcats FB (Pac-10)

Arkansas

Fayetteville

University of Arkansas
Barnhill Arena
Fayetteville, AR 72703
T: (501) 575-5255
F: (501) 575-4904
Barnhill Arena
Seating: 8, 500
Razorback Stadium
Seating: 53,000
Sports Use: U. AR Razorbacks (SEC)

Little Rock

Barton Coliseum
2600 Howard Blvd.
Little Rock, AR 72216
T: (501) 372-8341
F: (501) 372-4197
Seating: 10, 213
Sports Use: Arkansas Glacier Cats (WPHL), Twister (AFL2)
U. AR-Little Rock

War Memorial Stadium
Markham & Van Buren St.
Little Rock, AR 72205
T: (501) 663-0775
F: (501) 663-6387
Seating: 53, 500
Sports Use: UA- Little Rock FB

Ray Winder Field
PO Box 5599
War Memorial Park
Little Rock, AR 72215
T: (501) 664-1555
F: (501) 664-1834
Seating: 6, 156
Sports Use: AR Travelers
(TX Lg AA Baseball)

North Little Rock

Alltel Arena
312 Main Street
North Little Rock, AR 72114
T: (501) 340-5660
F: (501) 340-
www.alltelarena.com
Seating: 18,000
Sports Use: AR Riverblades (CHL)

California

Anaheim

Anaheim Edison Stadium
2000 Gene Autry Way
Anaheim, CA 92806
T: (714) 254-3100
F: (714) 254-3150
Seating: 48,000
Sports Use: Angels (MLB)

Arrowhead Pond
2695 E. Katella Ave.
Anaheim, CA 92806
T: (714) 704-2400
F: (714) 704-2443
Seating: 19, 400
Sports Use:
Mighty Ducks (NHL)

Bakersfield

Bakersfield Centennial Gardens
1001 Truxtun Ave.
Bakersfield, CA 93301
T: (661) 852-7300
F: (661) 861-9904
Seating: 9,000
Sports Use: Condors

Fresno

Selland Arena
700 M Street
Fresno, CA 93721
T: (559) 498-1511
F: (559) 488-4634
Seating: 11,000 (9,500 Hockey)
Sports Use: Falcons
Fresno State Univ. Bskb

Inglewood

Great Western Forum
PO Box 10
3900 W. Manchester Blvd
Inglewood, CA 90306
T: (310) 419-3100
F: (310) 419-3234
Seating: 18, 679

Long Beach

Long Beach Arena
300 E. Ocean Blvd.
Long Beach, CA 90802
T: (562) 436-3636
F: (562) 436-9491
Seating: 14, 500
Sports Use: Ice Dogs
LB State University

Los Angeles

Dodger Stadium
1000 Elysian park Ave
Los Angeles, CA 90012
T: (323) 224-1351
F: (323) 224-1269
Seating: 56,000
Sports Use: LA Dodgers

Home Depot Stadium
18400 Avalon Blvd.
Carson, CA 90746
T: (310) 630-2200
F: (310) 630-2250
Seating: 27,000
LA Galaxy (MLS), U.S. National Team

Los Angeles Memorial Coliseum
3939 S. Figueroa St.
Los Angeles, CA 90037
T: (213) 748-6136
F: (213) 746-9346
Seating: 92,000
Sports Use: USC Football, Int'l. Soccer

LA Staples Center
1111 Figueroa Street
Los Angeles, CA 90015
T: (213) 742-7100
F: (213) 742-7296
www.staplescenter.com
Seating:19,000
Sports Use: Kings (NHL), Lakers (NBA), Clippers (NBA), Avengers (AFL), Sparks (WNBA)

Los Angeles Sports Arena
3939 Figueroa St.
Los Angeles, CA 90037
T: (213) 748-6136
F: (213) 746-9346
Seating: 16,500
Sports Use: USC Basketball

Oakland

Oakland-Alameda County Coliseum
7000 Coliseum Way
Nimitz Freeway & Hegenberger
Oakland, CA 94621
T: (510) 569-2121
F: (510) 562-2754
Seating: 60,000
Sports Use: A's (MLB), Raiders (NFL)

Pasadena

Rose Bowl
1001 Rose Bowl Drive
Pasadena, CA 91103
T: (626) 577-3100
F: (626) 405-0992
Seating: 104,696
Sports Use: LA Galaxy (MLS), UCLA Football, NCAA Rose Bowl Game

Sacramento

Arco Sports Arena
1 Sports Parkway
Sacramento, CA 95834
T: (916) 928-0000
F: (916) 920-4388
Seating: 18,552
Sports Use: Kings (NBA), Monarchs (WNBA)

San Diego

Jack Murphy Field at Qualcom
9449 Friars Road
San Diego, CA 92108
T: (619) 283-5503
F: (619) 283-0460
Seating: 60,750
Sports Use: Chargers (NFL), Padres (MLB), SDSU Aztecs

San Diego Sports Arena
3500 Sports Arena Blvd
San Diego, CA 92110
T: (619) 224-4171
F: (619) 224-3010
Seating: 15,000
Sports Use: Gulls
SDSU Aztecs FB

San Francisco

Candlestick Park
PO Box 880232
Jamestown & Harney Way
San Francisco, CA 94124
T: (415) 467-1994
F: (415) 467-3049
Seating: 68,853
Sports Use: 49ers (NFL)

Pacific Bell Park
2nd & King Street
San Francisco, CA 94107
T: (415) 468-3700
Seating: 41,000
Sports Use: Giants (MLB),

San Jose

Municipal Stadium
PO Box 21727
South 10th & E. Azoca St
San Jose, CA 95152
T: (408) 297-1435
F: (408) 297-1453
Seating: 5,200
Sports Use: Bees (Cal. Lg. A Baseball), SJSU Spartans

San Jose Arena
525 W. Santa Clara St.
San Jose, CA 95113
T: (408) 287-7070
F: (408) 999-5797
Seating: 17,310
Sports Use: Sharks (NHL), Sabrecats (AFL), NLL Club

Spartan Stadium
San Jose State University
7th & Alma
San Jose, CA 95152
T: (408) 924-6360
F: (408) 924-6399
Seating: 37,500
Sports Use: Earthquakes (MLS), Cyberrays (WUSA), SJSU Spartans FB

Colorado

Boulder

Folsom Field Stadium
Univ. Colorado- Boulder
Campus Box 410
Regent Dr. & 28th St
Boulder, CO 80309
T: (303) 492-5316
Seating: 56,700
Sports Use: U. of Colorado FB

Colorado Springs

Broadmoor New World Arena
3185 Venetucci Blvd
Colorado Springs, CO 80906
T: (719) 477-2100
F: (719) 477-2199
Seating: 8,000
Sports Use:
Colorado College Hockey

Sky Sox Stadium
4385 Tutt Blvd
Colorado Springs, CO 80922
T: (719) 597-1449
F: (719) 597-2491
Seating: 6,100
Sports Use: Sky Sox (PCL BB)

Denver

Denver Coliseum
4600 Humboldt St
Denver, CO 80216
T: (303) 295-4444
F: (303) 295-4467
Seating: 11,500 (9,500 Bskb)

Coors Field
2001 Blake Street
Denver, CO 80205
T: (303) 292-0200
F: (303) 312-2319
Seating: 50,250
Sports Use: Rockies (MLB)

Mile High Stadium
1755 W. 17th Ave.
Denver, CO 80204
T: (303) 458-4850
F: (303) 458-4791
Seating: 76,000
Sports Use:
Broncos (NFL), Rapids (MLS)

Pepsi Center
901 Auraria Pkwy.
Denver, CO 80204
T: (303) 893-1999
F: (303) 893-
Seating:19,000
Sports Use: Avalanche (NHL),
Nuggets (NBA)

Connecticut

Hartford

Hartford Civic Center
1 Civic Center
Hartford, CT 06103
T: (860) 249-6333
F: (860) 241-4226
Seating: 14,758
Sports Use: Pride (CBA), Seawolves (AFL), Wolf Pack (AHL)

New Haven

New Haven Veterans Memorial Coliseum
PO Box 1857
275 S. Orange St.
New Haven, CT 06510
T: (203) 772-4200
F: (203) 772-4139
Seating: 10,500
Sports Use:

Storrs

Gampel Pavilion
Univ. of Connecticut
Div. of Athletics, Box U78
2111 Hillside Rd
Storrs, CT 06269
T: (203) 486-2277
F: (203) 486-1153
Seating: 9,000
Sports Use: U. Conn Basketball

District of Columbia

MCI Center
601 F Street NW
Washington, DC 20001
T: (202) 628-3200
F: (202) 661-5054
Seating: 23,000
Sports Use: Capitals (NHL), Wizards (NBA), Mystic (WNBA)

Robert E. Kennedy Memorial Stadium/Starplex
2001 E. Capitol Street
Washington, DC 20003
T: (202) 547-9077
F: (202) 547-7460
Seating: 54,497
Sports Use: DC United (MLS), Washington Freedom (WUSA)

Florida

Daytona Beach

The Ocean Center
101 N. Atlantic Ave.
Dayton Beach, FL 32118
T: (904) 254-4500
F: (904) 254-4512
Seating: 9,500

Fort Myers

Lee Civic Center
11831 Bayshore Blvd
Fort Myers, FL 33917
T: (941) 543-8368
F: (941) 543-4110
Seating: 7,500
Sports Use: FL Everblades (ECHL),
Sea Dragons (USBL), AFL2 Club

Jacksonville

Alltel Gator Bowl Stadium
One Alltel Stadium Place
Jacksonville, FL 32202
T: (904) 633-6100
F: (904) 633-6113
Seating: 82,000
Sports Use: Jaguars (NFL),
NCAA Gator Bowl Game

Veterans Memorial Coliseum
1145 E. Adams Street
Jacksonville, FL 32202
T: (904) 630-3900
F: (904) 630-3913
Seating: 11,676
Sports Use: Lizard Kings (ECHL),
Tomcats (AFL2)

Kissimee

**Osceola Co. Stadium &
Sports Complex**
PO Box 29979
1000 Osceola Blvd.
Kissimee, FL 32742
T: (407) 933-5400
F: (407) 847-6237
Seating: 55,130
Sports Use: Houston Astros
(Spring), Osceola Astros (FSL)

Miami

American Airlines Arena
6901 Biscayne Blvd.
Miami, FL 33132
T: (786) 777-1000
www.aaarena.com
Seating: 19,236
Sports Use: Heat (NBA),
Sol (WNBA)

Miami Arena
721 NW First Ave.
Miami, FL 33136
T: (305) 530-4400
F: (305) 530-4429
Seating: 16,640
Sports Use: Univ. of Miami
Hurricanes Bskb.

Orange Bowl Stadium
1501 NW Third Street
Miami, FL 33125
T: (305) 643-7100
F: (305) 643-7155
Seating: 74,177
Sports Use: U. of Miami
Hurricanes Football

Joe Robbie Pro Player Stadium
2269 NW 199th Street
Miami, FL 33056
T: (305) 623-6100
F: (305) 620-6596
Seating: 73,000
Sports Use: Dolphins (NFL),
Marlins (MLB), NCAA Bowl Game

Sunrise Arena
One Panthers Parkway
Sunrise, FL 33323
T: (954) 835-7000
Seating: 20,000
Sports Use: Florida Panthers (NHL),

Orlando

**Walt Disney Wide
World of Sports Complex**
PO Box 10000
Lake Buena Vista, FL 32830
T: (407) 363-6100
F: (407) 363-6601
The Ballpark (7,500)
The Fieldhouse (5,000)
Sports Use: Home of AAU,
Atlanta Braves Training Camp,
Harlem Globetrotters, Auto Racing

Orlando Centroplex
Orlando Arena
PO Box 151
600 W. Amelia St.
Orlando, FL 32801
T: (407) 849-2000
F: (407) 849-2329
Seating: 15,588
Sports Use: Magic (NBA), Predators (AFL)
Florida Citrus Bowl
Seating: 72,000
Sports Use: UCF Football, NCAA Citrus Bowl Game

Pensacola Civic Center
201 E. Gregory Street
Pensacola, FL 32593
T: (850) 432-0800
F: (850) 432-1707
Seating: 8,500
Sports Use: Ice Pilots (ECHL), Barracudas (AFL2)

St. Petersburg

Bayfront Center Arena
400 First Street S.
St. Petersburg, FL 33701
T: (727) 892-5798
F: (727) 892-5858
Seating: 6,500
Sports Use:

Tropicana Field & Thunderdome
One Tropicana Drive
St. Petersburg, FL 33705
T: (727) 825-3120
F: (727) 825-3111
Seating: 50,000 (Baseball)
Sports Use: Devil Rays (MLB), Storm (AFL)

Sarasota

Ed Smith Stadium
2700 12th Street
Sarasota, FL 34237
T: (941) 954-4101
F: (941) 365-1587
Seating: 7,500 (Baseball)
Sports Use: Chicago White Sox training, Sarasota Red Sox (FSL)

Tallahassee

Tallahassee-Leon County Civic Center
505 W. Pensacola St.
Tallahassee, FL 32302
T: (850) 487-1691
F: (850) 222-6947
Seating: 14,000
Sports Use: Thunder (AFL2), Florida State U. Seminoles, Florida A&M Rattlers

Tampa

The Ice Palace
501 E. Kennedy Blvd, Suite 1900
Tampa, FL 33602
T: (813) 223-4919
F: (813) 276-7348
Seating: 19,500
Sports Use: Lighting (NHL)

Raymond James Stadium
4201 N. Dale Mabry Pkwy.
Tampa, FL 33607
T: (813) 673-4303
Sports Use: Buccaneers (NFL)

West Palm Beach

West Palm Beach Auditorium & Stadium Complex
1610 Palm Beach Lakes Blvd
West Palm Beach, FL 33402
T: (561) 683-6010
F: (561) 683-6012
Seating: 7,000 (Arena)
       7,500 (Stadium)

Georgia

Athens

University of Georgia Coliseum
Athens, GA 30602
Seating: 10,500
Sanford Stadium
Seating: 85,450
Sports Use: U. GA Bulldogs (SEC)
T: (706) 542-9039
F: (706) 542-9339

Atlanta

Georgia Dome
One Georgia Dome Drive
Atlanta, GA 30313
T: (404) 223-9200
F: (404) 223-8011
Seating: 70,500 (42,000 Arena)
Sports Use: Falcons (NFL),
SEC FB Championship Game.

Phillips Arena
100 Techwood Drive NW
Atlanta, GA 30303
T: (404) 681-2100
Seating: 18,000
Sports Use: Hawks (NBA),
Thrashers (NHL)

Turner Field
755 Hank Aaron Drive SE
Atlanta, GA 30315
T: (404) 614-2310
F: (404)
Seating: 52,000
Sports Use: Atlanta Braves (MLB)

Macon

Macon Coliseum
200 Coliseum Drive
Macon, GA 31201
T: (912) 742-0901
F: (912) 742-4543
Seating: 8,100 (Hockey)
Sports Use: Macon Whoopee
(ECHL), Mercer University

Columbus

The New South Commons Complex
PO Box 1340
400 Fourth Street
Columbus, GA 31901
T: (706) 571-5889
F: (706) 571-5827
Civic Center
Seating: 10,000
Sports Use: Cottonmouths (ECHL),
Riverdragons (NBDL)
Golden Park
Seating: 6,000
Sports Use: Redstixx (SAL BB)

Savannah

Grayson Stadium
1401 E. Victory Drive
Savannah, GA 31414
T: (912) 351-9150
Seating: 7,300
Sports Use: Sand Gnats (SAL BB)

Savannah Civic Center
Martin Luther King, Jr. Arena
PO Box 726
Liberty at Montgomery
Savannah, GA 31401
T: (912) 651-6550
F: (912) 651-6552
Seating: 6,500 (Sports events)

Hawaii

Honolulu

Aloha Stadium
PO Box 30666
99-500 Salt Lake Blvd.
Aiea, HI 96701
T: (808) 486-9555
F: (808) 486-9520
Seating: 50,000
Sports Use: Univ. of Hawaii FB,
NFL Pro Bowl

Neal S. Blaisdell Center
777 Ward Avenue
Honolulu, HI 96814
T: (808) 527-5400
F: (808) 527-5499
Seating: 8,700 (Sports events)
Sports Use: U. Hawaii Rainbows

Idaho

Boise

Bank of America Center
245 S. Capitol Blvd.
Boise, ID 83702
T: (208) 424-2200
F: (208) 424-2222
Seating: 5,000
Sports Use: ID Steelheads

Boise State University Pavilion
1400 Bronco Lane
Boise, ID 83725
T: (208) 385-1600
F: (208) 385-1998
Seating: 12,300 (Basketball)
Sports Use: BSU Broncos sports

Moscow

University of Idaho Kibble ASUI Activity Center
Room 107
Moscow, ID 83844
T: (208) 885-7928
F: (208) 885-0562
Seating: 10,000 (Sports events)

Nampa

Idaho Center
16200 Can-Ada Road
Nampa, ID 83687
T: (208) 468-1000
F: (208) 442-3312
Seating: 12,000
Sports Use: Snake River Stampede Pro Rodeo

Pocatello

Idaho State University Holt Arena
550 Memorial Drive
Pocatello, ID 83209
T: (208) 236-2831
F: (208) 236-4089
Seating: 11,736 (8,000 Bskb)

Illinois

Chicago

Comiskey Park
333 West 35th Street
Chicago, IL 60616
T: (312) 793-1991
F: (312) 747-1975
Seating: 44,282
Sports Use: White Sox (MLB)

Soldier Field
425 E. McFetridge Drive
Chicago, IL 60605
T: (312) 747-1285
F: (312) 747-6694
Seating: 66,950
Sports Use: Bears (NFL), Fire (MLS),

United Center
1901 W. Madison Street
Chicago, IL 60616
T: (312) 455-4500
F: (312) 451-5519
Seating: 24,500 (hockey)
    20,800 (basketball)
Sports Use: Blackhawks (NHL), Chicago Bulls (NBA)

Wrigley Field
1060 W. Addison Street
Chicago, IL 60613
T: (312) 404-2827
F: (312) 404-4129
Seating: 39,012
Sports Use: Chicago Cubs (MLB)

Moline

The Mark of the Quad Cities
1201 River Drive
Moline, IL 61265
T: (309) 764-2001
F: (309) 764-6363
Seating: 10,500
Sports Use: Quad City Mallards (UHL), Thunder (CBA), Steemwheelers (AFL2)

Peoria

Peoria Civic Center
201 SW Jefferson Street
Peoria, IL 61602
T: (309) 673-8900
F: (309) 673-9223
Seating: 9,200 (hockey)
    10,400 (basketball)
Sports Use: Rivermen (ECHL), Pirates (AFL2), Bradley University

Rockford

MetroCentre
PO Box 437
300 Elm Street
Rockford, IL 61105
T: (815) 968-5600
F: (815) 968-5451
Seating: 10,000
Sports Use: Lightning (CBA), Icehogs (UHL)

Rosemont

Rosemont Horizon
6920 N. Mannheim Road
Rosemont, IL 60018
T: (847) 635-6601
F: (847) 635-6606
Seating: 17,500
Sports Use: Chicago Wolves (AHL), DePaul University Bskb.

Indianapolis

Conseco Fieldhouse
125 S. Pennsylvania St.
Indianapolis, IN 46205
T: (317) 917-2500
F: (317) 917-2599
www.consecofieldhouse.com
Seating: 19,000
Sports Use: Pacers (NBA), Fever (WNBA), Ice (CHL)

RCA Hoosier Dome
100 S. Capitol Avenue
Indianapolis, IN 46225
T: (317) 262-3410
F: (317) 262-3685
Seating: 60,500
Sports Use: Colts (NFL)

Notre Dame

University of Notre Dame
Joyce Ath. & Convocation Center
Notre Dame, IN 46556
T: (219) 631-5030
F: (219) 631-8596
Seating: 12,400
Notre Dame Stadium
Seating: 60,000

Iowa

Ames

Iowa State University
Ames, IA 50011
T: (515) 294-3347
F: (515) 294-3349
Hilton Coliseum
Seating: 14,000 (Bskb)
Cyclone Stadium
Seating: 53,000

Des Moines

Veterans Memorial Auditorium
833 Fifth Avenue
Des Moines, IA 50309
T: (515) 242-2946
F: (515) 242-2988
Seating: 11,700
Sports Use: IA Barnstormers (AFL)

Iowa City

University of Iowa
Carver Arena
Carver Hawkeye Arena
Iowa City, IA 52242
T: (319) 335-9410
F: (319) 351-6906
Seating: 16,000
Sports Use: IA Hawkeyes Sports

Sioux City

Sioux City Auditorium
401 Gordon Drive
Sioux City, IA 51102
T: (712) 279-4850
F: (712) 279-4903
Seating: 4,650
Sports Use: Musketeers (USHL), Attack (NIFL)

Kansas

Topeka

**Kansas Expocentre
Landon Arena**
One Expocentre Drive
Topeka, KS 66612
T: (785) 235-1986
F: (785) 235-2967
Seating: 7,400 (Sports Events)
Sports Use: Scare Crows (USHL),
Knights (NIFL)

Wichita

Kansas Coliseum
PO Box 9112
1229 E. 85th N.
Valley Center, KS 67147
T: (316) 755-1423
F: (316) 755-2869
Seating: 10,000
Sports Use: Thunder (CHL),
 Warlords (IFL)

Kentucky

Lexington

Rupp Arena
430 W. Vine Street
Lexington, KY 40507
T: (606) 233-4567
F: (606) 233-2718
Seating: 21,000
Sports Use: Univ. of KY Bskb

Louisville

**Kentucky Fair & Expo Center/
Freedom Hall Coliseum**
PO Box 37130
937 Phillips Lane
Louisville, KY 40209
T: (502) 367-5000
F: (502) 367-5139
Seating: 16,000
Sports Use:
Cardinal Stadium
Seating: 31,600
Sports Use: Redbirds (AABB),
U. of Louisville Football

Louisiana

Alexandria

Rapides Parrish Coliseum
5600 Coliseum Blvd.
Alexandria, LA 71303
T: (318) 484-2800
Seating: 6,500
Sports Use: Louisiana Rangers
(NIFL)

Baton Rouge

**LSU-Pete Maravich Assembly
Center**
LSU Campus
PO Box 25095
Baton Rouge, LA 70894
T: (504) 388-6606
F: (504) 388-1861
Seating: 16,500
Sports Use: LSU

Riverside Centroplex
275 S. River Road
Baton Rouge, LA 70802
T: (504) 389-3030
F: (504) 389-4954
Seating: 12,800
Sports Use: Kingfish (ECHL)

Lafayette

Cajundome
444 Cajundome Blvd.
Lafayette, LA 70506
T: (318) 265-2100
F: (318) 265-2311
Seating: 12,000 (Hockey)
Sports Use: LA IceGators (ECHL)

Lake Charles

Lake Charles Civic Center
900 Lakeshore Drive
Lake Charles, LA 70602
T: (318) 491-1256
F: (318) 491-1534
Seating: 6,000 (Hockey)
Sports Use:

Monroe

Monroe Civic Center
401 Lea Joyner Mem. Expwy.
Monroe, LA 71201
T: (318) 329-2225
F: (318) 329-2548
Seating: 6,260 (Sports events)
Sports Use: Moccasins

New Orleans

Louisiana Superdome
PO Box 52439, Sugar Bowl Dr.
New Orleans, LA 70112
T: (504) 587-3663
F: (504) 587-3840
Seating: 72,968
Sports Use: Saints (NFL),
Tulane University, NCAA
Sugar Bowl Game

Shreveport

Hirsch Memorial Coliseum
Louisiana State Fairgrounds
3701 Hudson Street
Shreveport, LA 71109
T: (318) 635-1361
F: (318) 631-4909
Seating: 8,290 (Hockey)
Sports Use: Mudbugs (CHL),
Bombers (NIFL)

Maine

Lewiston

Central Maine Civic Center
190 Birch Street
Lewiston, ME 04240
T: (207) 783-2009
F: (207) 783-3347
Seating: 6,200

Portland

Cumberland Co. Civic Center
One Civic Center Square
Portland, ME 04101
T: (207) 775-3481
F: (207) 828-8344
Seating: 9,150
Sports Use: Pirates (AHL)

Maryland

Baltimore Arena
201 W. Baltimore Street
Baltimore, MD 21201
T: (410) 347-2020
F: (410) 347-2042
Seating: 14,000
Sports Use: Blast (MISL)

Oriole Park at Camden Yards
333 W. Camden Street
Suite 500
Baltimore, MD 21201
T: (410) 333-1560
F: (410) 333-1888
Seating: 48,445
Sports Use: Orioles (MLB)

PSINet Stadium
1101 Russell Street
Baltimore, MD 21230
T: (410) 230-8000
F: (410) 230-8145
Seating: 55,000
Sports use: Ravens (NFL)

Landover

US Air Arena
1 Harry S. Truman Drive
Landover, MD 20785
T: (301) 350-3400
F: (301) 808-3005
Seating: 19,000
Sports Use: Georgetown U. Bskb.,
Washington Power (NLL)

Jack Kent Cooke Stadium
Raljon Road
Landover, MD 20785
T: (301) 772-8800
F: (301) 772-8529
Seating: 78,600
Sports Use: Washington Redskins (NFL)

Massachusetts

Boston

Fleet Center
150 Causeway Street
Boston, MA 02114
T: (617) 227-3206
F: (617) 227-8403
Seating: 19,600
Sports Use: Bruins (NHL),
Celtics (NBA)

Foxboro

Gillette Stadium
Route 1
Foxboro, MA 02035
T: (508) 543-8200
F: (508) 543-1409
Seating: 68,000
Sports Use: Patriots (NFL),
Revolution (MLS)

Springfield

Springfield Civic Center
1277 Main Street
Springfield, MA 01103
T: (413) 787-6610
F: (413) 787-6645
Seating: 8,900 (Hockey)
Sports Use: Falcons (AHL)

Worcester

Worcester Centrum
50 Foster Street
Worcester, MA 01608
T: (508) 755-6800
F: (508) 754-9972
Seating: 12,000 (Hockey)
Sports Use: Ice Cats (AHL)

Michigan

Auburn Hills

The Palace of Auburn Hills
2 Championship Drive
Auburn Hills, MI 48326
T: (248) 377-8222
F: (248) 377-2534
Seating: 21,454 (Basketball)
Sports Use: Pistons (NBA),
Shock (WNBA), FURY (AFL)

Detroit

Ford Field
2001 St. Antoine
Detroit, MI 48226
T: (313)
F: (313)
Seating: 65,000
Sports Use: Lions (NFL)

Joe Louis Arena/Cobo Arena
600 Civic Center Drive
Detroit, MI 48226
T: (313) 396-7600
F: (313) 396-7994
Seating: 19,275 (Joe Louis), 9,500
(Cobo), Sports Use: Red Wings
(NHL),
Rockers (MISL)

Comerica Park
2100 Woodward Avenue
Detroit, MI 48201
T: (313) 962-4000
Seating: 48,000
Sports Use: Detroit Tigers

Flint

I.M.A. Sports Arena
3501 Lapeer Road
Flint, MI 48503
T: (810) 744-0580
F: (810) 744-2906
Seating: 4,025
Sports Use: Generals (UHL)

Grand Rapids

Van Andel Arena
245 Monroe NW
Grand Rapids, MI 49503
T: (616) 456-3922
F: (616) 456-3995
Seating: 12,000
Sports Use: Griffins (AHL),
Rampage (AFL)

Kalamazoo

Wings Stadium
3600 Van Rick Drive
Kalamazoo, MI 49002
T: (616) 345-1125
F: (616) 345-6452
Seating: 5,100 (Hockey)
Sports Use: Mich. K-Wings (UHL)

Muskegon

Walker Arena
955 Fourth Street
Muskegon, MI 49440
T: (616) 726-2939
F: (616-726-4620
Seating: 5,178
Sports Use: Muskegon Fury (UHL)

Pontiac

Pontiac Silverdome
1200 Featherstone Road
Pontiac, MI 48342
T: (248) 858-7358
F: (248) 456-1691
Seating: 80,300
Sports Use:

Port Huron

McMorran Place
701 McMorran Place
Port Huron, MI 48060
T: (810) 985-6166
F: (810) 985-3357
Seating: 4,500
Sports Use: Border Cats (UHL)

Saginaw Civic Center
Wendler Arena
303 Johnson Street
Saginaw, MI 48607
T: (517) 759-1320
F: (517) 759-1322
Seating: 4,700
Sports Use:

Minnesota

Minneapolis

Hubert H. Humphrey Metrodome
900 S. Fifth Street
Minneapolis, MN 55415
T: (612) 332-0386
F: (612) 332-8334
Seating: 63,000
Sports Use: Twins (MLB),
Vikings (NFL), U. MN Gophers FB

Target Center
600 First Street
Minneapolis, MN 55403
T: (612) 673-1300
F: (612) 673-1370
Seating: 17,500
Sports Use: Timberwolves (NBA),
Lynx (WNBA)

Saint Paul

St. Paul Civic Center
143 W. Fourth Street
St. Paull, MN 55102
T: (651) 224-7361
F: (651) 224-1142
Seating: 16,000
Sports Use: Minnesota Wild (NHL)

Mississippi

Biloxi

Mississippi Coast Coliseum
PO Box 4676
2350 Beach Blvd.
Biloxi, MS 39531
T: (228) 388-8010
F: (228) 385-2412
Seating: 11,500
Sports Use: SeaWolves (ECHL),
Firedogs (NIFL)

Jackson

Mississippi Coliseum
1207 Mississippi Street
Jackson, MS 39202
T: (601) 961-4000
F: (601) 354-6545
www.mdac.state.ms.us/fairgrounds
Seating: 6,886
Sports Use: Bandits (ECHL)

Tupelo

Tupelo Coliseum
375 E. Main Street
Tupelo, MS 38801
T: (601) 841-6573
F: (601) 841-6413
Seating: 8,500 (sports events)
Sports Use: T-Rex (AWHL)

Missouri

Kansas City

Kemper Arena
1800 Genessee
Kansas City, MO 64102
T: (816) 274-6222
F: (816) 274-0306
Seating: 17,500
Sports Use: Comets (MISL),

Arrowhead Stadium
1 Arrowhead Drive
Kansas City, MO 64129
T: (816)
F: (816) 922-4287
Seating: 78,000
Sports Use: Chiefs (NFL),
Wizards (MLS)

Kauffman Stadium
PO Box 419969
One Royals Way
Kansas City, MO 64141
T: (816) 921-2200
F: (816) 924-0347
Seating: 40,625
Sports Use: KC Royals (MLB)

St. Charles

Family Arena
2002 Arena Pkwy.
St. Charles, MO 63301
T: (636) 896-4200
F (636) 896-4205
Seating: 10,000
Sports Use: River Otters (UHL)

St. Louis

Busch Stadium
300 Stadium Plaza
St. Louis, MO 63102
T: (314) 241-3900
F: (314) 982-7890
Seating: 56,250
Sports Use: Cardinals (MLB)

Kiel Center
1401 Clark Avenue
St. Louis, MO 63103
T: (314) 622-5400
F: (314) 622-5410
Seating: 18,500
Sports Use: Blues (NHL),
Steamers (MISL), Stampede (AFL)

Transworld Dome
701 Convention Center
St. Louis, MO 63101
T: (314) 342-5036
F: (314) 342-5040
Seating: 70,000
Sports Use: St. Louis Rams (NFL)

Montana

Billings

Metrapark Arena
308 Sixth Avenue N.
Billings, MT 59101
T: (406) 256-2400
F: (406) 2256-2479
Seating: 8,000
Sports Use: Bulls (AWHL),
Thunder Bolts (NIFL)

Butte

Silver Bow Civic Arena
1340 Harrison Avenue
Butte, MT 59701
T: (406) 723-3055
F: (406) 723-9689
Seating: 5,100 (Hockey)
Sports Use: Fighting Irish (AWHL)

Great Falls

Four Seasons Arena
400 Third Street NW
Great Falls, MT 59404
T: (406) 727-8900
F: (406) 452-8955
Seating: 4,700 (Hockey)
Sports Use: Pro Rodeo,
Americans (AWHL)

Nebraska

Lincoln

Bob Devaney Sports Center
University of Nebraska
Lincoln, NE 68588
T: (402) 472-1132
F: (402) 472-8832
Seating: 13,930
Sports Use: U. NE Bskb.

State Fair Colliseum
1800 State Fair Park Blvd.
Llincoln, NE 68501
T: (402) 473-4107
F: (402) 473-4114
Seating: 2,700
Sports Use: Stars (USHL),
Lightning (NIFL)

Omaha

AK-Sar-Ben Coliseum
6800 Mercy Road, Suite 100
Omaha, NE 68106
T: (402) 444-4000
F: (402) 444-3742
Seating: 8,000
Sports Use: Lancers (USHL),
Beef (NIFL)

Nevada

Las Vegas

Cashman Field
850 Las Vegas Blvd. N
Las Vegas, NV 89101
F: (702) 386-7100
F: (702) 386-7126
Seating: 9,300
Sports Use: LV   (PCL-AAA BB)

MGM Grand Garden Arena
3799 Las Vegas Blvd. S
Las Vegas, NV 89019
T: (702) 891-7800
F: (702) 891-7831
Seating: 15,000
Sports Use: Boxing, Basketball,
Hockey Events

Sam Boyd Stadium
4505 Maryland Parkway
Las Vegas, NV 89154
T: (702) 895-3727
F: (702) 895-1099
Seating: 42,500
Sports Use: UNLV Rebels FB,
NCAA Las Vegas Bowl

Thomas & Mack Center
4505 S. Maryland Pkwy
Las Vegas, NV 89154
T: (702) 895-3761
F: (702) 895-1099
Seating: 18,500
Sports Use: UNLV Rebels Bskb

Reno

Reno-Sparks Convention Center
4590 S. Virginia Avenue
Reno, NV 89502
T: (775) 827-7622
F: (775) 827-7686
Seating: 5,000

Lawlor Events Center
University of Nevada
1500 N. Virginia Street
Reno, NV 89557
T: (775) 784-4659
F: (775) 784-4428
Seating: 12,400
Sports Use: UNR Sports

New Jersey

East Rutherford

Giants Stadium
50 State Route 120
East Rutherford, NJ 07073
T: (201) 460-4204
F: (201) 460-4294
Seating: 76,891
Sports Use: Giants, Jets (NFL),
Metrostars (MLS), Rutgers U. FB

**Continental Airlines
Meadowlands Arena**
50 State Route 120
East Rutherford, NJ 07073
T: (201) 460-4296
F: (201) 460-4294
Seating: 20,000
Sports Use: Devils (NHL),
Nets (NBA), Red Dogs (AFL),
NJ Storm (NLL lacrosse)

Trenton

Soverign Bank Arena
550 S. Broad Street
Trenton, NJ 08611
T: (609) 656-3200
www.soverignbank-arena.com
E: mail@soverignbankarena.com
Seating: 7,900
Sports Use: Titans (ECHL),

New Mexico

Albuquerque Sports Stadium
1340 University Blvd. SE
Albuquerque, NM 87102
T: (505) 768-3520
F: (505) 768-2846
Seating: 10,510
Sports Use:

**Tingley Coliseum
State Fairgrounds**
PO Box 8546
San Pedro & Central Avenue
Albuquerque, NM 87198
T: (505) 265-1791
F: (505) 266-7784
Seating: 10,200
Sports Use: NM Scorpions (CHL)

University of New Mexico Arena
Athletics
1414 University Blvd, SE
Albuquerque, NM 87131
T: (505) 277-4800
F: (505) 277-011142
Seating: 18,100
University Stadium
Seating: 30,000

Las Cruces

Pan American Center
New Mexico State University
PO Box 30001
Las Cruces, NM 88003
T: (505) 646-4413
F: (505) 646-3605
Seating: 13,007
Aggie Memorial Stadium
Seating: 45,000

New York

Albany

Pepsi Arena
51 S. Pearl Street
Albany, NY 12207
T: (518) 487-2000
F: (518) 487-2020
Seating: 17,500
Sports Use: Firebirds (AFL2),
River Rats (AHL)

Binghamton

**Broom County Veterans
Memorial Arena**
One Stuart Street
Binghamton, NY 13901
T: (607) 778-1528
F: (607) 778-6041
Seating: 4,840 (Hockey)
Sports Use: Senators (AHL)

Bronx

Yankee Stadium
161st Street & River Avenue
Bronx, NY 10451
T: (718) 293-4300
F: (718) 293-8431
Seating: 57,545
Sports Use: Yankees (MLB)

Buffalo

HSBC Arena
One Seymour H. Knox III Plaza
Buffalo, NY 14203
T: (716) 855-4100
F: (716) 855-4176
Seating: 19,500
Sports Use: Sabres (NHL),
Bandits (NLL)

North AmeriCare Pilot Field
263 Washington Street
Buffalo, NY 14203
T: (716) 851-5663
F: (716) 851-4269
Seating: 21,500
Sports Use: Bisons (IL-AAA BB)

Flushing

USTA Arthur Ashe Stadium
Tennis Center
Flushing Meadow-Corona Park
Flushing, NY 11368
T: (718) 760-6200
F: (718) 592-9488
Seating: 20,000
Sports Use: U.S. Open Tennis

William A. Shea Stadium
123-01 Roosevelt Avenue
Flushing, NY 11368
T: (718) 507-6387
F: (718) 565-4382
Seating: 55,600
Sports Use: NY Mets (MLB)

Glens Falls

Glens Falls Civic Center
One Civic Center Plaza
Glens Falls, NY 12801
T: (518) 798-0366
F: (518) 798-0816
Seating: 8,000
Sports Use: Adirondack
Icehawks (UHL)

Lake Placid

Olympic Center
216 Main Street
Lake Placid, NY 12946
T: (518) 523-1655
F: (518) 523-9275
Seating: 8,000 (Hockey)
Sports Use: Basketball, Boxing,
Hockey Tournaments

New York City

Madison Square Garden
2 Pennsylvania Plaza
New York, NY 10001
T: (212) 465-6000
F: (212) 465-6789
Seating: 19,940
Sports Use: Knicks (NBA),
Rangers (NHL), Liberty (WNBA)

Orchard Park

Rich Stadium
1 Bills Drive
Orchard Park, NY 14127
T: (716) 648-1800
F: (716) 649-6446
Seating: 80,290
Sports Use: Buffalo Bills (NFL)

Rochester

Frontier Field
333 N. Plymouth Ave.
Rochester, NY 14608
T: (716) 262-2009
F: (716) 262-3453
Seating: 15,000
Sports Use: Raging Rhinos
(A-League Soccer), Red Wings
(IL-AAA Baseball), Rattlers (MLL)

Rochester War Memorial
100 Exchange Blvd.
Rochester, NY 14614
T: (716) 546-2030
F: (716) 546-3775
Seating: 9,337
Sports Use: Americans (AHL),
Knighthawks (NLL)

Syracuse

Onondaga Co. War Memorial
800 S. State Street
Syracuse, NY 133202
T: (315) 435-8000
F: (315) 435-8099
Seating: 6,200
Sports Use: Syracuse Crunch (AHL), Smash (NLL)

Carrier Dome
900 Irving Avenue
Syracuse University
Syracuse, NY 13244
T: (315) 443-4634
F: (315) 443-3724
Seating: 50,000
Sports Use: Syracuse

Uniondale

Nassau Veterans Memorial Coliseum
1255 Hempstead Turnpike
Uniondale, NY 11553
T: (516) 794-9303
F: (516) 794-9389
Seating: 17,000
Sports Use: Islanders (NHL), Saints (NLL)

Utica

Utica Memorial Auditorium
400 Oriskany Street W
Utica, NY 13502
T: (315) 738-0164
F: (315) 738-0198
Seating: 6,000
Sports Use:

North Carolina

Chapel Hill

Dean E. Smith Center
University of North Carolina
PO Box 2126
Bowles Drive
Chapel Hill, NC 27514
T: (919) 962-7777
F: (919) 966-3173
Seating: 21,572
Sports Use: UNC Tarheels

Charlotte

Charlotte Coliseum
100 Paul Buck Blvd.
Charlotte, NC 28266
T: (704) 357-4700
F: (704) 357-4757
Seating: 23,698
Sports Use:
Sting (WNBA)

Ericsson Stadium
800 S. Mint Street
Charlotte, NC 28202
T: (704) 358-7407
F: (704) 358-7619
Seating: 72,000
Sports Use: Carolina Panthers (NFL)

Durham Athletic Park
101 City Hall Plaza
Durham, NC 27701
T: (919) 560- 4355
F: (919) 560-4205
Seating: 5,000
Sports Use: Bulls (IL-AAA BB)

Fayetteville

The Crown Coliseum
PO Box 64549
1960 Coliseum Drive
Fayetteville, NC 28306
T: (910) 323-5088
F: (910) 323-0489
Seating 11,000 (Coliseum)
6,000 (Arena)
Sports Use: Patriots (NBDL)

Greensboro

Greensboro Coliseum
PO Box 5447
1921 W. Lee Street
Greensboro, NC 27403
T: (910) 373-7400
F: (910) 373-2170
Seating: 23,300
Sports Use: Prowlers (AFL2), ACC Basketball

Raleigh

Dorton Arena
1025 Blue Ridge Road
Raleigh, NC 27607
T: (919) 733-7400
F: (919) 733-5079
Seating: 7,000
Sports Use: Ice Caps (ECHL),
Cobras (AFL)

Reynolds Coliseum
North Carolina State University
103 Dunn Avenue
Raleigh, NC 27695
T: (919) 515-3050
F: (919) 515-1161
Seating: 11,400
Carter Finley Stadium
49,000
Sports Use: NCSU ACC Sports

Winston Salem

**Lawrence Joel Veterans
Memorial Coliseum Complex**
2825 University Parkway
Winston-Salem, NC 27105
T: (336) 727-2900
F: (336) 727-2922
Seating: 14,400
Sports Use: Icehawks (UHL),
Wake Forest Univ., W-S State Univ.

North Dakota

Bismarck Civic Center
PO Box 1075
601 E. Sweet Avenue
Bismarck, ND 58502
T: (701) 222-6487
F: (701) 222-6599
Seating: 9,100
Sports Use: Dakota Wizard (CBA),
Blaze (NIFL)

Fargo Dome
1800 N. University Drive
Fargo, ND 58102
T: (701) 298-2627
F: (701) 237-0987
Seating: 12,000
Sports Use: Beez (CBA),
Ice Sharks (USHL), Freeze (NIFL)

Minot

All Seasons Arena
2005 Burdick Expressway E.
Minot, ND 58701
T: (701) 857-7620
F: (701) 838-4168
Seating: 3,900
Sport Use: Muskies (AWHL)

Ohio

Cincinnati

Cincinnati Gardens
2250 Seymour Ave
Cincinnati, OH 45212
T: (513) 631-7793
F: (513) 631-2666
Seating: 10,830
Sports Use: Mighty Ducks (AHL)

The Crown Riverfront Coliseum
100 Broadway
Cincinnati, OH 45202
T: (513) 241-1818
F: (513) 333-3088
Seating: 18,000
Sports Use: Cyclones (ECHL)

Great American Ballpark
100 Main Street
Cincinnati, OH 45202
T: (513) 765-7000
F: (513) 765-7180
Seating: 60,000
Sports Use: Reds (MLB)

Paul Brown Stadium
One Paul Brown Way
Cincinnati, OH 45202
T: (513) 621-3550
F: (513) 621-3570
Seating: 63,341
Sports Use: Bengals (NFL)

Cleveland

Cleveland Browns Stadium
1085 W. Third Street
Cleveland, OH 44114
T: (440) 891-5001
F: (440) 891-5054
Seating: 73,200
Sports Use: Browns (NFL)

Gund Arena
100 Gateway Plaza
Cleveland, OH 44115
T: (440) 420-2000
F: (440) 240-2101
Seating: 21,000
Sports Use: Cavaliers (NBA),
Lumberjacks (IHL), Rockers
(WNBA), Barons (AHL)

Jacobs Field
2401 Ontario Street
Cleveland, OH 44115
T: (440) 420-4200
F:(440) 420-4550
Seating: 42,865
Sports Use: Indians (MLB)

Columbus

Nationwide Arena
200 W. Nationwide Blvd.
Columbus, OH 43215
T: (614) 246-2000
F:
Seating: 19,500
Sports Use: Blue Jackets (NHL),
Landsharks (NLL)

Ohio Stadium
410 Woody Hayes Drive
Columbus, OH 43210
T: (614) 292-7572
F: (614) 292-0506
Seating: 92,000
Sports Use: Ohio State Univ.
Buckeyes FB, Crew Stadium

Dayton

Hara Arena
1001 Shiloh Springs Road
Dayton, OH 45415
T: (513) 278-4776
F: (513) 278-4633
Seating 5,000
Sports Use: Skyhawks (NIFL)

Erin J. Nutter Center
3640 Colonel Glen Hwy.
Dayton, OH 45435
T: (513) 873-3498
F: (513) 873-2060
Seating: 12,000
Sports Use: Bombers (ECHL),
Wright State University

Toledo Sports Arena
One Main Street
Toledo, OH 43605
T: (419) 698-1598
F: (419) 693-3299
Seating: 5,800
Sports Use: Storm (ECHL)

Oklahoma

Oklahoma City

Myriad Gardens Arena
One Myriad Gardens
Oklahoma City, OK 73102
T: (405) 232-8871
F: (405) 236-2320
Seating: 14,000
Sports Use: Blazers (CHL),
Wranglers (AFL)

State Fair Arena
State Fair Park
PO Box 74943
Oklahoma City, OK 73147
T: (405) 948-6704
F: (405) 948-6821
Seating: 12,000
Sports Use: Blazers (CHL)

Tulsa Convention Center Arena
100 Civic Center Drive
Tulsa, OK 74103
T: (918) 596-7177
F: (918) 596-7155
Seating: 9,138
Sports Use: Oilers (CHL),
Talons (AFL2)

Oregon

Rose Garden
One Center Court, Suite 200
Portland, OR 97227
T: (503) 235-8771
F: (503) 234-4503
Seating: 20,300
Sports Use: Trail Blazers (NBA),
Memorial Coliseum
Seating: 13,000 Winter Hawks (WHL)

PGE Park
1844 SW Morrison
Portland, OR 97205
Seating: 31,000
Sports Use: Portland Timbers Soccer

Pennsylvania

Erie Civic Center
809 French Street
Erie, PA 16501
T: (814) 453-7117
F: (814) 455-9931
Seating: 7,500
Sports Use: Erie Otters (OHL),
Invaders (NIFL)

Harrisburg

Farm Show Arena
22301 N. Cameron Street
Harrisburg, PA 17110
T: (717) 787-5373
F: (717) 783-8710
Seating: 7,600
Sports Use: Heat (MISL)

Hershey Park Arena/Stadium
100 W. Hershey Park Drive
Hershey, PA 17033
T: (717) 534-3348
F: (717) 534-3113
7,500 (Arena), 16,000 (stadium)

Giant Center
Hersheypark Drive
Hershey, PA 17033
Seating: 10.500
Sports Use: Hershey Bears (AHL)

Johnstown

Cambria Co. War Memorial Arena
326 Napoleon Street
Johnstown, PA 15901
T: (814) 536-5156
F: (814) 536-3670
Seating: 4,000 (Permanent)
Sports Use: Chiefs (ECHL),
Jackals (NIFL)

Philadelphia

First Union Center
3601 S. Broad Street
Philadelphia, PA 19148
T: (215) 336-3600
F: (215) 389-9505
Seating: 20,000
Sports Use: Flyers (NHL),
76ers (NBA), Wings (NLL)

First Union Spectrum
3601 S. Broad Street
Philadelphia, PA 19148
T: (215) 336-3600
F: (215) 389-9579
Seating: 19,000
Sports Use: Kixx (MISL),
Phantoms (AHL)

Lincoln Field
Seating: 65,000
New home for Eagles (NFL)

Veterans Stadium
Broad Street & Pattison Ave.
Philadelphia, PA 19148
T: (215) 685-1500
F: (215) 463-2833
Seating: 66,300
Sports Use: Phillies (MLB)

Pittsburgh

Mellon Civic Arena
300 Auditorium Place
Pittsburgh, PA 15219
T: (412) 642-1800
F: (412) 642-1295
Seating: 17,000
Sports Use: Penguins (NHL)

Heinz Field
100 Art Rooney Avenue
Pittsburgh, PA 15212
T: (412) 432-7800
F: (412) 432-7878
Seating: 64,450
Sports Use: Steelers (NFL)

PNC Stadium
115 Federal Street
Pittsburgh, PA 15212
T: (412) 321-0650
F: (412) 321-1436
Seating: 60,000
Sports Use: Pirates (MLB)

University Park

Bryce Jordan Center
Pennsylvania State University
University Park, PA 16802
T: (814) 863-5500
F: (814) 863-5705
Seating: 19,000
Sports Use: PSU Sports

Wilkes-Barre

NE Pennsylvania Civic Arena
255 Highland Park Ave.
Wilkes-Barre, PA 18701
T: (570) 970-7600
F:
Seating: 8,000
Sports Use: Penquins (AHL)

Rhode Island

Providence Civic Center
One LaSalle Square
Providence, RI 02903
T: (401) 331-0700
F: (401) 751-6792
Seating: 14,500
Sports Use: Prov. Bruins (AHL), Providence College Basketball

South Carolina

Charleston

Clemson Memorial Stadium
Perimeter Road
Clemson, SC 29634
T: (864) 656-5815
F: (864) 656-5833
Seating: 81,473
Sports Use: Clemson University

Florence Civic Center
PO Box 6423
One Civic Center Plaza
Florence, SC 29502
T: (803) 679-9417
F: (803) 679-9429
Seating: 8,000 (Hockey)
Sports Use: Pee Dee Pride (ECHL),

Greenville

Bi-Lo Center
650 N. Academy Street
Greenville, SC 29601
T: (864) 241-3800
F: (864) 241-0409
Seating: 16,000
Sports Use: Grrowl (ECHL), Rhinos (AFL2), Groove (NBDL)

North Charleston Coliseum
5001 Coliseum Drive
North Charleston, SC 29418
T: (843) 529-5050
F: (843) 529-5010
Seating: 12,500
Sports Use: Stingrays (ECHL), Lowgators (NBDL)

South Dakota

Rushmore Plaza Civic Center
444 Mt. Rushmore Road N.
Rapid City, SD 57701
T: (605) 394-4115
F: (605) 394-4119
Seating: 10,000
Sports Use: Machine (NIFL)

Sioux Falls Arena
1201 West End Avenue N.
Sioux Falls, SD 57104
T: (605) 339-7288
F: (605) 338-1463
Seating: 8,000
Sports Use: Sky Force (CBA), Stampede (USHL), Cobras (NIFL)

Tennessee

Knoxville Civic Coliseum
500 E. Church Avenue
Knoxville, TN 37901
T: (423) 544-5399
F: (423) 544-5386
Seating: 7,250
Sports Use: Ice Bears (ACHL)

Memphis

Liberty Bowl
335 S. Hollywood St.
Memphis, TN 38104
T: (901) 278-4747
F: (901) 276-2756
Seating: 62,300
Sports Use: Univ. of Memphis FB, NCAA Liberty Bowl

Mid-South Coliseum
996 Early Maxwell Blvd.
Memphis, TN 38104
T: (901) 274-3982
F: (901) 276-8653
Seating: 12,000
Sports Use: River Kings (CHL)

The Pyramid
One Auction Avenue
Memphis, TN 38105
T: (901) 521-9675
F: (901) 528-0153
Seating: 22,500
Sports Use: Memphis Grizzlies (NBA),
U. of Memphis Bskb.

Nashville

Adelphia Coliseum
One Titans Way
Nashville, TN 37213
T: (615) 565-4305
F: (615) 565-4444
Seating: 67,000
Sports Use: TN Titans (NFL)

Nashville Arena
501 Broadway
Nashville, TN 37203
T: (615) 770-2000
F: (615) 770-2010
Seating: 20,000
Sports Use: Nashville Predators (NHL)

Nashville Municipal Auditorium
417 Fourth Avenue N.
Nashville, TN 37201
T: (615) 862-6390
F: (615) 862-6394
Seating: 7,000

Vanderbilt Stadium
Vanderbilt University
PO Box 120158
West End Avenue
Nashville, TN 37212
T: (615) 322-4727
F: (615) 343-8738
Seating: 41,000
Sports Use: Vanderbilt U. FB (SEC),
Tennessee Titans (NFL)

Texas

Amarillo Civic Center
401 S. Buchanan
Amarillo, TX 79101
T: (806) 378-4297
F: (806) 378-4234
Seating: 6,500
Sports Use: Rattlers (CHL)

The Ballpark at Arlilngton
PO Box 90111
1000 Ballpark Way
Arllington, TX 76011
T: (817) 273-5100
F: (817) 273-5264
Seating: 49,292
Sports Use: TX Rangers (MLB)

Austin

Frank Erwin Center
1701 Red River
Austin, TX 78724
T: (512) 471-7744
F: (512) 471-9652
Seating: 16,000
Sports Use: UT-Austin

Travis County Expo Center
7311 Decker Lane
Austin, TX 78724
T: (512) 473-9200
F: (512) 928-3710
Seating 6,500
Sports Use: Ice Bats (CHL)

Belton

Bell County Expo Center
PO Box 206
301 W. Loop 121
Belton, TX 76513
T: (817) 933-5353
F: (817) 933-5354
Seating: 9,076
Sports Use:

Corpus Christi

Bayfront Plaza Memorial Coliseum Arena
402 S. Shoreline Drive
Corpus Christi, TX 78469
T: (512) 884-8227
F: (512) 883-0788
Seating: 5,400
Sports Use: Ice Rays (CHL)

Dallas

Cotton Bowl
1300 Robert B. Cullum Blvd.
Dallas, TX 75315
T: (214) 670-8400
F: (214) 670-8907
Seating: 72,000
Sports Use: Dallas Burn (MLS),
SMU FB, Cotton Bowl Game

Reunion Arena
777 Sports Street
Dallas, TX 75207
T: (214) 939-2770
F: (214) 939-2872
Seating: 17,000
Sports Use: Mavericks (NBA),
Stars (NHL), Sidekicks (MISL)

El Paso

El Paso County Coliseum
4100 E. Paisano Drive
El Paso, TX 79997
T: (915) 534-4229
F: (915) 532-4048
Seating: 7,500
Sports Use: Buzzards (CHL)

Sun Bowl
UTEP Athletics
201 Baltimore
El Paso, TX 79968
T: (915) 747-5347
F: (915) 747-5162
Seating: 51,000
Sports Use: UTEP Miners FB,
NCAA Sun Bowl Game

Fort Worth/Tarrant County Convention Center Arena
1111 Houston Street
Fort Worth, TX 76102
T: (817) 884-2222
F: (817) 884-2323
Seating: 11,300 (Hockey)
Sports Use: Brahmas (CHL)

Houston

Reliant Stadium
2 Reliant Park
Houston, TX 77054
T: (832) 667-2000
F: (832) 667-2188
Seating: 69,500
Sports Use: Houston Texans (NFL)

Minute Maid Field
501 Crawford Street
Houston, TX 77002
T: (713) 259-8000
F: (713) 799-9832
Seating: 42,000
Sports Use: Houston Astros (MLB)

Rice Stadium
6100 S. Main Street
Houston, TX 77251
T: (713) 527-4077
F: (713) 527-6019
Seating: 70,000
Sports Use: Rice Univ. FB

The Compaq Center
10 Greenway Plaza
Houston, TX 77046
T: (713) 627-9470
F: (713) 552-1606
Seating: 17,064
Sports Use: Rockets (NBA),
Comets (WNBA), Aeros (AHL),
Thunderbears (AFL)

Irving

Texas Stadium
2401 E. Airport Freeway
Irving, TX 75062
T: (972) 438-7676
F: (972) 438-4171
Seating: 73,855
Sports Use: Dallas Cowboys

Lubbock Municipal Coliseum
1501 Sixth Street
Lubbock, TX 79401
T: (806) 767-2241
F: (806) 762-5803
Seating: 8,200 (Basketball)
Sports Use: Cotton Kings (CHL),
Texas Tech. University

Odessa

Ector County Coliseum
PO Box 4124
42nd & Andrews Hwy.
Odessa, TX 79762
T: (915) 366-5647
F: (915) 366-5647
Seating: 5,500 (Hockey)
Sports Use: Jackalopes (CHL)

San Angelo Coliseum
500 Rio Concho Drive
San Angelo, TX 76903
T: (915) 653-9577
F: (915) 659-0900
Seating: 5,000
Sports Use: Outlaws (CHL)

San Antonio

Alamodome
100 Montana Street
San Antonio, TX 78203
T: (210) 207-3663
F: (210) 207-3646
Seating: 32,500 (Arena)
  65,000 (Stadium)
Sports Use: Spurs (NBA),
Silver Stars (WNBA)

Freeman Coliseum
PO Box 200283
3201 E. Houston Street
San Antonio, TX 78220
T: (210) 226-1177
F: (210) 226-5081
Seating: 12,000
Sports Use: Iquanas (CHL)

Waco

Heart O' Texas Coliseum
PO Box 7581
4601 Bosque Blvd.
Waco, TX 76710
T: (254) 776-1660
F: (254) 776-1667
Seating: 10,000
Sports Use:

Utah

Salt Lake City

Delta Center
301 W. South Temple
Salt Lake City, UT 84101
T: (801) 325-2000-03-23
F: (801) 325-2516
Seating: 20,400
Sports Use: Jazz (NBA)

West Valley

The East Center
3200 S. Decker Lake Drive
West Valley, UT 84119
T: (801) 988-8800
F: (801) 988-7000
Seating: 11,000
Sports Use: Grizzlies (AHL)

Virginia

Hampton Coliseum
PO Box 7309
1000 Coliseum Drive
Hampton, VA 23666
T: (757) 838-5650
F: (757) 838-2595
Seating: 12,610

Norfolk Scope
PO Box 1808
201 E. Brambleton Ave.
Norfolk, VA 23510
T: (757) 441-2764
F: (757) 441-2150
Seating: 13,500
Sports Use: Admirals (ECHL),
Nighthawks (AFL2)
Harbor Park
Seating: 12,000
Sports Use: Tides (IL-AAA BB)

Richmond Coliseum
601 E. Leigh Street
Richmond, VA 23219
T: (804) 780-4970
F: (804) 780-4606
Seating: 13,553
Sports Use: UHL Club, Speed (AFL2),
VCU Bskb

Roanoke Civic Center
PO Box 13005
710 Williamson Road
Roanoke, VA 24016
T: (540) 981-2241
F: (540) 981-2748
Seating: 11,000
Sports Use: Express (ECHL), Steam (AFL2), Dazzle (NBDL)

Salem Civic Center
PO Box 886
1001 Roanoke Blvd.
Salem, VA 24153
T: (540) 375-3004
F: (540) 375-4011
Seating: 7,400

Washington

Kennewick

Tri-Cities Coliseum
7100 W. Quinault
Kennewick, WA 99336
T: (509) 783-8824
F: ((509) 735-4699
Seating: 7,500
Sports Use: Americans (WHL)

Seattle

Key Arena at Seattle Center
305 Harrison Street
Seattle, WA 98109
T: (206) 684-7202
F: (206) 684-7342
Seating: 17,107
Sports Use: Supersonics (NBA), Thunderbirds (WHL), Storm (WNBA)
Memorial Stadium
Seating: 22,000
Sports Use: Sounders (A-League)
Seattle Center Arena
Seating: 4,500

Safeco Field
1250 First Avenue
Seattle, WA 98134
T: (206) 346-4000
Seating: 47,116
Sports Use: Mariners (MLB)

Seahawks Stadium
First Avenue
Seattle, WA 98134
Seating: 72,000
Sports Use: Seattle Seahawks (NFL

Spokane Arena
West 720 Mallon Ave.
Spokane, WA 99201
T: (509) 324-7000
F: (509) 324-7050
Seating: 12,500
Sports Use: Chiefs (WHL)

Tacoma

Cheney Stadium
2525 Bantz Blvd.
Tacoma, WA 98411
T: (253) 752-7707
F: (253) 752-7135
Seating: 10,000
Sports Use: Rainiers (PCL-BB)

Tacoma Dome
2727 E. D Street
Tacoma, WA 98421
T: (253) 272-3663
F: (253) 593-7615
Seating: 23,000
Sports Use:

Yakima Sundome
1301 S. Tenth Street
Yakima, WA 98901
T: (509) 454-3663
F: (509) 248-8093
Seating: 6,150
Sports Use: Sun kings (CBA)

West Virginia

Charleston Civic Center
200 Civic Center Drive
Charleston, WV 25301
T: (304) 345-1500
F: (304) 357-7432
Seating: 13,500

Huntington Civic Arena
1 Civic Center Plaza
Huntington, WV 25727
T: (304) 696-5990
F: (304) 696-4463
Seating: 11,000
Sports Use: Blizzard (ECHL)

Wheeling Civic Center
Two 14th Street
Wheeling, WV 26003
T: (304) 233-7000
F: (304) 233-7001
Seating: 7600
Sports Use: Nailers (ECHL)

Wisconsin

Green Bay

Brown County Memorial Arena
1901 S. Oneida Street
Green Bay, WI 54304
T: (920) 494-3403
F: (920) 494-6868
Seating:
Sports Use: Gamblers (USHL),
Bombers (NIFL)

Lambeau Field
1265 Lombardi Avenue
Green Bay, WI 54307
T: (414) 496-5700
F: (414) 496-5738
Seating: 60,000
Sports Use: Packers (NFL)

La Crosse Center
300 Harborview Plaza
La Crosse, WI 54602
T: (608) 789-7400
F: (608) 789-7444
Seating: 6,000
Sports Use: River Rats (NIFL),
U. Wisc-La Crosse Bskb.

Madison

Dane County Expo Center
1881 Expo Mall E.
Madison, WI 53713
T: (608) 267-3976
F: (608) 267-0146
Seating: 10,250
Sports Use: Kodiaks (UHL),
Mad Dogs (NIFL)

Milwaukee

Bradley Center
1001 N. Fourth Street
Milwaukee, WI 53203
T: (414) 227-0400
F: (414) 227-0797
Seating: 20,000
Sports Use: Bucks (NBA),
Admirals (AHL), Mustangs (AFL),
Wave (MISL)

Miller Park
201 S. 46th Street
Milwaukee, WI 53201
T: (414) 933-4114
F: (414) 933-7111
Seating: 56,531
Sports Use: Brewers (MLB)

Wyoming

Casper Events Center
PO Box 140
One Events Center Drive
Casper, WY 82601
T: (307) 235-8441
F: (307) 235-8445
Seating: 10,452
Sports Use: Outlaws (AWHL),
Cavalry (NIFL)

Puerto Rico

San Juan Hiram Bithorn Sports Complex
Call Box 70179
Hato Rey, PR 00936
T: (809) 781-2258
Seating: 18,000
Sports Use: National basketball
team, boxing, volleyball events

Canadian Facilities

Alberta

Calgary Olympic Saddledome
555 Saddledome Rise SE
Calgary, Alberta T2G 2W1
T: (403) 777-2177
F: (403) 777-3695
Seating: 20,000
Sports Use: Flames (NHL),
Hitmen (WHL), Roughnecks (NLL)

Edmonton

Commonwealth Stadium
11000 Stadium Road
Edmonton, Alberta T5J 2R7
T: (780) 944-7561
F: (780) 944-7545
Seating: 60,160
Sports Use: Eskimos (CFL)

Northlands Coliseum
7300 116th Avenue
Edmonton, Alberta T5J 2N5
T: (780) 471-7159
F: (780) 471-7172
Seating: 17,500
Sports Use: Oilers (NHL)

Lethbridge

Canada Games Sportsplex
2510 Scenic Drive
Lethbridge, Alberta T1J 0P6
T: (403) 329-4737
F: (403) 327-3620
Seating: 5,300
Sports Use: Hurricanes (WHL)

Medicine Hat

Medicine Hat Arena
580 First Street SE
Medicine Hat, Alberta T1A 8E6
T: (403) 529-8344
F: (403) 529-1112
Seating: 5,000
Sports Use: Tigers (WHL)
Athletic Park
Seating: 3,000
Sports Use: Blue Jays (Pioner BB)

Red Deer Centrium
4847A-19th Street
Red Deer, Alberta T4R 2N7
T: (403) 343-7800
F: (403) 341-4699
Seating: 5,850
Sports Use: Rebels (WHL)

British Columbia

Kamloops

Riverside Coliseum
300 Lorne Street
Kamloops, B.C. V2C 1W3
T: (250) 828-3487
F: (250) 372-7529
Seating: 5,000
Sports Use: Blazers (WHL)

Prince George Multiplex
2188 Ospika Blvd.
Prince George, B.C. V2N 4W5
T: (250) 561-7777
F: (250) 561-8018
Seating: 6,000
Sports Use: Cougars (WHL)

Vancouver

B. C. Place
777 Pacific Blvd.
Vancouver, B.C. V6B 4Y8
T: (604) 669-2300
F: (604) 661-3412
Seating: 60,000
Sports Use: B.C. Lions (CFL)

General Motors Place
800 Griffiths Way
Vancouver, B.C. V6B 2M1
T: (604) 899-7400
F: (604) 899-7401
Seating: 20,000
Sports Use: Canucks (NHL),
Ravens (NLL)

Manitoba

Brandon

Keystone Centre
#1, 1175-18th Street
Brandon, Manitoba R7A 7C5
T: (204) 726-3500
F: (204) 727-5552
Seating: 5,000 (hockey)
Sports Use: Wheat Kings (WHL)

Winnipeg Arena
1430 Maroons Road
Winnipeg, Manitoba R3G 0L5
T: (204) 982-5400
F: (204) 774-4332
Seating: 15,393
Sports Use: Moose (AHL),
Cyclone (IBA)
Winnipeg Stadium
Seating: 33,893
Sports Use: Blue Bombers (CFL)

New Brunswick

Fredericton

Aitken Centre
University of New Brunswick
Fredericton, N.B. E3B 5A3
T: (506) 453-5078
Seating: 5,800
Use: Canadiens (AHL), UNB

Moncton Coliseum-Agrena
377 Killam Drive
Moncton, N.B. E1C 3T1
T: (506) 857-4100
F: (506) 859-2678
Seating: 8,800, Hockey 6,800
Sports Use: Wildcats (QMJHL)

Saint John

Harbour Station
99 Station Street
Saint John, N.B. E2L 4X4
T: (506) 632-6103
F: (506) 632-6121
Seating: 7,600
Sports Use: Saint John Flame (AHL)

Newfoundland

St. John's Memorial Stadium
PO Box 908
Lake Avenue
Saint John's, Nfld. A1C 5M2
T: (709) 576-7820
F: (709) 576-8467
Seating: 5,570
Sports Use: Maple Leafs (AHL)

Nova Scotia

Halifax Metro Centre
5284 Duke Street
Halifax, Nova Scotia B2Y 2T5
T: (902) 421-8686
F: (902) 422-2922
Seating: 10,000
Sports Use: Mooseheads (QMHL)

Sydney

Centre 200
481 George Street
Sydney, Nova Scotia B1P 6R7
T: (902) 564-2200
F: (902) 539-4598
Seating: 6,300, Hockey 4,600
Sports Use: Cape Breton
Screaming Eagles (QMJHL)

Ontario

Hamilton

Copps Coliseum
101 York Blvd.
Hamilton, Ontario L8R 3L4
T: (905) 527-7900
F: (905) 527-6856
Seating: 17,500
Sports Use: Bulldogs (AHL)

Kanata

Coral Centre/Palladium
1000 Palladium Drive
Kanata, Ontario K2S 1B9
T: (613) 721-4364
F: (613) 721-8138
Seating: 18,000
Sports Use: Senators (NHL),
Rebels (NLL)

Kitchener Memorial Auditorium
400 East Avenue
Kitchener, Ontario N2H 1Z6
T: (519) 745-0303
F: (519) 741-2649
Seating: 7,200, Hockey 6,100
Sports Use: Rangers (OHL)

London Gardens Ice House
4380 Wellington Road S.
London, Ontario N6E 2Z6
T: (519) 681-0800
F: (519) 668-7291
Seating: 6,200
Sports Use: Knights (OHL)

Ottawa

Lansdowne Park
Frank Clair Stadium
1015 Bank Street
Ottawa, Ontario K1S 3W7
T: (613) 564-1485
F: (613) 564-1619
Seating: 30,000
Sports Use: Renegades (CFL)
Civic Centre
Seating: 10,000
Sports Use: 67's (OHL)

Toronto

Air Canada Centre
40 Bay Street
Toronto, Ontario M5J 2X2
T: (416) 815-5600
Seating: 22,500
Sports Use: Raptors (NBA),
Maple Leafs (NHL), Rock (NLL)

The Skydome
One Blue Jays Way, Ste 3000
Toronto, Ontario M5V 1J3
T: (416) 341-3663
F: (416) 341-3102
Seating: 53,000
Sports Use: Blue Jays (MLB),
Argonauts (CFL)

Prince Edward Island

Charlottetown

Canada Games Centre
46 Kensington Road
Charlottetown, PEI C1A 5H7
T: (902) 368-8330
F: (902) 566-7701
Seating: 4,600
Use: Abbies (Maritime JHL)

Quebe

Montreal

Molson Centre
1260 Rue de la Gauchetiere W.
Montreal, Quebec H3B 5E8
T: (514) 932-2582
F: (514) 932-9296
Seating: 21,000
Sports Use: Canadiens (NHL),
Express (NLL)

Olympic Stadium
4141 Pierre-de-Coubertin
Montreal, Quebec H1V 3N7
T: (514) 252-4602
F: (514) 252-9401
Seating: 62,000
Sports Use: Expos (MLB)

Percival Molson Memorial Stadium
McGill University
475 Pine Avenue Quest
Montreal, Quebec H2W 1S4
T: (514) 398-7005
F: (514) 398-4901
Seating: 16,000
Use: McGill U., Alouettes (CFL)

Quebec City

Colisee de Quebec
2205 Ave. du Colisee
Quebec, P.Q. G1L 4W7
T: (418) 691-7110
F: (418) 691-7478
Seating: 15,250
Sports Use: Citadelles (AHL),
Remparts (QMJHL)

Sherbrooke

Palais de Sports
360 Parc Street
Sherbrooke, Quebec J1E 2J9
T: (819) 821-5855
F: (819) 822-6062
Seating: 5,500
Sports Use: Falcons (QMJHL)

Saskatchewan

Prince Albert Comuniplex
690-32nd Street E.
Prince Albert, Sask. S6V 2W8
T: (306) 953-4848
F: (306) 953_4855
Seating: 3,100
Sports Use: Raiders (WHL)

Regina

Agridome
PO Box 167
Exhibition Park
Regina, Sask. S4P 2Z6
T: (306) 781-9200
F: (306) 525-2535
Seating: 7,400, Hockey 6,200
Sports Use: Regina Pats (WHL)

Taylor Field
PO Box 1790
8th Ave. & Cameron St.
Regina, Sask. S4P 3C8
T: (306) 777-7394
Seating: 27,600
Sports Use: Saskatchewan
Roughriders (CFL), Regina
Rams (CJFL)

Saskatoon

Saskatoon Place
3515 Thatcher Ave.
RR4, GB 260
Saskatoon, Sask. S7K 3J7
T: (306) 975-3155
F: (306) 975-2907
Seating: 13,301, Hockey 11,300
Sports Use: Blades (WHL),
Hawks (CBA)

Swift Current

Centennial Civic Centre
2001 Chaplin Street E.
Swift Current, Sask. S9H 4X6
T: (306) 778-2734
F: (306) 773-5406
Seating: 3,000
Sports Use: Broncos (WHL)

International stadium & arena facilities may be found in the International Sports Directory

Arena & Stadium Services

Allied Speciality Insurance, Inc.
10451 Gulf Blvd.
Treasure Island, FL 33706
T: (800) 237-33555
F: (813) 367-1407

American Speciality Insurance Service, Inc.
142 N. Main Street
Roanoke, IN 46783
T: (219) 672-8800
F: (219) 672-8835

American Speciality Underwriters, Inc.
91 Montvale Ave.
Stoneham, MA 02180
T: (617) 438-2220
F: (617) 438-3120

Aramark Leisure Services
1101 Market Street
Philadelphia, PA 19107
T: (215) 238-3000
F: (215) 238-4099
P: Joe Pistone

Deloitte & Touche LLP
Two Hilton Court
Parsippany, NJ 07054
T: (973) 631-6821
F: (973) 631-6704
Dir: Stewart Rog

K&K Insurance Group, Inc.
1712 Magnavox Way
PO Box 2338
Fort Wayne, IN 46801
T: (800) 440-5580
F: (219) 459-5866
Dir Mkt: Tim Thoms

Leisure Management International
Eleven Greenway Plaza
Suite 3106
Houston, TX 77046
T: (713) 623-4583
F: (713) 722-4134

Marriott Concessions & Arena Management
4966 W. Baywood Street
Boise, ID 83703
T: (208) 331-2547
F: (208) 333-8509
Bruce.turner@marriott.com
Oper: Bruce Turner

Ogden Entertainment Services
Two Pennsylvania Plaza
New York, NY 01021
T: (800) 868-6211
F: (212) 868-8108
Sr VP Fac Mgt: Danny Zausner

Service America Corp.
PO Box 10203
100 First Stamford Plaza
Stamford, CT 06904
T: (203) 964-5044
F: (203) 351-8949
P: Larry Kilfoy

Spectacor Management Group
Independence Center
701 Market Street, 4th FL
Philadelphia, PA 19106
T: (215) 592-4100
F: (215) 592-6699
E: smgdev@aol.com
Dir: Valerie Digue

Sportservice Corporation
One Delaware North Place
Buffalo, NY 14202
T: (716) 858-5000
F: (716) 858-5125
Oper: Joe Trimboli, Jr.

Sports Facility Architects, Engineers, Planners & Consultants

Ellerbe Becket, Inc.
605 W. 47th St., Suite 200
Kansas City, MO 64112
T: (816) 561-4443
F: (816) 561-2863

Hastings & Chivetta Architects
700 Corporate Park Dr., Suite 400
St. Louis, MO 63105
T: (314) 863-5717
F: (314) 863-2823
www.hastingschivetta.com

HNTB Sports Architecture
1201 Walnut, Suite 700
Kansas City, MO 64106
T: (816) 472-1201
F: (816) 472-4060
E: tmiller@hntb.com

HOK Sports Facilities Group
323 W. 8th Street, Suite 700
Kansas City, MO 64105
T: (816) 221-1576
F: (816) 221-1578

NBBJ
631 S. Olive St., Penthouse
Los Angeles, CA 90014
T: (213) 243-1160
F: (213) 243-1159

Rosser International Sports
524 W. Peachtree St. NW
Atlanta, GA 30308
T: (404) 876-3800
F: (404) 872-9279
www.rosser.com

Sink Combs Dethlefs
1900 Grant St., Suite 1250
Denver, CO 80203
T: (303) 308-0200
F: (303) 308-0222
www.sinkcombs.com

A more complete listing may be found in the 2002 Encyclopedia Of Sports Business Contacts, available in November 2002.

Sports Agencies

Listed in this section are athlete & event management services, sports agents, event promotion, arena management, speakers bureaus and other sports agencies.

A complete listing of agencies will be listed in our new book, **The Encyclopedia of Sports Business Contacts**, available in July 2000

Advantage International
1751 Pinacle Drive, 15th FL
McLean, VA 22102
T: (703) 905-3300
F: (703) 905-4495
Managing Dir: Francis Craighill

Advantage Management, Inc.
303 Church St., Suite 202
Nashville, TN 37201
T: (615) 255-5374
F: (615) 256-1949
P: Steve Jones

Advantage Marketing Group
5215 N. O'Connor Blvd.
Suite 770
Irving, TX 75039
T: (972) 869-2244
F: (972) 869-9560
P: Werner Scott

Alan Taylor Communications
225 W. 34th St., Suite 610
New York, NY 10122
T: (212) 714-1280
F: (212) 695-5685
P: Alan Taylor

Allsport Photography USA, Inc.
17383 Sunset Blvd., 3 FL
Pacific Palisades, CA 90272
T: (310) 230-3400
F: (310) 573-7600
VP: Greg Walker

API Soccer/API Sponsorship
1775 Broadway, Suite 608
New York, NY 10019
T: (212) 841-1580
F: (212) 841-1598
P: Gary Hopkins

Arthur Anderson & Co.
Athlete Advisory Services
633 W. 5th Street
32nd Floor
Los Angeles, CA 90071
T: (213) 614-6552
F: (213) 614-8439
P: Kenneth Anderson

Athletes & Artists, Inc.
888 Seventh Ave., 37 FL
New York, NY 10001
T: (212) 728-2000
F: (212) 977-2456
P: Art Kaminsky

Athletic Resource Management
6075 Poplar Ave., Suite 920
Memphis, TN 38119
T: (901) 763-4900
F: (901) 763-3762
P: Kyle Rote, Jr.

Bevilaqua International, Inc.
1401 Peachtree St. NE
Suite 500
Atlanta, GA 30309
T: (404) 658-9988
F: (404) 607-0049
P: John Bevilaqua

Blumenfeld & Associates
397 Post Road
Suite 202
Darien, CT 06820
T: (203) 656-3300
F: (203) 655-7710
P: Jeff Blumenfeld

Burns Sports Celebrity Svc.
211 E. Chicago Ave.
Suite 710
Chicago, IL 60611
T: (312) 951-5400
F: (312) 649-0944
P: David Burns

Russ Cline & Associates
2310 W. 75th Street
Prairie Village, KS 66208
T: (913) 384-8920
F: (913) 384-8921
P: Russ Cline

Dennis Conner Sports, Inc.
720 Gateway Center Drive
Suite E
San Diego, CA 92102
T: (619) 263-0059
F: (619) 263-1495
P: Dennis Conner

Custom Event Marketing, Inc.
444 E. 75th St., Suite 10D
New York, NY 10017
T: (212) 288-6742
F: (212) 288-6639
P: Elizabeth Phillips

Delwilber & Associates
1410 Springhill Rd., Suite 450
McLean, VA 22102
T: (703) 749-9300
F: (703) 749-9301
P: Del Wilber

Ernst & Young
787 Seventh Avenue
New York, NY 10019
T: (212) 773-3000
F: (212) 773-2144
Sports Practice: Steven Seneca

EventsCorp
1st Floor
16 St. Georges Terrace
Perth, WA 6000, Australia
T: (61.9) 270.3311
F: (61.9) 270.3399

Falk Associates Management Enterprises (FAME)
5335 Wisconsin Ave. NW
Suite 850
Washington, DC 20015
T: (202) 686-2000
F: (202) 686-5050
CEO: David Falk

David Fishof Presents, Inc.
252 W. 71st Street
New York, NY 10023
T: (212) 757-1605
F: (212) 265-4234
Pres: David Fishof

Global Sports
15 E. Ridge Pike
Suite 320
Conshohocken, PA 19428
T: (610) 825-4000
F: (610) 825-4455
P: Jim Drucker

Global Sports Productions, Ltd.
1223 Broadway, Suite 102
Santa Monica, CA 90404
T: (310) 454-9480
F: (310) 454-6590
E: Globalnw@earthlink.net
P: Ed Kobak

Golden Bear Sports Management
11780 U.S. Hwy 1
North Palm Beach, FL 33408
T: (561) 626-3900
F: (561) 626-4104
VP: Steve Nicklaus

IEG Consulting
640 N. La Salle, Suite 600
Chicago, IL 60610
T: (312) 944-1727
F: (312) 944-1897
P: Lesa Ukman

ISL Marketing USA, Inc.
383 Main Avenue
Norwalk, CT 06851
T: (203) 840-7999
F: (203) 840-7996
www.islworld.com
P: Darren Marshall

ISL Worldwide, AG
Zentralstrasse 1, PO Box 3339
CH-6002 Lucerne, Switzerland
T: (41.41) 24.95.95
F: (41.41) 24.97.97
Managing Dir: Stephen Dixon

Integrated Sports International
One Meadowlands Plaza
Suite 1501
East Rutherford, NJ 07073
T: (201) 507-1122
F: (201) 507-5308
P: Frank Vuono

International Creative Management
40 W. 57th Street
New York, NY 10019
T: (212) 566-5600
Dir. of Sports: Marc Perman

International Management Group (IMG)
One Erieview Plaza
Suite 1300
Cleveland, OH 44114
T: (216) 522-1200
F: (216) 522-1145
P: Mark McCormack

International Management Group Football
801 W. 47th Street
Suite 200
Kansas City, MO 64112
T: (816) 531-5777
F: (816) 753-2332
P: Thomas J. Condon

International Sports & Entertainment Representation Group, Inc.
2000 L St. NW, Suite 200
Washington, DC 20036
T: (202) 833-3330
Pres: Dominick Pilli

Jim Kelly Enterprises
Gateway Park
Buffalo, NY 14206
T: (716) 892-1212
F: (716) 892-1211
CEO: Jim Kelly

Don King Productions, Inc.
871 W. Oakland Park Blvd.
Oakland Park, FL 33311
T: (954) 568-3500
F: (954) 568-3555
P: Don King

Laidlaw Sports Management
105 Harbor Drive, Suite 1??
Stamford, CT 06902
T: (203) 324-49??
F: (203) 32?-?005
P: Tom Laidlaw

The Landmark Group
277 Richmond Street W.
Toronto, Ontario M5V 1X1
T: (416) 593-1991
F: (416) 593-4984
P: J. Elliott Kerr

Lawton Sports & Financial
First Bank Place, Suite 3800
601 Second Ave. South
Minneapolis, MN 55402
T: (612) 376-2803
F: (612) 317-2400
P: Brian Lawton

The Lazin Group
1333 N. Kingsbury
Suite 307
Chicago, IL 60622
T: (312) 642-5600
F: (312) 642-4775
P: Terry Lazin

Bruce Levy Associates International, Ltd.
Two Pennsylvania Plaza
Suite 1500
New York, NY 10121
T: (212) 254-3222
F: (212) 505-5771
P: Bruce Levy

Butch Lewis Productions, Inc.
250 W. 57th Street
Suite 311
New York, NY 10019
T: (212) 582-4344
F: (212) 582-4848
P: Butch Lewis

Lifestyle Marketing Group
345 Park Ave. S., 2nd FL
New York, NY 10010
T: (212) 779-6600
F: (212) 685-0781
CEO: Donald Dixon

MVP Management Ltd.
1120 Grant Ave., Suite 206
Winnipeg, Manitoba R3M 2A6
T: (204) 475-3981
F: (204) 452-9746
Pres: Richard J. Van Walleghem

Main Event Productions, Inc.
811 Totowa Road
Totowa, NJ 07512
T: (201) 389-9090
F: (201) 389-9080
P: Dan S. Duva

Management Plus Enterprises
3110 Main Street
The Annex
Santa Monica, CA 90405
T: (310) 581-2100
F: (310) 581-5632
P: Leonard Armato, Esq.

Millsport
Stanford Towers
750 Washington Blvd.
Stamford, CT 06901
T: (203) 977-0500
F: (203) 977-0555
CEO: James Millman

Mitchell, Silverley, Knupp
11377 W. Olympic Blvd.
Los Angeles, CA 90061
T: (310) 312-3290
F: (310) 312-3786
Counsel: Marvin Demoff

Muhleman Marketing, Inc.
6000 Monroe Rd., Suite 300
Charlotte, NC 28212
T: (704) 568-2520
F: (704) 568-2904
P: Max Muhleman

National Media Group, Inc.
1790 Broadway, Suite 400
New York, NY 10019
T: (212) 307-5300
F: (212) 582-8655
CEO: Michael Goldberg

Network International
701 Market St., Suite 4400
Philadelphia, PA 19106
T: (215) 922-7818
F: (215) 922-7836
Sr. VP: Richard Sherwood

Newport Sports Management
201 City Centre Drive, Suite 601
Mississauga, Ontario, L5B 2T4
Canada
T: (905) 275-2800
F: (905) 275-4025
Contact: Donald E. Meehan

Nike Sports Management
One Bowerman Drive
Beaverton, OR 97005
T: (503) 671-6453
F: (503) 671-6300
P: Terdema Ussery

Ogden Allied Entertainment Services
2 Pennsylvania Plaza
New York, NY 10121
T: (212) 868-6211
F: (212) 868-8108
Sr. VP: Loris Smith

The Pearlman Group, Inc.
11755 Wilshire Blvd.
Suite 880
Los Angeles, CA 90025
T: (310) 473-9353
F: (310) 479-0043
CEO: Daniel Pearlman

People & Properties, Inc.
345 Park Avenue S.
New York, NY 10010
T: (212) 685-0615
F: (212) 685-0797
P: Tony Andrea

Photo File
5 O'dell Plaza
Yonkers, NY 10701
T: (914) 375-6000
F: (914) 375-6009
P: Charles Singer

Pro Counsel Sports Management Group, Inc.
255 Park Ave., Suite 1100
Worcester, MA 01609
T: (508) 755-4300
F: (508) 754-9541
P: Michael Sowyrda

Pro-Rep Entertainment Group
276 Midpark Way SE, Suite 113
Calgary, Alberta T2X 1J6
T: (403) 256-5858
F: (403) 256-8272
Contact: Art J. Breeze

Queensland Events Corporation
Level 25, Waterfront Place
1 Eagle Street
Brisbane, Qnsld, Australia
T: (61.7) 3221.1552
F: (61.7) 3221.1684

ProServ, Inc.
1620 L St. NW, Suite 600
Washington, DC 20036
T: (202) 721-7200
F: (202) 721-7201
CEO: Donald Dell

Bobby Rahal, Inc.
PO Box 39
Hilliard, OH 43026
T: (614) 777-2040
F: (614) 777-2045
Pres: Bobby Rahal

Thomas M. Reich & Associates
2370 One PPG Place
Pittsburgh, PA 15222
T: (412) 391-2626
F: (412) 391-2613
P: Tom Reich

Re: Search
270 Lafayette Street
Suite 512
New York, NY 10012
T: (212) 219-8700
F: (212) 219-8736
Research Rep: Shari Chertok
Reasearch & rights clearance firm

The Rodman Group
620 Newport Center Dr.
Suite 1050
Newport Beach, CA 92660
T: (949) 719-1966
F: (949) 719-1969
CEO: Dennis Rodman
P: Dwight Manley

SCA Promotions, Inc.
8300 Douglas Ave., Suite 625
Dallas, TX 75225
T: (888) 860-3717
F: (214) 860-3723
P: Robert Hamman

Mike Schechter Associates
10012 N. Dale Mabry, Suite 213
Tampa, FL 33618
T: (813) 960-7555
F: (813) 960-7595
CEO: Mike Schechter

Spectacor Management Group (SMG)
Independence Center, 4th FL
701 Market Street
Philadelphia, PA 19106
T: (215) 592-4100
F: (215) 592-6699
P: Wes Westley

The Sports Corporation
2735 Toronto-Dominion Tower
Edmonton Centre
Edmonton, Alberta T5J 2Z1
T: (780) 421-8777
F: (780) 425-6937
P: Rich A. Winter

Sports Etcetera
2 Pennsylvania Plaza
New York, NY 10121
T: (212) 465-6565
F: (212) 465-6525
P: Ella Musolino-Alber

Sports Professional Management, Inc.
117 Aspen Airport Center
Suite 214
Aspen, CO 81611
T: (970) 920-7644
F: (970) 920-9989
P: Lewis Gross

Sports Promotion, Inc.
4425 Corporation Lane
Suite 421
Virginia Beach, VA 23462
T: (757) 497-1583
F: (757) 497-3919
P: Ronald Del Duca

Sportstars, Inc.
1350 Ave. of the Americas
28th Floor
New York, NY 10019
T: (212) 757-4044
F: (212) 765-4833
P: Alan G. Herman

Steinberg & Moorad
500 Newport Center Drive
Suite 820
Newport Beach, CA 92660
T: (949) 720-8700
F: (949) 720-1331
Partner: Leigh Steinberg

Steiner Sports Marketing
49 W. 27th Street, 6th FL
New York, NY 10001
T: (212) 689-2609
F: (212) 689-9641
P: Brandon Steiner

Tellem & Associates
11911 San Vicente Blvd.
Suite 325
Los Angeles, CA 90049
T: (310) 440-2811
F: (310) 440-2819
P: Art Tellem

Top Rank Boxing
3980 Howard Hughes Pkwy.
Suite 580
Las Vegas, NV 89109
T: (702) 732-2717
F: (702) 733-8232
P: Robert Arum

Bob Woolf Associates, Inc.
101 Huntington Avenue
Suite 257
Boston, MA 02199
T: (617) 437-1212
F: (617) 437-1528
P: Gregg Clifton

Zucker Sports Management Group
33 N. Dearborn, 19th Floor
Chicago, IL 60602
T: (312) 551-1000
F: (312) 551-1111
P: Stephen W. Zucker

Look for a more complete listings of sports marketing firms, sports promotion firms, event management firms, sports agents and sports lawyers in our Encyclopedia of Sports Business Contacts

We have also moved the sections on Sporting Good Manufacturers and Corporate Sports Sponsors to the Encyclopedia of Sports Business Contacts as well.

Sports Collecting

Sports Card Manufacturers

Listed in this section are sports card manufacturers for the major & minor leagues, amateur leagues & collegiate sports and licensed collectibles.

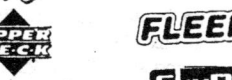

Action Packed/Pinacle Brands
1845 Wooddall Rodgers Fwy.
Suite 1300
Dalas, TX 75201
T: (214) 981-8100
F: (214) 981-8200
Also Racer's Choice, Score

Donruss Playoff Company
2300 E. Randolf Mill Road
Arlington, TX 76011
T: (817) 983-0300
F: (817) 983
www.donruss.com
www.playoff.com
www.scoreonline.com
Cardz, Donruss, Playoff, Prime, Score and WCW

Fleer Trading Cards
Executive Plaza
1120 Route 73, Suite 300
Mt. Laurel, NJ 08054
T: (856) 231-6200
F: (856) 727-9460
www.fleer.com

Fotoball USA, Inc.
6740 Cobra Way
San Diego, CA 92121
T: (800) 325-3686
F: (619) 467-9947
MLB licensed products

Grandstand Cards
22647 Ventura Blvd.
Suite 192
Woodland Hills, CA 91364
T: (818) 992-5642
F: (818) 348-9122
E: gscards@aol.com
Wholesale minor league card maker for independent baseball leagues

Highland Mint
4100 N. Riverside Drive
Melbourne, FL 32937
T: (800) 544-6135
F: (321) 777-9500
www.thehighlandmint.com

In the Game/Be A Player
22 St. Joseph Street
Toronto, Ontario M4Y 1J9 Canada
T: (416) 962-1991
F: (416) 925-2187
www.baptradingcards.com

JOGO Novelties, Inc.
1872 Queensdale Avenue
Gloucester, Ontario K1T 1K1
T: (613) 521-2457
F: (613) 244-5428
CFL card Sets

Kenyon Press, Inc.
12616 Chadron Ave.
Hawthorne, CA 90250
T: (800) 752-9395
T: (310) 331-4500
F: (310) 675-2358
cards & schedule cards to colleges

Pacific Trading Cards
18424 Highway 99
Lynwood, WA 98037
T: (800) 551-2002
F: (425) 775-0774
www.pacifictradingcards.com

Press Pass/Racing Champions/Ertl
9115 Harris Corners Pkwy, Ste. 200
Charlotte, NC 28269
T: (704) 942-3060
www.racingchampions.com
Race Cards

Starting Lineup
No other info on their website
www.startinglineup.com

Team Best
7115 Oak Ridge Pkwy, Suite 180
Austell, GA 30168
T: (770) 745-3434
F: (770) 745-3433
www.teambest.com
E: customerservice@teambest.com
Minor league card maanufacturer

Topps/Bowman Company
One Whitehall Street
New York, NY 10004
T: (212) 376-0300
F: (212) 376-0573
www.topps.com
Bazooka, Bowman, Parkhurst, Topps

Topps Canada
5409 Eglinton Ave. W.
Suite 210
Etobicoke, Ontario M9C 5K6
T: (416) 622-3425

Upper Deck Company
5909 Sea Otter Place
Carlsbad, CA 92008
T: (760) 929-6500
F: (760) 929-6548
www.upperdeck.com

Hobby Guides & Directories

The Athlete Address Book
International Sports Directory
Sports Address Bible
Encyclopedia of Sports Business
Global Sports
1223 Broadway, Suite 102
Santa Monica, CA 90404
T: (310) 454-9480
F: (310) 454-6590
E: Globalnw@earthlink.net

Baseball Card Price Guide
700 E. State Street
Iola, WI 54945
T: (715) 445-2214
F: (715) 445-4087
www.krause.com

The Charlton Standard Catalogue of Hockey Cards
Canadian Baseball Card Guide
Trajan Publishing Corp.
202-103 Lakeshore Road
St. Catharines, Ontario L2N 2T6
T: (800) 408-0352
T: (905) 646-7744
F: (905) 646-0995
www.cscmag.ca
www.trajan.ca
E: rscott@cscmag.ca
Editor: Richard Scott

The Encyclopedia of Baseball Cards
PO Box 137
Centereach, NY 11720
T: (516) 588-4533
www.19thcentury.com
Publisher: Lew Lipset

Matchcover Collector's Price Guide
PO Box 18481
Asheville, NC 28814
T: (828) 254-4487
F: (828) 254-1066

The Sports Americana Price Guides
Beckett Publications
15850 Dallas Parkway
Dallas, TX 75248
T: (972) 991-6657
F: (972) 991-8930
www.beckett.com

The Standard Catalog of Baseball Cards
700 E. State Street
Iola, WI 54990
T: (715) 445-2214
F: (715) 445-4087
www.krause.com

Foreign Reference Guides

The Catalog of British & Foreign Cigarette Cards
The London Cigarette Card Co.
Sutton Road, Somerton
Somerset TA11 6QP, England
T: (44.1458) 273 452
F: (44.1458) 273 515
www.londoncigcard.co.uk

Cigarette Card Values
Imperial Collections International
PO Box 10814
Lynchburg, VA 24506
T: (804) 832-1007
Publisher: Murray Cards Int'l. Ltd

Hobby Magazines

Listed first are the major publications followed by the smaller, but specialized publications & newsletters.

Beckett Publications
15850 Dallas Parkway
Dallas, TX 75248
T: (972) 991-6657
F: (972) 991-8930
www.beckett.com
Publishers of baseball, basketball, football, hockey monthly magazines & Future Stars

Canadian Sports Collector
103 Lakeshore Road, Suite 202
St. Catharines, Ontario L2N 2T6
T: (905) 646-7744
F: (905) 646-0995
www.cscmag.ca
E: rscott@cscmag.ca
Editor: Richard Scott

Krause Publications
700 E. State Street
Iola, WI 54990
T: (715) 445-2214
F: (715) 445-4087
www.krause.com/sports
E: sports@krause.com
Publisher: Hugh McAloon
Publishers of Sports Card Price Guide Monthly, **Sports Collectors Digest***, The Postcard Collector, Today's Collector,* **Tuff Stuff** *& other collector magazines & price guides.*

Paper Collector's Marketplace
PO Box 128, 470 Main Street
Scandinavia, WI 54977
T: (715) 467-2379
F: (715) 467-2243
www.pcmpaper.com
E: pcmpaper@gglbbs.com
Publisher: Doug Watson

Hobby Periodicals & Newsletters

Many of the publications listed here are sports hobby related or specialized hobby papers.

While we tried to verify each listing, it is possible that some publications may have ceased operations.

American Collectors Journal
206 W. 4th Street
PO Box 407
Kewanee, IL 61443
T: (309) 852-2602

The Autograph Collector
510-A S. Corona Mall
Corona, CA 91719
T: (909) 734-9636
F: (909) 371-7139
www.autographs.com

The Autograph Review
305 Carlton Road
Syracuse, NY 13207
T: (315) 474-3516
Publisher: Jeff Morey

Barr's Post Card news
70 S. Sixth Street
Lansing, IA 52151
T: (800) 397-0145
T: (319) 538-4500
F: (319) 538-4038

Collector's Chronicle
PO Box 10151
Oakland, CA 94610
T: (510) 428-2000

The Collector's Marketplace
Box 25
Stewartsville, NJ 08886
T: (908) 479-4614

Collectors News
506 Second Street
Grundy Center, IA 50638
T: (319) 824-5456

Combo
155 E. Ames Court
Plainview, NY 11803
T: (516) 349-9494
Non-sport cards

Crowncappers Exchange
4300 San Juan Drive
Fairfax, VA 22030
T: (703) 591-3060

Front Striker Matchcover Bulletin
PO Box 18481
Asheville, NC 28814
T: (828) 254-4487
F: (828) 254-1066

Hobbies
1006 S. Michigan Ave.
Chicago, IL 60605
T: (312) 939-4767

Journal of Sports Philately
PO Box 2286
La Grange, IL 60525
T: (619) 457-1656
P: Mark C. Maestrone
Editor: John La Porta

The Old Judge
PO Box 137
Centereach, NY 11720
T: (516) 588-4533
www.t206museu.com

Olympin Collector's News
1386 Fifth Street
Schenectady, NY 12303
T: (518) 355-6493
Largest Olympic memorabilia & pin club in the world

Paper Pile Quarterly
PO Box 337
San Anselmo, CA 94979
T: (415) 454-5552
F: (415) 454-2947
E: apaperpile@aol.com

Right On Schedule
204 N. Charro
Thousand Oaks, CA 91320
T: (805) 499-1918
E: keithgad@mindspring.com
Editor: Keith Gadbury

The Sked Connection
16315 Wagner Way #319
Eden Prairie, MN 55344
E: jbartolett01@gwhamline.edu
Editor: Judy Bartolett

The Skedder Times
1956 Naskapi Drive
Ottawa, Ontario K1J 8K3
T: (613) 745-7573
Editor: Richard Provencher

Uniformity
2319 Home Avenue
Berwyn, IL 60402
T:
Editor: Dave Miedema
Uniform & equipment newsletter

The Vintage & Classic Baseball Collector Magazine
PO Box 39366
Tacoma, WA 98439
T: (253) 582-3146
F: (253) 589-3363

While we have attempted to verify the following listings in the remainder categories of this sports collecting section, several requests for info went unanswered.

Foreign Collecting Periodicals

Card Times
70 Winifred Lane
Aughton, Ormskirk
Lancs. L39 5DL, England
T: (44.695) 423 470
Publisher: Magpie Pubs.

Cartophilic Notes & News
The Cartophilic Society of Great Britain
116 Hillview Road
Ensbury Park, Bournemouth
BH1O 5BJ England

Cigarette Card News & Trade Card Chronicle
The London Cigarette Card Co.
Sutton Road, Somerton
Somerset TA11 6QP, England
T: (44.1458) 273 452
F: (44.1458) 273 515
www.londoncigcard.co.uk

The Football Programme Directory
66 Southend Road
Wickford, Essex SS11 8EN, England
T: (44.1268) 732 041
Editor: David Stacey

Programme Monthly
46 Milton Road
Kirkcaldy, Fife KY1 1TL, England

Foreign Collecting Societies

Association of Football Badge Collectors
18 Hinton Street, Fairfield
Liverpool L6 3AR, England
T: (44.151) 260 0554
P: Keith Wilkinson

Australia Cartophilic Society
PO Box 378
Boronia, Victoria 3155, Australia
Secretary: Eve Pryor
Publishes bi-monthly newsletter

Ephemera Society of Australia
PO Box 479
Warragul, Victoria 3820, Australia

Federazione Italiana Collezionisti Materiale Calcio
PO Box 1515
I-20101 Milano, Italy

Great Britain Cartophilic Society
116 Hillview Road
Ensbury Park,
Bournemouth BH10 5BJ, England

New South Wales Post Card Collectors Society
PO Box 58
Paddington, NSW 2021, Australia

New Zealand Cartophilic Society
2 Cannon Street
New Plymouth, New Zealand
Secretary: Mrs. Lyn Gill
Publication: Card Lines

South African Cartophilic Society
84 Marathon Street
Kensington 2094, Johannesburg
South Africa
Secretary: Murray Morrison

Western Australia Card Collectors Society
PO Box 670
Subiaco, WA 6008, Australia

Collecting Clubs

Listed in this section are collecting clubs that specialize in collectibles in the sports hobby or a peripheral hobby.

American Matchcover Collecting Club
PO Box 18481
Asheville, NC 28814
T: (828) 254-4487
F: (828) 254-1066
President: Bill Retskin

Beer Can Collectors of America
747 Merus Court
Fenton, MO 63026
T: (314) 343-6486
Contact: Richard Johnson

Deltiologists of America
Box 8
Norwood, PA 19074
T: (215) 485-8572
Contact: James Lowe
Postcards

Ephemera Society of America
PO Box 175
Wynantskill, NY 12198
T: (516) 295-7978
Contact: Wm. Frost Nobley

**National Association of
Paper & Advertising Collectors**
PO Box 500
Mount Joy, PA 17552
T: (717) 653-4300

Olympin Collector's Club
1386 Fifth Street
Schenectady, NY 12303
T: (518) 355-6493
Largest Olympic lapel pin & memorabilia club in the world

Pin Collector's Club
3822 rue Saint Damase
Jonquiere, Quebec G7X 2K1
T: (418) 542-6631
Contact: Michel Tremblay

Postcard History Society
PO Box 1765
Manassas, VA 22110
Director: John McClintock

Mathkamp Matchcover Society
PO Box 8541, 30 Melody Lane
Slidell, LA 70459
T: (985) 643-3691
www.matchcover.org
E: pandamap@aol.com
Secretary: Mary Anne Pertius

Sports Philatelists International
2824 Curie Place
San Diego, CA 92122
T: (619) 457-1656
P: Mark C. Maestrone

International Games

International Olympic Committee (IOC)
Chateau de Vidy
C.P. 356
1007 Lausanne, Switzerland
T: (41.21) 621 61 11
F: (41.21) 621 62 16
X: 45 40 24 ACIO CH
Tg: CIO Lausanne
www.OLYMPIC.ORG
P: Jacques Rogge

Olympic Museum & Studies Centre
Villa Olympique
1, Quai d'Ouchy
1006 Lausanne, Switzerland
T: (41.21) 621 65 11
F: (41.21) 621 65 12
www.museum.olympic.org
E: museum@olympic.org

Olympic Games Committees

Athens 2004 Summer Olympics

Organizing Committee for the Olympic Games Athens 2004
7 Kifissias Avenue
115 23 Athens, Greece
T: (30.1) 20 04 000
F: (30.1) 20 04 004
www.athens.olympic.org/gr
E: athoc@otenet.gr
P: Gianna Angelopoulos-Daskalaki
VP: Haralambos Nikolaou
Mkt: George Bolos
14-29 August 2004

2006 Torino, Italy Winter Olympics

Organizing Committee for the XX Olympic Winter Games-Torino 2006
Via Nizza 262/58
10126 Torino, Italy
T: (39.11) 63 10 511
F: (39.11) 63 10 500
www.torino2006.it
E: organization@torino2006.it
P: Valentino Castellani
VP: Evelina Christillin
GM: Paolo Rota
11-26 February 2006, Torino Italy

2008 Beijing, China Summer Olympics
No contact info at presstime

International Games Organizing Committees

2003 Pan Am Games Santo Domingo, Dom. Rep.
Organizing Committee
Pedro Henriquez urena No. 129
La Esperilla
Santo Domingo, DN
Dominican Republic
T: (809) 732-7230
F: (809) 732-7220
www.santodomingo2003.org.do
E: yvonnebroberg@codetel.net.do
P: Jose Joaquin Puello
Dir of NOC Svcs: Yvonne Broberg
Dates:

2003 Special Olympics World Games, Dublin, Irl
Organizing Committee
4 FL, Park House, North Circular Rd
Dublin 7, Ireland
T: (353.1) 868 7201
F: (353.1) 868 7203
www.2003specialolympics.com
E: info@2003worldgames.com
16-20 June 2003

2003 Summer University Games- Daegu, South Korea
no address given as of presstime
T: (82.53) 429 2155
www.universiade.taegu.kr
21-31 August 2003

Multi-Sport Games & Organizations

Goodwill Games
One CNN Center, PO Box 105583
Atlanta, GA 30348
T: (404) 827-3400
F: (404) 827-1394
www.goodwillgames.com
www.turner.com
E: goodwill.games@turner.com
P: Mike Plant
2005: Calgary, Alberta, Canada

International Children's Games
Malgajeva 2, SI 2390 Ravne Na
Koroskem, Slovenia
T: (386.2) 821 54 14
F: (386.2) 821 54 13
www2.arnes.si/guest
E: jozef.sater@guest.arnes.si
P: Jozef Robert Sater

International Paralympic Committee (IPC)
Adenaueralle 212-214
DE-53113 Bonn, Germany
T: (49.228) 209 72 00
F: (49.228) 209 72 09
www.paralympic.org
E: info@paralympic.org
P: Dr. Robert D. Steadward
Sec Gen: Miguel Sagarra
Media: Dr. Susanne Reiff

International University Sports Federation
56 Ave. Franklin Roosevelt
1050 Brussels, Belgium
T: (32.2) 640 68 73
F: (32.2) 640 18 05
www.fisu.net
E: fisuhq@ulb.ac.be
P: George Killian

International World Games Association (IWGA)
Willem de Zwijgerlaan 72
NL-2582 ES Le Havre, Netherlands
T: (31.70) 351 27 74
F: (31.70) 350 99 11
E: iwga@hetnet.nl
P: Ron Froehlich

Masters Games International
Bellishaven 47
DK 2625 Vallensbaek, Denmark
T: (45.43) 262.002
F: (45.43) 262.628

Special Olympics International
1325 G Street NW, Suite 500
Washington, DC 20005
T: (202) 628-3630
F: (202) 824-0200
www.specialolympics.org
E: SOImail@aol.com
P: Tomothy Shriver

Commonwealth Games Federation
Walkden House, 3-10 Melton House
London NW1 2EB, England
T: (44.171) 383 55 96
F: (44.171) 383 55 06
www.thecgf.com

*Look for other listings in our new **International Sports Directory**, available through us (310) 454-9480*

Intercollegiate Athletics

College Athletic Associations

National Association of Intercollegiate Athletics (NAIA)
23500 W 105th St., PO Box 1325
Olathe, KS 66051
T: (913) 791-0044
F: (913) 791-9555
www.naia.org
E: sbaker@naia.org
P/CEO: Steve Baker

National Christian College Athletic Association
302 W. Washington Street
Greenville, SC 29601
T: (864) 250-1199
F: (864) 250-1141
www.bright.net/nccaa
Exec. Dir: Dan Wood

National Collegiate Athletic Association (NCAA)
PO Box 6222
Indianapolis, IN 46206
T: (317) 917-6222
F: (317) 917-6888
www.ncaa.org
Exec. Dir: Cedric Dempsey

National Junior College Athletic Association (NJCAA)
PO Box 7305
Colorado Springs, CO 80933
T: (719) 590-9788
F: (719) 590-7324
www.njcaa.org
E: info@njcaa.org
Exec. Dir: George E. Killian

National Small College Ath. Assn.
6752 Winchell Road
Warners, NY 13164
T: (315) 488-0073
F: (315) 488-0074
www.thenscaa.com
Commissioner: David Magee

NCAA Bowl Games

Alamo Bowl
100 Montana St., Suite 3D01
San Antonio, TX 78203
T: (210) 226-2695
F: (210) 704-6399
www.alamobowl.com
Exec. Dir: Derrick S. Fox

Aloha Christmas Football Classics
1110 University Ave., Suite 403
Honolulu, HI 96826
T: (808) 947-4141
F: (808) 941-9911
Exec. Dir: Marcia J. Klompus

Blue Gray All Star Classic
PO Box 94
Montgomery, AL 36101
T: (334) 265-1266
F: (334) 265-5944
www.bluegrayfootball.com
Exec. Dir: Charles Jones

Cotton Bowl Classic
PO Box 569420
Dallas, TX 75356
T: (214) 634-7525
F: (214) 634-7764
www.swbellcottonbowl.com
Exec. Dir: Rick Baker

East-West Shrine Bowl
1919 Elkhorn Court
San Mateo, CA 94403
T: (650) 372-9300
F: (650) 372-9530
www.shrinebowl.com
E: jeff@shrinebowl.com
Exec. Dir: Jeff Foster

Fiesta Bowl
120 S. Ash Avenue
Tempe, AZ 85281
T: (480) 350-0900
F: (480) 350-0915
www.tostitosfiestabowl.com
Exec. Dir: John Junker

Florida Citrus Bowl
One Citrus Bowl Place
Orlando, FL 32805
T: (407) 423-2476
F: (407) 425-8451
Exec. Dir: Charles Rohe

Gator Bowl
One Gator Bowl Blvd.
Jacksonville, FL 32202
T: (904) 798-1700
F: (904) 632-2080
www.gatorbowl.com
Exec. Dir: Rick Catlett

Heritage Bowl
1401 Peachtree S., Suite M102
Atlanta, GA 30309
T: (404) 870-8414
F: (404) 870-5952
Exec. Dir: Shea Haynes
Postseason Div I-AA

Holiday Bowl
PO Box 601400
San Diego, CA 92160
T: (619) 283-5808
F: (619) 281-7947
www.holidaybowl.com
Exec. Dir: John Reid
PR: John Dolak

Hula Bowl All Star Classic
Maui Mall #B9, 70 Kaahumanu Ave
Kahului, Maui, HI 96753
T: (808) 871-4141
F: (808) 871-4143
www.hulabowlmaui.com
Ex. Dir: Marcia J. Klompus

Humanitarian Bowl
7032 S. Eisenman Road
Boise, ID 83716
T: (208) 338-8887
F: (208) 338-3833
www.humanitarianbowl.org
P: Steven Wood
PR: Duffer Vick

Independence Bowl
PO Box 1723
Shreveport, LA 71166
T: (318) 221-0712
F: (318) 221-7366
www.independencebowl.org
Exec. Dir: Glen Krupica

Insight.com Bowl
120 S. Ash Ave.
Tempe, AZ 85281
T: (480) 350-0900
F: (480) 350-0915
www.tucsonfiestabowl.com
Exec. Dir: John Junker

Kickoff Classic
Giants Stadium, 50 Route 120
East Rutherford, NJ 07073
T: (201) 460-4361
F: (201) 460-4294
www.meadowlands.com
Exec. Dir: Michael Graimel

Las Vegas Bowl
4505 Maryland Pkwy, PO Box 450001
Las Vegas, NV 89154
T: (702) 895-2868
F: (702) 895-2867
www.lvbowl.com
Exec. Dir: Tina Kunzer-Murphy

Liberty Bowl
3767 New Getwell Road
Memphis, TN 38118
T: (901) 795-7700
F: (901) 795-7826
www.libertybowl.org
Exec. Dir: Steve Ehrhart

Mobile Alabama Bowl
6159 Omni Park Dr., Suite B
Mobile, AL 36609
T: (334) 635-0011
F: (334) 666-0355
Exec. Dir: Bud Ratliff

Motor City Bowl
1200 Featherstone Drive
Pontiac, MI 48342
T: (248) 456-1694
F: (248) 456-1691
www.motorcitybowl.com
Exec. Dir: Ken Hoffman

Music City Bowl
211 Commerce St., Suite 100
Nashville, TN 37201
T: (615) 743-3130
F: (615) 244-3540
www.musiccitybowl.com
Exec. Dir: Scott Ramsey

Orange Bowl
601 Brickell Key Dr., Suite 206
Miami, FL 33131
T: (305) 371-4600
F: (305) 371-4318
www.orangebowl.org
Exec. Dir: Keith Tribble

Outback Bowl
4511 N. Himes Ave., Suite 260
Tampa, FL 33614
T: (813) 874-2695
F: (813) 873-1959
www.outbackbowl.com
Exec. Dir: James P. McVay

Peach Bowl
235 International Blvd.
Atlanta, GA 30303
T: (404) 586-8500
F: (404) 586-8508
www.chick-fil-apeachbowl.com
P: Gary Stokan

Pigskin Classic
PO Box 16428
Cleveland, OH 44116
T: (440) 892-4000
F: (440) 892-4007
Exec. Dir: Michael Cleary

Rose Bowl
391 S. Orange Grove Blvd.
Pasadena, CA 91184
T: (626) 449-4100
F: (626) 449-9786
www.rosebowl.com
Exec. Dir: Kevin Ash

Senior Bowl
63 S. Royal St., Suite 100
Mobile, AL 36602
T: (251) 438-2276
F: (251) 432-0409
www.seniorbowl.com
Exec. Dir: Steve Hale

Sugar Bowl
1500 Sugar Bowl Drive
New Orleans, LA 70112
T: (504) 525-8573
F: (504) 525-4867
www.nokiasugarbowl.com
Exec. Dir: Paul Houlahan

Sunshine Football Classic
6360 NW Fifth Way, Suite 310
Fort Lauderdale, FL 33309
T: (954) 564-5000
F: (954) 564-8902
E: footballclassic@aol.com
Exec Dir: Mitch Morrall

Sun Bowl
4100 Rio Bravo
Suite 303
El Paso, TX 79902
T: (915) 533-4416
F: (915) 533-0661
www.sunbowl.org
Exec. Dir: Joyce Feinberg

Basketball Tournaments

Hall of Fame Tip-off Classic
46 Lakeside Drive
Monson, MA 01057
T: (413) 747-6340
F: (413) 731-5710

National Invitation Tournament
19 West Street, Suite 3505
New York, NY 10004
T: (212) 425-6510
F: (212) 785-0594
www.NIT.org
Exec. Dir: John J. Powers
PR: Chris Fallon

NCAA Division I & I-AA Conferences

Listed here are the NCAA Dvision I & I-AA conferences.

America East (I)
10 High Street, Suite 860
Boston, MA 02110
T: (617) 695-6369
F: (617) 695-6380
www.americaeast.org
E: americaeast@americaeast.com
Commissioner: Chris Monasch
PR: Matt Bourque
Members: Boston U., U Delaware, Drexel, U. Hartford, Hofstra U., U. Maine, U. New Hampshire, Northeastern, Towson, U. Vermont

Atlantic 10 Conference (I)
2 Penn Center, Suite 1410
Philadelphia, PA 19102
T: (215) 751-0500
F: (215) 751-0770
www.atlantic10.org
E: lbruno@atlantic10.org
Commissioner: Linda Bruno
PR: Ray Cella
Members: U. Conn.(FB) Dayton, Delaware (FB) Duquesne, Fordham, George Washington, James Madison (FB), La Salle, Maine (FB), Massachusetts, New Hampshire (FB) Northeastern (FB) Rhode Island, Richmond (FB) St. Bonaventure, St. Joseph's, Temple, Villanova (FB) VA Tech, Xavier, West Chester (Fld. Hky) Wm. & Mary (FB)

Atlantic Coast Conference (I, I-A)
PO Drawer ACC
4512 Weybridge Lane
Greensboro, NC 27417
T: (336) 854-8787
F: (336) 316-6097
www.theacc.com
Commissioner: John Swofford
Media: Amy Moore
Members: Clemson, Duke, Florida State, GA Tech, Maryland, North Carolina, North Carolina State, VA, Wake Forest

Big East Conference (I, I-A FB)
56 Exchange Terrace
Providence, RI 02903
T: (401) 272-9108
F: (401) 751-8540
www.bigeast.org
Commissioner: Michael Tranghese
PR: W. John Paquette, Jr.
Big East Members: Boston College, Connecticut, Georgetown, U. Miami, Notre Dame, Pittsburgh, Providence College, Rutgers U., St. John's U., Seton Hall, Syracuse U., Temple U (FB), Villanova, VA Polytech (FB), West Virginia

Big Sky Conference (I, I-AA FB)
PO Box 1459, 2491 Washington
Ogden, UT 84402
T: (801) 392-1978
F: (801) 392-5568
www.bigskyconf.com
Commissioner: Douglas B. Fullerton
PR: Ron Loghry
Members: CSU Northridge, CSU Sacramento, Eastern WA, Idaho St., Montana, Montana St., Northern Arizona, Portland State, Weber State

Big South Conference (I)
6428 Bannington Dr., Ste. A
Charlotte, NC 28226
T: (704) 341-7990
F: (704) 341-7991
www.bigsouth.org
Commissioner: Kyle Kallander
PR: Drew Dickerson
Members: Charleston Southern, Coastal Carolina, Elon, High Point, Liberty U., UNC Asheville, Radford, South Alabama (soccer), Winthrop U.

Big Ten Conference (I, I-A FB)
1500 W. Higgins Road
Park Ridge, IL 60068
T: (847) 696-1010
F: (847) 696-1150
www.bigten.org
E: jdelany@bigten.org
Commissioner: James Delany
PR: Sue Ryan
Members: Illinois, Indiana, Iowa, Michigan, Michigan St., Minnesota, Northwestern, Ohio St., Penn State, Purdue, Wisconsin.

Big 12 Conference (I, I-A FB)
2201 Stemmons Freeway, 28 FL
Dallas, TX 75207
T: (214) 742-1212
F: (214) 743-0145
Commissioner: Kevin Weiberg
Media: Bo Carter
Big 12 Members: Baylor, U Colo., Iowa St., Kansas, Kansas St., Missouri, Nebraska, Oklahoma, Oklahoma St., Texas, Texas A&M, Texas Tech.

Big West Conference (I, I-A FB)
2 Corporate Park, Suite 206
Irvine, CA 92714
T: (949) 261-2525
F: (949) 261-2528
www.Bigwest.org
Commissioner: Dennis Farrell
PR: Mike Daniels
Members: Boise St., Cal. Poly-SLO, CS Fullerton, UC Irvine, UC Santa Barbara, Idaho, Long Beach St., Nevada-Reno, New Mexico St., U. North Texas, U Pacific, Utah State.

Central Collegiate Hockey Association (I)
23995 Freeway Park Drive
Farmington Hills, MI 48335
T: (248) 888-0600
F: (248) 888-0664
www.ccha.com
E: ccha@ccha.com
Commissioner: Tom Anastos
PR: Sherry Skalko
Members: AK-Fairbanks, Bowling Green St, Ferris St, Lake Superior St, Miami (OH), Michigan, Mich. State, U. Nebraska-Omaha,Northern Mich., Notre Dame, Ohio State, Western Michigan U.

Colonial Athletic Association (I)
8625 Patterson Avenue
Richmond, VA 23229
T: (804) 754-1616
F: (804) 754-1830
www.caasports.com
Commissioner: Thomas E. Yeager
SID: Steve Vehorn
Colonial members: American U, East Carolina, George Mason, James Madison, UNC-Wilmington, Old Dominion, Richmond, Virginia Commonwealth, Wm. & Mary.

Conference USA (I, I-A FB)
35 E. Wacker Drive, Suite 650
Chicago, IL 60601
T: (312) 553-0483
F: (312) 553-0495
www.c-usa.org
E:confusa@aol.com
Commissioner: Michael Slive
PR: Erika Amstadt

C-USA Members: AL-Birmingham, Cincinnati, DePaul, E. Carolina (FB), Houston, Louisville, Marquette, Memphis, UNC Charlotte, St. Louis, U. So. FLA, Southern MS, Tulane, US Military (FB)

Eastern College Athletic Conference (I, I-AA FB)
PO Box 3
Craigville Beach Road
Centerville, MA 02632
T: (508) 771-5060
F: (508) 771-9481
www.ecac.com
E: ecac@ecac.com
Commissioner: Philip Buttafuoco
PR: John W. Garner, Jr.

Gateway Football Conference (I-AA FB)
1000 Union Station, Suite 105
St. Louis, MO 63103
T: (314) 421-2268
F: (314) 421-3505
www.mvc.org/gateway.htm
Comm: Patricia V. Viverito
Gateway Members: IL State, Indiana St, Northern Iowa, SIU-Carbondale, SW Missouri St, Western Illinois, Youngstown State

Hockey East Association (I)
654 S. Union Street
Lawrence, MA 01843
T: (978) 687-8535
F: (978) 687-6740
Commissioner: Joseph Bertagna
Media: Edward N. Saunders
Members: Boston College, Boston Univ,, Maine, U. Mass-Amherst, U. Mass.-Lowell, Merrimack Coll., New Hampshire, Northeastern, Providence College.

Ivy League (I, I-AA FB)
330 Alexander Street
Princeton, NJ 08544
T: (609) 258-6426
F: (609) 258-1690
www.ivyleague.princeton.edu
E: ivygroup@princeton.edu
Exec. Dir: Jeffrey H. Orleans
Members: Brown, Columbia U., Cornell, Dartmouth, Harvard, U Penn., Princeton, Yale.

Metro Atlantic Athletic Conference (I, I-AA FB)
1090 Amboy Avenue
Edison, NJ 08837
T: (732) 225-0202
F: (732) 225-2921
www.maac.org
E-mail: rich.ensor@maac.org
Commissioner: Richard J. Ensor
PR: Cathie Hughes
Members: Canisius, Duquesne, Fairfield, Georgetown (FB), Iona, Le Moyne, Loyola (MD), Manhattan, Marist, Mt. St. Mary's (Lacrosse), Niagara, Providence (FB/Lacrosse), Rider U., St. Johns (FB), St. Peters, Sienna, Wagner

Mid-American Conf. (I, I-A FB)
24 Public Square, 15 FL
Cleveland, OH 44113
T: (216) 566-4622
F: (216) 696-2622
www.midamconf.com
Commissioner: Rick Chryst
PR: Gary Richter
Members: Akron, Ball State, Bowling Green St, Buffalo, Central Mich, Eastern Mich, Kent State, Marshall, Miami (OH) Northern IL.,, Ohio U, Toledo, Western Michigan.

Mid-Continent Conference (I)
340 W. Butterfield Rd., Suite 3D
Elmhurst, Il 60126
T: (630) 516-0661
F: (630) 516-0673
www.mid-con.com
Commissioner: Jon A. Steinbrecher
PR: Nancy Smith
Members: Chicago State, Missouri-Kansas City, Oral Roberts, Southern Utah, Valparaiso, Western Illinois, Youngstown State.

Mid-Eastern Athletic Conf. (I, I-AA)
102 N. Elm Street, Suite 401
Greensboro, NC 27401
T: (336) 275-9961
F: (336) 275-9964
www.meacsports.com
E: meac@nr.infi.net
Commissioner: Charles S. Harris
PR: Bradford Evans, Jr.

MEAC Members: *Bethune-Cookman, Coppin State, Delaware State, Florida A&M, Hampton, Howard, Md-Eastern Shore, Morgan State, Norfolk State, NC A&T State, South Carolina State U.*

Midwestern Collegiate Conf. (I)
201 S. Capitol Ave., Suite 500
Indianapolis, IN 46225
T: (317) 237-5622
F: (317) 237-5620
www.mccnet.org
E: jlecrone@mccnet.org
Comm: Jonathan B. LeCrone
PR: Josh Lehman
Members: Butler, Cleveland State, Detroit-Mercy, IL-Chicago, Loyola-IL, WI-Green Bay, WI-Milw., Wright State

Midwestern Intercollegiate Volleyball Association (I)
Ohio State University
261 Northmoor Place
Columbus, OH 43214
T/F: (614) 262-3290
Comm: Bill Cooperrider

Missouri Valley Conference (I)
1000 Union Station, Suite 105
St. Louis, MO 63103
T: (314) 421-0339
F: (314) 421-3505
www.mvc.org
E: elgin @mvc.org
Comm: J. Douglas Elgin
PR: Mike Kern
Members: Bradley, Creighton, Drake, Evansville, Illinois State, Indiana State, Northern Iowa, SIU-Carbondale, SW MO State, Wichita State.

Mountain Pacific Sports Fed. (I)
800 S. Broadway, Suite 400
Walnut Creek, CA 94596
T: (925) 296-0723
F: (925) 296-0724
www.mpsports.org
E: abeaird@mpsports.org
Comm: Al Beaird
SID: Rick Hazeltine

Mountain West Conference (I)
1855 Testar Drive, USAA Bldg.
PO Box 35670
Colorado Springs, CO 80935
T: (719) 533-9500
F: (719) 533-9512
www.mountainwestconf.com
E: aturner@mountainwestconf.com
Comm: Craig Thompson
PR: Amy Turner
Members: Brigham Young U., Colo State U., U. of Nevada-Las Vegas, U. of New Mexico, San Diego St. U., U. of Utah, U. of Wyoming, U.S. Air Force Academy.

Northeast Conference (I)
220 Old New Brunswick Rd., Ste 201
Piscataway, NJ 08854
T: (732) 562-0877
F: (732) 562 8838
www.northeastconference.org
E: jiamarino @northeastconference.org
Commissioner: John Iamarino
PR: Ron Ratner
Members: Central CT State, Fairleigh Dickinson, LIU-Brooklyn, U. MD-Balt. Co., Monmouth U., Mt. St Mary's (MD), Quinnipiac, Robert Morris, Sacred Heart, St. Francis (NY), St. Francis (PA), Wagner.

Ohio Valley Conf. (I, I-AA FB)
278 Franklin Rd., Suite 103
Brentwood, TN 37027
T: (615) 371-1698
F: (615) 371-1788
www.ovcsports.com
E: dbeebe@ovc.org
Comm: R. Daniel Beebe
PR: Rob Washburn
OVC Members: Austin Peay State, Eastern IL, Eastern Kentucky, Middle TN, Morehead State, Murray State, SE Missouri State, TN-Martin, Tennessee State, Tennessee Tech, Western Kentucky (FB).

Pacific 10 Conference (I, I-A FB)
800 S. Broadway, Suite 400
Walnut Creek, CA 94596
T: (925) 932-4411
F: (925) 932-4601
www.Pac-10.org
E: thansen@pac-10.org
Commissioner: Thomas C. Hansen
PR: Jim Muldoon

Pac 10 Members: Arizona, Arizona State, Cal-Berkeley, UCLA, Oregon, Oregon State, U Southern California, Stanford, Washington, Washington State.

Patriot League (I, I-AA FB)
3897 Adler Place, Bldg. C, Ste. 310
Bethlehem, PA 18017
T: (610) 691-2414
F: (610) 691-8414
www.patriotleague.org
E: coh2@lehigh.edu
Exec. Dir: Todd A. Newcomb
PR: Suzanne Hoffman
Members: Bucknell, Colgate, Fordham (FB), Hobart (Lax), Holy Cross, Lafayette, Lehigh, Navy, Towson (FB), Ursinus (Fld. Hky.), U.S. Military Academy (Army).

Pioneer Football League (I, I-AA)
1000 Union Station, Suite 105
St. Louis, MO 63103
T: (314) 421-2268
F: (314) 421-3505
Commissioner: Patricia Viverito
PR: Cindy Kern
Members: Butler, Dayton, Drake, San Diego, Valparaiso.

Southeastern Conference (I, I-A)
2201 Civic Center Blvd.
Birmingham, AL 35203
T: (205) 458-3000
F: (205) 458-3031
www.SECsports.com
E: rkramer@sec.org
Comm: Roy F. Kramer
PR: Charles Bloom
SEC Members: Alabama, Arkansas, Auburn, Florida, Georgia, Kentucky, Louisiana State, Mississippi, Mississippi State, South Carolina, Tennessee, Vanderbilt.

Southern Conference (I, I-AA)
One West Pack Squ., Ste 1508
Asheville, NC 28801
T: (828) 255-7872
F: (828) 251-5006
www.soconsports.org
E: awhite@socon.org
Comm: Alfred White
Media: Heather Czeczok

SoCon Members: *Appalachian State, The Citadel, College of Charleston, Davidson, E. TN State, Furman, GA Southern, UNC-Greensboro, TN-Chattanooga, VA Military, Western Carolina, Wofford*

Southland Conference (I, I-AA)
8150 N. Central Expwy., Suite 930
Dallas, TX 75206
T: (214) 750-7522
F: (214) 750-8077
www.southland.org
E: gsankey@southland.org
Comm: Gregory Sankey
PR: Bruce Ludlow
Members: *Lamar, McNeese State, Nicholls St, NE LA, NW State, Sam Houston State, SE Louisiana, SW TX State, Stephen F. Austin State, TX-Arlington, TX-San Antonio*

Southwestern Athletic Conference (I, I-AA FB)
1500 Sugar Bowl Drive
New Orleans, LA 70112
T: (504) 523-7574
F: (504) 523-7513
www.swac.org
Comm: Rudy Washington
PR: Lonza Hardy, Jr.
Members: *Alabama A&M, Alabama State, Alcorn State, Arkansas-Pine Bluff, Grambling State, Jackson State, Mississippi Valley State, Prairie View A&M, Southern U-Baton Rouge, Texas-Southern*

Sun Belt Conference (I)
One Galleria Blvd., Suite 2115
Metairie, LA 70001
T: (504) 834-6600
F: (504) 834-6806
www.sunbeltsports.org
E: sunbelt@sunbeltsports.com
Commissioner: Wright Waters
PR: Dayna Wells
Members: *Arkansas-Little Rock, Arkansas State, Denver, Florida Int'l, Louisiana Tech, New Orleans, S. Alabama, SW LA, Western KY.*

Trans America Athletic Conference (I)
The Commons, Suite 108-B
3370 Vineville Avenue
Macon, GA 31204
T: (912) 474-3394
F: (912) 474-4272
www.taac.org
E: taac@taac.org
Commissioner: William C. Bibb
PR: Tom Snyder
Members: *Campbell, Central FL, FL Atlantic, Georgia St, Jacksonville State, Jacksonville U (FL), Mercer, Samford, Stetson, Troy State.*

West Coast Conference (I)
1200 Bayhill Drive, Suite 302
San Bruno, CA 94066
T: (650) 873-8622
F: (650) 873-7846
www.westcoast.org
E: wcc@westcoast.org
Comm: Michael M. Gilleran
PR: Don Ott
Members: *Gonzaga, Loyola Marymount, Pepperdine, Portland, St. Mary's (CA), San Diego, San Francisco, Santa Clara.*

Western Athletic Conference (I, I-AA FB)
9250 E. Costilla Ave., Suite 300
Englewood, CO 80112
T: (303) 799-9221
F: (303) 799-3888
www.wac.org
E: kbenson@wac.org
Comm: Karl D. Benson
PR: Dave Chaffin/Lisa Vad
WAC Members: *Fresno State, Hawaii, Rice, San Jose St, Southern ethodist, Texas Christian, Texas-El Paso, Tulsa*

Western Collegiate Hockey Association (I)
2190 S. High Street
Denver, CO 80208
T: (303) 871-4223
F: (303) 871-2600
E: bmcleod @ du.edu
Commissioner: Bruce McLeod
PR: Doug Spencer

WCHA Members: *Alaska-Anchorage, Colorado College, Denver, Michigan Tech, MN-Duluth, Minnesota, North Dakota, Northern Michigan, St. Cloud State, Wisconsin-Madison.*

NCAA Division II & III Conferences

Listed here are conferences that are Division II & III status.

American Southwest Conf. (III)
1221 W. Campbell Rd., Suite 217
Richardson, TX 75080
T: (972) 234-0033
F: (972) 234-8433
Comm: Fred Jacoby
Media: Michael Ziegler

California Collegiate Athletic Association (II)
800 S. Broadway, Suite 102
Walnut Creek, CA 94596
T: (925) 472-8290
F: (925) 472-8887
www.gocaa.org
E: rhiegert@goccaa.org
Comm: Robert J. Hiegert
PR: Joe Lang

Capital Athletic Conference (III)
224750 Marva Point Way
Hollywood, MD 20636
T: (301) 373-3293
F: (301) 373-3236
www.ycp.edu/cac
Commissioner: Richard Cook
PR: Scott Guise

Carolinas-Virginia Athletic Conference (II)
26 Cub Drive
Thomasville, NC 27360
T: (336) 884-0482
F: (336) 884-0315
www.cvac.net
E: cvac@northstate.net
Commissioner: Alan H. Patterson
PR: Joe Christy

Centennial Conference (III)
PO Box 3003
Franklin & Marshall College
Lancaster, PA 17604
T: (717) 399-4463
F: (717) 399-4480
www.centennial.org
E: s_ulrich @ centennial.org
Commissioner: Steven F. Ulrich
PR: megan Patruno

Central Intercollegiate Athletic Association (II)
303 Butler Farm Rd., Suite 102
PO Box 7349
Hampton, VA 23666
T: (757) 865-0071
F: (757) 865-8436
www.theciaa.com
E: ciaaoffice@aol.com
Commissioner: Leon G. Kerry
PR: Tonia G. Walker

City University of New York Athletic Conference (III)
250 Bedford Park Blvd. W.
Lehman College, The Apex, Rm 221
Bronx, NY 10468
www.bway.net/nysol/cunyac
T: (718) 960-7193
F: (718) 960-7194
Exec. Dir: Ted Hurwitz

College Conference of Illinois & Wisconsin (III)
Millikin University
1184 West Main Street
Decatur, IL 63522
T: (217) 420-6623
F: (217) 420-6629
Comm.: Merle W. Chapman
PR: David Wrath

Commonwealth Coast Conference (III)
Sunset Lane, Anna Maria College
Paxton, MA 01612
T: (508) 849-3446
F: (508) 849-3449
Comm.: Stephen Washkevich

Deep South Lacrosse Conference (II)
Gateway Plaza, Suite 130
226 North Park Drive
Rock Hill, SC 29730
T: (803) 981-5240
F: (803) 981-9444
Commissioner: Doug Echols

Dixie Intercollegiate Athletic Conference (III)
3101 Ellwood Avenue
Richmond, VA 23221
T: (804) 358-3543
F: (804) 358-0338
Comm: Michael J. Welch

Eastern Football Conference (II)
175 Forest Street
Bentley College
Waltham, MA 02154
T: (781) 891-2232
F: (781) 891-2648
E: rdefelice@bentley.edu
Comm: Robert DeFelice

Eastern Intercollegiate Volleyball Association (III)
42 Warren Street
Rutgers University
Newark, NJ 07102
T: (973) 353-5474 x 212
F: (973) 353-1431
E: rlarsen@andromeda.rutgers.edu
P: Ron Larsen

Eastern Intercollegiate Wrestling Association (I)
PO Box 3
Centerville, MA 02632
T: (508) 771-5060
F: (508) 771-9481
www.wrestlingreport.com/ewl
Comm: Rich Cole

Eastern Wrestling League (I)
PO Box 7436
University of Pittsburgh
Pittsburgh, PA 15213
T: (412) 648-8226
F: (412) 648-8225
President: Richard Cole

Empire Athletic Association (III)
RIT, 51 Lomb Memorial Drive
Rochester, NY 14623
T: (716) 475-2615
F: (716) 475-5675
P: Louis Spiotti

Freedom Football Conference (III)
Plymouth State College
Plymouth, NH 03264
T: (603) 535-2751
F: (603) 535-2558
E: sbamford@psc
Comm: Stephen R. Bamford

Great Lakes Football Conf. (II)
PO Box 869
Saint Joseph's College
Rensselaer, IN 47978
T: (219) 866-6157
F: (219) 866-6354
E: shannon@saintjoe.edu
P: Albert J. Shannon

Great Lakes Intercollegiate Athletic Conference (II)
3250 W. Big Beaver, Suite 300
Troy, MI 48084
T: (248) 649-2036
F: (248) 649-6847
Comm: Thomas J. Brown

Great Lakes Valley Conf. (II)
Pan Am Plaza
201 South Capitol Ave., Suite 560
Indianapolis, IN 46225
T: (317) 237-5636
F: (317) 237-5632
E: cmglvc@aol.com
Comm: Carl McAloose

Great Northeast Athletic Conference (III)
Daniel Webster College
20 University Drive
Nashua, NH 03063
T: (603) 577-6495
F: (603) 577-6001
Comm: Donna M. Ruseckas

Gulf South Conference (II)
4 Office Park Circle, Ste. 218
Birmingham, AL 35223
T: (205) 870-9750
F: (205) 870-4723
www.gulfsouthconference.org
E: gulfsout@ix.netcom.com
Comm: Nathan N. Salant

Heartland Collegiate Athletic Conference (III)
205 S. Madison Avenue
PO Box 425
Greenwood, IN 46142
T: (317) 882-8090
F: (317) 882-8086
Comm: Tom Bohlsen

Iowa Intercollegiate Athletic Conference (III)
608 33rd Street
West Des Moines, IA 50265
T: (515) 225-3021
F: (515) 221-2646
Comm: John Van Why

Lake Michigan Conference (III)
855 Woodrow Street
Madison, WI 53711
T: (608) 663-3249
F: (608) 663-6703
E: glarson@edgewood.edu
Comm: G. Steven Larson

Little East Conference (III)
University of Southern Maine
Hill Gymnasium
Gorham, ME 04038
T: (207) 780-5588
F: (207) 780-5182
E: albean@usm.maine.edu
Comm: Albert D. Bean, Jr.

Lone Star Conference (II)
1221 W. Campbell Road
Suite 217
Richardson, TX 75080
T: (972) 234-0033
F: (972) 234-4110
Comm: Fred H. Jacoby
Media: Brian Briscoe

Massachusetts State College Athletic Conference (III)
Bridgewater State College
Bridgewater, MA 02325
T: (508) 697-1352
F: (508) 697-1356
E: jharper@bridgew.edu
Commissioner: John C. Harper

Michigan Intercollegiate Athletic Association (III)
PO Box 643
1255 Hideway Lane
Hillsdale, MI 49242
T/F: (517) 439-0492
www.miaa.org
Comm: Sheila Kovalchik

Mid-America Intercollegiate Athletics Associaton (II)
10551 Barkley, Suite 501
Overland Park, KS 66212
T: (913) 341-3839
F: (913) 341-5887
E: miaasid@aol.com
Comm: Ralph McFillen

Middle Atlantic States Conference (III)
101 College Avenue
Lebanon Valley College
Annville, PA 17003
T: (717) 867-6395
F: (717) 867-5008
www.lvc.edu/mac
E: hopple@lvc.edu
Comm: Linda E. Hopple
PR: Jim Miller

Midwest Conference (III)
700 College Street
Belloit College
Beloit, WI 53511
T: (608) 363-2238
F: (608) 363-2140
El: peterson@beloit.edu
Comm: Ruth Peterson

Midwest Intercollegiate Football Conference (II)
3250 West Big Beaver, Suite 300
Troy, MI 48084
T: (248) 649-2036
F: (248) 649-6847
Comm.: Thomas J. Brown

Minnesota Intercollegiate
Athletic Conference (III)
2004 Randolph Ave., Mail #4014
College of St. Catherine
St. Paul, MN 55105
T: (651) 690-8734
F: (651) 690-8737
www.stkate.edu/miac
E: ccarter@admin.stkate.edu
Exec. Dir: Carlyle Carter

New England College
Athletic Conference (III)
1 Westwood Street
Burlington, MA 01803
T: (617) 272-9963
F: (617) 272-7250
Exec. Sec: Al Shields

New England College
Wrestling Association (III)
Weslyan University
Middletown, CT 06459
T: (860) 685-2896
F: (860) 685-2691
E: jbiddiscombe @ wesleyan.edu
Exec. Dir: John S. Biddiscombe

New England Collegiate
Conference (II)
PO Box 1307
Farmington, CT 06034
T: (860) 677-1269
F: (860) 674-8363
Comm: William M. Moore

New England Football
Conference (III)
Marine Maritime Academy
Pleasant Street
Castine, ME 04421
T: (207) 326-2451
F: (207) 326-2513
Comm: William J. Mottola

New England Small College
Athletic Conference (III)
Ferris Athletic Center
Trinity College
Hartford, CT 06106
T: (860) 297-2055
F: (860) 297-2492
E: richard.hazelton@mail.trincoll.edu
Commissioner: Richard J. Hazelton

New England Women's
& Men's Athletics Conf. (III)
100 Institute Road, WPI
Worcester, MA 01609
T: (508) 831-5243
F: (508) 831-5775
P: Ray Gilbert

New Jersey Athletic Conference (III)
Kean University
1000 Morris Avenue
Union, NJ 07083
T: (908) 527-2436
F: (908) 354-9423
P: Glenn Hedden

New York Collegiate
Athletic Conference (II)
3031 Arrowhead Lane
Norristown, PA 19401
T: (610) 825-5068
F: (610) 825-3676
Comm: Thomas Gallagher

New York State Women's
Collegiate Athletic Assoc. (III)
Union College, Alumni Gym
Schenectady, NY 12308
T: (518) 388-6546
F: (518) 388-6695
E: burtm@idol.union.edu
Exec. Dir: Mary Ellen Burt

North Central Intercollegiate
Athletic Conference (II)
Ramkota Inn, 2400 N. Louise
Sioux Falls, SD 57107
T: (605) 338-0907
F: (605) 338-1889
Comm: Mike Marcil

North Coast Athletic Conference (III)
24700 Center Ridge, #10
Westlake, OH 44145
T: (440) 871-8100
F: (440) 871-4221
E: ncacoffice @ aol.com
Exec. Dir: Dennis Collins

Northeast-10 Conference (II)
16 Belmont Street
South Easton, MA 02375
T: (508) 230-9844
F: (508) 230-9845
Comm: Dave Brunk

Northern Collegiate Hockey Association (III)
University of Wisconsin
127 Health Enhancement Center
Stevens Point, WI 54481
T: (715) 346-2694
F: (715) 346-4655
E: fobrien@uwsp.edu
P: Frank O'Brien

Northern Illinois-Iowa Conf. (III)
1550 Clarke Drive
Dubuque, IA 52001
T: (319) 588-6462
F: (319) 588-6666
P: Lon Boike

Northern Sun Intercollegiate Conference (II)
1901 University Avenue SE
Minneapolis, MN 55414
T: (612) 626-7680
F: (612) 626-7682
Comm: Kurt L. Patberg

Northwest Conference of Independent Colleges (III)
6059 SW Seville
Lake Grove, OR 97035
T: (503) 636-5376
F: (503) 697-4918
Comm: Arleigh R. Dodson

Ohio Athletic Conference (III)
8984 Darrow Road, #2B
PO Box 400
Twinsburg, OH 44087
T: (330) 963-0444
F: (330) 963-0459
E: oac@oac.org
Comm: Timothy W. Gleason

Old Dominion Athletic Conf. (III)
PO Box 971, 402 Idaho St.
Salem, VA 24153
T: (540) 389-7373
F: (540) 389-6196
E: odac1@roanoke.infi.net
Comm: Richard B. Bankston

Pacific West Conference (II)
PO Box 2002
Billings, MT 59103
T: (406) 657-2932
F: (406) 657-2934
Comm: Elwood B. Hahn

Peach Belt Athletic Conf. (II)
PO Box 204290
Augusta, GA 30917
T: (706) 860-8499
F: (706) 650-8113
www.peachbelt.com
Comm: Marvin Vanover

Pennsylvania Athletic Conf. (III)
Beaver College
Glenside, PA 19038
T: (215) 572-2194
F: (215) 572-2159
P: Shirley Liddle

Pennsylvania State Ath. Conf. (II)
114 Zimmerli Bldg.
Lock Haven University
Lock Haven, PA 17745
T: (717) 893-2780
F: (717) 893-2206
www.1hup.edu/psac
E: psac@eagle.lhup.edu
Commissioner: Stephen Murray

Presidents' Athletic Conf. (III)
Grove City College
100 Campus Drive
Grove City, PA 16127
T: (724) 458-2500
F: (724) 458-2190
www.pac.gcc.edu
P: John H. Moore

Rocky Mountain Athletic Conference (II)
1631 Mesa Avenue
Copper Bldg., Suite B
Colorado Springs, CO 80906
T: (719) 471-0066
F: (719) 471-0088
www.rmacsports.org
Comm: Thomas Wistrcill

St. Louis Intercollegiate Athletic Conference (III)
700 College Avenue
Blackburn College
Carlinville, IL 62626
T: (314) 968-6984
F: (314) 963-6092
P: Tom Hart

Skyline Conference (III)
Manhattanville College
2900 Purchase Street
Purchase, NY 10577
T: (914) 323-5281
F: (914) 323-5130
P: Karen Peterson

South Atlantic Conference (II)
Gateway Plaza, Suite 130
226 North Park Drive
Rock Hill, SC 29730
T: (803) 981-5240
F: (803) 981-9444
www.thesac.com
Comm: Doug Echols

Southern Calif. Intercollegiate Athletic Conference (III)
500 E. Ninth St., CMS Athletics
Claremont, CA 91711
T: (909) 607-3138
F: (909) 621-8336
Chair: Dave Jacobs

Southern Collegiate Athletic Conference (III)
3338 Gwinnett Plantation Way
Suite A-1
Duluth, GA 30096
T: (770) 495-9353
F: (770) 495-9363
www.scac-online.org
E: socolcon @ aol.com
Comm: Stephen P. Argo

Southern Intercollegiate Athletic Conference (II)
PO Box 92032
233 Peachtree Street NE
Suite 301
Atlanta, GA 30303
T: (404) 659-3380
F: (404) 659-7422
Comm: Wallace Jackson

SUNY Athletic Conference (III)
State University College
Fredonia, NY 14063
T: (716) 673-3105
F: (716) 673-3135
E: sunyac@fredonia.edu
Comm: Patrick R. Damore

Sunshine State Conference (II)
7061 Grand National Dr., Ste. 138
Orlando, FL 32819
T: (407) 248-8460
F: (407) 248-8325
E: sunshine_st_conf@msn.com
Comm: Don Landry

University Athletic Association (III)
668 Mount Hope Avenue
Rochester, NY 14620
T: (716) 273-5881
F: (716) 275-8322
E:dick_rasmussen@uaa.rochester.edu
Comm: Richard Rasmussen

Upstate Collegiate Athletic Conference (III)
William Smith College
Geneva, NY 14456
T: (315) 781-3500
F: (315) 781-3503
E: bassett@hws.edu
P: Susan Bassett

West Virginia Intercollegiate Athletic Conference (II)
1422 Main Street
Princeton, WV 24740
T: (304) 487-6298
F: (304) 487-6299
www.wviac.org
E: cnb00541@wvnum.wvnet.edu
Comm: Barry Blizzard

Western Water Polo Assn. (III)
580 Brambles Way
Orange, CA 92869
T: (714) 639-9106
E: montrella@ocweb.com
Comm: John J. Montrella

Wisconsin Intercollegiate Athletic Conference (III)
780 Regent Street
Madison, Wisconsin 53715
T: (608) 263-4402
F: (608) 265-3176
E: gkarner@ccmail.uwsa.edu
Comm: Gary F. Kamer

NCAA Division I, I-A & I-AA Member Colleges

Listed are members with Division I, I-A or I-AA status.

A=Athletic Director S=Sports Info.

Akron, University of
Akron, OH 44325
T: (330) 972-7080
F: (330) 972-5473
www.gozips.com
A: Michael Thomas
S: Jeff Brewer
MAC

Alabama, University of
Box 870323
Tuscaloosa, AL 35487
T: (205) 348-3697
F: (205) 348-2196
www.rolltide.com
A: Mal Moore
S: Larry White
SEC

Alabama A&M University
PO Box 1597
Normal, AL 35762
T: (256) 851-5365
F: (256) 851-5369
A: James A. Martin, Sr.
S: Ashley Balch
SWAC

Alabama-Birmingham, Univ. of
1530 3rd. Avenue South
Birmingham, AL 35294
T: (205) 934-7252
F: (205) 975-7286
www.uabsports.com
A: Herman Frazier
S: Grant Shingleton
Conference USA

Alabama State University
915 S. Jackson Street
Montgomery, AL 36104
T: (334) 229-4507
F: (334) 229-4992
A: Rob Spivey
S: Ronnie Johnson
SWAC

Alaska-Fairbanks, Univ. of
PO Box 757440
Fairbanks, AK 99775
T: (907) 474-7205
F: (907) 474-5162
www.uaf.edu
A: Randy Pitney
S: Ton Tragis
CCHA, Great Northwest

Alaska, University of
3211 Providence Drive
Anchorage, AK 99508
T: (907) 786-1230
F: (907) 786-1133
www.goseawolves.com
A: Steve Cobb
S: Nate Sagan/Kristi Palmer
Pacific West

Albany, University at
1400 Washington Ave.
Albany, NY 12222
T: (518) 442-3263
F: (518) 442-3031
www.albany.edu/sports
A: Dr. Lee McElroy
S: Brian DePasquale
America East, NEC (FB)

Alcorn State University
1000 ASU Drive #510
Alcorn State, MS 39096
T: (601) 877-6500
F: (601) 877-3821
www.alcorn.edu/athletics/default.htm
A: Robert Raines
S: Peter Forest
SWAC

American University
4400 Massachusetts Ave. NW
Washington, DC 20016
T: (202) 885-3000
F: (202) 885-3033
www.aueagles.com
A: Open
S: Jay C. Whipple
Patriot League

Appalachian State University
Owens Fieldhouse
Boone, NC 28608
T: (828) 262-4010
F: (828) 262-2556
www.appstate.edu
A: Roachel Laney
S: Kelby Siler
Southern Conference

Arizona, University of
PO Box 210096, Tucson, AZ 85721
T: (520) 621-2200
F: (520) 621-9690
www.arizcats.com
A: Jim Livengood
S: Tom Duddleston
Pacific-10

Arizona State University
Box 872505
Tempe, AZ 85287
T: (480) 965-3482
F: (480) 965-8219
www.thesundevils.com
A: Gene Smith
S: Mark Brand
Pacific-10

Arkansas, University of
Broyles Athletic Center
PO Box 7777
Fayetteville, AR 72701
T: (501) 575-6533
F: (501) 575-7481
www.hogwired.com
A: J. Frank Broyles
S: Kevin Trainor
SEC

Arkansas, University of
2801 S. University Avenue
Little Rock, AR 72204
T: (501) 569-3167
F: (501) 569-3030
A: Chris Peterson
S: Kevin Tankersley
Sun Belt

Arkansas State University
PO Box 1000
State University, AR 72467
T: (870) 972-3880
F: (870) 972-3886
A: Joe Hollis
S: Regina Bowman
Sun Belt

Auburn University
PO Box 351
Auburn, AL 36831
T: (334) 844-4750
F: (334) 844-9807
A: David Housel
S: Meredith Jenkins

Austin Peay State University
PO Box 4515
Clarksville, TN 37044
T: (931) 648-7903
F: (931) 648-7562
www.apsu.edu
A: Dave Loos
S: Brad Kirtley
Ohio Valley

Ball State University
2000 University Avenue
Municie, IN 47306
T: (765) 285-1671
F: (765) 285-5123
www.bsu.edu
A: Andrea Seger
S: Joe Hernandez
MAC

Baylor University
150 Bear Run
Waco, TX 76711
T: (254) 710-1234
F: (254) 710-2823
www.baylorsportsnet.com
A: Tom Stanton
S: Scott Stricklin
Big 12

Belmont University
1900 Belmont Blvd.
Nashville, TN 37212
T: (615) 460-6420
F: (615) 460-5584
www.belmont.edu/athletics
A: Michael Strickland
S: Matt Wilson
Trans America

Bethune-Cookman College
640 M. McLeod Bethune Blvd.
Daytona Beach, FL 32114
T: (904) 255-1401
F: (904) 253-4231
A: Lynn W. Thompson
S: Charles Jackson
MEAC

Boise State University
1910 University Drive
Boise, ID 83725
T: (208) 385-4214
F: (208) 385-1778
www.broncosports.com
A: Gene Bleymaier
S: Max Corbet
Big West

Boston College
140 Commonwealth Ave.
Chestnut Hill, MA 02167
T: (617) 552-8520
F: (617) 552-4903
www.bceagles.com
A: Gene DeFilippo
S: Mike Enright
Big East, Hockey East

Boston University
285 Babcock Street
Boston, MA 02215
T: (617) 353-4630
F: (617) 353-5286
www.gobu.com
A: Gary Strickler
S: Ed Carpenter
America East, ECAC,
Hockey East,

Bowling Green State Univ.
Perry Stadium
Bowling Green, OH 43403
T: (419) 372-2401
F: (419) 372-6969
www.bgsufalcons.com
A: Paul Krebs
S: J.C. Campbellr
CCHA, MAC

Bradley University
1501 W. Bradley Ave.
Peoria, IL 61625
T: (309) 677-2666
F: (309) 677-3626
www.bubraves.com
A: Kenneth Kavanagh
S: Bobby Parker
MVC

Brigham Young University
PO Box 22241, 106 Smith Fieldhouse
Provo, UT 84602
T: (801) 378-2096
F: (801) 378-5981
www.byucougars.com
A: Val Hale
S: Norma Collett
Mountain West

Brown University
Box 1932, 235 Hope Street
Providence, RI 02912
T: (401) 863-2211
F: (401) 863-1436
www.brownbears.com
A: David Roach
S: Christopher Humm
ECAC, Ivy League, NECAC

Bucknell University
Moore Avenue
Lewisburg, PA 17837
T: (570) 577-1232
F: (570) 577-1660
www.bucknellbison.ecom
A: John Hardt
S: Todd Newcomb
ECAC, Patriot

Buffalo, University at
(North Campus) 102 Alumni Arena
Buffalo, NY 14260
T: (716) 645-3141
F: (716) 645-3756
www.Ubathletics.buffalo.edu
A: Bob Arkeilpane
S: Paul Vecchio
Mid- American

Butler University
510 W. 49th Street
Indianapolis, IN 46208
T: (317) 940-9375
F: (317) 940-9734
www.butlersports.com
A: John C. Parry
S: Jim McGrath
Horizon, Pioneer, Great Western

California Polytechnic State University
1 Grand Avenue
San Luis Obispo, CA 93407
T: (805) 756-2923
F: (805) 756-2699
www.gopoly.com
A: John McCutcheon
S: Jason Sullivan
Big West

California State-Fullerton
PO Box 6810
Fullerton, CA 92834
T: (714) 278-3058
F: (714) 278-5396
www.sports.fullerton.edu
A: John Easterbrook
S: Mel Franks
Big West

California State-Northridge
18111 Nordhoff Street
Northridge, CA 91330
T: (818) 677-3208
F: (818) 677-4762
www.GoMatadors.com
A: Richard Dull
S: Ryan Finney
Big West, MPSF, PCSC

California State-Sacramento
6000 J Street
Sacramento, CA 95819
T: (916) 278-6481
F: (916) 278-5429
www.hornetsports.com
A: Debby Colberg
S: Brian Berger
Big Sky, Big West, MPSF

California, University of
115 Haas Pavilion
Berkeley, CA 94720
T: (510) 642-5316
F: (510) 642-3399
www.calbears.com
A: Stephen Gladstone
S: Kevin Reneau
Pacific-10

California-Irvine, University of
903 W. Peltason
Irvine, CA 92697
T: (949) 824-6931
F: (949) 824-8492
www.athletics.uci.edu
A: Dan Guerrero
S: Bob Olson
Big West, Mountain Pacific

California-Los Angeles, Univ. of
Morgan Center
Los Angeles, CA 90095
T: (310) 825-8699
F: (310) 206-7047
www.uclabruins.com
A: Peter T. Dalis
S: Mark Dellins
Pacific-10

California-Santa Barbara, U. of
Santa Barbara, CA 93106
T: (805) 893-3291
F: (805) 893-8640
www.ucsbgauchos.com
A: Gary A. Cunningham
S: Bill Mahoney
Big West, Mountain Pacific

Campbell University
Box 10, 89 Pope Street
Buies Creek, NC 27506
T: (910) 893-1325
F: (910) 893-1330
www.campbell.edu/athletics
A: Stan Williamson
S: Stan Cole
Trans America

Canisius College
2001 Main Street
Buffalo, NY 14208
T: (716) 888-2970
F: (716) 888-3174
www.canisius.edu
A: Timothy Dillon
S: Marc Gignac
ECAC, MAAC

Centennary College
Box 41188
Shreveport, LA 71134
T: (318) 869-5275
F: (318) 869-5145
E: dbedard@centenary.edu
A: David Bedard
S: Patrick Netherton
TAAC

Central Connecticut State U.
1615 Stanley Street
New Britain, CT 06053
T: (860) 832-3040
F: (860) 832-3087
www.ccsu.edu/athletics
A: Charles Jones
S: Gene Gkumbs
ECAC, NEC

Central Florida, Univ. of
PO Box 163555
4000 Central Florida Blvd.
Orlando, FL 32816
T: (407) 823-2256
F: (407) 823-5293
www.oir.ucf.edu/sports/main.html
A: Steve Sloan
S: John Marini
TAAC

Central Michigan University
Rose Center
Mount Pleasant, MI 48859
T: (517) 774-3041
F: (517) 774-5391
www.cmuchippewas.com
A: Herb Deromedi
S: Fred Stabley, Jr.
MAC

Charleston, College of
30 George Street
Charleston, SC 29424
T: (843) 953-5556
F: (843) 953-8296
A: Jerry Baker
S: Tony Ciuffo
Southern Conference

Charleston Southern University
PO Box 118087
Charleston, SC 29423
T: (843) 863-7678
F: (843) 863-7695
www.csusports.com
A: Hank Small
S: David Shelton
Big South

Chicago State University
9501 S. King Drive, JDC 201
Chicago, IL 60628
T: (773) 995-2448
F: (773) 995-3656
A: Al Avant
S: Terrance Jackson
Mid-Continent

Cincinnati, University of
PO Box 210021
Cincinnati, OH 45221
T: (513) 556-4603
F: (513) 556-5059
www.ucbearcats.com
A: Bob Goin
S: Tom Hathaway
Conference USA

The Citadel
171 Moultrie Street
Charleston, SC 29409
T: (843) 953-5070
F: (843) 953-6727
www.citadelsports.com
A: Les Robinson
S: Andy Solomon
Southern

Clarkson University
Box 5830, Alumni Gym
Potsdam, NY 13699
T: (315) 268-6616
F: (315) 268-7613
www.clarksonathletics.com
A: Geoff Brown
S: Gary Mikel
ECAC, UCAA

Clemson University
PO Box 31, 1 Perimeter Rd.
Clemson, SC 29634
T: (864) 656-1935
F: (864) 656-0299
www.clemsontigers.com
A: Bobby Robinson
S: Tim Bourret
ACC

Cleveland State University
2451 Euclid Ave.
Cleveland, OH 44115
T: (216) 687-5119
F: (216) 523-7257
www.csuohio.edu
A: John Konstantinos
S: Paulette Welch
MCC, EWL

Coastal Carolina University
PO Box 261954
Conway, SC 29528
T: (843) 349-2820
F: (843) 349-2893
A: Warren Koegel
S: Wayne White
Big South

Colgate University
13 Oak Drive
Hamilton, NY 13346
T: (315) 228-7611
F: (315) 228-7008
www.athletics.colgate.edu
A: Mark Murphy
S: Bob Cornell
ECAC, Patriot

Colorado, University of
Campus Box 368
Boulder, CO 80309
T: (303) 492-7931
F: (303) 492-7753
www.cubuffs.com
A: Richard Tharp
S: David Plati
Big 12

Colorado College
14 E. Cache La Poudre St.
Colorado Springs, CO 80903
T: (719) 389-6476
F: (719) 389-6873
www.coloradocollege.edu/athletics
A: Joel Nielsen
S: Dave Moross
WCHA (HKY), Independent

Colorado State University
McGraw Athletic Center
Fort Collins, CO 80523
T: (970) 491-5300
F: (970) 491-1348
www.csurams.com
A: Open
S: Gary Ozzello
Mountain West

Columbia University
3030 Broadway
Dodge Physical Fitness Ctr.
New York, NY 10027
www.gocolumbialions.com
T: (212) 854-4576
F: (212) 854-2988
A: Dr. John Reeves
E: jar14@columbia.edu
ECAC, Ivy League

Connecticut, Univ. of
2095 Hillside Road
Storrs, CT 06269
T: (860) 486-2725
F: (860) 486-1204
www.uconnhuskies.com
A: Lew Perkins
S: Tim Tolokan
Big East, ECAC, MAAC (Hky)

Coppin State College
2500 W. North Ave.
Baltimore, MD 21216
T: (410) 383-5607
F: (410) 669-6154
A: Ronald Mitchell
S: David Popham
MEAC

Cornell University
Teagle Hall, Campus Rd.
Ithaca, NY 14853
T: (607) 255-5220
F: (607) 257-5182
www.cornellbigred.fansonly.com
A: J. Andrew Noel
S: Laura Stange
ECAC, Ivy League

Creighton University
2500 California Plaza
Omaha, NE 68178
T: (402) 280-2720
F: (402) 280-5596
www.gocreighton.com
A: Bruce Rasmussen
S: Michael Molde
MVC

Dartmouth College
6083 Alumni Gym, Wheelock St.
Hanover, NH 03755
T: (603) 646-2465
F: (603) 646-3348
www.dartmouth.edu
A: Richard Jaeger
S: Kathy Slattery
Ivy League, ECAC

Davidson College
PO Box 1750, 200 Baker St.
Davidson, NC 28036
T: (704) 892-2800
F: (704) 892-2556
www.davidson.edu
A: James Murphy III
S: Rick Bender
Southern

Dayton, University of
300 College Park
Dayton, OH 45469
T: (937) 229-2100
F: (937) 229-4946
www.daytonflyers.com
A: Ted Kissell
S: Doug Hauschild
Atlantic 10, Pioneer

Delaware, University of
Bob Carpenter Center
Newark, DE 19716
T: (302) 831-4006
F: (302) 831-8653
www.udel.edu/sportsinfo
A: Edgar Johnson
S: Scott Selheimer
Amer. East, Atlantic 10 (FB) Colonial

Delaware State University
1200 North Dupont Hwy
Dover, DE 19901
T: (302) 857-6030
F: (302) 857-6034
www.dsc.edu
A: Hallie Gregory
S: Dennis Jones
ECAC, MEAC

Denver, University of
2201 E. Asbury Ave.
Denver, CO 80208
T: (303) 871-2275
F: (303) 871-3890
A: Dr. Diane Murphy
S: Maria Rodriguez
WCHA (HKY), Sun Belt

DePaul University
2323 N. Sheffield Avenue
Chicago, IL 60604
T: (773) 325-7526
F: (773) 325-7529
www.depaulbluedemons.com
A: Bill Bradshaw
S: Scott Reed
Conference USA

Detroit Mercy, Univ. of
PO Box 19900
Detroit, MI 48219
T: (313) 993-1700
F: (313) 993-2449
www.detroittitans.com
A: Brad Kinsman
S: Mark Engel
Horizon League

Drake University
25th & University
Des Moines, IA 50311
T: (515) 271-2889
F: (515) 271-3015
www.drakebulldogs.org
A: Dave Blank
S: Mike Mahon
Central Collegiate, MVC, Pioneer FB

Drexel University
3141 Chestnut Street
Philadelphia, PA 19104
T: (215) 895-1999
F: (215) 895-2037
www.drexel.edu/sports
A: Eric Zillmer
S: Jan Giel
Colonial Athletic Association

Duke University
PO Box 90555
Durham, NC 27708
T: (919) 684-2120
F: (919) 681-7866
www.goduke.com
A: Joe Alleva
S: Jon Jackson
ACC

Duquesne University
600 Forbes Ave.
Pittsburgh, PA 15285
T: (412) 396-6565
F: (412) 396-6210
www.duq.edu
A: Brian Colleary
S: Dave Saba
Atlantic 10, MAAC (FB)

East Carolina University
Ficklen Drive
Greenville, NC 27858
T: (252) 328-4600
F: (252) 328-4537
www.ecupirates.com
A: Michael Hamrick
S: Open
Conference USA (FB)

East Tennessee State U.
Box 70707, 325 W. Memorial Ctr.
Johnson City, TN 37614
T: (423) 439-4343
F: (423) 439-5294
www.etsubucs.edu
A: Todd Stansbury
S: Simon Gray
Southern

Eastern Illinois University
262 Lantz Bldg., Grant Street
Charleston, IL 61920
T: (217) 581-2319
F: (217) 581-7001
www.eiu.edu/~sprtinfo/
A: Rich Mc Duffie
S: Dave Kidwell
Ohio Valley

Eastern Kentucky University
521 Lancaster Ave.
Richmond, KY 40475
T: (606) 622-3654
F: (606) 622-1230
www.eku.edu/athletics
A: Chip Smith
S: Karl Park
OVC

Eastern Michigan University
Convocation Center
Ypsilanti, MI 48197
T: (734) 487-1050
F: (734) 487-6898
www.emich.edu/goeagles
A: Dr. David L. Diles
S: Jim Streeter
MAC

Eastern Washington University
207 Physical Ed. Building
Cheney, WA 99004
T: (509) 359-2463
F: (509) 359-2828
www.athletics.ewu.edu
A: Scott Barnes
S: David Cook
Big Sky

Elon College
2500 Campus Box
Elon College, NC 27244
T: (336) 584-2420
F: (336) 584-2443
www.elon.edu/athletics
A: Dr. Alan J. White
S: Matt Eviston
Big South

Evansville, University of
1800 Lincoln Ave.
Evansville, IN 47722
T: (812) 479-2237
F: (812) 479-2190
www.evansville.edu
A: Bob Gallman
S: Bob Boxell
MVC

Fairfield University
N. Benson Road
Fairfield, CT 06430
T: (203) 254-4000
F: (203) 254-4270
www.fairfield.edu
A: Eugene Doris
S: Jack Jones
ECAC, MAAC, Patriot

Fairleigh Dickinson University
1000 River Road
Teaneck, NJ 07666
T: (201) 692-2254
F: (201) 692-9361
A: Steve Hurlbut
S: Drew Brown
NEC Northeast

Ferris State University
210 Sports Drive
Big Rapids, MI 49307
T: (231) 591-2860
F: (231) 591-2869
www.ferris.edu/htmls/sports/
A: Tom Kirinovic
S: Joe Gorby
CCHA (HKY), GLIAC

Florida, University of
Gainesville, FL 32604
T: (352) 375-4683
F: (352) 377-8971
www.uaa.ufl.edu
A: Jeremy Foley
S: Matthew Ciciarelli
SEC

Florida A&M University
1500 Wahnish Way, Rm. 203 LSB
Tallahassee, FL 32307
T: (850) 599-3868
F: (850) 599-3810
A: Kenneth Riley
S: Alvin Hollins, Jr.
MEAC

Florida Atlantic University
777 Glades Rd.
Boca Raton, FL 33431
T: (561) 297-3710
F: (561) 297-3963
www.fausports.com
A: Tom Cargill
S: Katrina McCormack
TAAC

Florida International University
Tamiami Trail & SW 107th Ave.
Miami, FL 33199
T: (305) 348-2756
F: (305) 348-2963
www.fiu.edu/``Athletic
A: Rick Melloo
S: Rich Kelch
Sun Belt

Florida State University
PO Box 2195, Moore Athletic Center
Tallahassee, FL 32316
T: (850) 644-1079
F: (850) 644-7293
www.seminoles.com
A: Dave Hart, Jr.
S: Rob Wilson
ACC

Fordham University
411 E. Fordham Rd., Rose Hill
Bronx, NY 10458
T: (718) 817-4300
F: (718) 817-5588
www.fordham.edu/athletics
A: Frank McLaughlin
S: Joe DiBari
Atlantic 10, ECAC, Patriot

Fresno State University
5305 N. Campus Drive MS NG27
Fresno, CA 93740
T: (559) 244-2800
F: (559) 244-2945
www.gobulldogs.com
A: Scott Johnson (interim)
S: Steve Weakland
WAC

Furman University
3300 Poinsett Hwy
Greenville, SC 29613
T: (864) 294-2150
F: (864) 294-3059
www.furmanpaladins.com
A: Gary Clark
S: Hunter Reid
Southern

George Mason University
4400 University Drive, MS 3A5
Fairfax, VA 22030
T: (703) 993-3200
F: (703) 993-3239
www.sports.gmu.edu
A: Thomas O'Connor
S: Ben Trittipoe
IC4AAAA, CAA, ECAC

George Washington University
600 22nd Street NW, Suite 219
Washington, DC 20037
T: (202) 994-6650
F: (202) 994-6818
www.gwsports.com
A: Jack Kvancz
S: Brad Bower
Atlantic 10

Georgetown University
McDonough Arena
Washington, DC 20057
T: (202) 687-2435
F: (202) 687-5366
www.guhoyas.com
A: Joseph Lang
S: Mike Tuberosa
S: Bill Shapland (Men's Bskb.)
ECAC, Big East, IC4A, ECAC

Georgia Institute of Technology
150 Bobby Dodd Way, NW
Atlanta, GA 30332
T: (404) 894-5400
F: (404) 894-1248
www.ramblinwreck.com
A: David Braine
S: Mike Stamus
ACC

Georgia, University of
PO Box 1472, Butts-Mehre Bldg.
Athens, GA 30603
T: (706) 542-9037
F: (706) 542-9100
www.georgiadogs.com
A: Vince Dooley
S: Claude Felton
SEC

Georgia Southern University
PO Box 8082
Statesboro, GA 30460
T: (912) 681-5376
F: (912) 681-0095
www.georgiasoutherneagles.com
A: Sam Baker
S: Tom McClellan
Southern

Georgia State University
1 Park Place S., Suite 840
Atlanta, GA 30303
T: (404) 651-2722
F: (404) 651-0842
www.georgiastate.com
A: Greg Manning
S: Devlin Pierce
TAAC

Gonzaga University
E. 502 Boone Ave.
Spokane, WA 99258
T: (509) 323-4202
F: (509) 323-5787
www.gozags.com
A: Michael Roth
S: Oliver Pierce
WCC

Grambling State University
Box 868
Grambling, LA 71245
T: (318) 274-2634
F: (318) 274-2761
A: Albert Dennis
S: T. Scott Boatright
SWAC

Hampton University
Hampton, VA 23668
T: (757) 727-5641
F: (757) 727-5813
A: Dr.Dennis Thomas
S: Patricia Harvey
MEAC

Hartford, University of
200 Bloomfield Ave.
West Hartford, CT 06117
T: (860) 768-4658
F: (860) 768-5047
www.hartford.edu
A: Pat Meiser-McKnett
S: Tom Pincince
America East

Harvard University
65 N. Harvard St., Murr Center
Boston, MA 02163
T: (617) 495-4848
F: (617) 496-9950
www.fas.harvard.edu/~athletic
A: Robert Scalise
S: John Veneziano
ECAC, Ivy League, NECAC

Hawaii, University of
1337 Lower Campus Rd.
Honolulu, HI 96822
T: (808) 956-7301
F: (808) 956-4637
www.uhathletics.hawaii.edu
A: Hugh Yoshida
S: Lois Manin
WAC

High Point University
University Station, Montilieu Ave.
High Point, NC 27262
T: (336) 841-9276
F: (336) 841-9182
www.acme.highpoint.edu
A: Dr. Woody Gibson
S: Richard Hord
Big South

Hofstra University
Hempstead, NY 11550
T: (516) 463-6750
F: (516) 463-4860
www.hofstra.edu/sports
A: Harry Royle
S: Jim Sheehan
EAA, ECAC

Holy Cross, College of the
Worcester, MA 01610
T: (508) 793-2571
F: (508) 793-3863
www.holycross.edu
A: Richard Regan, Jr.
S: Frank Mastrandrea
ECAC, MAAC (Hky), Patriot

Houston, University of
3100 Cullen Blvd.
Houston, TX 77204
T: (713) 743-9370
F: (713) 743-9375
www.uhcougars.com
A: Chet Gladchuk
S: Chris Burkhalter
Conference USA

Howard University
6th & Girard Sts. NW
Washington, DC 20059
T: (202) 806-7140
F: (202) 806-9090
www.cldc.howard.edu
A: Sondra Norrell-Thomas
S: Edward Hill
MEAC

Idaho, University of
Kibbie-ASUI Activity Center
Moscow, ID 83844
T: (208) 885-0200
F: (208) 885-2862
www.uidaho.edu/athletics
A: Mike Bohn
S: Becky Paull
Big West (FB), Sun Belt

Idaho State University
Box 8173, Holt Arena
Pocatello, ID 83209
T: (208) 236-2771
F: (208) 236-4063
www.isu.edu/athletics
A: Dr. Howard Gauthier
S: Frank Mercogliano
Big Sky

Illinois, University of
1700 S. 4th Street
Champaign, IL 61820
T: (217) 333-3631
F: (217) 244-3269
www.fightingillini.com
A: Ronald Guenther
S: Kent Brown
Big Ten

Illinois-Chicago, University of
901 W. Roosevelt Rd.
Chicago, IL 60608
T: (312) 996-2772
F: (312) 996-8349
www.uicflames.com
A: James Schmidt
S: Anne Schoenherr
Horizon League

Illinois State University
2660 Redbird Arena, #213
Normal, IL 61790
T: (309) 438-3636
F: (309) 438-2323
www.redbirds.org
A: Perk Weisenburger
S: Kenneth Mossman
Gateway (FB), MVC

Indiana University
Athletic Department
1001 E. 17th Street
Bloomington, IN 47408
T: (812) 855-2794
F: (812) 855-0448
www.athletics.indiana.edu
A: Michaell McNeely
S: Jeff Fanter
Big Ten

Indiana Univ.-Purdue Univ.
901 W. New York St., Ste 105
Indianapolis, IN 46202
T: (317) 274-0622
F: (317) 274-0609
www.iupui.edu/~jagsport
A: Michael R. Moore
S: Kevin Buerge
Mid-Continent

Indiana State University
Terre Haute, IN 47807
T: (812) 237-4040
F: (812) 237-4157
www.indstate.edu/athletic
A: Andrea Myers
S: Kent Johnson
Gateway, MVC

Iona College
715 North Ave.
New Rochelle, NY 10801
T: (914) 633-2305
F: (914) 633-2072
www.iona.edu
A: Shawn Brennan
S: Mike Laprey
ECAC, MAAC

Iowa, University of
1 Elliott Drive
Iowa City, IA 52242
T: (319) 335-9327
F: (319) 335-9333
www.hawkeyesports.com
A: Bob Bowlsby
S: Phil Haddy
Big Ten

Iowa State University
1800 S. 4th St.
Ames, IA 50011
T: (515) 294-3662
F: (515) 294-0104
www.cyclone.com
A: Bruce Van De Velde
S: Tom Kroeschell
Big 12

Jackson State University
1325 John R. Lynch Street
Jackson, MS 39217
T: (601) 968-2291
F: (601) 968-7008
A: Roy Culberson
S: Samuel Jefferson
SWAC

Jacksonville University
2800 University Blvd. N.
Jacksonville, FL 32211
T: (904) 745-7400
F: (904) 743-0067
www.judolphins.com
A: Hugh Durham
S: Jamie Zeitz
TAAC

Jacksonville State University
700 Pelham Rd. N.
Jacksonville, AL 36265
T: (256) 782-5365
F: (256) 782-5666
www.jsu.edu/athletics
A: Tom Seitz
S: Mike Galloway
Southland (FB), TAAC

James Madison University
Harrisonburg, VA 22807
T: (540) 568-6164
F; (540) 568-3489
www.jmu.edu
A: Jeffrey T. Bourne
S: Gary Michael
Atlantic 10, Colonial, ECAC

John Hopkins University
3400 N. Charles Street
Baltimore, MD 21218
T: (410) 516-7490
F: (410) 516-5376
www.HopkinsSports.com
A: Tom Calder
S: Ernie Larossa
ECAC (Lacrosse), Centennial

Kansas, University of
Lawrence, KS 66045
T: (785) 864-3143
F: (785) 864-5035
www.jayhawks.org
A: Al Bohl
S: Doug Vance
Big 12

Kansas State University
1800 College Avenue
Manhattan, KS 66502
T: (785) 532-6910
F: (785) 532-2340
www.ksu.edu
A: Tim Weiser
S: Doug Dull
Big 12

Kent State University
Kent, OH 44242
T: (330) 672-5974
F: (330) 672-3806
www.kent.edu/athletics
A: Laing Kennedy
S: Will Roleson
MAC

Kentucky, University of
Memorial Coliseum
Lexington, KY 40506
T: (859) 257-8000
F: (859) 257-8570
www.ukathletics.com
A: Larry w. Ivy
S: Tony Neely
SEC

La Salle University
1900 W. Olney, PO Box 805
Philadelphia, PA 19105
T: (215) 951-1516
F: (215) 951-1694
www.lasalle.edu/athletic
A: Dr. Thomas Brennan
S: Kevin Currie
Atlantic 10, ECAC, MAAC (FB)

Lafayette College
Easton, PA 18042
T: (610) 330-5470
F: (610) 330-5702
www.goleopards.com
A: Open
S: Scott Morse
ECAC, Patriot

Lake Superior State University
Sault Ste. Marie, MI 49783
T: (906) 635-2627
F: (906) 635-2753
www.lssu.edu
A: Bill Crawford
S: Jill Rheaume
CCHA (Hky), GLIAC

Lamar University
PO Box 10066, 211 Red Bird Lane
Beaumont, TX 77710
T: (409) 880-2248
F: (409) 880-1814
www.athletics.lamar.edu
A: Dean Billick
S: Daucy Crizer
Southland

Lehigh University
Bethlehem, PA 18015
T: (610) 758-4300
F: (610) 758-6629
www.lehigh.edu
A: Joe Sterrett
S: Jim Marshall
ECAC, Patriot

Liberty University
1971 University Blvd.
Lynchburg, VA 24502
T: (804) 582-2100
F: (804) 582-2076
www.liberty.edu
A: Kim Graham
S: Todd Wetmore
Big South

Long Beach State University
1250 Bellflower Blvd.
Long Beach, CA 90840
T: (562) 985-4655
F: (562) 985-8197
A: Bill Shumard
S: Steve Janisch
Big West, MPSF

Long Island University
1 University Plaza
Brooklyn, NY 11201
T: (718) 488-1030
F: (718) 488-1669
www.liu.edu
A: John Suarez
S: Greg Fox
NEC

Louisiana State University
PO Box 25095
Baton Rouge, LA 70894
T: (225) 334-4578
F: (225) 388-2430
www.LSUsports.net
A: Stanley "Skip" Bertman
S: Michael Bonnette
SEC

Louisiana Tech University
PO Box 3046
Ruston, LA 71272
T: (318) 257-4111
F: (318) 257-4437
A: Jim Oakes
S: Dr. Malcolm Butter
Western Athletic Conference

Louisville, University of
Student Activities Center
Louisville, KY 40292
T: (502) 852-5732
F: (502) 852-0816
www.uoflsports.com
A: Tom Jurich
S: Kenny Klein
Conference USA

Loyola College
4501 N. Charles Street
Baltimore, MD 21210
T: (410) 617-5013
F: (410) 617-2008
www.loyola.edu/athletics
A: Joseph Boylan
S: David Rosenfeld
ECAC, MAAC

Loyola Marymount University
One LMU Drive, Gersten-MC8235
Los Angeles, CA 90045
T: (310) 338-2765
F: (310) 338-5915
www.lmulions.com
A: William Husak
S: John Shaffer
WCC

Loyola University
6525 N. Sheridan Rd.
Chicago, IL 60626
T: (773) 508-2560
F: (773) 508-3884
www.loyolaramblers.com
A: John Planek
S: Bill Behrns
Horizon League

Maine, University of
5747 Memorial Gym
Orono, ME 04469
T: (207) 581-1058
F: (207) 581-3297
E: sjtyler@maine.maine.edu
A: Dr. Suzanne Tyler
S: Joseph Roberts
America East, Atlantic 10,
Hockey East

Manhattan College
Manhaattan College Parkway
Riverdale, NY 10471
T: (718) 862-7227
F: (718) 862-8020
www.manhattan.edu
A: Robert Byrnes
S: Jeffrey Wyshner
ECAC, MAAC

Marist College
Poughkeepsie, NY 12601
T: (914) 575-3304
F: (914) 452-7028
www.marist.edu/athletics
A: Tim Murray
S: Kimberly Zivkovich
MAAC

Marquette University
PO Box 1881
Milwaukee, WI 53233
T: (414) 288-6303
F: (414) 288-7341
www.gomarquette.com
A: Bill Cords
S: John Farina
Conference USA

Marshall University
Huntington, WV 25715
T: (304) 696-5408
F: (304) 696-6448
www.herdzone.com
A: Lance West
S: Ricky Hazel
Mid-American

Maryland, University of
PO Box 295
College Park, MD 20741
T: (301) 314-7075
F: (301) 314-7149
www.umterps.com
A: Deborah A. Yow
S: Dave Haglund
ACC, ECAC

Maryland-Baltimore Co., Univ. of
1000 Hilltop Circle
Baltimore, MD 21250
T: (410) 455-2126
F: (410) 455-1159
www.umbc.edu/UMBCAthletics
A: Dr. Charles Brown
S: Steve Levy
ECAC, Northeast

Maryland-Eastern Shore, U. of
Princess Anne, MD 21853
T: (410) 651-6496
F: (410) 651-7600
www.umes.edu
A: Vivian Fuller
S: Open
MEAC

Massachusetts, University of
Amherst, MA 01003
T: (413) 545-2342
F: (413) 545-1727
www.umassathletics.com
A: Bob Marcum
S: Nick Joos
Atlantic 10, ECAC, Hockey East

Massachussets-Lowell, Univ. of
One University Ave., Costello Gym
Lowell, MA 01854
T: (978) 934-2310
F: (978) 934-2313
www.uml.edu/athletics
A: Dana Skinner
S: Chris O'Donnell
Northeast Ten

McNeese State University
PO Box 92735, Ryan Street
Lake Charles, LA 70609
T: (318) 475-5200
F: (318) 475-5202
A: Sonny Watkins
S: Louis Bonnette
Southland

Memphis, University of
570 Normal
Memphis, TN 38152
T: (901) 678-2335
F: (901) 678-5078
www.gotigersgo.com
A: R.C. Johnson
S: Bob Winn
Conference USA

Mercer University
1400 Coleman Ave.
Macon, GA 31207
T: (912) 752-2994
F: (912) 752-2061
www.mercer.edu
A: Bobby Pope
S: Kevin Coulombe
TAAC

Merrimack College
351 Turnpike Street
North Andover, MA 01845
T: (978) 837-5341
F: (978) 837-5032
A: Robert DeGregorio, Jr.
S: Tom O'Brien
ECAC, Hockey East, NE10

Miami, University of
5821 San Amaro Ddrive
Coral Gables, FL 33146
T: (305) 284-3822
F: (305) 284-2703
www.hurricanesports.com
A: Paul Dee
S: Mark Pray
Big East

Miami University
Millett Hall
Oxford, OH 45056
T: (513) 529-3113
F: (513) 529-6318
www.muredhawks.com
A: Joel Maturi
S: Mike Wolf
MAC

Michigan, University of
1000 S. State Street
Ann Arbor, MI 48109
T: (734) 647-2583
F: (734) 764-3221
www.mgoblue.com
A: William Martin
S: Bruce Madej
Big Ten

Michigan State University
248 Jenison Field House
East Lansing, MI 48824
T: (517) 355-9710
F: (517) 432-1047
www.msuspartans.com
A: Clarence Underwood
S: John Lewandowski
Big Ten

Michigan Technological Univ.
1400 Townsend Drive
Houghton, MI 49931
T: (906) 487-3070
F: (906) 487-1810
www.athletics.mtu.edu
A: Rick Yeo
S: David Fischer
WCHA, GLIAC, MIFC

Middle Tennessee State University
MTSU Box 77, 1500 Greenland Dr.
Murfreesboro, TN 37132
T: (615) 898-2450
F: (615) 898-5626
www.goblueraiders.com
A: James Donnelly
S: Mark Owens
OVC

Minnesota-Duluth, University of
10 University Drive
Duluth, MN 55812
T: (218) 726-8168
F: (218) 726-6529
www.umdbulldogs.com
A: Robert Corran
S: Bob Nygaard
WCHA, NSIC

Minnesota, University of
516 15th Ave SE, Rm. 226
Minneapolis, MN 55455
T: (612) 625-4838
F: (612) 626-7859
www.gophersports.com
A: Tom Moe
S: Bill Crumley
Big Ten, WCHA

Minnesota State U., Mankato
Mankato, MN 56001
T: (507) 389-6111
F: (507) 389-2904
www.mankato.msus.edu/dept/athletic
A: Donald Amiot
S: Paul Allan
NCC

Mississippi, University of
University, MS 38677
T: (662) 232-7241
F: (662) 232-7683
www.olemisssports.com
A: John Shafer
S: Langston Rogers
SEC

Mississippi State University
Mississippi State, MS 39762
T: (662) 325-2532
F: (662) 325-2563
www.mstateathletics.com
A: Larry Templeton
S: Mike Nemeth
SEC

Mississippi Valley State Univ.
14000 Highway 82 W. #7246
Itta Bena, MS 38941
T: (662) 254-3550
F: (662) 254-3639
www.mvsu.edu
A: Lonza Hardy, Jr.
S: Marlon Reed
SWAC

Missouri, University of
Hearnes Center, PO Box 677
Columbia, MO 65205
T: (573) 882-6501
F: (573) 882-4720
A: Michael Alden
S: Chad Moller
Big 12

Missouri-KC, University of
5100 Rockhill Rd.
Kansas City, MO 64110
T: (816) 235-1036
F: (816) 235-1035
www.umkckangaroos.com
A: Robert Thomas
S: Patrick Madden
Mid-Continent

Monmouth University
400 Cedar Avenue
West Long Branch, NJ 07764
T: (732) 571-3415
F: (732) 571-3535
www.monmouth.edu
A: Marilyn McNeil
S: Thomas Dick
ECAC, Northeast

Montana, University of
Missoula, MT 59812
T: (406) 243-5331
F: (406) 243-6859
www.montanagrizzlies.com
A: Wayne Hogan
S: Dave Guffey
Big Sky

Montana State University
Bozeman, MT 59717
T: (406) 994-4221
F: (406) 994-2278
www.msubobcats.com
A: Chuck Lindemenn
S: Bill Lamberty
Big Sky

Morehead State University
Morehead, KY 40351
T: (606) 783-2088
F: (606) 783-5035
www.morehead-st-edu/athletics
A: Mike Mincey
S: Randy Stacy
OVC

Morgan State University
1700 E. Coldspring Lane
Baltimore, MD 21251
T: (443) 319-3050
F: (443) 319-3221
www.morgan.edu
A: David Y. Thomas
S: Open
ECAC, MEAC

Mount St. Mary's College
16300 Old Emmitsburg Rd.
Emmitsburg, MD 21727
T: (301) 447-5296
F: (301) 447-5300
www.mountathletics.com
A: Harold Menninger
S: Eric Kloiber
NEC

Murray State University
Murray, KY 42071
T: (270) 762-6800
F: (270) 762-6814
www.goracers.com
A: E.W. Dennison
S: Steve Parker
OVC

Nebraska, University of
Lincoln, NE 68588
T: (402) 472-4224
F: (402) 472-9675
www.huskers.com
A: William Byrne, Jr.
S: Chris Anderson
Big 12

Nevada-Las Vegas, University of
PO Box 450001-LVNV
Las Vegas, NV 89154
T: (702) 895-4729
F: (702) 895-4468
www.unlvrebels.com
A: Charles Cavagnaro
S: Andy Grossman
Mountain West

Nevada, University of
Legacy Hall 232
Reno, NV 89557
T: (775) 784-6900
F: (775) 784-4497
www.nevadawolfpack.com
A: Chris Ault
S: Jamie Klund
WAC

New Hampshire, University of
145 Main Street, Field House
Durham, NH 03824
T: (603) 862-1850
F: (603) 862-3839
www.unhwildcats.com
A: Martin Scarano
S: Scott Stapin
Amer.East, ECAC, Hky East, EAGL
Atlantic Ten

New Mexico, University of
Dept. of Athletics, South Campus
Albuquerque, NM 87131
T: (505) 925-5500
F: (505) 925-5509
www.golobos.com
A: Rudy Davalos
S: Greg Remington
Mountain West

New Mexico State University
Las Cruces, NM 88003
T: (505) 646-4126
F: (505) 646-5221
www.nmsu.edu/~athletic
A: Brian Faison
S: Sean Johnson
Big West

New Orleans, University of
New Orleans, LA 70148
T: (504) 280-6239
F: (504) 280-3980
www.athletics.uno.edu
A: Bob Brown
S: Bob Boyle
Sun Belt

Niagara University
Niagara University, NY 14109
T: (716) 286-8600
F: (716) 286-8609
www.niagara.edu/sports
A: Mike Hermann
S: Mark Vandergrift
ECAC, MAAC, CHA

Nicholls State University
PO Box 2032
Thibodaux, LA 70310
T: (504) 448-4794
F: (504) 448-4814
www.nich.edu
A: Robert Bernardi
S: Ross Blacker
Southland

Norfolk State University
700 Park Avenue
Norfolk, VA 23504
T: (757) 823-8152
F: (757) 823-2566
A: Orby Z. Moss, Jr.
S: Randy Jones
MEAC

North Carolina, University of
One University Heights
Asheville, NC 28804
T: (828) 251-6459
F: (828) 251-6386
www.unca.edu.athletics
A: Dr. Joni Comstock
S: Mike Gore
Big South

North Carolina, University of
PO Box 2126
Chapel Hill, NC 27515
T: (919) 962-6000
F: (919) 962-6002
A: Richard Baddour
S: Steve Kirschner
ACC

North Carolina, University of
9201 University City Blvd.
Charlotte, NC 28223
T: (704) 547-4920
F: (704) 547-4918
www.uncc.edu/athletics
A: Judy Rose
S: Tom Whitestone
Conference USA

North Carolina, University of
PO Box 26168, 337 HHP Bldg.
Greensboro, NC 27402
T: (336) 334-5952
F: (336) 334-4063
www.uncgspartans.com
A: Nelson Bobb
S: Jake Keys
Southern Conference

North Carolina, University of
601 S. College Road
Wilmington, NC 28403
T: (910) 962-3232
F: (910) 962-3002
www.uncwil.edu/athletics
A: Margaret Bradley-Doppes
S: Joe Browning
CAA

North Carolina A&T State Univ.
Moore Gym
1601 E. Market Street
Greensboro, NC 27411
T: (336) 334-7686
F: (336) 334-7272
www.ncat.edu/~athletics
A: Alfonso Scandrett
S: Donol O. Ware
MEAC

North Carolina State University
Box 8501, Case Athletics Center
Raleigh, NC 27695
T: (919) 515-2101
F: (919) 515-3624
www.ncsu.edu/athletics
A: Lee Fowler
S: Annabelle Vaughan
ACC

North Dakota, University of
Box 9013, 2nd Ave. N.
Grand Forks, ND 58203
T: (701) 777-2234
F: (701) 777-4352
www.fightingsioux.com
A: Roger Thomas
S: Dan Benson
WCHA, NCIAC

North Texas, University of
PO Box 311397
Denton, TX 76203
T: (940) 565-3646
F: (940) 565-3470
www.unt.edu/meangreen/
A: Rick Villarreal
S: Sean Johnson
Sun Belt

Northeast Louisiana University
308 Stadium Drive, Malone Stadium
Monroe, LA 71209
T: (318) 342-5365
F: (318) 342-5367
www.ulmathletics.com
A: Bruce Hanks
S: Hank Largin
Southland

Northeastern Illinois University
5500 N. St. Louis Avenue
Chicago, IL 60625
T: (773) 794-6128
F: (773) 794-6244
A: Robert Krawchuk
S: Open
Mid-Continent

Northeastern University
219 Cabot Ctr., 360 Huntington Ave.
Boston, MA 02115
T: (617) 373-2672
F: (617) 373-8988
www.gonu.com
A: Ian Mc Caw
S: Jack Grinold
America East. ECAC, Hky East
Atlantic 10 (FB)

Northern Arizona University
Box 15400
Flagstaff, AZ 86011
T: (928) 523-5353
F: (928) 523-6035
www.nauathletics.com
A: Steve Holton
S: Jack Grinold
Big Sky

Northern Illinois University
101 Evans Field House
DeKalb, IL 60115
T: (815) 753-1295
F: (815) 753-7700
www.niu.edu/athletics
A: Cary Sue Groth
S: Michael Korcek
Mid-American

Northern Iowa, University of
Cedar Falls, IA 50614
T: (319) 273-3100
F: (319) 273-6112
www.uni.edu/athletic/
A: Rick Hartzell
S: Nancy Justis
Gateway, MVC

Northern Michigan University
1401 Presque Isle Ave.
Marquette, MI 49855
T: (906) 227-2105
F: (906) 227-2492
www.nmu.edu
A: Dan Spielmann
S: Jim Pinar
CCHA, GLIAC

Northwestern State University
Natchitoches, LA 71497
T: (318) 357-5251
F: (318) 357-4221
www.nsudemons.com
A: Greg Burke
S: Doug Ireland
Southland

Northwestern University
1501 Central Street
Evanston, IL 60208
T: (847) 491-3205
F: (847) 491-4659
www.nusports.com
A: Rick Taylor
S: Mike Wolf
Big Ten

Notre Dame, University of
Joyce Center
Notre Dame, IN 46556
T: (219) 631-6107
F: (219) 631-8231
A: Kevin White
S: John Heisler
Independent (FB), Big East, CCHA

Oakland University
Athletic Dept.
Rochester, MI 48309
T: (248) 370-3190
F: (248) 370-4056
www.oakland.edu/ouathletics
A: Jack Mehl
S: Amy Stabley-Hirschman
Mid-Continent

Ohio State University
410 Woody Hayes Drive
Columbus, OH 43210
T: (614) 292-7572
F: (614) 292-0506
www.ohiostatebuckeyes.com
A: Andy Geiger
S: Steve Snapp
Big Ten

Ohio University
Athens, OH 45701
T: (740) 593-1000
F: (740) 593-2420
www.ohiobobcats.com
A: Thomas Boeh
S: Open
MAC

Oklahoma, University of
Norman, OK 73019
T: (405) 325-8200
F: (405) 325-7632
www.soonersports.com
A: Joe Castiglione
S: TBA
Big 12

Oklahoma State University
Stillwater, OK 74078
T: (405) 707-7800
F: (405) 780-7734
www.okstate.com
A: Terry Phillips
S: Steve Buzzard
Big 12

Old Dominion University
Athletic Administration Bldg.
Norfolk, VA 23529
T: (757) 683-3375
F: (757) 683-3119
www.odusports.com
A: Dr. James Jarrett
S: Carol Hudson
Colonial

Oral Roberts University
7777 S. Lewis Avenue
Tulsa, OK 74171
T: (918) 495-7100
F: (918) 495-7123
www.oru.edu
A: Mike Carter
S: Cory Rogers
Mid-Continent

Oregon, University of
2727 Leo Harris Pkwy.
Eugene, OR 97401
T: (541) 346-4481
F: (541) 346-5031
www.goducks.com
A: William Moos
S: David Williford
Pacific 10

Oregon State University
Corvallis, OR 97331
T: (541) 737-2547
F: (541) 737-1790
www.osubeavers.com
A: Mitch Barnhart
S: Hal Cowan
Pacific 10

Pacific, University of the
3601 Pacific Ave.
Stockton, CA 95211
T: (209) 946-2472
F: (209) 946-2731
www.pacifictigers.com
A: Lynn King
S: Mike Millerick
Big West

Pennsylvania, University of
235 S. 33rd Street
Philadelphia, PA 19104
T: (215) 898-6121
F: (215) 573-2095
www.pennathletics.com
A: Steven Bilsky
S: Carla Shultzberg
Ivy League

Pennsylvania State University
University Park, PA 16802
T: (814) 865-1000
F: (814) 863-7955
A: Tim Curley
S: Jeff Nelson
Big Ten

Pepperdine University
24255 Pacific Coast Hwy.
Malibu, CA 90263
T: (310) 456-4150
F: (310) 456-7459
www.pepperdine.edu/athletics
A: Dr. John Watson
S: Mike Zapolski
WCC

Pittsburgh, University of
PO Box 7436
Pittsburgh, PA 15213
T: (412) 648-8200
F: (412) 648-8248
www.pittsburghpanthers.com
A: Steven Pederson
S: E.J. Borghetti
Big East, ECAC, EAGL, EWL

Portland, University of
5000 N. Willamette Blvd.
Portland, OR 97203
T: (503) 283-7117
F: (503) 978-8082
www.up.edu
A: Joe Etzel
S: Loren Wohlgemuth
WCC

Portland State University
PO Box 751
Portland, OR 97207
T: (503) 725-4000
F: (503) 725-5550
www.goviks.com
A: Tom Burman
S: Mike Lund
Big Sky (FB),
Pacific 10 (Wrestling)

Prairie View A&M University
PO Box 97
Prairie View, TX 77446
T: (409) 857-2127
F: (409) 857-2408
www.pvamu.edu/sports
A: Walter Redd
S: Harlan Stefann Robinson
SWAC

Princeton University
PO Box 71, Jadwin Gym
Princeton, NJ 08544
T: (609) 258-3534
F: (609) 258-4477
www.goprincetontigers.com
A: Gary Walters
S: Jerry Price
ECAC, Ivy League

Providence College
549 River Avenue
Providence, RI 02918
T: (401) 865-2500
F: (401) 865-2583
www.friars.com
A: John Marinatto
S: Tim Connor
Big East, ECAC, IC4A, MAAC
Hockey East

Purdue University
1790 Mackey Arena
West Lafayette, IN 47907
T: (765) 494-3189
F: (765) 496-1280
A: Morgan Burke
S: Tom Shott
Big Ten

Quinnipiac University
275 Mt. Carmel Ave.
Hamden, CT 06518
T: (203) 582-8620
F: (203) 582-8716
www.quinnipiac.edu/athletics
A: Jack McDonald
S: Al Carbone
ECAC, NEC

Radford University
Box 6913
Radford, VA 24142
T: (540) 831-5228
F: (540) 831-6095
www.runet.edu
A: Greig Denny
S: Aaron Barter
Big South, Colonial

Rensselaer Polytechnic Institute
Troy, NY 12180
T: (518) 276-6685
F: (518) 276-8997
www.rpi.edu/dept/athletics
A: Eddie Knowles
S: Kevin Beattie
UCAA, ECAC, NYSWCAA

Rhode Island, University of
Kingston, RI 02881
T: (401) 874-5245
F: (401) 874-2458
www.gorhody.com
A: Ron Petro
S: Mike Ballweg
Atlantic 10

Rice University
PO Box 1892, MS 548
Houston, TX 77251
T: (713) 527-4077
F: (713) 527-6019
www.rice.edu/owls
A: John R. "Bobby"May
S: Bill Cousins
WAC

Richmond, University of
Robins Center, College Road
Richmond, VA 23173
T: (804) 289-8371
F: (804) 287-1826
www.richmondspiders.edu.com
A: Jim Miller
S: Phil Stanton
Atlantic 10 (FB), CAA

Rider University
Lawrenceville, NJ 08648
T: (609) 896-5054
F: (609) 896-0341
www.rider.edu/athletics
A: Curtis Blake
S: Bud Focht
ECAC, ECWA, MAAC

Robert Morris College
Moon Township, PA 15108
T: (412) 262-8295
F: (412) 262-8557
www.robert-morris.edu
A: Dr. Susan Hofacre
S: Open
ECAC, NEC

Rutgers, The State Univ. of NJ
Piscataway, NJ 08854
T: (732) 445-8610
F: (732) 445-8616
www.athletics.rutgers.edu
A: Robert Mulcahy III
S: John Wooding
Big East, ECAC

Sacred Heart University
5151 Park Ave.
Fairfield, CT 06432
T: (203) 371-7917
F: (203) 365-7696
www.sacredheart.edu
A: C. Donald Cook
S: Mike Guastelle
ECAC, NEC

St. Bonaventure University
St. Bonaventure, NY 14778
T: (716) 375-2282
F: (716) 375-2280
A: Barbara Hick
S: Steve Mest
Atlantic 10, ECAC

St. Cloud State University
720 4th Ave. South
St. Cloud, MN 56301
T: (320) 255-3102
F: (320) 255-2099
www.stcloudstate.edu/~sports/sports
A: Dr. Morris Kurtz
S: Anne Abicht
WCHA Div 1, Div II

St. Francis College
180 Remsen Street
Brooklyn Heights, NY 11201
T: (718) 489-5490
F: (718) 797-2140
www.stfranciscollege.edu
A: Edward Alquilone
S: Jim Hoffman
ECAC, NEC

St. Francis University
PO Box 600, Maurice Stokes Ath. Ctr.
Loretto, PA 15940
T: (814) 472-3018
F: (814) 472-3209
www.saintfrancisuniversity.com
A: Jeffrey Eisen
S: Pat Farabaugh
ECAC, NEC

St. John's University
8000 Utopia Parkway
Jamaica, NY 11439
T: (718) 990-6217
F: (718) 990-2197
www.redstormsports.com
A: Dave Wegrzyn
S: Dominic Scianna
Big East, ECAC, ICAA. NEC (FB)

St. Joseph's University
5600 City Avenue
Philadelphia, PA 19131
T: (610) 660-1707
F: (610) 660-1716
www.sjuhawks.com
A: Don DiJulia
S: Larry Dougherty
Atlantic 10, Big 5, ECAC

St. Lawrence University
Canton, NY 13617
T: (315) 229-5421
F: (315) 229-5589
www.stlawu.edu
A: Margaret Strait
S: Wallly Johnson
ECAC, UCAA

St. Louis University
3672 W. Pine Mall
St. Louis, MO 63108
T: (314) 977-3177
F: (314) 977-3178
www.slu.edu
A: Doug Woolard
S: Doug Mclihagga
Conference USA

St. Mary's College
1928 St. Mary's Road
Moraga, CA 94556
T: (925) 631-4383
F: (925) 376-0829
www.stmarys-ca.edu
A: Rick Mazzuto
S: Rich Davi
WCC

St. Peter's College
2641 John F. Kennedy Blvd.
Jersey City, NJ 07306
T: (201) 915-9100
F: (201) 915-9102
A: William A. Stein
S: Tim Camp
ECAC, Metro Atlantic

Sam Houston State University
PO Box 2268
Huntsville, TX 77341
T: (936) 294-1726
F: (936) 294-3538
www.shsu.edu\~athletic
A: Bobby Williams
S: Paul Ridings
Southland

Samford University
800 Lakeshore Drive
Birmingham, AL 35229
T: (205) 726-2966
F: (205) 726-2132
www.samford.edu
A: Bob Roller
S: Craig Threlkeld
TAAC

San Diego, University of
5998 Alcala Park
San Diego, CA 92110
T: (619) 260-4803
F: (619) 260-2213
www.sa.acusd.edu/athletics
A: Tom Iannacone
S: Ted Gosen
Pioneer, WCC (FB)

San Diego State University
5500 Campanile Drive
San Diego, CA 92182
T: (619) 594-3019
F: (619) 582-6541
www.goaztecs.edu
A: Rick Bay
S: Kevin Klintworth
Mountain West, Mountain Pacific

San Francisco, University of
2130 Fulton Street
San Francisco, CA 94117
T: (415) 422-6891
F: (415) 422-2510
www.usfdons.com
A: William Hogan
S: Peter Simon
WCC

San Jose State University
One Washington Square
San Jose, CA 95192
T: (408) 924-1200
F: (408) 924-1291
www.spartans.sjsu.edu
A: Chuck Bell
S: Lawrence Fan
WAC

Santa Clara University
500 El Camino
Santa Clara, CA 95053
T: (408) 554-4063
F: (408) 554-6969
www.santaclarabroncos.com
A: Cheryl Levick
S: Richard Kilwien
WCC

Seton Hall University
South Orange, NJ 07079
T: (973) 761-9497
F: (973) 761-9675
www.shupirates.com
A: Jeff Fogelson
S: Marie Wozniak
Big East, ECAC

Sienna College
Loudonville, NY 12211
T: (518) 783-2551
F: (518) 783-2992
www.siena.edu/athletics
A: John D'Argenio
S: Jason Rich
ECAC, MAAC

South Alabama, University of
1107 HPELS Bldg.
Mobile, AL 36688
T: (251) 460-7121
F: (251) 460-6505
A: Joe Gottfried
S: Matt Smith
Big South (Soccer), Sun Belt

South Carolina, University of
1300 Rosewood Drive
Columbia, SC 29208
T: (803) 777-4202
F: (803) 777-8226
www.uscsports.com
A: Dr. Michael McGee
S: Kerry Tharp
SEC

South Carolina State University
Orangeburg, SC 29117
T: (803) 536-7242
F: (803) 533-3634
www.scsu.edu
A: Dr. Timothy Autry
S: Bill Hamilton
MEAC

South Florida, University of
PED 214, 4202 E. Fowler Avenue
Tampa, FL 33620
T: (813) 974-2125
F: (813) 974-4028
www.gousfbulls.com
A: Lee Roy Selmon
S: John Gerdes
Conference USA

Southeast Missouri State Univ.
1 University Plaza
Cape Girardeau, MO 63701
T: (573) 651-2227
F: (573) 651-2959
www.gosoutheast.com
A: Don Kaverman
S: Ron Hines
OVC

Southeastern Louisiana Univ.
Hammond, LA 70402
T: (985) 549-2253
F: (985) 549-3495
www.selu.edu
A: Frank Pergolizzi
S: Dart Volz
Southland

Southern California, University of
103 Heritage Hall
Los Angeles, CA 90089
T: (213) 740-3843
F: (213) 740-1306
www.usc.edu/athletics
A: Mike Garrett
S: Tim Tessalone
Pacific 10

Southern Illinois University
Carbondale, IL 62901
T: (618) 453-5311
F: (618) 453-5152
www.siu.edu/athletics
A: Paul Kowalczyk
S: Fred Huff
MVC

Southern Methodist University
6024 Airline Rd., PO Box 750216
Dallas, TX 75275
T: (214) 768-2864
F: (214) 768-2044
www.smumustangs.com
A: Jim Copeland
S: Chris Walker
WAC

Southern Mississippi, University of
Hattiesburg, MS 39406
T: (601) 266-5017
F: (601) 266-6595
www.southernmiss.com
A: Richard Giannini
S: Mike Montoro
Conference USA

Southern University & A&M
PO Box 9942
Baton Rouge, LA 70813
T: (225) 771-3170
F: (225) 771-4400
www.susportsinfo.com
A: Floyd Kerr
S: Kevin Manns
SWAC

Southern Utah University
Cedar City, UT 84720
T: (435) 586-1937
F: (435) 586-5444
www.suu.edu/webpages/athletics
A: Thomas Douple
S: Neil Gardner
Mid-Continent, Independent

Southwest Missouri State Univ.
Springfield, MO 65804
T: (417) 836-5244
F: (417) 836-6344
www.sports.smsu.edu
A: Bill Rowe
S: Mark Stillwellh
Gateway, MVC

Southwest Texas State University
Jowers Center
San Marcos, TX 78666
T: (512) 245-2114
F: (512) 245-8387
www.swt.edu
A: Greg LaFleur
S: Tony Brubaker
Southland

Southwestern Louisiana, Univ. of
201 Reinhardt Drive
Lafayette, LA 70506
T: (318) 482-5393
F: (318) 482-6649
www.swtbobcats.com
A: Nelson Schexnayder
S: Dan McDonald
Sun Belt

Stanford University
Stanford, CA 94305
T: (650) 723-4591
F: (650) 725-8642
www.gostanford.com
A: Edward Leland
S: Bob Vazquez
Pacific 10

Stephen F. Austin State University
Nacogdoches, TX 75962
T: (409) 468-3501
F: (409) 468-4070
www.athletics.sfasu.edu
A: Steve McCarty
S: Rob Meyers
Southland

Stetson University
Deland, FL 32720
T: (904) 822-8100
F: (904) 822-8148
www.stetson.edu
A: Jeff Altier
S: Chris Belvin
TAAC

StonyBrook, Univ. At
Stonybrook, NY 11794
T: (516) 632-7205
F: (516) 632-7122
www.goseawolves.org
A: Sandy Weeden
S: Robert Emmerich, Jr.
America East, ECAC, NECC

Syracuse University
Manley Field House
Syracuse, NY 13244
T: (315) 443-2385
F: (315) 443-3724
www.suathletics.com
A: Jake Crouthamel
S: Sue Cornelius Edson
Big East, ECAC

Temple University
Vivacqua Hall, PO Box 2842
Philadelphia, PA 19122
T: (215) 204-7447
F: (215) 204-7770
www.owlsports.com
A: David O'Brien
S: Merv Jones
Atlantic 10, Big East, ECAC

Tennessee, University of
615 McCallie Avenue
Chattanooga, TN 37403
T: (423) 755-4495
F: (423) 757-1710
www.utc.edu
A: Oval Jaynes
S: Jeff Romero
Southern

Tennessee, University of
1720 Volunteer Blvd.
Knoxville, TN 37996
T: (865) 974-1212
F: (865) 974-2060
www.utsports.com
A: Doug Dickey
S: Bud Ford
SEC

Tennessee, University of
Martin, TN 38238
T: (731) 587-7660
F: (731) 587-7962
www.utmsports.com
A: Phil Dane
S: Lee Wilmot
OVC

Tennessee State University
3500 John A. Merritt Blvd.
Nashville, TN 37209
T: (615) 963-5861
F: (615) 963-5911
www.tsutigers.com
A: Teresa Lawrence Phillips
S: Wallace Dooley
OVC

Tennessee Technological Univ.
Cookeville, TN 38505
T: (931) 372-3940
F: (931) 372-3114
www.tntech.edu
A: Dr. David Larimore
S: Robert Schabert
OVC

Texas, University of
Box 19079
Arlington, TX 76019
T: (817) 272-2261
F: (817) 272-5037
www.uta.edu
A: Pete D. Carlon
S: Mickey Seward
Southland

Texas, University of
Austin, TX 78713
T: (512) 471-4602
F: (512) 471-2378
www.texassports.com
A: DeLoss Dodds
S: John Bianco
Big 12

Texas, University of
500 W. University Avenue
El Paso, TX 79968
T: (915) 747-5347
F: (915) 747-5162
www.utep.edu
A: Robert Stull
S: Jeff Darby
WAC

Texas-Pan American, Univ. of
Edinburg, TX 78539
T: (956) 381-2221
F: (956) 381-2261
www.panam.edu/athletics
A: William Weidner
S: Open
Independent

Texas, University of
6900 N. Loop 1604 W.
San Antonio, TX 78249
T: (210) 458-4161
F: (210) 458-4813
www.utsa.edu/sports
A: Lynn Hickey
S: Rick Nixon
Southland

Texas A&M-Corpus Christi
6300 Ocean Drive
Corpus Christi, TX 78412
T: (361) 825-5541
F: (361) 825-3218
www.tamucc.edu
A: Dan Viola
S: John Gilger
Independent

Texas A&M University
College Station, TX 77842
T: (409) 845-5129
F: (409) 845-6825
www.aggieathletics.com
A: Wally Groff
S: Alan Cannon
Big 12

Texas Christian University
2800 Stadium Dr., Box 297600
Fort Worth, TX 76129
T: (817) 257-7965
F: (817) 257-7656
www.tcu.edu
A: Eric Hyman
S: Steve Fink
Conference USA

Texas Tech University
Box 43021, 6th & Boston
Lubbock, TX 79409
T: (806) 742-3355
F: (806) 742-1970
www.ttu.edu/~athletic
A: Gerald Myers
S: Chris Cook
Big 12

Toledo, University of
2801 W. Bancroft Street
Toledo, OH 43606
T: (419) 530-4184
F: (419) 530-4428
www.utoledo.edu/athletics
A: Mike Karabin
S: Paul Helgren
MAC

Towson University
8000 York Road
Baltimore, MD 21252
T: (410) 830-2759
F: (410) 830-4322
A: Dr. Wayne Edwards
S: Peter Schlehr
America East, EAGL, ECAC, Patriot

Troy State University
Troy, AL 36082
T: (334) 670-3480
F: (334) 670-3724
www.trojan.troyst.edu
A: Johnny Williams
S: Tom Strother
TAAC

Tulane University
James Wilson Jr. Center
New Orleans, LA 70118
T: (504) 865-5501
F: (504) 865-5512
www.tulanegreenwave.com
A: Rick Dickson
S: Donna Turner
Conference USA

Tulsa, University of
600 S. College Avenue
Tulsa, OK 74104
T: (918) 631-2381
F: (918) 631-3670
www.tulsahurricane.com
A: Judy MacLeod
S: Don Tomkalski
WAC

Union College
Alumni Gym
Schenectady, NY 12308
T: (518) 388-6284
F: (518) 388-6695
www.union.edu
A: Val Belmonte
S: George Cuttita
ECAC, UCAA

U.S. Air Force Academy
Air Force Academy, CO 80840
T: (719) 333-4008
F: (719) 333-2964
www.airforcesports.com
A: Col. Randall Spetman
S: Troy Garnhart
Mountain West

U.S. Military Academy
Bldg.639 Howard Road
West Point, NY 10996
T: (914) 938-2973
F: (914) 938-8707
www.goARMYsports.com
A: Rick Greenspan
S: Bob Beretta
Conference USA, ECAC, Patriot,
EIWL, MAAC (Hockey)

U.S. Naval Academy
Annapolis, MD 21402
T: (410) 268-6220
F: (410) 263-7390
www.navysports.com
A: Jack Lengyel
S: Scott Stasemeier
ECAC, Patriot

Utah, University of
1825 E. South Campus
Salt Lake City, UT 84112
T: (801) 581-8171
F: (801) 581-4358
www.utahutes.com
A: Chris Hill
S: Liz Abel
Mountain West

Utah State University
Logan, UT 84322
T: (435) 797-1850
F: (435) 797-1800
www.usu.edu
A: Rance Pugmire
S: Mike Strauss
Big West

Valparaiso University
Valparaiso, IN 46383
T: (219) 464-5230
F: (219) 464-5762
www.valpo.edu/athletics
A: Dr. William Steinbrecher
S: Bill Rogers
Pioneer, Mid-Continent

Vanderbilt University
2601 Jess Neely Dr
Nashville, TN 37212
T: (615) 322-4727
F: (615) 343-8738
www.vanderbilt.edu/athletics
A: Todd Turner
S: Rod Williamson
SEC

Vermont, University of
Patrick Gymnasium
Burlington, VT 05405
T: (802) 656-3074
F: (802) 656-0949
www.uvm.edu/~sportspr
A: Richard Farnham
S: Gordon Woodworth
ECAC, America East

Villanova University
800 Lancaster Avenue
Villanova, PA 19085
T: (610) 519-4110
F: (610) 519-7987
www.villanova.com
A: Vince Nicastrob
S: Dean Kenefick
Atlantic 10, Big East, ECAC, Patriot

Virginia, University of
Charlottesville, VA 22903
T: (434) 982-5000
F: (434) 982-5012
www.virginiasports.com
A: Craig Littlepage
S: Rich Murray
ACC

Virginia Commonwealth University
819 W. Franklin Street
Richmond, VA 23284
T: (804) 828-4000
F: (804) 828-7526
www.vcu.edu/vcurams
A: Dr. Richard Sander
S: Joseph Lehman
Colonial

Virginia Military Institute
Lexington, VA 24450
T: (540) 464-7251
F: (540) 464-7622
www.vmi.edu/athhome.htm
A: Donny White
S: Wade Branner
Southern

Virginia Polytechnic Institute
Blacksburg, VA 24061
T: (540) 231-6796
F: (540) 231-3060
www.hokiesports.com
A: Jim Weaver
S: Dave Smith
Atlantic 10, Big East (FB)

Wagner College
One Campus Road
Staten Island, NY 10301
T: (718) 390-3433
F: (718) 390-3347
www.wagner.edu
A: Walt Hameline
S: Bob Balut
ECAC, ECWA, NEC

Wake Forest University
PO Box 7265
Winston-Salem, NC 27109
T: (336) 758-5616
F: (336) 759-6090
www.wakeforestsports.com
A: Ron Wellman
S: Dean Buchan
ACC

Washington, University of
Graves Bldg., Box 354070
Seattle, WA 98195
T: (206) 543-2210
F: (206) 685-4668
www.gohuskies.com
A: Barbara A. Hedges
S: Jim Daves
Pacific 10

Washington State University
PO Box 641602
Pullman, WA 99164
T: (509) 335-0311
F: (509) 335-0328
www.wsucougars.com
A: Jim Sterk
S: Rod Commons
Pacific 10

Weber State University
Ogden, UT 84408
T: (801) 626-6500
F: (801) 626-6490
www.catsis.weber.edu/athletics
A: John Johnson
S: Brad Larsen
Big Sky

West Virginia University
Box 0877
Morgantown, WV 26507
T: (304) 293-5621
F: (304) 293-4105
www.MSNsportsNET.com
A: Ed Pastilong
S: Shelly Poe
Big East, ECAC, EWL, EAGL

Western Carolina University
Cullowhee, NC 28723
T: (828) 227-7338
F: (828) 227-7688
www.wcu.edu/athletics
A: Jeffrey Compher
S: Mike Cawood
Southern

Western Illinois University
103 Western Hall, 1 University Cir.
Macomb, IL 61455
T: (309) 298-1190
F: (309) 298-2009
www.wiu.edu
A: Tim Van Alstine
S: Doug Smiley
Gateway (FB), Mid-Continent

Western Kentucky University
One Big Red Way
Bowling Green, KY 42101
T: (270) 745-3542
F: (270) 745-6187
www.wku.edu/athletics
A: Pam Herriford
S: Paul Just
MVC (Soccer), Sun Belt, OVC (FB)

Western Michigan University
Read Fieldhouse
Kalamazoo, MI 49008
T: (616) 387-3120
F: (616) 387-3668
www.wmubroncos
A: Kathy Beauregard
S: Daniel Jankowski
CCHA, MAC

Wichita State University
1845 Fairmount
Wichita, KS 67260
T: (316) 978-3251
F: (316) 978-3336
A: Jim Schaus
S: Larry Rankin
MVC

William & Mary, College of
Williamsburg, VA 23187
T: (757) 221-3400
F: (757) 221-3412
www.tribeathletics.com
A: Terry Driscoll
S: Peter Clawson
Atlantic 10, ICAAA, ECAC, CAA

Winthrop University
Rock Hill, SC 29733
T: (803) 323-2129
F: (803) 323-2433
www.winthrop.edu
A: Thomas Hickman
S: Jack Frost
Big South

Wisconsin, University of
2420 Nicolet Drive
Green Bay, WI 54311
T: (920) 465-2145
F: (920) 465-2357
www.gbphoenix.com
A: Otis Chambers
S: Brian Nicol
Horizon League

Wisconsin, University of
1440 Monroe Street
Madison, WI 53711
T: (608) 262-1866
F: (608) 265-3036
www.wisc.edu/ath
A: Pat Richter
S: Steve Malchow
Big Ten, WCHA

Wisconsin, University of
3415 N. Downer Ave.
Milwaukee, WI 53201
T: (414) 229-5151
F: (414) 229-6759
www.uwmpanthers.com
A: Bud Haidet
S: Kevin O'Connor
Horizon League

Wofford College
Spartanburg, SC 29303
T: (864) 597-4090
F: (864) 597-4129
www.wofford.edu/athletics
A: David Wood
S: Mark Cohen
Southern

Wright State University
3640 Colonel Glenn Hwy
Dayton, OH 45435
T: (937) 775-2771
F: (937) 775-2368
www.wright.edu/athletics
A: Dr.Michael Cusack
S: Bob R.J. Noss
Horizon League

Wyoming, University of
Laramie, WY 82071
T: (307) 766-2292
F: (307) 766-5414
www.wyomingathletics.com
A: Wm. Lee Moon, Sr.
S: Kevin McKinney
WAC

Xavier University
3800 Victory Parkway
Cincinnati, OH 45207
T: (513) 745-3414
F: (513) 745-4390
www.xu.edu/athletics
A: Michael Bobinski
S: Tom Eiser
Atlantic 10

Yale University
Ray Tompkins House
PO Box 208216
New Haven, CT 06520
T: (203) 432-4747
F: (203) 432-7772
www.yale.edu/athletic/
A: Thomas A. Beckett
S: Steve Conn
ECAC, Ivy League

Youngstown State University
Youngstown, OH 44555
T: (330) 742-3478
F: (330) 742-2733
www.ysu.edu/sports/
A: Ron Stroilo
S: Trevor Parks
Gateway (FB), Horizon League

NCAA Division II Colleges

Abilene Christian University
ACU Station Box 27916
Abilene, TX 79699
T: (915) 674-2353
F: (915) 674-6831
www.acu.edu/sports
A: Stan Lambert
S: Lance Fleming
Lone Star

Adelphia University
South Avenue
Garden City, NY 11530
T: (516) 877-4240
F: (516) 877-4237
www.adelphia.edu/campus/athletics
A: Robert Hartwell
S: Daniel Booth
ECAC, NYCAC

Alamabam, University of
Spragins Hall
Huntsville, AL 35899
T: (256) 890-6144
F: (256) 890-7306
www.uah.edu/athletics
A: Jim Harris
S: Antoine Bell
GSC

Albany State University
504 College Drive
Albany, GA 31705
T: (912) 430-4754
F: (912) 430-1774
A: Dan Land
S: Edythe Bradley
SIAC

Alderson-Broaddus College
Campus Box 2062
Philippi, WV 26416
T: (304) 457-6262
F: (304) 457-6291
www.ab.edu
A: Paul A. Bennett
S: Marsha Denniston
WVIAC

American International College
1000 State Street
Springfield, MA 01109
T: (413) 747-6540
F: (413) 731-5710
A: Robert E. Burke
S: Doug Monson
ECAC, EFC, MAAC, NECAC, NE-10

Anderson College
Anderson, SC 29621
T: (864) 231-2029
F: (864) 231-5601
www.anderson-college.edu
A: Bobby Beville
S: Cobb Oxford
Carolinas Virginia Ath. Conf.

Angelo State University
2601 W. Avenue N Box 10884
ASU Station
San Angelo, TX 76904
T: (915) 942-2091
F: (915) 942-2277
A: Jerry Vandergriff
S: M.L. Hinkle
Lone Star

Arkansas, University of
Monticello, AR 71656
T: (870) 460-1058
F: (870) 460-1458
www.uamont.edu/~athletics
A: Alvy Early
S: Tim Munn
Gulf South

Arkansas Tech University
Tucker Coliseum, 1604 Coliseum Dr.
Russellville, AR 72801
T: (501) 968-0345
F: ((501) 964-0829
www.atu.edu
A: Dr. Earle Dorman
S: Larry Smith
Gulf South

Armstrong Atlantic State U.
11935 Abercom St.
Savannah, GA 31419
T: (912) 927-5336
F: (912) 921-5571
www.armstrong.edu
A: Dr> Eddie Aenchbacher
S: Dr. Michael Lariscy
Peach Belt Athletic

Ashland University
Ashland, OH 44805-3702
T: (419) 289-5441
F: (419) 289-5468
www.ashland.edu/athletics
A: Bill Goldring
S: Al King
GLIC, MIFC

Assumption College
500 Salisbury Street
Worcester, MA 01609-1265
T: (508) 767-7279
F: (508) 798-2568
www.assumption.edu
A: Rita Castagna
S: Steve Morris
NE-10, Eastern FB

Augusta State University
2500 Walton Way #10
Augusta, GA 30904
T: (706) 737-1626
F: (706) 737-1782
www.aug.edu
A: Clint Bryant
S: John Bush III
Peach Belt

Augustana College
2001 S. Summit Ave.
Sioux Falls, SD 57197
T: (605) 336-5298
F: (605) 336-5298
www.augie.edu
A: Bill Gross
S: Karen Madson
North Central

Barry University
11300 NE 2nd Ave.
Miami, FL 33161
T: (305) 899-3550
F: (305) 899-3556
www.barry.edu
A: Mike Covone
S: Fred Battenfield
Sunshine State

Barton College
Wilson, NC 27893
T: (252) 399-6514
F: (252) 399-6516
www.barton.edu
A: Gary Hall
S: John Hackney
Carolinas Virginia

Bellarmine College
2001 Newburg Rd.
Louisville, KKY 40205
T: (502) 459-2952
F: (502) 452-8450
www.bellarmine.edu
A: David O'Toole
S: Mark Mulloy
GLVC

Belmont Abbey College
100 Belmont Mount Holly Rd
Belmont, NC 28012
T: (704) 825-6809
F: (704) 825-6570
A: Eliane Kibbe
S: Br. Paul Shanley
Carolinas-Virginia

Bemidji State University
1500 Birchmont Dr. NE
Bemidji, MN 56601
T: (218) 755-2940
F: (218) 755-3898
www.bemidji.msus.edu
A: Doreen Zierer
S: Ron Christian
NSIC

Bentley College
Waltham, MA 02452
T: (781) 891-2256
F: (781) 891-2648
www.bentley.edu/sports/
A: Robert DeFelice
S: Dick Lipe
NE-10, ECAC, NECAC,
MAAC Hockey

Binghamton University
PO Box 6000
Binghamton, NY 13902
T: (607) 777-4255
F: (607) 777-4597
www.binghamton.edu
A: Joel Thierer
S: John Hartrick
NECC, ECAC

Bloomsburg University
Bloomsburg, PA 17815
T: (570) 389-4050
F: (570) 389-2099
www.bloomu.edu
A: Mary Gardner
S: Tom McGuire
PSAC, EWL (1), ECAC

Bluefield State College
Bluefield, WV 24701
T: (304) 327-4208
F: (304) 327-4179
www.bluefield.wnet.edu
A: Terry Brown
S: John Morris
WVIAC

Bowie State University
14000 Jericho Park Rd, James Gym
Bowie, MD 20715
T: (301) 464-6683
F: (301) 464-6110
www.bowiesyaye.edu
A: David Thomas
S: Scott Rouch
CIAA

Bridgeport, University of
120 Waldemere Ave.
Bridgeport, CT 06601
T: (203) 576-4059
F: (203) 576-4057
A: Joe DiPuma
S: David Scivines
ECAC

Brigham Young University
55-220 Kulanui Street
Laie, HI 96762
T: (808) 293-3764
F: (808) 293-3764
www.byuh.edu
A: Ken Wagner
S: Scott Lowe
Pacific West, NCAA

Bryant College
Smithfield, RI 02917
T: (401) 232-6070
F: (401) 232-6361
www.bryant.edu
A: Dan Gavitt
S: John White
ECAC, NE-10

Cal State Dominguez Hills
1000 E. Victoria Street
Carson, CA 90747
T: (310) 243-3893
F: (310) 217-6975
www.csudh.edu/athletics
A: Ron Prettyman
S: Pat Guillen
CCAA

Caldwell College
Caldwell, NJ 07006
T: (973) 618-3260
F: (973) 618-3370
www.caldwell.edu
A: Mark Corino
S: Michael Lamberti
CACC

California, University of
One Shields Ave.
Davis, CA 95616
T: (530) 752-1111
F: (530) 752-6681
www.ucdavis.edu
A: Greg Warzecka
S: Doug Dull
CCAA

California, University of
900 University Avenue
Riverside, CA 92521
T: (909) 787-5432
F: (909) 787-3569
www.ucr.edu/athletics
A: Cliff Dochterman
S: Tom Phillips
CCAA

California State Poly U.
3801 W. Temple Ave
Pomona, CA 91768
T: (909) 869-2810
F: (909) 869-2814
www.csupomona.edu
A: Karen L. Miller
S: Chris Ward
CCAA

California State University
9001 Stockdale Hwy.
Bakersfield, CA 93311
T: (661) 664-2188
F: (661) 664-2376
www.csubak.edu
A: Rudy Carvajal
S: Kevin Gilmore

California State University
Chico, CA
T: (530) 898-6470
F: (530) 898-4699
www.csuchico.edu
A: Don W. Batie
S: Teresa Clements
CCAA

California State University
5151 State University Drive
Los Angeles, CA 90032
T: (323) 343-3080
F: (323) 343-6535
A: Carol M. Dunn
S: Jacqueline Mejia
CCAA

California State University
5500 University Pkwy
San Bernardino, CA 92407
T: (909) 880-5011
F: (909) 880-5984
www.csusb.edu/athletics/coyote
A: Nancy Simpson
S: William E. Gray
CCAA

California State University
801 W. Monte Vista Ave.
Turlock, CA 95382
T: (209) 667-3566
F: (209) 667-3084
www.csustan.edu/athletics
A: Milton Richards
S: Will Keener
NCAC

California Univ. of PA
250 University Ave.
California, PA 15419
T: (724) 938-4351
F: (724) 938-5849
A: Dr. Thomas G. Pucci
S: Dave Smith
PSAC

Cameron University
Lawton, OK 73505
T: (580) 581-2306
F: (580) 581-5537
www.cameron.edu
A: Sam Carroll
S: Jason West
Lone Star

Carson-Newman College
Jefferson City, TN 37760
T: (423) 471-3360
F: (423) 471-3514
www.cn.edu
A: David Barger
S: Martin Curnutt
SAC

Catawba College
2300 W. Innes Street
Salisbury, NC 28144
T: (704) 637-4474
F: (704) 637-5705
www.catawba.edu
A: Dennis Davidson
S: Jimmy Lewis
South Atlantic

Central Arkansas, U. of
Conway, AR 72032
T: (501) 450-3150
F: (501) 450-3151
www.uca.edu/ucasports
A: Arch Jones
S: Steve East
Gulf South

Central Missouri State U.
500 Washington Street
Warrensburg, MO 64093
T: (660) 543-4250
F: (660) 543-8034
www.cmsu.edu
A: Jerry Hughes
S: Bill Turnage
MIAA

Central Oklahoma, Univ. of
Edmond, OK 73034
T: (405) 974-2501
F: (405) 974-3820
A: John Wagnon
S: Mike Kirk
Lone Star

Central Washington University
Ellensburg, WA 98926
T: (509) 963-1914
F: (509) 963-1485
www.cwu.edu
A: Gary Frederick
S: Bob Guptill
Columbia FB League

Chadron State College
1000 Main St., Armstrong Bldg.
Chadron, NE 69337
T: (308) 432-6344
F: (308) 432-6493
www.csc.edu
A: Brad Smith
S: Con Marshall
RMAC

Charleston, University of
2300 MacCorkle Ave. SE
Charleston, WV 25304
T: (304) 357-4823
F: (304) 357-4827
A: Tom Nozica
S: Ryan Brisbin
WVIAC

Cheyney, Univ. of PA
Campus Box 350, Cheyney Rd.
Cheyney,PA 19319
T: (610) 399-2287
F: (610) 399-2352
A: Dr. Gregory Smith
S: Tara Owens
PSAC, ECAC

Christian Brothers Univ.
650 E. Parkway S.
Memphis, TN 38104
T: ((901) 321-3370
F: (901) 321-3570
www.cbu.edu
A: Michael Daush
S: Roger McAfee
Gulf South

Clarion University
Wood St., Tippin Gym, Rm.112
Clarion, PA 16214
T: (814) 226-1997
F: (814) 226-2063
A: Bob Carlson
S: Rich Herman
PSAC

Clark Atlanta University
J.P. Brawley Dr. at Fair St. SW
Atlanta, GA 30314
T: (404) 880-8123
F: (404) 880-8397
A: Dr. Richard Cosby
S: Cecil McKay
SIAC

Clayton College & State U.
PO Box 285
Morrow, GA 30260
T: (770) 961-3450
F: (770) 960-5127
www.athletics.clayton.edu
A: Mason Barfield
S: J.D. Barlow
Peach Belt Athletic

Coker College
Hartsville, SC 29550
T: (843) 383-8073
F: (843) 383-8167
www.coker.edu
A: Tim Griggs
S: Cale Bigbee
Carolinas-Virginia

Colorado, Univ. of
PO Box 7150, Austin Bluffs Pkwy.
Colorado Springs, CO 80933
T: (719) 262-3575
F: (719) 26203131
www.uccs.edu
A: Ruben "Randy" Cubero
S: Jerry Cross
RMAC

Colorado Christian Univ.
180 S. Garrison St.
Lakewood, CO 80226
T: (303) 238-5388 ex 221
F: (303) 234-1217
A: Dave Foster
S: Jennifer Peiffer ex 225
Rocky Mountain

Colorado School of Mines
Volk Gym, 1500 Illinois St.
Golden, CO 80401
T: (303) 273-3360
F: (303) 273-3362
www.mines.edu/athletics
A: Marvin Kay
S: Jeff Duggan
RMAC

Columbia Union College
7600 Flower Ave.
Takoma Park, MD 20912
T: (301) 891-4195
F: (301) 891-4552
A: Rick Murray
S: Dr. Rick Herlinger
NCAA II Independent

Columbus State University
4225 University Ave.
Columbus, GA 31907
T: (404) 568-2204
F: (706) 569-3435
www.colstate.edu/athletics
A: Herbert Greene
S: Mike Peacock
PBAC

Concord College
Vermillion Street
Athens, WV 24712
T: (304) 384-5347
F: (304) 384-5117
A: Ron Macosko
S: Tom Bone
WVIAC

Concordia College
171 White Plains Rd.
Bronxville, NY 10708
T: (914) 337-9300 x 2447
F: (914) 395-4515
www.concordia-ny.edu
A/S: Ivan Marquez
ECAC, NYCAC, EIVA

Concordia University
IH 35 North
Austin, TX 78705
T: (512) 452-7662 ex 1164
F: (512) 302-4365
A: Linda Lowery ex 1162
S: Wendy Adams
Heart of Texas

Concordia University
275 Syndicate St. N
Saint Paul, MN 55104
T: (651) 641-8854
F: (651) 641-8787
www.csp.edu/csp/dept/_pages/athletics
A: Dan O'Brien
S: Pat Hample
UMAC

Dallas Baptist University
3000 Mountain Creek Pkwy.
Dallas, TX 75211
T: (214) 333-5234
F: (214) 333-5306
www.dbu.edu
A/S: Wayne Poage

Davis & Elkins College
100 Campus Dr.
Elkins, WV 26241
T: (304) 637-1251
F: (304) 637-1414
www.dne.edu
A: Will Shaw
S: Darlene A. Roy
WVIAC

Delta State University
PO Box A-3
Cleveland, MS 38733
T: (662) 846-4300
F: (662) 846-4297
www.deltast.edu
A: Dr. Jim Jordan
S: Fred Sington
Gulf South, New South (SWIM)

Dickinson State University
291 Campus Drive
Dickinson, ND 58601
T: (701) 483-2181
F: (701) 483-0501
www.dsu.nodak.edu
A: Roger Ternes
S: Dana Rae Andersoon
NDCAC

District of Columbia, U. of
4300 Connecticut Ave. NW
Washington, DC 20008
T: (202) 274-5024
F: (202) 274-5065
A; William S. Jones
S: Donald Huff
Independent

Dominican College
470 Western Hwy.
Orangeburg, NY 10962
T: (914) 398-9008
F: (914) 398-3042
A: Joe Clinton
S: Kathleen Rooney-Metcalf
CACC

Dowling College
1509 Idle Hour Blvd.
Oakdale, NY 11769
T: (516) 244-3019
F: (516) 244-3317
www.dowling.edu
A: Robert Dranoff
S: Dawn Havranek
ECAC, Nycac, Metro (tennis)

Drury College
Springfield, MO 65802
T: (417) 873-7265
F: (417) 873-7510
www.drury.edu
A; Dr. Bruce Harger
S: Dan Cashel
Independent

East Central University
E. 14th St.
Ada, OK 74820
T: (580) 332-8000 ex 314
F: (580) 332-8361
www.ecok.edu
A: Dr. Tim Green
S: Justin Tinder ex 258
Lone Star

East Stroudsburg Univ.
East Stroudsburg, PA 18301
T: (570) 422-3642
F: (570) 422-3306
A: Earl Edwards
S: Pete Nevins
PSAC

Eastern New Mexico Univ.
Greyhound Arena, Station 17
Portales, NM 88130
T: (505) 562-2153
F: (505) 562-2822
www.enmu.edu
A: Rosie Stallman
S: Robert McKinney
Lone Star

Eckerd College
4200 54th Ave. S
St. Petersburg, FL 33711
T: (727) 864-8251
F: (727) 864-8968
www.eckerd.edu
A: Jim Harley
S: Aaron Barter
Sunshine State

Edinboro University
Edinboro, PA 16444
T: (814) 732-2776
F: (814) 732-2190
www.edinboro.edu
A: Bruce Bakumgartner
S: Robert Shreve ex 234
PSAC

Elizabeth City State U.
1704 Weeksville Rd.
Elizabeth City, NC 27909
T: (252) 335-3388
F: (252) 335-3627
www.edsu.edu
A: Dr. Edward McLean
S: Randy Jones
CIAA

Embry-Riddle Aeronautical U.
University Fieldhouse
600 S. Clyde Morris Blvd.
Daytona Beach, FL 32114
T: (904) 226-6484
F: (904) 226-6435
www.db.erau.edu/campus/athletics
A: Steve Ridder
S: Todd Guilliams
Florida Sun

Emporia State University
12th & Commercial
Emporia, KS 66801
T: (316) 341-5354
F: (316) 341-5603
www.emporia.edu
A: Paul Sweetgall
S: J.D. Campbell
MIAA

Erskine College
PO Box 357
Due West, SC 29639
T: (864) 379-8859
F: (864) 379-2197
www.erskine.edu
A: J.H. "Chip" Sherer, Jr.
S: Jean Pinson
Carolinas-Virginia

Fairmont State College
Fairmont, WV 26554
T: (304) 367-4220
F: (304) 367-0202
A: David Cooper
S: Jim Brinkman

Fayetteville State Univ.
Newbold Sta. 1200 Murcheson Rd.
Fayetteville, NC 28301
T: (910) 486-1314
F: (910) 486-1241
A: Horace Small
S: Marion Crowe, Jr.
CIAA

Felician College
262 S. Main St.
Lodi, NJ 07644
T: (201) 559-6119
F: (201) 559-6188
www.felician.edu
A: Robert Symons
S: Ben Dinallo, Jr.
Independent

Findlay, Univ. of
Findlay, OH 45840
T: (419) 424-4663
F: (419) 424-4618
www.findlay.edu
A: Steven Rackley
S: David Faiella
GLIAC, CHA

Florida Southern College
Lake Hollingsworth Dr.
Lakeland, FL 33801
T: (863) 680-4244
F: (863) 680-4122
www.fsouthern.edu/sid
A: Hal Smeltzly
S: Wayne Koehler
Sunshine State

Florida Tech
150 W. University Blvd.
Melbourne, FL 32901
T: (407) 674-8032
F: (407) 984-8529
www.fit.edu
A: William Jurgens
S: Dean Watson
Sunshine State

Fort Hays State University
600 Park St
Hays, KS 67601
T: (785) 628-4050
F: (785) 628-4383
www.fhsu.edu/htmlpages/athletics/sports
A: Tom Spicer
S: Jack Kuestermeyer
RMAC

Fort Lewis College
1000 Rim Drive
Durango, CO 81301
T: (970) 247-7571
F: (970) 247-7655
A: J. R. Smith
S: Chris Aaland
RMAC

Fort Valley State University
Fort Valley, GA 31030
T: (912) 825-6209
F: (912) 825-6889
www.fvsu.edu
A: Ed Wyche
S: Russell Boone
SIAC

Frankllin Pierce College
PO Box 60, College Rd., RFD 119
Rindge, NH 03461
T: (603) 899-4087
F: (603) 899-4328
www.fpc.edu
A: Bruce Kirsh
S: Chris O'Donnell
New England Collegiate

Gannon University
University Square
Erie, PA 16541
T: (814) 871-7416
F: (814) 871-7794
www.gannon.edu
A: Michael Corbett
S: Open
ECAC, GLIAC, NCAA

Gardner-Webb Univ.
Boiling Springs, NC 28017
T: (704) 434-4340
F: (704) 434-4739
www.gardnerwebb.edu
A: Chuck Burch
S: Mark Wilson
SAC

Georgia College & State U.
CBX 065
Milledgevillle, GA 31061
T: (912) 445-6341
F: (912) 445-1790
A: Dr. Stan Aldridge
S: Brad Muller
Peach Belt

Georgia Southwestern
800 Wheatley Street
Americus, GA 31709
T: (912) 931-2222
F: (912) 931-2143
www.gsw.peachnet.edu/~athletics
A: Dr. Steve Cobb
S: Larry Thompson, Jr.
GAC

Glenville State College
Glenville, WV 26351
T: (304) 462-4102
F: (304) 462-5593
www.glenville.wvnet.edu
A: Steven Harold
S: Rick Simmons
WVIAC

Goldey Beacom College
4701 Limestone Rd.
Wilmington, DE 19808
T: (302) 998-8814
F: (302) 998-3467
www.goldey.gbc.edu
A/S: Linda M. Doran
Central Atlantic

Grand Canyon University
3300 W. Camelback Rd.
Phoenix, AZ 85017
T: (602) 589-2806
F: (602) 589-2529
www.grand-canyon.edu/sports.htm
A: Keith Baker
S: Dave Wahlstrom
CCAA

Grand Valley State Univ.
Allendale, MI 49401
T: (616) 895-3259
F: (616) 895-3232
www.gvsu.edu
A: Tim W. Selgo
S: Tim Nott ex 3275
GLIAC, MIFC

Harding University
Searcy, AR 72149
T: (501) 279-4305
F: (501) 279-4138
www.harding.edu
A: Greg Harnden
S: Scott Goode
Lone Star

Hawaii-Hilo, Univ. of
200 W. Kawili Street
Hilo, HI 96720
T: (808) 974-7520
F: (808) 974-7711
www.uhh.hawaii.edu/~athletics
A: Bill Trumbo
S: Kelly Leong
Pacific West

Hawaii Pacific Univ.
1060 Bishop St., # PH
Honolulu, HI 96813
T; (808) 544-0221
F: (808) 521-7998
www.hpu.edu
A: Anthony Sellitto
S: Trey Garman
Pacific West

Henderson State Univ.
PO Box 7630
Arkadelphia, AR 71999
T: (870) 230-5161
F: (870) 230-5408
www.hsu.edu
A: Ken Turner
S: David Worlock
Gulf South

Hillsdale College
201 Oak Street
Hillsdale, MI 49242
T: (517) 437-7341
F: (517) 437-7341
www.hillsdale.edu
A: Dr. Mike Kovalchik
S: Greg Younger
GLIAC, MIFC

Humboldt State University
Arcata, CA 95521
T: (707) 826-3666
F: (707) 826-5446
www.humboldt.edu/~hsujacks
A: Scott Barnes
S: Dan Pambianco
Pacific West

Incarnate Word, U. of the
4301 Broadway Street
San Antonio, TX 78209
T: (210) 829-6050
F: (21) 805-3574
www.univere.uiwtx.edu
A: Dr. Howard Patterson
S: Wayne Witt
Independent

Indiana U. of Pennsylvania
Indiana, PA 15705
T: (724) 357-2751
F: (724) 357-7991
www.iup.edu/athlet
A: Frank Condino
S: Michael Hoffman
PSAC

Indiana U.-Purdue U.
2101 E. Coliseum Blvd.
Fort Wayne, IN 46805
T: (219) 481-6643
F: (219) 481-6002
www.ipfw.edu/athletics
A: Dr. Walter Bowman
S: Michael Jewell
GLVC

Indianapolis, Univ. of
1400 E. Hanna Ave.
Indianapolis, IN 46227
T: (317) 788-3246
F: (317) 788-3472
www.uindy.edu
A: Dr. Dave Huffman
S: Joe Gentry
Midwest Intercollegiate FB,
Great Lakes Valley

Jarvis Christian College
Hawkins, TX 75765
T: (903) 769-5763
F: (903) 769-4842
A: Robert Thomas
Big State

Johnson C. Smith Univ.
100 Beatties Ford Rd.
Charlotte, NC 28216
T: (704) 378-1072
F: (704) 378-1073
www.jcsu.edu
A: Cathkerine Wright
S: Patricia Harvey
CIAA

Kennesaw State Univ.
1000Chastain Rd. NW
Kennesaw, GA 30144
T: (770) 423-6284
F: (770) 423-6665
www.kennesaw.edu/sports
A: Dr. Dave Waples
S: Steve Ruthsatz
Peach Belt

Kentucky State Univ.
E. Main Street
Frankfort, KY 40601
T: (502) 227-6011
F: (502) 227-6446
www.kysu.edu
A: Derrick Ramsey
S: Ronald Braden
SIAC

Kentucky Wesleyan College
PO Box 1039; 3000 Frederica St.
Owensboro, KY 42302
T: (270) 683-4795
F: (270) 684-5028
A: Dr. Bill Meadors
S: Roy Pickerill x 124
GLVC

Kutztown University
Kutztown, PA 19530
T: (610) 683-4094
F: (610) 683-1379
www.kutztown.edu
A: Clark Yeager
S: Josh Laibozz
PSAC, ECAC

Lander University
Stanley Avenue
Greenwood, SC 29649
T: (864) 388-8316
F: (864) 388-8889
www.lander.edu
A: Jeff May
S: Bob Stoner
PBAC

Lane College
545 Lane Ave.
Jackson, TN 38301
T: (901) 426-7568
F: (901) 421-7107
www.lanecollege.edu
A: Dr. J.L. Perry
S: Kim Walker
SIAC

Le Moyne-Owen College
807 Walker Avenue
Memphis, TN 38126
T: (901) 942-7327
F: (901) 942-6272
www.lemoyne-owen.edu
A: E.D. Wilkens
SIAC

Le Moyne College
Springfield Rd.
Syracuse, NY 13214
T: (315) 445-4450
F: (315) 445-4678
www.lemoyne.edu
A: Richard Rockwell
S: Mike Tuberosa
ECAC, NE-10, MAAC

Lees-McRae College
Banner Elk, NC 28604
T: (828) 898-8742
F: (828) 898-8742
www.imc.edu
A: Reid Estus
S: Craig McPhail
CVAC

Lenoir-Rhyne College
PO Box 7356
Hickory, NC 28603
T: (828) 328-7115
F: (828) 328-7399
www.lrc.edu
A: Dr. Jane Jenkins
S: Michael MacEachern
South Atlantic

Lewis University
Route 53
Romeoville, IL 60446
T: (815) 836-5247
F: (815) 836-5835
A: Paul Ruddy
S: Mickey Smith
GLVC

Limestone College
1115 College Drive
Gaffney, SC 29340
TL (864) 488-4568
F: (864) 488-0714
A: Dennis Bloomer
S: Patricia Norris
CUAC

Lincoln Memorial University
PO Box 2028, Cumberland Gap Pkwy
Harrogate, TN 37752
T: (423) 869-6285
F: (423) 869-6382
www.lumnet.edu
A: Jack Bondurant
S: Rusty Peace
Gulf South

Lincoln University
820 Chestnut Street
Jefferson City, MO 65102
T: (573) 681-5342
F: (573) 681-5998
www.lincolnu.edu
A: Theressa Ferguson
S: Walter Klein
Independent

Livingstone College
701 W. Monroe St.
Salisbury, NC 28144
T: (704) 797-1013
F: (704) 797-1012
A: Clifton Huff
S: Leonard Haynes
CIAA

Lock Haven University
Thomas Field House
Lock Haven, PA 17745
T: (570) 893-2102
F: (570) 893-2414
www.lhup.edu/sports
A: Sharon Taylor
S: Aaron Russell
PSAC, ECAC

Longwood College
Farmville, VA 23909
T: (804) 395-2057
F: (804) 395-2568
www.longwood.iwc.edu
A: Donald L. Lemish
S: Greg Prouty
NCAA II

Lynn University
Trinity Hall, 3601 Military Trl.
Boca Raton, FL 33431
T: (561) 237-7274
F: (561) 237-7283
www.lynn.edu
A: Richard Young
S: Jeff Schaly
Sunshine State

Mansfield University
Academy Street
Mansfield, PA 16933
T: (570) 662-4860
F: (570) 662-4116
A: Roger Maisner
S: Steve McCloskey
ECAC, PSAC

Mars Hill College
Mars Hill, NC 28754
T: (828) 689-1219
F: (828) 689-1501
www.mhc.edu
A: David Riggins
S: Rick Baker
SAC

Mary Hardin-Baylor, Univ. of
UMHB Box 8010, 9 th & College
Belton, TX 76513
T: (254) 295-4618
F: (254) 295-4614
www.umbh.edu/
A: Ben Shipp
S: Jon Wallin
American Southwest

Mercy College
555 Broadway
Dobbs Ferry, NY 10522
T: (914) 674-7220
F: (914) 674-7281
www.mercynet.edu
A: Neil D. Judge
S: Steve Balsan
ECAC, NYCAC

Mercyhurst College
501 East 38th Street
Erie, PA 16546
T: (814) 824-2228
F: (814) 824-2591
www.mercyhurst.edu
A: Pete Russo
S: John Leisering
Great Lakes

Mesa State College
1175 Texas Avenue
Grand Junction, CO 81501
T: (970) 248-1503
F: (970) 248-1980
www.mesastate.edu
A: Doug Schakel
S: Tish Elliot
RMAC

Metropolitan State College
PO Box 173362
Denver, CO 80217
T: (303) 556-8300
F: (303) 556-2720
www.mscd.edu
A: Joan McDermott
S: Steve Allen
Rocky Mountain

Midwestern State University
3410 Taft Blvd.
Wichita Falls, TX 76308
T: (940) 397-4767
F: (940) 691-8129
www.mwsu.edu
A: Dr. Bob McBee
S: Stan Wagnon
Lone Star

Millersville University
PO Box 1002, N. George St.
Millersville, PA 17551
T: (717) 872-3361
F: (717) 871- 2125
www.millersv.edu
A: Dan Audette
S: Greg Wright
PSAC, ECAC

Minnesota, University of
Sports Center
Crookston, MN 56716
T: (218) 281-8415
F: (218) 281-8430
www.crk.umn.edu/people/athletics/
A: Brad Kerr
S: Stephanie Reck
NSIC

Minnesota, University of
East 2nd Street
Morris, MN 56267
T: (320) 589-6425
F: (320) 589-6428
www.ynb.edu
A: Mark Fohl
S: John Griffin
Northern Sun

Minnesota State University
123 Highland Center
Mankato, MN 56001
T: (507) 389-6111
F: (507) 389-2904
www.mankato.msus.edu/dept/athletics
A: Donald Amiot
S: Paul Allan
NCIAC

Missouri, University of
Rolla, MO 65409
T: (573) 341-4175
F: (573) 341-4880
www.umr.edu/~sports
A: Mark Mullin
S: John Kean
MIAA

Missouri, University of
8001 Natural Bridge Road
Saint Louis, MO 63121
T: (314) 516-5661
F: (314) 516-5503
www.umsc.edu
A: Paatricia Dolan
S: Michael Deford
GLVC

Missouri Southern State College
3950 East Newman Road
Joplin, MO 64801
T: (417) 625-9317
F: (417) 625-9397
www.mssc.edu/athletics
A: Jim Frazier
S: Joseph Moore
MIAA

Missouri Western State
4525 Downs Drive
Saint Joseph, MO 64507
T: (816) 271-4481
F: (816) 271-5901
www.mwsc.edu
A: Pete Chapman
S: Pat Madden
MIAA

Molloy College
1000 Hempstead Ave.
Rockville Centre, NY 11570
T: (516) 256-2207
F: (516) 256-2210
A/S: Bob Houlihan
ECAC, Independent

Montana State University
1500 N. 30th Street
Billings, MT 59101
T: (406) 657-2369
F: (406) 657-2399
www.billings.edu
A: Michael Swan
S: Peter Yazvar
Pacific West

Montevallo, University of
Montevallo, AL 35115
T: (205) 665-6600
F: (205) 665-6586
www.montevallo.edu
A; Roy Culberson
S: DeWayne Peevy
Southern States

Moorhead State University
17th St. & 9th Avenue S.
Moorhead, MN 56563
T: (218) 236-2622
F: (218) 299-5825
A: Dr. Katy Wilson
S: Larry Scott
NSIC

Morehouse College
830 Westview Drive SW
Atlanta, GA 30314
T: (404) 215-2752
F: (404) 521-9073
www.morehouse.edu
A: Josh Culbreath
S: James Nix
SIAC

Morris Brown College
643 M. Luther King, Jr. Dr. NW
Atlanta, GA 30314
T: (404) 220-3615
F: (404) 220-0114
www.morrisbrown,edu
A: Gene Bright
S: Charles Mooney
SIAC

Mount Olive College
Mount Olive, NC 28365
T: (919) 658-5056
F: (919) 658-1753
www.mountolivetrojans.com
A: Dr. Mac Cassell
S: Benny Benton
Carolinas-Virginia

Nebraska, University of
Hwy 30 & 15 th Ave.
Kearney, NE 68849
T: (308) 865-8514
F: (308) 865-8832
A: Michael Sumpter
S: Aaron Babcock
Rocky Mountain

Nebraska, University of
6001 Dodge Street
Omaha, NE 68182
T: (402) 554-2305
F: (402) 554-2555
www.//cid.unomaha.edu~cybermav/
A: Bob Danenhauer
S: Gary Anderson
North Central

New Hampshire College
2500 North River Road
Manchester, NH 03106
T: (603) 645-9604
F: (603) 645- 9686
www.unh.edu
A: Joseph "Chip" Polak
S: Tom McDermott
NECC, ECAC

New Haven, University of
300 Orange Avenue
West Haven, CT 06516
T: (203) 932-7017
F: (203) 932-7470
www.newhaven.edu
A: Deborah Chin
S: Tom Pincince
ECAC, NECC

New Jersey Inst. Of Technology
University Heights
Newark, NJ 07102
T: (973) 596-3636
F: (973) 596-8295
A: Dr. James Catalano
S: Open
NYCC

Newberry College
2100 College Street
Newberry, SC 29108
T: (803) 321-5155
F: (803) 321-5169
A: Wm. Grafton Young, Jr.
S: Darrell Orand
South Atlantic

New York Inst. Of Technology
PO Box 8000
Old Westbury, NY 11568
T: (516) 686-7626
F: (516) 626-0750
www.nyit.edu
A: Clyde Doughty, Jr.
S: Thomas Riordan
ECAC, NYCAC

North Alabama, University of
Florence, AL 35632
T: (256) 765-4397
F: (256) 765-4685
www.unanov.una.edu
A: Dan Summy
S: Jeff Hodges x 4595
Gulf South

North Central University
910 Elliot Avenue
Minneapolis, MN 55404
T: (612) 343-4755
F: (612) 343-4778
www.northcentral.edu
A: Greg Hayton
S: Matt Hayton
Northern Athletic

North Dakota State University
16th Ave. & University Dr. N
Fargo, ND 58105
T: (701) 231-8982
F: (701) 231-8022
www.nodak.edu
A: Dr. Robert Entzion
S: George Ellis
NCIAC

North Florida, University of
4567 St. Johns Bluff Road S.
Jacksonville, FL 32224
T: (904) 620-2833
F: (904) 620-2836
www.unf.edu/sports/unfpage.html
A: Dr. Richard Gropper
S: Bonnie Senappe
Peach Belt

Northeastern State University
Tahlequah, OK 74464
T: (918) 458-2071
F: (918) 458-2339
www.nsuok.edu
A: Dr. Gil Cloud
S: Scott Pettusl
Lone Star

Northern Colorado, Univ. of
Greeley, CO 80639
T: (970) 351-2018
F: (970) 351-2018
www.uncbears.com
A: Jim Fallis
S: Dave Moll
NCIAC

Northern Kentucky University
Newport, KY 41099
T: (606) 572-5193
F: (606) 572-6089
www.nku.edu/~athletics
A: Jane Meier
S: Don Owen
GLVC

Northern State University
1200 South Jay Street
Aberdeen, SD 57401
T: (605) 626-2488
F: (605) 626-2238
www.northern.edu
A: James Kretchman
S: Bruce Bachmeier
NSIC

Northland Baptist Bible
Dunbar, WI 54119
T: (715) 324-5245 x 6900
F: (715) 324-6133
www.nbbc.edu
A: Dennis Scott
S: Paul Dickerson
Northern Athletic Conf.

Northwest Missouri State Univ.
800 University Drive
Maryville, MO 64468
T: (660) 562-1713
F: (660) 562-1493
A: James Redd
S: Andy Seely
MIAA

Northwest Nazarene University
623 Holly Street
Nampa, ID 83686
T: (208) 467-8876
F: (208) 467-8396
www.nwmissouri.edu
A: Dr. Scott Armstrong
S: Gil Craker
Cascade Collegiate

Northwood University
3225 Cook Road
Midland, MI 48640
T: (517) 837-4381
F: (517) 837-4484
www.northwood.edu/athletics
A: Dave Coffey
S: Dave Marsh

Nova Southeastern Univ.
3301 College Avenue
Fort Lauderdale, FL 33314
T: (954) 262-8250
F: (954) 262-3926
www.nova.edu
A: Corey Johnson
S: Mike Laderman
Florida Sun

Oakland City University
143 Lucretia Street
Oakland City, IN 47660
T: (812) 749-1264
F: (812) 749-1291
A: Mike Sandifar
S: Tory Horner
Independent

Ohio College
PO Box 450640
Westlake, OH 44145
T:
F:
A: Dr. Kimberly LaRue
S: Joe Rossati
Ohio Intercollegiate

Ohio Valley College
4501 College Pkwy
Parkersburg, WV 26101
T: (304) 485-7384
F: (304) 485-2106
A: Ron Pavan
Independent

Pace University
8612 Bedford Road
Pleasantville, NY 10570
T: (914) 773-3412
F: (914) 773-3441
www.//enrollment.pace.edu/athletics
A: Joseph O'Donnell
S: Nick Renda

Paine College
1235 15th Street
Augusta, GA 30901
T: (706) 821-8353
F: (706) 821-8376
A: Ron Spry
S: Shawn Parks
Independent

Panhandle State University
PO Box 430
Goodwell, OK 73939
T: (580) 349-2611 x 390
F: (580) 349-3375
www.opsu.edu
A: Kevin Emerick
S: Doug Bender x 369
Independent

Philadelphia University
School House Ln. & Henry Ave.
Philadelphia, PA 19144
T: (215) 951-2720
F: (215) 951-2775
www.philacol.edu
A: Tom Shirley
S: Tony Berich
ECAC, NYCAC

Pittsburg State University
1701 S. Broadway Street
Pittsburg, KS 66762
T: (316) 235-4389
F: 9316) 235-4661
www.pittstate.edu
A: Charles Broyles
S: Dan Wilkes
MIAA

Pittsburgh, University of
Sports Center
Johnstown, PA 15904
T: (814) 269-2000
F: (814) 269-2026
www.pitt.edu
A: Ed Sherlock
S: Chris Caputo
Independent

Post, C.W. –LIU
Post Campus
720 Northern Blvd.
Brookville, NY 11548
T: (516) 299-2288
F: (516) 299-3155
www.liu.edu/cwpsport.htm
A: Vincent Salamone
S: Brad Sullivan
ECAC, NYCAC

Presbyterian College
105 Ashland Avenue
Clinton, SC 29325
T: (864) 833-8242
F: (864) 833-8323
A: Allen Morris
S: Allen Ansley
SAC

Quachita Baptist University
Box 3788, 410 Quachita St.
Arkadelphia, AR 71923
T: (870) 245-5181
F: (870) 245-5598
www.obu.edu
A: David Sharpe
S: Mac Sisson
Lone Star

Queens College
1900 Selwyn Avenue
Charlotte, NC 28274
T: (704) 337-2529
F: (704) 337-2237
www.queens.edu
A: Jeannie King
S: Jeff Aumend
Carolinas-Virginia

Queens College
65-30 Kissena Blvd.
Flushing, NY 11367
T: (718) 997-2770
F: (718) 997-2799
www.quincy.edu
A: Dr. Richard Wettan
S: Neal Kaufer
NYCAC

Quincy University
1800 College Street
Quincy, IL 62301
T: (217) 228-5290
F: (217) 228-5473
www.quincy.edu
A: Jim Naumovich
S: J.D. Hamilton
Great Lakes Valley Conf.

Regis University
Athletic Dept., 3333 Regis Blvd.
Denver, CO 80221
T: (303) 458-4070
F: (303) 964-5499
www.regis.edu
A: Barbara Schroeder
S: Doug Montgomery
RMAC

Rockhurst College
1100 Rockhurst Road
Kansas City, MO 64110
T: (816) 501-4141
F: (816) 501-4119
www.rockhurst.edu
A: Frank Diskin
S: Sid Bordman
Independent

Rollins College
Winter Park, FL 32789
T: (407) 646-2366
F: (407) 646-1555
A: Phillip Roach
S: Dean Hybl
Sunshine State

Saginaw Valley State
7400 Bay Road
University City, MI 48710
T: (517) 791-7311
F: (517) 791-7793
www.svsu.edu/athletics
A: Robert Becker
S: Tom Waske
GLIAC, MIFC

Saint Andrews Presbyterian
Laurinburg, NC 28352
T: (910) 277-5274
F: (910) 277-5272
www.sapc.edu
A: Rick Johnson
S: Robert Simmons
CVAC

Saint Augustine's College
1315 Oakwood Avenue
Raleigh, NC 27610
T: (919) 516-4171
F: (919) 828-9731
A: George Williams
S: Leon Carrington
CIAA

Saint Edwards University
3001 S. Congress Avenue
Austin, TX 78704
T: (512) 448-8480
F: (512) 416-5834
www.stedwards.edu
A: Dr. John Knorr
S: John Schmidt
Heartland

Saint Joseph's College
PO Box 875
Rensselaer, IN 47978
T: (219) 866-6342
F: (219) 866-6140
www.saintjoe.edu
A: Martin Smith
S: Joe Danahey
GLVC, Independent (FB)

Saint Martin's College
5300 Pacific Avenue SE
Lacey, WA 98503
T: (360) 438-4372
F: (360) 412-6191
www.stmartin.edu
A: Bob Grisham
S: Michael Ostlund
Pacific West

Saint Mary's University
1 Camino Santa Maria St.
San Antonio, TX 78228
T: (210) 436-3528
F: (210) 436-3040
www.stmarytx.edu
A: Buddy Meyer
S: Dr. Steve Johnson
Independent

Saint Michael's College
Winooski Park
Colchester, VT 05439
T: (802) 654-2500
F: (802) 654-2497
www.smcvt.edu
A: Geri Knortz
S: David Caspole
ECAC, NE-10

Saint Paul's College
Lawrenceville, VA 23868
T/F: (804) 848-2001
A: Leslie Young
S: Keyonna Robinson
CIAA

Saint Rose, The College of
432 Western Avenue
Albany, NY 12203
T: (518) 454-5282
F: (518) 458-5457
www.strose.edu/
A: Catherine Haker
S: David Alexander
NYCAC, ECAC

Salem-Teikyo University
Salem, WV 26426
T: (304) 782-5286
F: (304) 782-5516
www.salem-teikyo.wvnet.edu
A: Mike Carey
S: Cheryl Ann Morgan
WVIAC

San Francisco State Univ.
1600 Holloway Avenue
San Francisco, CA 94132
T: (415) 338-2218
F: (415) 338-1967
www.sfsu.edu/~athletic
A: Dr. Michael Simpson
S: Maureen Arata
California Collegiate

Savannah State University
3219 College Street
Savannah, GA 31404
T: (912) 353-5181
F: (912) 353-5287
www.savstate.edu
A: Jerome Fitch
S: Lee Grant Pearson
SIAC

Seattle Pacific University
3307 3rd Avenue W.
Seattle, WA 98119
T: (206) 281-2085
F: (206) 281-2266
www.spu.edu/depts/athletics
A: Dr. Nancy Gerou
S: Gretchen Gove
PWC

Shaw University
118 East South Street
Raleigh, NC 27601
T: (919) 546-8218
F: (919) 546-8299
A: Al Carter
S: Ronnie Holloway
CIAA

Shepherd College
Shepherdstown, WV 25443
T: (304) 876-5481
F: (304) 876-3267
www.shepherd.wvnet.edu
A: Monte Cater
S: Chip Ransom
WVIAC

Shippensburg University
1871 Old Main Drive
Shippensburg, PA 17257
T: (717) 477-1711
F: (717) 477-4045
www.ship.edu
A: Dr. James Pribula
S: John Alosi
ECAC, PSAC

Slippery Rock University
102 Morrow Field House
Slippery Rock, PA 16057
T: (724) 738-2021
F: (724) 738-2626
www.sru.edu
A: Paul Lueken
S: John Carpenter
PSAC

Sonoma State University
1801 E. Cotati Avenue
Rohnert Park, CA 94928
T: (707) 664-2521
F: (707) 664-4104
www.sonoma.edu/athletics
A: Bill Fusco
S: Mitch Cox
CCAA

Southampton College of LIU
239 Montauk Hwy.
Southampton, NY 11968
T: (516) 287-8386
F: (516) 287-8188
www.southampton.liunet.edu
A: Mary Topping
S: Cindy Corwith
ECAC, NYCAC

South Carolina, University of
17 University Pkwy
Aiken, SC 29801
T: (803) 648-6851 x 3486
F: (803) 641-3441
www.aiken.sc.edu
A: Randy Warrick
S.: Lindy Brown x 3252
Peach Belt

South Carolina, University of
800 University Way
Spartanburg, SC 29303
T: (864) 503-5141
F: (864) 503-5130
www.uscs.edu
A: Mike Hall
S: Jeremy Richardson
PBAC

South Dakota, University of
414 E. Clark Street
Vermillion, SD 57069
T: (605) 677-5309
F: (605) 677-5618
www.usd.edu
A: Kelly Higgins
S: Kyle Johnson
NCIAC

South Dakota State Univ.
16th Ave. & 11th Street
Brookings, SD 57007
T: (605) 688-5625
F: (605) 688-5999
www.sdstate.edu
A: Dr. Fred Oien
S: Ron Lenz
NCIAC

Southeastern Oklahoma St. Univ.
University Blvd
Durant, OK 74701
T: (580) 924-0121 x 2311
F: (580) 920-7493
www.sosu.edu
A: Dr. Don Parham
S: Trenten Hilburn x 2773
Lone Star

Southern Colorado, University of
2200 Bonforte Blvd.
Pueblo, CO 81001
T: (719) 549-2711
F: (719) 549-2570
www.uscolo.edu
A: Stanley Perchan
S: Todd Kelly
RMAC

Southern Connecticut State Univ.
125 Wintergreen Avenue
New Haven, CT 06515
T: (203) 392-6000
F: (203) 392-6006
A: Darryl Rogers
S: Rick Leddy
NECC, ECAC, Eastern FB

Southern Illinois University
SIUE Box 1129
Edwardsville, IL 62026
T: (618) 650-2871
F: (618) 650-3369
www.siue.edu/athletic
A: Cindy Jones
S: Eric Hess
GLVC

Southern Indiana, University of
8600 University Blvd.
Evansville, IN 47712
T: (812) 464-1846
F: (812) 465-1129
www.usi.edu/athletic.htm
A: Steve Newton
S: Ray Simmons
GLVC

Southwest Baptist University
1600 University Avenue
Bolivar, MO 65613
T: (417) 328-1787
F: (417) 328-2009
www.sbuniv.edu
A: Dennis Roland
S: Stephen Schwepker
MIAA

Southwest State University
1501 State Street
Marshall, MN 56258
T: (507) 537-7271
F: (507) 537-6578
www.southwest.msus.edu
A: Butch Raymond
S: Kelly Loft
Northern Sun

Southwestern Oklahoma State University
100 Campus Drive
Weatherford, OK 73096
T: (580) 774-3068
F: (580) 774-7106
www.swosu.edu
A: Cecil Perkins
S: Chris Doyle
Lone Star

Stonehill College
320 Washington Street
Easton, MA 02357
T: (508) 565-1384
F: (508) 565-1460
www.stonehill.edu
A: Paula Sullivan
S: James Seavey
ECAC, NE-10, EFC

Tampa, University of
401 W. Kennedy Blvd, Box 1
Tampa, FL 33606
T: (813) 253-6240
F: (813) 253-6288
www.Utampa.edu
A: Larry Maftise
S: Gil Swalls
Sunshine State

Tarleton State University
Stephenville, TX 76402
T: (254) 968-9178
F: (254) 968-9831
A: Lonn Reisman
S: Reed Richmond
Lone Star

Texas A&M University
Kingsville, TX 78363
T: (361) 593-2411
F: (361) 593-3587
A: Ron Harms
S: Fred Nuesch
Lone Star

Texas A&M University
Commerce, TX 75429
T: (903) 886-5549
F: (903) 886-5365
www.yamu-commerce.edu
A: Paul Peak
S: Bill Powers
Lone Star

Texas Lutheran University
1000 W. Court Street
Sequin, TX 78155
T: (830) 372-8120
F: (830) 372-8135
www.txlutheran.edu
A: Bill Milller
S: Tim Clark
Independent

Texas Wesleyan University
1201 Wesleyan Street
Fort Worth, TX 76105
T: (817) 531-4210
F: (817) 531-4208
www.txwesleyan.edu
A: Dr. Skip Applin
S: Jason Jacobsmeter
Heart of Texas

Truman State University
Kirksville, MO 63501
T: (660) 785-4235
F: (660) 785-4189
www.truman.edu
A: Kathy Turpin
S: Melissa Ware
MIAA

Tusculum College
PO Box 5021, 2299 Tusculum Blvd.
Greeneville, TN 37743
T: (423) 636-7323
F: (423) 798-1636
A: Ed Hoffmeyer
S: Dom Donnelly
South Atlantic

Tuskegee University
Tuskegee Institute, AL 36088
T: (334) 727-8849
F: (334) 724-4233
www.tusk.edu
A: Rick Comegy
S: Arnold Houston
SIAC

Valdosta State University
Patterson Street
Valdosta, GA 31698
T: (912) 333-5890
F: (912) 333-5972
www.valdosta.edu
A: Herb Reinhard
S: Steve Roberts
Gulf South

Virginia State University
PO Box 9058
Petersburg, VA 23806
T: (804) 524-5030
F: (804) 524-5763
www.vsu.edu
A: Edward Cooper
S: Greg Goings
CIAA

Virginia Union University
1500 N. Lombardy Street
Richmond, VA 23220
T: (804) 321-0243
F: (804) 321-0287
A: James Battle
S: Paul Williams
CIAA

Washburn University
1700 SW College Avenue
Topeka, KS 66621
T: (785) 231-1134
F: (785) 231-1091
www.washburn.edu
A: Loren Ferre
S: Gene Cassell
MIAA

Wayne State College
111 Main Street
Wayne, NE 68787
T: (402) 375-7520
F: (402) 375-7120
www.wayne.edu
A: Greg McDermott
S: Kevin Ludwig
Northern Sun

Wayne State University
5101 John C. Lodge
101 Matthaei Bldg.
Detroit, MI 48202
T: (313) 577-4280
F: (313) 577-5997
www.wayne.edu
A: Bob Brennan
S: Lisa McCoy
GLIAC, MIFC

West Alabama, University of
Station 5
Livingston, AL 35470
T: (205) 652-3600
F: (205) 652-3600
www2.westal.edu
A: Dee Outlaw
S: Kevin Graber
Gulf South

West Chester University
Sturzebecker Health Science Ctr.
West Chester, PA 19383
T: (610) 436-3555
F: (610) 436-1020
www.wcupa.edu
A: Dr. Edward Matejkovic
S: Tom Di Camillo
PSAC, ECAC II

West Florida, University of
11000 University Pkwy
Pensacola, FL 32514
T: (904) 474-3003
F: (904) 474-3342
A: Richard Berg
S: Karen Harrell
Gulf South Conf.

West Georgia, State Univ. of
Maple Street
Carrollton, GA 30118
T: (770) 836-6533
F: (770) 836-6792
www.westga.edu/~wgbraves
A: Ed Murphy
S: Mitch Gray
Gulf South

West Liberty State College
Bartell Field House
West Liberty, WV 26074
T: (304) 336-8046
F: (304) 336-8304
www.wlsc.wvnet.edu/www/sports/
A: James Watson
S: Lynn Ullom
WVIAC

West Texas A&M University
WTAMU Box 60049
Canyon, TX 79016
T: (806) 651-2069
F: (806) 651-2688
www.wtamu.edu
A: Ed Harris
S: Bill Kauffman
Lone Star

West Virginia University
Inst. of Tech.
Route 61
Montgomery, WV 25136
T: (304) 442-3121
F: (304) 442-3499
A: Mike Neese
S: Rusty Melvin
WVIAC

West Virginia State College
Campus Box 181
Institute, WV 25112
T: (304) 766-3165
F: (304) 766-3364
www.wvsc.edu
A: Bryce Casto
S: Sean McAndrews
WVIAC

West Virginia Wesleyan
College Avenue
Buckhannon, WV 26201
T: (304) 473-8099
F: (304) 473-8056
www.wvwc.edu
A: Dr. George Klebez
S: Janet Crites
WVIAC

Western New Mexico Univ.
1000 W. College Avenue
Silver City, NM 88061
T: (505) 538-6218
F: (505) 538-6163
A: Scott Woodard
S: Alan Kirsch
Pac West

Western Oregon University
345 Monmouth Avenue N.
Monmouth, OR 97361
T: (503) 838-8252
F: (503) 838-8164
www.wou.edu
A: Jon Carey
S: Russ Blunck
CFA, Cascade Collegiate, Pac.West Cor

Western State College
of Colorado
1 College Heights
Gunnison, CO 81231
T: (970) 943-2079
F: (970) 943-2754
www.western.edu/athletics
A: Dr. Greg Waggoner
S: Keith Hawkins
RMAC

Western Washington Univ.
516 High Street
Bellingham, WA 98225
T: (360) 650-3109
F: (360) 650-3495
www.wwu.edu
A: Lynda Goodrich
S: Paul Madison
Independent

Westminster College
Market Street
New Wilmington, LPA 16172
T: (724) 946-7317
F: (724) 946-7021
www.westminster.edu/athletics
A: Jim Dafler
S: Joseph Onderko
Great Lakes

Wheeling Jesuit University
316 Washigton Avenue
Wheeling, WV 26003
T: (304) 243-2365
F: (304) 243-2265
www.wju.edu
A: Jay DeFruscio
S: Jack Regis
WVIAC

Wingate University
PO Box 3054, Camden Road
Wingate, NC 28174
T: (704) 233-8193
F: (704) 233-8170
A: Beth Lawrence Murray
S: David Sherwood
South Atlantic

Winona State University
PO Box 5838
Winona, MN 55987
T: (507) 457-5210
F: (507) 457-5479
www.winona.msus.edu
A: Larry Holstad
S: Michael Herzberg
NSIC

Winston-Salem State Univ.
601 Martin Luther King, Jr. Dr.
Winston-Salem, NC 27102
T: (336) 750-2141
F: (336) 750-2144
www.wssu.edu/athletics
A: Anne Little
S: Adrian Ferguson
CIAA

Wisconsin, University of
PO Box 2000, 900 Wood Road
Kenosha, WI 53141
T: (414) 595-2308
F: (414) 595-2225
www.uwp.edu
A: Lenny Klaver
S: Steve Kratochvil
GLVC

ARE YOU MOVING?
Please follow the instructions below:

Be sure to send us your new address so we may keep you informed of new editions!

Thank you!

Edward T. Kobak, Jr.

Global Sports Productions, Ltd.
1223 Broadway, Suite 102
Santa Monica, California 90404

Canadian Colleges & Universities

Canadian Interuniversity Athletic Union (CIAU)
110 Eglinton Ave. W., Suite 303
Toronto, Ontario M4R 1A3
T: (416) 482-9933
F: (416) 482-8676
E: national@ciau.ca
www.ciau.ca
CEO: Kerry Moynihan
Mkt & Comm: Mark Bartschat

Regional Associations

Atlantic Universities Athletic Association
5657 Spring Garden Road
4th Floor, Suite 403
Halifax, Nova Scotia B3J 3R4
T: (902) 425-4235
F: (902) 425-7825
E: kcameron@auaa.ca
Exec. Dir: Kevin Cameron

Canada West Universities Athletic Association
Intercollegiate Coordinator
University of British Columbia
Dept. of Athletics
272-6081 University Blvd.
Vancouver, BC V6T 1Z1
T: (250) 822-2295
F: (250) 822-6011
Director: Ms. Kim Gordon

Great Plains Athletic Conference
Director of Recreation & Athletics
Dept. of Athletics
3737 Wascana Parkway
Regina, Saskatchewan S4S 0A2
T: (306) 585-4048
F: (306) 585-4373
P: Dick White

Ontario Universities Athletic Association
OUA Office
50-A Jackson Street W.
Canadian FB Hall of Fame Bldg.
Hamilton, Ontario L8P 1L4
T: (905) 540-5148
F: (905) 540-5149
www.oua.org
Exec. Dir: Rick Morocco

Ontario Women's Intercollegiate A.A.
1185 Eglinton Ave. East
Suite 506
North York, Ontario M3C 3C6
T: (416) 426-7047
F: (416) 426-7386
Exec. Dir: Sheila Forshaw

Quebec Student Sports Federation
Stade Olympique
4545 ave. Pierre-de-Coubertin
C.P. 1000, Succursale M
Montreal, Quebec H1V 3R2
T: (514) 252-3300
F: (514) 254-3292
Director: M. Michel Carrieres

CIAU Members

* A: Athletic Director
* S: Sports Information

Acadia University
Box 99
Wolfville, Nova Scotia B0P 1X0
T: (902) 585-1552
F: (902) 585-1061
www.acadiau.ca
E: bruce.cohoon@acadiau.ca
A: Don Wells
S: Bruce Cohoon

University of Alberta
P220, Universiade Pavilion
Athletics & Recreation
Edmonton, Alberta T6G 2H9
T: (403) 492-3413
F: (403) 492-7307
www.bears.ualberta.ca
E: ireade@per.ualberta.ca
A: Ian Reade
S: Dan Carle

Bishop's University
Lennoxville, Quebec J1M 1Z7
T: (819) 822-9668
F: (819) 822-9600
www.ubishops.ca
A: Eddie Pomykala
S: Jeff Harris

Brandon University
270-18th Street
Brandon, Manitoba R7A 6A9
T: (204) 727-7405
F: (204) 727-6906
www.brandonu.ca
A: Tom Skinner

University of British Columbia
272-6081 University Blvd.
Vancouver, British Columbia V6T 1Z1
T: (604) 822-9466
F: (604) 822-6011
www.athletics.ubc.ca
A: Robert Philip
S: Jacquie Dyck

Brock University
St. Catharines, Ontario L2S 3A1
T: (905) 688-5550 ext. 3383
F: (905) 688-0541
www.arnie.pec.brocku.ca
A: Bob Davis
S: Murray Nystrom

University of Calgary
2500 University Drive NW
Calgary, Alberta T2N 1N4
T: (403) 220-3409
F: (403) 220-1503
www.kin.ucalgary.ca
E: neumann@acs.ucalgary.ca
A: Don Wilson
S: Jack Neumann

University College of Cape Breton
PO Box 5300
Sydney, Nova Scotia B1P 6L2
T: (902) 563-1657
F: (902) 539-4493
www.uccb.ns.ca
A: David MacLean
S: Wayne Clark

Carleton University
1125 Colonel By Drive
Physical Rec. - Rm. 201
Ottawa, Ontario K1S 5B6
T: (613) 520-5627
F: 613) 520-4466
www.carleton.ca
E: drew_love @ carleton.ca
A: Drew Love
S: David Kent

Concordia University
PA 104
7141 Sherbrooke St. West
Montreal, Quebec H4B 1R6
T: (514) 848-3867
F: (514) 848-8637
www.concordia.ca
E: zairnsh@alcor.concordia.ca
A: Harry Zarins
S: Catherine Grace

Dalhousie University
Dalplex, South Street
Halifax, Nova Scotia B3H 3J5
T: (902) 494-3752
F: (902) 494-2574
www.tigers.dal.ca
E: karen.moore@dal.ca
A: Karen Moore
S: Jim Charters

University of Guelph
Department of Athletics
Guelph, Ontario N1G 2W1
T: (519) 824-4120 ext. 8908
F: (519) 766-9563
www.uoguelph.ca
E: dcopp@ath.uoguelph.ca
A: David Copp
S: Peter Barnsley

Lakehead University
955 Oliver Road
Thunder Bay, Ontario P7B 5E1
T: (807) 343-8605
F: (807) 343-8944
www.lakeheadu.ca
E: stu.julius@lakeheadu.ca
A&S: Stu Julius

Laurentian University
935 Ramsey Lake Road
Sudbury, Ontario P3E 2C6
T: (705) 675-1151 ext. 1026
F: (705) 673-6502
www.laurentian.ca
E:spinfo@nickel.laurentian.ca
A: Dr. Patricia Pickard
S: Peter Ennis

Universite' Laval
SAS, Bureau 2254
Peps, Universite Laval
Cite' Universitaire, Quebec
Canada G1K 7P4
T: (418) 656-2807
F: (418) 656-5749
www.ulaval.ca
E: gilles.damboise@sas.ulaval.ca
A: Gilles D'Amboise
S: Yvan Breault

University of Lethbridge
4401 University Drive
Lethbridge, Alberta T1K 3M4
T: (403) 329-2380
F: (403) 329-2709
www.uleth.ca/anc.ath
E: slavsl @ gw.uleth.ca
A: Sandy Slavin
S: Dave Crook

University of Manitoba
Department of Athletics
124 Frank Kennedy Centre
Winnipeg, Manitoba R3T 2N2
T: (204) 474-9140
F: (204) 474-7634
www.umanitoba.ca
E: walt_mckee@umanitoba.ca
A: Walt McKee
S: Brad Woods

Mc Gill University
475 Pine Avenue West
Montreal, Quebec H2W 1S4
T: (514) 398-7000
F: (514) 398-4901
www.mcgill.ca
E: bobd@stuserv.lan.mcgill.ca
A: Robert Dubeau
S: Earl Zukerman

Mc Master University
1280 Main Street West
Hamilton, Ontario L8S 4K1
T: (905) 525-9140 ext. 23699
F: (905) 526-1573
www.athrec.mcmaster.ca
E: athlete@mcmaster.ca
A: Therese Quigley
S: Les Miller

Memorial University of Newfoundland
School of Phys. Edu. & Athletics
Elizabeth Avenue
St. John's, Newfoundland A1C 5S7
T: (709) 737-8669
F: (709) 737-3979
www.mun.ca
E: fbutler@morgan.ucs.mun.ca
A: Frank Butler
S: Heather Gibbons

Universite' de Moncton
Service des Sports Universitaires
CEPS Louis-J-Robichaud
Moncton, New Brunswick E1A 3E9
T: (506) 858-3773
F: (506) 858-4058
www.umoncton.ca
E: arsenag@umoncton.ca
A: Christine LeBlanc
S: Ghislaine Arsenault

Universite' de Montreal
Departement D'Education
Physique - Case Postale 6128
Succursale Centreville
Montreal, Quebec H3C 3J7
T: (514) 343-6166
F: (514) 343-2181
www.edphys.umontreal.ca
E: simarman@ere.umontreal.ca
A: Claude Alain
S: Manon Simard

Mount Allison University
50 York Street
Sackville, New Brunswick E4L 1C8
T: (506) 364-2400
F: (506) 364-2217
www.mta.ca
E: jtdrover @mta.ca
A: Jack Drover
S: Susan Seaborn

University of New Brunswick
PO Box 4400
Fredericton, New Brunswick E3B 5A3
T: (506) 453-5034
F: (506) 453-3511
www.unb.ca/web/vreds
E: jimborn@unb.ca
A: James Born

Nipissing University
100 College Drive
PO Box 5002
North Bay, Ontario P1B 8L7
T: (705) 474-3461 x 4249
F: (705) 474-6323
www.unipissing.ca
E: vitoc@admin.unipissing.ca
A: Vito Castiglione

University of Ottawa
Montpetit Hall, Rm. 361
125 University Avenue
Ottawa, Ontario K1N 6N5
T: (613) 562-5800 ext. 4336
F: (613) 562-5151
www.geegees.uottawa.ca
E: gelineau@uottawa.ca
A: Luc Gelineau
S: Stephen Partridge

University of Prince Edward Island
550 University Avenue
Charlottetown, P.E.I. C1A 4P3
T: (902) 566-0606 / 566-0432
F: (902) 566-0700
www.upei.ca
E: mullaly@upei.ca
A: Barb Mullaly
S: Ron Annear

Universite du Quebec `a Montreal
Case Postale 8888
Succursale Centre-Ville
Montreal, Quebec H3C 3P8
T: (514) 987-3000 x 1804
F: (514) 987-6819
www.unites.uqam.ca/sve/
E: vaillancourt.manon@uqam.ca
A: Manon Vaillancourt
S: Alain Giasson

Universite du Quebec `a Trois-Rivieres
3351 Boul. des Forges
C.P. 500
Trois-Rivieres, Quebec G9A 5H7
T: (819) 376-5254 x 4401
F: (819) 376-5193
www.uqtr.uquebec.ca
E: pierre_clermont@uqtr.uquebec.ca
A: Michel Morin
S: Pierre Clermont

Queen's University
Physical Education Centre
Union Street
Kingston, Ontario K7L 3N6
T: (613) 545-2666
F: (613) 545-6478
www.queensu.ca/athletics/index.html
E: qsports@post.queensu.ca
A: Dr. Joan Stevenson
S: Ken Kirkwood

University of Regina
3737 Wascana Parkway
Regina, Saskatchewan S4S 0A2
T: (306) 585-4048
F: (306) 585-4373
www.uregina.ca
E: dick.white@leroy.cc.uregina.ca
A: Dick White

Royal Military College of Canada
Athletic Department
PO Box 17000, STN Forces
Kingston, Ontario K7K 7B4
T: (613) 541-6000
F: (613) 541-6186
www.rmc.ca/athletics/english.htm
E: thibault-m @ rmc.ca
A: Joan Thibault

Ryerson Polytechnic University
350 Victoria Street
Toronto, Ontario M5B 2K3
T: (416) 979-5089
F: (416) 979-5211
www.acs.ryerson.ca/athletics/
E: bfullertt@acs.ryerson.ca
A: Bob Fullerton

St. Francis Xavier University
PO Box 5000
Antigonish, Nova Scotia B2G 2W5
T: (902) 867-2280
F: (902) 867-2455
www.stfx.ca
E: jmcfarla@stfx.ca
A: Dr. John McFarland
S: Paul Bowen

Saint Mary's University
Halifax, Nova Scotia B3H 3C3
T: (902) 420-5427
F: (902) 420-5844
www.stmarys.ca
E: lori-forbes@stmarys.ca
A: Larry Uteck
S: Lori Forbes

St. Thomas University
PO Box 4569
Fredericton, New Brunswick E3B 5G3
T: (506) 452-0409
F: (506) 452-0547
www.stthomasu.ca
E: cwadden@stthomasu.ca
A: LeRoy J. Washburn
S: Cathy Wadden

University of Saskatchewan
College of Kinesiology
105 Gymnasium Place
Saskatoon, Saskatchewan S7N 5C2
T: (306) 966-6490
F: (306) 966-6502
www.usask.ca/physed/huskies
E: wilsonr@duke.usask.ca
A: Ross Wilson
S: Ryan Parchman

Universite' de Sherbrooke
2500 Boul. de l'Universite'
Sherbrooke, Quebec J1K 2R1
T: (819) 821-7570
F: (819) 821-7576
www.usherb.ca
E: rene.roy@sportif.usherb.ca
A: Jean Poirier
S: Rene Roy

University of Toronto
Dept. of Phys. Edu. & Health
55 Harbord Street
Toronto, Ontario M5S 2W6
T: (416) 978-7379
F: (416) 971-2118
www.utoronto.ca/dar
E: liz.hoffman@utoronto.ca
A: Liz Hoffman

Trent University
PO Box 4800
Peterborough, Ontario K9J 7B8
T: (705) 748-1252
F: (705) 748-1447
www.trentu.ca
E: pwilson@trentu.ca
A: Paul Wilson

Trinity Western University
Dept. of Athletics
7600 Glover Road
Langley, BC V2Y 1Y1
T: (604) 513-2055
F: (604) 513-2065
www.twu.ca/athletics
E: hall@twu.ca
A: Murray Hall
S: Scott Stewart

University of Victoria
PO Box 3015
McKinnon Bldg., Room 181
Victoria, British Columbia V8W 3P1
T: (250) 721-8409
F: (250) 721-8956
www.stas.uvic.ca/athletics-recreation
E: wpm@uvic.cac.ca
A: Wayne MacDonald
S: Judy Joseph

University of Waterloo
University Avenue
Waterloo, Ontario N2L 3G1
T: (519) 888-4567 ext. 3663
F: (519) 746-2283
www.athletics.waterloo.ca
E: jamccrae@watserv1.uwaterloo.ca
A: Judy McCrae
S: Bob Copeland

The University of Western Ontario
Room 3165, Thames Hall
Richmond Street North
London, Ontario N6A 3K7
T: (519) 661-3088
F: (519) 661-3937
www.uwo.ca/athletics
E: semotiuk @ julian.uwo.ca
A: Darwin Semotiuk
S: Helen Vande Bovenkamp

Wilfrid Laurier University
75 University Ave. West
Waterloo, Ontario N2L 3C5
T: (519) 884-0710 x 2216
F: (519) 884-0203
www.wlu.ca
E: wgowing @mach1.wlu.ca
A: Peter Baxter
S: Mike Mc Kenna

University of Windsor
St. Denis Centre, College Ave.
Department of Athletics & Rec. Svcs.
Windsor, Ontario N9B 3P4
T: (519) 253-4292 x 5062
F: (519) 973-7058
www.uwindsor.ca/athletics
E: wizard @ uwindsor.ca
A: Dr. Joanne MacLean
S: Ian Harrison

University of Winnipeg
Duckworth Centre
515 Portage Avenue
Winnipeg, Manitoba R3B 2E9
T: (204) 786-9419
F: (204) 783-7866
www.uwinnipeg.ca/athletics
E: debbiesenyk@uwinnipeg.ca
A: Aubrey Ferris
S: Deborah Senyk

York University
4700 Keele Street
302 Tait McKenzie Centre
North York, Ontario M3J 1P3
T: (416) 736-5469
F: (416) 736-5702
www.yorku.ca/dept/physed/sport
E: sprtinfo@yorku.ca
A: Paticia Murray
S: Laurie Lyle

Canadian Colleges Athletic Association
Windmill Point
Cornwall, Ontario K6H 4Z1
T: (613) 937-1508
F: (613) 937-1530
www.ccaa.ca
E: smmacdon@slcsl.stlawrence.on.ca
Ex. Dir: Sandra Murray-MacDonnell

Interprovincial competition was initiated in 1971 when colleges in Alberta, British Columbia, Manitoba & Saskatchewan formed the 4-West Championships for competition.
In 1972, Ontario & Quebec initiated similar competition. The CCAA was formally established in 1973.

Member Colleges

Listed here are the colleges, with the Athletic Director listed as the contact person

Alberta Colleges Athletic Association
Percy Page Centre
11759 Groat Road
Edmonton, Alberta T5M 3K6
T: (403) 427-9269
F: (403) 427-9289
www.acac.ab.ca
E: i.strifler@acac.ab.ca
Ex. Dir: Irwin Strifler

Augustana University College
4901-46 Avenue
Camrose, Alberta T4V 2R3
T: (403) 679-1158
F: (403) 679-2485
www.augustana.ab.ca
A: Morten Asfeldt

Briercrest Bible College
510 College Drive
Caronport, Sask. S0H 0S0
T: (306) 756-3279
F: (306) 756-3366
www.briercrest.ca
A: James Clark

Concordia College
7128 Ada Blvd.
Edmonton, Alberta T5B 4E4
T: (780) 479-9321
F: (780) 479-5050
www.concordia.ab.ca
A: Bernie Masterson

Grande Prairie Regional College
10726-106 Ave.
Grande Prairie, Alberta T8V 4C4
T: (403) 539-2901
F: (403) 539-2811
www.gprc.ab.ca
A: Ron Thomson

Grant Mac Evan Community College
10700-104 Ave.
Edmonton, Alberta T5J 4S2
T: (780) 497-5291
F: (780) 497-5290
www.gmcc.ab.ca
A: Phil Allen

Keyano College
8115 Franklin Avenue
Fort McMurray, Alberta T9H 2H7
T: (403) 791-8901
F: (403) 791-4867
www.keyanoc.ab.ca
A: Wayne Thomas

Lakeland College
5707 47 Avenue West
Vermilion, Alberta T9X 1K5
T: (403) 853-8470
F: (403) 853-8711
www.lakelandc.ab.ca
A: Ingo Hentschel

Lethbridge Community College
3800 College Drive
Lethbridge, Alberta T1K 1L6
T: (403) 382-6912
F: (403) 327-1654
www.lethbridge.ab.ca
A: Tim Tollestrup

Medicine Hat College
299 College Dr. SE
Medicine Hat, Alberta T1A 3Y6
T: (403) 529-4823
F: (403) 504-3511
www.mhc.ab.ca
A: Rob Morgan

Mount Royal College
4825 Richard Road SW
Calgary, Alberta T3E 6K6
T: (403) 240-6516
F: (403) 240-8969
www.mtroyal.ab.ca
A: Mark Kosak

Northern Alberta Institute of Technology
11762-106 Street
Edmonton, Alberta T5G 2R1
T: (780) 471-7601
F: (780) 471-7463
www.nait.ab.ca
A: Gregg Meropoulis

Prairie Bible College
Box 4000
Three Hills, Alberta T0M 2N0
T: (403) 443-5511
F: (403) 443-5540
www.pbi.ab.ca
AD: Keith Harder

Red Deer College
PO Box 5005, 56 Ave. & 32 St.
Red Deer, Alberta T4N 5H5
T: (403) 342-3221
F: (403) 343-8840
www.rdc.ab.ca
A: Allan Ferchuk

Southern Alberta Instit. of Tech.
1301-16 Avenue, NW
Calgary, Alberta T2M 0L4
T: (403) 284-8033
F: (403) 284-7109
www.sait.ab.ca
A: Ken Babey

The King's University College
9125-50 Street
Edmonton, Alberta T6B 2H3
T: (780) 465-3500
F: (780) 465-3534
www.kingsu.ab.ca
A: Dr. Robert Day

Atlantic Colleges Athletic Association (NSSAF)
PO Box 3010
Halifax, Nova Scotia B3J 3G6
T: (902) 425-5450
F: (902) 425-5606
P: Ron O'Flaherty

University of King's College
6350 Coburg Rd.
Halifax, Nova Scotia B3H 2A1
T: (902) 422-1271 ext. 133
F: (902) 423-3357
www.ukings.ns.ca
A: Neil Hooper

Mount Allison University
50 York Street
Sackville, New Brunswick
Canada E0A 3C0
T: (506) 364-2400
F: (506) 364-2217
www.mta.ca
A: Jack Drover

Mount St. Vincent University
166 Bedford Hwy.
Halifax, Nova Scotia B3M 2J6
T: (902) 457-6370
F: (902) 457-1694
www.msvu.ca
A: June Lumsden

University of New Brunswick
PO Box 5050
Saint John, NB E2L 4L5
T: (506) 648-5520
F: (506) 648-5529
www.unbsj.ca
A: Bob Bonnell

Nova Scotia Agricultural College
PO Box 550, 20 Cumming Drive
Truro, Nova Scotia B2N 5E3
T: (902) 893-6661
F: (902) 897-0014
www.nsac.ns.ca
A: Judy Smith

Nova Scotia Community College
36 Arthur Street
Truro, NovaScotia B2N 3N2
T: (902) 893-5316
F: (902) 893-5390
www.nscc.ns.ca
A: Wilf MacCormack

University Sainte-Anne
RR#1 Church Point
Digby County, NS, B0W 1M0
T: (902) 769-2114
F: (902) 769-2930
www.ustanne.ednet.ns.ca
A: Pierre Norbert

St. Thomas University
PO Box 4569
Fredericton, NB Canada E3B 5G3
T: (506) 452-0409
F: (506) 452-0547
www.stthomasu.ca
A: Leroy Washburn

British Columbia College Athletic Association
Langara College, 100 West 49th Ave.
Vancouver, B.C. V5X 2X6
T: (604) 324-8025
F: (604) 324-3117
www.ouc.bc.ca/athletics/bccaa
SID: Andre Tee

British Columbia Instit. of Tech.
3700 Willingdon Avenue
Burnaby, B.C. V5G 3H2
T: (604) 432-8282
F: (604) 431-7261
www.bcit.bc.ca
A: Paul Fortier

Camosun College
3100 Foul Bay Rd.
Victoria, B.C. V8P 5J2
T: (250) 370-3601
F: (250) 370-3609
www.camosun.bc.ca
A: Graham Matthews

Capilano College
2055 Purcel Way
North Vancouver, B.C. V7J 3H5
T: (604) 983-7533
F: (604) 984-1736
www.capcollege.bc.ca
A: Joseph Iacobellis

Cariboo University-College
PO Box 3010
Kamloops, B.C. V2E 2P3
T: (250) 828-5273
F: (250) 371-5672
www.cariboo.bc.ca
A: Tracey Bilsky

Columbia Bible College
2940 Clearbrook Rd.
Clearbrook, B.C. V2T 2Z8
T: (604) 853-3567 ext. 311
F: (604) 854-1862
www.columbia.bc.edu
A: Tim Demant

Douglas College
700 Royal Avenue
New Westminster, B.C. V3L 5B2
T: (604) 527-5043
F: (604) 527-5032
www.douglas.bc.ca
A: Lou Rene Legge

University College of the Fraser Valley
33844 King Road
Abbotsford, B.C. V2S 7M9
T: (604) 854-4583
F: (604) 855-5936
www.ucfv.bc.ca
A: Jane Antil

Langara College
100 West 49th Avenue
Vancouver, B.C. V5Y 2Z6
T: (604) 323-5421
F: (604) 323-5664
www.langara.bc.ca
A: Theresa Hanson

Malaspina University College
900 5th Street
Nanaimo, B.C. V9R 5S5
T: (250) 741-2356
F: (250) 741-2586
www.mala.bc.ca
A: Rick Bevis

College of New Caledonia
3330-22nd Avenue
Prince George, B.C. V2N 1P8
T: (250) 562-2131
F: (250) 561-5816
www.cnc.bc.ca
A: Tina McComb-Tardif

Okanagan University College
3333 College Way
Kelowna, B.C. V1V 1V7
T: (250) 470-6030
F: (250) 470-6031
www.ouc.bc.ca
A: Rob Johnson

College of the Rockies
2700 College Way
Cranbrook, BC V5G 3H2
T: (250) 489-8201
F: (250) 489-1790
www.cotr.ba.ca
A: Chris New

Selkirk College
PO Box 1200
Frank Biender Way
Castlegar, B.C. V1N 3J1
T: (604) 365-1298
F: (604) 365-2132
A: Preston Zeeben

Trinity Western University
7600 Glover Road
Langley, BC V2Y 1Y1
T: (604) 513-2020
F: (604) 513-2065
www.twu.bc.ca
A: Murray Hall

Ontario Colleges A.A.
1185 Eglinton Avenue East
Suite 505A
North York, Ontario M3C 3C6
T: (416) 426-7043
F: (416) 426-7308
Exec. Dir: Loretta McKenzie

Algonquin College
1385 Woodroffe Ave.
Nepean, Ontario K2G 1V8
T: (613) 727-4723 x 5330
F: (613) 727-7631
www.algonquinc.on.ca
A: Ron Port

College Boreal
21, boulevard Lasalle
Sudbury, Ontario P3A 6B1
T: (705) 560-6673
F: (705) 521-6004
www.borealc.on.ca
A: Dan Landry

Cambrian College
1400 Barrydowne Rd.
Sudbury, Ontario P3A 3V8
T: (705) 566-8101 x 7450
F: (705) 524-6395
www.cambrianc.on.ca
A: Bob Piche

Canadore College
100 College Dr., PO Box 5001
North Bay, Ontario P1B 8K9
T: (705) 474-7600
F: (705) 474-2384
www.canadorec.on.ca
A: Linda Turcotte

Centennial College
41 Progress Court
PO Box 631, Station A
Scarborough, Ontario M1K 5E9
T: (416) 289-5000
F: (416) 439-9510
www.cencol.on.ca
A: Mary Zettel

Conestoga College
299 Doon Valley Drive
Kitchener, Ontario N2G 4M4
T: (519) 748-3512
F: (519) 748-4214
www.conestogac.on.ca
A: Ian James

Confederation College
1450 Nakina Rd., Box 398
Thunder Bay, Ontario P7C 4W1
T: (807) 473-6161
F: (807) 622-4842
www.confederationc.on.ca
A: Ron Fearon

Durham College
2000 Simcoe Street North
Box 385
Oshawa, Ontario L1H 7L7
T: (905) 721-3042
F: (905) 721-3117
www..durhamc.on.ca
A: Ken Babcock

Fanshawe College
1460 Oxford St. East
PO Box 4005
London, Ontario N5W 5H1
T: (519) 452-4430 x 4666
F: (519) 452-0656
www.fanshawec.on.ca
A: Michael C. Lindsay

George Brown College
20 King Street East
Toronto, Ontario M5A 3W8
T: (416) 415-2099
F: (416) 415-2653
www.gbrownc.on.ca
A: Alex Barbier

Georgian College
1 Georgian Drive
Barrie, Ontario L4M 3X9
T: (705) 728-1968
F: (705) 722-5181
www.georcoll.on.ca
AD: Michele McConney

Humber College
205 Humber College Blvd.
Etobicoke, Ontario M9W 5L7
T: (416) 675-6622
F: (416) 675-2833
www.humberc.on.ca
A: Doug Fox

Lambton College
1457 London Road
PO Box 969
Sarnia, Ontario N7T 7K4
T: (519) 542-7751
F: (519) 542-6667
www.lambton.on.ca
A: Dave Gotts

Loyalist College
Wallbridge-Loyalist Rd.
PO Box 4200
Belleville, Ontario K8N 5B9
T: (613) 969-1913 x 371
F: (613) 969-0175
www.layalistc.on.ca
A: Greg Gavin

Mohawk College
PO Box 2034
Fennell Ave. W & West 5th St.
Hamilton, Ontario L8N 3T2
T: (905) 575-2075
F: (905) 575-2372
www.mohawkc.on.ca
A: Mary Hrycay

Niagara College
300 Woodlawn Road
Welland, Ontario L3B 5S2
T: (905) 735-2211 x 7583
F: (905) 735-5904
www.niagarac.on.ca
A: Ray Sarkis

Nipissing University
100 College Drive
North Bay, Ontario P1B 8L7
T: (705) 474-3461
F: (705) 495-2850
www.unipissing.ca
A: Vito Castiglione

Redeemer College
777 Garner Road East
Ancaster, Ontario L9K 1J4
T: (905) 648-2131
F: (905) 648-2134
www.redeemerc.on.ca
A: Allan Brown

Royal Military College
PO Box 17000, Stn. Forces
Kingston, Ontario K7K 7B4
T: (613) 541-6000
F: (613) 541-6186
www.rmc.ca
A: Joane Thibault

St. Clair College
2000 Talbot Road W.
Windsor, Ontario N9A 6S4
T: (519) 972-2727
F: (519) 966-2737
www.stclairc.on.ca
A: Rosemary Smyth

St. Lawrence College
2288 Parkedale Ave.
Brockville, Ontario K6V 5X3
T: (613) 345-0556
F: (613) 345-7871
www.stlawrencec.on.ca
A: Tyler Forkes

St. Lawrence College
Windmill Point
Cornwall, Ontario K6H 4Z1
T: (613) 933-4693
F: (613) 937-1523
www.stlawrencec.on.ca
A: Shirley McGlynn

St. Lawrence College
King St. & Portsmouth Ave.
PO Box 6000
Kingston, Ontario K7L 5A6
T: (613) 544-5532
F: (613) 545-3920
www.stlawrencec.on.ca
A: Diana Drury

Sault College
PO Box 60
443 Northern Avenue
Sault Ste. Marie, Ontario
Canada P6A 5L3
T: (705) 759-2554
F: (705) 757-1319
www.sault.on.ca
A: Pat Story

Seneca College
1750 Finch Ave. E.
North York, Ontario M2J 2X5
T: (416) 491-5050
F: (416) 491-5446
www.seneca.on.ca
A: Linda Stapleton

Sheridan College
1430 Trafalgar Road
Oakville, Ontario L6H 2L1
T: (905) 845-9430
F: (905) 815-4014
www.sheridanc.on.ca
A: Dick Ruschiensky

Sir Sandford Fleming College
Albert St. S.
Box 8000
Lindsay, Ontario K9V 5E6
T: (705) 324-9144
F: (705) 878-9316
www.flemingc.on.ca
A: Steve McLaughlin

Sir Sandford Fleming College
Brealey Drive
Peterborough, Ontario K9J 7B1
T: (705) 749-5552
F: (705) 749-5532
www.flemingc.on.ca
A: Fred Batley

Federation Quebecoise du Sport Etudiant
C.P. 1000, Succ. M
Montreal, Quebec H1V 3R2
T: (514) 252-3110
F: (514) 254-3292
Sec. Collegial Dir: Jacques Cyr

College Ahuntsic
9155 rue St-Hubert
Montreal, Quebec H2M 1Y8
T: (514) 389-5921
F: (514) 389-4554
www.collegeahuntsic.qc.ca
A: Christian Moisan

College Andre-Grasset
1001 Boul. Cremazie
Montreal, Quebec H2M 1M3
T: (514) 381-4293
F: (514) 381-7421
www.grasset.qc.ca
A: Edith Morisseau

College Andre-Laurendeau
1111, rue Lapierre
Lasalle, Quebec H8N 2J4
T: (514) 364-3320
F: (514) 364-7130
www.claurendeau.qc.ca
A: Patrice Audy

Cegep Beauce Appalaches
1055-116 ieme rue est.
Ville de Saint-Georges, G5Y 3G1
Quebec
T: (418) 228-8896
F: (418) 228-0562
www.cegepbceapp.qc.ca
A: Gaetan Mathieu

College Bois-de-Boulogne
10555 Av. Bois-de-Boulogne
Montreal, Quebec H4N 1L4
T: (514) 332-3000
F: (514) 332-6145
www.colegebdeb.qc.ca
A: Real Gregoire

Champlain Regional College
Lennoxville, Quebec J1M 2A1
T: (819) 564-3666
F: (819) 564-5171
www.lennox.champlain.college.qc.ca
A: Tony Addona

Champlain Regional College
900 Riverside Drive
St. Lambert, Quebec J4P 3P2
T: (450) 672-7360
F: (450) 672-9299
www.champlaincollege.qc.ca
A: Andre E. LeBlanc

Dawson College
3040 Sherbrooke Street Ouest
Montreal, Quebec H3Z 1A4
T: (514) 931-8731
F: (514) 931-1864
www.dawsoncollege.qc.ca
A: John Davidson

CEGEP De Drummondville
960 rue Saint-Georges
Drummondville, Quebec J2C 6A2
T: (819) 478-4671
F: (819) 474-6859
www.cdrummond.qc.ca
A: Andre Gingras

College Edouard Montpetit
945 chemin de Chambly
Longueuil, Quebec J4H 3M6
T: (514) 679-2630
F: (514) 651-1491
www.collegeem.qc.ca
A: Monique Magnan

College Francois Xavier-Garneau
1660 boul. de l' Entente
Quebec, P.Q. G1S 4S3
T: (418) 688-8310
F: (418) 688-0087
www.cegep-fxg.qc.ca
A: Nicole Vachon

College Jean de Brebeuf
3200, ch. Cote Ste-Catherine
Montreal, Quebec H3T 1C1
T: (514) 342-1320
F: (514) 342-0130
www.brebeuf.qc.ca
A: Danielle Nadon

John Abbott College
Box 2000
21275 Lakeshore Road
Ste.-Anne de Bellevue,
Quebec H9X 3L9
T: (514) 457-6610
F: (514) 457-1427
www.johnabbott.qc.ca
A: Glenn Ruiter

College de Jonquiere
2505 rue Saint-Hubert
Jonquiere, Quebec G7X 7V2
T: (418) 547-2191
F: (418) 695-4489
www.cjonquiere.qc.ca
A: Langis Croft

Cegep de Limoilou
1300, 8e Ave., C.P. 1200
Quebec 3 Quebec G1J 5L5
T: (418) 647-6600
F: (418) 647-6795
www.climoilou.qc.ca
A: Louis Grou

College de Maisonneuve
3800, rue Sherbrooke est.
Montreal, Quebec H1X 2A2
T: (514) 254-7131
F: (514) 253-8909
www.cmaisonneuve.qc.ca
A: Stephane Dubreuil

Marianopolis College
3880 Cote des Neiges
Montreal, Quebec H3H 1W1
T: (514) 931-8792
F: (514) 931-6786
A: Louise McLellan

College Montmorency
475 boul. de Souvenir
Laval, Quebec H7N 1C6
T: (514) 975-6180
F: (514) 975-6153
www.cmontmorency.qc.ca
A: Michel Blanchette

College de L'Outaouais
333 boul. Cite des Jeunes
Hull, Quebec J8Y 6M5
T: (819) 770-4012
F: (819) 770-8167
www.coll-outao.qc.ca
A: Henri Pierre Caron

Cegep de Sainte-Foy
2410 Chemin Sainte-Foy
Sainte Foy, Quebec G1V 1T3
T: (418) 659-6600
F: (418) 658-0887
www.cegep-ste-foy.qc.ca
A: Marlene Levesque
    Robert Goulet

Cegep de Saint-Laurent
625 boul. Ste-Croix
St. Laurent, Quebec H4L 3X7
T: (514) 747-6521
F: (514) 747-0642
www.cegep-st-laurent.qc.ca
A: Yves Charron

College de Sherbrooke
475 rue Parc
Sherbrooke, Quebec J1H 5M7
T: (819) 564-6234
F: (819) 820-9688
www.collegesherbrooke.qc.ca
A: Georges Laurent

Cegep de Trois-Rivieres
3500, de Courval, C.P. 97
Trois-Rivieres, Quebec GPA 5E6
T: (819) 376-1721
F: (819) 693-9409
www.cegeptr.qc.ca
A: Denis Guillemette

Vanier College
821 Boul. St. Croix
Ville de St. Laurent, Quebec
Canada H4L 3X9
T: (514) 744-7133
F: (514) 744-7127
www.vaniercollege.qc.ca
A: Linda MacPherson

Cegep de Victoriaville
475, rue Notre Dame est
Victoriaville, Quebec G6P 4B3
T: (819) 758-6401
F: (819) 758-6026
www.cgpvicto.qc.ca
A: Yvon Pare

College Vieux Montreal
255, rue Ontario est
Montreal, Quebec H2X 3M8
T: (514) 982-3437
F: (514) 982-3448
www.cvm.qc.ca
A: Pierre Hubert

NAIA Member

Simon Fraser University
55 Harbord Street
Burnaby, B.C. V5A 1S6
T: (604) 291-3675
F: (604) 291-4922
www.SFU.ca/athletics-rec
A: Michael Dinning
S: Michael Kinghorn

Independent

**University of Toronto
at Mississauga**
3359 Mississauga Road
Mississauga, Ontario L5L 1C6
T: (905) 828-5269
F: (905) 569-4354
A: Amy Lobo
S: Jack Krist

National State High School Associations

National Federation of State High School Associations
PO Box 690
Indianapolis, IN 46206
T: (317) 972-6900
F: (317) 822-5700
www.nfhs.org
Executive Dir: Robert F. Canaby
PR: Bruce Howard

Alabama High School Athletic Associiation
PO Box 5014
926 Pelham Street
Montgomery, AL 36103
T: (334) 263-6994
F: (334) 240-3389
Exec. Dir: Daniel Washburn

Alaska School Activities Association, Inc.
4120 Laurel Street
Suite 102
Anchorage, AK 99508
T: (907) 563-3723
F: (907) 561-0720
E: asaa@alaska.net
Exec. Dir: Gary Matthews

Arizona Interscholastic Assoc.
7007 N. 18th Street
Phoenix, AZ 85020
T: (602) 385-3810
F: (602) 385-3779
www.aiahisch.org
Exec. Dir: Dr. Voie Stuart Coy

Arkansas Activities Association
3920 Richards Road
North Little Rock, AR 72117
T: (501) 955-2500
F: (501) 955-2600
www.ahsaa.org
Exec. Dir: Lamar Cole

California Interscholastic Federation
664 Las Gallinas
San Rafael, CA 94903
T: (415) 492-5911
F: (415) 492-5919
www.CIFstate.org
Exec. Dir: Jack Hayes
SID: Jim Duel

Colorado High School Activities Association
14855 East Second Ave.
Aurora, CA 80011
T: (303) 344-5050
F: (303) 367-4101
www.chsaa.org
Comm: Bob Ottewill

Connecticut Interscholastic Athletic Conference
30 Realty Drive
Cheshire, CT 06410
T: (203) 250-1111
F: (203) 250-1345
www.casciac.org
Exec. Dir: Michael H. Savage

Delaware Secondary School Athletic Association
John G. Townsend Building
Federal & Loockerman Streets
Dover, MD 19901
T: (302) 739-4181
F: (302) 739-4221
Exec. Dir: Robert A. Depew

D.C. Interscholastic Athletic Association
Public Schools Dept. of Athletics
800 Ingraham Street NW
Washington, DC 20011
T: (202) 576-7167
F: (202) 576-8505
Exec. Dir: Allen E. Chin

Florida High School Activities Association
515 N. Main Street
PO Box 1173
Gainesville, FL 32602
T: (352) 372-9551
F: (352) 373-1528
Comm: Ronald N. Davis

Georgia High School Association
150 S. Bethel Street
PO Box 271
Thomaston, GA 30286
T: (706) 647-7473
F: (706) 647-2638
www.alltel.net/~ghsa
Exec. Dir: Tommy Guillebeau

**Hawaii High School
Athletic Association**
PO Box 62029
Honolulu, HI 96839
T: (808) 587-4495
F: (808) 587-4496
Exec. Dir: Keith Amemiya

**Idaho High School
Activities Association**
8011 Ustick Road
PO Box 4667
Boise, ID 83704
T: (208) 375-7027
F: (208) 322-5505
Exec. Dir: Bill Young

Illinois High School Association
2715 McGraw Drive
PO Box 2715
Bloomington, IL 61702
T: (309) 663-6377
F: (309) 663-7479
www.ihsa.org
Exec. Dir: H. David Fry

**Indiana High School
Athletic Association**
9150 N. Meridian St.
PO Box 40650
Indianapolis, IN 46260
T: (317) 846-6601
F: (317) 575-4244
www.ihsaa.org
Comm: Bob Gardner

**Iowa High School
Athletic Association**
1605 South Story
PO Box 10
Boone, IA 50036
T: (515) 432-2011
F: (515) 432-2961
www.iahsaa.org
Exec. Dir: Bernie Saggau

**Kansas State High School
Activities Association**
520 SW 27th Street
PO Box 495
Topeka, KS 66611
T: (785) 235-9201
F: (785) 235-2637
www.kshaa.org
Exec. Dir: Gary Musselman

**Kentucky High School
Athletic Association**
2280 Executive Drive
Lexington, KY 40505
T: (606) 299-5472
F: (606) 293-5999
www.khsaa.org
E: khsaa@iglou.com
Comm: Louis Stout

**Louisiana High School
Athletic Association**
7905 Wrenwood Blvd.
Baton Rouge, LA 70809
T: (504) 925-0100
F: (504) 925-5801
Comm: Tommy Henry

Maine Principals Association
16 Winthrop Street
PO Box 2468
Augusta, ME 04338
T: (207) 622-0217
F: (207) 622-1513
www.mint.net/~mpa
Exec. Dir: Richard W. Tyler

**Maryland Public Secondary
Schools Athletic Association**
200 W. Baltimore Street
Baltimore, MD 21201
T: (410) 767-0376
F: (410) 333-2379
Exec. Dir: Edward F. Sparks

**Massachusetts Interscholastic
Athletic Association**
83 Cedar Street
Milford, MA 01757
T: (508) 478-5641
F: (508) 634-3044
www.miaa.net
Exec. Dir: Richard F. Neal

Michigan High School Athletic Association
1661 Ramblewood Drive
East Lansing, MI 48823
T: (517) 332-5046
F: (517) 332-4071
www.mhsaa.com
Exec. Dir: John E. Roberts

Minnesota State High School League
2100 Freeway Boulevard
Brooklyn Center, MN 55430
T: (612) 560-2262
F: (612) 569-0499
www.mshsl.org
Exec. Dir: David V. Stead

Mississippi High School Activities Association
1201 Clinton-Raymond Rd.
PO Box 244
Clinton, MS 39060
T: (601) 924-6400
F: (601) 924-1725
www.misshsaa.com
Exec. Dir: Dr. Ennis Procter

Missouri State High School Activities Association
1808 I-70 Drive, SW
PO Box 1328
Columbia, MO 65205
T: (573) 445-4443
F: (573) 445-2502
Exec. Dir: Becky Oakes

Montana High School Association
1 South Dakota Avenue
Helena, MT 59601
T: (406) 442-6010
F: (406) 442-8250
Exec. Dir: James C. Haugen

Nebraska School Activities Association
8230 Beechwood Dr.
PO Box 5447
Lincoln, NE 68505
T: (402) 489-0386
F: (402) 489-0934
www.nsaahome.org
Exec. Dir: James Riley

Nevada Interscholastic Activities Association
1 East Liberty Street
Suite 505
Reno, NV 89501
T: (775) 688-6464
F: (775) 688-6465
Exec. Dir: Dr. Jerry A. Hughes

New Hampshire Interscholastic Athletic Association
251 Clinton Street
Concord, NH 03301
T: (603) 228-8671
F: (603) 225-7978
www.nhiaa.org
Exec. Dir: James W. Desmarais

New Jersey State Interscholastic Athletic Association
Route 130, PO Box 487
Robbinsville, NJ 08691
T: (609) 259-2776
F: (609) 259-3047
www.njsiaa.org
Exec. Dir: Boyd. A. Sands

New Mexico Activities Association
6600 Palomas NE
Albuquerque, NM 87109
T: (505) 821-1887
F: (505) 821-2441
www.nmact.org
kExec. Dir: Dan Salzwedel

New York State Public High School Athlettic Association
88 Delaware Avenue
Delmar, NY 12054
T: (518) 439-8872
F: (518) 475-1556
www.nysphsaa.org
Exec. Dir: Dr. Sandra E. Scott

North Carolina High School Athletic Association
PO Box 3216
Finley Golf Course Road
UNC Campus
Chapel Hill, NC 27515
T: (919) 962-2345
F: (919) 962-4438
Exec. Dir: Charles H. Adams

North Dakota High School Activities Association
PO Box 817
134 NE Third Street
Valley City, ND 58072
T: (701) 845-3953
F: (701) 845-4935
E: rking@send-it.nodak.edu
Exec. Sec: Robert D. King

Ohio High School Athletic Association
4080 Roselea Place
Columbus, OH 43214
T: (614) 267-2502
F: (614) 267-1677
www.ohsaa.org
Comm: Clair Muscaro

Oklahoma Secondary School Activities Association
PO Box 14590
7300 N. Broadway Extension
Oklahoma City, OK 73113
T: (405) 840-1116
F: (405) 840-9559
Exec. Sec: Bill Self

Oregon School Activities Association
25200 SW Parkway Avenue
Wilsonville, OR 97070
T: (503) 682-6722
F: (503) 682-0960
www.osaa.org
Exec. Dir: Wes Ediger

Pennsylvania Interscholastic Athletic Association
PO Box 2008, 550 Gettysburg Rd.
Mechanicsburg, PA 17055
T: (717) 697-0374
F: (717) 697-7721
www.piaa.org
Exec. Dir: Bradley Cashman

Rhode Island Interscholastic League, Inc.
#6, R.I. College Campus
600 Mt. Pleasant Avenue
Providence, RI 02908
T: (401) 272-9844
F: (401) 272-9838
Exec. Dir: Richard B. Lynch

South Carolina High School League
121 Westpark Boulevard
PO Box 211575
Columbia, SC 29210
T: (803) 798-0120
F: (803) 731-9679
Exec. Dir: Ronnie Matthews

South Dakota High School Activities Association
PO Box 1217
204 N. Euclid
Pierre, SD 57501
T: (605) 224-9261
F: (605) 224-9262
Exec. Dir: Marlyn Goldhammer

Tennessee Secondary School Athletic Association
3333 Lebanon Road
Hermitage, TN 37076
T: (615) 889-6740
F: (615) 889-0544
Exec. Dir: Ronnie Carter

Texas University Interscholastic League
1701 Manor Road
Austin, TX 78722
T: (512) 471-5883
F: (512) 471-6589
www.utexas.edu/admin/uil/
Dir: William D. Farney

Utah High School Activities Association
199 East 7200 South
Midvale, UT 84047
T: (801) 566-0681
F: (801) 566-0633
Exec. Dir: Evan K. Excell

Vermont Principals' Association
Two Prospect Street
Suite 3
Montpelier, VT 05602
T: (802) 229-0547
F: (802) 229-4801
E: vpa@vpa.k12.vt.us
Exec. Dir: W. Scott Blanchard

Virginia High School League
1642 State Farm Blvd.
Charlottesville, VA 22911
T: (804) 977-8475
F: (804) 977-5943
www.vhsl.org
Exec. Dir: Ken Tilley

Washington Interscholastic Activities Association
435 Main Avenue S.
Renton, WA 98055
T: (425) 687-8585
F: (425) 687-9476
Exec. Dir: Mike Colbrese

West Virginia Secondary School Activities Commission
Route 9, Box 76
Parkersburg, WV 26101
T: (304) 485-5494
F: (304) 428-5431
Exec. Sec: Warren L. Carter

Wisconsin Interscholastic Athletic Association
5516 Vern Holmes Drive
Stevens Point, WI 54481
T: (715) 344-8580
F: (715) 344-4241
www.wiaawi.org
E: info@wiaawi.org
Exec. Dir: Douglas Chickering

Wyoming High School Activities Association
731 E. 2nd Street
Casper, WY 82601
T: (307) 577-0614
F: (307) 577-0637
www.coffey.com/whsaa
E: whsaa@coffey.com
Comm: Larry Klaassen

Canada

Alberta Schools' Athletic Assn.
11759 Groat Road
Edmonton, Alberta T5M 3K6 CAN
T: (780) 427-8182
F: (780) 415-1833
www.afternet.com/asaa
Exec. Dir: John Paton

British Columbia School Sports
#330, 1367 West Broadway
Vancouver, B.C. V6H 4A9, CAN
T: (604) 737-3066
F: (604) 737-9844
Exec. Dir: Marilyn Payne

Manitoba High Schools Athletic Association
200 Main Street
Winnipeg, Manitoba R3C 4M2, CAN
T: (204) 925-5640
F: (204) 925-5624
Exec. Dir: Morris Glimcher

New Brunswick Interscholastic Athletic Association
PO Box 143
Petitcodiac, N.B. EOA 2H0, Canada
T: (506) 756-2190
F: (506) 756-8455
Exec. Dir: Ron Hooper

Newfoundland-Labrador High School Athletic Federation
Provincial Recreation Centre
Bldg. 25, Torgay Airport
St. John's, Nfld. A1C 5T7, Canada
Exec. Dir: Karen Keough

Nova Scotia School Athletic Federation
PO Box 3010-S
5516 Spring Garden Road
Halifax, Nova Scotia B3J 3G6, CAN
T: (902) 425-5450
F: (902) 425-5606
www.nssaf.ednet.ns.ca
Exec. Dir: Ron O' Flaherty

Ontario Federation of School Athletic Associations
7880 Keele Street,
Suite 206
Concord, Ontario L4K 4G7, Canada
T: (905) 761-5540
F: (905) 761-5542
www.ofsaa.on.ca
E: schoolsport@ofsaa.on.ca
Exec. Dir: Colin Hood

Prince Edward Island School Athletic Association
Department of Education
PO Box 2000
Charlottetown, PEI C1A 7N8, CAN
T: (902) 368-4672
F: (902) 368-4663
Exec. Sec: Lyall Huggan

Quebec Student Sport Federation
4545 Ave. Pierre-de-Coubertin
C.P. 1000, Succursale M
Montreal, Quebec H1V 3R2, Canada
T: (514) 252-3105
F: (514) 254-3292
E: fqse@interlink.net
Director: Jacques Moffatt

Saskatchewan High Schools Athletic Association
425 Winnipeg Street
Regina, Sask. S4P 8P2, Canada
T: (306) 721-2151
F: (306) 721-2659
E: shsaa@sk.sympatico.ca
Exec. Dir: Bryan Matheson

Others

American Samoa High School Athletic Association
Division of Curriculum & Instruction
Department of Education
Pago Pago, American Samoa 96799
T: (684) 633-1246
F: (684) 633-5184
Exec. Dir: Jeff Chun

Bermuda School Sports Federation
PO Box HM 2511
Hamilton, HM BX, Bermuda
T: (441) 295-1983
F: (441) 295-3349
Exec. Dir: Clint Smith

Commonwealth Interscholastic Federation, Inc.
Caller Box 10007
Saipan, MP 96940
T: (670) 664-4200
F: (670) 235-2397
Chair: Ms. G.C. Borja-Robinson

Independent Interscholastic Athletic Association of Guam
PO Box FD
Agana, Guam 96310
T: (671) 734-2261
F: (671) 734-5738

Phillippine Secondary Schools Athletic Association
George Dewey High School
USNS Box 70
FPO San Francisco, CA 96651
Exec: Sec. John J. Stauffer

St. Croix Interscholastic Athletic Association
PO Box 3539
Frederiksted, St. Croix
US Virgin Islands, 00841
T: (340) 778-0123 x 219
F: (340) 778-3939
Exec. Dir: Gregory Tyler

St. Thomas - St. John Interscholastic Athletic Association
PO Box 11102
St. Thomas,
US Virgin Islands, 00801
Chairman: William I. Frett

National Congress of State Games
Box 7136
Billings, MT 59103
T: (406) 254-7426
F: (406) 254-7439
www.stategames.org
E: ncsg@aol.com
Exec Dir: Thomas Osborne

Alabama

Alabama Sports Festival
PO Box 20327
Montgomery, AL 36120
T: (334) 280-0065
F: (334) 280-0988
www.alagames.com
E: alagames@aol.com
Exec. Dir: Ron Creel

Alaska

Greatland Games
2075 Glenn Highway
Palmer, AK 99645
T: (907) 746-7153
F: (907) 746-2699
E: dean@statefair.org
Exec. Dir: Dean Phipps

Arizona

Grand Canyon State Games
1515 West University Dr., Ste. 101
Tempe, AZ 85281
T: (602) 517-9700
F: (602) 517-9739
Exec. Dir: Erik Widmark

Arkansas State Games
Univ. of Arkansas for Med. Science
4301 W. Markham, Slot 716
Little Rock, AR 72205
T: (501) 686-7950
F: (501) 686-5067
Exec. Dir: Larry Bone

California State Games
3073 Palm Street
San Diego, CA 92104
T: (619) 282-1360
F: (619) 282-1391
www.calstategames.org
E: Calgames@sosinet.net
Exec. Dir: Sandi Hill

Colorado State Games
9222 S. Rockport Lane
PO Box 260683
Littleton, CO 80163
T: (303) 791-3384
F: (303) 791-4686
www.Colo_Amateur_Sports.org
Exec. Dir: Tom Alison

Connecticut

Nutmeg State Games
290 Roberts Street
East Hartford, CT 06108
T: (860) 528-4588
F: (860) 291-8032
Exec. Dir: William Mudano

District of Columbia

Capital Games
PO Box 2196
Falls Church, VA 22042
T: (703) 560-3310
F: (703) 560-6699
Exec. Dir: Josh Henson

Florida

Sunshine State Games
1408 NW 6th Street
Gainesville, FL 32601
T: (352) 955-2120
F: (352) 373-8879
www.sunshinestategames.org
Exec. Dir: Jimmy Carnes

Georgia Games
1415 Barclay Cir. SE, Ste. F
Marietta, GA 30060
T: (770) 528-3580
F: (770) 528-3590
www.georgiagames.org
Exec. Dir: Nick Gailey

Hawaii

Aloha State Games
1110 University Ave. # 403
Honolulu, HI 96826
T: (808) 947-4141
F: (808) 947-6648
E: higames@aloha.net
Exec. Dir: Marcia Klompus

Idaho

First Security Games of Idaho
PO Box 873
Pocatello, ID 83204
T: (208) 233-0022
F: (208) 233-2106
Exec. Dir: Bette Cagen

Idaho Winter Games
PO Box 15214
Boise, ID 83715
T: (800) 442-3794
Exec. Dir: Will Simons

Illinois

Prairie State Games
First Financial Bank Bldg. #310
6550 N. Illinois Street
Fairview Heights, IL 62208
T: (618) 632-1002
F: (618) 632-1123
www.prairiestategames.com
Exec. Dir: Maureen Moore

Indiana

Hoosier State Games
Pan Am Plaza
201 S. Capitol Av. # 1200
Indianapolis, IN 46225-1069
T: (317) 237-5000
F: (317) 237-5041
Exec. Dir: Donna Billiard

Iowa Games
PO Box 2350
Ames, IA 50010
T: (515) 292-3251
F: (515) 292-3254
www.iowagames.org
E: iagames@netins.net
Exec. Dir: Jim Hallihan

Kansas

Sunflower State Games
1414 W. 6th St. # 200
Lawrence, KS 66044
T: (785) 842-7774
F: (785) 842-7731
www.sunflowergames.org
Exec. Dir: Kelly Mason

Kentucky

Bluegrass State Games
200 E. Main St, PO Box 1463
Lexington, KY 40507
T: (606) 255-0336
F: (606) 258-3022
Exec. Dir: Eric Ward

Louisiana State Games
New Orleans Centre
1400 Poydras, Suite 918
New Orleans, LA 70112
T: (504) 525-5678
F: (504) 529-1622
www.louisianagames.org
Exec. Dir: Ralph Morton

Maine

The Maine Event Sports Festival
PO Box 730
Old Orchard Beach, ME 04064
T: (207) 761-6504 x 33
F: (207) 934-7058
Exec. Dir: Brian Corcoran

Maryland State Games
100 Waterland Way
Frederick, MD 21702
T: (301) 663-3584
F: (301) 66307710
Exec. Dir: Michael Dunn

Massachusetts

Bay State Games
800 W. Cummings Park, Ste. 5550
Woburn, MA 01801
T: (781) 932-6555
F: (781) 932-3441
E: baystateg@aol.com
Exec. Dir: Linda Driscol

Michigan

Great Lakes State Games
PO Box 27187
Lansing, MI 48909
T: (517) 351-8959
F: (517) 351-7811
www.michiganfitness.org
Exec. Dir: Marilyn Lieber

Minnesota

Star of the North State Games
1700 - 105th Av. NE
Blaine, MN 55449
T: (612) 785-5634
F: (612) 785-5699
www.masc.state.mn.us/sgames
Exec. Dir: Barclay Kruse

State Games of Mississippi
PO Box 5866
Meridian, MS 39302
T: (601) 482-0205
F: (601) 483-0650
E: stgamiss@aol.com
Exec. Dir: david Stevens

Missouri

Show-Me State Games
404 Jesse Hall
Columbia, MO 65211
T: (573) 882-2101
F: (573) 884-4004
E: show4games@aol.com
Exec. Dir: Gary Filbert

Montana

Big Sky State Games
401 North 31st Street
Suite 620, Box 7136
Billings, MT 59103
T: (406) 254-7426
F: (406) 254-7439
www.bigskygames.org
Exec. Dir: Karen Sanford Gall

Nebraska
Cornhusker State Games
PO Box 82411
Lincoln, NE 68501
T: (402) 471-2544
F: (402) 471-9712
www.nestgames.com
Exec. Dir: Tom Ash

Nevada

Silver State Games
600 S. Rock Blvd., Ste. 21-B
Reno, NV 89502
T: (775) 856-3434
F: (775) 856-2200
Exec. Dir: Jim VandenHeuvel

New Hampshire

Granite State Festival of Athletes
305 Rimmon Street
Manchester, NH 03102
T: (603) 625-1436
F: (603) 624-2858
Exec. Dir: Edward Houle

New Jersey

Garden State Games
102 Park Avenue
West Caldwell, NJ 07006
T: (973) 228-6649
Exec. Dir: Michael Garamella

New Mexico

**First Security Games
of New Mexico**
PO Box 30627
Albuquerque, NM 87190
T: (505) 764-1510
F: (505) 764-1719
Exec. Dir: Fred Hultberg

New York

Empire State Games
Agency Building 1, 14th FL
Empire State Plaza
Albany, NY 12238
T: (518) 474-8889
F: (518) 474-7944
Exec. Dir: Fred Smith

State Games of North Carolina
PO Box 12727
Research Triangle Pk., NC 27709
T: (919) 361-1133
F: (919) 361-2559
www.ncsports.org
E: ncas@interpath.com
Exec. Dir: Chuck Hobgood

North Dakota

Prairie Rose State Games
1835 Bismarck Expressway
Bismarck, ND 58504
T: (701) 328-5357
F: (701) 328-5363
E: prsg@state.nd.us
Exec. Dir: Marnie Walth

Ohio Games
1468 West 9th St., Suite 220
Cleveland, OH 44113
T: (800) 487-6446
F: (216) 363-0698
E: GCSC@aol.com
Exec. Dir: Neal Neroni

Oklahoma

Sooner State Games
100 West Main St., Suite 287
Oklahoma, City, OK 73102
T: (405) 235-4222
F: (405) 232-7723
E: Snrstgms@aol.com
Exec. Dir: Robbie Robertson

State Games of Oregon
4840 SW Western Av. # 900
Beaverton, OR 97005
T: (503) 520-1319
F: (503) 520-9747
E: sgoduffy@aol.com
Exec. Dir: Kerry Duffy

Pennsylvania

Keystone State Games
PO Box 3131
Wilkes-Barre, PA 18753
T: (570) 823-3164
F: (570) 822-6558
www.keystonegames.com
E: keystones@aol.com
Exec. Dir: Owen Costello

Rhode Island State Games & Sports Festival
145 Black Hut Road
Harrisville, RI 02830
T/F: (401) 568-8955
Exec. Dir: Ken Milligan

South Carolina

Palmetto Sports Festival
2313 Reidville Rd., Ste. H
Spartanburg, SC 29301
T: (864) 574-2134
F: (864) 574-2130
Exec. Dir: Len Stubbs

South Dakota State Games
Box 286
Milbank, SD 57252
T: (605) 432-9137
Exec. Dir: Craig Haugaard

State Games of Tennessee
Memphis, Shelby Co. Sports
47 Union Avenue
Memphis, TN 38103
T: (901) 543-5319
F: (901) 543-5350
Exec. Dir: Ross Bartow

Games of Texas
PO Box 1789
Georgetown, TX 78627
T: (512) 863-9400
F: (512) 869-2393
Exec. Dir: Cliff Warrick

Utah Summer Games
351 W. Center Street
Cedar City, UT 84720
T: (435) 865-8422
F: (435) 865-8420
www.utahsummergames.org
Exec. Dir: Bryan Dangerfield

Utah Winter Games
1760 S. Fremont Drive
Salt Lake City, UT 84104
T: (801) 975-4515
F: (801) 974-9565
www.utahwintergames.org
Exec. Dir: Maria McNulty

Vermont

Green Mountain State Games
36 Lexington St., #3
Dover, NH 03821
T: (603) 749-3561
F: (802) 468-1179
Exec. Dir: Brian Burleigh

Commonwealth Games of Virginia
711-C 5th Street NE
Roanoke, VA 24016
T: (540) 343-0987
F: (540) 343-7407
www.commonwealthgames.org
Exec. Dir: Pete Lampman

State Games of Washington
816 Sumner Ave.
Sumner, WA 98390
T: (253) 863-1269
Exec. Dir: Carl Jones

West Virginia

Mountain State Games
540 5th Avenue
Huntington, WV 25701
T: (304) 525-5151
F: (304) 525-9685
Exec. Dir: Tom Hargis

Wisconsin

Badger State Games
PO Box 7788
Madison, WI 53707
T: (608) 226-4780
F: (608) 226-9550
www.badgerstategames.org
Exec. Dir: Janet Bell

Wyoming

Cowboy State Games
PO Box 3485
Casper, WY 82602
T: (307) 577-1125
F: (307) 577-8111
E: csg@trib.com
Exec. Dir: Eileen Ford

Senior Games

The Senior Games are not affiliated with the State Games.

National Senior Games Association
3032 Old Forge Drive
Baton Rouge, LA 70802
T: (225) 925-5678
F: (225) 216-7552
www.nsga.com
E: dhull@nsga.com
Director: D. Hull

Late Arrivals & Additions

Listed in this section are some late additions to the book.

New Brunswick Senior Baseball League
PO Box 563
Moncton, NB E1C 8L9 Canada
T: (506) 854-9288
E: donlivin@sympatico.ca
P: Don Mitchell
VP: Ron Wilson, Sr.
Sec/Treas: Don Livingstone

Chatham Senior BB Club
161 St. Thomas Street
Miramichi City, NB E1N 1Z1 Canada
T: (506) 778-6077
F: (506) 778-6158
P: Daryl Mitchell

Fredericton Royals
757 Union Street
Fredericton, NB EA3 2N1 Canada
T: (506) 444-2104
E: kevin.lunn@gnb.ca
P: Kevin Lunn

Moncton Mets
PO Box 1105
Moncton, NB E1C 8P6 Canada
T: (506) 386-1177
F: (506) 387-5008
E: rchamber@nbnet.nb.ca
P: Ralph Chambers

Newcastle Cardinals
281 Miller Avenue
Newcastle, NB E1Z 3B3 Canada
T: (506) 622-1833
F: (506) 622-2278
P: Gary Dunnett

Saint John Alpines
50 Fenton Drive
Saint John, NB E2M 4E7
T: (506) 635-1410
F: (506) 635-0209
E: silhunt@nb.sympatico.ca
P: Terre Hunter

Womens Football League
3640 Dickerson Pike
Nashville, TN 37207
T: (615) 612-0061
F: (615) 612-0061
E: wfleague@aol.com
www.womensfootballleague.com